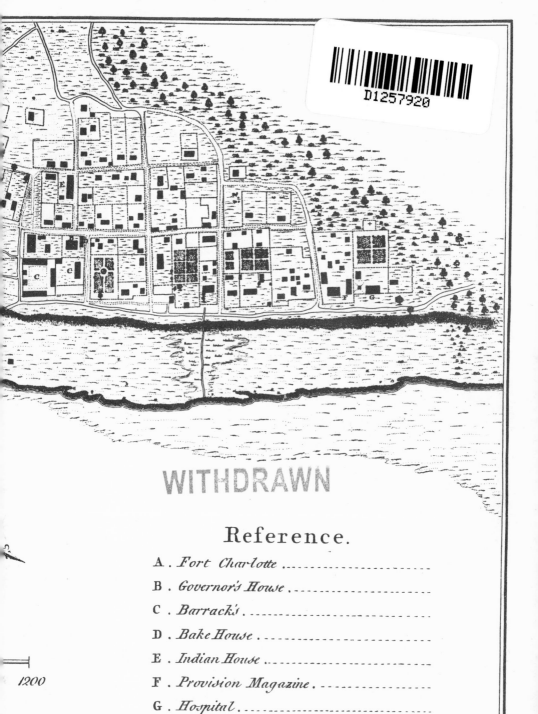

Reference.

A . Fort Charlotte ....

B . Governor's House ....

C . Barrack's ....

D . Bake House ....

E . Indian House ....

F . Provision Magazine. ....

G . Hospital ....

1200

ALABAMA

ALABAMA

A Documentary History to 1900

Revised and Enlarged Edition

LUCILLE GRIFFITH

The University of Alabama Press

University, Alabama

For my Griffith nephews
Ralph, John, Nicky,
Edwin, and Larry
With love

PREFACE

There has been extended debate as to whether this volume should be called a new edition of the *History of Alabama, 1540–1900* . . . published by Colonial Press in 1962. When it became apparent that it would be out of print soon, the decision was made to reprint it but with more narrative and interpretation so that it would be an independent volume and not merely a supplementary one. There were acknowledged weak spots in the earlier one that needed to be strengthened. When the writing got underway, new material not available earlier often appeared appropriate and so the work now contains much more and, in some instances, unpublished material. Less than half of this volume was in the earlier one. It is the hope of both the author and the University of Alabama Press that it will prove to be useful both to the general reader and to the student of Alabama history.

In selecting the topics to be used, I have tried to stay in the mainstream of Alabama history but by using more than the traditional sources. I have let all kinds of people, young and old, men, women and children, black and white, slave and free, educated and uneducated, governors and tenant farmer, from every section of the state have a part in this book. While I hope the reader will find it interesting, my chief concern has been accuracy, accuracy of fact and also of spirit. Therefore, most passages herein quoted could be duplicated many times over because they are typical of what was going on at the time. In short, I have made no attempt to use unique illustrations, only representative ones.

In preparing this volume I have accumulated many debts which I gladly acknowledge. The original idea came out of a conversation with the late Dr. Hallie Farmer before her retirement. It soon became apparent that the small volume of basic documents we envisioned would be inadequate and should be replaced by something more elaborate, so the project grew. Encouraged by the kind reception of the first edition and stimulated by suggestions for improvement, we now offer a new and enlarged version.

I owe a special debt to many people who have helped in many ways: to the personnel at the Department of Archives and History, Montgomery, and especially to Mrs. Virginia K. Jones and Mrs. Jessie Cobb; to Miss Mary Frances Tipton, reference librarian at the Carmichael Library, University of Montevallo, who good-naturedly complained I always gave her only the hard problems but who always came up with the right answer; to Mrs. Carolyn

M. Reid, Miss Susan Vaughn and Mr. Reuben Triplett, who helped with typing; to Dr. Lorraine Pierson, who has read the whole manuscript and made many wise criticisms of it; to Dr. Kermit Johnson and the University of Montevallo for a grant from the Faculty Research Fund; and to many individuals who have helped in lesser but nevertheless significant ways.

LUCILLE GRIFFITH

November, 1971

Acknowledgments

I wish to acknowledge with gratitude the permission of the following publishers and individuals to print in this book extracts from the following copyrighted material controlled by them:

American Historical Association: from Dwight L. Dumond, ed., *Southern Editorials on Secession* (1931).

Associated University Presses: from H. E. Sterkx, *Partners in Rebellion* (1970).

Architectural Book Publishing Company: from Ralph Hammond, *Antebellum Mansions in Alabama* (1951).

Barnes and Noble: from F.W. Hodge, ed., *Spanish Explorers in the Southern United States* (1907).

Birmingham Publishing Company: from *Early Days in Birmingham* (1911).

Clanahan Publications: from James F. Clanahan, *The History of Pickens County, Alabama, 1540–1920* (1965).

Confederate Publishing Company: from John L. Hunnicutt, *Reconstruction in West Alabama* (1959).

Doubleday and Company: from Booker T. Washington, *My Larger Education* (1910).

Dumond, Dwight L.: *Letters of James G. Birney* (1938)

Fleming, Mary Boyd: from Walter L. Fleming, ed., *Documentary History of Reconstruction* (1950).

Florida State University Press: from Weymouth T. Jordan, *Antebellum Alabama: Town and Country*. Florida State University Studies (1957).

Harper and Brothers: from W.W. Sweet, ed., *Religion on the Frontier: The Presbyterians* (1936).

Holt, Rinehart and Winston: from Norman R. Yetman, *Life Under the Peculiar Institution* (1970).

Houghton Mifflin: from George Washington, *Diaries* (1923).

Georgia Historical Society: from *Letters of Benjamin Hawkins* (1918) ; Benjamin Hawkins, *A Sketch of the Creek Country* (1948).

Hoole, W. Stanley: from *Alabama Tories: The First Alabama Cavalry, U.S.A., 1862–1865* (1960).

Louisiana State University Press: from Richebourg G. Williams, ed., *Fleur de Lys and Calumet* (1953) ; Richard B. Harwell, ed., *Kate: The Journal of a Confederate Nurse* (1959).

Mellown, Bennie Catherine: from *Memories of a Pre-Civil War Community*.

Mississippi Department of Archives and History: from *Mississippi Provincial Archives,* vols. 1, 2, 3; Eron Rowland, *Jefferson Davis, Constitutionalist* (1923).

McCowat-Mercer Press: from Robert S. Henry, *As They Saw Forrest* (1956).

McMillan, Malcolm: *Constitutional Development in Alabama* (1955) National Society of Colonial Dames of America in Tennessee: from James Adair, *The History of the American Indian* (1930).

Smith, Sydney C. and C. Carter Smith: from *Mobile, 1861–1865* (1964).

Starnes, Hugh: from "Madoc," *Birmingham News,* March 5, 1967.

University of Alabama Press: from Mitchell B. Garratt, *Horse and Buggy Days on Hatchet Creek* (1957); Allen J. Going, *Bourbon Democracy in Alabama* (1951); Malcolm C. McMillan, *Alabama Confederate Reader* (1963); Matthew Woodruff, *A Union Soldier in the Land of the Vanquished* (1969).

University of California Press: from John Walton Caughey, *Bernardo de Gálvez* (1934).

University of Chicago Press: from E.A. Botkin, ed., *Lay My Burden Down* (1945).

University of Florida Press: from Jacob R. Motte, *Journey Into Wilderness* (1953).

University of Oklahoma Press: from John Walton Caughey, ed., *McGillivray of the Creeks* (1938); Grant Foreman, *Indian Removal* (1932).

University of North Carolina Press: from Edwin C. Knight, ed., *A Documentary History of Education in the South Before 1860* (1952).

University of South Carolina Press: from Fletcher Green, ed., *The Lides Go South and West* (1952).

Vestal, Elizabeth Garth: from "Terror on the Eliza Battle," *Birmingham News,* October 5, 1969.

Viewpoint Publications: from Charles G. Summersell, *Alabama History for Schools* (1961).

CONTENTS

TO ALABAMA

I sigh for the scenes of my earlier years,
    For the sweet little cot that stood in the lawn,
For the loved one who then oft melted to tears
    At the tale of the griefs of my life's early dawn:
For the song of the birds which rang in the grove,
    For the rush of the streamlet o'er clustered with
        vines,
For the shadowing oak, whose deep branches wove
    A sigh to the whistle of the tall waving pines.

I sigh for the shades of thy woodlands and brakes,
    For thy mountains and valleys, rich in fruits
        and in flowers,
For the zephyrs that move on thy rivers and lakes;
    Thine odor-balmed dews, thy sweet-scented
        showers;
For thy wide-spread prairies, enamelled and green,
    For the chase of the wild deer that over them
        roam,
For the glow of thy sunset which sheds o'er each
        scene
    An halo of glory, like a vision of home.

I sigh for the girls, who, in health and in beauty,
    Are the fairest and loveliest that ever charmed
        youth,
Who in friendship or love—in virtue or duty,
    Are pure as the angels and stainless as truth;
I sigh for the flash of their bright beaming eyes,
    For the words of kind impact that fall from
        their lips,
For the romp and the ramble, 'neath the clear
        evening skies,
    Where the white lilies bloom and the honey-bee
        sips.

I sigh for the smile of those true-hearted friends,
    Whose kindly regard no clouds could o'ercast,
Whose mem'ry, like hope, now soothingly blends
    The visions to come, with the dreams of the past;
For the grasp of the hand I met with of yore,
    For the union of soul that linked us then,
For that pledge of the wine-cup, which opened the
        store
    Of emotions and feelings we'll ne'er know again.

Sweet clime of the South—may this be thy glory,
    In peace or in war—on land or on sea—
In laws and in letters—in legend or story—
    The foremost and proudest of this land of the
        free;
May thine be the garden—the Eden of earth,
    Where pleasure and plenty spring up from the soil:
Where religion and virtue preside o'er each hearth,
    Giving incense to love, and sweetness to toil.

July 1839   GEORGE D. SHORTRIDGE

Chapter 1

THE COLONIAL PERIOD

The Madoc Story

Spain was the first European nation to claim what is now Alabama, but there may have been white men in the area before the Spaniards. There is a persistent legend that Madoc, a Welsh prince of the twelfth century, landed somewhere on the Gulf coast, very possibly Mobile Bay, in 1170—some three hundred years before Columbus set foot on the western hemisphere. According to the legend:

Madoc, one of 17 sons of the ruler of Wales, could not stomach the possibility of a violent interfamily fight over the throne when their father died. Howel was the eldest son, he knew, but was basely born of an Irish woman. Next in line was David, and as sure as the fog rose from the castle moat every morning, David would not brook his brother's ascendance. A fight—perhaps even civil war—was inevitable.

Madoc himself was far down on the list, out of the running. And besides, Madoc seemed to be born for less petty things than fraternal blood-letting. The sea had always been his attraction, and to the icy waters of the North Atlantic he soon turned his eyes.

With four of his brothers and some women, including a sister, he gathered a small band and set out in 10 sailing ships—toward the unknown west.

The next land the adventurers saw, no one knows exactly how long later, was the gleaming white beach of the Gulf Coast. There they sailed until they discovered a magnificent bay, circled with such trees as they had never seen in Wales. The group landed and found the land to be gentle to them—fertile and pleasant. A land, Madoc said to his brothers, which any Welshman would be proud to live in.

He was excited—if he could convince others of his country to cross the sea, they could stop wasting their time vying for only a ragged

1

the mouth of the Mississippi River. As Pineda moved upstream, he counted forty Indian villages within the first six leagues. The exact circumstances under which the party set foot on Alabama soil are unknown, but they spent some forty days caulking their ships. No doubt, they kept an eye open for signs of gold; if they found anything valuable, there is no record of it.

Less than ten years later (1528) Pánfilo de Narváez, an experienced conquistador who had spent twenty-six years in the New World, made a forced landing on the banks of Mobile Bay. Narváez, described as tall, fair, of commanding person and agreeable address, had lost an eye when he led an expedition of 900 troops into Mexico to arrest the free-wheeling Hernando Cortez. Covey describes Narváez as a "grasping bungler" who by his "stupid decision to separate his cavalry and infantry from their sustaining ships sealed the doom of his expedition in Florida."

Narváez by 1527 was a veteran of enough distinction that the Council of the Indies appointed him governor with authority to conquer lands extending from the Rio de las Palmas (Rio Grande) to the Cape of Florida. He was to have the "routine titles and concessions" that came with the office. Setting out from Santo Domingo and after prolonged stays in Trinidad and Havana, he and his party of some 400 men and 80 horses landed at Tampa Bay on April 14, 1528. After many indecisions and much consultation between the governor and his subordinates, the party started westward, heading for Mexico. Having lost many of their ships (and using rafts the men had improvised from logs, horse hides, palmetto and horse hair for ropes, and even their shirts for sails), and encountering troubles with the natives whenever they ventured ashore, they reached the Mobile area in the late fall of 1528. Short of fresh water, the party under Commander Cabeza de Vaca landed at Mobile Bay early in November. Cabeza de Vaca, who proved to be the historian of the expedition, gives here an "unvarnished, soldierly account" of what they went through:

> Continuing along the coast, we entered an estuary [Mobile Bay] where we saw a canoe of Indians coming toward us. We hailed them and, when they drew close to the Governor's boat, he asked for water. They showed themselves willing to get some if we furnished containers. That Greek, Doroteo Teodoro . . . said he would go, too. The Governor and others failed to dissuade him. He took along a Negro, and the Indians left two of their number as hostages.
>
> It was night when the Indians returned, without water in the containers and without the Christians.
>
> When these returning Indians spoke to our two hostages, the latter started to dive into the water; but some of our soldiers held them back in the barge. The canoe sped away, leaving us very confused and de-

jected over the loss of our comrades.———Cabeza de Vaca, *Adventures in the Unknown Interior of America,* translated by Cyclone Covey (New York: The Crowell-Collier Publishing Co., 1961), pp. 50–51. First published in 1542.

Narváez later was lost when he was swept overboard by a storm; but Cabeza de Vaca, after many adventures in the effort to join his compatriots in Mexico, returned home to Spain in 1537.

Three months before he set foot on home soil, Hernando de Soto had been named governor of Florida, a post Cabeza longed for. The new governor was, like most of the big names in Spanish exploration, a veteran of earlier expeditions. He had followed Pedrarías de Ávila to the West Indies, served under him in Nicaragua (and eventually married his daughter, Doña Isabel), and had won great distinction under Pizarro in the conquest of Peru. By marriage he was a brother-in-law of Balboa; several of his own relatives would serve with him in his expedition through the interior of North America.

Even though de Soto had participated in several expeditions, he was only in his middle thirties. A man of above average height and a skilled horseman, he was an agreeable figure in court circles. He was blessed with a strong constitution, without which he would never have been able to endure the long marches and extended periods of privation in the wilderness. He had returned from Peru with great wealth, much of it "lavished on him" by the Inca Atahualpa who had been his royal captive. Surrounded by stewards, ushers, equerries, and pages, he lived in "all the glitter and pagent of a rich nobleman." However, the young man chafed under the restrictions of court life and sought new worlds to conquer. Emperor Charles V granted him "a royal asiento and capitulation to conquer, pacify, and people" in the territory between the Rio de las Palmas and the Cape of Florida. Furthermore, he was made governor of Cuba. The task of recruiting men for the expedition was made easy by the stories Cabeza de Vaca told of clothes made of cotton, wool, vast amounts of gold, silver, and precious stones which he had seen in the "richest country in the world." On April 6, 1558, de Soto set sail from San Lucar with a fleet of seven large and three small vessels, at least 600 soldiers, several monks, and the usual number of royal officials. By the latter part of May, he had reached Cuba, where he busied himself with arrangements to leave the island under the care of a lieutenant and with preparations for the exploration of Florida. Having learned from his subordinates who had been sent to reconnoiter the coast that Tampa Bay was the best place to land, he sailed on May 18, 1539; on June 3 he began his fateful journey into the wilderness. He led the first band of Europeans into the interior of Alabama.

Knowing that he would be cut off from any help and that he must therefore take with him the provisions and equipment he would need in his search for gold, de Soto was well supplied. In fact, it is astonishing that he could make any rapid progress encumbered with as much impedimenta as he was. Albert Pickett, an early historian of the state, summarizes the personnel and equipment of the expedition:

> His troops were provided with helmets, breastplates, shields and coats of steel to repel arrows of the Indians; and with swords, Biscayan lances, rude guns called arquebuses, crossbows, and one piece of artillery. His cavaliers, mounted upon two hundred and thirteen horses, were the most gallant and graceful men of all Spain. Greyhounds, of almost the fleetness of the winds, were ready to be turned loose upon the retreating savages; and bloodhounds, of prodigious and noted ferocity, were at hand to devour them, if the bloody Spaniards deemed it necessary. To secure the unhappy Indian, handcuffs, chains and neck collars abounded in the camp. Workmen of every trade, with their various tools, crucibles for refining gold, were in attendance. Tons of iron, and steel, and much other metal, various merchandise, and provisions to last two years, were provided by the munificence of the commander and his followers. A large drove of hogs, which strangely multiplied upon the route, together with cattle and mules, was also attached to the expedition. The establishment of the Catholic religion appears to have been one of the objects; for, associated with the army, were twelve priests, eight clergymen of inferior rank, and four monks, with their robes, holy relics, and sacramental bread and wine. Most of them were relatives of the superior officers. Never was an expedition more complete, owing to the experience of De Soto, who, upon the plains of Peru, had ridden down hundreds in his powerful charges, and had poured out streams of savage blood with his broad and sweeping sword!——Albert James Pickett, *History of Alabama* (Birmingham: The Webb Book Company, 1900), p. 19. The book was first published in 1853.

De Soto led his band through northern Florida, Georgia and finally Alabama, entering the state in what is now Jackson County, near Bridgeport. This was on July 2; in late December they crossed through Pickens County into what is now Mississippi. In those five months, the band of Spaniards had visited village after village, requiring food and guide service and taking hostages as well as slaves. Each village greeted them politely and sometimes even cordially, but each was anxious to be rid of them and sped them on their way with stories of gold further on. There was treachery and cruelty on both sides. There was skirmish after skirmish in which men of both races were killed. The one great battle was at Mauvilla (spelled several ways) when de Soto and the Spaniards met Tuscaloosa, probably a Choctaw, and his warriors in a mighty slaughter. This was October 18, 1540. The exact site of the battle is not known but the United States De Soto Expedition in 1939 decided it must be somewhere in Clarke County.

The Governor (as de Soto is always called in the four contemporary accounts of the expedition) was invited to visit Tuscaloosa. De Soto was told that he would find "service and obedience, friendship and peace" whenever he chose to pass through Tuscaloosa's territories. Instead, he met rebellion and disaster. The story of the encounter is told by a chronicler known only as the Gentleman of Elvas.

The cacique was at home, in a piazza. Before his dwelling, on a high place, was spread a mat for him, upon which two cushions were placed, one above another, to which he went and sat down, his men placing themselves around, some way removed, so that an open circle was formed about him, the Indians of the highest rank being nearest to his person. One of them shaded him from the sun with a circular umbrella, spread wide, the size of a target, with a small stem, and having deer-skin extended over cross-sticks, quartered with red and white, which at a distance made it look of taffeta, the colors were so very perfect. It formed the standard of the chief, which he carried into battle. His appearance was full of dignity: he was tall of person, muscular, lean, and symmetrical. He was the suzerain of many territories, and of a numerous people, being equally feared by his vassals and the neighboring nations. The master of the camp, after he had spoken to him, advanced with his company, their steeds leaping from side to side, and at times towards the chief, when he, with great gravity, and seemingly with indifference, now and then would raise his eyes, and look on as in contempt.

The Governor approached him, but he made no movement to rise; he took him by the hand, and they went together to seat themselves on the bench that was in the piazza. The cacique addressed him these words:—

POWERFUL CHIEF:
Your lordship is very welcome. With the sight of you I receive as great pleasure and comfort as though you were an own brother whom I dearly loved. It is idle to use many words here, as it is not well to speak at length where a few may suffice. The greater the will the more estimable the deed; and acts are the living witnesses of truth. You shall learn how strong and positive is my will, and how disinterested my inclination to serve you. The gifts you did me the favor to send I esteem in all their value, but most because they were yours. See in what you will command me.

The Governor satisfied the chief with a few brief words of kindness. On leaving he determined, for certain reasons, to take him along. The second day on the road he came to a town called Piache; a great river ran near, and the Governor asked for canoes. The Indians said they had none, but that they could have rafts of cane and dried wood, whereon they might readily enough go over, which they diligently set about making, and soon completed. They managed them; and the water being calm, the Governor and his men easily crossed. . . .

After crossing the river of Piache, a Christian having gone to look after a woman gotten away from him, he had been either captured or killed by the natives, and the Governor pressed the chief to tell what had been done; threatening, that should the man not appear, he would never release him. The cacique sent an Indian thence to Mauilla, the town of a chief, his vassal, whither they were going, stating that he sent to give him notice that he should have provisions in readiness and Indians for loads; but which, as afterwards appeared, was a message for him to get together there all the warriors in his country.

The Governor marched three days, the last one of them continually through an inhabited region, arriving on Monday, the eighteenth day of October, at Mauilla. He rode forward in the vanguard, with fifteen cavalry and thirty infantry, when a Christian he had sent with a message to the cacique, three or four days before, with orders not to be gone long, and to discover the temper of the Indians, came out from the town and reported that they appeared to him to be making preparation; for that while he was present many weapons were brought, and many people came into the town, and work had gone on rapidly to strengthen the palisade. Luis de Moscoso said that, since the Indians were so evil disposed, it would be better to stop in the woods; to which the Governor answered, that he was impatient of sleeping out, and that he would lodge in the town.

Arriving near, the chief came out to receive him, with many Indians singing and playing on flutes, and after tendering his services, gave him three cloaks of marten-skins. The Governor entered the town with the caciques, seven or eight men of his guard, and three or four cavalry, who had dismounted to accompany them; and they seated themselves in a piazza. The cacique of Tastaluça asked the Governor to allow him to remain there, and not to weary him any more with walking; but, finding that was not to be permitted, he changes his plan, and, under pretext of speaking with some of the chiefs, he got up from where he sate, by the side of the Governor, and entered a house where were many Indians with their bows and arrows. The Governor, finding that he did not return, called to him; to which the cacique answered that he would not come out, nor would he leave that town; that if the Governor wished to go in peace, he should quit at once, and not persist in carrying him away by force from his country and its dependencies . . . .

The Governor, presently as he found himself in the field, called for

a horse, and, with some followers, returned and lanced two or three
of the Indians; the rest, going back into the town, shot arrows from
the palisade. Those who would venture on their nimbleness came out a
stone's throw from behind it, to fight, retiring from time to time, when
they were set upon. . . . He and they were all badly wounded: within
the town five Christians were instantly killed. Coming forth, he called
out to all his men to get farther off, because there was much harm doing from the palisade. The natives discovering that the Christians were
retiring, and some, if not the greater number, at more than a walk,
the Indians followed with great boldness, shooting at them, or striking
down such as they could overtake. Those in chains having set down
their burdens near the fence while the Christians were retiring, the
people of Mauilla lifted the loads on to their backs, and, bringing them
into the town, took off their irons, putting bows and arms in their
hands, with which to fight. Thus did the foe come into possession of all
the clothing, pearls, and whatsoever else the Christians had beside,
which was what their Indians carried. Since the natives had been at
peace as far as to that place, some of us, putting our arms in the
luggage, had gone without any; and two, who were in the town, had
their swords and halberds taken from them, and put to use.

The Governor, discovering that if he remained there they could not
escape, and if he should order his men, who were outside of the town,
to come in, the horses might be killed by the Indians from the houses
and great injury done, he ran out; but before he could get away he fell
two or three times, and. . . .

*How the Governor set his men in order of battle and entered the town
of Mauilla.*

So soon as the advance and the rear of the force were come up, the
Governor commanded that all the best armed should dismount, of
which he made four squadrons of footmen. The Indians, observing
how he was going on arranging his men, urged the cacique to leave,
telling him, as was afterwards made known by some women who were
taken in the town, that as he was but one man, and could fight but as
one only, there being many chiefs present very skilful and experienced
in matters of war, any one of whom was able to command the rest, and
as things in war were so subject to fortune, that it was never certain
which side would overcome the other, they wished him to put his person in safety; for if they should conclude their lives there, on which
they had resolved rather than surrender, he would remain to govern
the land: but for all that they said, he did not wish to go, until, from
being continually urged, with fifteen or twenty of his own people he
went out of the town, taking with him a scarlet cloak and other articles
of the Christians' clothing, being whatever he could carry and that
seemed best to him.

The Governor, informed that the Indians were leaving the town,
commanded the cavalry to surround it; and into each squadron of foot

he put a soldier, with a brand, to set fire to the houses, that the Indians might have no shelter. His men being placed in full concert, he ordered an arquebuse to be shot off: at the signal the four squadrons, at their proper points, commenced a furious onset, and, both sides severely suffering, the Christians entered the town. The friar, the priest, and the rest who were with them in the house, were all saved, though at the cost of the lives of two brave and very able men who went thither to their rescue. The Indians fought with so great spirit that they many times drove our people back out of the town. The struggle lasted so long that many Christians, weary and very thirsty, went to drink at a pond near by, tinged with the blood of the killed, and returned to the combat. The Governor, witnessing this, with those who followed him in the returning charge of the footmen, entered the town on horseback, which gave opportunity to fire the dwellings; then breaking in upon the Indians and beating them down, they fled out of the place, the cavalry and infantry driving them back through the gates, where, losing the hope of escape, they fought valiantly; and the Christians getting among them with cutlasses, they found themselves met on all sides by their strokes, when many, dashing headlong into the flaming houses, were smothered, and, heaped one upon another, burned to death.————
The Narrative of the Expedition of Hernando de Soto by the Gentleman of Elvas, edited by Theodore H. Lewis, *Spanish Explorers in the Southern United States, 1528–1543* (New York: Charles Scribners Sons, 1907), pp. 187–91.

It is generally accepted that de Soto and the Spanish won, but the price of victory was high. The Gentleman of Elvas says that around two thousand five hundred perished, eighteen of this number being Spaniards. The slain included a brother-in-law and a nephew of de Soto and other men of "condition and courage." The wounded ran into hundreds. The material things lost by the Spanish in the fire were their clothing, the ornaments for saying mass, and the pearls—the one treasure they had gathered in all their wanderings. There is no further word about Tuscaloosa, who may have also perished.

Instead of going on to meet the waiting ships at Pensacola, de Soto turned northwestward and eventually died of fever and was buried in the Mississippi River.

After de Soto there were other Spanish interests in Alabama. Philip II believed that if he could plant a colony on Mobile Bay, he would be able to protect the galleons loaded with treasure from Peru and Mexico. Consequently he ordered the viceroy of Mexico, Don Luis Velasco, to send an exploring party into the area; Guido de los Bazares was the leader. He reported that his explorations of the Bay and Tensas River area proved that the region was suited admirably for a settlement. The soil was rich; there was some native stone and more clay suitable for making brick; the native plants would provide food for people and grazing for the animals; and there was abundant game, from birds to deer. Tristan de Luna, who was chosen to head the actual settlement, learned to his sorrow that Bazares spoke in hyperbole.

It would appear that this attempt at colony-making had good chance of success. Tristan, having spent nearly thirty years in the New World with Cortez and Coronado, was a seasoned *Conquistador;* he had several near relatives who were leading officials in Mexico and Central America; he was a close friend to Luis de Moscoso, who had led de Soto's bedraggled army back to New Spain and who had given him a copy of his report of the journey through the southeast. He also had other help: three, and possibly more, of the priests (all Dominicans) had been in "Florida" before. Tristan certainly knew the realities of exploring and colonizing. He had considerable wealth (much of which came from his wife, who had inherited immense property from two earlier husbands) and the enthusiastic backing of Viceroy Velasco, who appointed him in a ceremony of "medieval splendor" and accompanied him to Veracruz to give his departure official blessings.

For the first time the Spanish were making plans for a settlement on the northern shores of the Gulf of Mexico. They came well prepared. Herbert Ingram Priestley described the party that embarked on June 11, 1558.

> There were five hundred cavalry, arquebusiers, shield-bearers, and cross-bowmen, one thousand colonists and servants—men, women, and children, Negro men and women, friendly Indians—and two hundred and forty horses. . . . A full hundred of the faithful beasts were destined to be thrown overboard during the voyage, and much was the grief thereat and great the later need of them. Ample supplies of corn, biscuit, bacon, dried beef, cheese, oil, vinegar, wine, and cattle for breeding were . . . on board. There were tools for building and digging, so as to plant crops; axes and mattocks for the farmers, and "everything else necessary all of which was provided by command of the viceroy entirely."
> ——Herbert I. Priestley, *Tristan de Luna: Conquistador of the Old South* (Glendale, Calif.: Arthur H. Clark Co., 1936), pp. 102–103.

The destination was Achusi, which Priestley assumes to be Pensacola but others are sure it was a village on the eastern side of Mobile Bay. Regardless of the exact location (and the evidence is heavy for Mobile), a severe hurricane which struck on August 19 destroyed much of the fleet, food, and equipment even before the party had unloaded. The Spaniards looked at the results of the storm in disbelief; all but three of the ships were snapped from their moorings and sunk or blown ashore. How, they asked, could a vessel be blown inland "the distance of a arquebuse shot" and still be undamaged "without a pin missing"? The sea could not have done it, the good Father Davila Padilla recorded, so it must have been the work of demons. Later witnesses of tropical storms probably would find it easy to agree with him.

The storm was but a foretaste of the tragedy and failure that would follow. Nothing went right. The climate was bad and many came down with fever; the death toll was high. Tristan survived but for long priods of time he acted so irresponsibly that his captains feared his illness had done lasting brain damage. His decisions were often irrational and ill-advised and yet he would fly into a rage when his captains suggested he was too ill to continue in command.

Starvation proved to be their greatest enemy. The supplies they had brought for the first months were lost, therefore they had to live off the land. This was not easy to do. The Indians never had large surpluses and the avaible food in the Bay area was soon exhausted. Someone remembered that the de Soto party had found abundant food up the river. After bitter disagreement, which became characteristic, two hundred soldiers under Mateo del Sauz were dispatched to spend the winter at Nanipacana, a village near present day Claiborne. Eventually de Luna sent most of the people into the interior, many of them going as far as the place now called Childersburg, keeping only about sixty soldiers and some Negro slaves on the coast waiting for the expected relief ships. The Indians, while at first friendly, soon exhausted their supplies; the captains, the soldiers, the priests all quarreled with each other and with Tristan, who refused to honor their demands that the project be abandoned and the survivors be allowed to return to Mexico. On January 30, 1561, Velasco replied to Luna:

. . . In view of what you and the religious, the maestre de campo, and the captains write me, and understanding the dissensions, passions, and lack of conformity which have existed and still prevail between you and them, the little accomplishment effected by the expedition or to be expected from it, and the great amount which his Majesty has spent upon it; considering all this, and also the lack of health which you have experienced, and the desire which you express in one of your letters to get out of the country, it has seemed wise to me, after laying the case before this royal audiencia, the archbishop, the treasury officials of his Majesty, and certain other gentlemen and principal persons, to send you license to make the journey to Spain to give account to his Majesty of what has happened, or to come to this country to choose whatever may seem best to you.——Priestley, *Tristan de Luna,* p. 181, quoting an unidentified passage from *The Luna Papers.*

In April 1561, after nearly two years of agonizing effort to survive, de Luna's party sailed out of the bay, defeated chiefly because they had not solved the supply problem.

A few more Spaniards would visit Alabama but the de Luna fiasco was the only serious Spanish attempt to plant a colony in Alabama. It failed and consequently the first lasting settlement on our shores was not Spanish but French.

The French Period 1699–1763

It is a well-known fact in early American history that French interest in the Gulf of Mexico area predated the founding of Mobile in 1702. Some twenty years earlier (1678), Robert Cavalier of Rouen, known to history as LaSalle, ventured down the Mississippi River to its mouth, where he planted a standard, claiming for Louis XIV all the land drained by the river and its tributaries. He returned upstream to Canada convinced that this mighty river could become an important artery of French trade. Leaving Henri de Tonty (the "man with the iron hand") as his deputy in America, LaSalle returned to France to obtain official help for an expedition by water to the mouth of the Mississippi. Delayed by international complications, he did not start his return until 1685. For reasons not understood at the time, he missed the mouth of the river and landed on the Texas coast near Matagorda Bay. Having lost his ships and plagued by desertions, La Salle and a few of his followers set out for Canada on foot. They had not gone far when one of his men assassinated him. Thus ended the first French attempt to locate on the Gulf Coast.

The responsibility and honor of creating a colony fell to the Le Moyne family, native Canadians, some of whom had already distinguished themselves in the wars against the English. Count Maurapas, Minister of Marine to Louis XIV, in looking for ways to thwart the expansion of the English in America, determined to renew LaSalle's project of planting a settlement near the mouth of the Mississippi. To lead the new venture, he chose Pierre d' Iberville, who had seen active service at Hudson bay and Newfoundland. He was the eldest of four brothers who played important roles in the Biloxi-Mobile colony. Of these Bienville is the best known in Alabama because he served as governor after the death of Iberville and on three subsequent occasions.

Louis XIV favored the project and gave orders, often impossible to carry out, for the men to depart in a very short time. The actual work of equipping the expedition was turned over to Michel Régon; the ships were the *Badine* and the *Marin*. Iberville commanded the first and Bienville the second. At last, after many delays, on October 24, 1698, Iberville set out; on December 4 he was off the coast of Santo Domingo. After a stop for refreshment and revictualing, the expedition headed for Cuba before turning north to the American mainland. On January 26, 1699, the ships anchored off Pensacola Bay. There, to their surprise because they were on the alert for the English, they found two Spanish ships moored. The next day, Iberville sent one of his lieutenants ashore under the pretext of obtaining water and fuel to assess the situation. The Spanish, they discovered, had begun the fort (for it was little more than that) two years earlier and, while they seemed to hold it in contempt, they let the French know they had no intention of handing it over to them. Thereafter, the French, while wary of their European rivals, took great pains to cultivate cordial relations with the Spanish commandant.

Their next stop was at the mouth of Mobile Bay on January 31. Iberville took careful soundings the next two days before risking his large ships in the uncertain waters around Dauphin Island. However, the second night he spent on shore along with his brother Bienville and Sauvole, who would become the first royal governor of Louisiana but would succumb to yellow fever in 1701. Two days of intermittent heavy rains and high winds forced them to return to Dauphin Island (which Iberville had named Massacre Island because of the some sixty skeletons he had found there); but the skies having cleared, the Le Moyne brothers crossed over to Cedar Point on February 3. After going north about twelve miles Iberville climbed a big oak tree for a better view of the bay. He liked what he saw—fertile land with an abundance of oak, pine, and other trees of prodigious size and a large river flowing in from the north. Nevertheless, he was disappointed to find that the water was too shallow for his ships to enter. Therefore, he turned west and built his fort on Biloxi Bay. Three years later he decided to move it to Mobile, where he had better contact, via the rivers, with the interior.

One of several skilled workmen in that first settlement was a master carpenter by the name of Penicaut, whose Christian name very likely was André. He was present when the settlement was moved to Mobile.

> After we had rested for a week, M. d'Hyberville had two longboats loaded with provisions and took thirty men and one pilot with him, and we went to take soundings off Isle Massacre, following up M. de Sauvol's report to him that a good anchorage for ships would be found there. This was in fact found to be true. At the east end of Isle Massacre, where there is a small island off shore forming a crescent-shaped harbor, thirty ships could be sheltered. In getting in, one runs right along the ground, all mud, of Isle of Massacre. The channel to it and all adjacent waters were sounded and found to be good. We then went from

Isle Massacre to a bay five leagues wide that is only two leagues distant from Isle Massacre. We entered this bay and went as far as a river that is nine leagues up into the headwaters of the bay, into which it empties. We ascended it for one league and found a river that empties into it on the left side, and a league farther, still another river that also empties into it. The first river we got to we named Riviere St. Martin and the second Riviere-a-Boutin.

Twelve leagues upstream we found a settlement of savages named the Mobilients. They were not surprised at seeing us, because they had already learned that we had built a fort at Biloxi. They wanted to make preparations to sing the calumet of peace to M. d'Hyberville, but he told them that for the moment he did not have time to stop. He gave them several presents, anyhow, and left next day to go back down the Riviere de la Mobile. He took one of their chiefs with him to show him a spot on high ground, six leagues below their vallage on the right side going downstream. He told the chief he would order a fort to be built here and would have all the French come here to live. We then went down the river to the bay. On our way back to Fort Biloxi, two leagues from the Riviere de la Mobile we found a stream named Riviere-aux-Chiens; one league below, on the right, we found another named Riviere-aux-Chevreuils; and still a third, two leagues from Riviere-aux-Chevreuils, which we called Riviere-aux-Poulles. From there we went directly to our fort, where the illnesses were becoming frequent on account of the summer heat. This compelled M. d'Hyberville to speed up the construction of the fort on the Mobile. . . .

After the departure of M. d'Hyberville, M. de Boisbrian took sixty men and left for the Mobile to erect the fort on the spot that M. d'Hyberville had marked before his departure. During this time, M. de Sauvol, the commandant at Biloxi, who had fallen sick, died there.

M. de Bienville, who was with M. de St. Denis at the fort on the bank of the Missicipy, came down to see and took over the command of Fort Biloxi in the place of M. de Sauvol; and noticing that lack of water was the cause of the illnesses, he worked as fast as possible to move all the merchandise and the munitions from Fort Biloxi to the fort on the Mobile, where M. de Boisbrian, who was there, had already got the fort and the warehouses ready to hold everything securely. M. de Bienville then came to the Mobile and had the work on the fort concluded, both on the lodging for the *habitans* and on the fortifications.

This fort was sixty toises square. At each of the four corners there was a battery of six pieces of cannon which, protruding outside in a half circle, covered the sector in front and to right and left. Inside, within the curtains, were four fronts of buildings fifteen feet back from the curtains behind them. These buildings were to be used as chapel, as quarters for the commandant and the officers, as warehouses, as guardhouse. So, in the midst of these buildings there was a *place d'armes* forty-five toises square. Barracks for the soldiers and the Canadians were built outside the fort, to the left, one hundred and fifty steps away, on the bank of the Riviere de la Mobile. During the winter we were kept busy putting the finishing touches to all these buildings.——*Fleur de Lys and Calumet: Being the Penicaut Narrative of French Adventure in Louisiana,* Translated and edited by Richebourg Gaillard McWilliams (Baton Rouge, La.: Louisiana State University Press, 1953), pp. 56–59.

Two years later, Sieur de LaSalle who, Dunbar Rowland says, was the nephew of the great explorer, reported on the physical condition of the new colony. In taking the 1704 census La Salle says he was "performing the function of Commissary of the Navy" by order of the king.

Census of Louisiana by Nicholas de La Salle

Enumeration of everything, and the state in which the colony of Louisiana is at present according to the census of it that has been made by Sieur de La Salle, by order of the King performing the function of Commissary of the Navy.

FIRST, BUILDINGS BELONGING TO THE KING

The fort has four bastions in keeping with the plan sent by Sieur Le Vasseur in which there are mounted sixteen iron cannons of twelve and eight pounds calibre.

A house sixty-eight feet long by sixteen wide of one story of dressed timber laid piece on piece with a roof of framework covered with shingles and a gallery from one end to the other on the side of the river.

A storehouse forty feet long by sixteen wide covered with shingles.

Another house serving as a church, sixty-two feet long by sixteen wide of framework covered with shingles.

A guard-house forty feet long by sixteen wide of one story covered with shingles and of framework, two-thirds serving as a storeroom for arms and ammunition.

A shop for the forge in the town covered with palmetto leaves which are a kind of leaf as broad as a fan.

A shop for gunsmithery in the town with the same covering as above for the forge.

A little shop of piles standing on end in the town that serves for the laying-up of barks and other small vessels.

A hall to make bricks in the town with a kiln adjoining it. Barks, ship's boats and pirogues.

Two barks of fifty tons with everything that concerns the armament. One bark of fifty tons that has been in the ship-yard for nearly three years. It is only necessary to sheathe it to put it in condition. The rigging and sails have been sent from France on the ship the *Loire.* Three ship's boats one of which is a felucca. Seven wooden pirogues.

Number of the People Including the Garrison

One hundred and eighty men bearing arms, all armed with their guns. Twenty-seven French families that have only three little girls and seven young boys from one to ten years of age.

Six young Indian slave boys from twelve to eighteen years of age. Five Indian slave girls from fifteen to twenty years of age.

Cleared Ground in the Neighborhood of Fort Louis

One hundred and ninety arpents of land which form the enclosure of the town.

Eighty wooden houses of one story covered with palmetto leaves or straw, built on the streets laid out in a straight line (p. 470).

Animals of Every Kind

Nine oxen, five of which belong to the King and four to private persons.

Fourteen cows.

Four bulls, one of which belongs to the King.

Five calves.

One hundred pigs, or about that number, including the sows.

Three kids.

Four hundred hens.

Done at Fort Louis of Louisiana on the thirty-first of August, 1704.

                             de La Salle.

Endorsed: Number 10.

Mississippi Provincial Archives, 1701–1729, French Dominion, Dunbar Rowland and Albert G. Sanders, eds. (Jackson, Miss.: Mississippi Department of Archives and History, 1929), vol. 2, pp. 18–20.

The fort and surrounding settlements that Penicaut and La Salle are describing were not on the site of Mobile on the bay. Commonly called Fort Louis de la Mobile but later abbreviated to merely La Mobile, it was where Twenty-Seven Mile Bluff near Mount Vernon is at a later date. It has been described as the first "modern" French American city because it was not walled.

The new settlement had many difficulties. There were warring Indians whom the officers tried to bring to terms, Frenchmen killed on expeditions into the interior, sickness caused by the hot climate, shortages of food which sometimes were relieved by sending hunting parties among the Indians, at other times by borrowing supplies from the Spanish in Pensacola and by shiploads from the homeland. There was dissatisfaction but it was not until an unusual flood that threatened to wash away the site that D'Artaguette, commandant of Mobile, and Bienville, governor for the third time, decided to move the fortification to higher ground on the site of the modern city of Mobile. Penicaut tells the circumstances of 1709 which persuaded them. The removal was completed by 1711.

At the beginning of this year, Fort Mobile and the resident's settlement near the fort were so inundated by the overflow of the river that only high places were without damage.

MM. Dartaguet and de Bienville, seeing that, according to the accounts given them by the savages, we should often be in danger of such floods, decided to move Fort Mobile. They choose a place where we had located the Chaqtos savages—at the cove on Baye de la Mobile, on the right. The savages whose grounds we were taking were given another place to live, two leagues below on our right side going down to the sea, on the bank of Riviere-aux-Chiens.

M. Paillous, assistant adjutant, went with our officers to this place, where it had been decided to have the fort built. He laid out the outer wall of the fort requisite for the interior and then the distance for the empty spaces of the cleared-off area outside the fort; also, beyond those distances, he assigned to the residents each family's location, giving them each a plot of ground twelve toises wide by twenty-five long. At the same time he marked the place for the soldier's barracks. The residence of the priests was to the left of the fort and faced the sea. Work on this establishment continued through the whole year.

During that time, Mr. La Vigne Voisin, a captain of St. Malo, arrived at Isle Dauphine, where he dropped anchor; then he came to Mobile to call on MM. Dartaguet and de Bienville; and after stopping there for several days he asked them to permit him to have a fort built on Isle Dauphine. This pleased them. He did not fail to have the work started as soon as he got there. At his fort he had embrasures constructed to contain cannon which secured the entrance to the harbor from all ships that might come there with the purpose of making a landing.

Also, at the place where the residents of the island lived, he had a very pretty church built. The front of the church faced the harbor where the ships were, and people in the ships could come there in a moment and hear Mass. This was the reason that habitants of the environs of Mobile went to Isle Dauphine and settled. M. De Vigne returned to France a month later. . . .

The new Fort Mobile on the seashore being finished and the living quarters built, all the furniture and merchandise were moved there in boats. Some raftlike structures were made, on which the cannon were put and, in general, all supplies and effects that were at the old fort.

Likewise, the residents carried their possessions at the same time to the dwelling place that had been given them very close to the new fort; and the old one was entirely abandoned. Several days after we were well established at our new fort on the seashore, a ship came and anchored at the Isle Dauphine roadstead. This was the frigate named *La Renommee,* commanded by M. de Remonville, who was captain of it.

The Sieur de Waligny, an officer who had been a post adjutant from his youth, had come in that ship, bringing twenty-five Frenchmen to add to the garrison.

The munitions and food supplies were unloaded and stored in the warehouses in the fort on Isle Dauphine, and troops assigned to guard

them. Also, many people came and settled on the island. Something of
a little town developed, as all the free persons settled there who came
in the ships from France.———Penicaut, *Fleur de Lys and Calumet,* pp.
128–129, 132–133.

The new settlement was systematically planned and mapped
before the end of 1711.

DESCRIPTION OF THE CITY AND OF THE FORT LOUIS

Fort Louis, fortified with an exterior length from one point of bastion
to another 90 toises, and with this length they have given to the faces
of the bastion 23½ toises, to flanks 12½, to gorges 5 toises and to the
curtain 40 toises.

The fort is constructed of cedar stakes 13 ft. high, of which 2½ are
in the ground, and 14 inches square *de paisseur,* planted joined the one
to the other. These stakes end on top in points like palisades. On the
inside along the stakes runs a kind of banquette in good slope, two
feet high and one and a half wide.

There is in the fort only the governor's house, the *magasin* where
are the king's effects, and a guard-house. The officers, soldiers, and
residents have their abode outside the fort, as is indicated, being placed
in such manner that the streets are six toises wide and all parallel. The
blocks are 50 toises square except those opposite the fort, which are
60 toises wide and 50 deep, and those nearest the river, which are 50
toises wide and 60 deep.

The houses are constructed of cedar and pine upon a foundation of
wooden stakes which project out of the ground one foot and might be
called piling, because this soil is inundated, as you see marked on the
plan, in certain localities, in times of rain. Some people use to support
their houses stone which is kind of turf, very soft, and would be admirable for fine buildings. This stone is found 18 leagues above the new
establishment along the bank of the Mobile river. The houses are 18,
20, to 25 feet high or more, some lower, construction of a kind of
plaster (mortier) made of earth and lime. . . .

They give to all who wish to settle in this place land 12½ toises wide,
facing a street, by 25 deep.

The stone used to support the houses is scarce and not common for
lack of the means of water transportation, such as flat-boats, which
do not exist, nor are there persons who wish to go to the expense (of
building them). This would be a great aid, for those whose houses rest
only on wooden stakes are obliged to renew them every three or four
years, because they decay in the ground.———The map and translation
appear in Peter Hamilton, *Colonial Mobile* (Mobile, Alabama: First
National Bank of Mobile, 1952), pp. 86–87.

CHANGES IN MANAGEMENT

Louisiana, of which Alabama was a part, had been founded as a
royal colony. Louis XIV, under the influence of his great finance

minister, Jean Baptiste Colbert, believed that colonies that supplemented the economy of the mother country were in keeping with good mercantilist theories. Settlements along the Gulf of Mexico would produce semitropical goods, provide bases for expeditions into the interior in search of precious metals, serve as centers for trade with the Indians, and hinder the expansion of France's rivals, England and Spain.

In spite of the king's personal interest and the expenditure of thousands of livres, the new colony did not prosper. Louis, growing old (he died in 1715 after reigning for seventy-two years) and needing money, decided to lease the province, apparently to the highest bidder. Antoine Crozat, a wealthy merchant, became the new proprietor. Although his lease was for fifteen years, he kept it for only five, from 1712 to 1717. His domain included the southern regions but not the Illinois country or Canada. Cadillac replaced Bienville as governor. Penicaut witnessed his arrival on June 5, 1713.

Toward the beginning of this year, M. de la Mothe de Cadillac and M. Durigoüin arrived at Isle Dauphine, the first to serve as Governor-General of Louisiana and the second as director-general, their expenses paid by M. de Croisat, to whom His Majesty had ceded the commerce of Louisiana. They came on the ship named *Le Baron de la Fosse,* of which M. de la Jonquière was captain. On this ship, too, came M. Duclos as commissary-general. M. de la Mothe brought his wife with him, his sons and his daughters, with their servants. There were also twenty-five Breton girls, who had come of their own accord, and, in addition, a great supply of munitions and food, together with a great deal of merchandise, which M. Durigoüin, who was in charge of it, ordered to be stored both in the warehouses of Isle Dauphine and in those at Mobile.

M. de la Mothe had M. de Croisat's instructions to send detachments out both in the direction of the Spaniards, to sound them out over trade, and in the direction of the Illinois, to discover mines; and a few days after his arrival he sent M. de Jonquière, the captain of the ship, with M. Durigoüin, the director, to Vera Cruz among the Spaniards to trade the goods he had brought from France for livestock, which we badly needed. But the Governor of Vera Cruz would not even hear of any trade; he merely had M. de la Jonquière given some food supplies and some livestock, which he sent to his ship out at the roadstead, along with the order to set sail immediately and go home.

During this time M. de St. Denis, who was a very courageous officer and venturesome man on war parties as well as in the discovery of mines, was summoned down to Mobile by M. de la Mothe. When he got there, M. de la Mothe engaged him to go to the Nassitoches and from the Nassitoches by land to Mexico among the Spaniards to sound out the freedom of trade in that direction. M. de la Mothe made a contract with him in the name of the Company to stock him with ten thousand livres' worth of merchandise. We loaded five boats with it. He took also a passport from M. de la Mothe and twenty-two Frenchmen, of whom I was one. After he had embraced M. de la Mothe and M. Duclos, we got in our boats and rowed as far as Biloxi, where M. de St. Denis lived.—*Fleur de Lys and Calumet,* pp. 143–145.

The purpose of the new management (which seems never to have been called anything but The Company) was to make money. To that end, Cadillac had instructions to open up trade with the Spanish at Veracruz, Havana, and other ports, to encourage trade with the Indians, to search for mines, and to encourage immigration in order to increase the population to more than the estimated four hundred Frenchmen in the area. Duclos, the commissary general at Mobile, reported to Pontchartrain that there were no more than thirty-five heads of families in the Mobile–Dauphin Island settlements when he arrived in 1713.

Duclos, who appears to have been a realist, seems to have had a better understanding than did some of his contemporaries of the time it would take to make the venture pay.

I shall give warning . . . that the Company must not count at all on large returns from these goods for more than five or six years and especially on the silk even though the mulberry trees that are here in great numbers scattered in all directions. . . . It takes time to assemble and grow these mulberry trees and . . . to become acquainted with work of this sort . . .——Duclos to Pontchartrain, 1713, *Mississippi Provincial Archives,* vol. 2, p. 102.

Cadillac, the governor under Crozat, had served his country in Canada where he had, among other things, founded Detroit in 1701. Therefore he knew something about settlements in the wilderness. Nevertheless, his administration in Louisiana was a failure. His grandiose plans of trade with Spanish colonies came to naught; the authorities refused to break their own mercantile system to admit foreign goods and consequently sent several shipments back. The expeditions to the Red River and Mexico resulted in more geographical knowledge than commerce.

In the field of Indian affairs the Crozat period seems to have been fairly successful. The Indians were friendly and the French at Mobile cultivated good relations by building a fort named Toulouse (named for Crozat's native city), near the junction of the Coosa and Tallapoosa Rivers, not far from the modern city of Wetumpka, in an area long inhabited by the Alabamos. The "emperor" of the Alabamos and other head men, so the story goes, went to Mobile to invite the French to establish a post in their midst and promised, according to Bossu, to build the fort at their own expense. Bienville, second in command while Cadillac was on an extensive tour up the Mississippi, sent Captain de la Tour to carry out their request. The first commander was Marigny de Mandeville. The exact date has been the subject of much debate but very likely it was 1717. The fort and garrison, while never strong, would continue as a focal point of French trade and influence until the *fleur de lis* was pulled down in 1763.

The English in the Carolinas considered the fort an intrusion into their territory. Traders out of Charleston had been dealing with the Indians as far west as the Mississippi River since well before 1690 and did not take lightly the attempts of the French to gain control of their trade.

The French and the English agreed that the fort was important. At the time of its founding the French stocked it with ample supplies and provided adequate quarters for officers and troops because it was the corridor leading to and from Carolina. A French officer (nephew of Bienville) saw Fort Toulouse as the "key to the country." However, to Governor James Glen of South Carolina it was "an eyesore" to his province, a "thorn in the flesh." Besides being an encroachment on English territory (as the English insisted), the *fleur de lis* flag was the symbol of a foreign power being flaunted in their faces. It was the center of influence among the powerful, independent (or fickle, depending on the point of view) warlike tribes which seemed to be willing to sell their allegiance to the highest bidder. This fear is expressed again and again in the correspondence of the South Carolina governors. For example, in 1740 William Bull wrote to the Board of Trade of his concern "for the dangers that threaten this province by means of the powerful interest and influence the French have among the Indians." James Glen saw Fort Alabama as giving the enemy "a footing among those people and has emboldened them to demand of the Indians that they drive away the English traders."

It has been commonly accepted that the French had more finesse in dealing with the Indians than did the English. This may be true, but in trade the French considered their rivals superior and copied their methods and even their exchange rates.

At a somewhat later date, Bienville reported at length about the terms the Indians demanded.

Sieur Benoit informs me further that the Alabama Indians persist in asking for trade on the same terms that the English offer them, in consideration for which they promise to have no dealings with them and not to permit them to make any settlement on their territory. This officer adds that if we continue to refuse them this request, it is to be feared that these Indians may become alienated from our interests. The consideration that he causes me to give to the necessity of retaining the nations for ourselves, and the comparison that Mr. De Salmon and I have made of the proposed trade with that which has been in use until the present cause us to consent to their demand.

The English divide deerskins into three classes; large, medium and small. The large ones must weigh at least two pounds; the medium from one pound and a quarter to two pounds; and the small ones less than one pound and a quarter. They receive the medium ones only at the rate of two for one, and the small ones at the rate of three for one, but they receive very little of these last, which are of little use.

An ell and a half of limburg cloth, which here costs the King twelve livres, will be sold for five large skins or ten medium sized which at thirty sous a pound will bring at least fifteen livres at the rate at which they are sold today. Blankets of white wool are sold at the same rate. Guns that cost the store eleven livres are sold by the English for ten large skins, and a trade shirt that costs the store three livres will be sold for two large skins. There will be the same profit on the other small goods, and everything carefully considered, if your Lordship is so good as to order that there be sent to us limburg cloth of an inferior quality of the sort that we have had the honor to ask of him, inasmuch as at the present rates the costs absorb the profit on this sort of goods, I think that this manner of trading will be almost as advantageous to those who engage in it as that which has been in practice until the present, for it must be noticed that as there is no reference in our trading tariff to the weight of the skins but only to the number, the Indians carry the large ones to the English and the tariff can be accepted only at the rate of three for one large one, so that the twelve skins which the French received for an ell and a half of limburg cloth did not weigh ten to twelve pounds, the price of which was lower considering the difference in quality.

I think then that we can, without fearing that we will make our trade decline, grant the request that the Alabamas are making of us in this respect. I have even, before deciding upon it, consulted several traders who seemed to me to be convinced that they would find almost the same advantages in it, because the Indians would no longer carry their large skins to the English, and the colony will find its security in it by making the Indians more loyal to itself. By this means we shall drive away the English, who no longer having any hope of commerce with this nation, will find more difficulty in establishing themselves in it.
——*Mississippi Provincial Archives, French Dominion,* Vol. 2, pp. 261–62.

Relations between Cadillac and Bienville were not cordial. Cadillac found little to praise in the colony: the country was unproductive, there was no building stone near Mobile, the Canadians in the province were an unruly lot, there was a perpetual shortage of supplies, the mines were a myth, and the people in general were irreligious. Apparently the authorities in Paris wearied of his jeremiads and in March, 1716 they recalled him home. The next year Crozat, seeing no future gain, turned Louisiana back to the king. While it appeared that little progress had been made in the five years, the population had almost doubled and in 1717 numbered around seven hundred. Within a short time, however, it became the proprietary of John Law, who organized a joint stock company called variously the Western Company, the Company of the Indies, and the Mississippi Company.

Law is one of the most colorful figures associated with our early history; he has been classed as one of the greatest promoters of all times. "Scotch gambler, outlaw from England, introducer of the game of faro, French banker, intimate of the notorious regent, the Duke of Orleans, head of the Mississippi Bubble, outlaw again, then a wanderer on the face of the earth until his death"—thus Peter Hamilton described him.

In the beginning it appeared that Law may have had long-range rather than immediate plans for developing Louisiana into a paying plantation. He appointed Bienville governor and emphasized agriculture (which Bienville had tried to do earlier) so that the settlers could at least feed themselves. He advertised for settlers and imported slaves for a dependable labor supply and sought for marketable products. But in the end he tried to do too much in too short a time. The company became more and more speculative and the "Mississippi Bubble," as it was called, "burst" leaving a trail of ruined creditors across Europe. Claiborne says this company lost 20 million livres.

For Alabama, however, the Law period was not without some results. The population increased considerably, and slavery had become an established institution. Certain semitropical fruits like figs and oranges were grown in the Bay area. The capital was moved from Mobile to New Orleans in 1722.

After Law's company surrendered the province in 1732, Louisiana was a royal province until France lost all her claims in America in 1763. Bienville would continue as governor.

Under the French system, the governor had a number of other royal officials like the commissaries general, the commandants, and members of the administrative council, but there was no popular government. Government was for, but not by, the people.

CASSETTE GIRLS

There was a shortage of women in Mobile as in every new settlement. Several of the colonists had their wives with them and there were a few servant girls but never many young women for the single men, many of them Canadians. To encourage permanent

homes and to discourage alliances with Indian women, the French
sent several shiploads of marriageable young women to Fort Louis.
The first, the famous *Cassette* girls, came in 1704, but there were
others later. A shipload of them arrived in 1728 but few of them
stayed in Mobile; there were greater opportunities for them in
New Orleans. Pontchartrain, Minister of Marine and Colonies,
wrote Bienville from Versailles that he was sending these young
women as a part of the "regular assistance" to the colony.

> The King is sending to Louisiana the vessel *Pelican* commanded by
> Sieur Ducoudray, a captain of artillery, who is bringing you the regular
> assistance of the colony. Mr. Begon will send you the statements of it
> by the same vessel. It will be necessary for you to see to it that all of
> it that is put ashore is put in a place of safety and employed according
> to the purpose for which it was intended. By this same ship his
> Majesty is sending twenty girls to be married to the Canadians and
> others who have begun to make themselevs homes on the Mobile in
> order that the colony may be firmly established. All these girls have
> been brought up in virtue and piety and know how to work. This will
> make them very useful to this colony by showing the daughters of the
> Indians what they can do, and in order that none at all may be sent
> except those of recognized and irreproachable virtue his Majesty has
> directed the Bishop of Quebec to obtain them from places that cannot
> be suspected of any dissoluteness. You will be careful to establish them
> as best you can and to marry them off to men capable of supporting
> them with some sort of comfort. By the same vessel his Majesty is send-
> ing a midwife with the wages of four hundred livres per year and some
> workmen of different occupations who can teach their trades not only
> to the French but also to the Indians, and in order to work on his
> Majesty's works. It is necessary that you distribute them in such a way
> that they may be employed usefully according to his intentions. He is
> also sending you two companies of soldiers of fifty men each to guard
> the fort of Mobile and to serve in the enterprises that will be carried
> out for his Majesty's service. . . .——Pontchartrain to Bienville, Jan-
> uary 30, 1704, *Mississippi Provincial Archives,* Dunbar Rowland, ed.
> (Jackson, Miss.: Department of Archives and History, 1932) vol. 3,
> pp. 15–16.

Writers of song and story have reveled in spinning romances
about the arrival of these young women. The historian, however,
has to be content with a single entry in Penicaut's narrative.

> In fourteen days we reached Fort Mobile, where we found a ship
> that had arrived from France bringing us food supplies. This ship,
> named *Le Pelican,* was under the command of M. du Coudray. He had
> brought twenty-six girls from France. These were the first ones that
> came to Louisiana. They were quite well behaved, and so they had
> no trouble finding husbands. They were in the care of a priest named M.

Huet, who remained in Louisiana as much to instruct the French as to convert the savages.——Penicaut, *Fleur de Lys and Calumet,* pp. 96–97.

The only enlightening detail about them as people is that they objected to a diet of corn bread and threatened to rebel!

In addition to the Cassette girls there was a shipload of German women, one of whom was reputed to have been a Russian-born princess whose story lightens the somewhat drab picture of early Alabama.

She came to Alabama about 1721. When a shipload of German immigrants docked at Mobile, a sad-faced, royally-dressed woman stepped ashore and introduced herself as the daughter of Wolfenbuttel, Duke of Brunswick. But she had not come as a royal visitor, she explained, she had come as a refugee, for she was also the disowned wife of Czarowitz Alexis Petrowitz, a Russian prince, and she had come to the New World to escape his persecution.

Having already heard of how the dissolute playboy prince had married and then soon disowned an unfortunate European woman, the French officials did not find it too difficult to understand her flight to America. But they questioned her story, for according to international rumors the unfortunate woman had died. How was it then that this woman could claim to be the princess? Had she returned from the grave?

"Not really from the grave," she replied, "but from the coffin."

According to her explanation, when the cruel prince made her life intolerable she faked symptoms of acute illness for several weeks. When at the opportune time she feigned death, a few of her loyal servants prepared her for burial with much pretended mourning and lamentation. Then while the court made ready for the funeral, those same servants helped her to escape from the coffin and the palace. Slowly she made her way across Europe and obtained passage on the first ship for the New World.

"C'est formidable," muttered the French officials. "How do we know you are tell us the truth?"

A young French officer, the Chevalier D'Aubant, had been staring at the woman. Suddenly he stepped forward. "I'll vouch for her identity," he declared. "As you know, I was once in St. Petersburg and while there I was received in the court. During that reception I met the beautiful princess. So I assure that this woman is indeed the same beautiful princess. Besides, who else but the princess would dare leave Russia with so many of the royal jewels?"

The young Chevalier had eyes for the "princess" (and for the jewels, some said). So after a short courtship he married her and began a marriage that lasted more than forty years. And never once during those years did he doubt that his wife was the Russian princess.

Although seemingly used to the highest luxuries of Europe, the "princess" adapted without complaint to the crude life of the French colonists and devoted all her time (and jewels) to making a good life for the Chevalier. Unafraid of the untamed New World, she often accompanied him on inspection tours of the outposts in the far wilderness.

After he had been sent to faraway Fort Toulouse, she made the long trip up the rivers to join him. There she lived in a comfortable little cabin built especially for her visit. For many years, the Indians talked of the kind white woman who lived near the fort and played games with their children.

Eventually the Chevalier was returned to France. When he died in 1765 she moved to Paris to live with a daughter, their only child. As the remainder of her royal fortune dwindled, her station in life diminished until she was reduced to poverty. She died in 1771.——Ernest Shubird, "Princess or Imposter?" *Birmingham News Magazine,* October 10, 1969.

Historians have never agreed as to who she was, whether a genuine princess or an imposter, but she was a good wife and a colorful figure in a drab wilderness.

THE CHURCH

The French settlers in Louisiana were required to be Roman Catholics. All Protestants, including the Huguenots, were forbidden from emigrating to a French colony. Mobile and other parishes, as they evolved, were under the jurisdiction of the Bishop of Quebec. At the inception of Fort Louis there had been at least two clergymen present, Douge and Davion, the latter ministering regularly. The first curé, la Vente, arrived on the *Pelican.* The oldest known document relating to the Church in Alabama is on page one of the baptismal record of the church in Mobile. This document created a parish and inducted La Vente as its priest.

I, the undersigned priest and missionary apostolic, declare to all whom it may concern, that, the 28th day of September in the year of Salvation 1704, in virtue of letters of provision and collation granted and sealed July 20 of last year, by which Monseigneur, the most illustrious and reverend bishop of Quebec, erects a parochial church in the place called Fort Louis of Louisiane, and of which he gives the cure and care to M. Henri Roulleauz De la Vente, a missionary apostolic of the diocese of Bayeus, I have placed the said priest in actual and corporal possession of the said parochial church and of all the rights belonging to it, after having observed the usual and requisite ceremonies, to wit, by entrance into the church, sprinkling of holy water, kissing the high altar, touching the mass book, visiting the most sacred sacrament of the altar, and ringing the bells, which possession I certify that no one has opposed.

Given in the church of Fort Louis the day of month and year above, in the presence of Jean Baptiste de Bienville, lieutenant of the king and commandant of the said fort, Pierre du Q. de Boisbriant, major, Nicolar de la Salle, clerk and performing function of commissary of the marine.

(Signed) DAVION, BIENVILLE, BOISBRIANT, DE LA SALLE.
——quoted in Peter Hamilton, *Colonial Mobile* (1952), pp. 67–68.

Sieur de la Vente did not find his parish easy. Part of his trouble lay in his quarrel with the governor, described in the following report written by la Vente to Pontchartrain.

The missionaries who are at Mobile all ask to return because Sieur de Bienville, instead of helping them, opposes them in everything that he can, causes them difficulties, makes them odious to everybody, has riotous assemblies against them held at night, has petitions drawn up in them in which they are calumniated, refuses them all justice and persecutes those who are attached to them.

The said Sieur de Bienville has prevented Sieur de La Vente from embarking in order to come and render an account of his conduct under the pretext that he could not leave without doing a wrong to the colony, however, they could very easily have done without him if he was as incapable and as much hated by the people as he wished to make people believe, so much the more because there are three other priests who could have performed his functions.

The bad treatment that the said Sieur de Bienville gives these priests comes from the fact that they have been obliged to warn him about a too great familiarity that he had with a woman which scandalized the entire colony, and although this woman has died, this commandant has not become pacified in regard to these missionaries. The said Sieur de Bienville has made use of a Jesuit who [has come] from Illinois, in order to hold the position of chaplain of the fort. He has had the salary given to him and has had him say mass at hours that disturbed the curate in his parochial mass.

The said Sieur de La Vente writes that he interdicted the chapel of the fort only after having several times called the attention of the said Sieur de Bienville to the indecency that there was in celebrating mass in it because it was not closed.

If there is an intention to reestablish the Jesuits in Louisiana, they petition that they be informed of it in order that they may bring back the missionaries whom they have there, but if the intention is that they remain there, they ask in what time the King will send a vessel there in order that they may prepare some missionaries to go and assist those who are there.

It is necessary to issue an ordinance to forbid the French of Mobile from taking Indian women as slaves and especially from living with them under the same roof in concubinage. They say that it is men of this sort who do not receive the Sacrament at Easter and that the missionaries think that they ought not to admit them to it.——*Mississippi Provincial Archives, French Dominion*, vol. 2, pp. 30–31.

MAKING PITCH

In every American colony, the settlers searched for some marketable product that would bring prosperity to it as tobacco had to Virginia. Diron d' Artaguette, who wrote the following letter about the production of pitch, was commandant at Mobile from 1728 to 1738 and lived in the colony even longer.

Mr. De Salmon has done me the honor to write to me to induce the colonists of Mobile to make pitch because the King was taking it at an advantageous price and because half would be paid here and the other half after it had been received at the port of Rochefort. His Majesty could not choose a better way to establish this colony quickly since this is the only profitable return that it can furnish in the present situation. But he informed me in the next place that they would accept only that which could be shipped in the King's vessels; so that those who were preparing to work at it were in part disgusted with it at the prospect of so small a business and of the preference that they imagine persons in favor or in authority will always have. Whereupon I have thought it my duty, my lord, to represent to you for the interest of this post, which for a long time has been languishing in inaction, that neither it nor the others will prosper at all if his Majesty is not so good as to receive this pitch in the colony or to oblige the merchants who come there each to take a certain quantity proportioned to their tonnage in consideration of the forty francs per ton that they have as a subsidy, at least until the exportation of this pitch gives the colonists the means to obtain vessels of their own to transport it to France at their own risk, which would be a matter of at most three or four years if one received what they might produce, without turning aside from the cultivation of the fields. Then the colony would be in a position to support itself and to increase by itself, but I do not think that without that it can make any progress. I have informed Messrs. De Bienville and de Salmon of these ideas and they will not fail to add their sound reflections to them.——Diron d' Artaguette to Pontchartrain, March 25, 1734. *Mississippi Provincial Archives, French Dominion,* vol. 1, p. 248.

There were other economic interests besides farming but most of them were connected with the soil. With the help of slaves the French raised cattle and made the hides into leather; several merchants handled both the import and export trade; soldiers, priests, and others did civilian jobs; and there were also a surprising number of artisans. Charles G. Summersell says that even by 1718 Alabama had

at least one clerk, cooper, musketeer, domestic servant, cook, shoemaker, tobacco worker, carpenter, joiner, tailor, laborer, brewer, locksmith, soldier, wheelwright, baker, miner, wig-maker, surgeon, bookkeeper, weaver, stone-cutter, flax-dresser, paper-maker, vine-dresser, sailor, rope-maker, goldsmith, maker of gold and silver cloth, thatcher, anvil-maker, tile-maker, silk worker, butcher, farrier, miller, "edge-toolmaker," puppet-maker, turner, carter, and coppersmith.——*Alabama History for Schools* (Northport, Ala.: Colonial Press, 1961), p. 93, citing the passenger list of a ship bound for Mobile.

The French period came to an end with the Treaty of Paris in 1763. For half a century the English and French had glared at each other in the Coosa-Tallapoosa valley, each hoping to oust the other. By threats, treaties, conferences, presents, honors, and trade they had wooed the fickle Creek Indians. Historians are inclined to credit the French with greater finesse in maintaining friendship with the savages, but in Alabama, especially around Fort Toulouse, they were little, if any, more successful in this respect than their English rivals.

If there was any drama connected with the French withdrawal from Fort Tombeckbee (which they had established in 1735 in what is now Sumter County), it is unrecorded. When they abandoned Fort Toulouse, however, the French slipped away in the night to save their Creek friends from embarrassment. As a final act of defiance, the officer in charge spiked the cannons, broke off the trunions, and threw all their provisions and military effects into the river. Then they slipped down the bank of the Coosa and embarked for Mobile, to join their fellow countrymen in the surrender to the English.

British West Florida 1763–1783

The fears of the French and the ambitions of the English were fulfilled when by the Treaty of Paris (1763) England received all the French territory east of the Mississippi River (with the exception of the Isle of Orleans) and Spanish Florida in exchange for Cuba, which had been seized during the latter part of the war. For twenty years thereafter much of what is now Alabama was part of British West Florida. It was an eventful period which saw many changes that included the introduction of Anglo-Saxon institutions, growth in population, material progress, and tensions created by a war raging along the eastern seaboard.

English officialdom had only the vaguest knowledge of the extent and nature of their new territory. Therefore, early in May 1763, the Earl of Egremont submitted a number of questions of a practical nature to the Board of Trade, the answers to which would not only enlighten the government but would help in formulating future policies and activities. What, for instance, were the physical assets of soil and climate? Since the French inhabitants had not been accustomed to English law, what kind of government should be established? What should be done about the Indians so recently separated from their allies and who now somehow had to be convinced that George III was their king and the English their allies? These and other questions plagued the officials. Some of them were satisfactorily answered, others not.

The government created two provinces out of the southern district; East Florida included the peninsula and West Florida a strip of land extending from the Appalachicola (Chattahoochee) River westward to the Mississippi River. The thirty-first parallel, set by proclamation on October 7, was the northern boundary. Since no one in London knew much about the area, the line was admittedly arbitrary and temporary. And temporary it was for within a few months (on March 23, 1764) it was moved north to 32° 28′ on a line that ran eastward from the mouth of the Yazoo River on the Mississippi. This would remain the boundary until the end of the British period.

ENGLISH TAKE MOBILE

The Treaty of Paris was signed on February 10, 1763; on the following October 20, Major Robert Farmar, after stops in Jamaica and Pensacola, took possession of Mobile for the English. He reported the event to Egremont.

> I have the honor to inform your Lordship that on the 20th day of October last, with his majesty's 22nd and 34th regiments, I took possession of the fort and town of Mobile, and on the 6th of November detached a subaltern and thirty men in five battoes for Tombeckbay who arrived there on the 22nd and the same day relieved the French troops. . . .
> A corporal and six men I have sent to Island Dauphin to be assisting to the pilot in going off the ships, as the bar is very dangerous, and no inhabitants upon the island.——Farmar to Egremont, January 24, 1764, quoted in Dunbar Rowland, ed., *Mississippi Provincial Archives, English Dominion, 1763–1766* (Jackson, Mississippi: Department of Archives and History, 1911), volume I, pp. 137–138.

Peter Hanibal Develle, Commander of the Port of Mobile and Réne John Gabriel Fezende, Marine Commissary, represented Kerlerec, governor of Louisiana, in handing over the province to Farmar.

Having taken possession of the province, within a few days Major Farmar reported on conditions in Mobile. He found little that pleased him.

> The Fort at Mobille is a Square, with four Bastions nearly regular, of about 90 yards each Front, the Scarp wall is built of Brick and is

about 16 feet in height from the bottom to the Cordon, the Parapet which is also of brick and very thin, is raised about 4½ feet above the Cordon, all of which want new faceing and painting, the bricks being very much wasted, the Embrazures likewise want repairing; under the Rampart of the Curtains of the three Fronts, are small Casemates Arched with brick, but are very much out of repair and let in Rain, the Rampart having been neglected for some time past were all Covered with Long grass and Shrubs that lodged the Rain, which has very much Destroyed the bricks that cover the tops of the Casemates, and that from the Terre plain of the Rampart, but is now cleared away. The front and side walls of the Casemates want new Facing with brick and pointing, besides doors and window Shutters. Some of the Platforms, the Sleepers being rotten want entirely to be new Laid and others to be repaired with Planks.

The powder Magazine wants repairing and new doors.

There are Barracks within the Fort for about 216 men allowing 12 men for each room the whole in very bad repair & wants to be rebuilt, and enlarged by adding another Storry—There is only one officers room besides the Guard room in the Fort, both in very bad repair.

A Bake-House in the Interior part of the North west Bastion, in brick work, and Oven of the same, entirely useless at present.

There is a Covert way and Glascis round the Fort which is faced with brick and Pallisaded some of the Gates very bad and many of the Pallisades rotten, which together with the rest of the works want to be cleared of brush and Cleaned out.

The Officers Barracks are detached from the Fort about 100 yards, and want a good many Repairs the Floors being mostly rotten, as are many of the windows, they are sashed but mostly all the panes broke. ——Ibid., pp. 19–20.

There were two bake houses with only part of the ovens in workable condition. The mill for hulling rice, however, seems to have been in good repair.

A year later, Lord Adam Gordon, an officer in the Sixty-sixth Regiment of Foot, on a tour of America, found conditions little better. However, he did believe the Bay area had greater economic promise than the other southern ports he had seen.

The English early decided to abandon Fort Toulouse but to hold Tombeckbee. Lt. Thomas Ford of the 34th Regiment took it over within a few weeks after Farmar entered Mobile.

I arrived here on Tuesday Morning last about Eleven o'Clock after a verry fateigueing passage of Seventeen days, without the least accident or misfortune, my party being in good health; I surveyed the Fortifications and Buildings the same day, which I found much better than I expected, the Stockade is all whole, but the south Curtain wants a great deal of Reparation, The Powder Magazine is excessively bad, and will never do for the purpose until it is entirely new Built, the Oven,

which is a material Article wants a great deal of Repairing; the Inter-
preters appartment is very bad and must be pulled down and rebuilt,
the Shed which is intended for a Store house, wants a great deal of
Repairs; the Mens Barracks, Guard House, and Prison in very good
Condition. The Grainery and the other Store house Joyning in good
Condition, the building for the Officers in good Condition, the House
out of the Fort, intended for the Savages, in very good Condition, ten
Pieces of Cannon fit for service, but the greatest part very old, all their
Magazine Stores, I have Returned very bad, except those that were
never used, there is three Gates to the Fort, two with Locks and Keys
very bad, therefore hope you will be so good as to send some Strong
ones for the Garrison Gates, the locks that are on, being very difficult
to Lock and Unlock, the Gate that Faces the River is but very weak,
the Land port Gate is very good, the East and South Curtains, stand
upon a Rock, about forty yards in height, the East defended by a River,
and the South by surprising Ditch, the north and west by a fine Campaign Country, cleared for two miles every way; I am happy so far,
they cannot surprise me any way; an addition of Ten men more would
make me very happy, as I should then have ten men for each Bastion:
The Country here on both sides of the River is very well Cleared for
about a large mile quite round the fort. The Indians call'd the Ichactaws
who are all settled here abouts, are full six thousand Strong, they have
a large Town within Musquet Shot of the Fort; the Commandant and
Mr. Baurans have behaved Excessive politely, and gave me all the
information that lay in their power, they give the Chief and his Son a
very bad Character, and not in the least to be depended upon, but
Strongly advise me to keep in with him if possible, as he has great sway
amongst the whole; but he is either out a hunting, or at Mobile.——
Ibid., pp. 22–23.

Until a royally-appointed governor arrived, Robert Farmar was
the highest ranking official in Alabama and performed the duties
that usually fall to one. To implement the terms of the Peace of
Paris, Farmar issued a proclamation to the local inhabitants, which
among other things required that they either take the oath of
allegiance to the English king or leave the province.

Whereas, by a Definitive Treaty of Peace signed the 10th of February
    and ratified the 10th of March 1763, that portion of Louisiana lying
    to the left-hand side, or on the Eastern bank of the Mississippi River,
    from its source to the Iberville River, and across Lakes Maurepas
    and Pontchartrain to the sea, is ceded in full possession to His
    Britannick Majesty.
By these presents it is commanded, and required of all persons
    engaged in the administration of Civil Law, to discontinue all pro-
    ceedings, suits instituted and defended, nor to sue henceforth at law,
    or pleadings, in the form and practice of the Laws of France, the
    present inhabitants having become subject to the Laws of England, by

which they shall be peaceably protected in their rights and properties, and in order that the courts of Justice may suffer no delay or retard, all cases, suits and subjects of complaint shall be submitted in writing to the Commander at Mobile, and all trivial disputes to the Commanding Officer of the Posts nearest the aggrieved parties.

The inhabitants by these presents may rest assured of being protected in their rights and properties, and not at all bothered or inconvenienced in any manner, without grounds, by the Troops, and it is expected that on their part they shall behave likewise towards the Troops, furnishing them with the things they may need and the country produces for which they shall be paid in ready money.

To prevent as far as may be possible all frauds and disputes with reference to purchases or sales of lands and real property, all landed estates shall be recorded within one year of the publication of these presents, and it shall not be at all permissible to dispose of any lands or real property until the titles and tenure to said property can be verified by the recording thereof, and approved by the commanding Officer.

Those among the French inhabitants who shall choose to remain in their diverse abodes and live under the laws of England and His Britannick Majesty's government, as soon as may be possible shall repair to Mobile there to take oath of allegiance. Those who will not at all comply hereunto within three months of the date of these presents shall be dispossessed and compelled to quit this portion of the country ceded to the English Nation. Those complying hereunto shall be protected in their property and their religious rights as stipulated in the peace treaty, they having themselves peacefully, without plotting any designs to the detriment of other subjects of His Britannick Majesty or its government. But whenever it shall be discovered that they are guilty of maliciously prejudicing the Indians to the disadvantage of the English, or act in any manner to their detriment, or should make attempts to overthrow the English government, they shall be proceeded against as rebels.

Those among the inhabitants who shall be possessed of an inclination to quit their present abodes and withdraw from this portion of the country, shall be afforded secure and safe transportation of their chattels as provided by the peace treaty.

These presents shall be read in the Church of each parish by the Rector, or whomsoever should officiate for him, for four consecutive Sundays, and shall be posted on the doors of the Churches and all other public places that no person may plead ignorance thereof.——
Ibid., pp. 61–63.

Of the approximately 350 inhabitants of Mobile when Farmar arrived, only eight had taken the oath by April 1764. Many of the French, fearing for their religion and land, hastily disposed of their possessions and joined their fellow-countrymen in New Orleans. The Spanish regime there they found incompatible, however, and began returning to Mobile. Farmar reported that over a hundred families had come back and taken the oath by the time the governor arrived.

GOVERNOR JOHNSTONE

George Johnstone (1730–1787) was the first royal governor of West Florida. The Scotsman, a native of Dumphries, was a career navy man. Although only in his early thirties when he became governor, Johnstone had already seen action in every part of the world, including the West Indies. He seems to have had a "fiery and tempestuous" nature; he had fought several duels and had acquired a reputation of being overbearing and difficult to get along with.

His appointment, supposedly through the influence of Lord Bute, a fellow Scotsman who was Prime Minister, raised a great furor in the British press. In the verbal battle that ensued, the fitness of Johnstone for the post was seriously questioned. Most of the criticism centered in a publication called *The North Briton*. Johnstone was furious and tried to hunt down the publishers in order to challenge them to a duel. The anonymous editor made fun of the challenge in an open letter to Johnstone.

> I begin to doubt (entre nous) whether a Hyde Park encounter was your real desire. Hum! let me see! A gentleman imagines his character attacked in a public paper on the 17th, writes a challenge to the author on the evening of the 20th, appoints a meeting the very next morning at six; not being met (for I have the charity to suppose he was there) as appointed, returns in violent hurry to the publisher at noon, is told the party did not receive it till after the time; insists on an answer directly, is assured he will certainly have one that day, orders his equipage home, the letter is absolutely sent that very afternoon and yet in so very critical situation, this *Passionate, Injured* gentleman, so tenacious of his honor and so hot for an answer, goes cooly out of town and does not return till *Five Days After!* Indeed, Mr. Johnstone, this tale hangs but clumsily together!——*The North Briton,* no. LXVIII, October 27, 1763.

Johnstone ended up the fiasco with a fist fight with the man he supposed to be the author.

His two years in America were equally stormy; he quarreled with Chief Justice William Clifton over the authority of the Council and with Farmar over the question of civil versus military authority. David Widderburn, commandant at Mobile, wrote of this dispute to his brother, Alexander. The date is April 14, 1765.

I really believe that my coming to Mobile was one of the luckiest things that could have happened to Johnston in the Settlement of his Province: You I fancy never saw the meek, moderate, patient, ill-treated Johnston; and really I could not have believed, that any man, would have submitted so quietly, as he had done, to the treatment, he had met with. I shall not trouble you with a detail of the Mobilian Politickes, as I know you hate long storys, either about Law affairs, or military discipline. Major Farmar who had taken possession of this place when it was ceded by France, continued to act as Governor, 'till Johnston arrived; I am much afraid, it will appear upon an Examination that he had neither acted, so much like a man, an Officer, or a Magistrate, as might have been expected when one of the Kings Field Officers, would not allow him the powers, which he undoubtedly has. He desired Farmar to mark his own line, and that he would be satisfied, 'till dispute was otherwise determined: Farmar not knowing his own powers, gave one point up today, & took it back the next, Said, and unsaid, puzzled, and quibbled 'till every part of civil & military Government, was thrown into a most terrible confusion. *Tantas componere lities,* to settle the line between Civil Authority, and military command, to draw light and precision, out of darkness and confusion, to make anarchy produce Government, was reserved for Your Brother; how he had done this will appear from the Courtmartial at which Johnston will certainly prosecute Major Farmar. I have the pleasure of finding a more ample sanction of my conduct, in some orders, which are arrived from Genl. Gage within these few days; you will think me more a puppy than ever, by this panegyrick upon myself, but I think it will appear less so, when I account for my having carried on my business so perfectly well with Johnston, by saying, that I firmly believe, he & I had one and the same point in view; the prosperity of the colony, and the general good of our Master's Service. It was a difficult situation, I stood in, had I given up the smallest hairsbreadth of military dignity, & Command, which has been supported by old Officers; I should have been much hurt in my military Character: but, I think, I contrived very quietly, and without giving umbrage to the Civil Governor, to carry the point of Command even further than my Predecessor.——Printed in *Alabama Review,* vol. 7, pp. 222–23, original in William R. Clements Library, Michigan State University.

STAMP ACT CRISIS

The climax of Johnstone's troubles, however—the one that he believed ruined his whole administration—was the Stamp Act and the consequences of it. Johnstone recognized the poverty of the colony but considered stamp duties the "best and most equitable mode of taxation," the "easiest and most efficacious" form of revenue to collect. But there were those in Mobile and Pensacola who resisted the measure on the basis that the act had not been promulgated in the province and that the stamp master (agent) had not received his commission prior to November 1, 1765, when the act went into effect. The governor explained that this situation was due to the distance and slow communication, but the protestors were not satisfied. There may not have been any physical violence but, wrote Johnstone,

> This has been the occasion of a torrent of abuse. Many of the inhabitants would not . . . take out their grants. Several now lie in the office which are refused. Masters of ships were afraid to proceed to their destined homes with such badges of slavery, as they term it. In short, I have been obliged to publish notifications that in case the grants are not taken up, the land will be given to others; which with one or two examples, has had the proper effect. . . .——Johnstone to John Pownal, Public Record Office, Colonial Series 5/574, quoted in C. N. Howard, *The British Development of West Florida, 1763–1769,* p. 124.

Already "unjustly deprived of the control of the troops and differing in opinion with the chief justice, and the lieutenant governor being very willing to occupy" his place, the Stamp Act was almost too much for Johnstone to bear. Sure that someone would report to the Board of Trade, he asked only that he be allowed to state his side of the case before judgment was made. On December 17, 1766, he resigned.

On the positive side, Johnstone had carried out two assignments with credit. One was in handling Indian affairs and the other was in initiating civil government.

CIVIL GOVERNMENT

West Florida was a royal colony under British rule. It was to be governed by a royally-appointed governor, a council of twelve who were nominated by the governor but appointed by the king in council, and a lower house elected by the free holders. There were the usual administrative offices and courts, headed by men who, like the council members, were nominated by the governor but appointed by the king. One of Johnstone's instructions was to initiate a civil government as soon as practical. Until an assembly was elected, administration centered in the governor working with the council.

The capital of the province was Pensacola; but so much of the business, especially that involving Indians and foreign trade, centered in Mobile, that three members of the first council lived there. They were Jacob Blackwell, Francis Morcier, and Robert Crook. Blackwell was collector of customs and was later named collector of stamp duties.

Not until Johnstone had been in the colony a year and a half did he call an assembly and only then on petition from some inhabitants of Mobile. Six of the fourteen members of the first assembly were from that settlement. An election was held in the fall of 1766 and the first session of the assembly met on November 3, 1766. It is of interest to Alabamians that Francis Poussatt of Mobile was the first speaker of the house. There were long intervals in which the assembly did not meet, usually for want of a quorum. When in session, it dealt with problems of Indians, trade, taxation, defense, jails, roads, and others that any growing frontier area of the time encountered. Relations between the assembly and the governors were often stormy, but British institutions and practices managed to weather personal conflicts.

INDIAN CONGRESSES

In order to promote friendly relations with the Indians, John Stuart, Superintendent of Indian Affairs, and Governor Johnstone held a series of meetings, called congresses, with the leaders of the principal tribes. The one with the Creeks met in Pensacola; the one with the Choctaws and Chickasaws in Mobile. In a joint letter to Lord Halifax, Johnstone and Stuart wrote of conditions when they arrived in October 1764.

> . . . There was the greatest reason to apprehend a general insurrection of Indians . . . against his majesty's arms. Three very superior characters [Pontiac to the north; Mortor, chief of the Creeks; and old Alabama Mingo, leader of the Choctaw nation] in their way had conspired to bring about this event, by strongly instilling into the minds of the various nations . . . that the English intended first, totally to surround them and next, to extirpate them from the face of the earth by cutting off their supplies.——Johnstone and Stuart to Halifax, June 12, 1765, *Mississippi Provincial Archives, English Dominion,* p. 184.

Believing this, the red men must therefore unite against their common foe, the English. It was to combat this danger by turning these enemies into allies or as Johnstone said, to induce them to "give up their French medals and commissions and to accept . . . others from his majesty," that the officials held these meetings.

The records of these congresses should dispel forever the misconception of the Indians as a solemn people given to little besides hunting and fighting, or sitting around in silence, smoking. The principal men of the Choctaw and Chickasaw nations, upwards of two thousand of them, met for nearly two months beginning on March 26, 1765, and, as Johnstone said at the conclusion, with "no damage worthy of notice."

The meeting opened with due formalities; the governor and the superintendent smoking the calumet and the Reverend Samuel Hart reading prayers before Johnstone made the first speech. The chieftains "behaved with great decency and listened with utmost attention." In the days that followed Stuart and many of the chief men spoke at length, in exaggerated, but often poetic language. Mingo Huma spoke on one of the last days.

> Last year when the French governor took his leave of us he advised me to give my hand to the English commandant, which I did. I have waited with impatience for the sight of my new father, I now have the pleasure of seeing the governor and superintendent who came over the great waters, they have suprisingly arrived safe in pieces of wood joined together. At which we rejoice.
>
> The medal which I wear was given to me by the French governor as a token of power and authority to govern my people, but he . . . has gone away and left me destitute. I am sensible it is impossible for a child to have two fathers; I now acknowledge you to be my father, in token of which I deliver you my commission and medal. I hope you will replace them with others as good and honorable.——Ibid., p. 245.

And indeed they did and more. In exchange for medals and other presents, the tribes and the English made a treaty of seven articles in which the principal men had agreed,

> . . . to grant to the province a tract of rich, convenient, and extensive land [in what is now Mobile and Washington Counties]; to agree to render blood for blood; to restore Negroes and other deserters; and to refrain from plundering the inhabitants; to submit to the regulations of trade. . . .——Ibid., p. 186.

Cecil Johnson, the modern authority on British West Florida, describes Johnstone's administration as full of "aggressiveness and action," in which

> . . . civil government was inaugurated, the assembly was established, Pensacola was laid out, meetings were held with the Indians and treaties were negotiated, efforts were made to tap the Spanish trade.—— Cecil Johnson, *British West Florida, 1763–1783* (New Haven: Yale University Press, 1943), p. 60.

In spite of these evidences of progress, the period was marred by angry bickering between the governor and his associates.

BROWNE AND ELIOT

The troubles of the Johnstone administration were only a foretaste of what was to come in the next few years. When Johnstone left for England, Montfort Browne, the lieutenant governor who had allied himself with Johnstone's opposition, became acting governor. Because of his enmity toward the governor, he had not been part of the ruling circle and knew little about the administration of the colony. However, he undertook several constructive measures for the public welfare and succeeded in quieting the Creeks, who had been less than happy with Governor Johnstone. However, Browne's accounts were under investigation even before his replacement, Governor John Eliot, arrived. That worthy gentleman may never have been in Mobile; after taking the required oaths as governor on April 2, 1769, in Pensacola and conducting business for a short time, he committed suicide and Browne became governor again, to serve until the arrival of Peter Chester. Browne, like Johnstone, was a cantankerous individual who seemed to invite controversy.

PETER CHESTER

Peter Chester, the last of the royal governors, and whose personal life is little known, was appointed in 1770 and served until the Spanish captured the area in 1780. Officially, he was governor until the treaty of 1783, but he had returned to England before then, probably in the early months of 1780.

As governor, Chester had his difficulties. The Indians, who had come to expect preferential treatment, were a nuisance expecting more and more presents, and it became necessary to hold another congress with the Choctaws and Chickasaws in 1771. The settlements in West Florida were widely scattered and communications difficult; rivalry between the civil and military authorities continued. The General Assembly, still new at its job of law-making, was often at odds with Chester; the Spanish in New Orleans were a constant threat to the safety of the Gulf settlements; there were frequent rumors of "rebel" plots to invade West Florida and one significant invasion.

James Willing, a "rebel" who had led a raid down the Mississippi River, did real damage in the Natchez district and at Manchac, destroying property, arresting citizens, and confiscating slaves. Although the story does not seem to be well authenticated, Willing is reported to have appeared (1778) in the Tensas settlements above Mobile with a copy of the Declaration of Independence, the first the Gulf settlers had seen, hoping in vain to enlist the people in his cause. He was promptly confined in Fort Charlotte, where he stayed until the end of 1779.

Many of the troubles Chester had were attributable to tensions caused by the war going on in the Atlantic colonies. Generally speaking, his opposition caused only annoyance until 1779 when 130 "leading citizens," about half of them from Mobile, signed a petition to the king, asking for the removal of the "weak-minded, avaricious" Chester as governor. "From the origin [of the rebellion]," the petition stated, "we have in many instances severely felt its fatal effects . . . mingled with bad police and mismanagement of Peter Chester. . . ." The charges said that he granted lands, often in large amounts, without the consent of the council and often to his favorites, among whom were retired "military personnel of reduced rank," some of the choicest going to Philip Livingston, Jr., his private secretary. Many of the other complaints centered around Livingston, whose loyalty to the king was suspect because he was the son of a leading patriot in New York. Young Livingston, in addition to his job as secretary, held nine other offices (including collector of customs at Mobile) from which he collected fees. Chester, furthermore, was charged with increasing old fees and initiating new ones; of "borrowing" out of the Indian goods provided for presents, to clothe his and Livingston's plantation Negroes; and of being "soft" toward the rebels within the province and neglectful of its defenses.

In his replies Chester explained or denied the allegations but significantly pointed out that many of the accusations were caused by the frontier conditions. Capable men were few, settlements far apart, the extensive borders hard to defend, and the people restless. Chester gave little credence to the complaints in the petition, dismissing them as the protestations of factions, parties, dissatisfied or disappointed office seekers, or disgruntled merchants, many of whom were hardly known in the province. Nevertheless, among the signatures are several names prominent in the military and economic life of the region. Whether this was a pro-American, anti-British, or simply anti-Chester movement is a difficult question, but it does indicate considerable unrest in West Florida.

From the petitioners' viewpoint the hassle was a failure. The petition reached London in early August 1779 and was given a hearing on the 19th, but the king did not remove the governor.

TORIES IN WEST FLORIDA

The retention of Chester in West Florida may have been due to his activity in attracting and providing for Loyalist (Tory) refugees from the theaters of the American war. West Florida became a Tory refuge in 1775 when Chester declared the province open to any person who found it impossible to live in the midst of the patriots. On November 11, the governor laid before the council a letter from the Earl of Dartmouth which contained a request that he afford every possible protection to the king's subjects in the rebellious colonies who were "too weak to resist the violence of the times and too loyal to concur in the measures" of the rebels. As a further inducement to potential refugees, the council granted lands to each person applying. Each petition told the home of applicant, the size of the family he brought with him, the land he was given, and often the wealth he had lost to the rebels. For example, Thomas Bassett from Georgia came seeking asylum on June 21, 1776. He brought with him a wife, two children, and 14 Negroes. Two hundred acres of the land assigned him was on the Tombigbee River, one-fourth mile from the McIntosh Bluffs, and 750 acres elsewhere.

Bassett came from Georgia but others came from every other colony. The total number in Alabama is not known and while not as great as those in the Natchez area of West Florida it was still considerable. Most of them had their lands on Mobile Bay, the Tensas River, the Tombigbee, or tributaries of these. Some of them returned home after the peace treaty, but others remained to be permanent citizens. Probably their greatest contribution during the war was to bolster the loyal Britons, thus discouraging any latent rebellion from becoming active.

Even before General Cornwallis surrendered at Yorktown, Pensacola and Mobile fell to the Spanish, who entered the war as allies of France. On March 12, 1780, Bernardo de Gálvez, the young and ambitious governor of Louisiana, entered Mobile.

I have the satisfaction of relating to you how on the twelfth instant, four days after the opening of the trench, the fort of Mobile with three hundred men of the garrison who have remained prisoners of war, thirty-five cannon, and eight mounted mortars, has surrendered to the forces of the king. This capture has cost us some loss and much more time than was expected, because in addition to its being a fort presenting plenty of resistance, for four months the enemy had done nothing but fortify it, giving its parapets seven feet more thickness than they had in the time of the French. The resistance they made was vigorous, and although this alone would not fail to give sufficient merit to the capture made by troops fatigued, scantily clad, and saved from shipwreck, there is another circumstance which I believe merits your bringing it to the consideration of his majesty.

This circumstance is, that after the notice of our shipwreck reached Pensacola with the exaggeration that we had lost 700 men, General Campbell resolved to leave a small garrison there and to come to attack us by land with the greater part of his forces, with the purpose of deciding here the fate of the province. He put into practice and came with 1100 men within nine leagues of our camp. His vanguard was in sight before we had finished opening the trenches; because, having lost most of the launchers in the shipwreck, we consequently had to use those that remained to carry supplies for our subsistence and had transported munitions too slowly.

You can understand our situation, on the verge of having our food give out, with very little munitions (for the greater part was lost in the shipwreck), with 1100 men in sight from whose muskets their general had removed the flints in order to attack us with cold steel, with 300 in the fort, who with those of General Campbell totaled 1400, a number equal to ours, and with the country on their side, and the protection of a fort.

The whole disagreeable prospect did not take away from our officers and troops the least part of their confidence and hope of victory. On the contrary, believing that new efforts were necessary, they persevered in their labors, opened the trench, established the battery, attacked and conquered the fort in view of the vanguard of the enemy and of General Campbell, who contented himself with observing us. For eight days he was a witness of the valor and courage of our troops, with which, having changed his mind, he broke camp to return to Pensacola with his army, from whose rear guard one of our parties took prisoner a captain and twenty men.

I cannot give expression to the sentiments with which all the individuals of my small army saw the retreat of General Campbell without coming to grips with us, nor could we reflect without sadness that if the expedition from Havana had arrived to join with us we could have succeeded over the English the same as at Saratoga. And so that you may know whether this belief is well or ill founded, I would have you know that General Campbell set out with only enough bread for eight days and the meat which was to be found in the houses, counting on arriving at the fort before it was taken; that the road by which they are returning is seven leagues longer than the one we would have taken to cut off the retreat and block the crossing of the Perdido River, indispensable for their return to Pensalcola.——Gálvez to José de Gálvez, March 20, 1780, quoted in John Walton Caughey, *Bernardo de Gálvez* (Berkeley, California, 1934), pp. 183–85.

The English commandant at Mobile, Lieutenant Governor Elias Durnford, sent a terse note about his surrender to General John Campbell, his military superior.

[GEN.] CAMPBELL.
   Sir,
   It is my misfortune to inform you that this morning my small but brave Garrison marched down the Breach and surrendered themselves Prisoners of War to General Bernardo de Galvez's Superior Arms. I write for your information and request you will do me the favor to inform Mrs. Durnford that I am in good health and that she ought to be under no uneasiness at my fate, when it is in my power to send you the Capitulation and state preceeding it for a few days will do it;

in the mean time I assure you Sir that no man in the Garrison hath stained the Luster of the British Arms.

I have the honor to be &c.

[Signed] ELIAS DURNFORD.

FORT CHARLOTTE, MOBILE, 14th March 1780.

The number by return of killed, wounded, and prissoners, 304.——— *American Historical Review,* vol. I. (July 1896), p. 699.

Not long after the fall of British West Florida there occurred an incident which has lent itself to dramatic retelling. In the summer of 1781, a band of some one hundred Natchez loyalists, unwilling to live under Spanish domination, set out by land to join their friends in Savannah, Georgia. Following a circuitous route northeastward in Mississippi and, according to Pickett, coming into Alabama from Aberdeen, they crossed the Warrior River at Tuscaloosa Falls. Pickett believed that the band, fearing for their safety if they followed known routes, wandered aimlessly into Blount County and northward. A chance meeting with a trader turned them southeastward. They crossed the Coosa River and eventually spent some days with Alexander McGillivray near Wetumpka. After sufficient rest, the party moved on and finally reached Georgia. Pickett ends his account by saying,

> Strange to say, no one died, or was killed upon the whole route from Natchez which was accomplished in one hundred and forty-nine days.———Albert James Pickett, *History of Alabama* (Sheffield, Alabama: Robert C. Randolph, 1896), p. 351.

Pickett was writing in the 1840's. A later historian, Peter Brannan, agrees that the journey exhibited great courage but denies that it was aimless or that the meeting with McGillivray was accidental. He says the refugees followed the Great Path used by the Indians for centuries and they had planned to stop at McGillivray's, where they knew they would receive sympathy and supplies. Whatever the details, it was a dramatic incident in the Revolutionary War period.

The Second Spanish Period 1783–1799

While the fall of Mobile on March 14, 1780, ended for all practical purposes English rule in Alabama, the Spanish did not officially own it until the Treaty of Paris was signed in 1783. By this treaty Spain regained both East and West Florida with the 31st parallel as the northern boundary from the Mississippi River to the Appalachicola. This boundary, however, was subject to dispute. There had been some behind-the-scenes consultations between the British

and Americans in which they had agreed that, if England retained
the district, the boundary would remain where it was (at 32°28′),
but if it reverted to Spain the more southerly line would be the
northern limit. This decision the Spanish challenged, saying the
two nations had no power to determine the matter. The line would
be the subject of much dispute and negotiations as long as Spain
owned any of the area. North of the disputed line, development was
similar to most other frontier areas with Georgia claiming the land,
organizing it into Bourbon County (1785), and in the 1790's disposing of much of the land (still occupied by the Indians) through
the four Yazoo Land Companies, which eventually led to the Supreme Court case of Fletcher vs. Peck. Although land speculators'
attempts to develop the area around Muscle Shoals came to little,
pioneers flocked in so that by 1813, when the Spanish finally left
the area, there were several thriving settlements. But the area south
of the line has a history of intrigue between the Spanish and the
Indians and of encroachments by the Americans.

The government of Spanish Florida was much like that of the
French, having none of the popular features of the English. The
capital was in New Orleans but there were officers and garrisons
in Mobile and Pensacola. Colonel Esteban Miró became governor of
Louisiana when Bernardo de Gálvez was appointed Captain-General
of Cuba in 1784 (and in 1785 Viceroy of New Spain). Miró held the
office until 1791 to be followed by Baron de Carondelet who was in
office at the time of the Pinckney Treaty. Gayoso de Lemos and
Marquis Casa Calvo were later governors, but their influence was
greater in the Mississippi Valley than in Alabama.

Miró's ambition was to strengthen the Spanish provinces in North
America. One of the means to that end was to promote good will
among the Indians. In the eastern part of his province, the Creeks
were potentially the most powerful ally since they had been pro-
British (and therefore anti-American) during the American
Revolution. The key man among the Creeks was Alexander Mc-
Gillivray.

Alexander McGillivray (1759–1793), son of a Scots father and
Creek mother, was known as the "Talleyrand of Alabama." He had
lived his early years at his father's trading post on the banks of the
Tallapoosa and when he was about fourteen he was sent to Charleston to learn the merchant's trade; he lived there and at Savannah
until after the Revolutionary War. Because he was a Loyalist and
actually fought on the British side, his property was confiscated
by the Americans. After the war he returned to the Creek country
and the plantation at Little Talassee (near Fort Toulouse) that he
inherited from his father, Lachlan McGillivray. From 1784 until
his death in 1793, he spent his time working for the welfare of his

people. He was especially active in trying to organize a southern confederacy among the Indian tribes. During these years he "touched the life of the Old Southwest at many important points, and his rare career possessed international significance. He was courted by merchants, land speculators, and fiilibusters, and by the governments of Georgia, the United States and Spain." At one time he was the agent of the Spanish government in its attempt to maintain a monopoly of the trade among the Creeks. McGillivray was paid special attention by the Georgia land speculators who hoped to win the favor of this mighty man among the Indians whom they hoped to move out.

One of the best contemporary descriptions of him is by Arturo O'Neill, the Spanish official who probably knew him best, in a letter to Josef de Ezpeleta, governor of Havana.

My Dear Sir:

About the middle of last month there arrived here Alexander Maguilberi, half-breed son of a Scotchman and an Indian woman of the Wind Clan, a sister of the Indian chief named Red Shoes, who, though formerly under our monarch, put to the sword the Spanish settlers on the Escambia River and in other habitations in this vicinity because of some differences existing at the time between the governor of this town and the Indians. The said Maguilberi, I am well informed, has more influence among the Creek Nations than any other person; therefore, and because he was educated at Charleston, the English named him commissary for the Upper Creek Nations. But when the English retired from the Florida Coast he was called to St. Augustine, his accounts adjusted and his salary paid, and the English bade him farewell, as he preferred to remain in his own land with the Indians, his wife, and his family. He has informed me that the English General MacArthur, who was in St. Augustine, urged him to hold the Indians in readiness to recommence the war, and that in case they were called anew to such activity it would be for the good of the Indians. At the same time Maguilberi assured me that he preferred peace, and to this end, accompanied by other Indian chiefs, he had come to solicit the establishment of a trade with them for the purchase of their deer-skins, offering his services to enlist the friendship of the different towns his neighbors. He as well as various other Indians friendly to us will refuse to gather at a congress offered them by the Americans in Augusta and Savannah.

He has a great number of cattle and negroes in his town on the Cosita, and a sister married to an Indian half-breed named Duran, whose father was French, and they are actually on the road with a good herd of cattle and some forty slaves to settle on the Escambia River eighteen leagues from here.

In regard to the foregoing I must explain to you that it seems to me advisable to keep the friendship of Maguilberi and other creoles living in the nations and of such Englishmen as are married and have Indian children, since in what other fashion can we be assured of the trade and friendship of the Indians, who at present are strongly opposed to the name of Americans. Of this situation I shall inform the provisional governor of New Orleans and Colonel Gilberto Maxent.

The Indian chief named Red Shoes, Maguilberi's uncle, has asked me for a medal and promises to protect all the Spanish subjects who are established on the Escambia. I would not have acceded except that without his consent they would be restrained from cultivating, because his town is nearer than those of the other chiefs of the nation

May God keep you many years, Pensacola, October 19, 1783. ——Quoted in John Walton Caughey, ed., *McGillivray of the Creeks* (Norman, Okla.: University of Oklahoma Press, 1938), pp. 62–63.

Having suffered great loss of property to the Americans, McGillivray looked to the Spanish as the protector of his people. To acquaint the officials with his scheme, he wrote O'Neill in Pensacola:

I shall Say Something on what methods ought to be taken to frustrate the americans Schemes. One Principal Consideration Should be a plentiful Supply of Goods Should be carried to trade in the Nation on the footing that the English used to do, for Indians will attach themselves to & Serve them best who Supply ttheir Necessities. There is a Stipulation made for that in the articles for delivering up East Florida to his Most Catholic Majesty, the Indian Trading Merchants remain and carry on their trade as usual but it is much more convenient for this upper Nation to have the trade from West Florida, for which purpose I have to pray for leave to be given me to be allowed to Bring a Quantity of Indian Goods from St. Augustine to Mobile from whence I could Supply my People by Water Carriage preferable to pack Horses.

I had no desire to Carry on a trade but that I had engaged my Nation in the Cause of Loyalty & to Which they Stood Stedfast to the last, I consider myself obligated to Support them for their fidelity. . . .

I likewise herewith beg leave to offer my Services as an Agent for Indian Affairs on the part of his Most Catholic Majesty, in which capacity I have Served his Brittanick Majesty for very near Eight years past.——Ibid., pp. 65–66.

All the time McGillivray was in correspondence with the Spanish; and, even holding office as commissary for that government in his nation, he was dealing with the Americans in Georgia as is shown in his letter of November 20, 1784.

The other day the lame King arrived from Augusta & I have the Satisfaction to Inform Your Excellency that the americans have given a very Satisfactory answer. The Governor & assembly have forbid the Settling of thos lands in the Strongest Manner, so that the apprehensions I had that we Shoud be obliged to go to war with them to defend our lands in now at an end. But I must observe to Your Excellency that the americans are very uneasy that this Nation has entered into an alliance with the Spanish Nation, & that they have granted leave to English Merchants to Supply this Nation with a trade from the Floridas, because such Measures have made the Indians Independent, & not beholden to the americans for trade, so that they cant have the Sway of the Indians but have lost it, by this Stroke of Policy in the King of Spains offices, who held the Congress with this nation in Pensacola. These are the true reasons that makes the americans pretend to be so moderate to us, tis out of their Jealousy to Spain, & I do not thank them for it. . . .——Ibid., pp. 84.

The Americans, too, were aware of the importance of good relations with the Creeks and therefore wooed McGillivray. Shortly after his inauguration, President George Washington sent three commissioners to Georgia to hold talks with the chiefs. McGillivray attended but somewhat unceremoniously left before any business had been transacted. Later he decided to accept Washington's invitation to go to New York. The new president recorded in his diary the meeting with the Indian representatives.

Had a good deal of conversation in the evening with the above Commissioners on the more minute part of their transactions at the Treaty with the Creek Indians—and their opinion with respect to the real views of Mr. McGillivray, the principles of whose conduct they think is self-interest, and a dependence for support on Spain. They think also, that having possessed himself of the outlines of the terms he could treat with the United States upon, he wished to postpone the Treaty to see if he could not obtain better from Spain. They think that, though he does not want abilities, he has credit to the full extent of them, and that he is but a short sighted politician. He acknowledges, however, that an alliance between the Creek Nation and the United States is the most natural one, and what they ought to prefer, if to be obtained on equal terms.—— George Washington, *Diaries* (Boston: Houghton Mifflin, 1925), vol. 4, p. 54, Sunday, November 22, 1789.

The Treaty of New York (1789) contained many compromises. The modern biography of McGillivray describes it thus:

McGillivray held out against an acknowledgement of American sovereignty except over the parts of the nation that were within the limits of the United States. The effect of this provision was to make the ultimate disposition of the Creeks depend upon the settlement of the disputed boundary between the United States and Spain. If all or part of the Creek territory should be found to lie north or east of the ultimate line, it would be under American protection; any part south or west of the line would be under Spanish protection as specified in the Treaty of Pensacola of 1784. The Spaniards subsequently criticized this article bitterly, but McGillivray insisted, and correctly, that it was not a breach of faith with Spain.

Similarly the boundary laid down between the Creeks and the citizens of the United States was not entirely satisfactory. McGillivray had to relinquish that part of the disputed area on which the Georgians had already settled. To move them out would have been practically impossible. On the other hand, Georgia did not get the boundary set as far west as she had claimed, and the Indians gained a valuable hunting area on the Altamaha. Financial compensation was included for the territorial claims that the Creeks surrendered. Knox strove hard to get an American trade authorized, but McGillivray was true to Panton and would only consent to an arrangement for an emergency trade in case an English war closed the existing channels. This item was put in a secret article. It was provided also that the question of trade might be brought up again after two years had elapsed.

The other provisions were of less significance, with the exception of the secret commission of McGillivray as a brigadier with a salary set at $1200 a year.——Caughey, *McGillivray of the Creeks,* p. 44.

This treaty did not solve some of the thorny problems of the United States with either the Indians or the Spanish. With the mouth of the Mississippi River and Mobile Bay in the hands of the Spanish, the Americans in the interior had difficulty getting their produce to market; since each nation claimed a different boundary line, the Americans often lived in disputed territory. The United States tried to clear up these and other questions in the Treaty of San Lorenzo (Pinckney's Treaty) in 1795.

A commission to determine the exact location of this line was headed up by Andrew Ellicott, who began his work on the Mississippi River in the fall of 1797 and, after innumerable delays caused often by the Spanish authorities in Natchez and New Orleans, finally completed the survey in 1799. The problems involved in crossing the area above Mobile were described by Ellicott in his journal.

On our arrival at the end of the compass line on the Mobile river, one serious difficulty presented itself, that was the continuation of the line through the swamp, which is at all times almost impenetrable; but at that season of the year absolutely so: being wholly inundated:—But fortunately we found in the neighbourhood of our camp a small hill, the summit of which was just elevated above the tops of the trees in the swamp. From the top of this hill, we could plainly discover the pine trees on the high land, on the east side. Upon ascertaining this fact, we sent a party through to the other side, (along the water courses, by which the swamp is intersected in various directions), with orders to make a large fire in the night with light-wood; the same was likewise to be done on the hill before mentioned, to obtain nearly the direction from one place to the other.—The atmosphere was too much filled with smoke, to discern a flag, or other signal,—the woods being on fire on both sides of the swamp.—It happened unfortunately that the day before our fires were to be lighted, the fires in the woods had extended over almost the whole of the highlands, on both sides of thé swamp; by which so many dead trees were set on fire, that there was no possibility of discriminating between them, and our fires.—It was then agreed that the parties should light up, and extinguish their fires a certain number of times; making stated intervals. This succeeded so well, that we became certain of not taking a wrong fire in determining the angles.—Contrary to our expectation, a heavy rain fell on the same night, a short time after we had finished the experiment, and extinguished all the fires in the woods.— The storm cleared off with a strong north-west wind, which carried off all the smoke, and enabled us to determine the angles in the day, by erecting signals, which was accomplished on the second day of April.—This work was connected with the observatory in the following manner. At the observatory A (see Fig. G, plate V.) a meridional line was traced, by taking the greatest elongations of *a* Ursæ Minoris, both east, and west, with the transit and equal altitude instrument:—equal distances were carefully measured in each direction, and a fine mark placed at the termination of each measurement,—the distance between those marks was accurately bisected, and a fine mark placed at tthe point of bisection for the meridian. The same operation was performed a second time, and although the differences in the results, appeared too trifling to need any attention, it was nevertheless bisected, and that point of bisection taken for the meridian. . . .—*The Journal of Endrew Ellicott* (Philadelphia: William Fry, 1814), Appendix, p. 83.

The Spanish erected Fort St. Stephens as a stronghold on the Tombigbee River in 1789 and occupied it the next year. Although the Ellicott survey proved it to be north of the thirty-first parallel and therefore lost to them, it prospered as a settlement and became the seat of government for territorial Alabama. The fort in Mobile was rebuilt in brick and some other improvements made in the port city, but except for officials few Spanish citizens seem to have moved into the area.

It is easier, however, to see the international intrigue and conflict that centered in the region than to point to positive gains. Spain and the United States were the principal rivals but England was often more than a disinterested bystander. The Indians, although often mere pawns in the games, were a vital part of the conflict. To their sorrow redmen found that their allies, whether Americans or Spanish, spoke to them with "forked tongues" and that their position was becoming untenable.

In the end it was the restless American frontiersman who won the international chess game here. Paying little attention to Indian claims or international boundaries and respecting little beyond his own ambitions for rich land, he pushed into the west.

The history of the last Spanish period is essentially the history of the whole colonial period. In it there were three factors at work: rivalry between European nations, the Indians, and land. In the end land won.

Chapter 2

ALABAMA AS A TERRITORY
1798–1819

Political Evolution

In 1798, shortly after the Pinckney Treaty and even before the completion of the Ellicott survey, the United States organized the Mississippi Territory. Alabama remained a part of it until 1817 when the western half became the state of Mississippi. The Alabama Territory lasted but a brief two years before it, too, was ready for statehood. These years would witness many changes in every phase of life.

Mississippi, the first organized territory in the southwest, followed the pattern outlined in the Northwest Ordinance of 1787. This plan provided that the transition from unorganized and sparsely settled land to statehood would proceed in three stages. In the first stage, the government should be carried on by a governor, a secretary and three judges, all appointed by the president and confirmed by Congress until the population reached five thousand free adult males. At that time it entered phase two. The freeholders then could elect a house of representatives who, in turn, were to nominate ten men from whom the president would choose five to form a legislative council functioning as an upper chamber. In this stage, the territory was represented at the national capital by a delegate who sat in the House of Representatives and could enter into debate, appear before committees, present petitions, and do most things a Congressman could, except vote. He was in effect a lobbyist, looking after the interests of his constituents. This system continued until the district had a total population of sixty thousand when the people, through their legislature, could petition for statehood. Alabama went through these stages, first as a part of the

Mississippi Territory and later as the Alabama Territory. It was admitted as a state on December 14, 1819.

Four governors served the Mississippi Territory. The first was Winthrop Sargent (1798–1801), a Federalist from Massachusetts, a holder of two degrees from Harvard College, who was appointed by President John Adams. Previously Sargent had been secretary of the Northwest Territory and acting governor during the long absences of Governor Arthur St. Clair. He was, therefore, no stranger to territorial administration or frontier conditions. However, his three years in Natchez, the territorial capital, were turbulent and filled with controversy with the local inhabitants, who were mostly Jeffersonians in politics. The records of the territory hold many petitions of the inhabitants showing dissatisfaction with the high-handed chief executive. They objected, for example, to the total use of the code of Northwest Territory, which, they said, left them no self-government. They found fault with the fact that these laws were "proclaimed" rather than "enacted." Among his enemies were two powerful planters of the Natchez districts, Cato West and Anthony Hutchins, who eventually succeeded in getting Sargent removed but only when the Federalists lost power.

W.C.C. Claiborne was President Thomas Jefferson's choice for the post, but he served only a short time before becoming governor of the newly created Louisiana Territory. Cato West expected to be named governor, but Jefferson appointed Robert Williams, an experienced North Carolina legislator, who had been in Mississippi on a land claims commission. Although there seem to be fewer recorded objections to him, he fought a running battle with Sargent's old foes, frequently proroguing and even dissolving the territorial legislature—the last governor to use these powers. In 1809 he resigned and was replaced by David Holmes, who remained in office until Mississippi became a state. Holmes, a native of Pennsylvania who had early moved to Virginia, was the first elected governor of the new state (1817–1820) and later served in the United States Senate. He was the first governor to pay much attention to the eastern part of his territory. Generally he was a popular governor. His vigorous actions during the Creek War help to account for his popularity but so does his cooperative disposition.

However, a memorial to Congress from the territorial legislature in 1814, in which its members were pleading for "the rank of a Sister State of the Union," shows the attitude toward the kind of government they had.

Your memorialists will not fatigue your honorable bodies, with a minute and critical examination of the various objections which exist to a territorial form of government. The powers of the executive are limited only by the responsibility which he owes to the president of the United States. Our legislative authority is but a cypher without his concurrence. He is commander in chief of our militia, possesses without control the authority to appoint all officers, civil and military, who hold their appointments during his will and pleasure. He is also possessed of an absolute veto on all laws passed by the other two branches of the legislature and may prorogue or dissolve the General Assembly whenever in his opinion it may be expedient and there is none who can demand of him the reasons for his conduct.——*Territorial Papers of the United States,* Clarence E. Carter, ed. (Washington: U. S. Government Printing Office, 1938), vol. 5, p. 486, December 27, 1814.

In the earliest stage of territorial development, the government was constituted by the judges, along with the governor and secretary. After the election of a legislature, the judges were not so necessary to the existence of government but nevertheless played important roles. Malcolm C. McMillan says that there were nineteen different territorial judges from 1798 to 1817. Some of these men resigned, others died in office, and a few served long terms. Among the latter was Judge Harry Toulmin.

In 1804, Congress passed a law giving a judge to Washington County, a part of which was in Alabama; Toulmin was appointed to the office by President Thomas Jefferson, whom he had met through Joseph Priestley, a mutual friend. He brought with him an impressive record and proved to be one of the most prominent early Alabamians.

Toulmin, an Englishman by birth and a dissenting preacher with Unitarian leanings by calling, had migrated to America in 1793, settling in Virginia before moving west to Lexington, Kentucky, where he became president of Transylvania University. Later while he was secretary of state for Kentucky, he compiled several volumes of transactions of that state. As judge he was especially interested in developing order on the restless frontier and in helping to straighten out land claims in the Tombigbee-Tensaw area. But he was more than a judge. His biographer, Dunbar Rowland, says that he also served as "postmaster, preached and officiated at funerals and marriages, made Fourth of July orations, practiced medicine gratuitously, and in general was head of the settlements."

The territory was divided in 1817 but only after repeated petitions to have it done and about as many counter petitions to prevent it. Northern congressmen were inclined to let it come in as one state, southern ones wanted to divide it. At times the residents themselves were in disagreement over the matter. At one point Huntsville was so desirous of statehood that she favored running the dividing line east and west about middle way between Mobile and the Tennessee state line. Finally, on March 3, 1817, Congress passed an act creating the Alabama Territory.

William Wyatt Bibb (1781–1820), the only governor Alabama Territory had in the fifteen months of its existence, was a native Virginian but had lived his adult life in Georgia. In Alabama he, along with Charles Tait, J. W. Walker, and others, formed the "Georgia Machine" in politics. When Alabama became a state, he was elected the first governor but lived only about eight months after taking office. On May 20, 1820, he died from the effects of a fall from his horse, which became frightened during a severe thunderstorm. He had extensive land holdings in Autauga County. His commission as governor is dated September 25, 1817.

Whether Alabama had enough people to become a state in 1817 was debatable, but the population was growing rapidly and even an incomplete census of 1818 showed a total of 67,594, well over the required minimum. Not having to go through the first stage, territorial history was short. The general assembly met only twice, both occasions in 1818; the first session was made up of members who had been in the Mississippi legislature. These two sessions wrangled over representation between the northern and southern counties (prophetic of the rivalry that became characteristic), chose Cahaba to be the permanent capital, and created some new counties in addition to passing routine legislation. James Titus, formerly Speaker of the House in Mississippi, was president of the Legislative Council (upper house); and John W. Walker, a native of Virginia who had moved to Georgia, was Speaker of the House of Representatives. John Crowell was the delegate to Congress.

Because of the rapidly growing population, it was well known that statehood would not be long delayed. Consequently, petitions to that end date from the early days of the territory. Speaker Walker, a resident of Huntsville since 1810, transmitted the memorial of the legislature along with a copy of the recent (November 1818) census returns from eighteen counties.

To the Honorable, the Senate & House of Representatives of the United States, in Congress assembled:

The memorial of the Legislative Council and House of Representatives of the Alabama Territory, in General Assembly convened, respectfully represents.—

That the good people of said Territory have been long subject of their present form of government; and have borne the many privations attending it, with patience & submission. They have witnessed the recent admission of the State of Mississippi, with which they were once connected, without a murmur; solacing themselves by the anticipation of the speedy approach of the period, which would entitle them, also, to the full enjoyment of a free constitution. They confidently believe, that *that* period has, now, arrived. Although your memorialists are unable, owing, as they believe, to accidental Causes, to afford actual evidence of the full number of "free inhabitants", necessary to found a claim to admission into the Union, *as matter of right,* they believe, it may be made appear, to the satisfaction of your Honorable bodies, that its present population, and the practise pursued in similar cases, fairly and justly entitle the Territory of Alabama to "form a permanent Constitution & State government, consistent with the general interest of the confederacy".

It appears, by returns of the census of said Territory, recently made by sworn officers, in conformity to law, that it contains sixty seven thousand, five hundred & ninety four souls; of which number, there are forty six thousand, two hundred and ten "free inhabitants". Add to the number, last named, twelve thousand and, eight hundred & twenty eight, being three fifths of our Slaves, and it will augment our *federal* population to fifty nine thousand and thirty eight; excluding the number contained in the Counties of Lawrence and Marion; from which counties, owing to causes not within the knowledge of your memorialists, no return has, yet, been received. It is moreover, a fact generally notorious, that complete returns have not been made from *some,* if *any,* of the Counties; which deficiency has arrisen from the great extent of some, and the extraordinary ferment produced, in others, by sales of public land, and disturbances on our frontier. No rational doubt can be entertained, but that the whole federal population of Alabama, if correctly ascertained, would amount to, considerably, more than sixty thousand; which brings us, at least, within the *spirit* of the provision of the ordinance, requiring that number—

Your memorialists, further, represent that, in eighteen hundred & sixteen, the present Territory of Alabama, then composing a part of the Mississippi Territory, contained, only, twenty eight thousand six hundred & seven souls.—Taking into view the deficiency of returns occasioned by the causes before mentioned, it is fair to estimate our present number at seventy thousand; showing an increase of more than forty one thousand souls, in the short period of two years. From those facts, it is rational to conclude, that the unparalleled tide of emigration, invited by the general fertility of our soil and the happy temperature of our Climate, and which is daily flowing into the bosom of our Territory, would augment its number of "free inhabitants" to more than sixty thousand, before it would be possible to form a constitution.—

Your memorialists would, further, beg leave to call the attention of your Honorable bodies to the policy, recently pursued by the national Legislature, toward the States of Indiana, Mississippi and Illinois, neither of which are believed to contain at present, a more numerous population, than that of our Territory. The population of Indiana is not, now, distinctly recollected; but the State of Mississippi, on her admission, contained, only, about forty seven thousand *inhabitants,* of *all description;* amounting to about eight hundred more, than our *free population.*—

By an act of your last Session, Illinois was authorized to "form a permanent constitution and state government" with a population of forty thousand.—

With such examples of your recent liberality before them, your memorialists would be impeaching your high sence of impartiality and Justice, were they to doubt the success of their present application.—Your memorialists cannot conceive, how it could promote the interest of the national government, longer, to withhold from the people of Alabama the right they solicit; for whilst it grants them a boon, it relieves itself of a burthen. In common with their countrymen, in other portions of the Union, do *they* appreciate the advantages and happiness to be enjoyed under the auspices of a republican form of government.—Coming, as *they* have done, principally, from the original States, where every man's rights were guaranteed by a free constitution, of paramount authority; and accustomed to consider themselves the legitimate source of all political power, it is not matter of surprise, that they should be impatient of the restraints & privations inseparable from a Territorial form of Government. They look forward with no ordinary solicitude to the period, which they trust is rapidly approaching, when they will be disenthralled from principles which deprive them of their most important political rights, and entitled to their voice and weight in the councils of the nation.—

Your memorialists, therefore, for, & in behalf of, the good people of said Territory, respectfully pray, that an Act may be passed, authorising them to form a Constitution and State Government.—

J. W. WALKER, Speaker of the House of Representatives.
JAMES TITUS, President of the Legislative Council.
—*Territorial Papers,* vol. 18, pp. 459–61

An editorial in the *Alabama Republican* (Huntsville) for January 16, 1819, explained to its readers the terms of the bill before Congress.

EDITORIAL ON STATEHOOD LEGISLATION
[January 16, 1819]

We have received a copy of the bill for the admission of Alabama into the union, as reported by the committee.

The bill was introduced into the senate by Mr. Tait from Georgia, on the 18th December, and on the 21st it passed a second reading; on the 23rd it was taken up again and on a motion to amend it, it was postponed to monday the 28th when it would probably pass. We understand the proposed amendment was to restrict the limits of the state to Tombeckbee river, being the same proposition which Congress rejected at the last session.

The bill embraces every thing, which the people of the territory could wish; it provides for the election of members to the convention, according to the late apportionment of representatives to the Territorial Legislature; the election to be held on the first monday in May, and the convention to meet on the first monday in July next at Huntsville.

The bill proposes a grant of all salt springs to the state, for the use of the people thereof subject to the regulation of the Legislature; it also proposes to appropriate *five percent* of the net proceeds of sales of land, after the 1st of September next, to improvements of roads and inland navigation—also an additional entire township for the use of a College, which is to be reserved by the secretary of the Treasury either in a body or in tracts of two sections each, to be appropriated by the Legislature and instead of one entire section for the seat of Government which was granted at the last session, 1150 acres on both sides of the Alabama river at the mouth of Cahaba are substituted.

These are the leading features of the bill, which we hope 'ere long to present to our readers in the form of a law.

It is a subject of much congratulation that so large a proportion of public lands as 72 sections or 46,000 acres should be granted to the state for the support of a seminary of learning; at the present prices of land, this donation will enable the state of Alabama to found and support one of the first literary institutions in the union.—Printed in ibid., pp. 534–35.

The text of the acts which admitted Alabama into the union was signed on December 14, 1819.

Resolution declaring the admission of the State of Alabama into the Union

Whereas, in pursuance of an act of Congress, passed on the second day of March, one thousand eight hundred and nineteen, entitled "An act to enable the people of the Alabama Territory to form a Constitution and State government, and for the admission of such state into the Union on an equal footing with the original States", the people of the said territory did, on the second day of August, in the present year, by a Convention called for that purpose, to form for themselves a Constitution and State government, which Constitution and State government so formed is republican, and in conformity to the principles of the articles of Compact, between the original States, and the people and States in the Territory North West of the river Ohio, passed on the thirteenth day of July, one thousand seven hundred and eighty-seven, so far as the same have been extended to the said Territory by the articles of agreement between the United States and the State of Georgia:

Resolved by the Senate and House of Representatives of the United States of America, in Congress assembled, That the State of Alabama shall be one, and is hereby declared to be one of the United States of America, and admitted into the Union on an equal footing with the original States, in all respects whatever.

H. CLAY Speaker of the House of Representatives,

JAS BARBOUR President of the Senate, pro tempore.

December 14, 1819

Approved JAMES MONROE

Ibid., Vol. 18, p. 753.

Alabama was launched on her way as a state but prior to reaching this point she had had to hurdle several obstacles. One of these was the perplexing relations with the Spanish in Mobile.

Pinckney's Treaty and the subsequent Ellicott's survey had determined the line between the two territories but the port of Mobile and most of what is now Mobile and Baldwin Counties was south of that line. Separated by hundreds of miles of wilderness to either Natchez or the Georgia settlements, the Americans north of Mobile felt the inconvenience, and what they considered the injustice, of the situation. Ephriam Kirby at Fort Stoddert wrote President Jefferson that

> these people can have no commercial intercourse with any part of the world, but by descending the River, and gaining the Ocean, through the Bay of Mobile.—This pass is commanded by the Spanish government of West Florida.—By recent orders, no article, whether it be the produce of the country, or of foreign production or manufacture is permitted to go by the port of Mobile, either to or from this country, without paying twelve per centum, on its value, as estimated by the Spanish officers of the revenue. An exaction so exorbitant and unreasonable, amounts in effect to a prohibition of exports or imports of every description.—Thus situated the condition of these people is truly distressing.—April 20, 1804, *Territorial Papers,* vol. 5, pp. 317–18.

Americans in the area were certain that the Spanish (and the British in Pensacola) were stirring up the Indians and supplying them with arms and ammunition. Furthermore, most Americans, including Thomas Jefferson and his successor in the presidency, James Madison, believed that the United States had bought that part of West Florida that extended to the Perdido River along with Louisiana in 1803.

The efforts of the United States to purchase all of Florida were complicated by the passage of the "Mobile Act" in November 1803. The act, introduced in the House of Representatives by John Randolph of Roanoke, added to the Mississippi customs district "all the navigable waters, rivers, creeks, bays and inlets lying within the United States which empty into the Gulf of Mexico east of the River Mississippi." This certainly seemed to include Mobile. Furthermore, it gave the president discretionary power to create a separate customs district that included "the shores, waters, and inlets of the bay and river of Mobile. . . ."

The measure caused a minor international crisis. Yrujo, the Spanish minister in Washington, vigorously defended his country's title to West Florida, asserting that the treaty of San Ildefonso (Pinckney's) was one of "retrocession" and Spain had restored to France "all the territory which she had received from her." There followed several months of consultations between the officials of the United States, Spain, and Great Britain. Jefferson temporarily side-stepped the issue by making Fort Stoddert, a few miles north of the international boundary, a port of entry, thus keeping the provision of the treaty that such a port should be within the boundaries of the United States.

This may have quieted international objections but it did not satisfy the disgruntled Americans living in the area between the Tombigbee and Pearl Rivers. Impatient with the slowness of the presidents in implementing the Mobile Act, they began to organize for direct action. Rumors of such a plan circulated for several years before anything specific took place. In 1810, Governor David Holmes sent Major John Hanes at Fort Stoddert directions on how he was to deal with any outbreak of hostilities.

> Sir, for some time past a rumour has been in circulation here, that a combination was forming in your part of the Territory for the purpose of attacking Mobile. The extravagance and folly of such an attempt— the ruinous consequences that would certainly result to the individuals who might be so unfortunate as to become the subjects of such delusion, and the impossibility of procuring any desirable object that could be attained even if the attempt should prove successful are circumstances which renders it difficult for me to believe that anything of the kind is seriously intended; yet as I may possibly be mistaken, I have thought it proper to direct the respective Col of the Regiments in Washington, Wayne and Baldwin, to aid the civil authority in suppressing any unlawful expedition that may be undertaken.
>
> The subject generally of the relative situation of West Florida to the United States will no doubt occupy the attention of Congress at their next session. Nothing therefore could be attended with more injurious consequences to the interest of the Citizens of Tombigbee, than an attempt of this nature. I wish you to inform me by the earliest opportunity whether you think any project of the kind is still in contemplation.— *Territorial Papers,* vol. 6, p. 119.

The Spanish, however, were more willing to make concessions (short of actual surrender) than most residents seem to have realized. James Innerarity, connected with the powerful merchant firm of Leslie, Panton and Forbes, which had important trading posts at Mobile, Pensacola, and other ports, reported that, after an interview with Governor Vicente Folch of West Florida, he felt that the situation was still gloomy but that he still hoped their exertions would not prove "altogether unsuccessful."

> Governor Folch arrived here yesterday afternoon. I have had some interesting conversation with him today. He opened himself the subject of our present critical situation and informed me of some decisive steps

that he had taken of which I was previously ignorant, but which you will have learnt from a letter written to you by my brother in his name, and which he now tells me to confirm to you in all points. He desires me moreover to add that provided no succours of any kind are given directly or indirectly by any of the inhabitants of your district to the agents of the Convention in their intended attack upon these parts of the province, he will abolish the duties paid at this port on American goods passing up and down the river and the said abolition shall take effect from the day on which he receives from you a notification that the expedition under Kemper and Kennedy is entirely laid aside and abandoned by all the inhabitants of your three counties.—Innerarity to Harry Toulmin, Nov. 22, 1810.—Printed in *American Historical Review,* vol. 2 (July 1897), p. 703.

Two years later the situation had intensified. Governor Holmes, in agreeing with Brigadier General James Wilkinson's opinion that the "safety and interest of an important portion of this territory would be greatly advanced" with the possession of Mobile, gave his own evaluation.

The Situation of East & West Florida was brought before Congress at the last Session, and was discussed & considered with closed doors. In the House of Representatives a bill to authorize the President to occupy East and West Florida was brought in by Mr Troup, a Gentleman know to be friendly to the Administration. This Bill was passed and sent to the Senate for their concurrence. On the 3rd of July the Bill was returned by the Senate *rejected.* The proceedings took place long after the passage of the law for annexing a part of West Florida to this Territory. You will find them in the 2nd Volume of the journals of the last Session, pages 77 and 97 secret journal. After Congress having thus refused to give an unconditional authority to take complete possession of West Florida, I presume the President will consider himself confined to the restrictions contained in the Law passed in 1811. That Law gives the power to occupy East & West Florida upon the happening of certain events only. In all probability the Senate at the approaching Session will see this subject in a different light. We may then be authorized to act.

Remonstrances and petitions have been presented to me stating the danger to be apprehended from the Negroes & Indians, should the Militia be marched out of the Territory. To these representations I have given no answer. But I am of opinion that if you can dispense with the service of the Cavalry, and furnish us with two hundred Muskets for the use of the Militia that will remain at home, it would make the Country secure against any probable difficulties, and quiet the fears of many good citizens.—*Territorial Papers,* vol. 6, p. 328.

The leader of the group which actually precipitated an independence movement in Baton Rouge and other settlements extending to beyond the Pearl River was Colonel Reuben Kemper, a native of Virginia, "a man of marked individuality, undaunted courage, and great physical strength"—and great aversion to the Spanish. One of his chief agents in the Tombigbee settlements was J.P. Kennedy.

To General James Wilkinson fell the "honor" of actually taking the Mobile district. It is ironic that he should be the man because he had played a very devious role in American-Spanish relations for more than a decade. A career army officer, who previously had seen service in nearly every major campaign in the northeast during the Revolutionary War, he had been stationed at many posts on the frontier, including Fort Adams, Baton Rouge, and New Orleans on the Mississippi River. It is known that he was in close contact with the Spanish authorities and that following the Jay treaty with England (1795) Governor Corondelet offered Wilkinson not only pensions (he demanded $20,000) but the opportunity to "aspire to the same position in the west that Washington had attained in the East." Since many of the agreements were oral, it is not certain what they were but seemed to have involved a movement to dislodge large portions of the country from the United States. It is known that he did accept money as an agent of Spain, probably around $4,000 annually; at one time he admitted receiving $17,000 from Spain in three payments. There is convincing evidence to show that he exposed Aaron Burr in order to divert attention from his own dual role as army officer and foreign agent. Later he was court-martialed but acquitted (February, 1812). Although many of his weaknesses of character and his dealings with Spain were exposed, he knew there was no available documentary evidence of the latter since all Spanish public records had been transferred to Havana. He was given what one writer called "a spotted coat of white wash."

However, within two months he was assigned to duty at New Orleans. With the declaration of war against England, he urged occupation of both Mobile and Pensacola. During the spring of 1813 pressure was building up to embark on such a campaign. Wilkinson's order to attack Mobile was dated February 16, but only after many delays did he embark from New Orleans. He landed below Mobile with six hundred men; he knew the Spanish had only sixty in the garrison. On April 12 Wilkinson sent a note to Cayetano Pérez, commandant at Mobile.

The troops of the United States under my command do not approach you as enemies of Spain, but by order of the President they come to relieve the garrison which you command from the occupancy of a post within the legitimate limits of those States. I therefore hope, sir, that you may peacefully retire from Fort Charlotte, and from the bounds of the Mississippi Territory [and proceed] east of the Perdido River with the garrison you command. . . .—Quoted, without source, in Peter J. Hamilton, *Colonial Mobile* (Mobile: First National Bank of Mobile, 1952),p. 411.

The terms of the surrender were agreed to on April 13 and the Spanish evacuated the garrison and the town on April 15, 1813, "without the effusion of a single drop of blood." Alabama now had the boundaries that had been claimed since the Louisiana Purchase in 1803.

Arrest of Aaron Burr

Former vice-president Aaron Burr, another prominent American involved in western intrigue, also figured in Alabama history during these years. Burr, the son of a Princeton University president and grandson of Jonathan Edwards, had played a central role in several questionable deals even while he was vice-president to Thomas Jefferson. After fatally wounding Alexander Hamilton in a duel (1804), he fled west, where he presently became involved in some dubious schemes—just exactly what they were is still being debated. First apprehended near Natchez, he escaped and fled toward Spanish Florida. On the night of February 19, 1807, he was arrested near Wakefield, Washington County. Nicholas Perkins, a young lawyer who was agent at the local land office and the man responsible for Burr's arrest, testified at the first day of the trial in Richmond.

On the night of the 18th or 19th of February last he was at Washington Courthouse. At about eleven o'clock, as he was standing at the door of the house occupied by the sheriff, he observed two men coming down the road. The moon afforded light enough . . . to see objects at some distance. The foremost man, who was thirty or forty yards before his companion and who turned out to be Colonel Burr, passed near the door without stopping or speaking. Burr's companion stopped and inquired the way to Major Henson's; the way was pointed out, but Perkins informed him that the major was from home and that in consequence of a late rise in the waters, he would experience some difficulty in getting there that night. The stranger, however, went on. Perkins, struck with this midnight journey, the silence of the person who had first passed, the unwillingess of the travellers to stop at a public place where they and their horses might have been accommodated and their determination to continue their route to Henson's after information was given that he was from home, communicated to the sheriff his suspicions that these men must be under the influence of some extraordinary motive. Possibly they might be robbers, or perhaps one of them was Burr endeavoring to effect his escape. . . . Impressed by these suspicions, he urged the sheriff, who had gone to bed, to rise and go with him to Henson's. After some time the sheriff agreed to accompany him and they went to Henson's, where they found both travellers. Burr, who had been in the kitchen to warm himself, soon came into the room where his companion and Perkins were. He spoke very little and did not seem willing to be observed. Perkins eyed him attentively but never got a full view of his face. He discerned that Burr once glanced his eye at him, apparently with a view to ascertain whether Perkins was observing him, but withdrew it immediately. The latter had heard Mr. Burrs eyes mentioned as being remarkably keen, and this glance from him strengthened his suspicions. He determined immediately to take measures for apprehending him. He accordingly left the place, after mentioning in a careless manner the way he meant to take. The way he indicated was opposite to the course he thought Burr would pursue. After getting beyond the reach of observation, he took the road to Fort Stoddard and obtained the aid of the commandant and four soldiers. The circumstances of the arrest have been already stated to the public—*Report of the Trials of Colonel Aaron Burr for Treason and For a Misdemeanor* (Philadelphia: Fry and Kammerer, 1808), vol. 1, p. 2.

Land Laws

It was land that beckoned most newcomers to the Alabama area. Therefore the land policy of the United States was of prime importance to them. Like other frontiersmen, they favored a liberal policy. The early settlers around Mobile acquired their land titles from either the French, the English, the Spanish, or the Indians. In November 1803 some seventy residents petitioned Congress to take under their "wise consideration their true situation" and either repeal an act that they feared would deprive them of their possessions or take some measures to indemnify them if they were forced to surrender their lands. The situation was complicated further by the Yazoo land sales. Georgia, which had sold most of Alabama and Mississippi to four land companies in 1795, claimed the area until 1814 when Congress awarded the claimants against the state forty-eight million dollars.

PETITION TO CONGRESS BY INHABITANTS ON ALABAMA RIVER

To The Honorable The Senate and House of Representatives of the United States of America in Congress Assembled

Your Humble Petitioners, Living on and Claiming Lands on the Alabama River, and on the East Side of the River and Bay of Mobile (all within the Mississippi Territory), to which the Indian Claims have Long since been extinguished, Humbly represent to your Honorable Body that a number of us and our Ancestors have Lived on and cultivated those Lands, for almost a Century, without the least molestation, In the course of which time, we have undergone, three several Changes of Government, by all of which till the present, we have been confirmed in our Titles,—

The eldest of our claims, we derived from the French Government, by whom those Lands for the enjoyment of which we Humbly solicit your Patronage, was Granted to our Ancestors—When this place, comprehending all, the settlement on the Alabama River below the mouth of the Cutt off, extending down that river to the Junction with Mobile and so to the Spanish Line, together with that Large Fertile Island Formed by the First water communication from the Alabama to the Tombeckbee river previous to the Junction of their principle branches, commonly called the cut off but sometimes called Curries Island, known by the Name of the Tensaw Settlement we obtained those first Grants— And when the province of West Florida was abandoned by the French, we, resolving to continue our possessions and property regardless of who might be our Sovereign, Continued to inhabit and Cultivate those Lands under the British Government, under whom a number of us migrated to this place and procured Grants from the British Government, and we enjoyed the unmolested possession of those Lands until the province of West Florada was surrendered to the Spaniards; when a number of British subjects, chosing rather to exchange their Country than their master, left us; But we your Memorialists, could not reconcile to ourselves to sacrifice our (as we thought Legal and natural) rights, continued the free enjoyment of our Lands, and Immigrants procured new titles under the Spanish Government, untill we experienced the third and happy Change to the Free Government of the United States of America. A Large number of your Memorialists have migrated to this place since October seventeen hundred and ninety five, from other parts of the United States and purchased those Lands at a vast expense from the Grantees in full confidence, that they would be secured in their Titles, by the beneficent Government of the United States—Your Memorialists Claim at present chiefly under Spanish Warrants of Survey, tho they have a number English and some French Grants. Your Memorialists further observe to your Honorable Body, that from any information they have had in their power to collect, from Tradition or otherwise, no Tribe of Indians, since the first settlement of this place had or pretended to have any title to the Tensaw Settlement And your Petitioners further observe to your honorable Body, that they have ever since the Government of the Mississippi Territory has been established and Organised, paid and this settlement comprehends the most valuable of the County of Washington.

But your Memorialists have observed in the Latter end of the eighth Section of the Act of Congress, approved the third day of March eighteen hundred and three entitled an Act regulating this Grants of Lands, and providing for the disposal of the Lands of the United States, South of the State of Tennessee, a provision that no certificate shall be Granted, for Lands lying East of Tombeckbee River, by which provision your Memorialists seem to be excluded from the same advantages, rights and privileges, that are secured to all others in the Mississippi Territory who claimed Lands, precisely in the same situation.—*Territorial Papers,* vol. 5, pp. 292–95.

During the territorial period most settlers purchased their lands under the terms of the Land Act of 1800; not until 1820 would there be another major land law. Under this act the settler could purchase a tract as small as one hundred sixty acres. After title to lands had been acquired from the Indians and the lands surveyed, the agent in charge of the local land office (St. Stephens had the first but eventually there were others in the state) was to sell, in three weeks, the lands to the highest bidder. Thereafter the unsold lands could be purchased at two dollars an acre. There was no limit to the amount of land an individual could buy; and, since the credit was extended for four years, there was considerable speculation although speculating companies *per se* seem to have played little part in early Alabama.

It is not quite clear what is the basis of the complaints made by Clabon Harris of "Munrow Coundty." It may have been the Intrusion Act of 1807, which set penalties for unregistered squatters, or the fact that the neighbors he spoke for had settled on Indian lands before they had been properly surveyed and offered for sale. Internal evidence points to the latter.

MISSISSIPPI TERRITORY MUNROW COUNDTY January 20th 1816
    Dear Sir in viewing our last Papers we find it very Distressing news for us to be obliged to move all of the Public lands,—which will Distress Not less than 500 families—in order for your Honour to be in possession of our Distress Situation I thought Proper to inform you we are at least 300 Milds from any State the news Reached us two late to Purchase lands on the tombigee—and all that is werth living on has been Sold—had we had Knowledg of this we would a have had land two—but general Jackson encouraged us to Settle on the allebarmer—there is also a Number of People from North & South Carolina & georgia and a grate Number of them has sold there Carages waggon & &—and Now how to get back god only knows—there is also a Number of Poore widows that has lost there Husbands in the late war with the British & Indians and is Not able to Move of—there assembled also about 70 Indians on the allebarmer Near the Standing Peach tree and states that the treaty between the Americans & British gave them there lands, and the Mean to work it—if we leave our Plantations the Indians will be shore to burn them the People in this Country are New Settlers and Mostly Poore People that has been already Ruined by the Indians—and Now to leave there Crops of wheat gardens & turnips will Compleetly Distress them over agian a grate Number of Citizens Scearcely Made bread last year oweing to the Invation with the British & Indians—I

am of the opinion that there Has been Some Rong Misrepresentations made to your Honour in Regard to the Public Lands—there has been a Stop to Cutting Down timber for Several Months which was obeyed all the lands that that was Improved Sold Considerably better then that was Not is went to 6–8 & 10 Dollers Pr achre that was good and that was Not Improved went genner lly at govenment Price I will also state to your Honour that if there in Not Preemptions allowd to the Citizens of this Cuntry that the Yazzo Company will Purchase all the good land from the Head to the Mouth of the allebarmer it will take all the good land to Pay five Million of Dollers—if your Honour should think Proper to Let us Stay till we make a Crop it would be a Blessing to some— Particular to those widows & Children that there Husbands has been Masicreed by the Savages—it is Impossible for us at this Hour to go and bui Land & build Houses and open land time Enought to make a Support—it is one of the Most Destressing News that we Even heard of it is worse then the Indian & British war. The feellings of our Citizens is very much Hurt Particualr those who fought Brave to obtain this Cuntry and Now Cannot Injoy it if the thing Could be Rightly Constrewed to our government I Cannot but think but what the orders would be Countermanded though I am always willing to Concur on my Part with any law that Govement will adopt—if your Honour would be so good as to favour me with an answer when Convenient and Direct your Letters to Fishers Post office on the allebarmer Near Fort Claibourne.— Clabon Harris to the President, *Territorial Papers,* vol. 6, pp. 647–48.

Clabon Harris may have known little about spelling or sentence structure but he still could plead his cause eloquently. There is something heartening about the fact that a frontiersman of his limited learning felt that he could appeal directly to the President of the United States.

A President Visits Huntsville

A political and social event of major importance in north Alabama in the late territorial period was the visit of President James Monroe to Huntsville in June 1819.

ARRIVAL OF THE PRESIDENT

On Tuesday last the President of the United States with Mr. Governeur, his private Secretary, and Lieut. Monroe of the Army, very unexpectedly arrived in Huntsville, and put up at the Inn. No intimation of his intention to visit our town had been received by any individual in it; but the citizens solicitous to show their respect to the Chief Magistrate of the Union, appointed a committee to wait upon his Excellency and invite him to a public dinner on which occasion C. C. Clay, esq. addressed him nearly in the following words:

SIR: In behalf of the citizens of Huntsville, we have the honor to wait upon your excellency and to communicate the joy with which we hail the arrival of the Chief Magistrate of the nation, in our remote and humble village. Be assured, sir, we duly appreciate the motives which have prompted you to a repetition of the labors we have seen you perform in the North, by your visit to the southern portion of the United States. We are sensible of the great advantage of adding practical observation to that extensive information which we have before seen so happily illustrated.

Permit us to congratulate you on the general tranquility and prosperity which have prevailed, and on the valuable acquisition of territory which has been made, in our vicinity, under your enlightened administration. We assure you that we contemplate with feelings of national pride the happy result of a policy founded in principle, and which has for its sole object the exhaltation of our country. If, sir, your time and convenience will permit, we should be happy to give you some feeble testimony of our respect and affection, and to have the honor of your Excellency's company at a public dinner on tomorrow.

To which the president answered in substance that he had undertaken the task of visiting different portions of the United States, more particularly with a view of examining the situation of the fortifications and of selecting suitable sites to be put in a state of defense against foreign aggression in the event of a future war which, he was happy to say, there was no immediate prospect of; that he conceived it the duty of the chief magistrate of the Union to acquaint himself with a knowledge of the interior country over which he presided, and as far as was practicable to ascertain the state of society and of improvement in agriculture, manufactures, &c, and also to enquire into the condition of the Indian tribes which were dispersed through the western portion of the Union. . . . He stated it was necessary for him to return to Washington by the 15th of July, when it was probable the Spanish treaty ceding the Floridas, to the United States would be received, at which time his presence at the seat of government would be indespensable . . . and concluded by accepting the invitation to dinner.

On Wednesday at 4 o'clock, the President and suite, together with more than one hundred of the most respectable citizens of Madison County, sat down to a sumptuous entertainment prepared by Capt. Toby Jones, at which Col. LeRoy Pope acted as President, assisted by C. C. Clay and Henry Minor, Esqrs., as Vice-Presidents. After the cloth was removed the following sentiments were drunk, accompanied by the discharge of cannon and appropriate songs.

TOASTS

1. Our Country.—She has proved that man is not incapable of self-government; may her example have its influence throughout the world.
2. The Constitution of the United States;—a legitimate form of government, instituted by express compact, and supported by the affections of the people.

[There were twenty-one in all. They included "our distinguished guest," Major General Andrew Jackson, General John Coffee, the late treaty with Spain, education, the people of the territories west of the

Mississippi, the friends of freedom in South America, and last, "Our
Fair Country Women—They feel the glow of patriotism in common with
those who defend them."]

BY THE PRESIDENT OF THE UNITED STATES:

The Territory of Alabama—may her speedy admission into the
Union advance her happiness, and augment the national strength and
prosperity. . . .

The company rose from the table about sunset, highly delighted with
the entertainment they had received and the opportunity they had enjoyed of demonstrating their great regard and affection for Mr. Monroe,
who now appeared to them more like a plain citizen than the Chief
Magistrate of a great nation. . . .

The President left this town on the ensuing day, 3rd inst. for Nashville
and was escorted by a number of respectable citizens several miles of
his way. The whole company being on horseback, he conversed freely
with those who were nearest him, and after exchanging the most cordial
expressions of respect and good will separated from them. . . .—*Alabama Republican,* June 5, 1819, printed in *Transactions of the Alabama
Historical Society, 1898–1899,* vol. 3, pp. 154–58.

Huntsville, named for John Hunt who built a cabin near Big
Springs in 1802, had taken an early lead among settlements in the
Tennessee River Valley. Madison County, of which it was the seat
of government, was the oldest county in the northern part of the
territory. It was organized in 1808 out of lands obtained by treaty
from the Cherokees in 1805. Six months after Mr. Monroe's visit,
another Virginian, Mrs. Anne Royall, arrived for what proved to
be a prolonged stay. She liked Huntsville and predicted that one
could "expect something from this flourishing town." She wrote a
friend back home in western Virginia that

The land around Huntsville, and the whole of Madison County . . .
is rich and beautiful as you can imagine, and the appearance of wealth
would baffle belief. The town stands on elevated gound, and enjoys a
beautiful prospect. There is a large square in the center of town . . .
and facing this all the stores, twelve in number. These buildings form
a solid wall though divided into apartments. The workmanship is the
best I have seen in all the states, and several of the houses are three
stories high and very large. There is no church. The people assemble in
the Court House to worship. Huntsville is settled by people mostly from
Georgia and the Carolinas—though there are a few from almost every
part of the world—and the town displays much activity. The citizens
are gay, polite, and hospitable, and live in great splendor.—Anne Royall,
Letters From Alabama, Lucille Griffith, ed. (University: University of
Alabama Press, 1969), p. 119.

The Vine and Olive Colony

Most settlements in early Alabama were typical of the American frontier. The French colony at Demopolis, however, is a colorful exception. It is also an example of the way international events have affected this state's history.

These Frenchmen, the first of whom arrived in 1818, were Bonapartists who, following Napoleon's final defeat at Waterloo in 1815, were in danger of their lives. The Bourbon monarchy of Louis XVIII had proscribed several officers and nearly forty of the leading Bonapartists had been ordered to leave Paris within three days. Others were exiled. In each of these groups were persons who fled to America and eventually settled in Alabama.

Appealing to certain prominent Americans, among them William Lee and Henry Clay, the French leaders were able to get Congress to grant them 92,160 acres of public land on the Tombigbee River. The settlers were to pay $2.00 per acre but had fourteen years in which to do it. The largest group of these Frenchmen went from Philadelphia to Mobile aboard the *McDonough*. Count Charles Lefebvre Desnouettes was the leader of the expedition. Colonel Nicholas Simon Parmentier, secretary to the colonizing company who was on the *McDonough*, wrote a letter from White Bluff (Demopolis) on July 14, 1817. In it he described their arrival in Mobile.

> We reached Mobile on the 25th ult., and found that our arrival was expected. The officers of the government, those who would be benefited by the increase of inhabitants and the augmentation of the price of produce, those who were friendly to the prosperity of the country, and, indeed, all who were not actuated by a jealousy as short-sighted as pitiable, were favorably disposed towards our settlement. Mr. Gibson, a public agent, and a man of liberal education, Mr. John Toulmin, brother of Judge Harry Toulmin, and Mr. (Addin) Lewis, the collector of the port, distinguished for their merit and affability, treated us with the greatest possible attention and introduced us to the first houses of Mobile, from whom we obtained very particular information of the country we were about to traverse. Mr. Lewis offered us the use of the revenue cutter, which we accepted, so that our first excursion up the country was made under the United States flag.—Quoted in Gaius Whitfield, Jr., "The French Grant in Alabama, A History of the Founding of Demopolis," *Transactions of the Alabama Historical Society,* vol. 4 (1904), p. 328.

After stopping at Fort Stoddert, where they were met by Harry Toulmin, and Fort Montgomery, where they were presented to

Toulmin's son-in-law, E.P. Gaines, who had helped apprehend Aaron Burr, Parmentier and the other officials followed Gaines' advice to settle at White Bluff.

> We have explored the country situated on the east side of the Tombigby, above the line called the Choctaw boundary, and we have resolved to fix ourselves on the spot known by the name of the White Bluff, about three-fourths of a mile below the junction of the Black Warrior and Tombigby rivers, as part of our grant. It remains to say in what shape the four townships are to be laid out, and this we will do as soon as the meridian line shall be continued twelve miles above the White Bluff, and the lines of demarcation shall be marked as far as the said Bluff. The season is already advanced and no resource would be left to a number of individuals during the ensuing winter in the benevolent intentions of the government towards us are not administered with some celerity. White Bluff is one of the finest situations I ever saw in my life. Nature here offers us everything. If we know how to profit by these advantages we must be happy.—Ibid., p. 330.

The four contiguous sections of land surveyed for the French were mostly in Marengo County but some of it was in Greene, including some very good land around Greensboro. The French had dfficulty about their location and, finding they were on land other than their own, had to move from their clearings three times. In February 1827, William L. Adams, agent of the Treasury department, reported what was being done toward growing vines for wine and olives for oil as the original plans called for.

> From my own examination, and the best information I could obtain, there are seven thousand four hundred and fourteen acres cultivated in vine, corn, cotton, small grain, etc. The quantity of land planted and cultivated in vine within the four townships granted is two hundred and seventy-one and one-half acres, and the manner of planting the vine is by putting the vines ten feet apart in one direction and twenty the other, and fastening the vine to a stake put in the ground for that purpose, of a size and height to suit the vine. The plantings are in their cotton fields, and are cultivated in the same manner as their cotton is. The number of olive trees planted within the four townships granted has been three hundred and eighty-eight, some of them about six years ago, and the latest three years since. Two hundred trees were imported, and perished on the way, and twenty-five thousand seed have been planted. The tree perishes with every winter's frost, but puts up fresh shoots in the spring, which also perish with the succeeding winter's frost; and I feel confident in the belief that the tree will not succeed in this climate.—Ibid., 348.

About the same time, Frederick Revesies, "agent for the Tombeckbee Association," explained why the French had not carried out their part of the bargain.

It will be recollected that the members of our association were chiefly composed of officers and merchants, possessing an extremely limited knowledge of either the science or practice of agriculture; that the region of country to which they were to remove was a perfect wilderness; and, under circumstances like these, it is to be expected that very many unforeseen and unexpected difficulties would present themselves; and as the common necessaries and means of support must be obtained before an entrance could be made upon the principal object of the association (the culture of the vine), we have, in many instances, been obliged to neglect the performers of our contract, and yield to the more immediate and pressing demands upon our industry for a bare competency and support. Many of the grantees, unfortunately for themselves, came prematurely to their lands, they came to the trackless desert or country, almost impervious to the approach of man, without a road or passway; consequently, the means of transportation to their particular allotments of land was so impracticable and expensive that many persons upon their arrival were compelled to settle, temporarily, on their small allotments around the town of Aigleville, where their funds were exhausted and they became unable to make a second settlement upon their large allotment. The surveyor's report of these lands will exhibit the difficulty of passing through the country, their notes showing that for many days they could not proceed more than 2 or 3 miles per day.

Many of us were obliged to pay as much as four or five dollars per bushel for corn, and a proportionate price for many other articles of provisions, which prices were very frequently doubled by the difficulties of transportation to their residences. 40 or 50 dollars have often been paid for a cow and a calf, which can now be purchased for 8 or 10 dollars. Thus commenced our strangers to the language, the manners, and habits of the people of this country, we have been greatly retarded from making the rapid progress, which perhaps the citizens of the United States would have made.

In addition to those natural difficulties under which we labored, we had other and more serious ones to encounter; for upon almost all that part of our grant which was the easiest to settle and cultivate, the squatter, who is the pioneer of all new countries, settling a new country, at once became hostile to our claims and sternly refused possession to the grantees, in some instances denying the right of the emigrant and in many others threatening the most violent and determined vengeance upon any person who would interfere with his settlement. From these circumstances many were deterred coming to their lands and in many instances those difficulties exist until this day, there having been as yet but one decision upon the subject, which was in 1825, which judged to the grantee the right of possession and entry, but many continue wrongfully to hold our lands, and refuse possession.

Again many of the allotments, from their natural locality, being within the prairie country, admit of no settlement, on account of the impracticability of procuring water, many having dug a great depth unsuccessfully; these still remain unsettled and unimproved. I further will remark that for several years the colony was remarkably unhealthy, scarcely a family escaped sickness, and many of the grantees died. These, sir, are some of the reasons why failures have occurred in regard to the conditions of settlements, etc. You will now permit me to mention some of the causes which have produced the failure in the condition relative to the vine; and here some of the same reasons present themselves that have been previously stated—the necessity of first acquiring the means of subsistence; the difficulty and length of time required in preparing and clearing land for that, that the 7 years had nearly elapsed before this was accomplished; yet very early importations of the vine were made long before the time necessary for planting them. But a large quantity of those first imported arrived out of season; and when we consider the lateness of the season in Europe when the cutting must be taken, and the early time at which they must be planted here, it will be seen that and delay in the arrival of vessels must prove fatal to the vines, and they will arrive out of due season. Many more vines have been shipped in due time, and had they all safely arrived, those would have been more than requisite to comply with the condition of the contract, upon all of the allotments, by the time required. All that have arrived alive have been carefully planted, and none wasted; as evidence of which they sold at first for 25 cts, a piece, then twelve and a half, and the last year at six and a quarter cents. A great number died after planting, owing as we believe to the newness of the soil on which we were obliged to plant. The vine required old land which we have not; and at first, not knowing the cause, the result was discouraging. Those planted in older soils grew better, and are not so apt to die. Again, many kinds of the vine have been imported which do not succeed in this country, and it is but very lately that we are enabled, in some degree, to ascertain the quality and kind of vine best adapted to this climate. At this time the great question seems to be the proper mode of cultivation, and, instead of seven, perhaps seventy years may be required to ascertain this fact. This will be readily conceded when it is known that in France, in many places, the mode of cultivation is radically different on opposite sides of the same river or mountain, and on farms differently situated in the same country. Your excellency is well aware how many years, nay centuries, Europe has required to obtain this experience and perfection. We can assert that from our own experience, seven years are not sufficient to enable us to cultivate the vine successfully in an old country, and much more so in a wilderness.—Ibid., pp. 338–50.

The colony was a failure from the start. The French were unable to grow either vines or olives in any profitable way. Furthermore, they were continually annoyed by American squatters who settled on their lands with no legal right and who found their ways strange and, at times, amusing. Anne Royall, visiting in central Alabama about 1822, was much entertained by stories of these Frenchmen. A young merchant from Demopolis, for example, explained how they cleared their land.

When they first began to clear their vinyard, they sent five men three miles for a rope and having previously provided axes, about 25 or 30 in a body proceed to the business [of cutting down a tree]. In the first place one ascends the tree . . . and ties the rope hard and fast to the top. He then descends and ten or a dozen of them take the end of the rope whilst the others commenced cutting and perform a portion of the task in rotation. They cut all round, up and down crossways and lengthways the tree. Meantime the rope division kept pulling. At length down came the tree, killed two and crippled several. From that day to the present, no entreaty or persuasion can prevail on them to resume the business of clearing. . . .—Anne Royall, *Sketches of History, Life and Manners in the United States, By a Traveller* (New Haven, 1826), pp. 24–26.

Consequently, they had only patches for raising their vegetables. If they had to have a tree cut down for firewood or some other reason, they simply hired Americans to do it for them. Mrs. Royall's informant said they had no more judgment about farming than children and that the government was adopting measures to get rid of them and "let those have the land who may turn it to better account."

Gradually the French moved to Mobile, joined relatives in New Orleans, or returned to France. By 1830 there were very few of the original families (347 families had been granted land) left in the Demopolis area. While it lasted, however, it had been a bright spot in the wilderness. A. J. Pickett described the French as happy "in the midst of their trials and vicissitudes."

Being in the habit of much social intercourse, their evenings were spent in conversation, music, and dancing. The larger portion were well educated, while all had seen the world, and such materials were ample to afford an elevated society. Sometimes their distant friends sent them rich wines and other luxuries, and upon such occasions parties were given. . . . The female circle was highly interesting. They had brought with them their books, guitars, silks, parasols and ribbons, and the village . . . resembled at night a miniature French town.—A. J. Pickett *History of Alabama* (Sheffield, Alabama, 1896), p. 663. Pickett used information he gained from conversations with George N. Stewart of Mobile, who had been secretary of the French Vine Company.

Today most of the evidence of their few years in Alabama is in place names. Demopolis and Aigleville are the names they gave to their settlements; Marengo County is named for a battle in which most of them had participated. There are a few olive trees that mutely remind us that they expected to develop an economy similar to that of southern Europe.

The territorial years had been eventful. The people, with the help of the federal government, had developed a workable political system; the economy had taken the form it would keep for upwards of a century; an occasional visit from an important figure added spice to frontier life; there had been one major Indian war and innumerable skirmishes and raids; and, most of all, the American pioneers, generally from Georgia, the Carolinas, and Tennessee, came in a steady stream.

By 1819 towns, often booming, had grown up north and south. Mobile was the oldest and largest but Blakeley across the bay and St. Stephens, Jackson, and Claiborne up the river were thriving. In the north, Huntsville was the leading center but Florence, Courtland, and others were developing in the rich Tennessee Valley. In between, there were scattered settlements.

By and large, international problems affecting Alabama had been settled. But white Americans still had to cope with red Americans, as they had been doing since early Spanish days.

Chapter 3

THE INDIANS

The natives of Alabama were red men. As every school child knows, when Columbus first saw the inhabitants of the Caribbean islands he started calling them Indians. Convinced that he had reached the sought-for Indies, he naturally assumed the people to be Indians, and Europeans have persisted in perpetuating the misnomer.

The Indians held a strange fascination for Europeans. For the early explorers they were a strange breed of men; they were neither Caucasian, Mongoloid, nor Negroid, the racial types with which they were familiar. Who, then, were they? There were many theories, but the most persistent one was that they were descendants of the "ten lost tribes of Israel." According to Biblical history, after the return from exile the two tribes of Judah and Benjamin remained the only people in the Promised Land, the others disappearing into oblivion. In all probability, they were absorbed into the other Semitic tribes in the Fertile Crescent, but there continued persistent legends about the fate of the tribes. That these tribes had reached the North American continent after wandering over Asia for several centuries was the theory of James Adair, Scottish Indian agent for the British government, who spent upwards of forty years (presumably from 1735 to 1775) among the natives of the Southeast. After these years of close contact with the Indian Americans he was convinced they were

. . . lineally descended from the Israelites, either while they were a maritime power, or soon after the general captivity; the latter however is the most probable. This descent, I shall endeavour to prove from their religious rites, civil and martial customs, their marriages, funeral ceremonies, manners, language, traditions, and a variety of particulars.— James Adair, *History of the American Indians* (Johnson City, Tennes-

see: The Watauga Press, 1930), pp. 14–15. This book was first
published in London in 1775.

The author then spends nearly five hundred pages defending his
thesis of the "copper colored American Hebrews." Although Adair
belabors his point, his work is extremely valuable for his observations on every phase of Indian life.

For Alabamians historic Indian times began in 1519 when the
Spanish explorer Pineda spent forty days in the Mobile area repairing his ships. He found a large Indian village on the bay and
some forty more in the 15 miles he explored up the Mobile River.

Before Pineda, however, were thousands of years of Indian life
in this area; just how long the experts do not agree, but it now
seems to be longer than formerly supposed. It is commonly accepted that the Indians were of Asiatic origin and came to this
continent by way of the Bering Strait some 40,000 to 50,000 years
ago. An Indian legend says it poetically, "In a remote period of
time our ancestors dwelt in a country far distant toward the
setting sun." Just when they arrived in the section east of the
Mississippi River is not known, but recent discoveries prove that
there was human life along the Tennessee River at least 10,000 to
12,000 years ago. Two sites have been of particular interest to
archeologists: the Stanfield-Worley Shelter in Colbert County near
Tuscumbia, and Russell Cave in Jackson County, near Bridgeport.
The Stanfield-Worley Shelter was excavated by the University of
Alabama in 1961. Work at Russell Cave was begun in 1954 by
the University of Chattanooga but later was taken over by the
Smithsonian Institution and National Geographic Society. It has
been declared a public monument and is now administered by the
National Park Service, Department of the Interior. From study
which continues of these and other locations in the state, scientists
believe that the human inhabitants of Alabama went through at
least six ages before the arrival of the first Europeans. The earliest
(before 8000 B.C.) was Paleolithic man, who "clothed in skins,
armed with stone weapons, did battle with beasts and the elements."
Stone spears and meat dressing tools such as he might have used
are found in all parts of Alabama. From 8000 to 7000 B.C. man
was living in a transition period from the Paleolithic to Archaic
ages. This is the age in which the Stanfield-Worley culture developed. The Archaic age was a long one, from about 7000 B.C. to
2000 B.C., during which man improved his tools, became a gatherer
as well as a hunter, and began decorating his stone utensils with
carvings. During the later part of this period he began making
pottery, an invention which had far reaching consequences. It is
believed that about this time (ca. 2000 B.C.) man began his first

efforts at domesticating plants which was a natural step to the
period archaeologists call "Woodland" (2000 B.C. to 800 A.D.). The
people in this age made pottery, carved rather elaborate stone objects, and decorated them with intricate designs. In the prehistoric
period (800 A.D. to 1500 A.D.) the inhabitants were the Mississippi Indians whom the Spanish discovered. They had villages and
complicated systems of religion and government and built mounds.

The Mound Builders

Mound builders, common to the eastern part of the United
States, lived in many sections of Alabama. These prehistoric people
erected earth and stone mounds for burial grounds, lookout positions, ceremonial sites, and locations for temples and the dwellings
of their chief men. The ones in Alabama are on river banks, making
one wonder if they did not serve as places of refuge in times of
high water. Marengo County has a big cluster of mounds on the
banks of the Tombigbee River; Baldwin and Mobile Counties
have earth mounds in addition to the shell mounds found only along
the coast. Clark, Montgomery, and Elmore Counties also have
mounds. In Dallas County excavations have unearthed burial urns,
covered with inverted pots of like design, holding single skeletons,
and one holding the skeletons of several infants.

The most important group of mounds, however, is near Moundville, south of Tuscaloosa, on the border between Hale and Tuscaloosa Counties on the Warrior River. Here are forty mounds, some
rectangular, some oval, arranged in a rough circle. They are on
a 315 acre tract which was named Mound State Monument in 1938;
in 1961 the Monument became a division of the University of Alabama. The Archeological Museum, dedicated in 1939, has an
elaborate display of objects excavated in the mound area, including
several graves showing skeletons in their original positions.

These mound builders were of medium height and build who considered a flattened head a mark of beauty. Their garments were of
skin and woven vegetable fabrics; their ornaments consisted of ear
plugs, bracelet arm bands, and beads made of copper, bone, shell
and stone. They lived in houses built of logs and poles with walls
of reeds and canes, plastered with thick coatings of sand and
clay. The roofs were thatch and the floors sand. They lived on meat
from the forest and fish from the rivers and vegetables (corn,
squash, beans and pumpkins) from their fields. In addition to their
tools for gathering food and making shelter and clothing, they devised nets for catching fish, bone awls and needles, chisels and
pestles. Religion was of prime importance to these mound builders;
the mounds on which they worshipped are lasting evidence to this

fact. Their religious ceremonies were elaborate and colorful; the priests were attired in symbolic costumes, copper breast plates, stone discs and pendants, delicately and beautifully carved. They buried their dead with care and respect. Probably their greatest achievement besides the mounds themselves was the pottery, especially their nonutilitarian ware, exquisitely decorated using the finest clay available. The potter shaped bowls, pots, shallow dishes and effigy vessels in the forms of frogs, ducks, beaver, rabbit, owl, shell and even human beings. Nowhere have there been found any objects of European origin, a fact which indicates that the culture lay entirely within the prehistoric period.

Just what the relationship was between the various people who lived in the area is not fully understood. Some scientists have doubted that the mound builders were Indians at all; it was once believed that cultures like those at Russell Cave and Moundville flourished for a time and then ended for some unexplained reason. It is now generally believed that each age was parent of the next and that the early inhabitants were ancestors of the Indians.

Historic Indians

The Europeans found four general tribal groupings in the area between the Chattahoochee and the Tombigbee Rivers. The Creeks, divided into Upper and Lower, occupied the eastern half. The Western, or Overhill, Cherokees lived in the northeastern corner, the Chickasaws in the northwest, and the Choctaws in the west.

No single major tribe lived wholly within the boundaries of this state. Most Cherokees were in North Carolina and eastern Tennessee, a majority of the Chickasaws and Choctaws in Mississippi, and Georgia shared the Creeks with the regions of the west. It was in Alabama, however, that these four tribes had a common even if shadowy boundary. There were many small subtribes of a few towns each that were all within the area, names of which appear often in early descriptions—Coosadas, Uchees, Coosas, Alabamos, and many others. The Indians differed in language, dress, customs, and appearance, but had many traditions in common.

INDIAN MYTHS

The Indians had numerous legends, which, like the myths of ancient Greece, attempted to explain natural phenomena. The flood, creation, and eclipses were favorite subjects. There were many versions of the origin of corn, their most important food. One was that it was the gift of a child, another that a crow brought a single grain from a distant land and presented it to an orphan child, and still another that it was the gift of "The Unknown Woman." Charles

Lanman, writer and amateur explorer, recorded the version given here:

It was in olden times, and two Choctaw hunters were spending the night by their watch-fire in a bend of the river Alabama. The game and the fish of their country were with every new moon becoming less abundant, and all that they had to satisfy their hunger on the night in question, was the tough flesh of a black hawk. They were very tired, and as they mused upon their unfortunate condition, and thought of their hungry children, they were very unhappy, and talked despondingly. But they roasted the bird before the fire, and proceeded to enjoy as comfortable a meal as they could. Hardly had they commenced eating, however, before they were startled by a singular noise, resembling the cooing of a dove. They jumped up and looked around them to ascertain the cause. In one direction they saw nothing but the moon just rising above the forest trees on the opposite side of the river. They looked up and down the river, but could see nothing but the sandy shores and the dark waters. They listened, and nothing could they hear but the murmur of the flowing stream. They turned their faces in that direction opposite the moon, and to their astonishment, they discovered standing upon the summit of a grassy mound, the form of a beautiful woman. They hastened to her side, when she told them that she was very hungry, whereupon they ran after their roasted hawk, and gave it all into the hands of the strange woman. She barely tasted of the proffered food, but told the hunters that their kindness had preserved her from death, and that she would not forget them when she returned to the happy grounds of her dear father, who was Hosh-tal-li, or Great Spirit of the Choctaws. She had one request to make, and this was, that when the next moon of midsummer should arrive, they should visit the spot where she then stood. A pleasant breeze swept among the forest leaves, and the strange woman suddenly disappeared.

The hunters were astonished, but they returned to their families, and kept all that they had seen and heard, hidden in their hearts. Summer came, and they once more visited the mound on the banks of the Alabama. They found it covered with a new plant, whose leaves were like the knives of the white man. It yielded a delicious food, which has since been known among the Choctaws as sweet toncha or Indian maize.— *Adventures in the Wilds of the United States and British American Provinces* (Philadelphia: J. W. Moore, 1856), vol. 2, pp. 463–64.

CHARACTERISTICS OF THE INDIANS

What were Indians like? How did they look? What were their personal characteristics? What kind of houses did they live in? What were their ideas of family life? of religion? of government? How did they "make a living"? What did they do for entertainment? How did the various tribes compare? It seems that every literate visitor to this area tried to answer these questions for his friends, thus providing voluminous material for posterity.

While differences among the tribes were more obvious to the
Indians than to the Europeans, there were certain common physical
characteristics: copper colored skin, black eyes and straight black
hair, high cheek bones, erect posture, athletic build, and grace in
movement. Men had sparse beards and "shaved" by plucking out
whiskers with clamshell "tweezers." Women had surprisingly small
hands and feet.

Samuel Cole Williams has collected many descriptive statements
about the Chickasaws from contemporary English, French, and
Spanish observers. Indians, whom James Adair called "cheerful
and gallant" friends, were "brave as ever trod the ground and
faithful under greatest dangers even unto death."

> The nation of the Chickasaws is very warlike. The men have regular
> features, well shaped and neatly dressed; they are fierce, and have a high
> opinion of themselves. The nations who border upon them who speak
> the Chickasaw language best value themselves upon it.
>
> They are accounted and esteemed the bravest Indians upon the main,
> which makes good the common observation that the bravest soldiers are
> generally the most civil to prisoners.
>
> They are the most indefatigable and most valiant of all the Indians.
>
> Not so numerous as the Choctaws, but more terrible on account of
> their intrepidity. The Chickasaws are tall, well made, and of an un-
> paralleled courage.
>
> A brave warlike people; tall, well-shaped and handsome featured.
>
> These brave Indians, our ancient allies and steady friends; irrecon-
> cilable enemies of the French.
>
> There is no Indian nation on the continent near so handsome as the
> Chickasaws; they have always been distinguished for their gallant actions
> and feats of heroism which have rendered them, even individually to be
> particularly respected throughout all the nations of North America. For
> which reason Chickasaw guides are more sought after and are more
> serviceable than those of any other nation.
>
> The most intrepid warriors of the South.
>
> The bravest of the brave. Admirably proportioned, athletic, active
> and graceful in their movements, and possessed of open and manly
> countenances.
>
> Their courage exceeded that of all other aborigines. Neighboring
> tribes found them invincible.
>
> Through all the epochs of colonial history the Chickasaw people main-
> tained their old reputation for independence and bravery.
>
> The ancient Chickasaws have justly been regarded as the bravest and
> most skillful warriors among all the American Indians.
>
> The smallest of the Southern nations, but they were also the bravest
> and most warlike.
>
> Noted from remote times for their bravery, independence and warlike
> disposition.—Adair, *History of the American Indians*, pp. 341–42,
> n. 178.

Although the Choctaws are estimated to have been the largest tribe in the Southeast, many of them lived in Mississippi, leaving more Creeks than any other people in the area that was to become Alabama. In all probability, more than half the estimated 30,000 Indians living here at the advent of the white settlers were Creeks. Lord Adam Gordon, who wrote the following description of the Creeks, visited the Gulf of Mexico area in the late summer of 1764:

. . . They [the Creeks] are a hardy well made Set of people, calculated seemingly to bear fatigue, their features are manly and expressive, and with the advantages of European Education and Address, would equal them in many particulars.—They early rub themselves over with grease and some juice of an Herb, which renders their faces and bodies of a dunn copper tint—they pluck all the hair off their beards, and value high foreheads,—what hair remains they plait or braid behind wearing a variety of things mixt with it, such as Strings, Shells, and feathers; some wear pieces of Metal and Shells to their Ears, which are almost always cut or Slit in uncommon Shapes, others have rings in the gristle of the Nose, and others large broad Bracelets round their Arms and Wrists.—The young Children that attend them down go naked, their Squaws and them selves are fond of having their faces painted with vermillion and black, in strange manners—when they come down it is always on Horse back, and when they return they carry their Kegs of Rum, which they call Taffy, upon their own backs, on Horseback, as well as much of the other presents, the most usual of which are as follows. Rum, Fire Arms, Flints, Powder and ball, Knives, Razors, Blankets, Shirts of all sorts, Beads, looking-glasses, and many other trifles; for these and such like they barter Skins—mostly Deer Skins.— "Journal of Lord Adam Gordon," Newton D. Mereness (ed.), *Travels in the American Colonies* (New York: The Macmillan Co., 1916), p. 385.

He (James Adair) found the Choctaws attractive in appearance:

The Choktah are in general more slender than any other nation of savages I have seen. They are raw-boned, and surprisingly active in ball-playing; which is a very sharp exercise, and requires great strength and exertion. In this manly exercise, no persons are known to be equal to them, or in running on level ground, to which they are chiefly used from their infancy, on account of the situation of their country, which hath plenty of hills, but no mountains; these lie at a considerable distance between them and the Muskohge.—Adair, *History of the American Indians,* p. 328.

In personal characteristics Adair considered the Choctaws

. . . the craftiest, and most ready-witted, of any of the red nations I am acquainted with. It is surprising to hear the wily turns they use, in persuading a person to grant them the favour they have in view. Other nations generally behave with modesty and civility, without ever lessening themselves by asking any mean favours. But the Choktah, at every season, are on the begging lay. I several times told their leading men, they were greater beggars, and of a much meaner spirit, than the white-haired Chikkasah women, who often were real objects of pity. I was once fully convinced that none was so fit to baffle them in those low attempts without giving offence, as their own country-men.—*Ibid.,* p. 325.

Their dress, while it may have varied slightly from tribe to tribe, was made of native materials and was designed to serve the needs of a wilderness people. Contact with Europeans resulted in strange (and at times ludicrous) combinations of dress, but before that time standard everyday dress was a breech clout and moccasins of deer skin for men and loose petticoat of skins for women. What else each wore varied with the weather and personal taste. Deer skins, treated until they were soft and pliable, were used for shoes, leggins, breeches, shirts, skirts, and many other items; fiber from certain plants and the soft inner bark of some trees could be woven into a coarse cloth; skins of bears, buffaloes, beavers, and other animals were sewn together for shawls or blankets.

James Adair, William Bartram, and many others who lived among the aborigines for considerable time found much to praise, but others found traits of cruelty, revenge, blood-thirstiness, and treachery. It is a well known fact that the Indians attacked isolated white individuals and at times massacred whole settlements; what is less publicized is that they made equally vicious attacks on rival Indian tribes whom they pursued relentlessly and attacked ruthlessly; they led scalping parties against both races.

Many observers were convinced that the savage nature of the aborigines was brought out by intoxicating liquors. The Indians seem to have had little, if any, alcoholic drinks in their native state, and they succumbed too easily to a taste for white man's rum and corn "likker." Governments, humanitarians, and apprehensive people on the frontier tried to control the sale of whiskey to them, but unauthorized traders and even legitimate merchants found that it was easy to obtain valuable skins and furs from drink-crazed hunters. To their ultimate sorrow, they discovered that a drunk Indian was a dangerous Indian.

In an attempt to protect its residents, the General Assembly of Mississippi Territory passed an act (December 6, 1816) ". . . to prevent the sale of spiritous liquors to Indians." Each person who was granted a license to serve liquor took an oath that he would not sell to Indians, nor would he knowingly permit it on his premises.

Even when the Indians were sober and peaceful, whites found

them difficult to understand as they did not fit into the European way of doing things. More than one writer agreed with Adair's description of them:

> They are a very dilatory people, and noted for procrastinating every thing that admits of the least delay: but they are the readiest, and quickest of all people in going to shed blood, and returning home; whence the traders say, "that an Indian is never in haste, only when the devil is at his arse." This proverb is fully verified by their method of building; for while the memory of the bleak pinching winds lasts, and they are covered with their winter-blackened skins, they turn out early in the spring, to strip clap-boards and cypress-bark, for the covering of their houses: but in proportion as the sun advances, they usually desist from their undertaking during that favourable season; saying, "that in the time of warm weather, they generally plant in the fields, or go to war; and that building houses in the troublesome hot summer, is a needless and foolish affair, as it occasions much sweating," which is the most offensive thing in life to every red warrior of manly principles.—Adair, *History of the American Indians,* p. 448.

There were other ways in which the Indian way of thinking differed from the white man's. Having no written language, no method of keeping accounts, and little concept of numbers, they developed a vague terminology that exasperated those trying to do business with them and provided ample room for the dishonest to take advantage of the red men. There is the simple matter of telling time.

> They *divide* the year into spring—summer—autumn, or the fall of the leaf—and winter. . . . They number their years by any of those four periods, for they have no name for a year; and they subdivide these, and count the year by lunar months . . . They count the day also by the three sensible differences of the sun. They subdivide the day, by any of the aforesaid three standards—as half way between the sun's coming out of the water; and in like manner by midnight, or cock-crowing, &c. . . . They begin the year, at the first appearance of the first new moon of the vernal equinox. . . . They pay a great regard to the first appearance of every new moon, and, on the occasion, always repeat some joyful sounds, and stretch out their hands towards her—but at such times they offer no public sacrifice. . . . When they lack a full moon, or when they travel, they count by sleeps.—Ibid., pp. 79–80.

Furthermore, the red men had no concept of private ownership of land or houses. An individual "owned" a field or house as long as he used it; he abandoned "title" to it when he vacated it. Land belonged to a whole tribe, and no chief had the right to sell it or sign it away by treaty.

A myth about the red men, popularized by entertainment media, is that they were a laconic people, speaking only in monosyllables.

It is true that all Indians had a high sense of public decorum and would never interrupt a speaker. However, they were eloquent orators when the occasion demanded it. A man might indulge in much frivolity when enjoying the society of his friends but

> . . . the moment he entered a public council of his people as a member of it, his countenance immediately assumed a grave and solemn air and he bore himself with a stern and exalted dignity. . . . No matter how much the speakers might differ in their views, none were interrupted (in council) and all were listened to in the most respectful silence. The speaker stood in addressing his audience. When he had finished, after a few moments pause, another arose and delivered his talk around the circle of councilmen until all that wished to speak had given his views.—H.S. Halbert, *History of the Choctaws,* Ms. Department of Archives and History, Montgomery, Alabama, Folder 25.

In summary, there were many contradictions in their personal traits. John R. Swanton has summarized them:

> They are ingenious, witty, cunning, and deceitful; very faithful indeed to their own tribes, but privately dishonest, and mischievous to the Europeans and Christians. Their being honest and harmless to each other, may be through fear of resentment and reprisal—which is unavoidable in case of an injury. They are very close and retentive of their secrets; never forget injuries; revengeful of blood, to a degree of distraction. They are timorous, and, consequently, cautious; very jealous of encroachments from their Christian neighbor; and, likewise, content with freedom, in every turn of fortune. They are possessed of a strong comprehensive judgment,—can form surprisingly crafty schemes, and conduct them with equal caution, silence, and address; they admit none but distinguished warriors, and old beloved men, into their councils. They are slow, but very persevering in their undertakings—commonly temperate in eating, but excessively immoderate in drinking.—They often transform themselves by liquor into the likeness of mad foaming bears. The women, in general, are of a mild, amiable, soft disposition: exceedingly modest in their behavior, and very seldom noisy, either in the single, or married state.—John R. Swanton, *Indians of the Southeastern United States* (Washington, Government Printing Office, 1946), pp. 231–32.

HOUSING

Another common misconception is that Indians ordinarily lived in wigwams and tepees. They may have used them when families went on the fall hunt, in much the same way that later Americans used campers, but their usual dwellings were permanent homes. In the middle of the eighteenth century, James Adair observed that

Most of the Indians have clean, neat, dwelling houses, white-washed within and without, either with decayed oyster-shells, coarse-chalk, or white marly clay; one or other of which, each of our Indian nations abounds with, be they ever so far distant from the sea-shore: the Indians, as well as the traders, usually decorate their summer-houses with this favourite white-wash.—The former have likewise each a corn-house, fowl-house, and a hot-house, or stove for winter: and so have the traders likewise separate store-houses for their goods, as well as to contain the proper remittances received in exchange.—Adair, *History of the American Indians,* p. 443.

THE ECONOMY OF THE RED MEN

Hunting was the central activity and mainstay of Indian economy. Although long past the hunting stage of their more primitive ancestors, they still hunted mostly for food but partly for skins and pelts to be used in trade with the whites. Their prowess in the woods, stalking deer or other game, was proverbial. Bernard Romans, an English captain sent into the Tombigbee River basin in the early 1770's, described the method the Chickasaws used to stalk deer:

They hunt like all their neighbors with the skin and frontal bone of a deer's head, dried and stretched on elastic chips; the horns they scoup out very curiously, employing so much patience on this, that such a head and antlers often do not exceed ten or twelve ounces; they fix this on the left hand and imitating the motions of the deer in sight, they decoy them within sure shot; a Choctaw Indian, who was hunting with one of these decoys on his fist, saw a deer, and thinking to bring it to him, imitated the deer's motions of feeding and looking around in a very natural way, another savage within shot, mistaking the head for a real one, shot the ball through it, scarcely missing the fingers of the first. . . .—Bernard Romans, quoted in Swanton, *Indians of the Southeastern United States,* p. 315.

A similiar incident was recounted by H. B. Cushman:

Years ago I had a Choctaw (full-blood) friend as noble and true as ever man possessed. . . . Oft in our frequent hunts together, while silently gliding through the dense forests ten or fifteen rods apart, he would attract my attention by his well known ha ha (give caution) in a low but distinct tone of voice, and point to a certain part of the woods where he had discovered an animal of some kind; and though I looked as closely as possible I could see nothing whatever that resembled a living object of any kind. Being at too great a distance to risk a sure shot, he would signal me to remain quiet, as he endeavored to get closer. To me that was the most exciting and interesting part of the scene; for then began those strategic movements in which the most skillful white hunter

that I have ever seen, was a mere bungler. With deepest interest, not un-
mixed with excitement, I closely watched his every movement as he
slowly and steadily advanced, with eyes fixed upon his object; now crawling noiselessly upon his hands and knees, then as motionless as a stump;
now stretched full length upon the ground, then standing erect and
motionless; then dropping suddenly to the ground, and crawling off at an
acute angle to the right or left to get behind a certain tree or log, here
and there stopping and slowly raising his head just enough to look over
the top of the grass; then again hidden until he reached the desired tree;
with intense mingled curiosity and excitement, when hidden from my
view in the grass, did I seek to follow him in his course with my eyes.
Oft I would see a little dark spot not larger than my fist just above the
top of the grass, which slowly grew larger and larger until I discovered
it was his [seemingly] motionless head; and had I not known he was
there somewhere I would not have suspected it was a human head or the
head of anything else; and as I kept my eyes upon it, I noticed it slowly
getting smaller until gradually it disappeared; and when he reached the
tree, he then observed the same caution, slowly rising until he stood
erect and close to the body of the tree, then slowly and cautiously peep-
ing around it, first on the right, then on the left; and when, at this juncture, I have turned my eyes from him, but momentarily as I thought, to
the point where I thought the game must be, being also eager to satisfy
my excited curiosity as the kind of animal he was endeavoring to shoot,
yet, when I looked to the spot where I had just seen him—lo! he was
not there; and while wondering to what point of the compass he had
so suddenly disappeared unobserved, and vainly looking to find his
mysterious whereabouts, I would be startled by the sharp crack of his
rifle in a different direction from that in which I was looking for him, and
in turning my eye would see him slowly rising out of the grass at a point
a hundred yards from where I had last seen him.—H. B. Cushman,
quoted in John R. Swanton, ed., *Source Materials for the Social and
Ceremonial Life of the Choctaw Indians,* pp. 50–51.

Hunting was done at anytime the family larder needed replenish-
ing. In the spring a deer "call" was used to entice the prey. This
device, made of a hollow horn, was "fitted with a wooden mouthpiece which contains a small brass vibrating tongue"; when blown
it gave off a "rather shrill but weak sound" that could be modified
by blowing softly or violently. Soft tremulous tones made by moving the palm of the hand over the opening of the horn sounded
like the cry of a fawn which would attract does and curious bucks
to within gun- or bowshot. A similar "call" was used for turkeys.

The big hunt, however, came in the late fall, after the leaves
had fallen, when large numbers of hunters went out together, often
"many days' journey" from home. Sometimes they went alone; at
other times the women and children accompanied them, returning
about March with their smoked and dried venison. Usually some
of the older men remained in the village to hold possession of it.

Hunting was primarily for food but produced a by-product, skins, that answered many needs of clothing and household equipment. Furthermore, deerskins were the most important item Indians had to sell to the English, and later, the French, in exchange for European-made goods. As early as 1690 Englishmen out of Charleston were trading as far west as the Mississippi River. So far as is known, there was never an English fort in Alabama; however, Okfushee, now under the waters of Lake Martin in Tallapoosa County, was an important trading post. There were others at places where trails crossed.

By the time European settlers came into the lower South, Indians were well past the primitive hunting and fishing stage and were living in permanent dwellings and farming lands which they cleared in much the same manner that white pioneers learned to use. Farming was primarily for providing food for the family or tribe; little was raised for a market, although Adair says that the Indians around Pensacola and Mobile sold peas, squash, corn, pumpkins, melons, and potatoes to the local inhabitants. Bernard Romans noted that in 1770 Indians raised and sold to the white settlers leeks, garlic, cabbage, and several kinds of corn, including popcorn. All tribes hunted, all raised corn, all gathered, and preserved for later use, berries, plums, nuts of various kinds; all grew beans, peas, pumpkins, and various kinds of squash in addition to at least four main kinds of corn.

The Choctaws were considered the best farmers. Thanks to Bernard Romans, James Adair, Jean-Bernard Bossu, William Bartram, Henry S. Halbert, and others, we have considerable knowledge about their agricultural methods and products.

Clearing lands was man's work; planting corn was work for all; but once the seed was in the ground, the crops were worked by the women. The men hunted or went on the warpath. The women, on whom much sympathy has been lavished, seemed not to have considered their work unreasonably heavy. The soil was loose, and work in the fields provided a welcome opportunity for companionship with other women. Many observers mention the chatter that went on among the women hoeing corn.

All Alabama Indians in the early days had a system of communal fields called "the out fields." Under this system the law required every town to work together in a body in planting its own communal field which was never enclosed. "All distinctions of rank," wrote H. S. Halbert who had lived among Choctaws, "were laid aside, the greatest war chief working side by side with common warrior." Work was made light by "the jest, the humorous stories and songs of an orator, the singing accompanied with the beating of a drum." The Creeks and Chickasaws continued cultivating a common field until well into the nineteenth century, each family depositing a part of their corn in a common crib before filling their own. The Choctaws, however, had abandoned the system in favor of individual plots. Nevertheless, they worked simultaneously, but each in his own plots, a truck patch near his house, a special patch for pumpkins, squash, potatoes, and the larger corn fields farther away. Corn fields, unlike truck patches, were not enclosed and therefore had to be watched to scare off animals and birds. This task fell to boys and old women.

Although Indians raised and used a great variety of agricultural products, corn was by far the most important. According to Halbert, Choctaws in common with all other Indians had four kinds: early corn called "tanchuse," a truck patch corn which ripened in six weeks; the yellow flint corn, "tanchi hlimishko," used for hominy; white corn "tanchi tohbih," for making bread; and pop corn, "tanchi bohanli" for entertaining visitors. Green corn could be eaten without much preparation, but after the grain became hardened it required much time-consuming work to turn it into usable form. This was women's work.

To make corn meal the cook used a mortar which had been fashioned from a small log that had been hollowed out by burning and scraping. She filled the mortar about two-thirds full of dried shelled corn and then poured about a pint of water in on the corn before starting to pound with the pestle. The friction of the pounding caused the grain to become warm and dry, and more water might have to be added to make the corn soft and loosen the husk. The cook continued pounding until the corn was sufficiently fine and thoroughly dry. She next sifted it, pouring a small amount in a sifter which was more like a flat bottomed basket than a modern sifter. She tossed the meal around, all the time blowing out the husks. It was then ready for use in many ways in bread and stews. The coarser corn was boiled and mixed with vegetables and meat, and the finer was used as thickening. Bread generally was baked in "pones" on hot stones or part of an earthen pot or wrapped in leaves and dropped into boiling water. Choctaws used dumplings made of many materials mixed with corn—cooked beans, potatoes, chestnuts, and even wild turnip roots and the inside of the maypop. Puddings of dried sunflower seed and hickory nut meats were common, and to satisfy the "sweet tooth" they turned to fruits, fresh or dried or cooked, as in the case of persimmon bread or cake. The pulp of ripe persimmons, made into "pancakes" some 12 to 18 inches in diameter, would keep indefinitely and was one of the first items of trade between the Choctaws and the French in the Mobile area.

Europeans reacted differently to Indian foods, some praising the great variety of dishes the native cooks were able to make, equal, one writer believed, to the foods produced by the English, "or perhaps French cooks." However it was prepared, it was "grateful to a wholesome stomach." Another said their bread was wholesome and well-tasted except to "the vitiated palate of an epicure."

Needless to say, there were others who could not "stomach" Indian food. General James Robertson, visiting among the Choctaws in the early 1800's, was offered a "peace pipe, big hominy and ashcake and mixed meats."

> We do not remember the term or word to express these "confounded mixtures," (he wrote long afterwards) but whatever it is, it concentrates in its meaning all the essences and all the odors which would make a delicate stomach "abhor all meats" and induce one to vom with St. Paul that as "these brethren offend me with their meats, I will eat meat no more as long as the world standeth lest I encourage these my brethren to sin." After one of these dishes, I tried to turn myself inside out and I came within an inch of doing it, and within half an inch of losing my life.—H.S. Halbert, History of the Choctaws, Ms, Department of Archives and History, Montgomery.

Most southeastern Indians, while well past the barbarian stage, lived in exceedingly primitive conditions. It is a fact, well-known to historians if not to the general public, that by 1800 there were some Indians living on big plantations in pretentious houses, owning Negro slaves and large herds of livestock, sending their children to school and serving as leaders among their people. Even more common were the white men, whether French, Dutch, Spanish, English or Scotch, who married native wives and reared half-breed families, many of whom became leaders in their various tribes. Some well-known sons of such unions were: Alexander McGillivray, William McIntosh, Hugh McQueen, and the children of Robert Grierson who lived near the town of Hillibees on the present boundary of Clay and Tallapoosa Counties. When Benjamin Hawkins, Indian agent, visited him in December 1796, he found the family busily picking and ginning cotton.

MARRIAGE AND THE FAMILY

The records of war and diplomacy would indicate that Indian society was dominated by males who left to women inferior roles of mistress, wife, cook, housekeeper, and field hand. It is true that most tribes excluded women from their councils, but the Cherokees and Creeks had a group known as "the Beloved Women" whose voice was heard in matters of war and peace. There are a few instances when the wife of an emperor or chief influenced affairs of state. Furthermore, in most tribes descent was matrilinial although even before the removal of the Indians in the 1830's, more and more chiefs, especially those carrying the title of emperor, were designating their sons as their heirs, contrary to the practice of inheritance through the son of the chief's eldest sister.

Most Indian maidens were reported to be pretty—and promiscuous. Visitor after visitor commented on the "looseness" of the women who as an act of hospitality offered themselves for a night or longer to any guest. There were others who accepted pay for their services and still others who pursued men with great ardor. In the last category falls the case of four women who cornered Leclerc Milfort in a loft and forced him to "demonstrate his manhood" to prove to the women that "a French warrior is well worth a Creek warrior." Milfort ends his account of the incident by saying, "I came out of the combat with honor and my adventure was soon generally known." [Leclerc Milfort, *Memoirs*, p. 201.]

However, most writers point out that such sexual freedom ended with marriage. Most husbands were jealous of the behavior of their wives, and the penalties for adultery (on the part of women) were severe, including a public thrashing by everyone in her village.

Marriages were never made with members of the same clan. Courtship may have been indirect as when a young brave, upon taking a liking to a particular maiden, arranged for one of his relatives to approach one of the girl's close relatives to see if his suit would be acceptable. Other times the young man took a more direct approach as the one recorded by Halbert.

When a young Choctaw . . . sees a maiden who pleases his fancy, he watches his opportunity until he finds her alone. He then approaches within a few yards of her and gently casts a pebble towards her, so that it may fall at her feet. He may have to do this two or three times before he attracts the maiden's attention. If this pebble throwing is agreeable, she soon makes it manifest; if otherwise, a scornful look and a decided "ekwah" indicate that his suit is in vain. Sometimes instead of throwing pebbles the suitor enters the woman's cabin and lays his hat or handkerchief on her bed. This action is interpreted as a desire on his part that she should be the sharer of his couch. If the man's suit is acceptable the woman permits the hat to remain; but if she is unwilling to become his bride, it is removed instantly. The rejected suitor, in either method employed, knows that it is useless to press his suit and beats as graceful a retreat as possible.

When a marriage is agreed upon, the lovers appoint a time and place for the ceremony. On the marriage day the friends and relatives of the prospective couple meet at their respective houses or villages, and thence march towards each other. When they arrive near the marriage ground—generally an intermediate space between the two villages—they halt within about a hundred yards of each other. The brothers of the woman then go across to the opposite party and bring forward the man and seat him on a blanket spread upon the marriage ground. The man's sisters then do likewise by going over and bringing forward the woman and seating her by the side of the man. Sometimes, to furnish a little merriment for the occasion, the woman is expected to break loose and run. Of course she is pursued, captured and brought back. All parties now assemble around the expectant couple. A bag of bread is brought forward by the woman's relatives and deposited near her. In like manner the man's relatives bring forward a bag of meat and deposit it near him. These bags of provisions are lingering symbols of the primitive days when the man was the hunter to provide the household with game, and the woman was to raise corn for the bread and hominy. The man's friends and relatives now begin to throw presents upon the head and shoulders of the woman. These presents are of any kind that the donors choose to give, as articles of clothing, money, trinkets, ribbons, etc. As soon as thrown they are quickly snatched off by the woman's relatives and distributed among themselves. During all this time the couple sit very quietly and demurely, not a word spoken by either. When all the presents have been thrown and distributed, the couple, now man and wife, arise, the provisions from the bags are spread, and just as in civilized life, the ceremony is rounded off with a festival. The festival over, the company disperse, and the gallant groom conducts his bride to his home, where they enter upon the toils and responsibilities of the future.—Quoted in Swanton, *Source Materials*, pp. 131–32.

Jean-Bernard Bossu, in describing life among the Alabama Indians near Fort Toulouse in 1759, said that marriage was "natural and took no form other than mutual agreement of the parties involved."

The future groom gives gifts of furs and food to his bride's family. After the presents have been accepted, there is a feast to which the whole village is invited. When the meal is over, the guests dance and sing of the battle exploits of the groom's ancestors. The next day, the oldest man in the village presents the bride to her husband's parents.—Jean Bossu, *Travels in the Interior of North America* (Norman, Okla.: University of Oklahoma Press, 1962), p. 132.

That was the whole ceremony. Although only one wife was the general rule, a man was permitted to have more than one, and some did—for example, Alexander McGillivray, who had one at Tuckabatchee and another at Tensas.

Within a family the role of each person was clearly defined by custom. Also, certain taboos were observed such as the fact that a husband ate no salt or pork during his wife's pregnancy. Child bearing was a simple matter, as Bossu observed:

The women never bring forth their children in the cabin; they do this in the woods without assistance from anyone. Immediately after they are delivered, they wash their infants themselves. The mothers also apply to their foreheads a mass of earth in order to flatten the head and as fast as they can bear it they increase the load. It is considered beautiful by these people to have a flat head. They do not swathe their children nor tie them down in clothing with bands. They do not wean them until they are tired of the maternal breast. I have heard very strong children say to their mothers "Sit down so that I may nurse," and the mother immediately sat down. Their cradle is made of canes. The mothers lay their children in these so that the heads are three or four finger-widths lower than their bodies. That is why one never sees crooked or hunch-backed children among the savages.—Ibid. p. 171.

Children were loved but not pampered. Even while they were still nursing babies, they were bathed in cold water and soon afterwards slept on the ground. Such treatment was designed to make their bodies no more sensitive to cold than were their hands and feet. Discipline was a matter for the mother, but education was the responsibility of both parents; the father made good hunters and warriors out of his sons and the mother instructed her daughters in the arts that would make them good wives. Family life seems to have been fairly stable.

RELIGION

The fact that Indians were a religious people can be demonstrated again and again. But determining what of their religious ceremonies were "religious" or secular, spiritual or superstitious, governmental or economic is well-nigh impossible. In fact, it appears that the religion of the Indians was like the religion of other peoples in that it touched every phase of their lives.

All tribes seem to have believed in a "great spirit." The "Great Medal chief Took-au-batche" called him E-sau-ge-tuk E-mis-see, the master of breath, who gave Indians their customs and protected them in war and difficulties. The Creek supreme deity was known as Hisagita-imisi, the preserver of breath, or Ibofanaga, "the one sitting above" who bore a close relationship to the sun but was not the sun itself. The Cherokees shared the same belief in the near-deity of the sun and the moon. Chickasaw religion was similar; there was a supreme being living in the sky-world, connected with both the sun and moon and represented on earth by fire. Bossu found the Alabama Indians believing in a supreme being and, like all other tribes, in a hereafter:

When I asked them what they thought of the hereafter, they replied that, if they had not taken someone else's wife, stolen, or killed during their lives, after death they would go to a very fertile land where there would be plenty of women and hunting grounds and where everything would be easy for them. If, on the other hand, they had acted foolishly and had disrespected the Great Spirit, they would go to a barren land full of thorns and briars where there would be no hunting and no women.—Bossu, *Travels,* p. 145.

The Alabamas buried their dead in a sitting position. A dead man was given a pipe and tobacco so he could make peace with the people in the next world. A warrior was buried with his arms and paint (vermillion) that he could apply to himself within the spirit world. The Chickasaws thought souls traveled west; that the good ones climbed to the sky to live with the supreme being but that the evil spirits remained in the western quarter "from which witchcraft emanated."

Early explorers report stone idols in the southeast, but the main writers of the eighteenth century apparently made no mention of them. However, Indians believed in a form of animism which gave special life and spirit to animals such as the snake, the screech owl, and the eagle, and to certain plants and places like high mountains and waterfalls. They believed in magic and witchcraft and taboos. They also believed in "medicine," and medicine men held high positions in all tribes. They seem to have been of two kinds, prophets and "physics," both of whom used "medicine" to cure the sick, win victories, and protect their people from stronger "medicine" of other tribes. The duty of the medicine man was to invoke the spirits, to incite a tribe to a frenzy on the eve of battle, and to assure protection to warriors.

Many of the ceremonies were associated with religion. The busk or green corn dance lasting five days in the latter part of July was the occasion for cleaning the private homes and the council house, for lighting a new fire, and for sacrificing seven kernels in gratitude for the gift of corn. The purification ceremony, was held on many important occasions; the following one was observed at Fort Mitchell in the 1830's by a young Harvard-trained native of Charleston, South Carolina.

Occasionally I found time to ride to Echo Hadjo's camp of friendly Indians, five miles off. On one of my visits I found their head men in full assembly and going through the ceremony of taking the black-drink. This is only done on very important occasions, such as the declaration of war, etc., of which this was one, for they were met in council to deliberate upon the expediency of going to Florida to fight against the Seminoles. The place of assembly was a large square area, bounded on the four sides by long open sheds, under which, upon a platform of canes raised three feet from the ground were reclining the dignitaries in various attitudes; some sitting cross-legged like a taylor [tailor], others resting upon their elbows, while not a few were stretched off at full length upon their backs, and all decked out in their savage finery. In the center of the square was a fire, over which was suspended from a cross-stick a large earthen pot, containing the ingredients of the black-drink. Two men who superintended the process of preparation, were engaged with long ladles in skimming off the froth which rose to the surface of the liquid in considerable quantity. After a due time had elapsed in this way, the ladles were supplanted in the hands of the two masters of ceremony by gourds with long handles and an aperture on one side an inch in diamitre [diameter]. Having filled these with the precious liquid, they proceeded to opposite sides of the area and commenced handing it round. As soon as the hole in the gourd and the mouth of the drinker came in contact, an apparent rivalship commenced between the two waiters, in a singular song of but one note, consisting of the sound ah-ah-a-a prolonged with a shrill key without drawing breath until the drinker finished his task. This they seemed in a great hurry to do, for the drink is said to be remarkably bitter and nauseous. I was told that the reputation of the drinker for eloquence was always measured by the number of mouthfuls he took; he who stood at the top of the ladder of oratory always drank the longest, while the occupant of the lower round could not take more than one swallow. The drink had the reputation of clearing their minds and making bright ideas flow, preparatory to making a speech. From its effect upon the stomach I do not doubt its capability of purifying the brain; for after swallowing a dose, the poor orators seemed much distressed as if laboring under the operatory of an emetic, with this difference only, that instead of discharging the nauseous stuff at once, they would sit for an hour after swallowing it, belching up the contents of their bread-baskets every five minutes into their mouths, and from there, discharge it with a squirt towards the centre of the square. The sight was extremely ludicrous after the drink had made the entire circuit, to see so many grave and dignified figures sitting around in perfect silence, engaged in squirting from all directions towards one spot. [Can this, however, be considered as presenting any more disgusting sight than the practice in all our legislative assemblies of squirting filthy tobacco juice over the floor? The savages indeed have the better claim to wisdom, for theirs is a purifying process; and by clearing the stomach, bring their minds to a proper condition for business; whereas tobacco chewing can produce no other effect than endangering the health, and weakening the intellectual faculties. Of the two practices let us rather adopt that of the Indians as far more civilized, and refined, and characteristic of wise people.] Observing a singular appearance of stripes upon the legs of all the men, I was induced to inquire the cause, was told that it was a universal custom with them to scratch their legs with needles fixed into a piece of wood, until the blood flowed. They asserted that when fatigued this operation afforded them immediate relief and considerable pleasure.—Jacob Rhett Motte, *Journey into Wilderness* (Gainesville, Florida: University of Florida Press, 1953), pp. 25–27.

Indians loved to dance, and they had dances for many different occasions. They also had games which they played with great gusto. The most famous was a form of ball which has been described as a cross between tennis, hockey, and lacross; if there were a national sport, this "chunkey," as they called it, was it. There are many accounts of it; the following was written by Jean-Bernard Bossu about 1759:

They have a game similar to our long racket game at which they are very skilful. Neighboring villages invite one another, inciting their opponents with a thousand words of defiance. Men and women gather in their finest costumes and pass the day singing and dancing; indeed they dance all night to the sound of the drum and rattle. Each village has its own fire lighted in the middle of a wide prairie. The day following is that on which the match is to come off. They agree upon a goal 60 paces distant and indicated by two large poles between which the ball must pass. Usually they play for 16 points. There are forty players on a side, each holding in his hand a racket two and a half feet long, of almost the same shape as ours, made of walnut [hickory] or chestnut wood and covered with deer skin.

In the middle of the ball ground an old man throws up a ball made by rolling deer skin together. At once each player runs to try to catch the ball in his racket. It is a fine sight to observe the players with their bodies bare, painted in all sorts of colors, with a tiger tail fastened behind and feathers on their arms and heads which flutter as they run, giving a remarkable effect. They push. They tumble over one another. He who is skillful enough to catch the ball sends it to the players on his side. Those on the opposite side run at the one who has seized it and return it to their own party, and they fight over it, party against party, with so much vigor that shoulders are sometimes dislocated. The players never become angry. The old men present at these games constitute themselves mediators and consider that the game is only a recreation and not something over which to fight. The wagers are considerable; the women bet against one another.

After the players have finished, the women whose husbands have lost assemble to avenge them. The racket which the women use differs from that of the men in being bent. They play with much skill. They run against one another very swiftly, and shove one another like the men, being equally naked except for the parts which modesty dictates they shall cover. They merely redden their cheeks, and use vermillion on their hair instead of powder.—Quoted in Swanton, *Source Materials,* pp. 141–42.

Betting was intense and the stakes high. Cushman tells of one game in which the ownership of the area between the Warrior and Tombigbee Rivers was settled by a ball game—but neither side kept its part of the bargain.

WAR

The most serious game of all was, of course, war; it was more art than game. Every tribe practiced it against neighboring red men and against the whites. Bossu observed that,

> The Chactas love war and have some good methods of making it. They never fight standing fixedly in one place; they flit about; they heap contempt upon their enemies without at the same time being braggarts, for when they come to grips they fight with much coolness. Some women are so fond of their husbands that they follow them to war. They keep by their sides in combat holding a quiver of arrows and encourage them by crying out continually that they must not fear their enemies but die like true men.
> The Chactas are extremely superstitious. When they are about to go to war they consult their Manitou, which is carried by the chief. They always exhibit it on that side where they are going to march toward the enemy, the warriors standing guard about. They have so much veneration for it that they never ate until the chief has given it the first portion.
> As long as the war lasts the chief is scrupulously obeyed, but after they have returned they have consideration for him only proportionate to his liberality with his possessions.
> It is an established usage among them that, when the chief of a war party has taken booty from the enemy, he must divide it among the warriors, and the relatives of those who have been killed in combat, in order, say they, to wipe away their tears. The chief retains nothing for himself except the honor of being the restorer of the nation. . . .
> If the chief of a Chacta party does not succeed in the war he loses all his credit; no one has confidence in his leadership any longer, and he must descend to the rank of a common warrior. However, consider the varying views of different nations! Among these warlike peoples it is no shame to desert. They attribute the desertion to a bad dream. If the chief of a big party himself, having dreamed the night before that he would lose some of his people, assures his warriors that he has had a bad dream, they turn back immediately to their village. After they have returned, they make medicine, for they use it on all kinds of occasions. Then they return toward the enemies. If they encounter any of them on their way, they kill five or six and then go home as well pleased as if they had subjugated a great empire.
> A general who should win a victory with the loss of many people would be very badly received by his nation, because these people consider a victory of no account when it is won at the price of the blood of their relatives and their friends. So the war chiefs take great pains to save their warriors and to attack the enemy only when they are sure to win, either on account of their numbers or natural topographical advantages, but as their adversaries have the same skill and know as well as they how to avoid the snares which are laid for them, the most cunning is the one who conquers. For that reason they hide themselves

in the woods during the day and travel only at night, and if they are not discovered, they attack at daybreak. As they are usually in wooded country, the one who goes in advance sometimes holds a very thick bush in front of him, and, as all follow in a line, the last effaces the marks of those who have gone ahead, so arranging the leaves, or the earth over which they have passed, that there remains no trace that might betray them.

The principal things which serve to reveal them to their enemies are the smoke of their fires, which they scent at a great distance and their tracks which are recognized in an almost incredible manner. One day a savage showed me, in a place where I perceived nothing, the footprints of Frenchmen, savages, and Negroes who had passed that way, and told me how long before they had been by. I confess that this knowledge appeared to me miraculous. One must admit that when the savages apply themselves to a single thing they excel at it.

The art of war, among them, as you see, consists in watchfulness, care to avoid ambuscades and in taking the enemy unawares, patience and endurance to withstand hunger, thirst, the inclemency of the seasons, the labors and the fatigues inseparable from war.

He who has struck a blow in war, carries off the dead man's scalp as a trophy, and has a record pricked or outlined on his body. Then he goes into mourning, and during that time, continuing for a month, he must not comb his hair, so that if his head itches, he is permitted to scratch himself only with a little stick fastened to his wrist for that particular purpose.—Bossu, *Travels,* pp. 164–66; quoted in Swanton, *Source Material etc.*

They had no compunctions about talking the scalps of women and children because it required courage to go into enemy territory to get them.

GOVERNMENT

Describing Indian government is like trying to pick up the proverbial mercury—both are elusive. Beyond the fact that it was tribal, government varied so greatly that generalization is extremely difficult. To be sure there was at least one head chief called variously a mico, mingo, or micko, but his power waxed and waned with public events, fate of war, and his personal prestige. Among the Cherokees there were two governments in existence at the same time—the white for peace and the red for war. Under ordinary circumstances the white chief was head of a town, but when war was undertaken, the red chief assumed the highest office until hostilities were over. Each chief had his own set of advisors known as Beloved Men. Among the Choctaws conditions described by an anonymous Frenchman are somewhat similar:

This nation is governed by a head chief whose power is absolute only so far as he knows how to make use of his authority, but as disobedience

is not punished among them. and they do not usually do what is requested of them, except when they want to, it may be said that it is an
ill-disciplined government. In each village, besides the chief and the war
chief, there are two Tascamingoutchy ["made a war chief"] who are
like lieutenants of the war chief, and a Tichou-mingo ["assistant chief"]
who is like a major. It is he who arranges for all of the ceremonies, the
feasts, and the dances. He acts as speaker for the chief, and oversees
the warriors and strangers when they smoke. These Tichou-mingo
usually become village chiefs. They (the people) are divided into four
orders, as follows. [The first are] the head chiefs, village chiefs, and
war chief; the second are the Atacoulitoupa [Hatakholitopa] or beloved
men (hommes de valleur); the third is composed of those whom they
call simply tasca or warriors; the fourth and last is atac emittla. . . . They
are those who have not struck blows or who have killed only a woman
or a child.—Ibid., pp. 90–92.

Among the Creeks government was somewhat the same. In 1789
William Bartram considered the mico "the first man in dignity and
power" and the supreme civil magistrate; yet he was in fact "no
more than president of the national council of his own tribe and
town and had no executive power independent of the council" that
met everyday in the public square.

The mico in each Creek town was always chosen from one clan;
the mico of Tuckabatchee for example was always from the Eagle
clan. A mico who was appointed for life, could, and often did, choose
a bright young man to train as a leader. At council meetings the
mico was flanked by various groups who had appointed seats: great
warriors, young war leaders, and beloved men or respected elder
statesmen who had won renown in some activity, most likely war.

The evidence seems to point to the fact that government was
conducted by an assembly of leaders from several age groups; some
held office by virtue of exploits in war, some by age, and some by
inheritance. These governmental activities seem to have been confined mostly to decisions of war and peace and affairs with other
tribes and the Europeans. They seem not to have passed laws
in the usual sense. Most acts considered crimes were controlled
by custom, and punishment was most often meted out by the family.

Although the Indians in Alabama never numbered more than a
few thousand, they occupied all parts of the state. They had long
since passed beyond the hunting and fishing stage, and by the 1830's
represented many levels of cultural development. Most of them
were living under a simple economic system, but others had advanced to a plantation life equal to many of their white neighbors.
Among the more affluent were half-breeds, sons of English, Scotch,
or French fathers but who considered themselves Indians and often
held important positions of leadership within the tribes.

The debt of the whites to the redmen included such foods as peas, beans, potatoes, pumpkins, squash, and, of course, corn. They gave us, too, many place names, words full of soft vowel sounds that roll easily off the tongue such as Tuscaloosa, Tallapoosa, Notasulga, Nanafalya, and Pushmahata.

The Indians' way of living was changed in many ways by contact with white culture. No longer did the redmen hunt with bows and arrows but with guns from the trading posts. Gradually they learned to use tools and utensils they could buy instead of depending on those they had learned from their ancestors how to make. As it became more and more evident that Americans were moving into the region to stay, some of the tribes, notably the Creeks and Cherokees, tried to modernize in order to deal with them on terms of equality. The Creeks strengthened their central government; Sequoya, reportedly born in what is now DeKalb County, developed a remarkable Cherokee alphabet of some 85 characters. Within a few years people of his tribe became the most literate in the area. The churches, too, through missions did much to elevate and educate them.

Unfortunately, the Indians were also prone to succumb to the more undesirable traits and weaknesses of the intruders—their diseases, their addiction to alcohol, their disregard for the rights of others.

In the end it was land that was their undoing, the land they loved and that had been theirs for untold generations, but which the white pioneers now coveted. Although the Indians are a colorful part of our past, by 1840 all of them had been removed from the state. The story of that removal is the subject of the next chapter.

Chapter 4

INDIAN WARS AND REMOVAL

With the coming of white settlers the position of the Indians became insecure in the land where their ancestors had hunted for untold generations. Perceptive Indians anticipated impending trouble, but during most of the eighteenth century they had been able to keep a reasonable balance of power by playing the European rivals (and other Indians, for that matter) against each other. Men like Alexander McGillivray tried to organize the natives into forces that would stop the encroaching whites; they saw no natural end to the surging flood of Americans sweeping over their land. After 1800 the number of Americans was even greater. Settlers from Georgia, Tennessee, Virginia, the Carolinas, and even more distant states were migrating to the Mobile Bay and Tombigbee areas in the south and the Tennessee Valley, where Huntsville was the principal settlement in the north. Almost without exception, the "intruders," as friends of the Indians were wont to call the whites, were seeking land which the red men had in abundance.

An historian once remarked that it took Americans seventy-five years of effort and two-hundred fifty treaties to get the Indians out of Alabama but that they finally made it! While the statement may be somewhat exaggerated, it does indicate that the process was long and involved—and finally successful.

One of the temptations that the historian must avoid is writing of the past in light of current ideas and attitudes. Take the question of Indian removal. In the twentieth century the Indian and his treatment in the nineteenth century is on the public conscience. It is an easy phrase that, after all, the red man was here first and that greedy whites did him a great injustice in pushing him off his land. He was duped into signing papers which he did not understand but which stripped him of his heritage and his proud independence. He has become a romantic object of our pity.

To the residents of the Alabama frontier before the 1830's this kind of thinking would have seemed strange indeed. To them, the Indians were savages and enemies. To be sure, there were friendly relations between some reds and whites and in some instances the half-breeds, of which there were many, bridged the gap between the races, but generally suspicion and hostility existed between them. The Americans moved in because they wanted land which they saw being unused. It was a sin and a crime, some said, for the heathen to be controlling idle land that Christians wanted to farm. For the white settlers, the stealthy Indian was a menace even after he had given up large parts of the state. The memories of attacks on settlements like Fort Mims and Sinquefield and on isolated individuals remained vivid in the minds of Alabamians until well toward the Civil War. Many families had stories of a father shot in the field, of a mother tomahawked at the spring, of a cabin set on fire, or of the dreaded warwhoop. Even the rumor of an Indian raid would panic a community.

Anne Royall, one of the early sympathizers of the Indians, recounted an incident of the Creek War.

> During the Creek War . . . some mischievous ill disposed man reported that there was a large body of Indians within a day's march of Huntsville, coming to take the town. The citizens of Huntsville, and the whole of Madison County, were instantly panic struck and immediately flew towards Nashville. Some left their calves fastened up in the pens, and some their horses in the stable, some their horses in the plow, most of them taking their flight on foot. Others . . . mounted their horses without saddles or bridles. Of these were four young ladies on one horse, riding like gentlemen, without saddle or bridle, and making good speed by applying their heels to the horse's sides. One man took another man's child and left his own . . . Some of the women mistook other men for their husbands and some husbands mistook other men's wives for theirs. One stout fat woman, though she had horses and slaves in abundance, picked up her youngest child and, taking it in her arms, on foot outstripped every man and horse in the company! . . .—Anne Royall, *Letters from Alabama,* pp. 243–44.

The fat lady walked about twenty-five miles without halting before one of her servants finally caught up with her to tell her that the whole episode was based on a false rumor. While Mrs. Royall tells the story in a humorous manner, one should not overlook the fact that the panic was so great that all but two men ("well charged with whiskey and courage") fled the settlement. Of all the problems facing the frontiersman, the Indian was the most frightening and the most vexing. Not until the red man was eliminated, it was generally believed, could the white man live in peace.

While it was not called such, the removal of the Indians had been going on for a long time. Treaties by which a "foreign" government gained exclusive use of a piece of Indian land predate the national history of the United States. The Spanish and French were interested in trade rather than agriculture and seem to have made no land treaties. The English, however, held congresses in Mobile and Pensacola (1765) by which the Choctaws ceded to them a section which included what is now Washington County and the Creeks ceded a strip along the Gulf Coast. Some of the early treaties between the United States and the tribes merely reconfirmed the English treaties; some applied to a horse path through an area or a wagon road, and others renounced Indian claims to land and opened it to white settlement. Between 1786, when the United States made its first treaty with the Choctaws, and 1835, when the New Echota Treaty provided for the removal of the Cherokees to the west of the Mississippi River, the tribes in Alabama ceded all their lands to the United States government.

The Creek War of 1813–1814

There had been trouble between the races at earlier periods, but the first (and probably the greatest) open conflict was the Creek War, which was fought entirely in Alabama. It was really a war within a war because it came during the War of 1812 with England and it arose in part from the larger conflict. It seems to be a well-established fact that the English were instigating (and supplying) depredations of the Creeks and giving encouragement to the northern leaders who were trying to stop the advance of the Americans.

Tecumseh was a Shawnee warrior from north of the Ohio River whose mother was allegedly born in Tuckabatchee on the banks of the Tallapoosa. In 1811 he visited the southern tribes in an effort to stir them into making a stand against the whites. After several days of talks with the Choctaws, most of which took place in Kemper County, Mississippi, and where Chief Pushmataha opposed any hostile acts against the whites, Tecumseh and his party moved on to the Creeks. In a statement sworn before Judge Harry Toulmin on August 2, 1813, Samuel Manac recounted the visit of the northern Indians to Tuckabatchee.

The Deposition of Samuel Manac, of lawful age, a Warrior of the Creek Nation

About the last of October, thirty Northern Indians came down with Tecumseh, who said he had been sent by his brother, the prophet. They attended our council at the Tuccabache, and had a talk for us. I was there for the space of two or three days, but every day whilst I was there, Tecumseh refused to deliver his talk, and on being requested to give it, said that the sun had gone too far that day. The day after I came away, he delivered his talk. It was not till about Christmas that any of our people began to dance the war dance. The Muscogees have not been used to dance before war, but after. At that time about forty of our people began this Northern custom, and my brother-in-law, Francis, who also pretends to be a prophet, was at the head of them. Their number has very much increased since, and there are probably now more than half of the Creek nation who have joined them.— Quoted in H. S. Halbert, *The Creek War* (University, Alabama: The University of Alabama Press, 1969), p. 91.

But Tecumseh finally did speak and in a memorable manner as Sam Dale, intrepid pioneer and Indian fighter of both Alabama and Mississippi, recalled.

All this time not a word had been uttered; everything was still as death: even the winds slept, and there was only the gentle rustle of the falling leaves. At length Tecumseh spoke, at first slowly and in sonorous tones; but soon he grew impassioned, and the words fell in avalanches from his lips. His eyes burned with supernatural luster, and his whole frame trembled with emotion; his voice resounded over the multitude— now sinking in low and musical whispers, now rising to its highest key, hurling out his words like a succession of thunderbolts. His countenance varied with his speech: its prevalent expression was a sneer of hatred and defiance; sometimes a murderous smile; for a brief interval a sentiment of profound sorrow pervaded it; and, at the close, a look of concentrated vengeance, such, I suppose, as distinguished the arch-enemy of mankind.

I have heard many great orators, but I never saw one with the vocal powers of Tecumseh, or the same command of the muscles of his face. Had I been deaf, the play of his countenance would have told me what he said. Its effect on that wild, superstitious, untutored, and war-like assemblage may be conceived: not a word was said, but stern warriors, the "stoics of the woods," shook with emotion, and a thousand tomahawks were brandished in the air. Even the Big Warrior, who had been true to the whites, and remained faithful during the war, was, for the moment, visibly affected, and more than once I saw his huge hand clutch, spasmodically, the handle of his knife. All this was the effect of his delivery; for, though the mother of Tecumseh was a Creek, and he was familiar with the language, he spoke in the northern dialect, and it was afterwards interpreted by an Indian linguist to the assembly. His speech has been reported, but no one has done or can do it justice. I think I can repeat the substance of what he said, and, indeed, his very words.

Tecumseh's Speech

In defiance of the white warriors of Ohio and Kentucky, I have travelled through their settlements, once our favorite hunting grounds. No war whoop was sounded, but there is blood on our knives. The Palefaces felt the blow, and knew not whence it came.

Accursed be the race that has seized our country, and made women of our warriors! Our fathers, from their tombs, reproach us as slaves and cowards; I hear them now in the wailing winds.

The Muscogee was once a mighty people. The Georgians trembled at your war whoop, and the maidens of my tribe, on the distant lakes, sung the prowess of your warriors, and sighed for their embraces. Now your blood is white; your tomahawks have no edge; your bows and arrows were buried with your fathers. Oh, Muscogees, brush from your eyelids the sleep of slavery; once more strike for vengeance, once more for your country. The spirits of the mighty dead complain. The tears drop from the weeping skies. Let the white race perish.

They seized your lands; they corrupt your women; they trample on the ashes of your dead.

Back, whence they came, upon a trail of blood, they must be driven.

Back! back, ay, into the great water whose accursed waves brought them to our shores!

Burn their dwellings! Destroy their stock! Slay their wives and children! The Red Man owns the country.

War now! War forever! War upon the living! War upon the dead! Dig their very corpses from the grave. Our country must give no rest to a white man's bones!

This is the will of the Great Spirit, revealed to my brother, his familiar, the Prophet of the Lakes. He sends me to you.

All the tribes of the north are dancing the war-dance. Two mighty warriors across the seas will send us arms.

Tecumseh will soon return to his country. My prophets shall tarry with you. They will stand between you and the bullets of your enemies. When the white men approach you the yawning earth shall swallow them up.

Soon shall you see my arm of fire stretch athwart the sky. I will stamp my foot at Tippecanoe, and the very earth shall shake.

When he resumed his seat the northern pipe was again passed round in solemn silence. The Shawnees then simultaneously leaped up with one appalling yell, and danced their tribal war-dance, going through the evolutions of battle, the scout, the ambush, the final struggle, brandishing their war-clubs, and screaming in terrific concert an infernal harmony fit only for the regions of the damned.—Quoting Sam Dale in J. F. H. Claiborne, *Life and Times of General Sam Dale, the Mississippi Partisan* (New York: 1860), pp. 50–62.

While it can be questioned whether Tecumseh said these exact words, the effect of them was powerful indeed.

In the bloody Creek War with the Red Sticks (the war party

led by High Head Jim, Josiah Francis, Menawa, Peter McQueen, and the most famous of all, William Weatherford) and the Americans (led by Big Sam Dale, Jere Austill, John Coffee, Davy Crockett, Sam Houston, George S. Gaines, and, of course, Andrew Jackson) the first important incident was the Battle of Burnt Corn in Baldwin County, July 27, 1813. The battle was an apparent surprise to both sides, caused by an accidental meeting on the road. But the Indians at least knew that such an encounter was planned. Samuel Manac told of the plot as he knew it.

High-Head told me that when they went back with their supply, another body of men would go down for another supply of ammunition, and that ten men would go out of each Town, and that they calculated on five horse loads for every Town. He said that they were to make a general attack on the American Settlements—that the Indians on the Tombigby and Alabama, particularly the Tensaw and Fork Settlements.—That the Creek Indians, bordering on the Cherokees, were to attack the people of Tennessee, and that the Seminoles and lower Creeks were to attack the Georgians.—That the Choctaws also had joined them and were to attack the Mississippi Settlements.—That the attack was to be made at the same time in all places where they got furnished with ammunition. I found, from my sister, that they were treated very rigorously by the Chiefs, and that many, particularly the women among them, (two daughters of the late Gen. McGillivray, who had been induced to join them to save their property,) were very desirous to leave them, but could not.

I found, from the talk of High-Head, that the war was to be against the whites and not between Indians themselves,—that all they wanted was to kill those who had taken the talk of the whites, viz.: the Big Warrior, Alex. Cornells, Capt. Issac, Wm. McIntosh, the Mad Dragon's son, the little Prince Spoko Kange and Tallasee Thicksico.

They have destroyed a large quantity of my cattle, and burnt my houses on my river plantation, as well as those of James Cornells and Leonard McGee.—Deposition of Samuel Manac, in H. S. Halbert, *The Creek War,* pp. 92–93.

The Battle of Burnt Corn occurred when several hundred Indians under Peter McQueen, High-Head Jim, and Josiah Francis were returning from Pensacola where they had bought (or had been given, the whites believed) supplies and ammunition. They were attacked by a volunteer force under Colonel James Collier at the bend in Burnt Corn Creek. The description of the battle was told to A. J. Pickett by Colonel G. W. Creagh of Clarke County.

Information [had] been received in Clarke, Washington and Baldwin [Counties] that a party of Indians had gone to Pensacola for the purpose of getting powder and lead to destroy the citizens in Clarke, more particularly on Bassett's Creek.

Col. James Collier, the then commander of all the militia east of Pearl River in the Mississippi Territory, having received information of the Indians in the territory, made a call on Clarke, Washington and Baldwin for volunteers. Col. Collier, having assembled the volunteers in Washington, came on to Clarke, was jointed at Jackson by Capt. Bradbury's Company & Capt. William McGrew's Company & Robert Collier's Company. They then proceeded to the Citizen's Fort on the frontier of Clarke. On arriving at that place he was joined by Capt. Sam Dale and Capt. Thomas Phillips, all volunteer companies. From the Citizen's Fort we commenced our march to Sizeman's Ferry (now Guins Town) where we [encamped?] the first night. The next day we crossed the men over the river in canoes and crossed the horses by swimming. . . . The command [then] proceeded to David Tait's cow pen where we encamped for the night. The next day we awaited the troops from Baldwin under the command of Captain Dickson Bailey. After the arrival of the troops under Bailey the command of Col. Collier's was nearly two hundred strong and now in the first degree, some few of the officers having been in service. Col. Collier the next day after the arrival of the troops from Baldwin took up the line of march to the Burnt Corn Spring. Arriving there before night, he advanced the troops to the Wolf Trail on the direct route to Pensacola where we made our last encampment in the Nation.

The morning of the 29th of July, 1813, was clear and cloudless. The troops commenced the march on the trail leading to Pensacola. At or about 11 o'clock A.M. we met the first of the Indians; on that day Capt. Benjamin Smith of Washington & Capt. Samuel Dale of Clarke and their companies composed the vanguard. . . . The troops proceeded on until we arrived at the crossing of the Burnt Corn Creek. . . . A part of the Indians crossed over and was on the east bank of the creek when the attack was made. The first onset we took 8 or 10 pack horses loaded with powder, lead and blankets which was not done but at the risk of our lives, for whilst carrying the horses up the bank, the Indians shot a hole through a kettle on the back of the horn over the head of the Writer (Creagh). . . . The horses were then [taken and turned] back into the midst of our troops by the advanced guard in which service Capt. Saml Dale received a ball below the left nipple, the ball striking a rib and [being] carried back to the backbone. After [this] he assisted to do all in his power to keep the troops in their proper position. After taking the pack horses we were just entering the swamp to engage the Indians in the swamp when the order was to fall back—fatal order, for it put it out of the power of the commander to restore order again, although he had done all that man could do to prevent the flight of a part of his command. As soon as the first order to fall back had been given, Major Phillips left with a portion of his, and some of the other Battalions left the battle ground and looked out for their safety in flight, taking with them the greater part of the pack horses and their loads. The remaining troops acted with more determination and maintained the action for a considerable time. Although a part had left . . .

the remainder kept the field against some three hundred Indians. At the close of the fight the writer was struck by an Indian ball in the left coat pocket, and having a silk handkerchief and a pair of buckskin gloves in the same, the gloves on the outside, the ball entered them and deadened the hip joint so that it was impossible to mount my horse. Patrick May . . . was kind enough to bring my horse to me and to assist me on him. . . . Just as the last of our troops were leaving, a man by the name of Bullard was killed by the Indians. David Glass, a private in Dale's Company fired the last gun on the murderer of Bullard. The Indians took the direction of Pensacola, our troops the direction of Burnt Corn Spring, each willing to close the labors of the day. Our loss was two killed and 18 or 20 wounded. The Indians say that they had 20 killed and a good many wounded. The command of Dale's Company devolved on me Lieut., and with Benjamin S. Smoot's company brought up the rear from the fight, keeping the wounded in advance. We came to Dale's ferry where the Clarke and Washington troops made their way to their respective homes.—A. J. Pickett Papers, Department of Archives and History, Montgomery, Alabama.

Following the Battle of Burnt Corn, settlers in the Tensaw district flocked to the stockaded home of Sam Mims, usually called Fort Mims, in Baldwin County, for protection. The attack, which took place on August 30, 1813, has been called the bloodiest in American frontier history. The narrator of the following story was Dr. Thomas G. Holmes, one of the few survivors, whom A. J. Pickett interviewed on June 3, 1847, in preparation for writing his history of Alabama.

FORT MIMS

The Indians came within 400 yds of the fort where there was a thick ravine in which they secreted themselves by laying flat on the ground, until the 12 o'c drum beat having received information by a very intelligent negroe named Ive, belonging to Capt. Zacharia McGist that if they would await until that hour, that the officers, soldiers & citizens would all be engaged at dinner, which was the fact, and at that awful moment they made a general rush and undiscovered until they surrounded the fort, and were in possession of three fourths of the port holes before the men assigned to defend them could get to them. The work of death now commenced with all the horror. The brave Capt. Dixon Baily got with his command to the Bastion on the north side of the fort as will appear by reference to the plan of the fort. Scarcely arrived before the Bastion was charged, by 150 of these inhuman monsters using all the contortions that their fanaticism could stimulate them to, little expecting to meet the fate they received from the unerring rifle of the whites. Capt. Baily very judiciously had supplied himself with rifles and extra guns most of them double barrels, soon as the first discharge from Baily's troops was made, the guns were withdrawn from the port holes and the extra put in their place which inflicted such a deadly fire that they passed around with out being able to occupy the port holes of which Dixon B. had command. But a little time elapsed before with an undivided number and with horible contorsions & painted faces, those hell hounds came as though certain of their prey but again they met the same disappointment, for the inmates of the Bastion instead of relaxing they seemed to be nerved with a spirit of defence never to yield, about this time, Mr. James Baily, Mr. Daniel Baily and some several others got up into the roof of Mimms large house placed in the centre, pulled off some shingles which they used as port holes, where by the by they from time to time kept at a deadly fire upon the Indians on the outside of the fort shooting over the pickets—after several rounds from this position, the Indians again made a violent attack upon the Bastion commanded by Capt. Baily and were again repulsed with much loss-from time to time they kept up attack after attack upon this Bastion each time with equal loss until about 4 o'clock when they seemed to have abandoned the attempt to take the Bastion-in the early part one solitary man of Capt. Jack's company of regulars that got into the half finished block house with his yauger charged and twenty cartridges in his cartridge box, this brave and worthy soldier some several days after the fall of the fort was found laying on his back with one hand griped to the ram rod the other to the yauger, his head perforated with a ball and the brains running therefrom with the last load from his box about half ramed down in his yauger, with 23 dead indians laying on their backs killed by said yauger for reason that they were in reach of the block house & no possibility for those Indians to have been killed by any other than by this brave man, who had sold his life with so much honor to himself nay to his country and so very dearly to the enemy-after his death, the Indians succeeded in cutting the pickets on the south side of the Fort covered by two large houses represented in the drawing as a kitchen and smoke house, & succeeded in communicating fore to both of these houses where the conflagration raged in the houses the wind sprang up and communicated the fire to the large building of Saml Mimms in the centre—then it was that horror and dismay was to be seen in every face within the fort even that brave & worthy soldier Capt. Dixon Baily was heard to give up—that his large family were all to be butchered by the savages there was no alternative left, then it was that Dr. Thomas G. Holmes a surgeon in the garrison determined to cut two of the pickets as soon as the conflagration became general and the brave fellows and citizens who were protected by the house in the centre had to flee therefrom tho Bastion commanded by Baily was the only place that they could flee to with any prospect of safety. There was little to be found there, for such was the fact when they all crowded together, there was no chance of defence—escape was the only alternative—those pickets previously cut by Dr. Holmes were thrown down, when the brave Dixon Baily ordered his negro man Tom to take up his favorite son Ralph, 14 years old, who had long been sick and carry him on his back. The negro in obedience to the order of his master forthwith went out of the fort through the pickets, followed by his master with his enemies rifle in hand, and followed by his intimate friend Dr. Holmes & the most rapid flight took place—soon after passing the north west corner of the fort 150 Indians attempted to cut off their retreat when by the by as they ran Capt. B. gave them a fire from his rifle and Dr. Holmes from both barrels of his gun. Baily had boiled his bullets in oil with the buck skin patch sowed over them to make them go down easy—So far the informant Dr. Holmes knows not how the others escaped after he left but presumes by the same breach in the walls. There were 1200 warriors when they were discovered & the discovery was known to the Commandant, he rushed sword in hand to the gate and attempted to shut it, but owing to its being made of very heavy materials it had much swaggered again the gate was planted on the declivity of the slope & from several heavy rains the earth had washed considerably against said gate and rendered it impossible for Major Beasly with all his phisical powers to shut it—five of the principle prophets rushed with all their infuriated fanaticism to the centre of the fort over the body of Beasly who had been dispatched with a war club— after reaching the centre of the fort, they got to dancing in defiance of the citizen soldiers, for they had assured their deluded followers, that they could dance in defiance of American powder or ball for reason if they attempted to shoot them, that their balls would split, but to their great disappointment they met their fate and that very suddenly for they were all five shot down which it was said dampened the feelings of the whole Indian army—for much confidence had been placed in whatever they said, those deluded followers had evidence that they could not split the balls, for before five o'clock 500 had been pierced by American lead. The destruction of the fort is horrible to tell. There were 553 citizens and soldiers and among the number about 453 women & children and only 13 escaped. The way that many of the unfortunate women were mangled and cut to pieces is shocking to humanity, for very many of the women who were pregnant had their unborn infants cut from the womb and lay by their bleeding mothers—They were stripped of every article of apparel not satisfied with this, they inhumanly scalped every solitary one—not satisfied with scalping in the ordinary manner but took from the skin of the whole head so as to make many scalps—for the Spaniards with more barbarous feeling than the in- human Indian had promised them $5 for every scalp they would bring them, thus they took the whole skin to make many scalps—again Amhiester & Woodbine claiming as they did all the advantages of a religious education had the barbaraty to offer a like reward to the Indians. Col. Nicols an officer of high grade, from England, assured the Indians that he was authorized by his government to pay the same price for scalps—The Indians had the cunning to make many scalps from each killed white that they murdered. They carried them on poles each town had a pole heavy with scalps and danced and sang & shouted in horrid yells on their way to Pensacola, after the fall of Fort Mims— where they went to tell of their victories to sell the scalps and receive

more supplies—after the battle was over they encamped that night outside of the remains of the fort where they trimmed and fixed the scalps.
There were many acts of bravery on the part of the females—Mrs.
Daniel Beasly loaded guns during the whole engagement for the de-
fenders of the Bastion—There was a Sargent Mathews taken with violent
chill, & struck like a man with a third day fever & ague and from his
sweating the water ran from him as freely as though he had been
deluged with water from a river—his teeth chattering together as though
he was freezing. This brave Mrs. Baily urged him from time to time to
get up & fight like a man and defend the women and children that
were in the fort—he refused to do so, she earnestly assured him that
if he did not fight that she would certainly bayonnett him which by
the by she done some 15 or 20 times in his rump, all to no purpose for
he lay like an ox—afterwards he made his escape and fled & reached
Mount Vernon where Claiborne was in Command and then reported
to the Gen. that he had killed 20 odd Indians—it so raised him in the
estimation of the Gen. & the officers that they one and all recommended
him to a commission in the army which it was probable he would have
gotten if Dr. Holmes had not prevented this unworthy man from succeeding by his false statements to the general—when Dr. H. charged
him with lying, he persisted in it until the Dr. proved by the marks on
his panteloons that Mrs. Baily had bayonetted him.

Again, all the females acted with great heroism and bravery and if
they were not remarkable in feats as Mrs. Baily, they nevertheless displayed the greatest coolness. From 12 o'clock until 5 not a scream
was heard. The blood was shoe deep in the Bastion about 3 o'clock it
was thought the Indians were whipped. They took a great deal of the
baggage out of the additional part of the fort where were encamped
the officers and suddenly retreated and went to the House of Mrs. O'Neal
about 300 yds distant and for a short time appeared to be packing up
with a disposition to be off. Suddenly a conspicious Indian warrior
supposed to be William Weatherford dashed up on a horse and appeared
to be harranging them for about 30 minutes, when their baggage was
suddenly laid down, and they returned with a rush yelling & screaming
like perfect demons—when they again charged the Bastion such was
their horrible appearance that it required all the nerve of the soldier to
meet them, but the inmates of the bastion pored upon them a deadly
fire—again & again they charged until about 4 o'clock they quit all
further assaults upon the Bastion.

Every Indian was provided with a gun, war club a bow and arrows
pointed with iron spikes. With few excepitons they were naked—around
the waist was drawn a girdle from which was tied a cows tail running
down the back and almost dragging the ground. It is impossible to imagine people so horribly painted. Some were painted half red & half
black. Some were adorned with feathers—their faces were painted so as
to show their terrible contortions. Rishbury, a soldier, died from pure
fear after the fall of the fort; the Indians burnt and destroyed every house

in the neighborhood.—Pickett Papers, Department of Archives and History, Montgomery.

The massacre sent shivers of fear throughout the whole southwest and, not suprisingly, brought retaliatory action from the army. Brigadier General Thomas Flounoy of the Military District sent the following instructions to Brigadier General F. L. Claiborne October 3, 1813, just over a month after the Fort Mims Massacre.

You will proceed to the towns of the Indians, which lie on or are contiguous to the waters of the two streams aforesaid, and literally burn, kill, and destroy. This mode of warfare it is true is considered to be contrary to the practice, which ought to obtain among civilized nations. But when we consider that the British nation has conducted itself in the present contest, in a manner which characterizes the savage, & that our Indian enemies, urged by their examples, and acting under their auspicies, pursued a system of ferocity which leads to an indiscriminate destruction of all ages, sexes, and conditions. I feel that I am not only excusable but justifiable in giving these instructions.

All negroes, horses, cattle, corn & other property that cannot be conveniently brought in, must be destroyed. All ammunition, arms, clothing, blankets, forage & provisions, must be secured for the service of the United States, pursuant to the 58th article of war. All other property, will wait the decision of the Secretary of War.—Copy in Pickett Papers, Department of Archives and History, Montgomery, Alabama.

When word of Fort Mims reached Andrew Jackson in Nashville, he was confined to his bed with his left shoulder shattered by a slug and with a bullet embedded in the upper arm, both the result of a duel with Jesse Benton, younger brother of Thomas Hart Benton with whom he had a feud of long-standing. The news struck terror in the hearts of Jackson and his fellow Tennesseans who knew only too well the horrors of Indian warfare. Although Fort Mims was several hundred miles away, fighting could quickly spread to their very doorsteps. A committee of public safety called at the Hermitage to see what could be done to punish the culprits and keep the ravages from spreading. As Marquis James said, "Jackson was too weak to leave his bed, but he was strong enough to make war." Already John Coffee, close friend and nephew to Jackson by marriage, had his cavalry in the field. Jackson quickly reported that "The health of your general is restored; he will command in person." While his beloved wife and others close to him knew that the first part of his statement was far from true, they had no doubt but that he would command.

On October 7, 1813, Jackson took command of the volunteer troops at Fayetteville, Tennessee; four days later he broke camp and headed south, marching thirty-two miles in nine hours. The next day he joined Coffee at Ditto's Landing on the Tennessee River to the south of Huntsville. Twenty-four miles farther on he threw up breastworks for Fort Deposit which would be his main base for the next several weeks. Chopping out a road over Raccoon Mountain, his army moved into hostile territory along the Coosa River. He defeated the Red Sticks under William Weatherford in battles at Tallushatchee and Talladega within six days (November 3 and 9). In the weeks that followed, Jackson had to cope with wholesale desertions among his troops; inadequate and even at times nonexisting supplies; insufficient forces to guard what supplies they had and to care for the wounded; and to keep Governor Willie Blount, under whose command he was, convinced that the operation against the Red Sticks was valid and should not be abandoned. He wrote the wavering Blount that he would perish before he would "retrograde." In January he again met the enemy at Emuckfaw and Enolochopco as he pressed toward Horseshoe Bend on the Tallapoosa River where he knew the Creeks were concentrating their forces.

The Battle of Horseshoe Bend was the greatest during the war with the Creeks and ranks along with the Battle of New Orleans in importance for the southwest. It made Andrew Jackson a hero and broke the power of the Creeks. Thereafter, victory for the whites was certain.

The following description of Horseshoe Bend is the official report of Andrew Jackson to Governor Willie Blount of Tennessee. Jackson was leading Tennessee volunteer troops.

"BATTLE OF TEHOPISKA, OR THE HORSE SHOE."
REPORT OF JACKSON TO GOVERNOR BLOUNT
FT. WILLIAMS, March 31, 1814.

His Excellency, Willie Blount,

Sir, I am just returned from the expedition which I advised you in my last I was about to make to the Tallapoosa; and hasten to acquaint you with the good fortune which attended it.

I took up the line of march from this place on the morning of the 24th instant, and having opened a passage of fifty two and a half miles over the ridges which divide the waters of the two rivers, I reached the bend of the Tallapoosa, three miles beyond where I had the engagements of the 22d January and at the southern extremity of New Youka, on the morning of the 27th. This bend resembles in its curvature that of a horse shoe, and is thence called by that name among the whites. Nature furnishes few situations so eligible for defence; and barbarians have never rendered one more secure by art. Across the neck of land which leads into it from the North, they had erected a breast-work, of greatest compactness and strength—from five to eight feet high, and prepared with double rows of port-holes very artfully arranged. The figure of this wall, manifested no less skill in the projectors of it, than its construction: an army could not approach it without being exposed to a double and cross fire from the enemy who lay in perfect security behind it. The area of this peninsular, thus bounded by the breast-works includes, I conjecture eighty or a hundred acres.

In this bend the warriors from Oakfuskee, Oakchaya, New Youka, Hillabees, the Fish ponds, and Eufaula towns, apprised of our approach, had collected their strength. Their exact number cannot be ascertained; but it is said, by the prisoners we have taken, to have been a thousand. It is certain they were very numerous; and that relying with the utmost confidence upon their strength—their situation, and the assurances of their prophets, they calculated on repulsing us with great ease.

Early on the morning of the 27th having encamped the preceding night at the distance of six miles from them—I detailed Genl. Coffee with the mounted men and nearly the whole of the Indian force, to pass the river at a ford about three miles below their encampment, and to surround the bend in such a manner that none of them should escape by attempting to cross the river. With the remainder of the forces I proceeded along the point of land which leads to the front of the breast-work; and at half past ten o'clock A.M. I had planted my artillery on a small eminence, distant from its nearest point about eighty yards, and from its farthest, about two hundred and fifty; from whence I immediately opened a brisk fire upon its centre. With the musquetry and rifles I kept up a galling fire whenever the enemy shewed themselves behind their works, or ventured to approach them. This was continued with occasional intermissions, for about two hours, when Capt. Russell's company of spies and a part of the Cherokee force, headed by their gallant chieftain, Col Richard Brown, and conducted by the brave Col. Morgan, crossed over to the extremity of the peninsular in canoes, and set fire to a few of their buildings which were there situated. They then advanced with great gallantry towards hte breast-work, and commenced firing upon the enemy who lay behind it.

Finding that this force notwithstanding the determined bravery they displayed, was wholly insufficient to dislodge the enemy and that General Coffee had secured the opposite banks of the river, I now determined upon taking possession of their works by storm. Never were men better disposed for such an undertaking than those by whom it was to be effected. They had entreated to be led to the charge with the most pressing importunity, and received the order which was now given, with the strongest demonstration of joy. The effect was such, as this temper of mind foretold. The regular troops, led on by their intrepid and skillful commander Co. Williams, and by the gallant Major Montgomery were presently in possession of the nearer side of the breast-work; and the militia accompanied them in the charge with a vivacity and firmness which could not have been exceeded and has seldom been equalled by troops of any description. A few companies of General Doherty's Brigade on the right, were led on with great gallantry by Co. Bunch—the advance guard, by the Adjutant General Sitler, and the left extremity of the line by Capt. Gordon of the Spies and Capt. McMurray, of Gen'l Johnston's Brigade of West Tennessee Militia.

Having maintained for a few minutes a very obstinate contest, muzzle to muzzle, through the port-holes, in which many of the enemy's balls were welded to the bayonets of our musquets, our troops succeeded in gaining possession of the opposite side of the works. The event could no longer be doubtful. The enemy altho many of them fought to the last with that kind of bravey which desperation inspires, were at length entirely routed and cut to pieces. The whole margin of the river which surrounded the peninsular was strewd with the slain. Five hundred and fifty seven were found by officers of great respectability whom I had ordered to count them; besides a very great number who were thrown into the river by their surviving friends, and killed in attempting to pass by General Coffee's men stationed on the opposite banks. Capt. Hammond who with his company of spies occupied a favorable position opposite the upper extremity of the breast-work did great execution and so did Lieu't Bean who had been ordered by Gen'l Coffee to take possession of a small Island fronting the lower extremity.

Both officers and men who had the best opportunities of judging, believe the loss of the enemy in killed, not to fall short of eight hundred and if their number was as great as it is represented to have been by the prisoners, and as it is believed to have been by Col. Carrol and others who had a fair view of them as they advanced to the breastworks, their loss must even have been more considerable—as it is quite certain that not more than twenty can have escaped. Among the dead was found their famous prophet Monahoee—shot in the mouth by a grape shot; as if Heaven designed to chastise his impostures by an appropriate punishment. Two other prophets were also killed—leaving no others, as I learn, on the Tallapoosa. I lament that two or three women and children were killed by accident. I do not know the exact number of prisoners taken; but it must exceed three hundred, all women and children except three or four.

The battle may be said to have continued with severity for about five hours; but the firing and the slaughter continued until it was suspended by the darkness of the night. The next morning it was resumed and sixteen of the enemy slain who had concealed themselves under the banks.

Our loss was twenty six white men killed and one hundred and seven wounded—Cherokees, eighteen killed, and thirty six wounded, friendly Creeks five killed and eleven wounded. The loss of Col. Williams' reg't of Regulars is seventeen killed and fifty five wounded; three of whom have since died. Among the former were Major Montgomery, Lieut' Somerville, and Lieut' Moulton, who fell in the charge which was made on the works. No men ever acted more gallantly, or fell more gloriously.

Of the artillery company, commanded by Capt. Parish, eleven were wounded; one of whom, Sam'l Gaines, has since died; Lieutenants Allen and Ridley were both wounded. The whole company acted with its usual gallantry. Capt. Bradford, of the U. S. Infantry, who acted as chief engineer, and superintended the firing of the cannon, has entitled himself, by his good conduct to my warmest thanks. To say all in a word the whole army who achieved this fortunate victory, have merited by their good conduct, the gratitude of their country. So far as I saw, or could learn there was not an officer or soldier who did not perform his duty with the utmost fidelity. The conduct of the militia on this occasion has gone far towards redeeming the character of that description of troops. They have been as orderly in their encampments and on the line of march, as they have been signally brave in the day of battle.

In a few days I shall take up the line of march for the Hickory Grounds; and have every thing to hope from such troops.—John Spencer Bassett, ed., *Correspondence of Andrew Jackson* (Washington, 1926), vol. 1, pp. 489–92.

It would be difficult to overestimate the importance of the Creek defeat at Horseshoe Bend. Not only did The Nation, as it was often called, lose a vast area in the heart of Alabama, but also the Creeks were so weakened that thereafter they gave little more than token resistance to the whites. In the treaty of Fort Jackson (on the site of old Fort Toulouse) they formally signed a treaty with the United States with Andrew Jackson as commissioner and Benjamin Hawkins and R. J. Meigs and some others as witnesses. Not a single important leader signed for the Creeks. Some were dead, Menawa was in hiding; Peter McQueen, the Prophet Josiah Francis, the Durants, and young Osceola had escaped to the Seminoles. A modern student of the battle, the late W. H. Brantley, Jr., wrote:

. . . This treaty has been called the Treaty of Conquest, for by it the Creeks ceded to the United States all of their lands within the territories of the United States lying west, south, and southeastwardly of the Coosa River and of a line to be run by a person appointed by the President of the United States from agreed points on the Tallapoosa River southeastwardly to the mouth of the Summochies Creek on the Chattahoochie River, and continuing thence east to the line then dividing the lands claimed by the Creek Nation, and those claimed and owned by the State of Georgia. This was the end. The Creeks no longer had contact with the outside world. They were confined between the Coosa and the State of Georgia and cut off from Florida by a tremendous expanse of land which lay between the lands retained by them and the Spanish colony of Florida. The existence of the Creek Nation as a sovereign power challenging the authority of the sovereign United States was forever ended. . . .—"The Battle of Horseshoe Bend in Tallapoosa County, Alabama," Pamphlet of Horseshoe Bend Battle Park Association, 1955, p. 16.

In recognition of its importance the area was designated as a national military park, by President Dwight D. Eisenhower, who signed the measure on July 25, 1956.

The Creek War, like all wars, has its stories of human interest. Among the men who lost their lives was Major Lemuel P. Montgomery for whom the city of Montgomery is named; his grave is in a lonely spot not far from where he fell. Jackson was touched by the sight of a small Indian child clinging to his dead mother's breast; he sent the boy home and reared him as his son Lincoyer. Menawa escaped by floating down the river in a canoe, apparently dead. Although he survived, he was not present for the signing of the treaty. As a result of the war he was impoverished. Most dramatically, William Weatherford surrendered to Jackson.

Weatherford, the "destroyer of Fort Mims," was an unusual man. Although the leader of the Red Sticks, he was more white than Indian. His mother was a Tait, half sister to Alexander McGillivray, his father a Scotch trader. The only Creek blood in his veins came from his beauteous groundmother, Sehoy, who was herself half French. Thomas S. Woodward knew him well and attributed to him many of the traits accredited to his half uncle Alexander McGillivray.

> He was a man of fine sense, great courage, and knew much about our government and mankind in general—had lived with his half brother, Davy Tate, who was an educated and well informed man—had been much with his brother-in-law, Sam Moniac, who was always looked upon as being one of the most intelligent half-breeds in the Nation, and was selected by Alexander McGillivray for interpreter at the time he visited Gen. Washington at New York.—*Woodward's Reminiscences of the Creek or Muscogee Indians, Contained in Letters to Friends in Georgia and Alabama* (Tuscaloosa, 1939), p. 94. First published in 1859.

There are several versions of Weatherford's final humiliation in surrendering to General Jackson; the one here was provided by Mr. William Letford of the Department of Archives and History; its origin is unknown.

WILLIAM WEATHERFORD'S SPEECH TO GENERAL ANDREW JACKSON AT TOHOPEKA ON THE TALLAPOOSA RIVER WHEN HE SURRENDERED MARCH 28, 1814

I am in your power. Do (with) me as you please. I am a soldier. I have done the white people all the harm I could. I have fought them and fought them bravely. If I had an army, I would yet fight and contend to the last, but I have none. My people are all gone. I can now do no more than to weep over the misfortunes of my nation. Once I could animate my warriors to battle, but I can not animate the dead. My warriors can no longer hear my voice. Their bones are at Talledaga, Emuckfau, and Tohepeka. I have not surrendered myself thoughtlessly. Whilst there was a chance of success I never left my post nor supplicated peace. But now I ask it for my nation and not for myself. On the miseries and misfortunes brought upon my country, I look back with deepest sorrow and wish to avert still greater calamities. If I had been left to contend with the Georgia army I could have raised my corn on one bank of the river and fought them on the other, but your people have destroyed my nation. You are a brave man and I rely upon your generosity. You will exact no terms of a conquered people but such as they can accede to, whatever they may be it would be madness and folly to oppose. If they are opposed you will find me one of the sternest enforcers of obedience. Those who hold out can be influenced only by a mean spirit of revenge and to this they must not and shall not sacrifice the last remnant of their people. You have told us where we might go and be safe. This is a good talk and my nation ought to listen to it. They shall listen to it. I shall say no more.

According to a biographer of Jackson:

Jackson poured his guest a cup of brandy. He promised to help the women and children. Weatherford promised to try to persuade the remaining braves to peace. General Jackson extended his hand. Red Eagle took it and strode from the ruined fort in which his mother had been born—vanishing from the view of the astonished soldiery, and from history, a not entirely graceless figure.—Marquis James, *The Life of Andrew Jackson* (New York: Bobbs-Merrill Co., 1938), p. 173.

A somewhat more realistic account of the incident is given by Thomas S. Woodward, who knew Weatherford personally.

Gen. Jackson said to Weatherford, that he was astonished at a man of his good sense, and almost a white man, to take sides with an ignorant set of savages, and being led astray by men who professed to be prophets and gifted with a supernatural influence. And more than all, he had led the Indians and was one of the prime movers of the massacre at Fort Mimms. Weatherford listened attentively to the General until he was through. He then said to the General, that much had been charged to him that he was innocent of, and that he believed as little in Indian or white prophets as any man living, and that he regretted the unfortunate destruction of Fort Mimms and its inmates as much as he, the General, or any one else. He said it was true he was at Fort Mimms when the attack was made, and it was but a little after the attack was made before the hostile Indians seemed inclined to abandon their undertaking; that those in the Fort, and particularly the half breeds under Dixon Bailey, poured such a deadly fire into their ranks as caused them to back out for a short time; at this stage of the fight he, Weatherford, advised them to draw off entirely. He then left to go some few miles to where his half brother, Davy Tate, had some negroes, to take charge of them, to keep the Indians from scattering them; after he left, the Indians succeeded in firing the Fort, and waited until it burnt so that they could enter it with but little danger. He also said to the General that if he had joined the whites it would have been attributed to cowardice and not thanked. And moreover, it was his object in joining the Indians, that he thought he would in many instances be able to prevent them from committing depredations upon defenseless persons; and but for the mismanagement of those that had charge of the Fort, he would have succeeded, and said, "Now, sir, I have told the truth, if you think I deserve death, do as you please; I shall only beg for the protection of a starving parcel of women and children, and those ignorant men who have been led into the war by their Chiefs."—Woodward, *Reminiscences of the Creeks,* pp. 92–93.

The removal of the Indians, which operated in a haphazard manner for many years, became established as a national policy with the election of Andrew Jackson to the presidency in 1829. By the end of his eight years in the White House, most of the Indians east of the Mississippi River had been moved west; there were only a scattered few left in Alabama. The Dancing Rabbit Creek Treaty (1830) arranged for the final removal of the Choctaws; Cusseta Treaty (1832) of the Creeks, and New Echota Treaty (1835) of the Cherokees. There is no big name treaty with the Chickasaws, but a series of treaties between 1826 and 1832 by which members of this tribe gained comparatively generous terms. The half-breed George Colbert, of Colbert's Ferry, and his brothers George and Pitman, played important roles in these negotiations. By 1830 most of the Indians left in this state were Creeks, and their fate was of the greatest interest to both settlers and politicians.

Even before removal treaties, Alabama (like Georgia and Mississippi) took steps to extend state jurisdiction over the coveted lands. They felt encouraged to do so by the election of Jackson who in his first inaugural address (March, 1829) asserted that the "old states" already exercised judisdiction over the tribes within their boundaries and that there was no "constitutional, conventional, or legal provision which allows [Alabama and Georgia] less power over the Indians within their bounds than is possessed by Maine or New York. . . . A state cannot be dismembered by Congress or restricted in the exercise of her constitutional power." Alabama specifically exempted Indians from taxation, jury and military duty, and road work, but she went further than the other states in making it easy for frontier citizens to move onto Indian lands before the United States government had acquired title to them. Before there had been any negotiations with the Creeks, the state passed legislation for the erection of county governments in their territory in Alabama; Barbour, Russell, Macon, Chambers, Tallapoosa, Coosa, Talladega, Randolph, and Benton (now Calhoun) counties were all created in 1832. County governments made it virtually necessary for white men to live within the bounds of the county, if for no more reason than to fill the offices. Settlers felt that they, too, had a right to be there and they went in great numbers. This led to much trouble between the Indians and whites locally and to a real struggle between the federal and state governments.

While the purpose of the Treaty of Cusseta was the removal of the Creeks to the west, the expressed terms did not say that. It provided that each head of a family and each orphan child of the Creeks was to receive 320 acres of land. Each of the ninety chiefs of the town was to have 640 acres; they were given an additional 16,000 acres to be sold for the benefit of the whole tribe. Each Indian was given a certificate of ownership, and the federal government sent a "locating agent" into the nation to help the natives get "located" on their lands. This was felt to be necessary since Indians had no experience in private ownership. However, before the agent got around, many of the Indians had lost or worn out or sold their certificates; one writer estimates that fully half of the Creeks disposed of their certificates without getting any benefit from them. In the absence of certificates, unprincipled Indians, halfbreeds, whites and their Negro agents, acting in collusion, got the agents to approve many fraudulent sales of land. The activities of these land speculators helped to bring on the war of 1836.

Article five of the treaty (Cusseta) stated that all white intruders on the ceded lands were to be removed until the lands were surveyed and the Indians settled on lands of their choice. Exceptions were made of those whites who had planted crops; they could wait until after harvest. It is a well-known fact that they refused to leave, others poured in, and trouble ensued.

Governor John Gayle, a native of South Carolina, defied the authority of the federal government to remove the settlers from their homes. The proclamation, signed October 7, 1833, appeared in the Philadelphia *Examiner*.

A PROCLAMATION
BY THE GOVERNOR

To the Citizens of the Counties in the Creek Nation.

The Secretary of War, by direction of the President of the United States, instructed the Marshall of the Southern District of Alabama, to remove all white persons from the territory ceded by the Creek Indians by the treaty of March, 1832, which territory is composed of the counties of Benton, Talladega, Randolph, Coosa, Tallapoosa, Chambers, Russell, Macon, and Barbour.

These counties have been established and organized by the General Assembly, in conformity with the views and policy of the Federal Government, and in pursuance of the Constitution of the State.

The order, if executed, will result in a destruction of property belonging to the inhabitants of these counties, . . . and inflict upon them great and irreparable injuries, not less calamitous than those which would mark the invasion of a public enemy.

By virtue of this treaty, the Government of the United States have assumed the right of removing by armed forces, not only all persons who have settled upon the public lands, but those also who, in the opinion of the agents, have committed trespasses upon the improvements of the Indians, which are their private property, thereby undertaking, without any lawful authority and in violation of our common Constitution to regulate matters which belong exclusively to the laws and tribunals of this state.

The order for the removal of the settlers must necessarily be attended with the expulsions of our civil officers, the suppression of our courts and, in fact, the destruction of the State Government throughout these counties. . . .

The course which the General Government has adopted, and is now pursuing, is a palpable and indefensible invasion of the acknowledged rights of this State, and in its tendency utterly subversive of our free and happy government.

There are now thirty thousand of our people alarmed at the horrors of starvation on one side and of military execution on the other. In this hour of their affliction I recommend and exhort them to look with abiding and undoubting confidence to the majesty of the law. It will cover them over with a shield, impenetrable to the sword or bayonet.

In order, therefore, that the laws may be faithfully executed, and by virtue of the power and authority in me vested, I hereby require all civil officers in the counties aforesaid, to be attentive to the complaints of the people upon whom any crimes may be committed . . . by issuing all such warrants and other process as may be necessary to bring offenders to justice, particularly such as are guilty of murder, false imprisonment, house burning, robbery, forcible entries, and all such like heinous offences.

And all good citizens are required, when duly called upon, to aid and assist in the execution of such process as may be issued by the competent authorities and according to the law of the land. And, furthermore, it is enjoined upon the citizens in the counties aforesaid to yield a ready obedience to any precept or process that may issue from the court of the United States or of this State; and especially to abstain from acts of unlawful violence towards the Indians, who being ignorant of our laws and of their rights, should be taught to look upon their more intelligent neighbors for information and protection.

The authorities of Alabama are obviously the proper tribunals for

the decision of this question. Alabama has offered to take cognizance
of suits entered against the intruders, but the General Government . . .
complains that such a course would not be sufficiently summary and
certain, and prefers the sword. Accordingly, twenty-five thousand of
our fellow freemen . . . are to be driven, at the point of a bayonet, from
their smiling farms and happy homes. . . .—*Philadelphia Examiner,*
November 13, 1833.

The contest over these lands had political overtones, and notices
of it appeared in the press throughout the country. The following
editorial was in a Philadelphia paper.

THE ALABAMA CASE

This controversy is one of startling and appalling importance. The
General Government and one of the states are directly at issue. Both
parties are determined upon the arbitrament of the sword. The principles
involved are vital; the result, whatever it is, must be deplorable.

The history of the case is plain. The United States owns lands in
Alabama. The established policy of the General Government has been
to encourage the settlement and cultivation of all public lands by giving
the settlers the right of pre-emption. The lands in controversy have been
accordingly thus settled, as the public land was in this and other states
first settled. The tract in question comprises nine counties and contains
a population of 25,000 persons. It has been, by the Legislature of
Alabama, organized so as to put the entire machinery of the State
Government into full operation. This measure was adopted as well in
conformity with the well-known views and wishes of the President as
in persuance of the Constitution and State of Alabama.

Such is the condition of the tract when the President directs the immense population to leave the land—to abandon their houses and fields
and go beyond the boundary lines of the public lands.

The settlers are of the opinion that they have not a title to the land,
but a legal right to remain upon it until sold and then become bidders
for it. They are willing to pay for the land, but not give it up. Under
these conditions they refuse to abandon it.

The President answers that he is bound by a treaty with the Creeks
to clear the land from intruders. The means of doing this have been
pointed out, he says, by an Act of Congress passed in 1807; they are
Military Force!

He therefore orders a portion of the army of the United States to
march into Alabama and drive out the whole white population from
these nine counties at the point of the bayonet.

The results would be the depopulation of nine counties; the driving
into the wilderness of 25,000 free citizens of the state; the annihilation
of the State Government in these nine counties and the substitution of
military force.

Alabama spurns the thought of submission. She sees in these acts of
the General Govenment an annihilation of State Sovereignty. Her Gover-

nor has placed the state in a posture of defence, and the instant the General Government resorts to force she will be resisted by force.

The questions which occur are, first, is the course adopted by the General Government necessary or humane, and, secondly, is it authorized by the Constitution.

Upon the first point we will only refer to the facts. It must be a peculiar obligation which would require the expatriation of twenty-five thousand free citizens and the entire depopulation of nine counties. . . .

Governor Gayle describes the harsh results of the course of the Administration in the following paragraphs:

"The great object of the settlers this year has been to raise a sufficiency of corn and other provisions to supply the wants of the next season, and also to obtain the necessary quantity of cattle, hogs, and other stock. It is well known that the first business of settlers in a new country is to exchange their transportation for the means of subsistence, and this has actually been done by the greater portion of the population in the Creek nation. Their wagons, carts, horses, &c are gone, and very many cannot possibly leave the country within the time specified in your instructions to the marshal.

"The agricultural labors of the people have been crowned with sucess, and their crops of corn, peas, potatoes, &c will place them during the ensuing year above the difficulties produced by the scarcity of the last.

"Imagine for a moment the almost total destruction of these crops, the loss of much of the stock, and the destitute condition of thousands of women and children, and you will have a faithful picture of scenes which your orders, if carried out, will spread over the entire region.

"It seems to me that the obligations resting upon the President to avert from this large community so dire and overwhelming a calamity are as 'imperative in their character' as any which have been 'assumed in the Creek treaty'. . . ."

But there is another inquiry of ten-fold greater importance. *Is this measure authorized?* or is it a direct and appalling violation of the Constitution—an act in its character severe—perhaps tyrannical; and in its results wholly destructive of the rights—nay, of the existence of the States?

The General Government explicitly disclaims *jurisdiction* over the lands in controversy. It only claims the naked right of ownership. It is a mere landholder, and has no right, as such, which other landholders do not share. Can it then, within the territory of a sovereign State, take the laws regulating property into its own hands, and execute its own decrees? It disclaims jurisdiction, yet prostrates and defies the jurisdiction of the State. . . . Do other landholders possess these rights? This is not pretended; but the General Government does it under the authority of a treaty. Alabama denies the constitutionality of this treaty; and sustains her position by arguments the most conclusive. The powers of the General Government are confined to the grant made by the following clause in the Constitution—

'Congress shall have power to dispose of and make all needful rules and regulations respecting the territory or other property of the United States.'

If this was designed to give the General Government unlimited power within the boundary lines of lands owned by it in the States, we cannot conceive what rights are left to the States. Governor Gayle justly says:—

"If the General Government has the right to regulate the conduct of our people in relation to their land—if it can rightfully expel a citizen who trespasses upon the landed possessions of his neighbor, by the summary interposition of a military guard . . . what is to restrain it from the exercise of the same power in relation to trespasses upon personal property? . . . . If by the treaty-making power, the ordinary operation of our laws upon the persons and property of our own citizens can be suspended, as will be the case if the fifth article of the treaty is executed in the mode prescribed in your late order to the Marshall, the whole field of state jurisdiction may be considered as occupied, and State sovereighty, the reserved rights of the States . . . are but meaningless sounds. . . .—*The Examiner and Journal of Political Economy,* November 18, 1833.

The strong states' rights position of Governor Gayle led to an impasse with the administration forces. Finally, the federal government sent Francis Scott Key to Fort Mitchell near where one Hardeman Owens had been killed when the United States deputies were trying to remove him from the Creek lands, and to Tuscaloosa (then the state capital) as mediator. On March 4, 1834, Key wrote to Gayle:

. . . . I find by a letter from Mr. Elliott that your legislature has adjourned, leaving Alabama and the U. States in statu ante bellum— without determining who was right or wrong in the quarrel. As this was the way in which I always wished the business to terminate, I have felt much gratified.

Key had been able to "satisfy" Governor Gayle and the state of Alabama and at the same time save face for Jackson in such a way as to make it appear that "Old Hickory" was not backing down. Frank L. Owsley, Jr., says that the whole controversy was almost certainly the result of a misunderstanding by all parties. While the matter was settled (and the Indians sent west), the episode made a rift in state politics, and John Gayle and others became Whigs. The breach between him and Jackson was never healed.

The War of 1836

The refusal of the whites to leave the still unsurveyed land, the defiance of the governor, and the pressure on the Creeks to leave combined to put the Indians in an intolerable position. This led to an actual outbreak of hostilities in east Alabama in 1836. The account of this second Creek war as one man remembered it is told by Rev. F. L. Cherry in his "History of Opelika," fifty years after the event.

When the war broke out in earnest, Uncle Blake Thomas and his servants were in the field plowing. This was on the 9th day of May, 1836. He had made one crop on his new place in the Indian country, and had made many friends among the Indians, and, as far as he knew, no enemies; though there were one or two of his immediate neighbors whose conduct incited to diligent watchfulness. He knew nothing definite of the Indian hostile movement. Early that morning, he discovered Tuskoo-na Fix-a-ko and his son driving their cattle out of the swamp, towards the council house, or his wigwam. This was something unusual, but he had plowed on until the noon hour. While at dinner, he related the circumstance to his wife, whereupon she informed him that old Katy Marthley had been there that morning and told her to go back to her father's house in Georgia, that her people were going to fight the whites and kill all who would not go away. Now, it appears that Mrs. Thomas had been kind to this Indian woman, and, as kindness will tell on every heart, savage or civilized, when properly extended, this untutored squaw could not stand listlessly by and see her destroyed without giving her timely warning and a chance to escape, though she did this at the peril of her own life, for if the Indians had the least suspicion of what they would consider a traitor in their camp, instant death would follow the object of such a suspicion. Old Katy Marthley call Mrs. Thomas *"ink-lis"* —a good squaw—and she did not want to see her killed. Mr. Joseph Thomas, Uncle Blake's brother, was out on the Crawford road that day and found the people leaving, or preparing to leave. George W. Elliott, the sheriff of the county, was living at Crocketville, a mile east of Crawford, and, at that time, his was the only house on what is now known as the Crawford road, between Uncle Blake's and Columbus. Joseph learned that the Indians had burned the bridge across the Big Uchee creek, on the old Federal road, killed Mr. McKizzie and his wife and fired into Mr. Hartwell D. Green's wagon, killing the mules, destroying the wagons and plunder, except what they appropriated to their own use. Mr. Greene and his servants managed to make their escape. His family, who were in the carriage, about a quarter a mile in the rear, hearing the guns firing and the Indians yelling, turned about, and by another route crossed the creek and made their escape.

This all occurred on the 9th of May. Joseph returned home about night and notified the neighborhood of what had occurred. Every man for himself and family. After agreeing upon some concert of action, and standing not upon the order of agreement, the house of Mr. John Perry, who lived on the north side of the creek, on the hill near where Mr. William Long now lives, was the point agreed upon to meet. About 9 o'clock p.m., they all started from that point, where they had collected. The caravan composed, as now remembered by Uncle Blake, Rev. Michael Thomas, Mr. Joseph Thomas, Mr. Harlin Blaylock. Mr. Isaac

Hill—the well known "Uncle Isaac"—Mr. James Cox, Rev. William Robinson, and his aged parents, Mr. J. Perry, Dr. Cone, Mr. Stutstill, Mr. James Jeter and their respective families. Others, whose names are not now remembered joined them as they advanced. The route they followed passed by where Judge E. A. Garlick now lives, the Duncan place, the F. C. Slappey place, turned to the left at the Digby place, followed the ridge, passed between the John D. Green place and the A. R. Tiller place, crossed the present road leading from Concord Church towards Crawford between Mr. Leslie's and Mrs. Burton's places and the Stroud creek a short distance above a little mill built by the late James Story. From there they struck what is now the Columbus and Salem road between Mt. Zion and what is now Mott's Mill, following that road until it forked near what is now Smith's Station. Here they turned towards the river passing the Black Dirt hill the Wm. Lowther place and touched the river at Hardaway's Ferry about daylight on the 10th of May. The women and children were crossed over first, after which the men, with the wagon and teams followed; all reaching the eastern side a little after sunrise. Then, and not until then, did they feel safe. Here they separated, each family turning in the direction of their respective friends along the border settlements of Georgia.

The next day Uncle Blake, after placing his wife with her father's family, started back to his place, by way of Columbus. On reaching the town he found the entire country people from the west side of the river collected there and intense excitement prevailing. Columbus was a small town then. They earnestly warned him and endeavored to persuade him not to attempt crossing the Indian country, saying that it would be foolhardiness—walking into the very jaws of death. In addition to his other property, he had left a negro woman and her two children there unprotected, with the promise that he would return to them as soon as he possibly could, and he was resolved to redeem that promise. In company with his two brothers, Mike and Joseph, and Mr. Stutstill, they crossed the river at the Girard bridge and struck out on what was known as the Old We-tum-ka Trail, which led by the Eli Stroud place. Here this trail turned to the left and touched the Little Uchee, about where Moffett's Mill was afterwards built, and running up the south side of the creek, passed the Cotton place and from there on west. Uncle Blake and his companions did not go that route, though it was the nearest, on account of its close proximity to an Indian town, where Tus-koo-na Fix-a-koo, who was supposed to be one of the most active chiefs in inaugurating the trouble, lived; but took the Chewacla Trail until he reached the trail followed on the refugee trip. This last mentioned was called the Joe Marshall trail. No trouble was met on this return trip. Uncle Blake had left everything he had, except the clothes he and his wife wore and the ponies they rode. On his return he found everything just as he had left it. His servant was in the field hoeing corn, and her two children nursing each other in the middle of the rows. She was overjoyed to see him for she always felt safe when "Mars Blake" was about, Indians or no Indians, but never was satisfied when he was away under any circumstances. He immediately loaded his ox-wagon with furniture, meat and as much corn and fodder as he could carry, with his negroes, and started back on the trip the same day, following the out-going route and crossed the river about 8 a.m., the next day, traveling all night. A cloudless mid May full moon favored him. His brothers and Mr. Stutstill returned with him. This was the 12th day of May and on that day, Tus-koo-na Fix-a-koo and his warriors—all of whom were his neighbors—way-laid and burned the stages, three in number, on their way from Montgomery to Columbus. The reason why there was more than the usual number of coaches on the line that day, was, the management was bringing out their stock from off the line, out of danger, in view of the forthcoming trouble. In addition to the usual team of four horses to the coach, there were several led, attached to the straps from behind. According to the best recollection available, there were about twenty-two horses, and "stage horses" in those days were selected from the best stock the country could produce. There was considerable treasure also in the coaches. This with the horses, was all lost. It is said by some that the famous Jim Henry, who was employed by a mercantile firm in Columbus as salesman, in order to secure a monopoly of the Indian trade from the west side of the river, was Tus-koo-na's informant as to the exact day that these horses, and treasure were to be brought out. It is also supposed by some that Jim Henry instigated the burning of Roanoke, and, by virtue of his situation in Columbus, being able to acquire information, reported the same to his people across the river, aiding and abetting their warlike movement to the best of all his ability, at the same time retaining the confidence of white friends. Others say, personally, Jim Henry was a coward and never fired a hostile gun in his life, and wonder why he has gone into history as "the famous Jim Henry." There was the usual complement of passengers that day, all of whom were fortunate enough to escape, except Mr. Lackey, who lived in Harris County, Ga. He was acting as agent for some orphan children, who held an interest in some property in Macon county, Ala. He had transacted the business and was on his way home. He had twelve or fifteen hundred dollars with him, belonging to the orphans, which was lost. Among the passengers was a soldier, who was on his return home from Mexico, after a long imprisonment by Santa Anna, in the U.S. trouble, on account of Texas territory. This soldier's name was Hard-away. Being well armed and game as a Spartan, he fought his retreat at his leisure, killing several reds before he left the scene. When he saw that it would be self-murder to remain longer, he turned to retreat. By this brave conduct, the other passengers had time to escape, all but Mr. Lackey, who being somewhat corpulent, was overtaken just before reaching the ford of Brush creek, a half a mile from the scene, and was killed. He was buried about a hundred yards west from where this tragedy occurred, and a weather-worn slab stood at the head of his grave a few years ago, and may still mark the spot. It should be renewed, at the expense of the Government, that the scene of this, one of the remarkable events of the war of 1836, should not be obliterated. A vigorous young hickory has sprung up near the grave within a few years. Mr. Hardaway reached the creek and hid himself in the canebrake, which was thick and rank at time. An Indian would scent him, cautiously approach, peering through the cane. Mr. Hardaway would wait patiently and motionless until he came within easy range of his deadly revolver; when a crack, a puff of smoke, a gutteral groan and that Indian ceased at once to struggle and live. Hardaway would then change his position and wait for his pursuers, who, directed by the report of his pistol, were soon on his track. He waited until his game was near enough to see him plainly through the thick reeds, pop away and down came another red. In this way, he killed three in the canebrake, some say four, though only three were found afterwards; directed by the buzzards. The last one was said to have been a burly fellow, and very anxious to be shot, and Mr. Hardaway thought it prudent to give him a good opportunity. So he waited until he got within a few feet of him and was discovered, upon which the Indian shouted, "Waugh!!" It was his last whoop, and down he went. All this occurred fifteen miles from Opelika, south, and only forty-eight years ago, the 12th of May, next. Mr. Hardaway reached Columbus after dodging the Indians three days, nearly naked, hungry and physically exhausted, but in spirit as game as ever. The good people of Columbus received him kindly, carried him to a clothier, supplied him with a complete suit of clothes, and means to meet his immediate wants, purchased a ticket for stage passage to Macon, and sent him home to his friends.—*Alabama Historical Quarterly,* vol. 15, pp. 291–95.

The inevitable happened and the Indians were forced to leave their lands. They went in groups, accompanied by agents of the Alabama Emigrating Company and by representatives of the army. One unidentified visitor in Tuscaloosa (January 20, 1835) saw a party of four hundred Choctaws "of all ages and all sexes" pass through the city on their way to Arkansas. These Choctaws under the direction of Captain Page of the United States Army were "with their horses, a miserable, squalid set."

Dr. Jacob Rhett Motte, a South Carolinian stationed with the army at Ft. Mitchell in Russell County, kept the following account of the departure of a band of Creeks, July, 1836.

It was a melancholy spectacle as these proud monarchs of the soil were marched off from their native land to a distant country, which to their anticipations presented all the horrors of the infernal regions. There were several who committed suicide rather than endure the sorrow of leaving the spot where rested the bones of their ancestors. One old fellow was found hanging by the neck the night before he was to leave Fort Mitchell for the far West; preferring the glorious uncertainty of another world, to the inglorious misery of being forced to a country of which he knew nothing, but dreaded every thing bad. This indifference to life was displayed by the Indians on many occasions; for though apparently great in open battle, yet death by their own hands presented no terror to them . . . .

One of this very party of emigrating Indians on his arrival at Montgomery (Alabama) attempted his escape; but when caught and secured in a waggon, by some accident got possession of a very dull knife; with this he made several ineffectual efforts to cut his throat, but it not proving sharp enough, he with both hands forced it into his chest over the breast-bone, and by successive violent thrusts succeeded in dividing the main artery, when he bled to death. Similar instances of suicide were very common, and served forcibly to exhibit how strong the "amor patriae" burned in their breasts. With them their country was life, and without the former the latter was valueless . . . .

A party of five hundred who had been taken captive, and brought to Fort Mitchell, were necessarily sent off in chains. The men were handcuffed two together, and a long chain passing between the double file connected them all together. The stoical disposition of these forest philosophers was strongly displayed, for neither their physical nor mental sufferings could elicit from them the least indication of distress, except occasionally the utterance of an emphatic "ta" whenever two of them pulling in opposite directions would jerk one another by the wrists. The women followed drowned in tears, and giving utterance to most distressing cries; the children joined in from sympathy, for they were yet too young to participate in the unenviable feelings of their parents. The smaller ones were comfortably disposed of in the waggons, which followed in the rear . . . .

On the 11th of July we left Fort Mitchell and proceeded in a westwardly direction on the old Federal road, directly through the heart of the hostile nation. All along the road was presented a repetition of the devastated scenes which met the eye at Roanoke. Bridges destroyed; houses burnt; and new made graves, where the murdered travellers had been hastily buried beside the road; half-burnt remains of stages and waggons that had been pillaged by the Indians blocked up the way; and in one spot the road was filled with empty coffins, scattered in all directions by the Indians, who had taken them from a wagon, set out for the purpose of bringing in the dead for burial.

We reached before dark the only house left by the Indians on the road; there we found Col. Brooks of the artillery with his command encamped; and there we concluded to stop for the night. This house was occupied by a man named Stone, and by a signboard which swung from a tree in front, I inferred that it had been a tavern in times of peace under the title of "Creek Stand."—*Journey into Wilderness* (Gainesville, Fla.: University of Florida Press, 1953, pp. 19–21.

A much longer (but here much abbreviated) account of the actual process of removing the Indians was kept by Lieutenant J. T. Sprague who accompanied a band west to their destination.

The following day, I assembled all the chiefs and explained to them the necessary arrangements to embody their town, in order to transfer them to the charge of the Alabama Emigrating Company upon such a day as might be designated by the commanding general. They gave no other than a silent acquiescence to my wishes, but expressed among themselves strong feelings of dissatisfaction. I promised them every assistance in disposing of what little they had, but assured them that upon the day fixed for their departure they must be ready.

The necessity of their leaving their country immediately was evident to everyone; although wretchedly poor they were growing more so every day they remained. A large number of white men were prowling about, robbing them of their horses and cattle and carrying among them liquors which kept up an alarming state of intoxication. The citizens of the country had no security, for though these Indians had professed the most friendly feelings, no confidence could be placed in them, as the best informed inhabitants of the country believed them to be allied with those who had already committed overt acts of hostility. Some families which had fled for safety were afraid to return until the country was rid of every Indian. Public indignation was strong against them, and no doubt the most serious consequences would have resulted, had not immediate measures been adopted for their removal.

In this state of things, however indignant their feelings or however great the sacrifice, it was but justice to get them out of the country as soon as possible. On the 23rd, inst. I received orders from the Commanding General to move the Party on the 29 inst. The time, however, was prolonged five days, to the 3rd of September. On the 1st of September I had in camp near two thousand ready for removal. This number comprised the whole of the two towns, excepting a few who had been secreted in a swamp from the commencement of the Creek War. These sent an express to know if I would receive them as friends, should they come in. I assured them they would be treated as the rest. I heard no more from them until the ninth night of our march, when they joined the train with their women and children. Their number I could never learn, as they kept themselves aloof lest they might be treated as hostiles; but from other Indians, who were silent on the subject, I learnt there were from one hundred to one hundred and fifty.

The 3rd of September I placed all the Indians under my charge in care of Mr. Felix G. Gibson and Charles Abercrombie, members of the Alabama Emigrating Company, and on the morning of the 5th the Party started for Arkansas, arranged to wagons according to the contract. The train consisted of forty-five wagons of every description, five hundred ponies and two thousand Indians. The moving of so large a body necessarily required some days to effect an arrangement to meet the comfort and convenience of all. The marches for the first four or five days were long and tedious and attended with many embarrassing circumstances. Men, who had never had claims upon these distressed beings, now preyed upon them without mercy. Fradulent demands were presented and unless some friend was near, they were robbed of their houses and even clothing. Violence was often resorted to keep off these depredators to such an extent, that unless forced marches had been made to get out of this and the adjoining counties, the Indians would have been wrought to such a state of desperation that no persuasion would have deterred them from wreaking their vengeance upon the innocent as well as the guilty.

As soon as time and circumstances would permit, proper arrangements were made to secure to the Indians, regularly, their rations and transportation. A large herd of cattle were driven ahead of the train which supplied the Party with fresh beef. Two days rations were issued every other day, while corn was issued every day. The Party moved on without any serious inconvenience, other than the bad state of the roads and frequent drunken broils, until the 22nd, when from the warmth of the weather and the wearied condition of the Indians, I deemed it expedient to halt for a days rest. Tuch-e-batch-ehadjo, the principal chief, had been desirous of stopping sooner, and had expressed his determination to do so. The situation of the camp at this time was not a desirable one for a halt, nor was I inclined to indulge him. I ordered the train to proceed. He, with reluctance, came on.

From the first days march, I saw a dispostion in the Indians, among both old and young, to remain behind. From their natural indolence and from their utter disregard for the future, they would straggle in the rear, dependent upon what they could beg, steal or find for support. I used every entreaty to induce them to keep up but finding this of no avail I threatened them with soldiers and confinement in irons. This had a salutary effect, and was the means of bringing most of them into camp in good season. On the night of the 24th inst. the party encamped at Town Creek, Ala. after twenty days march averaging about twelve miles a day. I waited on the contractors and requested them to halt the party the following day. To this they gave unqualified disapprobation and denied my authority to exercise such a power. Their expenses they said were from six to seven dollars per day, and if such authority was given or implied in the Contract, their hopes of making anything were gone. I assured them, that from the condition of the Indians, the common decency calls of humanity and forbearance. I ordered the Indians to halt, and told the Contractors they could act on their own pleasure; either go on with their empty wagons—or remain. The party halted and resumed the journey on the following morning, the 25th. The Indians and horses were evidently much relieved by the days rest.

From this period to the fifth of October our marches were long, owing to the great scarcity of water; no one time, however, exceeding twenty miles. The Indians in large numbers straggled behind, and many could not get to Camp till after dark. These marches would not have been so burdensome had proper attention been paid to the starting of the Party in the morning. It was necessary that their baggage, as well as their children, should be put in the wagons, and the sick and feeble sought out in the different parts of the camp. But this was totally disregarded. I reminded the Contractors that the party now required the utmost attention, that unless they were strictly seen to, we should not at night have more than half the Indians in Camp. To this they were indifferent, saying, that "they must keep up or be left". Early in the morning the wagons moved off, the Agents at the head, leaving those behind to take care of themselves; they are men it is true, but it is well known that they are totally incapable of it, and it's proverbial that they will never aid each other.

To this course of proceeding I remonstrated, and the tenth article of the Contract which authorizes the officer to make any expenditure contributing to the comfort and convenience, etc., I put in execution, which relieved the Indians from the destitute situation in which they would otherwise have been placed. My letters to the Contractors accompanying this report embrace this period and will explain to you more fully the course I was compelled to adopt. It, however, affords me pleasure to say, that upon a better knowledge of their obligations, they very readily consented to pay the expenses which accrued in keeping up the rear. . . .

On the 20th inst. the officer of the Government appointed to receive the Emigrating Creeks, acknowledged the receipt of my entire party. . . . After the Indians had received their blankets in compliance with the treaty, I proceeded with the larger portion of them to the country assigned them. Thirty five miles beyond Fort Gibson I encamped them upon a prairie and they soon after scattered in every direction, seeking a desirable location for their new homes. . . .

The excessive bad state of the roads, the high waters, and extreme cold and wet weather, was enough to embarrass the strongest minds. The distance traveled by the party from Chambers County, Alabama, to their last encampment, was eight hundred miles by land, and four hundred and twenty-five by water; occupying ninety-six days. The health of the Indians upon the entire route was much better than might have been anticipated.

Twenty nine deaths were all that occurred; fourteen of these were children and the others were the aged, feeble and intemperates. The unfriendly disposition of the Indians towards the whites from the earliest history of our country, is known to everyone. To what an extent this feeling existed in the party under my charge, I cannot with confidence say, for it was seldom expressed but when in a state of intoxication. But if this be a fair criterion, I have no hesitation in contradiction to the well known history of the Creeks for the last two years. They were poor, wretchedly, and depravedly poor, many of them without a garment to cover their nakedness. To this there was some exceptions, but this was the condtion of a large portion of them. They left their country, at a warm season of the year, thinly clad and characteristically indifferent to their rapid approach to the regions of a climate to which they were unaccustomed, they expended what little they had for intoxicating drinks or for some gaudy article of jewelry.

So long a journey under the most favorable auspices must necessarily be attended with suffering and fatigue. They were in a deplorable condition when they left their homes, and a journey of upwards of a thousand miles could not certainly have improved it. There was nothing within the provisions of the contract by which the Alabama Emigrating Company could contribute to their wants, other than the furnishing of rations and transportation, and strict compliance with the demands of the officer of the Government; these demands, unquestionably, must come within the letter and spirit of the contract. All these they complied with. The situation of the officers of the Government, at the head of these parties, was peculiarly responsible and embarrassing. They were there to protect the rights of the Indians and to secure to them all the Government designed for them. These Indians, looking up to the officers as a part of the Government, not only appealed for their rights, but their wants. They could sympathize with them, as every one must who saw their condition, but could not relieve them. They had nothing, within their power, for in a pecuniary point they were scarcely better off than those they were willing to assist. All that the contract granted was secured to them. But all this could not shield them from the severity of the weather, cold sleeting storms, and hard frozen ground.

Had a few thousand dollars been placed at the disposal of the officer which he could have expended at his discretion, the great sufferings which all ages, particularly the young, were subjected to, might have been in a measure avoided. But as it was, the officer was obliged to listen to their complaints without any means of redress.

Many exaggerated reports are in circulation, respecting the miserable condition of these emigrating Indians. Let these be traced to the proper source and it will be found that the white-men with whom they have been associated for years past have been the principal cause. There is enough in support of this opinion. It is only necessary to advert to the allegations in many instances, well established, of the lands of the Indians having been purchased by some of these citizens at prices much below their real value, or of the purchase money having been in whole or in part, withheld, the prosecution of valid or fictitious debts, commenced at the moment of their departure for the west, and thereby extorting from them what little money they had.

Had they been permitted to retain the fair proceeds of their lands they would have had the means of procuring any additional supplies for their comfort. The stipulations of the treaty were fairly executed; all that was to be furnished the Indians was provided, and if these were inadequate to their comfortable removal and subsistence, no blame can be attached to the agents of the Alabama Emigrating Company or to the officers of the government.—Grant Foreman, *Indian Removal* (Norman, Oklahoma: University of Oklahoma Press, 1932) pp. 166–68, 174–76.

With the departure of the emigrating parties in 1836 almost no Indians remained in this state. Unlike the Choctaws, who continued in large numbers in east-central Mississippi, the Creeks left. Only an undertermined number of people of mixed blood continued the

Indian race in Alabama. It was a sad day for the Indians but a time of relief for Alabamians who could now settle down to developing the whole state. For Americans, and especially the Jacksonians, it was a mission completed. They had treated the tribesmen like white men, even if in the process they had destroyed tribal governments and fragmented tribal domains. In the eyes of most Americans, the removal policy was moral since it provided payment for eastern land and allotments of western land. Furthermore, it was practical since it opened up new lands for white settlement and speculation. Only much later did these agreements significantly prick the public conscience.

Chapter 5

ECONOMIC DEVELOPMENT TO 1860:

AGRICULTURE AND SLAVERY

In the early decades of the nineteenth century, there was a recognizable disease prevalent in many neighboring states known as "Alabama fever." It was caused by a strong desire to own some of the good rich land lying within the bounds of the state. It compelled people, sometimes whole families and sometimes only the men, in Georgia, the Carolinas, Virginia, Tennessee, and even places farther away to "pull up stakes" and move to the new country. The population figures give an indication of how fast the new settlers were arriving. In 1800 the part of Mississippi Territory that was to become Alabama recorded 1,250 black and white residents; ten years later there were 9,046. The first state census (1820) showed that Alabama's population had reached 127,901. By 1830 there were 309,525. After 1820 the population increased about 200,000 each decade so that by 1860 there was a total of 964,201. The biggest rush of newcomers came in the years following the Treaty of Fort Jackson (1814), by which larger tracts of Indian lands were opened up to white settlers. In those years, many writers (often newspaper editors) observed an almost constant stream of wagons crossing the Chattahoochee River from Georgia, scores of families coming across the Tennessee river into western Alabama, and droves of hogs and cattle being driven west. Anne Royall noted that frequently there were strangers boarding at the same taverns where she stayed who were looking for land in north Alabama. In the early decades, most settlements were in that region or along the lower reaches of the Alabama and Tombigbee Rivers; not until the 1830's did farmers learn enough about handling the heavy soil in the Black Belt for many to move there.

Some of the excitement—and hazards—of the period is caught by Joseph G. Baldwin, a native of Winchester, Virginia. He practiced law in Kemper County, Mississippi, before moving to Sumter County, Alabama, in 1839 and had observed at first hand many of the features he wrote about.

This country was just settling up. Marvellous accounts had gone forth of the fertility of its virgin lands; and the productions of the soil were commanding a price remunerating to slave labor as it had never been remunerated before. Emigrants came flocking in from all quarters of the Union, especially from the slaveholding States. The new country seemed to be a reservoir, and every road leading to it a vagrant stream of enterprise and adventure. Money, or what passed for money, was the only cheap thing to be had. Every crossroad and every avocation presented an opening,—through which a fortune was seen by the adventure in near perspective. Credit was a thing of course. To refuse it—if the thing was ever done—were an insult for which a bowie-knife were not a too summary or exemplary a means of redress. The State banks were issuing their bills by the sheet, like a patent steam printing-press its issues; and no other showing was asked of the applicants for the loan that an authentication of his great distress for money. Finance, even in its most exclusive quarter, had thus already got, in this wonderful revolution, to work upon the principles of the charity hospital. If an overseer grew tired of supervising a plantation and felt a call to the mercantile life, even if he omitted the compendious method of buying out a merchant wholesale, stock, house and good will, and laying down, at once, his bullwhip for the yard-stick—all he had to do was to go on to New-York, and present himself in Pearl-street with a letter avouching his citizenship, and a clean shirt, and he was regularly given a through ticket to speedy bankruptcy.—Joseph G. Baldwin, *Flush Times in Alabama and Mississippi* (New York: Sagamore Press, 1957), p. 60, first published in 1853.

Pioneering

The Indians had left some clearings but generally speaking the new country was covered with heavy timber that had to be removed before farms and plantations could be developed. The problems of pioneers were much the same whether they moved to Huntsville in 1810, to Claiborne a decade later, or to Dallas County in the 1830's. The newcomers had to clear the land, plant a crop, erect buildings, and do whatever else was necessary to get a foothold in the new country.

Sarah Haynesworth, later the wife of Governor John Gayle and the mother of Amelia who married Josiah Gorgas, was a young child of about six when her family left South Carolina for Fort Stoddert. In her old age she recorded her memories for her descendants.

I can remember but little of our journey from South Carolina, commenced in, I think, March, 1810. It was a wild road, I know, and we were often attended by the Indians, in whom we had no confidence. Pah slept with arms under his head, and any stir among the horses at night, roused all and put them on their guard. Sometimes I rode on a pack horse, but was always in a glee when mounted on one by myself, and allowed to follow my humour in keeping the path (for road there was none in places) or wandering off at short distances amongst the undisturbed shade of trees which encroached on the track we traveled. At night I remember being always the busiest in running from the tent to the fires where supper was preparing. The coffee in a tin cup was delicious. We arrived at Fort Stoddert then occupied by the military, commanded by Capt., now Major-Gen'l E.P. Gaines from whom we received the kindest attentions. How great was my ecstacy when I saw for the first time the regularity and discipline, or what was more to me, the polished arms and uniform dresses of the soldiers! I flew from place to place, and when Mah became uneasy and sent a servant for me I was found at the guard house, seated on a soldier's knee giving and receiving delight; for all was new and I was the only child but one in the fort. The officers fancied me and took me with them to the parade and all other military exercises. I was frank and lively—fearless they endeavored to make me and partly succeed for the time. They would place me on the wheel of the cannon, and encourage me to stand the report without shrinking. At one time I sprung back, and in catching at the one who stood near me, seized something in his bosom, which proved a dirk, handsomely mounted in silver, which he gave me, and tied around me with a profusion of green ribbon. With this little weapon, I used for many years afterward to mingle with the officers on parade, mounting a gentle pony, a present of my father's low enough for me to spring from the ground to the saddle. They delighted to humor all of my childish whims, and indulged as I was at home and abroad, no wonder they were not a few.—Mrs. Sarah Haynesworth Gayle, "Diary," *Alabama Historical Quarterly*, vol. 5, pp. 164–67.

E. A. Powell (1817–1892) was about thirteen years of age when his family arrived in Tuscaloosa County in 1830. In 1888–89, Mr. Powell wrote a series of articles about these early days that was published in the Tuscaloosa *Gazette*.

My first entrance in Tuskaloosa County was about the last of February 1830. It was what I then thought to be about the end of the long wagon journey from South Carolina. We came down the old Huntsville road from Elyton. Elyton was the first town I ever saw in Alabama. It was there I saw the first Stage Coach I had ever seen. To me it was rather a big sight to see one man holding the reins of four horses, and they nearly at full speed and the driver cracking his long whip at every jump. I said I thought that we were at our journeys end, but I was mistaken. We came down to about opposite the Asylum. There my father had the wagon stopped, and he and mother and my two oldest brothers talked for nearly an hour. I well remember how impatient I was to get to see the 'Big Town.' But after a long talk, the wagon was turned around in the road and we took the back track for some eighteen miles, then turning to the right and finally on the ninth day of March, we passed up about twenty miles north of Selma.

That year under all the circumstances may be said to have been a prosperous one. But never will I forget the complete break down of Mother, when we drove up to the very poor apology for a cabin in which we were to live that year. She had been used to the comforts of life, and being in feeble health, the contrast seemed more than she could bear, and to use a common phrase, she just let go.

But the kind old gentleman from whom father had rented some land, came to the cabin, at once took in the situation, and spoke words of kindness and encouragement to mother; told her there was a better time coming, and for her not to give way.

The old gentleman's cropper soon came up with what was then considered a full outfit of carpenter's tools for a farmer, to-wit: a hand saw, auger and draw knife. He told mother that he would show her how to make an Alabama bedstead. A few heart pine rails, and some old boards filled up the timber bill, and in a very short time he had improvised a bedstead standing on one leg in each corner of the backend of the cabin, and mother put up her beds. By this time the genuine kindness and pleasant remarks of the man, uncultivated as they were, had produced a happy change in mother's feelings, and I don't think that I ever saw her in after life, come so near giving up again.

At the end of the year we moved to Fayette county, passing through Tuskaloosa County on the way. I had never before seen so large a town as Tuskaloosa. We got to the city on Saturday evening, a very cold evening in the first week of January. The river was then crossed only by means of the ordinary ferry boat, and from the crowd on the bank, it looked like it would be late in the night before we could get over. But owing to the earnest entreaties of Col. Johnson, who knew my father, and the kindness of old uncle Joe Cleveland, who gave us his turn in crossing, we got over in good time. These acts of kindness, boy as I was, made a deep impression upon my mind, and I have since remembered them with pleasure.

We spent that Saturday night in the celebrated little town of Kentuck. On the next morning, I heard the ring of the first church bell I had ever heard.

If the reader should be curious to know something more of the locality, appearance and character of Kentuck, let him just imagine, a low, or rather a squatty looking frame building, right on top of the river bank, just opposite Dodson's Warehouse, with a long piazza in front. A little store in front of that almost in the road. A cotton shed ware-house with post planted in the ground. On the opposite side of the road, at the place now covered by Dodson's Warehouse and a small shed store room of rough lumber at the north side of the ware-house, over the door of which was the sign, "Charles Snow & Co., Cash Store," he will have a very correct view of what was then known as Kentuck. These three places represented the commerce of that side of the river. The whole place did not extend fifty yards from the river.

Nearly all of what is now the town of North Port, particularly the lower parts, was a dense canebrake. There was a small cabin at the forks of the road where the store of T. J. Foster now stands, the most attractive feature of which to me was a pet bear chained in the yard. This last place was settled by the father of our very worthy citizen, Mr. W. L. Christian.—"Fifty-five Years in West Alabama," *Alabama Historical Quarterly,* vol. 4, pp. 545–47.

Both Mrs. Gayle and Mr. Powell were young when they came to Alabama and wrote about their arrival many years later. On the other hand, Sarah Jane Lide Fountain (aged 37), widowed daughter of the James Lide family, kept a diary as the family moved from South Carolina to Dallas County in the mid-1830's. Her account gives a sense of the "daily-ness" of such a trek. The Lides settled in Carlowville.

(17th. Thurs) day. Passed through Columbus, not very much pleased with its appearance, tho' a pretty smart little town, saw a good many Indians there, crossed the Chatahoochee river, and entered the Indian nation with gloomy feelings, traveled 10 miles over a dreadful road and have now taken up camp near a grog-shop where the Indians are making a great noise.

18th. Friday. Find the roads very rough and hilly today, oxen failing, getting on rather slowly, traveled only 15 miles. Indians so far more civil than I expected.

19th. Saturday. Warm and cloudy this morning, very much like rain. Got along very badly today, roads rough and muddy, my oxen give out, and little waggon broke down, tied it so as to get al (ong) but badly, feel very gloomy here in the midst of the Indians, tho' they seem pretty friendly. Now took up camp near the Indian town, where we expect to spend the Sabbath, traveled about 12 miles.

20th. Sabbath. Several of the negroes sick, weather cloudy and gloomy, we all met at 12 o'clock and had prayer meeting. Quite a thunderstorm tonight, rained very hard, tents leaked a good deal.

21st. Monday. A very gloomy morning. Pa sold one team of oxen for a little Indian pony this morning, saw a good many Indians today, and the most of them drunk, but appeared innocent, roads sloppy and muddy, crossed Caleba swamp, a very bad place, a long (rough) causeway, and steep bank on (the other side), and water deep, a dark drizly day, traveled about 17 miles.

22nd. Tuesday. Still cloudy and gloomy, but not rainy, see a good many Indians, crossed Line creek, now through the Nation, feel very much relieved that we have all got through safe, got to Mount Meggs, and spent the night at Mr. Temple's traveled 16 miles today.

23rd. Wednesday. A very pleasant day, left Mr. Temple's about 8 o'clock passed through Montgomery, quite a splendid looking town, oxen give out feel very much discouraged, traveled about 11 miles.

24th. Thursday. Crossed Catomac creek this morning, then passed over a prairie which was a dreadful bad road, then crossed the Pint Colly creek, dined near an old gentleman's house who was (very) kind, invited Pa and Ma to go and take a cup of warm coffee, and gave them some potatoes, met with Mr. DuBose and Mr. Prince, made me feel a little more cheerful to see an acquaintance once more, crossed the Talahassy creek this evening which was a pretty bad place, traveled about 17 miles today.

25th. Friday. A cloudy gloomy morning, with some rain, crossed Big swamp, water pretty deep, but the bottom good, passed through a little village called Church hill, roads very rough and hilly, a drizly day, traveled about 18 miles.

26th. Saturday. Weather more favourable. Set out about 5 o'clock this morning crossed Old town creek, passed over (some) long muddy hills, crossed Mush creek, passed through Pleasant hill, and have at length after a tedious journey of five weeks and two days reached our place of destination, feel worse than I have done since I left home, every thing seems gloomy and melancholly to me. Oh! how I would rejoice if I were only back to good old Darlington again, traveled 14 miles today.—*The Lides Go South, and West,* Fletcher M. Green, ed. (Columbia, S. C.: University of South Carolina Press, 1952), pp. 6–8.

There were constant vexations on any trip west, but the ones which a group of Georgians endured on their way to Crumly's Chapel in western Jefferson County seem to have been compounded. Twelve adults and thirty children travelling in covered wagons took ten days. The caravan left on Sunday and covered only twelve miles that day and encountered "countless troubles."

First Jesse Miller's horse had run away and torn up the wagon necessitating leaving it on the spot. Jonas Wheeler's horse got sick enroute and the caravan was halted while it was treated. Next, Lawson Young's steer balked and John Wheeler got up a trade with a settler encountered on the road and traded it off for one that would pull its share of the load. The next trouble on the same day came when Jim Glasgow's bow for his yoke of steers broke and the band was held up until it could be repaired. Then while they were halted at Cave Springs, Georgia to repair damages, the children scattered pellmell in the woods to pick up chestnuts, and the women of the group were almost in hysterics for fear some would get lost in the woods.—Mrs. W. C. Ferrill, *The Miller History,* quoted in Bennie Catherine Mellown, *Memoirs of a Pre-Civil War Community* (privately printed, 1950), p. 17.

One member of the party, John Y. Miller, was a Methodist preacher who attributed their hard luck to the fact they had started on Sunday. Therefore, he declared that there would be no more traveling on the Lord's day!

Pioneer families followed different plans in choosing spots to settle. Those going to Crumly's Chapel (which was quite late in the period) were joining relatives and friends who had preceded them to Jefferson County. There seem to have been many others, like the Powells who went west with no specific destination in mind, expecting to look around for suitable available land before making a decision. If they did not find what they wanted in Alabama, they could move one step farther west to Mississippi. Still many others sent a scout to choose a desirable place before leaving the old home. The Lide family had followed this plan and, after selecting the place, had sent some of the men, both white and black, to make a crop the year before the whole family migrated. This policy of making advance preparations for a move seems to have been more common among people who had large holdings in slaves, livestock, and household equipment than among those of little property.

The preparation made by the Tait family in moving from Elbert County, Georgia, to Alabama Territory in 1817 illustrates the care with which migrating families planned their departure. Senator Charles Tait had close connections with the territory. In February, 1817, James S. Tait, son of Senator Tait, left Georgia accompanied by his wife's father and brother to select a home site in the new country. The elder members of the family had agreed that such a site must combine fertile soil, healthful climate, and good navigation. There were other desirable factors such as:

> A stream near at hand for a mill and machinery—a never failing spring at the foot of a hillock on the summit of which a mansion house can be built in due time; that it have an extensive back range where our cattle and hogs can graze and fatten without the aid of corn houses, that on the right and left there is an extensive body of good land where will settle a number of good neighbors and from whom the pleasure and benefits of society will soon be realized.—Charles Tait to James A. Tait, January 20, 1819, Tait Papers, Department of Archives and History, Montgomery, quoted in Frank L. Owsley, *Plain Folk of the Old South* (Baton Rouge: Louisiana State University Press, 1949), pp. 64–65.

Such a place they found near Fort Claiborne in Monroe County on the bluffs of the Alabama River. They were soon joined there by other Georgians who furnished "the pleasure and benefits of society."

The most immediate problem facing the new arrival was clearing the land. The pioneers followed the method, used by the red men before them, which Philip Gosse observed in Dallas County.

The mode of clearing forest land for agriculture, called girdling, is almost universally practised here. An incision is made around the trunk of a tree with an axe, so that the inner bark is completely severed all round. The ascent of the sap being thus prevented, though no perceptible change is immediately manifested, death inevitably takes place in the course of the season. The scanty underbrush of scattered shrubs and slender saplings is torn up with an instrument called a grubbing hoe; and in the ensuing spring (a fence of oak rails having been run through the forest in the winter), this forest land is planted with Indian corn. No plough has turned up the soil, nor even a harrow scratched its surface; so soft and mellow is it with the accumulated vegetable mould of ages, that it needs but a hole to be made with the hoe, and the seed-corn deposited, to ensure an abundant harvest. No further trouble is taken with the trees; the branches decay and drop off piecemeal, and by-and-by the sapless trunks themselves, one at a time, come down with a crash, and scatter the earth beneath them.

This custom of girdling the trees instead of cutting them down gives the fields a most singular appearance. After the twigs and smaller boughs have dropped off, and the bark has dried and shrunk, and been stripped away, and the naked branches have become blanched by the summer's sun and winter's rain, these tall dead trunks, so thickly spread over the land, look like an army of skeletons stretching their gaunt white arms, clothed with long ragged festoons of Spanish moss across the field. They are not unattended with danger, but the risk of damage to the crop, and even to human life, is not considered to counter-vail the great saving of labour attending this mode of clearing; and they chiefly fall in the storms of winter, when the labours of the field are suspended. They form an unfailing resource for the Wood-peckers, all kinds of which, from the noble Ivory-billed to the little Downy, are incessantly tapping at their sapless trunks. The Red-tailed Hawk frequently chooses them as his watch tower, whence his large fiery eye gleams on his prey below, and now and then, as if impatient of rest, he flies from one to another with a sudden scream. But more especially the Turkey Vultures are fond of sitting on them; for, being totally destitute of foliage to intercept vision, their topmost branches form a convenient observatory for reconnoitering the surrounding country.—Philip Henry Gosse, *Letters from Alabama* (London: Morgan and Chase, 1859), pp. 87–88.

It is a truism that agriculture was the basis of economic life in antebellum Alabama. Family farms, of varying sizes, and plantations, also of varying sizes, had spread over the state by 1860. Farms greatly outnumbered the plantations, but the plantations furnished the social, economic, and political leaders of the state. Although only a small fraction (at best estimate, about twenty percent) of all Southerners had any connection whatever with the plantation slavery system, the plantation became the symbol of the old South. Evidently, it furnished the goal for most ambitious men. Young doctors, lawyers, schoolmasters, and even clergymen, arriving in the new country, usually either forsook their professions for planting or added it to their economic interests. Rarely did a man rise in public life without a plantation.

To differentiate between a farm and a plantation is not easy. To say that a plantation is a large farm is only avoiding the question. There were many large farms that were never called anything else but there were also small plantations. Furthermore, in north Alabama most holdings, regardless of size, were called farms. One caustic Wetumpka editor said the difference between farmers and planters was "that one supports a family and the other supports pride until pride gets a fall." Thomas P. Abernethy, writing about early Alabama, described two systems of agriculture: the planter raised cotton with corn as his subsidiary crop and the farmer raised corn with cotton as his subsidiary crop. Since there can be no absolute rule, the standard that U.B. Phillips used is as good as any. A farm, he said, was cultivated by the owner, his family, and possibly a few slaves. But when the size of the work force reached twenty and the acreage five hundred, it was a plantation. Most family holdings were easily recognized as one or the other; only the borderline cases cause any confusion, and probably more to the historian than to the residents of Alabama before 1860.

The definitive study of the farmer in Alabama remains to be made. Dr. Frank L. Owsley had begun work in this field before his death but he would have been the first to say that he had only scratched the surface. The "plain" folk left few personal papers and therefore any study of them must be based on other sources. Fortunately for diligent students like Dr. and Mrs. Owsley, the census returns (especially for 1850) contained much valuable information about land holdings, personal property, livestock, crops and other relevant items. Choosing certain key counties for his study, Dr. Owsley checked 2,351 landowners in Alabama's Black Belt, finding that 65.04 percent of them had less than 500 acres and another 20.54 percent owned from 501 to 1000 acres. In five sample counties in the uplands, he found 78.19 percent owning less than 500 acres. In his *Plain Folk of the Old South,* Dr. Owsley makes a strong case for his thesis that the Old South had a large class of farmers between the planters and the poor whites. Men in this class may have had relatively few acres but they were far from poor. They raised a variety of crops—peas, sweet potatoes, and corn—but depended chiefly on their herds of cattle and droves of hogs for their income. These animals fed on the open range and were of almost no expense to the farmer.

In the absence of extensive papers on men of this station, family memories become as reliable as anything. The composite "plain" man appears to have been a Democrat rather than a Whig in politics, although better acquainted with Jackson than with Jefferson; a member of one of the evangelical sects; a hardworking, unpretentious, fiercely independent individual. The chances were good that he was of Scotch-Irish ancestry. Many of them remained farmers but others bought land, improved it, started raising cotton in great quantities, purchased more slaves, and became planters.

The Plantation

The plantation is one of the best documented institutions in the South. For business reasons, if for no other, planters kept detailed and extensive records, many of which are still in existence. Some planters kept detailed journals of plantation activities; other recorded little beyond the weather and the work that was done each day. The William Proctor Gould Plantation Diaries fall in the second category but do show what took place on an Alabama plantation. Gould lived near Boligee in Greene County.

August 1 [1836] This has been a very hot day—a light shower about two o'clock—Work as yesterday—Heavy thunder and lightning in the S. E. late in the afternoon and a very dark cloud—but no rain

2d Cloudy occasionally—distant thunder—no rain. Two wagons went to Cook's mill for plank and paling—other hands as yesterday—& making rails

3 Warm day and no rain—work same—

4 Appearance of showers all day—but none came

5 Sunday—a very hot day Th 94.—thunder afternoon— and a bare sprinkle of rain

6 Fore part of the day very warm—afternoon a fine shower—Hoes in new ground—men getting rails and laying worm—pasture fence.—

7 There has been a light rain today—work as yesterday— Went to Erie with Mr. Nott on business relating to Squire Hays' Estate.—

8 Rode over the Crop this morning for the first time in a week—Cotton improving rapidly—ground sufficiently moist. —Examined Corn and concluded fodder would not be fit to pull until Monday. No change in work.—

9 A glorious rain this afternoon and evening—work as heretofore

August 10 Thunder and a light shower late in the afternoon—All hands working on Road.—

11 Worked on road again today—Killed a beef and gave the

people a week's rations—Weather continues very warm—
Thermometer from 90 to 94. day after day.—

12   Sunday.—Forenoon very warm—afternoon thunder
some heavy clouds but no rain.—

August 13   Began to pull fodder this morning—weather clear—
morning much cooler than usual—Went to Erie today.—

14.15.16   Continued pulling fodder—weather fine—this afternoon
it has been cloudy and I fear we will have rain soon.—

17 & 18   Two more fine days for saving fodder—we have twelve
stacks safe—Morning cool—after 10 o'clock the Sun was
oppresively hot Gave the people a months rations of
Bacon.—

19   Sunday—Middle of the day cloudy—a light shower afternoon—not enough to injure fodder

20   Continued pulling fodder.—there was another light
shower this afternoon,—that did not harm the fodder.

21   Finished pulling fodder in Big Prairie this forenoon and
went to Redd field. We have nineteen fine double stacks put
up—exclusive of what is pulled in the cut this side the
mound.—This forenoon I rode over the Cotton field for
the first time in several days and was much pleased with
the prospect until I went over the Branch;—there I saw a
great many squares spread open—and on getting down to
examine for the cause, found the worm was committing
great ravages.—On a more careful examination I found
this to be the case more or less in all parts of the plantation.
—Having never suffered in this way before, I cannot anticipate the extent of danger, but cannot help fearing the
injury will be very serious.—A heavy shower after sunset.

22   The worms continue the work of destruction—I find this
morning they are attacking full grown bolls—where it will
end is more than I can imagine—I will hope for the best,
but should not be surprised if the entire crop were to be
destroyed.—A fine day for fodder—morning & evening
cool.

23   Worms increasing—as far as I have heard their ravages
are general through the settlement—Another fine day for
fodder; finished pulling this forenoon.—

24   Finished stacking fodder this afternoon—We have 35
large stacks—Women spinning wool,—Men making rails—
children picking cotton for Spinning Jenny.—Worms continue to increase.—

August 25   A clear and very warm day—hands jobbing as yesterday
—Killed a large Beef—dried the greater part—Gave the
people 2 days rations.

26   Sunday—Another very warm day—Went to Burton's Hill
Church to hear Dr Manly and others;—was delighted with

Dr Manly—cannot say as much of Mr Baptist and Professor
Keenan.—

27   This has been the hottest day this Summer.—Thermometer 97° afternoon.—Hands continue jobbing as on Saturday.—

28   Another very warm day Th. 96°—afternoon cloudy—
and some hope of rain—Worms continue their work of dis-
tructions.—

29   Very hot again—Some clouds but no rain—

30   Morning cloudy—with a few drops of rain—became clear
and very hot during the forenoon.—Continue jobbing as
before.—

31   Thermometer 97 this afternoon.—Work as usual.—
Mimeographed (1938) by Department of Archives and
History. Journals cover years 1828–1864.

THE OVERSEER

To most planters a good plantation was one where the "number
of Negroes steadily increased, where enough was raised to feed
both people and stock abundantly, where the productive quality of
the land constantly improved, and where all equipment, mules,
horses, and fences were placed in condition by Christmas." If a
planter's establishment became too large for him to handle personally, he hired an overseer to supervise the work. There were never
enough overseers to fill the needs of Alabama planters and notices
similar to the following appeared frequently.

The subscriber, living near Russellville, Franklin County, Alabama,
wishes to employ an overseer for 1837. A man without a family, who
can come well recommended as a sober, steady, and industrious man,
and one who understands managing negroes and the cultivation of
cotton, can get liberal wages by an early application to William S.
Jones—*Democrat* (Huntsville), May 19, 1847, quoted in James B.
Sellers, *Slavery in Alabama* (University: University of Alabama Press,
1950), p. 52.

In spite of the promise of "liberal wages," salaries were seldom
large and often, but not always, based on the production of cotton.
Frederick L. Olmsted noted in the 1850's that Alabama overseers
received from $200 to $600 annual wage; C. C. Clay, Jr. employed
John Tanner, "highly recommended for industry, sobriety, and
honesty" for $185; James Tait at Claiborne hired three in one year
for $250, $275 and $375 each. Late in the period wages went as
high as $1000 but this amount was exceptional. John Brown, the
young man to whom the following instructions were given, was
hired for $180 for twelve months. But if he produced 100 or more

bales of cotton he would have $200. Usually there were fringe benefits such as a house, a horse, a servant, and allotments of staple groceries.

Because the position of the overseer was both important and difficult, many planters wrote out explicit instructions for their overseers. John Horry Dent, who instructed his young overseer in the following passage lived at Good Hope, Barbour County.

LETTER TO A YOUNG OVERSEER, UNEXPERIENCED

To: John Brown,

As by your acknowledgement to me, you have selected the occupation of an overseer as your future choice for a livelihood until circumstances may cause a change in your business, I shall take this method of giving you some admonitory hints which my experience, and as your employer, justifies in my so doing. And I trust the advice I give you may be correct and prudent, although by yourself, may be considered binding and unnecessarily rigid. But believe me, in the end, if you are governed by system, discipline, and requisite rigour, and at the same time my example to you corresponding with such instructions and discipline as I set forth, you will receive more knowledge, your course and duty to perform regular, and at the same time, your own duty is plain and unchangeable before you.

My advice in the first place shall be explicit and plain, so there can be no misunderstanding. Regularity and punctuality to be your first and most important steps. Be candid and have the instructions of your employer enforced promptly and as nearly as compatible with his views and orders as possible. Never be idle in the field before your labourers, for by so doing, the example you set them causes an indolent habit among them, and they soon believe that you are yourself careless and negligent to the business of your employer, consequently they feel themselves at liberty to be indolent.

If you give an order, see that it is promptly and properly obeyed, not left to their judgment, whether your order has been half executed or done to suit their convenience. Also in giving an order, let it be well understood by the one or they would have to execute it. So if it be improperly done, they can have no reasonable excuse to deter you from causing such punishment as the case may require or deserve. Be careful to review yourself any work or order executed before you say anything to those engaged in executing it. By such a course you will always feel assurance in yourself and avoid the disagreeable feeling [that] must prevail between yourself and employer when he has detected you in error. Indolence or negligence for one of the above faults must exist where any occurance of the kind takes place. The same perseverance and attention is requisite with you in all work done on the plantation.

Next deserving your special care is attention to your mules and the lot. Method is indispensible in the performance of this particular duty, as by negligence you not only break down and kill up stock, but is encouraging wasteful habits and cruelty in your lot boys and inhumanity to animals whose value and services to a plantation cannot be too highly appreciated. Every ear of corn fed away should be given under your own eyes—and allowance every mule or horse with so many ears—and so many bundles of fodder. By so doing you can form a correct idea what it requires to keep your animals in good order. For overfeeding is not only wasteful, but by gorging animals you destroy the appetite, and poor animals in the consequence where you have a plenty & the most wasteful way of destroying provisions.

Regular salting must be attended to every Sunday, and your troughs cleansed. Twice a week if the weather is favourable before day of a morning your hoe hands as well as the lot boys should scrape up the manure and collect it in a pile which will be of vast importance for two reasons. The first, the value of manure. The second, a clean lot keeps mules clear of scratches and other diseases produced by filth and negligence. Also make each plough hand attend regularly to the mule he ploughs. Never let them change a mule with each other, unless it be done for some necessary reason given by yourself—for if they are allowed to plough or work each others mules, abuse and negligence will be the result and it will be difficult to ascertain correctly by whom the animal is mistreated. Each ploughing and attending to his own constantly can be made responsible for the condition of his animal. The same exactness and system must be adopted with the gear and ploughs.

Next your crib and lots. Your lot be kept clean, all shucks placed in sheltered pens, and cobs thrown in the horse lot for manure. The keys of your cribs to be kept constantly by you, and the door never to be locked or unlocked except by yourself or employer. What corn is taken out should be used only by your own knowledge. By trusting Negroes with the keys to give out or take out corn is only leading them into temptation, and, by so doing, they will soon pilfer, waste, and make use of corn, in a way thievish.

Next to be attended to is lots made for different stock and kinds, hog lots, sows and pigs. Each should have separate lots suitable to their respective size and ages. For if they be fed in one lot, the larger hogs would consume all from the smaller which would result in the death of the smaller sizes. Range hogs should never be enticed more than twice a week to the pens, if possible, for if they are accustomed to be fed regularly, they would soon be made lazy and dependent on what you would give them and never go in quest of food in their usual range.

Lots must also be appropriated for sheep and so constructed as a division can be easily made when the ewes are having their lambs, for it is necessary the ewes and lambs should be separated from the wethers and rams at that period as, in fondness for the young lamb by the wether, they are apt to paw them in token of affection which the delicate habits of the young cannot stand. Also have shelters and troughs in each lot for feeding and salting. The last should be done regularly once a week. Some pains should be taken to save the manure from a sheep lot which is among the richest of manures for gardens &c.

Next are the cowpens which must be attended to from the plans of your employer. As circumstances occur relative [to] manuring fields or lots transpires. Consequently I will not note down this department with the others that must be constant and regularly attended to.

Such as the regular system and mode of working in preparing lands for the crops designed, or working the crop, harvesting and housing it, I cannot in this place give you my ideas or views in part or in full, as it must be taught you practically and in the field. But if you pay attention to orders and have them promptly and punctually fulfilled as recommended to you, in the first part of this letter, you will soon become expert and fully acquainted with the duties requisite to one in the occupation of an overseer.

In conclusion let me give you some advice relative to a young man pursuing steadily and soberly our business, and do not pretend to change annually your occupation, believing or risking that another kind of business is preferable or money can be more easily obtained than the one you have now selected and engaged in, for by so doing. If you can not be well assured of the success to attend your new occupation, you may be again displeased and desire another change. So many successive changes is apt to result in loss of time and money and the most to be feared is producing a vassalating mind, a restless disposition and finally fit you for no occupation or business—as men will lose all confidence in your stability, believing you to be a "jack-of-all-trades and master of none." Therefore, pursue steadily the business you are now engaged in with pride, energy, perseverence and a determination to obey the orders of your employer, and have your orders to the Negroes properly and punctually obeyed and executed, making them fear you and respect you and, depend upon it, your future success is in your own hands—and with ease to yourself. For so soon as you have enforced among your Negroes discipline and system, all business will be conducted with ease and pleasure. Without discipline and system everything will be attended with uncertainty, trouble, and confusion. Ill-success and ruin the result. JOHN H. DENT—*Farm Journal,* No. 1 (1841), John Horry Dent Collection, University of Alabama.

In some areas overseers were sons of "piney woods folks,"; in others, sons of small planters who wanted the experience of running a large plantation before they launched one of their own. There seems to have been very few overseers, and in some parts of the state none, from the northern states. As a class they have received much criticism for their cruel treatment of the slaves, for pushing them beyond their physical limits in their zeal to produce cotton, for the waste of the soil and for general incompetence. Much of this criticism was deserved, but there were humane and intelligent men in managerial positions—and lucky were both the planter and slaves to have one.

PLANTATION EQUIPMENT

Every planter who left instructions for an overseer stressed the importance of caring for the tools and equipment. Since the average person in the last third of the twentieth century has little knowledge of what this equipment consisted of, an inventory of John Horry Dent's plantation is given here.

Plough stocks	12
Trace chains in order	9 pr.
Hames and collars	11
Heel pins	9
Shovels in order	9
Skooters	7
Sweeps	4
Clevis & pins	10
Plough singletrees	10
1 large turning plough	1
Plough lines made for each plough to be made.	5 sweeps, 2 skooters
Hoes, weeding	15
grubbing	11
Axes	11
Spades	2
Cross cut saw	1
Frow	1
Carpenters & Black Smith's Tools	
Broad ax	1
Hatchet	1
Jack plains	2
Fore plains	2
Smoothing plains	1
Chisels	
Auguers	
Brace & bits, full set	1
Adz	1
Hand saws	2
Pannel saws	1
Squares	2
Smith tools, complete set	

At this time, Dent had fifty-five slaves which he classified as able hands, able female hands, "hef" hand, superannuated (2) and children (18).

Cotton

It would be hard to overestimate the importance of cotton in the history of antebellum Alabama. Few, if indeed any, planters raised cotton to the exclusion of all other crops, but some sections raised it in great quantities. The Tennessee River Valley, the Black Belt, and the Alabama-Tombigbee basin were the cotton producing areas. Cotton was the cash crop and if the crop was good and the price high everyone prospered—the planter, the merchant, the factor in Mobile or New Orleans, and, equally, when prices were low, people dependent on one staple fell deeply in debt, sometimes so deeply that bankruptcy—or emigration to the rich lands in Texas—was the only solution. Visitors complained that it was difficult to talk to Alabamians, men or women, on any topic other than cotton. One unidentified wit observed that

> Mobile is a cotton city of some thirty thousand inhabitants—where people live in cotton houses and ride in cotton carriages. They buy cotton, sell cotton, think cotton, eat cotton, drink cotton, and dream cotton. They marry cotton wives and unto them are born cotton children. In enumerating the charms of a fair widow, they begin by saying she makes so many bales of cotton. It is the great staple, the sum and substance of Alabama. It has made Mobile and all its citizens.

Cotton was well suited to be the staple crop for the southern planter. It grew well in most soils but especially so in the Black Belt and river bottoms. It found a ready market in England and in our own northeast. It could be cultivated by semiskilled, or even unskilled, labor of all ages. Furthermore, the work required to produce cotton was spread over a big part of the year so that there was no long period of idleness for the hands. Preparations for planting the crop began in February or early March and, except for a "laying by" time in July after the last cultivation, there was work every month until harvesting was over, often around Christmas.

Philip Henry Gosse described the cotton picking season as it appeared to one seeing it for the first time.

> The grand occupation of autumn is cotton picking. It commenced in the early fields more than a month ago, is now far advanced, and by the end of this month will be pretty nearly over. I have already spoken of the beauty of the cotton-plant when in full blossom; scarcely less beautiful is the appearance of a field of cotton at this season, when the produce is ripe. The fine dark-green foliage is relieved by the bunches of downy cotton of the purest white, bearing a curious resemblance to a meadow on which a light shower of snow has just fallen.

The pods open chiefly during the night. If one is opened by force, the cotton-fibres are found to be closely packed into a hard dirty-white mass, as scarcely to be recognised, and no manipulation will make them assume a downy appearance. When the capsules, which are three, or occasionally four-celled, burst naturally, the cotton springs out, and swells to four or five times the bulk of the pod, assuming the most beautiful softness, and the most delicate whiteness, and forming three oval bunches of snowy down, each about as large as a hen's egg. As soon as the sun has exhaled the dew, these are fit for picking; and the night's opening should be picked if possible on the next day, or it will be lost.

In the evening the negroes,—men, women, and children,—bring in the produce of their picking, in large deep baskets, to the gin-house, when the overseer weighs each one's lot. As every negro has an allotted task, differing according to the ability of the individual, it is a matter of anxiety to see whether this is accomplished or not; if it falls short, the whip may pretty certainly be expected, especially if the overseer is a rigorous disciplinarian. . . .

The cotton has now to undergo a very interesting process. In the picking, the workpeople pull out the whole bunch from the pod, and drop it into the basket. If we examine one of these bunches, we shall see that it consists of several oval seeds densely clothed with fine long white hairs, which are the cotton. In the variety chiefly grown here, the seeds are black, but are covered with a very short underclothing of green silky down, among the bases of the white fibres. The latter adhere to the seed with considerable force, but must of course be removed before they are fit for the manufacture. This separation of the fibre from the seed is accomplished by an effective and ingenious machine, the cotton-gin.

The following description will give you an idea of this valuable machine and of its operation.

The hopper is a long box with one side perpendicular and the other diagonal: the latter is of iron bars about an inch wide, and set with interstices about one-eighth of an inch apart, and the angle at the bottom is not closed, but allows a narrow admission into a box below. Behind the slope of the hopper are two cylinders running the whole length, and revolving in the frame-work of the machine. One cylinder is of solid wood, and carries some fifty or more circular saws of sheet iron, a foot in diameter, so fixed that the teeth enter a little way into the hopper, between the sloping bars.

The cotton is thrown into the hopper from above, and the wheel which communicates motion to the cylinders is set going by means of mules. The teeth of the saws now catch hold of the fibres, and drag them through the interstices, but as these are separated and the naked seeds fall down through the crevice at the bottom. The teeth of the saws come forth loaded with the cotton fibre, which are taken off the action of the second cylinder. This is a hollow drum, the surface of which is covered with brushes, and being made to revolve with a greater rapidity than the saws, and in the opposite direction, the cotton is brushed off, and falls in downy lightness and purity into a receiver below. With such a machine as this, one man will clear three hundred pounds of cotton a day. The seeds are thrown in heaps, that fermentation may destroy the germinating principle, and are then used as manure.

The cotton is packed into bales for exportation by the aid of powerful screws. The bale is put within a strong frame, around which the open mouth is firmly fastened. When the bag is so full that you think not another handful can be received, a pile of cotton nearly equal in height to the whole length of the bale is laid on the top, and by the force of the jack-screw is gradually pressed down into the bale.—Philip H. Gosse, *Letters From Alabama* (London: Morgan & Chase, 1859), pp. 277–80.

The price of cotton on the New York and Liverpool markets varied from year to year, reflecting the state of the economy, the size of the crop, and the amount of foreign competition. The average New York price per pound paid for middling upland cotton for each five years from 1820 to 1860 was:

1820	17.00 cents
1825	18.59
1830	10.04
1835	17.45
1840	8.92
1845	5.63
1850	12.34
1855	10.39
1860	11.00

Stuart Bruchey, ed., *Cotton and the Growth of the American Economy, 1790–1860* (New York: Harcourt, Brace and World, 1967), pp. 15–17.

Alabama produced an increasing amount of cotton.

1821	20 million pounds
1826	45 million pounds
1833	65 million pounds
1839	117.1 million pounds
1849	225.8 million pounds
1859	440.5 million pounds

Ibid., p. 20.

All cotton bales did not weigh the same but at Mobile the average was 500 pounds each.

The crop grown in the northern part of the state went by the Tennessee-Mississippi River route to New Orleans to be exported; most of the remainder by the Alabama-Tombigbee Rivers to Mobile. The figures for the south Alabama crop sold in the latter city are easily available. In 1830, for example, 102,684 bales were sold there, five years later, 197,847. In 1840 the output was 445,

725 bales; in 1845, 517,550 bales. In 1850, 350,297 (a decrease), in 1855, 454,593 bales and in 1860, 843,012 bales.

The percentage of the national crop also varied. In 1821, Alabama grew 11.3 percent of all the cotton in the United States; in 1826, 13.6 percent; in 1834, 18.6 percent; in 1849, 22.9 percent; and in 1859, 21.7 percent. Whatever the portion of the nation's crop, cotton production in Alabama increased each decade. To illustrate, in 1849, the output was 92.4 percent greater than it was in 1839. By 1860 there were seven counties (Madison County and the Black Belt) producing more than 45,000 bales each annually and four more between 35,000 and 45,000 bales. It was indeed big business.

Slavery

Such rapid expansion of cotton production would have been impossible without Negro slaves. This is not to say that cotton could not be grown with free labor. Free farmers were raising cotton in the uplands but only in small quantities. But raising it on the expanding scale as Alabama planters were doing required an adequate and stable supply of cheap labor. The only such labor available was slave.

The question of slavery is a thorny one. People of the twentieth century see the "peculiar institution" as a blight on the body politic. But so did many residents of Alabama even while it was still legal. For most Southerners in the early part of the nineteenth century, slavery was based primarily on economic necessity and was inextricably tied to the plantation system. But long before the end of the era, it had become a burning moral and political issue. The most vocal politicians and newspaper men were proslavery in their views, but there was an occasional nonconformist who saw the system as either immoral or uneconomical. As 1860 drew near, however, the voices of such dissidents grew fewer and fainter. Not until after the war broke out was there much evidence of any great discontent with the system.

Slavery was rooted in the colonial past. The Spanish had some blacks with them when they explored Mobile Bay and Narváez in 1528 left one of them as a hostage, but the French were the first to introduce Negro slavery into Alabama. Bienville urged the importation of blacks because he needed labor to develop the area. The first slave ships arrived at Mobile in 1721: the *Africane* in March with 120 Negroes, later the *Marie* with 338 and even later that year the *Neridi* with 238. After 1721 slave ships from Africa arrived regularly. Slaves became so numerous that King Louis XV issued the "Edict Concerning the Negro Slaves in Louisiana," commonly called the "Black Code." This was in 1724. The preamble began

Louis, by the Grace of God, King of France and of Navarre, to all present and to come, greeting. The Directors of the Company of the Indies having represented to us that the Province and colony of Louisiana is considerably established, by a large number of our subjects, who use slaves for the cultivation of the lands, we have judged that it behooves our authority and our justice, for the preservation of this colony, to establish there a law and certain rules, to maintain there the discipline of the Catholic Apostolic and Roman Church and to order about what concerns the state and condition of the slaves. . . .

The code contained, besides the preamble, fifty-five articles, protecting both the slaves and the masters. All slaves were to be instructed and baptized in the Roman Catholic faith; any other religion was forbidden; no slaves were to be worked regularly on Sunday and other holy days; marriages between slaves and free persons were forbidden. Certain articles of clothing and food were named as standard for slaves but they could not own property and their testimony in legal matters was not acceptable. Slave families (with young children) belonging to the same master could not be separated by sale nor could slaves be seized for debt. There were limits to the amount of punishment and the grounds on which manumission could take place. Tutors for a master's children, for example, were to be set free.

After 1763, the English continued the importation of slaves, transferring them from the ocean-going vessels in Mobile Bay to smaller boats that could go up river to Monroe, Clark, and Washington Counties. The number of blacks was augmented also by Tory refugees from the seaboard colonies who sought safety and land in West Florida. Slave laws were strict but not strictly enforced and manumission was fairly common.

During the territorial period the number of blacks continued to grow. In December 1816, just three years before statehood, the existing counties had both slaves and free blacks.

County	Whites	Free blacks	slaves	Total
Baldwin	411	43	709	1,163
Clarke	2,763	16	1,338	4,117
Greene	996	0	729	1,725
Monroe	3,593	72	1,603	5,268
Madison	10,000	0	4,200	14,200
Washington	1,888	0	671	2,559
Mobile	867	0	433	1,300

Territorial Papers of the United States, vol. 6, p. 730.

When the first federal census was taken (1820) Alabama had 127,-901 inhabitants, of whom 42,450 were slaves. By 1860 of the 964,201 total, 437,770 were slave, one of every two. In 1819 there were about 500 free blacks; in 1860 there were 2,690. Most of them lived in Baldwin, Mobile, Tuscaloosa, Madison, and Montgomery Counties where they found work as barbers, painters, blacksmiths, draymen, cooks, or laborers in the towns. There was little opportunity for the free black in a rural society.

The legal status of the slave in the state of Alabama was defined in the Slave Code of 1852. It was based on a code laid down during the first decades of statehood, laws regarding runaways, emancipation, sale, and other matters pertaining to slaves.

ARTICLE I

SLAVES

1005. No master, overseer, or other person having the charge of a slave, must permit such slave to hire himself to another person, or to hire his own time, or to go at large, unless in a corporate town, by consent of the authorities thereof, evidenced by an ordinance of the corporation; and every such offence is a misdemeanor, punishable by fine not less than twenty nor more than one hundred dollars.

1006. No master, overseer, or head of a family must permit any slave to be or remain at his house, out house, or kitchen, without leave of the owner or overseer, above four hours at any one time; and for every such offence he forfeits ten dollars, to be recovered before any justice of the peace, by any person who may sue for the same.

1007. Any owner or overseer of a plantation, or householder, who knowingly permits more than five Negroes, other than his own, to be and remain at his house, plantation, or quarter, at any one time, forfeits ten dollars for each and every one over that number, to the use of any one who may sue for the same, before any justice of the peace; unless such assemblage is for the worship of almighty God, or for burial service, and with the consent of the owner or overseer of such slaves.

1008. No slave must go beyond the limits of the plantation on which he resides, without a pass, or some letter or token from his master or overseer, giving him authority to go and return from a certain place; and if found violating this law, may be apprehended and punished, not exceeding twenty stripes, at the discretion of any justice before whom he may be taken.

1009. If any slave go upon the plantation, or enter the house or out house of any person, without permission in writing from his master or overseer, or in the prosecution of his lawful business, the owner or overseer of such plantation or householder may give, or order such slave to be given, ten lashes on his bare back.

1010. Any railroad company in whose car or vehicle, and the master or owner of any steamboat, or vessel, in which a slave is transported or carried, without the written authority of the owner or person in charge of such slave, forfeits to the owner the sum of fifty dollars; and if such slave is lost, is liable for his value, and all reasonable expenses attending the prosecution of the suit.

1011. In any action under the preceding section, it devolves on the defendant to prove that the owner has regained possession of the slave.

1012. No slave can keep or carry a gun, powder, shot, club, or other weapon, except the tools given him to work with, unless ordered by his master or overseer to carry such weapon from one place to another. Any slave found offending against the provisions of this section, may be seized, with such weapon, by any one, and carried before any justice, who, upon proof of the offence, must condemn the weapon to the use of such person, and direct that the slave receive thirty-nine lashes on his bare back.

1013. Any justice of the peace may, within his own county, grant permission in writing to any slave, on the application of his master or overseer, to carry and use a gun and ammunition within his master's plantation.

1014. No slave can, under any pretense, keep a dog; and for every such offence must be punished by any justice of the peace with twenty stripes on his bare back. If such dog is kept with the consent of the owner or overseer, he must pay five dollars for every dog so kept, to the use of any person who will sue for the same before any justice; and is also liable to any person for any injury committed by said dogs.

1015. Riots, routs, unlawful assemblies, trespasses, and seditious speeches by a slave, are punished, by the direction of any justice before whom he may be carried, with stripes not exceeding one hundred.

1016. Any person having knowledge of the commission of any offence by a slave against the law, may apprehend him, and take him before a justice of the peace for trial.

1017. Any slave fire hunting in the night time, must be punished with thirty-nine lashes, by order of any justice before whom he may be carried. If such fire hunting by the slave is by the command of the master or overseer, the slave must not be punished, but the master or overseer forfeits the sum of fifty dollars, one half to the county, and the other half to any person who may sue for the same before any justice of the peace.

1018. No slave can own property, and any property purchased or held by a slave, not claimed by the master or owner, must be sold by order of any justice of the peace; one half the proceeds of the sale, after the payment of costs and necessary expenses, to be paid to the informer, and the residue to the county treasury.

1019. Any slave who writes for, or furnishes any other slave with any pass or free paper, on conviction before any justice of the peace, must receive one hundred lashes on his bare back.

1020. Not more than five male slaves shall assemble together at any place off the plantation, or place to which they belong, with or without passes or permits to be there, unless attended by the master or overseer of such slaves, or unless such slaves are attending the public worship of God, held by white persons.

1021. It is the duty of all patrols, and all officers, civil and military, to disperse all such unlawful assemblies; and each of the slaves constituting such unlawful assembly, must be punished by stripes, not exceeding ten; and for the second offence, may be punished with thirty-nine stripes, at the discretion of any justice of the peace before whom he may be brought.

1022. Any slave who preaches, exhorts, or harangues any assembly of slaves, or of slaves and free persons of color, without a license to preach or exhort from some religious society of the neighborhood, and in the presence of five slaveholders, must, for the first offence, be punished with thirty-nine lashes, and for the second, with fifty lashes; which punishment may be inflicted by any officer of a patrol company, or by the order of any justice of the peace.

1023. Runaway slaves may be apprehended by any person, and carried before any justice of the peace, who must either commit them to the county jail, or send them to the owner, if known; who must, for every slave so apprehended, pay the person apprehending him six dollars, and all reasonable charges.

1024. Any justice of the peace receiving information that three or more runaway slaves are lurking and hid in swamps, or other obscure places, may, by warrant, reciting the names of the slaves, and their owners, if known, direct a leader of the patrol of the district, and if there be none, then any other suitable person, to summon, and take with him such power as may be necessary to apprehend such runaway; and if taken, to deliver them to the owner or commit them to the jail of his proper county.

1025. For such apprehension and delivery to the owner, or committal to jail, the parties so apprehending shall be entitled to twenty dollars for each slave, to be paid by the owner.

1026. The justice committing a runaway, must endeavor to ascertain from the slave, and from all other sources within his reach, the true name of the slave, and his owner's name, and residence; and must include all such information in the commitment, which must be preserved and filed by the justice.

1027. On the reception of a runaway slave, the sheriff must, without delay, cause advertisement to be made in a newspaper, published in the county, if there be one, if not, in the one published nearest to the court house of such county, giving an accurate description of the person of the slave, his supposed age, the information contained in the warrant in relation to the slave, and his owner, and such other facts important to the identification of the slave, as the sheriff may be able to obtain from the slave, or from any other source, which must be continued for six months, once a week, if the slave is not sooner reclaimed by the owner.

1028. If the slave is not reclaimed within six months, the sheriff must advertise and sell him for cash, in the manner slaves are sold under execution. The proceeds of the sale, after all expenses are paid, must be paid to the county treasurer for the use of the county.

1029. The owner may regain the possession of the slave before sale, or the proceeds after sale, by appearing before the judge of probate of the county, and proving, by an impartial witness, his title to the slave; which proof must be reduced to writing, sworn to, subscribed, and filed in the office of the probate judge.

1030. Thereupon, and upon the payment by the owner of the costs of advertising, and all other expenses attending the imprisonment, the judge of probate must, by order in writing, direct the jailor, if the slave has not been sold, to deliver him to the applicant. If he has been sold, then the order must be directed to the county treasurer, to pay him over the proceeds of such sale received in the treasury.

1031. The title of the purchaser of such slave is not affected by the claim of the owner, or by an irregularity in the advertisement or sale.

1032. The fee of probate judge is two dollars, and the sheriff is allowed the same commissions as on sales under execution.—*Alabama Code of 1852* (Montgomery: 1852), pp. 237–40.

The work required of the slave varied with his age, his skill, his status in the black hierarchy (whether he was a house servant or field hand) and the season of the year. The house servants—the nurses, cooks, personal servants, gardeners, butlers, coachmen and their various helpers and apprentices—held favored posts. Their work was considered lighter and on the market they brought higher prices than any except prime field hands. Since they came in daily contact with their masters, they acquired more of the white man's culture than did the field hands. Often snobs, the house servants considered themselves superior to the field hands and a threat to send a wayward servant to the fields was often sufficient discipline.

Just as planters had rules for their overseers, they had regulations for their slaves, a black code of their own. In them they outlined the duties of the various workers, stated the allowable rations of food and clothing, the premises, cited punishment to be expected for infractions of the rules, and gave basic regulations to maintain good health. The details varied by the principles were acknowledge by all good planters.

Doubtless most planters preferred to increase their work force from the people born on the plantation or by private purchase. At times, however, necessity drove them to patronize a slave trader who brought in gangs from distant states or to make purchases at public auctions. There were unfeeling (or financially embarrassed) masters who would allow families to be separated but generally the rule to sell them only as a unit was observed. Alabamians generally considered slave trading degrading and most of the dealers were from out of state. However, there were exceptions. In the 1840's Peter Stokes who made his home in Sumter County was clearing more than $2,000 a year trading slaves.

It seems to be a little known fact that slaves were often hired out to other planters who needed extra laborers by a master with a surplus of workers.

HIRING DAY

The first day of January is a very important day in this region of the country,—and especially with those who have to hire Negroes. Greensboro usually presents a more active, business-like appearance on that day, than on any other during the year. The crowd here on Monday last was quite large, even for that day; and the competition for Negroes hired at public hiring, as great as it has been for many years past, whilst prices were fully equal—if not a little superior—to those of last year.

Negro men ranged, generally, from $150 to $200,—though $175 was about the price paid at public hiring for choice field hands. Women and boys brought generally from $90 to $100.—*Alabama Beacon* (Greensboro), January 5, 1855.

There were cases where a skilled workman was allowed to hire himself out, paying his master a part of his income. Until the laws on manumission became stringent, it was possible for a man to purchase his freedom in this manner.

It is not widely known that free Negroes also owned slaves. While too little is known about this phase, it appears that when a free Negro owned only one slave, it was his wife whom he had purchased or, since the ages on the following table are high, parents. This will not explain, however, men like P. T. Harris of Clarke County who had twenty-five slaves. Presumably, they were laborers.

One of the problems facing the slave owner was the runaway. Slaves escaped for various reasons: to see their wives on other plantations, to return to former homes, to escape bondage or, which seems to have been most common, to avoid work during the rush season. Men (few women seem to have tried to get away) of this last category were no permanent loss because usually many came back of their own choice after a few days in the woods, when they no longer cared to subsist on the food they were able to gather there.

There seems to be no statistics on the number of slaves that were lost permanently and certainly it was less than in the border states where freedom was only a short distance away and organized agencies made concerted efforts to help the Negroes escape. However, the number was considerable as the advertisements in the newspapers indicate. Only two are given here.

FIFTY DOLLARS REWARD

Ran away from the subscriber, on the 27 of November last, a country born Negro about 25 years old, five feet four inches high; black skin with good white teeth; speaks tolerably good English. Had on when he went away, homespun pantaloons and a short coat of white plain and no hat. He stole a small canoe that had been lately finished and pitched over.

Any person that will apprehend said Negro and deliver him to me where I live shall receive the above reward. ROBERT PARKER—Alabama *Courier* (Claiborne), March 19, 1819.

Committed to the Tuscaloosa County jail the 17th of July, 1838, a runaway Negro fellow who calls his name Nelson, and says he belongs to John C. Faris of Sumter County, Ala. Nelson is 27 or 28 years old, 5 feet, 7 inches high, black, and weighs about 155 or 60 pounds, a blemish in his left eye, his back severely scarred. The owner is requested to come forward, prove property, pay charges, and take him away as the law directs.—*Flag of the Union* (Tuscaloosa), July 25, 1838.

FREE NEGROES OWNING SLAVES
ALABAMA

Name	Slaves	Total	Age	Name	Slaves	Total	Age
CLARKE COUNTY				Chastang, Basil	1	10	55–100
Meggs, James	1	2	36–55	Chastang, Bastiste	1	3	36–55
Harris, P. T.	24	25	55–100	Chastang, Zane	1	3	55–100
Hatcher, William	2	3	36–55	Chastang, Zeno	5	15	36–55
Stapleton, Joseph	1	2	36–55	Chastang, Louisa	14	19	55–100
Monack, David	27	28	55–100	Nicholas, Jasma	3	5	24–36
DALLAS COUNTY				*City of Mobile*			
Smith, Tom	4	14	36–55	Rutgeron, Frances	1	2	24–36
				Ferer, Clara	4	6	24–36
LAWRENCE COUNTY				Laurendine, Benjamin	1	7	24–36
Royall, Lewis	1	3	55–100	Rozieste, Burnadoz	14	32	24–36
				Guile, Mad. O.	4	10	55–100
MADISON COUNTY				Chastang, Frances	1	7	55–100
First and Second Ranges				Gregg, Frances	2	8	24–36
of Townships				Mary, Mad	6	8	36–55
Davis, Betsey	1	7	36–55	Rozieste, Peir	6	14	24–36
Stewart, James F.	2	3	36–55	Boshong, Madam	16	23	36–55
Third and Fourth Ranges				**MONROE COUNTY**			
of Townships				Sizemore (?), Arthur	3	8	55–100
Robinson, John	4	7	24–36	Sizemore (?), Susanna	2	7	36–55
Blanks, Paschal	2	4	24–36				
Hunt, Lewis	1	4	24–36	**MONTGOMERY COUNTY**			
Hunster, Nancy	1	8	36–55	Fowler (de), Oxey	1	3	55–100
Findley, Jenny	1	2	24–36	Lanton, Joseph (F. of C.)	2	11	55–100
Evans, John	1	3	36–55				
Winn, Andrew	2	3	55–100	**PERRY COUNTY**			
				Thomas, Frederick V.	1	8	55–100
MOBILE COUNTY							
Minnie	1	6	36–55	**SHELBY COUNTY**			
Key, Lawrence	4	11	24–36	Hadsen, Isah	1	12	36–55
Chastang, Theresa	2	3	100–				
Simore, Felix	1	10	55–100	**WASHINGTON COUNTY**			
Colderen, Simore	3	8	24–36	Saunsha, John	2	3	36–55
Andre, Sylvester	2	10	36–55				
Andre, Madomitian	6	15	36–55	**WILCOX COUNTY**			
Simore, Jane	10	13	36–55	Martin, John	1	3	36–55

Carter G. Woodson, ed., *Free Negro Owners of Slaves in the United States in 1830.* (Washington, D. C.: The Association for the Study of Negro Life and History, 1924), p. 1.

Ads such as these give much information about Negro clothing, skills, and characteristics.

What was slavery like? The answers are as diverse as the people who gave them. There were good masters and bad ones; there were diligent slaves and lazy ones; there were some slaves who were cherished as friends and members of the family and others who were considered little better than brutes. Slavery looked different to a person who was seeing it for the first time than to a person who had grown up with it. And it also appeared even more different to the slave himself although there are few if any contemporary accounts of what he thought about it. The following passages are chosen to show some of the contemporary opinions.

Harriet Martineau, English writer and reformer, found here little except food and hospitality which she admired.

> Slavery is nowhere more hopeless and helpless than in Alabama. The richness of the soil and the paucity of inhabitants make the labourer a most valuable possession; while his distance from any free state . . . makes the attempt to escape desperate. All coloured persons travelling in the slave states without a pass—a certificate of freedom or of leave— are liable to be arrested and advertised, and, if unclaimed at the end of a certain time, sold in the market.—Harriet Martineau, *Retrospect of Western Travel* (London: Saunders & Otley, 1838), p. 243.

Then she recounted the story of two Alabama slaves who worked hard and saved the "profits of their labor at over-hours," and hid their money until they had enough to hire a "mean white man" to impersonate a gentleman, equipped themselves with proper clothing as a coachman and footman, bought a carriage and travelled north in style. When they reached the Canadian border, they paid off the white man, sold their carriage, and lived in safety across the border.

Miss Martineau described her feelings at seeing the "quarters."

> We visited the negro quarter; a part of the estate which filled me with disgust, wherever I went. It is something between a haunt of monkeys and a dwelling-place of human beings. The natural good taste, so remarkable in free negroes, is here extinguished. Their small, dingy, untidy houses, their cribs, the children crouching round the fire, the animal deportment of the grown-up, the brutish chagrins and enjoyments of the old, were all loathsome. There was some relief in seeing the children playing in the sun, and sometimes fowls clucking and strutting round the houses; but otherwise, a walk through a lunatic asylum is far less painful than a visit to the slave quarter of an estate. The children are left, during working hours, in the charge of a woman; and they are bright, and brisk, and merry enough, for the season, however slow and stupid they may be destined to become.

On the other hand, many (probably most) masters and mistresses took a kindly interest in their people, looking after them in illness and old age, seeing that they were clean and properly clothed and fed, teaching them the principles of religion (often from the catechism), keeping them as content as they could. A contended, healthy hand worked better than a mistreated one and it was to the material advantage of the master to treat his people well. This is probably the best argument in support of the thesis that slaves were more often treated well than ill.

One of the kindest pictures of slavery in print is given by Mrs. Victoria V. Clayton in her autobiography, *Black and White Under the Old Regime*. Mrs. Clayton was born in South Carolina but when she was two years old her father migrated to Barbour County because he had heard "many marvelous stories of the great productiveness of the land." Later she married Henry D. Clayton, a young man "recently graduated with highest honors from a college in Virginia." After serving in the Confederate army, Mr. Clayton became a judge of the Circuit Court and later (1888) president of the University of Alabama. Clayton, Alabama, is named for the family. Mrs. Clayton spent her entire life in the South. Her autobiography covers the "most eventful and stirring period in the nation's history." She remembered the prosperity of the prewar days and knew "experimentally and by observation what slavery was" and realized its "happiness and sorrow."

> Upon his return to Irwinton, my father began to put his house in order, arranging for the white family in the village, and for the most part of the colored families on the plantation. The plantation lay on the banks of the Chattahoochie River, about two miles from the village. Here the greater number of his slaves lived. My father was a slave-holder by inheritance, never knowing anything else. "Our thoughts, our morals, our most fixed beliefs, are consequences of our place of birth."
>
> When fond memory carries me back to my childhood's happy days, these colored friends on the old plantation occupy a very important place. I recall the commodious carriage, the bay horses, and old Uncle Abram seated on the driver's seat to take us, the children, through the beautiful woods, to make a visit to the old "maumers" down on the plantation. Our mother taught us to respect age in whatever position we found it, and we always called the older women "maumers" as marks of respect due their years.
>
> Every slave family possessed a garden, truck patch, chicken house and a lot of hens, and, from these sources, always had something nice to present to us, their young "misses." We cherished these humble presents, peanuts, fresh eggs, and the like, as though they were of intrinsic value. Their little cottages were arranged so as to form streets. After making the round of visits, not slighting any, but going in to see every one at home, sitting and chatting with all, we usually finished our calls

at Uncle Sam's house. He was the foreman on the plantation, and had a more pretentious home. His wife, maum Flora, would entertain us most royally with bread and milk under the grand old oaks that sheltered the space around the door. The old man was a Methodist preacher, and close by his house stood a neat little building, in which he gathered all the children on Sunday morning to teach them their duty to God and man. Later in the day the adults assembled for worship. Frequently a visiting preacher would assist Uncle Sam in ministering to these people on a Sunday. The old man could read the Bible, but his education did not extend much beyond that and weighing the cotton as it was gathered from the fields, and putting down the weights for my father's inspection. Uncle Sam was, I believe, a good Christian man, and these people looked up to him with almost reverence.

My father was a kind, indulgent master, and I think I have never in the world met with happier people than were these simple uneducated blacks. . . .

After two years' stay at boarding school, I returned to the old homestead and found my father all alone except the faithful family slaves. In those days, with the better class of citizens, such servants were numerous, and each had his special charge. In our household there were Middleton, who waited on my father and kept the dining room in order; the cook, maum Louisa; the washwoman, maum Kate; and Uncle Abram, the man-servant who cared for the horses. There were all these servants with so little to occupy them; yet they were cared for as members of the family, fed and clothed, and attended by the family doctor when sick. They were not taken on social equality with their owners, any more than the servants at the North would be. My father's slaves all looked up to him with loving respect. On my return home, a girl of twelve summers was brought in from the plantation for my special service. . . .

In our dear old home I found the management of domestic duties in the hands of the Negroes. I at once proceeded to take the supervision of the household into my own hands, not only the little every-day matters about the house, but also the weighing-out and providing supplies to be sent down to the plantation. All these things had been entrusted to the Negroes by my father.

I stayed close at home attending to these duties. I did not know that any one in town was taking note of my conduct. A young man recently graduated with the highest honors from a college in Virginia, came to Eufault for the purpose of studying law, and hearing of me, he remarked, "Must seek her acquaintance; she will make a good wife." This young man studied law, was admitted to the bar, and soon procured the position of assistant in the Circuit Clerk's office at Clayton, the county seat. He bought a home there and finally asked me to share it with him.

On the ninth day of January, in the year of 1850, we were married at my father's house in Eufaula. I was in my eighteenth year and Mr. Clayton in his twenty-second, a youthful couple, happy and joyous, full of hope for the long future that lay before us.

He took me to a dear little home in Clayton where we began house-
keeping, with three servants; my cook, Harriet, inherited from my
mother's estate; a boy, Ned, given my husband by his father; and little
Annie, Harriet's daughter.

We lived in this house two years, when my husband having saved
up enough money, purchased a farm near by, and we came into the
inheritance of more slaves. We sold our dear little first home and moved
to the farm. We gathered together our slaves and began a new life.
Rules were made and everything was organized with reference to the
comfort of all and profit to ourselves.

We had only eight grown Negroes. One woman did the cooking for
the whole household and the washing for the white family. I, with the
help of my little girl, Annie, discharged the other duties of the house.
The Negroes were all called up early in the morning and went to the
field before breakfast. The breakfast was prepared and sent to them.
Their breakfast generally consisted of meat, ordinarily bacon, sometimes beef, hot coffee, and bread. At twelve o'clock they all returned
to the house to feed the mules, eat their midday meal, and rest. The
dinner consisted of meat, vegetables of different kinds, and bread, often
fruit pies, especially in the summer season, and old fashioned pot pies
cooked in a big oven. Apples baked with honey was a great dish for
all at our house. After two hours' rest, the slaves returned to the field
and remained until the setting sun warned them of the near approach
of night. The evening meal was generally lighter than the others, milk
taking the place of meat. Many of our farmers weighed out the rations
weekly to their hands, letting them prepare their own meals; but my
husband adopted his father's way of doing; having their meals cooked
for them, so that time allotted for rest could be spent literally at rest.

By and by the family became large, both through natural increase of
the Negroes, and because my husband, at the close of each year, having
saved up money enough to invest in something to increase our income,
was naturally disposed to invest in slaves as being then the most available and profitable property in our section of the country.

We never raised the question for one moment as to whether slavery
was right. We had inherited the institution from devout Christian parents. Slaves were held by pious relatives and friends and clergymen to
whom we were accustomed to look up. The system of slave-holding
was incorporated into our laws, and was regulated and protected by
them. We read our Bible and accepted its teachings as the true guide
in faith and morals. We understood literally our Lord's instructions to
His chosen people, and applied them to our circumstances and surroundings. . . .

We simply and naturally understood that our slaves must be treated
kindly and cared for spiritually, and so they were. We felt that we were
responsible to God for our entire household.

I found it necessary to keep two cooks now instead of one, as heretofore. Every morning I would take my key basket on my arm and make
the rounds, giving out to each cook the various articles of food to be

cooked for both white and colored families for the ensuing day. I gave the preparation of the food my careful attention. And their clothes were comfortable, each garment cut out with my own hands.

In these days of plenty there was a meat house filled with good home-cured meat, a cellar filled with sugar, syrup, wine, vinegar, and soap, a potato house filled with sweet potatoes, and also a store room containing the breadstuffs, and so forth.

Every Sunday morning the mothers brought their little ones up to see me. Then I could satisfy myself as to the care they gave them, whether they had received a bath and suitable clothing for the holy day. Later the larger children presented themselves to be taught the Catechism. I used the little Calvary Catechism, prepared by Mrs. D. C. Weston. The adults were permitted to attend the different churches in town as they pleased, but when the sun hid himself behind the western hills, all were compelled to return home to feed and care for the horses, cows, etc. When the evening meal was over my dining room was in readiness for the reception of all the grown members of the family. They gathered there and took their respective seats. They were taught the Creed of the Holy Apostolic Church, the Lord's Prayer, and the Ten Commandments; that is, all who could be taught, for some of them never could learn to repeat them, but understood the meaning sufficiently to lead a right life. Sometimes I would read a short sermon to them. They sang hymns, and we closed with prayer to our Heavenly Father.

Here we lived in this quiet country home. . . .—Victoria V. Clayton, *Black and White Under the Old Regime* (Milwaukee, 1899), pp. 17–60, passim.

Southerners were fond of contrasting the advantages of their own slaves to the plight of the "wage slaves" of the industrial North.

Joab, a slave belonging to Senator Fitzpatrick . . . brought his cotton to Wetumpka on last Saturday and sold it to Bryant and Carter for one hundred and sixty dollars in clean cash. This case makes a very pretty contrast to the one reported in the New York papers where thousands of women and children gathered together to seek bread where there was no bread. This is Joab's spending money; there is no need of his laying up for old age or decrepitude. The hand of a kind master stands between him and want, and no visions of famished wife and starving children haunt his future.—*Dallas Gazette,* December 21, 1858.

As to what the slaves themselves thought of their state of bondage we have only their accounts given long after emancipation. Most of the narrators were past one hundred. John Brown, born in Talladega County, was eighty-seven. He remembered some of the older Negroes on his master's plantation who had come from Africa.

Most of the time there was more'n three hundred slaves on the plantation. The oldest ones come right from Africa. My grandmother was one of them. A savage in Africa—a slave in America. Mammy told it to me. Over there all the natives dressed naked and lived on fruits and nuts. Never see many white mens. One day a big ship stopped off the shore and the natives hid in the brush along the beach. Grandmother was there. The ship men sent a little boat to the shore and scattered bright things and trinkets on the beach. The natives were curious. Grandmother said everybody made a rush for them things soon as the boat left. The trinkets was fewer than the peoples. Next day the white folks scatter some more. There was another scramble. The natives was feeling less scared, and the next day some of them walked up the gangplank to get things off the plank and off the deck. The deck was covered with things like they'd found on the beach. Two-three hundred natives on the ship when they feel it move. They rush to the side but the plank was gone. Just dropped in the water when the ship moved away.

Folks on the beach started to crying and shouting. The ones on the boat was wild with fear. Grandmother was one of them who got fooled, and she say the last thing seen of that place was the natives running up and down the beach waving their arms and shouting like they was mad. The boat men come up from below where they had been hiding and drive the slaves down in the bottom and keep them quiet with the whips and clubs. The slaves was landed at Charleston. The town folks was mighty mad 'cause the blacks was driven through the streets without any clothes, and drove off the boat men after the slaves was sold on the market. Most of that load was sold to the Brown plantation in Alabama. Grandmother was one of the bunch.

The Browns taught them to work. Made clothes for them. For a long time the natives didn't like the clothes and try to shake them off. There was three Brown boys—John, Charley, and Henry. Nephews of old lady Hyatt who was the real owner of the plantation, but the boys run the place. The old lady, she lived in the town. Come out in the spring and fall to see how is the plantation doing. She was a fine woman. The Brown boys and their wives was just as good. Wouldn't let nobody mistreat the slaves. Whippings was few and nobody got the whip unless he need it bad. They teach the young ones how to read and write; say it was good for the Negroes to know about such things.

Sunday was a great day around the plantation. The fields was forgotten, the light chores was hurried through, and everybody got ready for the church meeting. It was out of the doors, in the yard fronting the big lot where the Browns all lived. Master John's wife would start the meeting with a prayer and then would come the singing—the old timey songs. But the white folks on the next plantation would lick their slaves for trying to do like we did. No praying there, and no singing.

The master gave out the week's supply on Saturday. Plenty of hams, lean bacon, flour, cornmeal, coffee, and more'n enough for the week. Nobody go hungry on that place! During the growing season all the slaves have a garden spot all their own. Three thousand acres on that place—plenty of room for gardens and field crops.—Norman R. Yetman, ed. *Life Under the "Peculiar Institution:" Selections from the Slave Narrative Collection* (New York: Holt, Rinehard and Winston, 1970), pp. 45–46.

John Brown stayed on the place until the last Brown died and then he went to Oklahoma.

Cato, who was one hundred at the time he told his story, was a mulatto, the son of his master's brother. He lived his slave years near Pineapple. If his memory did not play him false, he led a pleasant life but realized others were less fortunate than he.

Back in Alabama, Missy Angela took me when I was past my creeping days to live in the big house with the white folks. I had a room built on the big house, where I stayed, and they was always good to me, 'cause I's one of their blood. They never hit me a lick or slapped me once, and they told me they'd never sell me away from them. They was the best-quality white folks and lived in a big, two-story house with a big hall what run all the way through the house. They wasn't rough as some white folks on their niggers.

My mammy lived in a hewn-oak log cabin in the quarters. There was a long row of cabins, some bigger than t'others, 'count of family size. My massa had over eighty head of slaves. Them little old cabins was cozy, 'cause we chinked 'em with mud and they had stick chimneys daubed with mud, mixed with hog-hair.

The fixings was just plain things. The beds was draw-beds—wooden bedsteads helt together with ropes drawed tight, to hold them. We scalded moss and buried it awhile and stuffed it into ticking to make mattresses. Them beds slept good, better'n the ones nowadays.

There was a good fireplace for cooking, and Sundays Missy gave us niggers a pint of flour and a chicken, for to cook a mess of victuals. Then there was plenty game to find. Many a time I've kilt seventy-five or eighty squirrels out of one big beech. There was lots of deer and bears and quails and every other kind of game, but when they run the Indians out of the country, the game just followed the Indians. I've seed the biggest herds of deer following the way the Indians drifted. Whenever the Indians left, the game all left with them, for some reason I dunno.

Talking 'bout victuals, our eating was good. Can't says the same for all places. Some of the plantations half-starved their niggers and 'lowanced out their eating till they wasn't fitting for work. They had to slip about to niggers on other places to piece out their meals. They had field calls and other kinds of whoops and hollers, what had a meaning to 'em.

Our place was fifteen hundred acres in one block, and 'sides the crops of cotton and corn and rice and ribbon cane we raised in the bottoms, we had vegetables and sheep and beef. We dried the beef on scaffolds we built, and I used to tend it. But best of anything to eat, I liked a big fat coon, and I always liked honey. Some the niggers had little garden patches they tended for themselves.

Everything I tells you am the truth, but they's plenty I can't tell you. I heard plenty things from my mammy and grandpappy. He was a fine diver and used to dive in the Alabama River for things what was wrecked out of boats, and the white folks would git him to go down for things they wanted. They'd let him down by a rope to find things on the bottom of the riverbed. He used to git a piece of money for doing it.

My grandmammy was a juksie, 'cause her mammy was a nigger and her daddy a Choctaw Indian. That's what makes me so mixed up with Indian and African and white blood. Sometimes it mattered to me, sometimes it didn't. It don't no more, 'cause I'm not too far from the end of my days.

I had one brother and one sister I helped raise. They was mostly nigger. My white folks told me never to worry 'bout them, though, 'cause my mammy was of their blood and all of us in our family would never be sold, and sometime they'd make free men and women of us. My brother and sister lived with the niggers, though.

I was trained for a houseboy and to tend the cows. The bears was so bad then, a 'sponsible person who could carry a gun had to look after them.

My massa used to give me a little money 'long, to buy what I wanted. I always bought fine clothes. In the summer when I was a little one, I wore lowerings, like the rest of the niggers. That was things made from cotton sacking. Most of the boys wore shirttails till they was big yearlings. When they bought me red russets from the town, I cried and cried. I didn't want to wear no rawhide shoes. So they took 'em back. They had a weakness for my crying. I did have plenty fine clothes, good woolen suits they spinned on the place, and doeskins and fine linens. I druv in the carriage with the white folks and was 'bout the most dudish nigger in them parts.

I used to tend the nursling thread. The reason they called it that was when the mammies was confined with babies having to suck, they had to spin. I'd take them the thread and bring it back to the house when it was spinned. If they didn't spin seven or eight cuts a day, they'd git a whupping. It was considerable hard on a woman when she had a fretting baby. But every morning them babies had to be took to the big house, so the white folks could see if they's dressed right. They was money tied up in little nigger young-uns.

They whupped the women and they whupped the mens. I used to work some in the tannery, and we made the whups. They'd tie them down to a stob, and give 'em the whupping. Some niggers, it taken four men to whup 'em, but they got it. The nigger driver was meaner than the white folks. They'd better not leave a blade of grass in the rows. I seed 'em beat a nigger half a day to make him 'fess up to stealing a sheep or a shoat. Or they'd whup 'em for running away, but not so hard if they come back of their own 'cordance when they got hungry and sick in the swamps. But when they had to run 'em down with the nigger dogs, they'd git in bad trouble.

My massa never did have any real 'corrigible niggers, but I heard of 'em plenty on other places. When they was real 'corrigible, the white folks said they was like mad dogs and didn't mind to kill them so much as killing a sheep. They'd take 'em to the graveyard and shoot 'em down and bury 'em face downward, with their shoes on. I never seed it done, but they made some the niggers go for a lesson to them that they could git the same.

But I didn't even have to carry a pass to leave my own place, like the other niggers. I had a cap with a sign on it: "Don't bother this nigger, or there will be hell to pay." I went after the mail, in the town. It come in coaches and they put on fresh hosses at Pineapple. The coachman run the hosses into Pineapple with a big to-do and blowing the bugle to git the fresh hosses ready. I got the mail. I was a trusty all my days and never been 'rested by the law to this day.

I never had no complaints for my treatment, but some the niggers hated syrup-making time, 'cause when they had to work till midnight making syrup, it's four o'clock up, just the same. Sunup to sundown was for field niggers.

Corn-shucking was fun. Them days no corn was put in the cribs with shucks on it. They shucked it in the field and shocked the fodder. They did it by sides and all hands out. A beef was kilt, and they'd have a regular picnic feasting. They was plenty whiskey for the niggers, just like Christmas.

Christmas was the big day. Presents for everybody, and the baking and preparing went on for days. The little ones and the big ones were glad, 'specially the nigger mens, 'count of plenty good whiskey. Massa Cal got the best whiskey for his niggers.

We used to have frolics, too. Some niggers had fiddles and played the reels, and niggers love to dance and sing and eat.

'Course niggers had their serious side, too. They loved to go to church and had a little log chapel for worship. But I went to the white folks' church. In the chapel some nigger mens preached from the Bible but couldn't read a line no more than a sheep could. My white folks didn't mind their niggers praying and singing hymns, but some places wouldn't 'low them to worship a-tall, and they had to put their heads in pots to sing or pray.

Most the niggers I know, who had their marriage put in the book, did it after the breaking-up, plenty after they had growed children. When they got married on the place, mostly they just jumped over a broom and that made 'em married. Sometimes one the white folks read a little out of the Scriptures to 'em, and they felt more married. . . .

They used to cry the niggers off just like so much cattle, and we didn't think no different of it. I seed them put them on the block and brag on them something big. Everybody liked to hear them cry off niggers. The crier was a clown and made funny talk and kept everybody laughing.

When Massa and the other mens on the place went off to war, he called me and said, "Cato, you's always been a 'sponsible man, and I leave you to look after the women and the place. If I don't come back, I want you to always stay by Missy Angela!" I said, " 'Fore God, I will, Massa Cal." He said, "Then I can go away peaceable."—E. A. Botkin, ed., *Lay My Burden Down* (Chicago: University of Chicago Press, 1945), pp. 84–87.

Jenny Proctor had few such pleasant memories of her childhood as a slave. Born in 1850, she would have been fifteen at the time she was freed.

I's hear tell of them good slave days, but I ain't never seen no good times then. My mother's name was Lisa, and when I was a very small child I hear that driver going from cabin to cabin as early as 3 o'clock in the morning, and when he comes to our cabin he say, "Lisa, Lisa, git up from there and git that breakfast." My mother, she was cook, and I don't recollect nothing 'bout my father. If I had any brothers and sisters I didn't know it. We had old ragged huts made out of poles and some of the cracks chinked up with mud and moss and some of them wasn't. We didn't have no good beds, just scaffolds nailed up to the wall out of poles and the old ragged bedding throwed on them. That sure was hard sleeping, but even that feel good to our weary bones after them long hard days' work in the field. I 'tended to the children when I was a little gal and tried to clean the house just like Old Miss tells me to. Then soon as I was ten years old, Old Master, he say, "Git this here nigger to that cotton patch."

I recollects once when I was trying to clean the house like Old Miss tell me, I finds a biscuit, and I's so hungry I et it, 'cause we never see such a thing as a biscuit only sometimes on Sunday morning. We just have corn bread and syrup and sometimes fat bacon, but when I et that biscuit and she comes in and say, "Where that biscuit?" I say, "Miss, I et it 'cause I's so hungry." Then she grab that broom and start to beating me over the head with it and calling me low-down nigger, and I guess I just clean lost my head 'cause I knowed better than to fight her if I knowed anything 't all, but I start to fight her, and the driver, he comes in and he grabs me and starts beating me with that cat-o'-nine-tails, and he beats me till I fall to the floor nearly dead. He cut my back all to pieces, then they rubs salt in the cuts for more punishment. Lord, Lord, honey! Them was awful days. When old Master come to the house, he say, "What you beat that nigger like that for?" And the driver tells him why, and he say, "She can't work now for a week. She pay for several biscuits in that time." He sure was mad, and he tell Old Miss she start the whole mess. I still got them scars on my old back right now, just like my grandmother have when she die, and I's a-carrying mine right on to the grave just like she did.

Old master, he wouldn't 'low us to go fishing—he say that too easy on a nigger and wouldn't 'low us to hunt none either—but sometime we slips off at night and catch possums. And when Old Master smells them possums cooking 'way in the night, he wraps up in a white sheet and gets in the chimney corner and scratch on the wall, and when the man in the cabin goes to the door and say, "Who's that?" he say, "It's me, what's ye cooking in there?" and the man say, "I's cooking possum." He say, "Cook him and bring me the hindquarters and you and the wife and the children eat the rest." We never had no chance to git any rabbits 'cept when we was a-clearing and grubbing the new ground. Then we catch some rabbits, and if they looks good to the white folks they takes them and if they no good the niggers git them. We never had no gardens. Sometimes the slaves git vegetables from the white folks' garden and sometimes they didn't.

Money? Uh-uh! We never seen no money. Guess we'd-a bought something to eat with it if we ever seen any. Fact is, we wouldn't-a knowed hardly how to bought anything, 'cause we didn't know nothing 'bout going to town.

They spinned the cloth what our clothes was made of, and we had straight dresses or slips made of lowell. Sometimes they dye 'em with sumac berries or sweet-gum bark, and sometimes they didn't. On Sunday they make all the children change, and what we wears till we gits our clothes washed was gunny sacks with holes cut for our head and arms. We didn't have no shoes 'cepting some homemade moccasins, and we didn't have them till we was big children. The little children they goes naked till they was big enough to work. They was soon big enough though, 'cording to our master. We had red flannel for winter underclothes. Old Miss she say a sick nigger cost more than the flannel.

Wedding? Uh-uh! We just steps over the broom and we's married. Ha! Ha! Ha!

Old Master he had a good house. The logs was all hewed off smooth-like, and the cracks all fixed with nice chinking, plumb 'spectable-looking even to the plank floors. That was something. He didn't have no big plantation, but he keeps 'bout three hundred slaves in them little huts with dirt floors. I thinks he calls it four farms what he had.

Sometimes he would sell some of the slaves off of that big auction block to the highest bidder when he could git enough for one.

When he go to sell a slave, he feed that one good for a few days, then when he goes to put 'em up on the auction block he takes a meat skin and greases all round that nigger's mouth and makes 'em look like they been eating plenty meat and such like and was good and strong and able to work. Sometimes he sell the babes from the breast, and then again he sell the mothers from the babes and the husbands and the wives, and so on. He wouldn't let 'em holler much when the folks be sold away. He say, "I have you whupped if you don't hush." They sure loved their six children though. They wouldn't want nobody buying them.

We might-a done very well if the old driver hadn't been so mean, but the least little thing we do he beat us for it and put big chains

round our ankles and make us work with them on till the blood be cut
out all around our ankles. Some of the masters have what they call
stockades and puts their heads and feet and arms through holes in a
big board out in the hot sun, but our old driver he had a bull pen.
That's only thing like a jail he had. When a slave do anything he
didn't like, he takes 'em in that bull pen and chains 'em down, face up
to the sun, and leaves 'em there till they nearly dies.

None of us was 'lowed to see a book or try to learn. They say we
git smarter than they was if we learn anything, but we slips around
and gits hold of that Webster's old blue-back speller and we hides it
till 'way in the night and then we lights a little pine torch, and studies
that spelling book. We learn it too. I can read some now and write a
little too.

They wasn't no church for the slaves, but we goes to the white
folks' arbor on Sunday evening, and a white man he gits up there to
preach to the niggers. He say, "Now I takes my text, which is, Nigger
obey your master and your mistress, 'cause what you git from them
here in this world am all you ever going to git, 'cause you just like the
hogs and the other animals—when you dies you ain't no more, after
you been throwed in that hole." I guess we believed that for a while
'cause we didn't have no way finding out different. We didn't see no
Bibles.

Sometimes a slave would run away and just live wild in the woods,
but most times they catch 'em and beats 'em, then chains 'em down in
the sun till they nearly die. The only way any slaves on our farm ever
goes anywhere was when the boss sends him to carry some news to
another plantation or when we slips off way in the night. Sometimes
after all the work was done a bunch would have it made up to slip
out down to the creek and dance. We sure have fun when we do that,
most times on Saturday night.

All the Christmas we had was Old Master would kill a hog and
give us a piece of pork. We thought that was something, and the way
Christmas lasted was 'cording to the big sweet-gum backlog what the
slaves would cut and put in the fireplace. When that burned out, the
Christmas was over. So you know we all keeps a-looking the whole
years round for the biggest sweet gum we could find. When we just
couldn't find the sweet gum, we git oak, but it wouldn't last long enough,
'bout three days on average, when we didn't have to work. Old Master
he sure pile on them pine knots, gitting that Christmas over so we could
git back to work.

We had a few little games we play, like Peep Squirrel Peep, You
Can't Catch Me, and such like. We didn't know nothing 'bout no New
Year's Day or holidays 'cept Christmas.

We had some corn-shuckings sometimes, but the white folks gits
the fun and the nigger gits the work. We didn't have no kind of cotton-
pickings 'cept just pick our own cotton. I's can hear them darkies now,
going to the cotton patch 'way 'fore day a-singing "Peggy, does you
love me now?"

One old man he sing:

> Saturday night and Sunday too
> Young gals on my mind.
> Monday morning 'way 'fore day
> Old Master got me gwine.
> Peggy, does you love me now?

Then he whoops a sort of nigger holler, what nobody can do just like them old-time darkies, then on he goes:

> Possum up a 'simmon tree,
> Rabbit on the ground.
> Lord, Lord, possum,
> Shake them 'simmons down.
> Peggy, does you love me now?

> Rabbit up a gum stump,
> Possum up a holler.
> Git him out, little boy
> And I gives you half a dollar.
> Peggy, does you love me now?

We didn't have much looking after when we git sick. We had to take the worst stuff in the world for medicine, just so it was cheap. That old blue mass and bitter apple would keep us out all night. Sometimes he have the doctor when he thinks we going to die, 'cause he say he ain't got anyone to lose, then that calomel what that doctor would give us would pretty nigh kill us. Then they keeps all kinds of lead bullets and asafetida balls round our necks, and some carried a rabbit foot with them all the time to keep off evil of any kind.

Lord, Lord, honey! It seems impossible that any of us ever lived to see that day of freedom, but thank God we did.—Ibid., pp. 89–93.

Life was not always as harsh as Jenny Proctor pictured it. There were some diversions as many observers point out. On many plantations Christmas was a prolonged holiday with presents, extra rations of food and drink, dancing and other "frolicking" that lasted until the yule log was completely burned up. There were barbecues and other events where there was a minimum of white supervision and of course any communal task could be a combination of work and fun.

There probably was never a bona fide abolitionist resident in Alabama. In fact, many Alabamians (especially after 1840) were defending slavery on religious, constitutional, economic, or scientific grounds. This does not mean, however, that everyone was of one mind about the institution and what should be done about it. For example, there was considerable acrimony over the proposal, taken quite seriously, to limit the number of slaves brought into the state from Virginia and Maryland. The Eufaula *Democrat* and other

papers took the position that those who advocated restrictive measures were "very unfairly and dishonestly appealing to the deep
prejudice of southern people against Negro traders and their
trade." The goals that the advocates of restriction sought were in
the editor's opinion the same as those abolitionists who advocated
restricting slavery by the Wilmot Proviso.

The strongest organization in the South seeking a solution to the
slavery question was the American Colonization Society. Simply
stated, its purpose was to purchase slaves, or take the Negroes
already free, and send them back to Africa, locating them in Liberia.
Southern planters and politicians approved the scheme, partly
because it removed freedmen (considered trouble-makers) from
their midst, but mostly (at least on theoretical grounds) because
it did no violence to property rights in slaves.

While there were local chapters and even a state organization of
the national society and many prominent men lent their names to
the movement, most members took little interest in its affairs. However, an Alabamian, James G. Birney, was its national agent for
three years. Birney, Kentucky born, moved to Huntsville in 1818
where he became a prominent lawyer, planter, and mayor of the
city. His interest in seeking a solution to the slavery question led
to an offer from the national society. In a letter acknowledging his
commission as agent for the southwestern district, he outlined some
of the goals he sought.

> The first step that should be taken in this District, where jealousy
> of the Society exists from an apprehension that its object is an inter-
> ference with the rights of property, is to gain the good will, at least,
> of the Legislatures. This being done, the Agent will not be looked upon,
> in the *country,* as "Raw-head and bloody bones", and all undue fear of
> his influence upon the Slaves will be removed. I have sketched out for
> myself the following plan, —Attend upon the meeting of the Legisla-
> ture of Mississippi at Jackson early in November—thence, to New
> Orleans, for the purpose of addressing the Legislature of Louisiana,
> which will assemble *this year* on 3. Monday in November—to superin-
> tend there the contemplated expedition to Liberia—thence to Tuska-
> loosa to operate, if possible, upon the Legislature of this State. I deem
> it altogether important that the subject be first fully discussed before
> these people, before it is introduced elsewhere among the people, unless
> very peculiar and favorable circumstances should call for a different
> course. . . .
>
> The Society in this place [Huntsville], considered by me one of the
> most important in this whole region, has been recently in rather a
> languid condition. We are making an effort to revive it at our Anni-
> versary which will occur about the middle of next month. The object of
> the Society has been always well received here, and good success may
> be ensured by activity and attention. I cannot but trust, my dear Sir,

that the Sun of prosperity is about to break out with great warmth and brilliancy upon the cause of unhappy Africa, and that this cause so intimately connected with the progress of Truth and its triumph in the world will be signally blessed. That God may use us for his glory in alleviating the burden of human woe is the very earnest wish of J.G.B.— Birney to Ralph R. Gurley, August 23, 1832, Dwight L. Dumond, ed. *Letters of James G. Birney* (New York: D. Appleton-Century, 1938), vol. 2, pp. 20–23.

In 1835 he resigned as agent and thereafter devoted his energies to the anti-slavery movement. Most of his later life was spent in the free states. In 1840 he was the presidential candidate for the Free Soil party.

One of the favorite topics for discussion by economists and historians is the profitableness of the plantation-slave system in the Old South. Did the planter really make money, they ask, or did the system merely provide unlimited credit? Was slavery on the way out because the end of good cheap land suitable for plantation economy was already in sight? These and other related questions have been debated *ad infinitum*.

There can be no doubt that some planters were making money. The two most prosperous periods appear to have been in the 1820's when the price of slaves was low and in the late 1850's when, although the price of slaves was high, the established planters had already acquired their work force and therefore had to expand very little in new purchases. Good land was still available although in some of the older sections constant cropping without systematic fertilizing was exhausting the soil. C. C. Clay, Jr. of Huntsville in an address to the Chunnennuggee Horticulture Society pointed out that cotton was rapidly depleting the soil.

I can show you, with sorrow, in the older portions of Alabama, and in my native county of Madison, the sad memorials of the artless and exhausting culture of cotton. Our small planters, after taking the cream off their lands, unable to restore them by rest, manures, or otherwise, are going further west and south, in search of other virgin lands, which they may and will despoil and impoverish in like manner. *Our wealthier planters, with greater means and no more skill, are buying out their poorer neighbors, extending their plantations, and adding to their slave force. The wealthy few, who are able to live on smaller profits, and to give their blasted fields some rest, are thus pushing off the many, who are merely independent. . . .*

In traversing that county one will discover numerous farmhouses, once the abode of industrious and intelligent freemen, now occupied by slaves, or tenantless, deserted, and dilapidated; he will observe fields, once fertile, now unfenced, abandoned, and covered with those evil harbingers—foxtail and broom-sedge; he will see the moss growing on the mouldering walls of once thrifty villages; and will find "one only master grasps the whole domain" that once furnished happy homes for a dozen white families. Indeed, a country in its infancy, where, fifty years ago, scarce a forest tree had been felled by the axe of the pioneer, is already exhibiting the painful signs of senility and decay, apparent in Virginia and the Carolinas; the freshness of its agricultural glory is gone; the vigour of its youth is extinct, and the spirit of desolation seems brooding over it.—DeBow's Review, December 1855, p. 725.

Interest in Scientific Agriculture

Generally speaking, Alabama farmers were little interested in soil conservation or agricultural improvements. There were some, however, who experimented with new varieties of cotton, new crops, new tools, new fertilizers, and new methods of cultivation. They were pioneers in scientific agriculture in the state. To promote their cause they urged the formation of agricultural societies and conventions. After several abortive attempts, a group of men including Dr. N. B. Cloud of Macon County organized the State Agricultural Society (January 10, 1855) to "improve the conditions of agricultural, mechanic, and domestic arts and manufacturers."

There were many county societies. The letter to the editor of the Greensboro *Alabama Beacon* (July 13, 1855) emphasizes the advantage for a local organization.

Mr. Editor: Allow me through the columns of your paper, to call the attention of the farming population of the country, to the subject of improvement, in that occupation. In this age of improvement, this "go-a-head" generation of the nineteenth century, the farmers must not be idle, but must keep pace with the improvements of the day. Whilst we are prosecuting plans, for the construction of railroads and manufactories, the founding of Seminaries, and Institutions of learning, the building of fine houses, and the embellishing of our places of abode, let us not neglect farming, the foundation and most important of all employments, the most independent and honorable, and the primitive occupation of man.

From what I have said above, the question suggests itself, "how can its improvement be promoted?" I answer; by establishing an "Agricultural Society" among us.

I think this might be established and maintained, among as intellectual and wealthy a class of citizens as that of Greene county. We have fine lands, if they are improved; and our county is generally acknowledged as the "Goshen" of the State. If we could succeed in this, there would be a surprising change in the improvement of farming in our county in a few years. Their westward emigration would be retarded, and they would stay at home, and improve their farms. It would create a competition among the farmers, and they would vie with each other, in raising cattle, horses, hogs, &c., in growing fruit trees, in cultivating their gardens, in improving their lands and in making as large an amount as possible on a small piece of land.

I recommend that a meeting be held, as early as practicable, in the town of Eutaw, where all parts of the county shall be represented by their ablest & most influential men, & that the subject be discussed before the meeting by speakers appointed for the purpose. I hope our sister counties will join with us in endeavoring to establish an Agricultural Society. But if they will not join us let Old Greene try it single handed and alone, for we know she can do it, and let one of the county papers be enlarged, and one side of it at least, be devoted exclusively to the subject of Agriculture. I hope our brother farmers, and all those who feel interested on this subject, will come out and give us their views and their advice, both of this and of the adjoining counties; but you especially Mr. Editor. We hope to meet with good luck, as well as the favor and approbation of the press, as we believe our cause to be a good one.

AGRICOLA.

In spite of all the efforts of the leaders, farming methods were little changed until motorized tools were introduced in the twentieth century.

During the whole antebellum period, the price of both cotton and slaves fluctuated, with the price of slaves forging ahead. Perhaps the profits to be made from planting have been exaggerated. The planter who was making the substantial profits was not necessarily the largest producer of cotton but the one who was raising corn and other foodstuffs at home so that he did not have to buy them. From the point of view of economics it is not certain whether slavery was a sound investment. However, the forces that would have led eventually to its downfall were already at work and emancipation merely cut the time short.

Chapter 6

COMMERCE, INDUSTRY, AND TRANSPORTATION BEFORE 1860

Alabamians did not confine their economic interests to agriculture, however important that was; nor did all of them live on plantations. Some, although a much smaller number, lived in towns, engaged in commerce, developed industry, built several hundred miles of railroads, and were always talking about ways of improving their production so that they could be independent of the "Yankee" manufacturer.

Antebellum Towns

Historians generally have neglected the several towns in antebellum Alabama. The United States census of 1860 listed fifteen communities as towns although several of them were little more than villages. Ashville, for instance, had only 116 white inhabitants. On the other hand, Mobile had 20,854 white residents (a total of 29,284); Montgomery had 4,341; Huntsville, 1,980; Tuscaloosa, 1,520; Marion, 623; Florence, 807; and Selma 1,809. There was a total of 38,246 whites listed as living in towns. Few of these places were more than country towns, yet all of them were trading-centers for the surrounding area, shipping ports for the planters, the seats of local government, and the residence of lawyers, newspaper editors, and other professional men.

ST. STEPHENS

St. Stephens was the capital of Alabama Territory. It promised to be an important center of life in south Alabama.

The town of St. Stephens, at the head of ship navigation of the Tombigbee, is advancing with a rapidity beyond that of any place, perhaps in the western country. It has at this moment at least thirty new houses commenced; many of them wou'd vie with those generally built in the United States. It has an academy supported by the voluntary contributions of the citizens; with two teachers and sixty or seventy students; who have since their commencements, made progress highly honorable to the institution. There is a Steam Boat on the stocks, in size and force, calculated in an eminent degree to give greatest facility to our commerce to the ocean. It is intended, as occasion may require, to run from thence to New Orleans, and return up either the Tombigbee or Alabama, as high as Fort Claiborne. The navigation of the Tombigbee, as high as this place is perfectly secure, to vessels of any size that can enter Mobile at, any season of the year. The annual amount of merchandize, brought and vended at this place, is not less than five hundred thousand dollars, and is still increasing.—*Alabama Republican* (Huntsville), September 30, 1817.

At the time that Alabama became a state Claiborne was a prosperous town on the Alabama River. It had a newspaper, *The Alabama Courier,* which carried ads for grocers, for an auctioneer appointed by Governor W. W. Bibb, for Benjamin Levy & Co., for booksellers and stationers, for general merchants (at least six of them) who advertised everything from silks to steel, for one tailor, and one printer. There were also notices of dissolution of a partnership, and the settling of estates. A fifty dollar reward was offered for a runaway Negro.

The editor in the passage below was discussing the progress made since the Treaty of Fort Jackson (1814) and making predictions for the future. He was understandably optimistic about his home town.

. . . Huntsville has already attained its acme, and so has St. Stephens— Mobile and Blakeley must continue to thrive; so must the town at the Falls of the Black Warrior, and Philadelphia or Alabama. Cahaba's prosperity appears to depend on contingencies. But the town of Claiborne has natural advantages that will always insure its prosperity. It is situated equidistantly from Mobile, Blakeley, and Pensacola, to all of which places the best roads can be had with no more labor and expense than cutting down the natural growth of the country. Its elevation of two hundred feet above the water in the Alabama River gives it an appearance truly romantic; the view from it to the west and northwest is equally picturesque and pleasing. It is watered by innumerable springs of clear water which issue from the bluff and precipitate themselves into the river below, forming beautiful cascades—five considerable streams of water empty into the river within eight miles of the place, affording large tracts of fertile land which are now settled by rich and respectable planters from the Carolinas and Georgia. Experienced and able merchants from Boston and New York, aware of the importance of the place, have settled themselevs permanently here and are realizing the profits of their foresight. Two thousand inhabitants, thirty stores, two female seminaries and a grammar school afford ample proof of the eligibility of the site for a town and the capacity of a neighboring country to support it.—*The Alabama Courier* (Claiborne), March 19, 1819.

HUNTSVILLE

Huntsville was the oldest setlement in the oldest county in north Alabama. Settled by familes of means and education, it rapidly became the best-known place in Alabama after Mobile. Every visitor to the area visited it. Anne Royall, arriving there on Christmas Eve, 1817, liked the place and the people from the beginning.

You will expect something of this flourishing town. It takes its name from a man called Captain Hunt, who built the first cabin on the spot, where the Court House now stands, in 1802. In front of this cabin, which was built on a high bluff, there was a large pond, which is now nearly filled up by the citizens. Captain Hunt cleared a small field west of his cabin, the same year. This was between his cabin and the Huntsville Spring. He spent much of his time in wageing war with the rattlesnakes, who were very numerous in his day, and had entire possession of the Bluff at the Spring. Thousands of them, it appears, were lodged amongst the rocks, and the Captain would shoot hundreds of a day, by thrusting long canes filled with powder, into the scissures of the rocks.

Whether Hunt, or the snakes acquired the victory, I have not heard, as he was compelled to abandon his settlement to a more successful rival, who purchased the land. This was Colonel L. Pope, who, in company with Dr. Maning, and others, purchased the land at a Land Office opened in Nashville; and though this sale did not stand, these gentlemen at this time own vast bodies of land around Huntsville, and are the wealthiest men in the Territory. Colonel Pope, it is said, tried hard to have the name changed, to *Twickenham,* after the residence of his namesake (and from whom it is said he is descended) in England. But, places, somehow or other, will retain their first names. The land around Huntsville, and the whole of Madison county, of which it is the capital, is rich and beautiful as you can imagine; and the appearance of wealth would baffle belief. The town stands on elevated ground, and enjoys a beautiful prospect. It contains about 260 houses, principally built of brick; has a bank, a courthouse, and market house. There is a large square in the centre of the town, like the towns in Ohio, and facing this are the stores, twelve in number. These buildings form a solid wall, though divided into apartments. The workmanship is the best I have seen in all the states; and several of the houses are three stories high, and very large. There is no church. The people assemble in the Court House to worship. Huntsville is settled by people mostly from Georgia and the Carolinas—though there are a few from almost every part of the world; —and the town displays much activity. The citizens are gay, polite, and hospitable, and live in great splendor. Nothing like it in our country.— Lucille Griffith, ed., *Letters from Alabama 1817–1822* (University: University of Alabama Press, 1969), pp. 118–19.

FLORENCE

St. Stephens and Claiborne, for all the hopes of their early settlers, have long since passed their glory. Huntsville and Florence,
in the 1960's and '70's, are among the fastest growing centers of
the state. Anne Royall was among those who foresaw the development of the Tennessee River Valley.

Florence is one of the new towns of this beautiful and rapidly rising
state. It is happily situated for commerce at the head of steamboat navigation, on the north side of Tennessee River, in the County of Lauderdale, five miles below the port of Muscle Shoals, and ten miles from the
line of the state of Tennessee.
Florence is to be the great emporium of the northern part of this
state. I do not see why it should not; it has a great capital and is patron-
ized by the wealthiest gentlemen in the state. It has a great state to its
back, another in front and a noble river on all sides, the steamships pouring every necessary and every luxury into its lap. Its citizens, bold,
enterprising, and industrious—much more so that any I have seen
in the state.
Many large and elegant brick buildings are already built here (although it was sold out but two years since), and frame buildings are
putting up daily. It is not uncommon to see a framed building begun
in the morning and finished by night.
Several respectable mercantile houses are established here and much
business is done on commission also. The site of the town is beautifully
situated on an eminence, commanding an extensive view of the surrounding country and Tennessee river, from which it is three quarters of a
mile distant. . . . Florence has communication by water from Mississippi,
Missouri, Louisiana, Indiana, Illinois, Ohio, Kentucky, West Pennsylvania, West Virginia and East Tennessee, and very shortly will communicate with the Eastern States through the great canal! The great
military road that leads from Nashville to New Orleans, by way of Lake
Ponchartrain, passes through this town, and the number of people who
travel through it, and the numerous droves of horses for the lower country for market, are incredible. Florence contains one printing press, and
publishes a weekly paper called the *Florence Gazette;* it is ably patron-
ized and edited by one of our first men, and said to be the best paper
in the state. Florence is inhabited by people from almost all parts of
Europe and the United States; here are English, Irish, Welch, Scotch,
French, Dutch, Germans, and Grecians. The first Greek I ever saw was
in this town. I conversed with him on the subject of his country, but
found him grossly ignorant. He butchers for the town and has taken
to his arms a mulatto woman for a wife. He often takes an airing on
horseback of a Sunday afternoon, with his wife riding by his side, and
both arrayed in shining costume.
The river at Florence is upwards of five hundred yards wide; it is
ferried in a large boat worked by four horses and crosses it in a few
minutes.

There are two large and well kept taverns in Florence and several doggeries. A doggery is a place where spirituous liquors are sold; where men get drunk, quarrel and fight as often as they choose, but where there is nothing to eat for man or beast. Did you ever hear of a better name? "I swear!" said a Yankee pedlar, one day, with both his eyes bunged up, "that are doggery be rightly named. Never seed the like on't. If I get hum agin it'll be a nice man'll catch me in these parts. Awfullest place one could be at." It appears the inmates of the doggery inticed him under pretense of buying his wares, and forced him to drink, and then forced him to fight, but the poor little Yankee was sadly beaten. Not content with blacking up his eyes, they overturned his tin cart and scattered his tins to the four winds, frightened his horse and tormented his very soul out about lasses, etc. . . .

. . . One of the largest buildings I ever saw is in Florence. It was built by a company of gentlemen and is said to have cost $90,000 and is not yet finished . . .—Ibid., pp. 227–29.

MONTGOMERY

Among the many foreigners to visit Alabama in the antebellum period was George W. Featherstonhaugh, English author and scientist. In 1835 he made a trip from Mobile to Montgomery by water and from there through the Creek country to Fort Mitchell. As the following passage shows, he found Montgomery little to his taste:

From the landing we had to walk a mile to Montgomery, a small straggling town with a population of from two to three thousand inhabitants. . . .

The two principal streets are very broad, in the style common to all the southern towns, and from the great number of stores in them, amounting at least to one hundred, it would seem to be a place of extensive inland business; but of all the horrid filthy places into which I ever entered in any country, I think the principal hotel here, which was the one to which we were directed by common consent of all those we made inquiries of, bears the dirty palm. Everything about it seemed to breathe of whiskey and tobacco, and the walls of the bed-room to which I was shown were so incommunicably squirted over with a black-coloured tobacco-juice, and with more disgusting things, that it was evident the visitors to the place were, as to manners, but little raised above the inferior animals. There was an unfinished hotel then building opposite, but what the other hotels were which were not "principal," I had not time to ascertain. I regretted much, however, that I had not gone to one of them, upon the very chance that they could not be worse. . . .—Quoted in Walter B. Posey, *Alabama in the 1830's* (Birmingham, Ala: Birmingham-Southern College, 1938), p. 27.

MOBILE

Mobile was of course the oldest town and throughout the antebellum period was the metropolis of the state. After New Orleans, it was the most important Gulf port. Early visitors, however, found it small and struggling, and it was not until the American period that it attained any considerable size.

The description given here is by Charles Lanman and is only one of many that could be used.

> I like Mobile much. It has a substantial as well as a dashing appearance, and the business habits and manners of the people remind me of old Gotham. It's "Battle House" would be the boast of any city, and, like most of the better hotels in the South, is kept by a Yankee. Mobile is an opulent place, and has been made so almost exclusively by the cotton interest. It is an extravagant, joyous and free and easy town; so that sporting characters, thoroughbred and fast horses, and lovely women are as "familiar as household words." Warmhearted, it seems to me, are all its citizens. . . . With the market of this city I have been particularly pleased and it is deservedly the centre of attraction to all strangers. The building itself is commonplace, but as a depot for all the good things of this bountiful land, and as a congregating place for queer characters, it is worthy of a frequent visit. The butchers and hucksters are usually of French or Spanish extractions, and when you add to these their wives and daughters, negroes of every age and shade of color and an occasional group of Choctaw Indians, you have a sufficient variety. Fruit of every kind peculiar to the tropics is found here in greatest profusion; so also it is with game, deer, wild turkeys, ducks and birds of the partridge tribe being the staples in this line; and as to the fish, the following are what I noted during a single walk through the market, viz; saltwater trout, rockfish or stripped bass, black bass, bream, sunfish, pike, redfish or red horse, sheepshead, saltwater mullet, buffalo or drum, flounder and flat fish, the common sucker, and catfish of every imaginable size. The number of Indians who spend much of their time in Mobile, but who live in the neighboring pine woods, is estimated at one thousand. The men, some of whom are fine looking, do a little hunting for the market, but their principal business is to deck themselves in bright colors and hang about the market or hotels, very much after the manner of their brother snobs in our Northern cities who loitre about the church doors on Sunday; but the women are industrious, and manage to keep themselves quite comfortable by selling bundles of fat pine for lighting fires, and beautiful willow baskets.—Charles Lanman, *Adventures in the Wilds of the United States and British American Provinces* (Philadelphia: J. W. Moore, 1856), vol. 2, pp. 153–54.

What happened in the cities and towns of Alabama and what kinds of cases came before the law enforcement officers? The best way to find out is to read the newspapers. The Report of Mayors Court of Mobile (1859) gives the answers to some of these questions.

MAYOR'S COURT.—Monday, July 24.—Before His Honor Jones M. Withers, Mayor.

A man who cursed another, was fined $25 therefor.

A man found drunk on the side-walk by night, was fined $5 therefor.

A man who made a noise, was fined $5 therefor, and a man who struck him and tore his shirt off, was fined $10 therefor.

A man who perseveringly pursued another, hitting him whenever he could get a chance was fined $5 therefor—do, for being drunk, and the other who told him that he had sold his vote for two bitts and a drink of whiskey, was—after an argument by the Mayor—fined $10 therefor.

Two men who took a friendly fight in a bar-room without troubling anybody, were fined $10 each therefor.

A boy who hit another a smack " 'side o' th' head" and kicked him in the nose was fined $10 therefor.—making, with $50 hereinafter to be noticed $140 for the city, if ever she gets it.

No application having come from Pensacola for McGregor, arrested as a deserter, the Mayor threatens to discharge him soon.

In the sidewalk case, the Mayor decided from his own inspection that the request for a few shovel-fulls of dirt was reasonable, and the refusal by the Deputy Boss Dirt-Digger was unreasonable and churlish, (doggish he might have said,) but then the accused had called him a son of a b . . . h. The accused stated that there was very provoking language first used towards him, which he could not prove except by the testimony of ladies; in consideration of which His Honor will hear the case privately, if it becomes necessary.

A negro taken in the fish-market with the manner, that is with his hand in a money box, and the money in his hand, was, with his agent's consent ordered fifty stripes, twenty five a day.

Two saucy looking negro women found abroad with fictitious passes, were ordered twenty very good stripes apiece, and the police were directed to hand the passes to the masters, that they might take such actions as they see fit. The passes, from whomsoever they came, respecting which there is no legal proof, but only the women's statements are from a fictitious place, and signed in a cramped hand with a fictitious name.

A woman who was found drunk in a church, yesterday, was represented to be very poor, a widow of a few months, with a child, and honest, but disposed to drink. The Mayor dismissed her with a reproof.

William Verneuille was arrested for striking Thomas Smith with a stone. Between 11 and 11½ o'clock he came into the Verandah bar-room, showed a disposition to elbow people and make himself disagreeable generally, took a drink and smashed the tumbler against the counter. Smith spoke to him about his behavior, telling him it would not be permitted, &c. Verneuille—like all men (politicians included) who mean to raise a fuss under a false issue—said he was willing to pay for the tumbler, but Smith told him "never mind that," but he must not behave as he was doing; and then passed out with the man with whom he was conversing, Verneuille followed him, tapped him on the arm, and said he wanted to speak with him; but Smith excused himself, as being engaged. Verneuille then withdrew some twenty or thirty feet, picked up a stone of about four pounds weight, threw it at Smith, whose back was turned, and walked away. The stone struck Smith on the back of the head and knocked him down. The testimony of different witnesses was direct as to seeing him pick up and throw the stone, and the stone being found on the pavement. Verneuille, who has already been in the penitentiary for killing a man by coming behind his back, was held to bail in $1,000 for assault with intent to commit murder.

J. Doherty, Thomas Brown and . . . . . . Lewis were complained of by P. Dumas for attacking him with sundry and divers bottles, slung-shot, brickbats, &c. We have only room to report the result, which was, that upon satisfactory evidence Doherty was held to bail in $500, for assault and battery, (with a bottle of whiskey;) Brown ditto, for assault and battery with a slung shot, and Lewis, respecting whom nothing was proved beyond disorderly conduct, was sentenced to $50 or 30 days.

We have ascertained in part why that affair of the policemen did not come up in court. The policeman principally in fault did enter the charge against himself upon the book; but His Honor extends the ladies' rule, above referred, to the policemen, and tries them in private; but this case has not been tried yet.—*The Daily Mercury* (Mobile), July 26, 1859.

The Store

The large planters shipped their cotton and made their purchases through factors in Mobile or New Orleans, but there were small planters and farmers who purchased what they could not produce at home from a local merchant. Therefore, merchants played an important economic role. The advertisements in state papers show that merchants offered for sale an amazing variety of merchandise. Moore and Jones in Huntsville offered to trade for cash or cotton and either wholesale or retail.

NEW & CHEAP GOODS.
MOORE & JONES,

Have just received from Philadelphia and New York, and are now opening in the Brick store at the S. W. corner of the public square, an extensive & well selected assortment of
MERCHANDISE,
among many others are the following articles now in demand
Superfine London Blue and Black Broad clothe
Mixed, Drab, Gray & fancy cold. do
Double Milled, Drab Blue Black & Grey Casimeres,
Superfine Peleese cloths,
Maroon Blue and other fancy colors
Double Milled Drab cloths,
Drab Coatings, bearskins
Forest and Kersey cloths asd.
Black Blue Grey and White,
Plains and negro Cottons
Flannels & baizes of all colors,

Rose, point and Duffle Blankets
Figured and plan Bumbazetts
Bambazines and Rattinetts
Velvet and Manchester chords
Swansdown, Tiolnetts Moleskin and Florentine Vestings
Woollen, cotton & silk Hoseries asd.
Boots and shoes well assorted
Ladies dressing Cases & paint Boxes
Bandana, Barcelona and striped Silk Handkerchiefs
Marino Laventine & plain silk shawles
Black and white Lace Veils
Shawls and Capes
Muslin Ruffs with coleretts
Sattin Laventine
Lutestrong and Senshaw Silks
Figured and plain
Domestic stripes, plaids & ginghams
Damask and diaper
Table linen
Madapallam Shirting
Cambrics and Irish linen
4-4 and 6-4 figured and plain
Cambrics and dimity do.
India mull and Jaconet muslins
Furniture dimity
Ladies straw and Beaver Hats, late fashion full trimed
Figured parasols with Ivory handles
Gents. Fine Beaver, Castor and Roram white and Black Hats
China tea sets by the box or half doz.
Glass and Queens ware assorted
Liverpool do plates and dishes
Sugar, Coffee teas and spices
Irish whiskey, Rum, Brandy, and Wines
Molasses Raisins and Almonds
Hardware and Cutlery well assorted
Iron Castings and Salt
4 to 20 penny Cut & Wrought nails
A few kegs of horse shoe nails

All of which we are determined to sell unusually low, wholesale or retail for Cash or Cotton, and on their usual credits to punctual men.

Country merchants and others desirous to have an additional assortment, are particularly invited to call and judge for themselves.—The *Alabama Republican* (Huntsville), April 18, 1818.

Commerce

Alabama had more navigable rivers than any state in the nation, most of them emptying into Mobile Bay. It was only natural, therefore, that Mobile became Alabama's "metropolis by the sea." As a Gulf coast port it was second only to New Orleans. Not all products that Alabamians shipped found their way to Mobile, however; residents of north Alabama found it convenient to send their boats to New Orleans by way of the Tennessee and Mississippi Rivers. In the eastern and south eastern parts of the state, some planters used the Chattahoochee and Escambia Rivers. But still Mobile handled the bulk of the state's export business.

Cotton, of course, was the most important item in Mobile trade, but there were others in quantity. The list is long: tar, turpentine, pitch, resin shingles, deck planks, empty barrels, staves, cedar logs and many other wood products; iron, tallow, hides, leather, bones; sugar, corn; brick, lime, and many others. These products were shipped to many ports, Great Britain and France getting the bulk, but quantities also going to Amsterdam, Bremen, St. Petersburg, Stockholm, Gibraltar, Havana, Genoa, Trieste and other far-flung places. New York and Boston, Providence and Baltimore received most of the domestic shipping.

DeBow's Review reported the extent of the Mobile trade in 1850–51.

COMMERCE OF MOBILE, 1850-51.

In accordance with custom, we present . . . our annual review of the business of the commercial year, ending the 31st of August, 1851, with tabular statements of trade and commerce in our city. The transactions in our great staple for the year under review have been made on a scale of prices the very reverse of that which marked prices the preceding year. In 1850 the prices steadily advanced; in 1851, they as steadily declined. . . . A declining market is one in which the dealers suffer more or less. But whatever may have been their losses, not a single disastrous failure has occurred among our merchants. . . . A decline of 5 or 5¾ cents per pound in the price of cotton necessarily affects all interests in a country and a commodity so dependent on this article for their prosperity as we are in Alabama. But in the face of this adverse influence our city has advanced in population, wealth and prosperity. New branches of industry have been introduced, and the activity of those before established increased. The cotton factories . . . are now in successful operation, and turning out thousands of yards of goods weekly. Our anticipations of the advancement of the Mobile and Ohio Railroad have been nearly met, and the cars will be running to Citronelle, thirty-three miles, by Christmas. . . . The number of buildings completed is greater than any preceding year, and still, so great is the demand for them, rents are advancing. Public buildings are now under contract in the city, the estimated cost of which is over half a million dollars. Nine new steamboats are also building for the Mobile trade the coming season. Much of this city activity is doubtless owing to the increase in the receipts of cotton at this port of over 100,000 bales, and to the uninterrupted health which has uniformly prevailed.

Cotton.—At the commencement of the year under review, middling cotton sold at 12½ & 12⅝ cents; it closes with middlings at 8 cents. Market dull and inactive. This fall has been experienced without the agency of any disturbing cause in Europe, and seems to have been brought about solely by the operation of the laws of supply and demand. The receipts of cotton at this port for the year ending today are 433,646 bales, against 332,896 bales last year—being an increase of 100,850 bales. The stock on hand is 27,797 bales. The amount exported reaches 418,525 bales, being an increase of 92,984 bales. The crop of the United States will be about 2,350,000 bales; that of last year was 2,096,706 bales. . . .

Of the receipts at this port, 480 bales are new crop—401 bales from the Alabama and 79 from the Bigbee river, against 91 received at the same date last year. . . .

Lumber, Timber, and Staves.—. . . The exports in these matters have fallen off to some extent from those of last year. There has not been as much lumber shipped by about 450,000 feet, as much timber by about one-half, and the exports of staves last year doubled those of the season just closed. While the exports of lumber to Cuba and to Mexican ports are larger, the deficiency to coastwise and to other foreign ports make the total deficiency upwards of 450,000 feet. . . . There has been very little variation in prices, $9 per M. having been the ruling rate for assorted cargoes of lumber throughout the past year. . . .

Naval Stores.—The trade in these articles has been carried on for about three or four years, and with marked success. A better article of spirits of turpentine is now made, and improvements have also been made in the manufacture of the other articles, so that they command a higher price than heretofore. Our receipts have been mostly disposed of by shipments made to New Orleans, St. Louis, and New York, at prices ranging from 37½ @ 50 cents per gallon for spirits turpentine; 18 @ 20c per gallon for bright varnish; $1.50 @ $1.75 per bbl. for crude turpentine; $1.10 @ $2.50 for rosin, Nos. 1 and 2; $2 @ 2.25 per bbl for tar; $1.75 per bbl for pitch. Total receipts for season 1,133 bbls. spirits turpentine, 205 do. crude, 4595 do. rosin, 358 do. tar, 131 do. pitch, 20 do. bright varnish.

Comparative Exports of Cotton from Port of Mobile, from September 1 to date, in the following years:

	G. Britain	France	Other Foreign Ports	U. S.
1851	250,118	46,005	26,373	96,029
1850	162,189	39,973	11,972	111,452
1849	290,836	63,290	44,525	140,993
1848	228,329	61,812	29,070	120,350
1847	131,156	39,293	19,784	116,674
1846	208,047	66,821	26,824	115,164
1845	269,037	68,789	52,811	130,701
1844	204,242	49,611	15,885	195,714
1843	285,029	53,645	26,903	113,768

—*DeBow's Review,* December 1851, pp. 647–48.

Mobile harbor was shallow and sea-going vessels had to lie some thirty miles below the city, but as an agricultural market it had a thriving business. As a modern scholar pointed out, Mobile had shipped 13,355,588 bales of cotton from 1817 to 1861. This was not a one-way traffic because the merchants shipped agricultural supplies upstream. This made business for many factors and commission merchants.

In 1859 cotton and supplies were bought and sold by more than 150 factors and commission agents. In the same year the city supported 3 local banks and 16 insurance companies. Steamboats were making more than 700 official landings or stops along the Alabama, Tombigbee, and Warrior rivers. Six pilot boats and 23 pilots were working the waters in and near the city. Three lighthouses were in operation and between 1826 and 1857 the federal government appropriated more than $200,000 to improve the harbor. The Mobile and Ohio Railroad, projected by Mobile business leaders, was in operation, and the Mobile and Ohio Telegraph Company was incorporated in 1859. At various times during the 1850's consuls representing 16 foreign governments were stationed in the city.—Weymouth T. Jordan, *Antebellum Alabama: Town and Country* (Tallahassee, Florida: The Florida State University, 1957), pp. 20–21.

To conclude that Alabamians gave all their attention to cotton is a gross mistake.

Infant Industries

There were no factories in Alabama that compared with those in the northeast, but there were some. The products going through the port of Mobile, and those used at home, were made by amateurs in small quantities. *DeBow's Review* encouraged experimenters to report their methods and successes as an incentive to others, always hoping to balance the economy.

The almost unlimited stands of pine timber in the southern part of the state led to efforts to produce tar, turpentine and resin. Although turpentine manufacture was in its infancy, C. Krout reported that he made 150 barrels of turpentine in 1849.

PRODUCTION OF TURPENTINE IN ALABAMA

I herewith comply with your request and give you such information as I think would be of interest to those who design engaging in the turpentine business. Select about 200 acres to the hand where it is well timbered with pitch pine—it should be as level as possible. Commence cutting boxes about the first of November, and be careful to have them all one size—say to hold about a quart. You may cut from 1 to 3 boxes in a tree, according to the size of your trees. A hand can cut from 50 to 100 boxes per day—but a green hand could not average more than 60 or 65 per day. You may continue cutting boxes till the sap begins to rise, which is generally about the first or middle of March. You will then divide your boxes—8,000 to the hand—and proceed to gauging your trees which is done with the common broad ax. Here you ought to be very particular that you get your gauge deep and the face wide enough. The gauge ought to be about 1½ inches deep and the face 18 or 20 inches wide. One hand ought to gauge 300 boxes per day. After you are done gauging, which will be about the first of April, your boxes will then be full and ready for dipping, unless there has been a very severe winter. After the first dipping you should commence round shaving and round shave about once a week until the boxes have again filled, which will be about four weeks, provided you have good trees and an ordinary season. . . . If the work is well done, you ought to get 40 or 50 barrels at a dipping; one hand can dip six barrels per day.

The season is for eight months, and in that time you will get six dippings, which will yield, at a safe calculation, 200 barrels to the hand.

If you wish to distill the crude turpentine, you ought to have your still up by the first of April, and distill as fast as you gather it, as it will yield more spirits and make better resin. The still should be located on some stream where water could be conveyed to the condensing tube without carrying by hand. The barrels for the spirits should be of the best quality, made of well seasoned white oak, iron hooped, and well glued inside with three coats of glue. . . . The crude turpentine will yield from 6 to 8 gallons spirits per barrel, owing to how soon it is distilled, its cleanness, and a sufficiency of cold water. The general calculation is 5 gallons crude to 1 of spirits. . . .—*DeBow's Review,* December 1849, pp. 560, 562, quoting the *Mobile Planter.*

There were other attempts to use the abundant supply of virgin timber; carpenters, cabinet makers and other skilled workmen made furniture, spinning wheels, handles for axes, hoes, shovels, and other tools and farm machinery. Almost all of these establishments were small. It would be many years before Alabamians (along with other Americans) would come to appreciate the true value of their woodlands.

COTTON INDUSTRY

Processing cotton began in Alabama as early as 1796. In December of that year, Benjamin Hawkins, Indian agent, visited the farm of Robert Grierson near Hillibees in eastern Alabama where he found Grierson's half-breed family (and the Indian women he could hire) picking cotton. He noted that Grierson had a "treadle-gin, well made, sent to him from Providence, [Rhode Island]." It should be noted that this was only three years after Eli Whitney had invented his gin. The Pierce brothers at Tensas left school teaching to erect a gin in 1799 and Abraham Mordicai (either a Jew or Pennsylvania Dutchman) built one near Coosada on the Tallapoosa River in 1802. Thereafter, new gins were established rapidly wherever cotton was raised.

The honor of putting cotton that was ginned in Alabama to commercial use apparently goes to Charles Cabiness and Company whose spinning factory was near Huntsville. It advertised its wares in early 1818.

COTTON SPINNING FACTORY
Charles Cabiness and Co.

Respectfully informs their friends and the public in general, that they have their Cotton Factory now in complete operation, and will sell thread at the following prices:

400	at	$0.50	per pound
500	at	0.62½	per pound
600	at	0.75	per pound
700	at	0.87½	per pound
800	at	1.00	per pound
900	at	1.12½	per pound
1000	at	1.25	per pound

N.B. They will also exchange thread for raw cotton.

Robert Fletcher, Manager
—*Alabama Republican*, February 17, 1818.

Although raw cotton was turned into thread for sale during the territorial period, it was not until later that the state had a cotton factory of any great significance. The best known of these early mills was Bell Factory incorporated by Patton-Donegan and Company in 1832. It was reportedly called the Bell Factory because a bell rather than a whistle was used to mark the work day. It was located some ten miles northeast of Huntsville on Flint River; water power was used to operate its three thousand spindles and one hundred looms. A typescript in the Huntsville Public Library states that slave labor was used "almost exclusively" in the operation of the mills. Whether the factory owned some of the slaves or hired all of them is not clear but in 1827 two Negroes (a boy and a girl) belonging to Ezek Moore were hired for $70 (plus clothing) for twelve months. This date indicates that the mill was operating before it was incorporated. It produced sheetings, osnaburgs, ticking, and yarns. It operated, under successive owners, until 1885.

The oldest cotton mills in operation today are in Tallassee. Chartered by the Alabama legislature in 1841 as the Tallassee Falls Manufacturing Company, they were erected on the east bank of the Tallapoosa River. The charter was made to Barent DuBoise ("a Frenchman of mixed blood") Heckerson Burnham and their associates but Thomas M. Barnett and William M. Marks were responsible for the industrial development of Tallassee. It is interesting to local historians that Benjamin Hawkins, in 1798, had described the site as ideal for an industrial town. It had building stone, a fall in the river of ten feet in twenty feet that would produce unlimited water power. The narrow, flat margin between the hills and the river was convenient he said for a canal for the mills on an extensive scale.

The Tallassee mills manufactured both cotton and wool yarn and cloth. In 1854 highest cash prices were offered for raw wool. According to an ad, the mill had one woolen machine in operation and would manufacture linsey or twilled jeans on shares or for cash. Two years later the company ran an ad which said:

Terms for Manufacture
For making all wool sent into light or heavy linsey as directed, 15¢ per yd. Making all twilled jeans, 20¢ per yd., or make up one half wool sent us and take other for pay.—Unidentified newspaper ad, quoted in Virginia Noble Golden, *A History of Tallassee for Tallasseeans* (Tallassee, Ala.: Tallassee Mills, 1949), p. 21.

In the last year, the notice said, the mill had doubled its capacity.

During the decade before the Civil War, the textile mill prospered. The company, as a service to the community, operated grist and flour mills, a saw mill, a gin, a foundry, and a blacksmith shop. During the crucial war years, the mill took farm supplies like bacon in lieu of money which it turned over to the Confederacy. For the first two years of the war the plant manufactured cloth for uniforms and thereafter became an armory for the manufacture of carbines for the Confederate army. Unlike the Bell Factory, the Tallassee mills used free white labor from the neighboring small farms.

The paternalism that became characteristic of the southern textile industry was already present in Alabama as the description of the Scottsville village shows.

AN ALABAMA MANUFACTURING VILLAGE

There is an entire village in Alabama devoted exclusively to manufactures. It is called Scottsville and is situated in the northwestern portion of Bibb County, near the river Cahawba, between Centerville and Tuscaloosa and to the southeast of the latter place, some fifty or sixty miles. . . .

Scottsville was originally known as the Tuscaloosa Manufacturing Company. It was incorporated by the Alabama Legislature in 1837 with a capital stock of $36,000 which sum was quickly subscribed by a number of capitalists in Tuscaloosa.

In May, 1837, the mills got to work, making coarse cotton cloths, but for some years made no money. The company and the locality soon changed names and management; the latter coming into the hands of Mr. Scott as principal owner and director; and the place itself took the name of Scottsville. He immediately went to work making improvements and additions to the buildings and machinery and the mills soon paid dividends. The first $2,200, realized in 1841, was expended in a family of Negroes to work in the factory. The family has so increased that the company values them at $10,000, and most of them are now working in the factory and are very useful. The company have made several purchases of Negroes with the profits of the factory, and Negro labor is much employed by them.

The principal mill is a large brick building of three stories with two wings, filled with the best machinery, and employing over one hundred hands, of whom three-fourths are females. A large overshot wheel, driven by water, is the principal motor of the machinery. There are about 25,000 spindles and 50 looms at work.

Wool and cotton are both spun. The consumption of cotton averages 35,000 pounds per month, and $1,000 worth of yarns in the same time, together with a large quantity of linseys and a superior article of sewing thread.

In 1841, the sum of $40,000 capital stock had been paid in. Every year since then a dividend of ten per cent has been declared which has been laid out in buying Negroes, land, &c, adding to the buildings and machinery in the village, until the capital stock has increased to $117,000, of which $25,000 is in Negroes, and about $16,000 in goods in the company's store.

The company owns 3,000 acres of land and all the buildings on the place, which consist of the factory, a large hotel, a store, blacksmith, carpenter, wheelwright, and boot and shoe shops, a saw mill, grist mill, large flouring mill, a church, and a large number of cottages. No liquor is permitted in the village, and the company will not sell an inch of its land to any one. Its stock has long been over par, and its dividends this year will be at least twelve per cent.—*DeBow's Review,* December 18, 1858, p. 717.

Balancing Agriculture With Industry

It was widely accepted in all parts of the South that the North prospered at the expense of the South by manufacturing the goods the South had to buy. Daniel Pratt, one of the strongest advocates of home industries, became Alabama's first great industrialist and made Prattville the best known industrial center before the war. A transplanted "Yankee" from New Hampshire, he settled in Autauga County in 1838.

A representative of the *Cotton Planter,* published by Dr. N. B. Cloud in Montgomery from 1853 on, visited Daniel Pratt in Prattville and gave a full description of his extensive operations. The reporter may well have been the editor himself.

A DAY WITH DANIEL PRATT

Mr. Pratt had long, long ago invited us to visit him and examine his manufacturing establishment at Prattville, in Autauga county, some fourteen miles west of Montgomery. . . . Prattville is a thrify and handsomely situated manufacturing village, on Autauga creek, about four miles from Washington, on the Alabama river. This village has been built up by the industry and energy of Mr. Daniel Pratt, mainly, whose name it bears, within the last few years, probably eighteen. We arrived at Prattville as the sun was going down, when everything inanimate, with the operatives in the various factory departments, were, with the setting sun, closing the performances of the day. We found Mr. Pratt at home with his family, with whom we spent the evening to a late hour, in various conversations on the subject of agricultural improvement, agricultural machinery and Southern manufacturing, in all of which Mr. Pratt is deeply and practically interested. And we found Mrs. Pratt also, who is a lady of unusual intelligence and social vivacity, instructingly interesting on every subject appertaining to improvements about the homestead, such as tastefully arranged shrubbery, fine fruit and vegetable gardens and terraced vineyards, which contribute so essentially to the comfort, content and true pleasure of home, sweet home!

In the morning we commenced early after breakfast, as we had a great day's work before us. We spent the first hour in Mr. Pratt's gallery of paintings. Many hours we could have remained there, had time permitted, in contemplating the canvassed scenes of passed grandeur and greatness. Its beauty cannot be appreciated in description, however; it must be seen to be fully enjoyed. From the gallery we proceeded to the gin factory, which one of Prattville might easily imagine to be the pet of Mr. Pratt's ambition.

As you enter the door of the first floor you have in full view a line of shafting 250 feet long, on which, at suitable distances apart, are over seventy drums for driving the various machines used in the manufacture of gins. This room is 250 by 50 feet, fitted with machines adapted to the different kinds of work and material employed in the construction of gins.

The second floor is used for breasting and finishing gins. It has a large room partitioned off for the purpose of testing gins with seed cotton. Fifty pounds are run through each gin, and a note made of the time required to gin it. If the speed is not sufficient, or there is any other defect found in the performance, it is remedied at once. No gin is allowed to leave the shop until it performs satisfactorily.

The third floor is all in one room—probably the largest in the State— 250 by 50 feet. Here the gins are painted and varnished, and put in order for boxing and shipping. There is an elevator large enough to receive the gins, which raises and lowers them from one floor to another by the aid of machinery.

In the garret is a cistern, kept full of water, which is raised from a spring underneath the shop by machinery. From this cistern each room is supplied with pure cold water by means of pipes. The waste water from the cistern is conveyed to the centre of the square in front of the shop, where it jets thirty feet, and falls into a large circular reservoir.

Connected with the gin shop by a railway is a brick lumber-house, 172 feet long by 40 feet wide. In this house the lumber for manufacturing the gin stands is carefully stacked away, where it remains two years to season before it is used. An iron foundry is also connected with the shop, which works up about a hundred tons of iron annually. The gin shop turns out about $160,000 worth of gins annually.

Adjoining the gin shop is a brick building, three stories high and 250 feet long, which is used for a grist-mill, a sash, door and blind factory, a machine shop, a shop for making horse mills, and a carriage and wagon shop, all furnished with suitable machinery for these various branches of business the machinery in both buildings is driven by one breast wheel of sixty-horse power.

There are fifty hands actively employed all the time in the gin factory and foundry together, many of whom are slaves, that seem to be well skilled in the performance of this work.

There is also quite an extensive and flourishing cotton factory here, a large share of the stock of which is owned by Mr. Pratt. It contains twenty-eight hundred spindles, one hundred looms, and is worked by one hundred and fifty hands, several of them slaves. It works up twelve hundred bales of cotton, and turns out two thousand bales of osnaburgs annually. The company contemplate at an early period putting up a new and greatly enlarged building for increasing their spindles and looms.

At a short distance below the gin factory—perhaps a half mile—Mr. Pratt has fitted up a large two-story brick building, in which he has already received and is putting up machinery of the latest improvement for carding and spinning wool, to be manufactured into kerseys, in another department of the cotton factory.

After examining the various factories and machinery, we took a stroll with Mr. Pratt through his garden, orchard and vineyard, where we found the same skill, industry and improvement of the soil; in a rich and well-cultivated vegetable garden, a beautiful orchard of fine fruit trees, embracing various varieties of the apple, peach, pear, plum and fig, all healthful and thrifty, and a vineyard of perhaps three to five acres of Scuppernongs and Catawbas, terraced in the most picturesque style to the summit level of a high and very steep hill, perhaps one hundred feet or more perpendicular, the upper terrace above the lower or first. The vines are all kept up by castiron posts, set along on the terraced embankments, and wire railings from post to post. This vineyard plat, so favorably located, contains, in all, twenty-five acres of land, and enclosed by a substantial brick and picket fence.

From the vineyard we returned to the mansion, where Mrs. Pratt had prepared for us an elegant dinner, with which we had the pleasure of testing several specimens of fine Autauga wine, the pure juice of the grape, and fruit of the vineyard we had just before examined. Of this wine Mrs. Pratt had several casks, the vintage of last year.

Thus closed one of the most interesting social visits it had been our good fortune to enjoy for years past.

Of Mr. Pratt's gins, we can say to our readers in want of a first-rate stand, unhesitatingly—and we say so without prejudicing any other factory—that, with all his late improvements and the advantages afforded by his large factory arrangements, he is able to furnish the neatest, most complete and best cotton gin stand in America.—*The Cotton Planter,* n.d. quoted in Mrs. S.F.H. Tarrant, ed., *Hon. Daniel Pratt* (Richmond, Va.: Whittet and Shepperson, 1904), pp. 62–66.

The gin works sustained the reputation set by Mr. Pratt and eventually became the Continental Gin Company of the twentieth century.

The extent of Mr. Pratt's interests is further illustrated by his own statement of the business done in one year.

The following is a statement of the business of Prattville for the year 1857:

Cotton Gin Manufactory,	$144,000 00
Prattville Manufacturing Co.,	151,724 00
Sash, Door and Blind Manufactory,	13,360 00
Corn Mill (Horse-Power),	17,160 00
Foundry,	11,432 00
Carriage,	6,500 00
Tin,	3,050 00
Machine and Blacksmith's Shops,	8,694 00
Printing Business,	8,000 00
Mercantile Business,	155,249 00
Total,	$519,169. 00

DANIEL PRATT

Prattville, January, 1858.—From an advertisement issued by Pratt, quoted in ibid., p. 68.

By 1850, Alabama had 12 cotton mills, employing 715 people and processing 5,208 bales of cotton each year. Ten years later the number of mills was only 14 but the amount of cotton being raised had doubled and the number of workers had increased. Alabama was making strides in textile manufacturing, by 1860 ranking fourth among the southern states, but even then the state (along with the other southern states) was doing little to free its residents from their dependence on northern goods.

MINING

Coal and iron are the best known of the many minerals to be found in the state. A mineral that attracted much more attention for a time however was gold. Although the amount extracted was never great (probably not over a total of a million dollars) in comparison to other gold fields, it was an important factor in east central Alabama in the 1830's and 1840's.

It is ironic that De Soto and his forces, looking for gold, tramped over the very lands where it was hidden. There is no evidence that the Spanish discovered it. Apparently, however, later intruders on Indian lands did find it in promising amounts. The exact date when it was discovered, or by whom, seems to be unknown but it was shortly before the New Echota treaty (1832), while negotiations were going on. In fact, the discovery of the precious metal may have hastened the cession of Creek lands. The first gold rush (1835–36) centered in Cleburne County at Arbacoochee where there were deposits on some six hundred acres. Michael Toumey, the first state geologist, reported that the placer mines employed 600 workers and supported a community of 5000 persons. In 1842, a rich outcropping was found at a place that became known as Goldville in Tallapoosa County. The mines, which are still there, were worked down to the water level before they were abandoned. There were dozens of small mines, usually known by the owner's name or the Indian term for the area, worked in Cleburne, Talladega, Clay, Randolph, Tallapoosa, Coosa and Chilton counties. Most of the deposits had been exhausted or abandoned as uneconomical by 1850. When word of the rich strikes in California reached the east, many of the seasoned gold miners from Alabama and Georgia went west, becoming the nucleus of the "49 ers."

COAL AND IRON

Before 1860 the great mineral beds in the Birmingham area were as yet undeveloped and largely undiscovered. Nevertheless, mining in other parts of the state was being developed which, while never extensive, proved to be of great worth to the Confederacy during the 1860's.

In the antebellum period little use was made of coal. Mobile and Montgomery residents, for example, preferred to heat their homes with wood fires. This preference prompted one coal producer to send a workman along with a barge of coal to show Mobilians how to make fires with it. Blacksmiths, however, used most of it. Coal was being produced in Jasper County around Cordova (Warrior field) and in Bibb and Shelby Counties (Cahaba field). Tradition has it that Montevallo white ash coal was the first coal sold in Alabama under a trade name.

IRON

Alabama from its earliest days had many blacksmiths. According to Ethel Armes they used imported bar iron for making horseshoes and other essentials of a frontier society. Not until Alabama Territorial days did this region begin producing its own raw iron. In

1818 a blast furnace at Cedar Creek was opened and the commercial production of pig iron was begun.

Cedar Creek furnace was in Franklin County some three miles from Russellville. It was on a tract of land that a scout for General Andrew Jackson had spotted as having mining potential. Joseph Heslip, however, an iron worker who seemingly had no connection with the Jackson scout, opened these first iron works. He bought the land directly from the federal government (it having just passed into government hands through the Chickasaw Cession of 1818) for $2.00 an acre. Heslip selected a furnace site on a sharp bend of the creek where there were quick rapids and began construction of his "rough jacket-clad" furnace.

> This furnace was rudely constructed . . . . It must have been lined inside with some kind of fireproof brick, but certain it is that the greater portion of the building was limestone rock quarried from the bluffs near by. The furnace proper was somewhat conical in shape, being from twenty-five to thirty feet in diameter at the base and narrowing at a height of about twenty-five feet into a short smokestack. The furnace and smokestack together were not over fifty feet high. The blast which heated the furnace was supplied by a kind of bellows run by water power. One of the most interesting features of the plant was a large forge hammer weighing five hunded pounds. It was lifted by water power and let fall by its own weight upon the piece of iron to be forged, thus doing the work . . . later done by the rolling mills.—Ethel Armes, *The Story of Coal and Iron in Alabama* (Birmingham, Ala.: The Chamber of Commerce, 1910), p. 28, quoting L. K. Pounder.

This huge hammer was used to break up the boulders of iron ore that were too bulky for the furnace. Nearly a century later there were people who remembered the "incessant throb and ring of the big hammer, sounding day and night over the country for miles and miles."

Within a short time, Mr. Heslip added a Catalan forge, a foundry, and a crude sort of rolling mill, warehouses, and tenants' shacks. In the beginning he used surface ore (Lafayette formation limonite) that the farmers were glad to give away to get out of their fields. State geologist Toumey later pronounced the ore of excellent quality but observed the ore below the surface was superior to the loose boulders.

From this simple beginning developed the great iron industry in Alabama. By 1850, as reported by *DeBow's Review*, the industry had grown considerably.

IRON AND OTHER MINERAL PRODUCTS OF ALABAMA

At this moment the manufacture of iron is attracting the attention of our citizens, and as so much depends on a good beginning, these hints are offered with the view of directing inquiry in the proper channel. . . .

There are eight bloomeries in the state, two of them are on Talladega Creek, and the others on the waters of the Cahawba.

Of the two high furnaces, one is in Bibb Cunty; it has but recently been erected, so that its operations are, as yet, confined to the manufacture of pig iron and hollow ware; the blast is urged by steam power, and the boiler is heated directly from the trundle head. These works are situated within eight or ten miles of the Coosa, and from the convenience and good quality of the ore, and the abundance of fuel, they can scarcely fail of success, under ordinary good management.

The Benton works are situated on Crane Creek, a short distance from the river; they have been for years in successful operation. An extension of the works, the introduction of the hot blast, and various other improvements are contemplated, which, when accomplished, will place this among the most complete establishment in the South. The following brief statement was furnished by one of the proprietors:

Polkville, Benton Co. Alabama
September 26, 1849

"We have a blast furnace, a puddling furnace, and a forge in operation. We turn out daily about 6000 pounds of iron; 2000 pounds of which are put into hollow ware and machinery castings; 2000 pounds into bar iron, and 2000 into pigs. We use 600 bushels of charcoal every 24 hours. Our iron ore beds (some of them) are within 600 yards of the furnace. Our limestone is at the furnace and in abundance. The nearest stone coal beds that have been worked are thirteen miles off. We are now preparing to put up a rolling mill, and think that in a short time we will be able to roll iron successfully. Our establishment is five miles east of the Coosa River, opposite the Ten Islands, and eleven miles from Greensport. We ship our iron down the Coosa in flat boats to Wetumpka, Montgomery, and Mobile. We have found the articles we produce here of ready sale in either of those markets. We are prepared to make, turn off and fit up all kinds of machinery, except fine castings for cotton mills, and will be very soon ready to furnish these."

[The article also reports on other minerals in Alabama: beds of red ochre near Bucksville; lead ore in Clarke and Benton Counties; peroxide of manganese in great quantities; limestone and marble around Montevallo, Six Mile, Tuscaloosa, Jonesborough, and on Big Sandy Creek.]—*DeBow's Review,* October 1851, p. 717.

Dr. Charles G. Summersell summarizes the number of ironworks at the outbreak of the Civil War.

In 1860 there were four furnaces making pig iron, four foundries making cast iron and 27 manufacturers of sheet iron, tin, and copper products. In addition there were 18 manufacturers of agricultural implements, many of which were of iron. The leading counties in iron manufacturing were Benton, later called Calhoun (which contained the Cane Creek Iron Works), Talladega (where the Riddle Brothers made iron castings), Bibb (Little Cahaba Furnace), Cherokee (Round Mountain Furnace), Lamar (Hale and Murdock Furnace), Tuscaloosa (Tannehill Furnace), and Shelby (Shelby Iron Works).—C. G. Summersell, *Alabama History for Schools* (Northport, Alabama: Colonial Press, 1961), p. 222.

These were not all of the furnaces but do give an indication of parts of Alabama where iron was being produced.

As has been said so many times, agriculture was more important than all the manufacturing that was done in the antebellum period. Nevertheless by 1860 there were 7,889 workers in 1,459 manufacturing plants (most of them no more than shops) which had a capital investment of $9,000,000. While the number of both workers and plants was on the increase, the average factory had no more than five employees.

Travel and Transportation

ON WATER

Those of us living in the twentieth century find it exceedingly difficult to imagine a time, a mere two centuries ago, when all travel was by footpath or water. Since Alabama had an abundance of navigable streams and travel on them was easy and quick, early Alabamians used water whenever possible. Instead of being barriers, streams were bonds that held widely separated settlements together. A recent visitor to the site of old St. Stephens remarked on the inaccessibility of the spot. "Why in the world," he asked, "did they choose a place so far from everywhere?" The answer, of course, is that at the head of schooner traffic on the Tombigbee River, St. Stephens in 1789 was the center of the Alabama upcountry. On other rivers a similar break in water transportation was responsible for the establishment of Claiborne, Tuscaloosa, Montgomery, Florence, and Wetumpka.

Indians plied the streams with their canoes and dugouts and crossed the large streams on crude ferries. Early European pioneers used the same methods but by the American period they were transporting their goods downstream on flatboats, and on keelboats (larger, better built, and more expensive) if they had to take goods on the return trip. If at all possible, the boatmen went back home on foot because poling the keelboat upstream was not only backbreaking, it was time-consuming. A boat could float downstream from Montgomery to Mobile in about two weeks, but it took from four to six weeks to make the trip back. Consequently, Alabamians, and especially those in the northern half of the state, often bought their goods from Charleston which could be brought through Georgia by way of the Federal Road, or down one of the tributaries of the Tennessee River to within a few miles of the headwaters of the Coosa River. In the dry summer months the rapids at Muscle Shoals posed a problem, but when water was high they could be navigated, even by steamboats.

It is interesting to note that proposals to unite the Tennessee River with the Gulf of Mexico were made as early as the territorial period. Instead of trying to connect the Tennessee with the Tombigbee in the western part of the state as is being done in the 1970's, the residents of eastern Tennessee and western Virginia, as well as Alabamians, favored joining the Hiwassee with the Coosa. This was not deemed impossible since the portage between the two rivers was a mere twelve miles. In 1824, John C. Calhoun, Secretary of War, reported on the Hiwassee-Coosa canal but it was judged of less importance than the Muscle Shoals canal and it "died a lingering death." The canal around the shoals was dug. On February 24, 1837, the *North Alabamian* (Tuscumbia), announced that they were happy to learn that the canal was "ready for the reception of the water." All that remained to be done before the canal could be opened was to obtain some iron fixtures for the locks which were then being prepared. The editors congratulated all those who had had a part in completing that portion of the canal which would "obviate the most of the formidable obstructions on the muscle shoals" and inspire other enterprising men to finish the "whole improvement according to the original plan of Congress." However, it was never a navigable success.

The hazards of navigating the shoals were pointed out in a letter to the editor of this same paper. It had been reported that the steamer *Hark-Away* had passed the rapids and was on its way to Knoxville. An unsigned member of the crew, probably the pilot, wrote:

> On Saturday we made a start to go through the muscle shoals. We were three days going over Shoal Creek bar and one day and night going over Poor Horse bar. We attempted to go further, but the water was falling so fast that Capt. Russell concluded it would be better to lay up immediately above Poor Horse bar than run the risk of going further and striking on the rocks. Where she is lying now there is a smooth gravel bar, and I expect she is out of danger of straining herself if properly attended to.—*North Alabamian* (Tuscumbia), March 17, 1837.

With the advent of the steamboat, conditions were vastly different. Goods and people could be transported upstream as easily as down. There seems to be some question as to the exact date a steamboat first appeared on Alabama waters but it was before 1819 when the *Mobile*, built in Boston, went up the Tombigbee as far Demopolis. Dr. Charles G. Summersell says that the St. Stephens Steamboat Company built the *Alabama* at St. Stephens in 1818 and that the *Tensas* was built in Blakeley the next year. Thereafter new boats and new routes were frequent. The *Harriet* (1821–1822) could make the trip from Mobile to Montgomery in five and one-half days, even after making the necessary stops. Steamboats were the most dependable form of transportation in antebellum Alabama and, carrying both passengers and freight, contributed much to the economic and social life of the state.

Some of the boats were small and unimpressive; others were commodious and luxuriant. The *Amaranth,* on which Sir Charles Lyell rode on the Alabama River in the 1840's, was in the latter class.

> . . . A vessel of such dimensions [as the Amaranth] makes a grand appearance in a river so narrow as the Alabama at Montgomery. . . . The principal cabins run the whole length of the ship on a deck above that on which the machinery is placed, and where the cotton is piled up. The upper deck is chiefly occupied with a handsome saloon, about 200 feet long, the ladies' cabin at one end, opening into it with folding doors. Sofas, rocking-chairs, tables, and a stove are placed in this room, which is lighted by windows from above. On each side of it is a row of sleeping apartments, each communicating by one door with the saloon, while the other leads out to the guard, as they call it, a long balcony or gallery, covered with a shade or verandah, which passes around the whole boat. The second class, or deck passengers, sleep where they can on the lower floor, where besides the engine and the cotton there are prodigious heaps of wood, which are devoured with marvellous rapidity by the furnace, and are as often restored at the different lands, a set of negroes being purposely hired for that work.
>
> These steamers, nothwithstanding their size, drew very little water. . . . They cannot quite realize the boast of a Western captain, 'that he could sail wherever it was damp; but I was assured that some of them could float in two-foot water. The high-pressure steam escapes into the air by a succession of explosions alternately from the pipes of the two engines. It is a most unearthly sound, like that of some huge monster gasping for breath; and when they clear the boilers of the sediment collected from the river water, it is done by a loud and protracted discharge of steam. . . . Every stranger who has heard of fatal accidents by the bursting of boilers believes, the first time he hears this tremendous noise, that it is all over with him and is surprised to see that his companions evince no alarm. . . .—Sir Charles Lyell, *Second Visit to the United States* (London: J. Murray, 1849), vol. 2, p. 46.

Most of the early steamboats were woodburning sidewheelers, requiring little space in which to turn, a distinct advantage at sharp bends in the river.

Cotton, of course, was the most important item of freight carried

on the steamers. Passengers often complained that so many bales
were taken on deck that they were cramped for space. Even more
passengers were impressed with the skill with which Negro dock-
hands loaded the cotton. Charles Lanman, an Englishman, described
the scene at Claiborne.

[There were no less than two hundred landings where cotton was
taken aboard steamers between Montgomery and Mobile.] In the time of
high freshets, however, the lowlanders, who constitute the majority, are
compelled to haul their cotton for shipment to the bluffs of their more
fortunate neighbors, the highlanders. Upon these spots are generally
erected spacious ware-houses, some of which are shed-like in their appearance and a hundred yards long; while others built up from the ordinary watermark, are many stories high. Long and steeply-inclined
planes are necessary appendages to all these storehouses, down which
the heavy bales are slidden with wonderful dexterity by the plantation
negroes, and tiered up on the steamers by the negro boatmen to the
number sometimes of two thousand bales. To the traveller who is in a
hurry, this important business of taking on cotton is a great bore, but to
those who can take pleasure in witnessing athletic feats, or have a taste
for the picturesque, it is full of interest. The negroes, as individuals or
in gangs, are always amusing to contemplate or talk with, and it needs
but little sagacity to discover that, if they are low in intellect, they are
often far from deficient in humanity and moral culture which cannot
always be said of the plantation overseers and steamboat mates who
superintend the loading of cotton. The whole aspect of an Alabama bluff
when a steamer is shipping cotton at night is truly beautiful; for then
it is that pitch-pine torches illuminate the entire scene and, while the
gay passengers are dancing and feasting in the gilded saloon of the
steamer, the loud and plaintive singing of the negroes give animation
and cheerfulness to all whose lot it is to toil. In managing the heavy
bales the negroes invariably work in pairs, and an iron hook, which
each man always carries about his person, is the unmistakable badge
of his profession. A hard time of it for a few weeks in the winter do
these fellows have; but then they seem to be quite happy. Hardly ever,
for even an hour, are they permitted to sleep undisturbed upon their
own beds, the cotton bales, and at all times are they summoned by the
perpetually ringing bells to their severe labor. They are well-fed, however; and I notice that they were usually supplied with a moderate but
comfortable quantity of grog. Their wages vary from thirty to thirty-five
dollars per month, with one dollar and a half for Sunday wages. The
freight upon a bale of cotton for any distance is one dollar.—Charles
Lanman *Adventures in the Wilds of America* (Philadelphia: J. W.
Moore, 1858), vol. 2, pp. 167–68.

An exciting by-product of steamboating was rivalry between
captains which resulted in an occasional race such as took place
between the *Senator* and *Southern Republic* on the Alabama River.

Almost imperceptibly our speed slackens, the thin dark column creeps nearer round the trees on the point in our wake; at last the steamer bursts into sight, not a pistol shot astern.

There is a sharp click of our pilot's bell, a gasping throb, as if our boat took a deep, long breath; and just as the "Senator" makes our wheel we dash ahead again, with every stroke of the piston threatening to rack our frail fabric into shreds.

The river here is pretty wide and the channel deep and clear. The "Senator" follows in gallant style, now gaining our quarter, now a boat's length astern—both engines roaring and snorting like angry hippopotami; both vessels rocking and straining til they seem to paw their way through the churned water.

Talk of horse-racing and rouge-et noir! But there is no excitement that can approach boat-racing on a southern river! One by one people pop up the ladders and throng the rails. First come the unemployed deck-hands, then a stray gentleman or two, and finally ladies and children, till the rail is full and every eye is anxiously strained to the opposite boat.

She holds her own wondrous well, considering the reputation of ours. At each burst, when she seems to gain on us, the crowd hold their breath; as she drops off again there is a deep-drawn, gasping sigh of relief, like wind in the pines. Even the colonel has roused himself from dreams of turtle at the St. Charles, and red fish at Pensacola; coming on deck in a shooting jacket and glengary cap, that make him look like a jaunty Fosco. He leans over the stern rail, smoking his cabana in long, easy whiffs as we gain a length; sending out short, angry puffs at the "Senator" as she creeps up on us.

Foot by foot, we gain steadily until the gap is widened to three or four boat-lengths, though the "Senator" piles her fires till the shores behind her glow from their reflection; and her decks—now black with anxious lookers-on—send up cheer after cheer, as she snorts defiantly after us.

Suddenly the bank seems to spring up right under our port bow! We have cut it too close! Two sharp, vicious clicks of the bell; our helm goes hard down and the engines stop with a sullen jar, as I catch a hissing curse through the set teeth of the pilot.

A yell of wild triumph rises from the rival's deck. On she comes in gallant style, shutting the gap and passing us like a race-horse, before we can swing into the channel and recover headway. It is a splendid sight as the noble boat passes us; her black bulk standing before out in the clear moonlight against the dim, gray banks like a living monster; her great chimneys snorting out volumes of massive black smoke that trail out level behind her, from the great speed. Her side toward us is crowded with men, women and children; hats, handkerchiefs and hands are swung madly about to aid the effort of the hundred voices.

Close down to the water's edge—scarce above the line of foam she cuts—her lower deck lies black and undefined in the shadow of the great mass above it. Suddenly it lights up with a lurid flash, as the furnace-doors swing wide open; and in the hot glare the negro stokers

—their stalwart forms jetty black, naked to the waist and streaming with exertion that makes the muscles strain out in great cords—show like the distorted imps of some pictured inferno. They, too, have imbibed the excitement. With every gesture of anxious haste and eyeballs starting from their dusky heads, some plunge the long brakes into the red mouths of the furnace, twisting and turning the crackling mass with terrific strength; others hurl in huge logs of resinous pine, already heated by contact till they burn like pitch. Then the great doors bang to; the Yo! ho! of the negroes dies away and the whole hull is blacker from the contrast; while the "Senator," puffing denser clouds than ever, swings round the point a hundred yards ahead!

There is a dead silence on our boat—silence so deep that the rough whisper of the pilot to the knot around him is heard the whole length of her deck: "Damnation! but I'll overstep her yit, or—bust!"

"Good old man!" responds Styles—"Let her out and I'll stand the wine!"

Then the old colonel walks to the wheel; his face purple, his glengary pushed back on his head, his cigar glowing like the "red eye of battle", as he puffs angry wheezes of smoke through his nostrills.

"Damned hard! sir—hard! Egad! I'd burn the last ham in the locker to overtake her!"—and he hurls the glowing stump after the "Senator," as the Spartan youth hurled their shields into the thick of the battle ere rushing to reclaim them.

On we speed, till the trees on the bank seem to fly back past us; and round the point to see the "Senator," just turning another curve!

On still, faster than ever, with every glass on board jingling in its frame; every joint and timber trembling, as though with a congestive chill!

Still the black demons below ply their fires with the fattest logs, and even a few barrels of rosin are slyly slipped in; the smoke behind us stretched straight and flat from the smoke-stack.

Now we enter a straight, narrow reach with the chase just before us. Faster—faster we go till the boat fairly rocks and swings from side to side, half lifted with every throb of the engine. Closer and closer we creep—harder and harder thump the cylinders—until at last we close; our bow just lapping her stern! So we run a few yards.

Little by little—so little that we test it by counting her windows—we reach her wheel—pass it—lock her bow, and run nose and nose for a hundred feet!

The stillness of death is upon both boats; not a sound but the creek and shudder as they struggle on. Suddenly the hard voice of our old pilot crashed through it like a broadaxe:

"Good-bye, Sen'tor! I'll send yer a tug!"—and he gives his bell a merry click.

Our huge boat gives one shuddering throb that racks her from end to end—one plunge—and then she settles into a steady rush and forges rapidly and evenly ahead. Wider and wider grows the gap; and we wind out of sight with the beaten boat five hundred yards behind us.

The cigar I take from my mouth, to make way for the deep, long sigh, is chewed to perfect pulp. A wild, pent-up yell of half-savage triumph goes up from the crowded deck; such as is heard nowhere besides, save where the captured work rewards the bloody and often repeated charge. Cheer after cheer follows; and, as we approach the thin column of smoke curling over the trees between us, Styles bestrides the prostrate form of the still sleeping professor and makes the calliope yell and shriek that classic ditty, "Old Gray Horse, come out of the Wilderness!" at the invisible rival.

I doubt if heartier toast was ever drunk than that the colonel gave the group around the wheel-house, where Styles "stood" the wine plighted the pilot. The veteran was beaming, the glengary sat jauntily on one side; and his voice actually gurgled as he said:

"Egad! I'd miss my dinner for a week for this! Gentlemen, a toast! Here's to the old boat! God bless her— —soul!"—Thomas C. DeLeon, *Four Years in Rebel Capitals* (Mobile: Gossip Printing Co., 1890), pp. 45–48.

Occasionally in such contests boats ran aground and boilers exploded. But the greatest tragedies were caused by fire. The *Alabama,* loaded with a considerable amount of gunpowder, burned to the water's edge at Mt. Vernon; the *General Brown* caught on fire at the foot of Dauphin Street in Mobile; the *H. L. Smith* with 60 passengers, 1000 bales of cotton and other freight aboard burned in the Chattahoochee with the loss of several lives. Probably the worst disaster was the burning of the *Eliza Battle* on the Tombigbee near Pickensville in December 1854.

About two hundred passengers boarded the ill-fated vessel in Columbus, Mississippi, that eventful day and a few others joined at later stops. Some were couples who married in time to take advantage of the excursion for a wedding trip to Mobile. This was a gala occasion; the luxury boat boasted well-appointed staterooms, a large ballroom, and it was decorated with banners and lights. There were two bands aboard to provide music for the dancing that began at twilight. The boat was obviously overloaded.

And the pilot was frankly worried. This had been a good cotton year and the lower decks of the *Eliza Battle* were piled to the top with bales for the Mobile market. A heavy cargo and an excessive number of passengers created a dangerous situation. Captain Daniel Eppes seemed to have had misgivings from the beginning, but was relieved when he reached the bend in the river below Vienna; the greatest hazards were now behind him, he thought.

It was after midnight, but the orchestra played on, and the ballroom was still filled with dancers. Suddenly above the laughter and music there was a sharp cry. Fire! Stop the music! Then a shriek and a chorus of voices. Fire! Fire! The music stopped abruptly. There was a rush for the decks and pandemonium. Men and women fell sprawling over each other in a desperate effort to reach the exits. Tongues of flame leaped out into the darkness. The cargo of cotton was on fire, and within a few moments the steamer was ablaze from stem to stern.

A few passengers crowded into the small number of life boats available. Others leaped from the boat into the icy waters, and tried to swim ashore, but in many instances they were drowned in the swift current. Some threw blazing cotton bales into the river and tried using them to keep afloat. The water extinguished the flames, and some passengers survived in this way, but many more were lost when the bales struck trees and underbrush and were overturned. The blazing boat drifted downstream leaving behind it darkness and death. Through the night men and women who were still alive clung desperately to trees praying to survive until dawn.—Elizabeth Garth Vestal, "Terror on the Eliza Battle," Birmingham *News,* October 5, 1969.

Of the more than two hundred registered passengers only about eighty survived.

ON LAND

Long before Europeans came, Indians had well-defined trails. They were used as paths to hunting grounds and roads between the principal towns, but seldom as trade routes because there was little exchange of goods. Later the English traders took advantage of these trails to meet with the red men to exchange skins. Oakfuskee, for example, was at a crossroads. High Town Path, across north Alabama and Wolf Trail to Pensacola were but two of the Indian trails.

The French preferred to use the waterways and therefore the English were the first to build a road in the Gulf coast area. It went from Mobile to Pensacola over the route Highway 90 follows today. The Americans had intense interest in better land transportation and early agitated for roads through Indian lands.

The first federally projected road through Alabama was the Natchez Trace which cut across the northwest corner. In 1801 Brigadier General James Wilkinson, Benjamin Hawkins, and Andrew Pickens signed a treaty with the Chickasaw nation to permit the president of the United States to "lay out, open and make a convenient waggon road through their land between the settlements of Mero District in the state of Tennessee and those of Natchez in the Mississippi Territory in such a way and manner as he may deem proper. . . ." The highway, a link between the lower Mississippi and, through Kentucky, the great National Road, was to be open to citizens of the United States and the Chickasaws alike. It crossed the Tennessee River at Colbert's Landing, a few

miles below Muscle Shoals, and the Tombigbee at Cotton Gin Port.
It was an important route from the Ohio Valley and the upper
South into the Old Southwest.

The isolation of the Tombigbee settlements was eased somewhat
in 1811 when an earlier (1805) horsepath through the Creek lands
was widened into a wagon road. The work was done by troops
stationed in the several forts in the region. This federal road was
sometimes called the Three-Chopped Way because of the blazes the
surveyors had used to mark the course. It entered Alabama at Fort
Mitchell on the Chattahoochee and ran west and southwest to St.
Stephens by way of Mt. Meigs and Montgomery, Fort Deposit and
Burnt Corn and then northerly to St. Stephens. A branch of this
road ran from Burnt Corn to Mims' Ferry on the Alabama. Later
this federal road was extended from St. Stephens to Natchez. Dr.
A. B. Moore says that Congress, by a series of contracts that ended
only in 1838, appropriated a total of $79,565.50 for these two roads.
Early maps show the Huntsville Road running southward through
the center of the state, crossing the Tennessee at Ditto's Landing
and eventually joining the Old Federal Road at St. Stephens. Andrew Jackson was responsible for two of its early roads: in the
east during the Creek War his men cut a road from Ditto's Landing to Fort Strothers and Fort Williams on the Tallapoosa River
and eventually Old Fort Toulouse which he renamed Fort Jackson.
In the west he cut a similar but more important road on his way
to New Orleans in 1815. This is known as Jackson's Military road;
it roughly paralleled the Natchez Trace but was some miles to the
east of it.

The local county roads were little more than excuses for
thoroughfares; they were built and maintained (if one can presume
to use that word) by local people who thus worked out their road
tax. In an effort to provide better transportation, enterprising businessmen built toll roads, usually called turnpikes. Some of these
turnpike companies also ran a stage line over their roads, thus adding to their income. Others operated toll bridges and ferries. Contracts were awarded to a group of associates for a specified period
of time, usually ten to twenty years, and named specific rates they
could charge. In 1819 John Byler and his associates, for example,
were authorized to operate a toll road from Shoal Creek in Lauderdale County to Tuscaloosa at these rates:

On a four-wheel carriage and team, seventy-five cents; on a two-wheel
carriage, fifty cents; on a man and horse, twelve and one-half cents;
on each pack horse, six and a fourth cents; for each head of cattle,
one cent; for each head of hogs and sheep, a half a cent—Quoted in

A.B. Moore, *History of Alabama* (University, Alabama: University Supply Store, 1934), p. 297.

These turnpikes were praiseworthy projects but few of them succeeded for long. They needed financial backing that they never received and were unable to maintain their roads in good condition. The roads were universally bad and everyone, both visitors and residents, often complained of the hardships they underwent when they were forced by circumstances to use them.

Rough roads, uncomfortable travel and inhospitable inns were all common to the American frontier. Tyrone Power, a prominent Irish comedian who visited America in the 1830's, passed through Alabama from the east. The "Sodom" he mentioned was later renamed Phenix City.

A little before midnight (December 23, 1834), my two New York *campagnonds du voyage* and myself took our seats in the mail for Montgomery on the Alabama river. We found ourselves the sole occupants of the vehicle, and were congratulating each other on the chance, when we heard directions given to the driver to halt at Sodom, for the purpose of taking up a gentleman and his lady.

It was dark as pitch and raining hard when we set out: a few minutes found us rumbling along the enclosed bridge, amidst the mingled roar of the rain, our wheels, and the neighboring falls: the flood passing below us had in the course of the last ten hours risen nearly twenty feet: its rush was awful.

At one of the first houses in the redoubtable border village the stage halted, and a couple of trunks were added to our load; next a female was handed into the coach, followed by her protector. The proportions of neither could at this time be more than guessed at; and not one syllable was exchanged by any of the parties. In a few minutes we were again under way, and plunging through the forests.

We reached Fort-Mitchell about daylight, where formerly a considerable garrison was kept up: the post is now, however, abandoned. Here an unanticipated treat awaited us, for we were compelled to leave our, by this time, tolerably warm stage, for one fairly saturated with the rain that had fallen during the night. Our luggage was pitched into the mud by the coachman, who had only one assistant: so we were fain to lend a hand, instead of standing shivering by, until the trunks were fished out, and disposed of on the new stage. A delay here of an hour and a half enabled me, however, to stroll back, and take a look at the deserted barrack. By this time too the day was well out. . . .

We halted for a late breakfast at a solitary log-tavern kept by Americans, where we were received with infinite civility, and where the lady of the *auberge* was inclined to be amiable and communicative,—not an every day rencontre in these parts. She informed me that the means they could command for the mere necessaries of living very were limited; that the butcher's meat was only attainable at Columbus, and that any attempt to rear a stock of poultry was ridiculous, as the Indians of the country invariably stole every feather.

After breakfast the driver made his appearance, and desired us to come down to the stable and fix ourselves as well as we could on the *Box*. Conceiving he alluded to me, I asked if the stage was ready, but received for reply an assurance that it was not intended the stage should be any longer employed by the service; but that, by the agent's order the BOX was to be tagen on from this point, and that those who liked might go on with it, and those that did not might stay behind.

This was (un) pleasant, but all appeared desirous of trying the BOX. I confess that a mail conveyance bearing a name so novel excited my curiosity; so, sallying forth, I walked down to the starting-place, where ready-hardnessed and loaded, stood literally the BOX, made of rough fir plank, eight feet long by three feet wide, with sides two feet deep: It was firmly fixed on an ordinary coach-axle, with pole, and etc. The mails and luggage filled the box to overflowing, and on the top of all we were left to, as the driver said, "fix our four quarters in as little time as possible."

Now this fixing, in any other part of the globe, would have been deemed an impossibility by persons who were paying for a mail conveyance, but in this spot we knew redress was out of the question—the choice lay between the Box and the forest. We however, enjoyed the travellers' privilege,—grumbled loudly, cursed all scoundrel stage agents . . . (and then) we next laughed at our unavailing ill-humour, which the driver bore with the calmness of a stoic, and finally, disposed of our persons as best we could; not the least care having been taken in the disposition of the luggage, our sole care, in fact, was to guard against being jolted off by the movement of the machine; any disposition in favour of ease or comfort was quite out of the question. . . .

Thus we progressed till the evening advance, when the clouds gathered thick, and then began to roll towards the north-west in the dark threatening masses, right in the teeth of a brisk, fitful breeze.

"We'll get it presently," observed our driver, eyeing the drift, "hot as mush and most as thick, by the looks of't."

All at once the wind lulled; then it shifted round to the southeast, and blew out in heavy gusts that bent the tall pines together like rushes; upon this change, lightning quickly followed, playing in the distance about the edges of the darkening horizon. For about two hours we were favoured with these premonitory symptoms, and thus allowed ample time for conjecture as to the probable violence of the storm in active preparation.

In this uncertainty I resolved to consult our driver's experience; so, coming boldly to the point, demanded, "I say, driver, do you calculate that we shall be caught in a hurricane?"

"I'll tell you how that'll be exact," replied our oracle: "If the rain comes down pretty (hard), we sha'n't have no hurricane, if it holds up dry, why, we shall."

Henceforth never did ducks pray more devoutly for rain than did the crew of the BOX, although without hope or thought of shelter.

. . . . At last, our prayers were heard; and we all, I believe, breathed more freely as the gates of the sky opened, and the falling flood subdued and stilled the hot wind whose heavy gusts rushing among the pines had been the reverse of musical.

The thunder-clouds, hitherto confined to the southern horizon, now closed down upon the forest, deepening its already darkness; at a snail's pace we still proceeded, and luckily found an Indian party encamped closed by a sort of bridge lying across a swamp. It would have been impossible, as the driver assured us, to have crossed without a good light. . . .

My New York companions and I had out-walked the Box; but when about half way across the rain extinguished our torches, which were rather too slight for the service, when, as we had perceived in our course that many of the planks were unshipped or full of holes, we thought it best to halt for the coming up of our baggage.

I can never forget the effect produced by the blaze of the huge bundle of light wood borne aloft by our Creek guide: I entirely lost sight of the discomfort of our condition in the pleasure I derived from the whole scene.

Let the reader imagine a figure dressed in a deep-yellow shirt reaching barely to the knees, the legs naked; a belt of scarlet wampum about the loins, and a crimson and a dark-blue shawl twisted turban—fashion round the head; with locks of black coarse hair streaming from under this, and falling loose over the neck or face; fancy one half of such a figure lighted up by a very strong blaze, marking the nimble tread, the aware cold features, sparkling eye, and outstretched muscular arms of the red-man,—the other half, meantime, in the blackest possible shadow: whilst following close behind just perceptible through wreaths of thick smoke, moved the heads of the leading horses; and, over all, flashed at frequent intervals red vivid lightning; one moment breaking forth in a wide sheet, as though an overcharged cloud had burst at once asunder; the next, descending in zigzag lines, or darting through amongst the tall pines and cypress trees; whilst the quick patter of the horses' hoofs for a time heard loudly rattling over the loose hollow planks, and then again drowned wholly by the crash of near thunder. . . .

Having cleared the swamp we took our places on the Box, still lighted by our friendly Creek; and in about half an hour gained the log-house where the mail agent to whose (in) considerate order we owed our change of vehicle, and consequent added discomfort, dwelt: here, however, a clean comfortable meal of tea, chops, fowls, and hot bread of every denomination awaited us.—Tyrone Power, *Impressions of America* (Philadelphia: R. Bentley, 1836), vol. 2, p. 91ff.

Some wag is said to have posted up in these early days a bulletin by the side of one of the Alabama quagmire roads, which read:

> This road is not passable
> Not even jackassable.

So when you travel
Take your own gravel.
Alderman and Armstead Churchill Gordin, *J. L. M. Curry* (New York:
MacMillan Co., 1911), p. 40.

PLANK ROADS

Faced with the problem of poor roads, citizens of several communities (some of them former turnpike promoters) turned to plank roads. These were roads "paved" with planks attached to parallel stringers. Many residents were optimistic that this smooth surface would solve transportation difficulties. In a period of two years, the state legislature chartered twenty-four plank roads. One of these was the Central Plank Road Company of Montgomery which was offering stock for sale.

. . . We are decidedly in favor of city aid to the plank road enterprises diverging from the concentrating at this point. [But] that aid we only wish to see extended to a moderate limit. The road to Wetumpka will be built without any assistance; so also will the one to the Tennessee River. But there are two roads, the completion of which is intimately connected with the welfare and progress of Montgomery, that should be pushed to completion as soon as the one from here to Wetumpka. . . . To effect this object in the short space allowed makes the temporary aid of the city indispensable; we allude to the Montgomery and Union Springs Road, and the Montgomery South plank road. The city ought to subscribe fifteen or twenty thousand dollars to each of those two roads—fifteen thousand to each would, we think, be sufficient to ensure their immediate undertaking and completion. The thirty thousand dollars . . . would, with the other works that are sure to be completed, do more toward permanently building up and making a large city of Montgomery than any other possible project that could be named. It would be returning also a regular dividend to the city for its outlay. We paid out $80,000 for the Capitol. It was money well laid out, and it was never expected to bring any direct reurn. Here is little more than one third the outlay with a certainty that it will pay for itself in four years, and add to the aggregate of city wealth, city population and city property, at least two fold. . . . It would be a vast accommodation to planters, who now trade here and who desire to trade there, and who would aid efficiently to the construction of these works themselves. Let Montgomery falter now, and a few years will build up other points that will divide the trade with her, or take it from her. Let her step forward now, even with the limits named . . . and we may well defy any point in the state to affect us or compete with us.

The city council of Wetumpka subscribes thirty thousand dollars to one plank road; Selma subscribes fifty thousand dollars to one railroad; Huntsville fifty thousand to one railroad; Mobile, we believe, one hundred thousand to her railroad. Shall Montgomery lie still now and see her sister cities outstrip her in their interest and subscriptions to works designed to benefit them?—*Daily Alabama Journal* (Montgomery), February 22, 1850.

The railroad was destined to be the solution of most of the transportation problems in the antebellum nation. Alabama built the first one south and west of the Appalachian Mountains yet it lagged behind many other states. By 1860 it had only 743 miles of track in operation. The state had too many good waterways and too little available capital to build railways very quickly. The first railway was in the Tennessee Valley and its purpose was to overcome or bypass the rapids at Muscle Shoals.

The state legislature granted a charter to the Tuscumbia Railway Company on January 16, 1830. In less than two and a half years the line was in operation; it had cost $9,500.00. The Huntsville *Southern Advocate* reported the activities of opening day.

On the 12th inst. the Tuscumbia Railway was opened in conformity with previous arrangements. At an early hour a large concourse had assembled to witness the operation of the first railroad in Alabama.

The cars were in motion throughout the day for the accommodation of visitors. A procession was formed at eleven o'clock a.m. of the cars drawn by one horse, crowded with the beauty and the fashion of the County and accompanied with a band of music. The procession passed to the foot of the road where an extensive collation had been prepared for the occasion. Several thousand persons partook of the hospitality of the railroad company. The utmost harmony and good humor prevailed. The whole scene was gay and animating and the celebration creditable to the company. It was truly novel and interesting to witness the rapid and graceful flight of the "majestic cars" in a country where but yesterday the paths of Indians were the only traces of human footsteps.— *Southern Advocate* (Huntsville), June 23, 1832, quoting *Florence Gazette*.

Ethel Armes says that the railway may have used horse drawn cars, but it did have a "little George Stephenson" engine which it used at times.

Major David Hubbard, whose cotton plantation was near Tuscumbia, had been the moving spirit behind the project. Hearing of a line in Pennsylvania that was moving coal, he visited it to see how it worked. When he returned, he organized a company to build the Tuscumbia line. Benjamin Sherrod was the president. Big planters in the Tennessee Valley were the chief promoters and subscribers of the project.

Two years later the Tuscumbia, Courtland, and Decatur railroad was chartered. It was forty-six miles long, reaching around the rapids that separated the eastern and western segments of the Tennessee river. It absorbed the earlier Tuscumbia road. This road illustrates the basic idea for all the early railroads: they bypassed natural hindrances or tapped areas where there were no streams, acting as feeders to water ports.

Interest in railroads grew rapidly. In the decade of the 1830's, the state legislature chartered twenty-five lines; reflecting the financial situation following the panic of 1837, it chartered only seven in the 1840's and there is no evidence that actual work was done on any of them; however, times in the 1850's were better as indicated by the fact that the state chartered seventy-three lines. Few of these were started and none was completed by the outbreak of the war. The most ambitious lines were the Mobile and Ohio that was intended to link the port city with the midwest. The principal east-west line was the Charleston and Memphis which connected Chattanooga, Huntsville and points west. The rail centers were Montgomery, Opelika, and Anniston.

One of the reasons so many lines that were chartered died aborning was the lack of money. However elaborate and detailed the charters, unless money was forthcoming lines could not be built nor rolling stock purchased. Money for the roads that were built came from many sources: loans, sale of stock, gifts from municipalities, local taxes, and aid from the state although there was considerable opposition to the last method. More came indirectly from the federal government. When Alabama became a state, one of the terms was that it should have a percentage of the sales of all public lands within the bounds of the state. The money accruing from this two and three percent (the amount varied) was to be used for internal improvement. In the 1820's some had been used in building canals and clearing streams. Later railroads were considered eligible. Almost a million dollars from this fund was used for railroads. The federal government also made donations of lands to the state for these roads, eventually a total of 3,171,373 acres. The Selma, Rome, and Dalton was the recipient of the largest amount, 858,515 acres. Many Alabamians approved of this policy. G. T. Yelverton, of the *State Rights Democrat* (Elba) editorially praised the president for setting aside land for the railroads and said he would be "glad to see all the public lands donated to the states for the great purposes of internal improvements and education." (July 12, 1856)

Roads and equipment were of poor quality. Little grading was done; iron rather than steel, was used for rails, cars were rough and uncomfortable, and the engines unsafe. Consequently, accidents were all too frequent. Nevertheless, Alabamians welcomed the trains as a satisfactory form of rapid transportation and many of them recorded their first experience with them. William Frierson Fulton II had gone by stage to Montgomery where he boarded a train for college at Milledgeville, Georgia.

This was my first railroad experience. The big engine with its long train of cars puffing and wheezing on the track looked like some huge animal, and the whole thing was too big for me to comprehend except by degrees. After riding for hours and hours I began to feel at home and was fixing myself for a nap when there was a mighty rumbling, jerking and a sudden crash, the passengers being hurled here and there, and then a complete stop. Our car had run off the track. Fortunately no one was hurt.—*Family Record and War Remeniscences,* p. 36.

The following amusing and probably fictitious account comes from the *Alabama Beacon* (Greensboro) February 4, 1853. It quotes an unidentified issue of the *Flag of the Union* (Tuscaloosa).

We have often thought that to a person who first saw a train of cars in motion, the sight must be most miraculous and astounding. As Jack Downing once said,—"twas queer to see a hull lot of wagons chuck full of people, and things agoing off in that ere speed, and no hoss to draw em." A genius of the sort referred to, lately made his experimental trip. He was a greenhorn, a genuine backwoodsman, who feared nothing in the shape of man or beast, but any thing that he could not understand puzzled him even more than it did, perhaps, the ordinary run of his fellows. Well, he came to Cartersville a short time since, for the purpose of taking his first railroad trip.

He's hearn tell on 'em, but didn't believe, he said, half of the nonsense folks said about 'em. When the cars arrived at the place, our hero was elated in anticipating his intended ride. As the cars approached, he stood gazing with wonder and awe at the engine, puffing and smoking. Following the example of others, as soon as the cars stopped he hurried aboard, with his saddle bags upon his arms, and seated himself near a window. Then looking around at the passengers, manifesting much surprise, he put his head out the window to see the 'critter start;' while in this position, watching with much anxiety, the whistle sounded. Our hero, much surprised, and evidently a little alarmed, drew back his head with a motion that might be called a jerk, and turning to a gentleman sitting near him, said:

'Well, stranger did you ever hear such a snort as that?'

'The engine,' suggested the other.

'Well, I don't know what it is, but—hallow, how she goes!'

'Guess you are not acquainted with railroad traveling?'

'Hang it no! haint they ran away? Creation how it jerks!'

'It's all safe enough, you may rely, the cars are starting.'

'That's all; well stranger, I ain't afraid, you know, but kinder surprised like, that's all,' said the mountain boy, half ashamed. 'I golly, stranger, did you hear that ere snort? It beats dad's jack-ass, and he's a roarer, no mistake. Whew, how it does puff; somethin' bustin,' I'm sure.'

'O' fudge! It's all right,' said the other, settling himself for a nap.

'Iswow! I don't see how you can sleep, darned if I do!'

'Nothing like getting used to it,' said the other. You've heard of the eels that have been skinned so many times they rather liked it, and used to come ashore every few days to get their hides taken off, hav'nt you?'

'You're gassin, stranger.'

The bell rang, the engine moved off, away went the cars at rapid speed, and before our hero had recovered from the shock which the 'snort' produced, the cars were moving slowly over Etowa bridge. Discovering a change in its gait, he popped his head out of the window again, 'to see how it moved,' saw that it was distant from the ground and supposing the 'critter' was flying, swooned, and fell from his seat speechless. Several gentlemen sitting near caught hold of him, raised him up, shook him and rubbed him until he revived a little.

'The man's crazy,' suggested some of the bystanders, sagely.

'No, he's not' answered he, who had before spoken, 'he's frightened.'

'Frightened?'

'Yes, scared half to death.'

'About what?'

'The cars; he never was in a train before; he told me so.'

A hearty laugh ran through the car about the half-fainting man, which had the effect to arouse him to consciousness, at least partially so, for his breath began to come and go more regularly, and at last he opened his eyes as large as saucers, and seeing several of the gentlemen who had just come to his assistance about him, he looked up most beseechingly in the face of one of them, and said—

'Stranger, has it lit?'

Chapter 7

THE CHURCH

The Roman Catholic Church was the first to establish itself in Alabama. Priests came with the Spanish and French explorers and in 1704 Mobile was designated a parish. That parish church grew into the Church of the Immaculate Conception and has the longest continuous history of any religious body in the state. But its growth was painful. The following report to Abbé Raguet was written in 1725, but it could apply to almost any year of the colonial period.

I come, Sir, to the points about which you do me the honor of asking me for information. In the first place . . . about the state of religion in general. This is a matter that is so little advanced that I scarcely dare to say that it is begun. It is true that there have been bad priests who instead of repressing disorders have authorized them by their scandals, but there have also been some very good ones whose zeal has remained fruitless for want of protection in the exercise of their ministry, the officials from whom they were to expect it having always been extremely indifferent on this point. Their pretext was that at the beginning of a colony it is necessary to be easy-going with people and to tolerate many things that would not be tolerated in a country already established. This false beginning caused every sort of impunity to be found for disorders. Concubinage, extortion, public impiety were safe against censure. The commands of God and of the church were transgressed with so much license that it seemed that they were no longer binding when they had crossed the seas. Almost no difference between feast days and Sundays and workdays, between Lent and Carnival, the Easter season and the rest of the year. That is, Sir, the condition in which we found things on our arrival. The change that we notice is not very considerable as far as the essence of religion is concerned; there is a little in the exterior. The majority of the great disorders cease to be public. There is a larger attendance at the religious services and at [religious] instruction. The number of those who attend the sacraments

217

at Easter and at solemn feasts is increasing although more than half are still failing to do their duties therein. If we had had churches in which to assemble the faithful, instruct them and exhort them, there is great probability that things would be on a better basis, but the places in which we have hitherto held religious services have had so little space that we have not yet been able to gather one-third of our parshioners in them at the same time.—Brother Raphael, Capuchin Priest, Vicar General to Abbé Raguet, *Mississippi Provincial Archives* (Jackson, Miss.: Dept. of Archives of History), vol. 2, pp. 478–79.

The Catholic Church was strong among the French settlers in the environs of Mobile but had little following elsewhere until much later.

The Protestant Church came to Alabama with the English shortly after the Treaty of Paris. The Reverend Samuel Hart, presumably from England, was reading prayers at the Indian Congress in Mobile in 1765. It is not known whether he was a sickly man at his arrival or whether the climate in Mobile, "that graveyard of Britons," was responsible for his poor health, but after a short time he left for Charleston, South Carolina, where he soon died. His successor, the Reverend Nathaniel Cotton, a graduate of Jesuit College, Cambridge, was appointed in February 1768, and served the Mobile congregation until his death in 1771. In his correspondence with the Earl of Hillsborough, Secretary of State, he repeatedly requested prayer books and Bibles and received at least one shipment of them from the Bishop of London. He noted that there was a large number of Presbyterians in the Mobile area. In May 1769, the General Assembly of West Florida authorized the choosing of vestrymen at Pensacola and Mobile "for the greater decency and the better regulation of the said towns." With the end of the British period, the number of Anglicans presumably declined; a permanent Episcopal Church was not formed until 1822 when Christ Church in Mobile was organized.

One of the first, if not the very first, Protestant preachers outside of Mobile was the Reverend Lorenzo Dow who visited the Bigbee settlements in 1803 on his way to the Natchez District on the Mississippi. Dow, who became a member of the Methodist Conference in his native Connecticut in 1798, has been evaluated in conflicting ways by historians of Methodism. Anson West in his *History of Methodism in Alabama* calls Dow an eccentric whose ministry was "accidental, irregular, occasional, only a sermon now and then preached in passing to and fro on contingent trips thru the land." West sees no positive results of his haphazard ministry and even questions his connection with the Methodist Church.

John G. Jones, author of *History of Methodism in Mississippi*, sees Dow in an entirely different light. If to call him eccentric meant that "he could not be trammeled by any Conference ties, but claimed the right to follow Providence and to labor when, how, and where he could be useful," then the word applied. Dow was generous to a fault, giving away his clothing and even selling his watch to help a church; he was little concerned with mundane affairs. That he was a pious, zealous man, attacking "sin, skepticism, Calvinism, and all other anti-Arminianisms," no one can deny.

Dow seems to have traveled wherever Providence, not the Church, directed. The first Methodist minister sent to Alabama by the Church was Matthew P. Sturdivant. At the January 1807 meeting of the South Carolina Conference, Bishop Francis Ashbury recorded in his journal that Sturdivant, who had "volunteered his services to Bigbee as a missionary was received and elected to the eldership." He became the forerunner of Methodism in the area. In his first conference report he "had no legion of souls converted to God over which to rejoice but he had, nevertheless, a thrilling narrative to recite"—a narrative of crossing flooded rivers and creeks, of camping in the wilderness, of cold nights spent on the ground, of days of hunger and thirst, of the growl of the bear, the howl of the wolf, the scream of the panther, and of the "significant whoop of the Indian savage." Conference was so impressed with his story that the officials returned him to the field and this time with a helper, Michael Burdge. In 1810 John Kennon was appointed junior preacher to Burdge.

It is not certain which Methodist church was first organized. Sturdivant and Burdge reported from the Bigbee settlements that in December 1809 there were 86 members, 71 white and 15 colored, but did not name a church. Whether these were members of an organized church or merely Methodists by profession is not certain. The next year there were 102 white and 14 colored members "in Society." Thereafter the number grew steadily until by 1860 there were 777 churches.

A state-wide Methodist Conference was organized in Tuscaloosa in 1832, when there were over 12,000 members.

The Baptists seem to have the honor of having established the first Protestant Church in what was to become Alabama. Among the pioneer families there were many Baptists, but it was not until 1808 that Flint River Church in north Alabama was organized. Two years later the Bassett Creek Church was established near Choctaw Corner in Clarke County. The church on Flint River was organized by the Rev. John Nicholson at the home of James Deaton with a membership of about twelve. Rev. James Courtney was instrumental in organizing the Bassett Creek Church. There were other organizations about the same time: Enon Church became the First Church in Huntsville; Rev. Joseph McGee and Rev. Jacob

Parker organized churches in Sumter County, and there were others elsewhere in rapid succession. The Baptist Church spread so rapidly that long before 1820 there were several local associations (Flint River Association in 1814 being the first) which in 1823 formed the state convention. Rev. James A. Ranaldson, a North Carolinian who had moved to south Alabama, was the man behind the movement to form a central state convention; he was elected recording secretary and Rev. Charles Crow the president. Noteworthy is the fact that many obscure women's missionary societies sent gifts to this meeting at Salem Church in Greensboro. The denomination before long became the largest in the state, having 805 congregations and 53,649 members by 1860.

The Presbyterian Church was the third largest in the state. Most historians give Huntsville First Church, established in 1818, credit for being the oldest of the denomination in Alabama, but there were Presbyterian ministers functioning in the Huntsville area long before that. In 1808 Rev. Thomas Calhoun was sent there by Church officials in Tennessee; it is said he preached in John Hunt's house before it was finished. The next year Rev. Robert Donnell was sent to the area; he was ordained by the Cumberland Presbytery in 1813. Delegates from the Huntsville, Herman, and Kelly's Creek churches sent delegates to presbytery meeting at Suggs' Creek in Wilson County, Tennessee, in 1812. To be sure after 1810, these men were Cumberland Presbyterians with separate organizations, but they were Presbyterians just the same and had many churches in central and north Alabama. It was the Presbyterian Church whose headquarters were at Philadelphia that established Huntsville First Church, Bethel Church in Tuscaloosa, and in 1822 Valley Creek Church in Dallas County. The Presbytery of Alabama was organized in Cahaba in 1821, the Synod of Alabama in Tuscaloosa in 1835 with R. M. Cunningham as its first moderator. By 1860 there were 135 Presbyterian churches in Alabama.

Starting a Church

How did a new church start? What did a congregaiton do at an official meeting? The answers differ, of course, with the type of church government. With the Baptists, constituting a church was done by simple agreement. Standards for their ministers were equally simple. Pioneer farmers like their members, the preachers were men of minimal education. They depended on a "call" from the Lord, memorized passages of scripture, natural eloquence, and pious fervor to carry on their ministry which they often did admirably.

This extract from the Record of Providence (Baptist) Church, Dallas County, illustrates the method of organizing, the accepted doctrines, and the events in congregational meetings. I am indebted to the late Dr. A. G. Moseley, Orville, who shortly before his death, allowed me to copy from the manuscript book. The original is now in the Samford University Library.

ORGANIZATION OF PROVIDENCE CHURCH
13th June A.D. 1820

We the brethren on Boguechitto Creek, Dallas County, Ala., having met together and taking into consideration our scattered situation and believing it to be our duty to become a constituted body and not forsake the assembling ourselves together, do agree to call a Presbytery to constitute us into a church. Brethren Issac Suttles and Wm. Harwood who are duly authorized ministers having met as a Presbytery for the above purpose at the house of Joseph Vann the 13th of June A. D. 1820 and the following named brethren Joseph Vann, Johnson Hayman, Henry Avery, Joseph McIlroy, Davenport Greaves, Lucy Vann and Jane Hayman being present and on examination found sound and orthodox in faith were by the above named Presbytery constituted a church known by the name of Providence Baptist Church of Christ.

This church is constituted on the following abstract of principles:

1st. We believe in one only true and living God, namely the Father, Word and Holy Ghost.

2nd. We believe the Scriptures of the Old and New Testament are the word of God and the only rule of faith and practice.

3rd. We believe in the doctrine of Election and that God chose his people in Christ before the foundation of the world.

4th. We believe in the doctrine of Original Sin.

5th. We believe in man's impotency to recover himself from the fallen state he is in by nature, by his own free will and ability.

6th. We believe that sinners are justified in the sight of God only by the imputed righteousness of Christ.

7th. We believe that God's elect are called, regenerated and sanctified by the Holy Spirit.

8th. We believe that the Saints persevere in grace and never fall finally away.

9th. We believe that Baptism and the Lord's Supper are ordinances of Jesus Christ and that true believers are subjects and that Immersion is the true mode of baptism.

10th. We believe in the Resurrection of the Dead and General Judgment, that the Punishment of the Wicked and Joys of the Righteous shall be eternal.

11th. We believe that only those ministers have a right to administer the ordinances as are regularly baptized, called and come under the imposition of hands by the Presbytery.

12th. We believe that only regularly baptized members have the right to commune at the Lord's Table.

. . . .

July 22, 1820. The Church of Christ at Providence met agreeable to appointment and after singing exhortation and prayer by Brother Issac Coleman, came together in conference and chose Brother Coleman as moderator, Brother D. Greaves, Clerk. Stated meeting to be held 4th Sundays in each month and Saturday before. No further business, adjourned.   D. Greaves, C.C.

Aug. 29th, 1820. No meeting on Saturday but met on Sunday and after singing and prayer by Brother I. Coleman proceeded to business in conference. Resolved to apply to the Alabama Association by letter and messengers. Brethren Joseph Vann, Henry Avery and Josiah Mc-Ilroy were chosen messengers and Brother Greaves to write the letter. Agreed to send one dollar for minutes of the Association. Adjourned.

D. Greaves, C.C.

May 1823. Met according to appointment and after preaching by Brethren Ray and McLimore proceeded to business in conference. Received by experience Sister Elizabeth Hitt. Took up the reference concerning missionary operations; decide in favour of Domestic mission. . . . Bro Jno Adams accused himself of having drunk too much spirits, laid over. Took up reference relating to the ordination of Bro Wm Moseley, Bro Wm Moseley is hereby ordained and set apart to the ministry.

July 1836. Took up case of Bro Thos McGill for getting drunk and fighting. Laid over till next meeting. Appointed Bro. Cochran and Bro. . . . Deacons a committee to visit Bro. McGill and report at next meeting.

Aug. 1836. The committee appointed to visit Bro McGill report that he professes to be sorry for acting as he has.

Sept. 1836. Took up Bro McGill's case and he failing to give satisfaction has this day been excluded by the church.

Oct. 1836. Bro Thos McGill came forward and made acknowledgement to the church which were satisfactory and he was restored to fellowship—

Dec. 1836. A report being in circulation that Bro. Thos. McGill has been drunk. Apptd a committee . . . to visit Bro. Thos. McGill and cite him to our next conference.

Jan. 1837. Took up Bro McGill's case. The committee not being ready to report the case was laid over till next meeting.

Feb. 1837. On motion agreed to lay Bro McGill's case over till next conference. March 1837. Took up Bro McGill's case and after some deliberation excluded him.

February, 1841. Met agreeable to appointment and after sermon by Bro. Jesse Hartwell met in conference, Bro. Parks, moderator. Granted a letter of dismission to Sister Sarah Taylor. Dispensed with all the usual business and took up the difficulty existing between this church and Concord relative to a resolution passed by this church against their pastor J. Reeves. The church being nearly equally divided, one part being in favor of rescinding said resolution and the other opposed to it. The church then agreed to a friendly division, and the brethren who were opposed to rescinding the resolution. The church agree that two disinterested men shall be appointed to value the meeting house and should they not agree, to call in a third person who shall then decide. Then the church shall pay one half the value to the brethren who have withdrawn. The church appointed Bro. Willis Nunnalee on her part and Bro. H. Avery was appointed on the other side. The church then rescinded the resolution against Bro. Reeves of Concord. . . .

The Methodist Church with its centralized organization and administration was somewhat more complex and required a bishop. At the annual conference, among other functions, he made the appointments to churches each year.

For a time all Methodist churches in this area were under the jurisdiction of the Mississippi Conference. A division was made, and the Alabama Conference held its organizational meeting in Tuscaloosa on December 12, 1832. An unnamed young minister described the second conference meeting in Montgomery.

. . . In due time we were at Montgomery, and homes assigned us. My sleeping apartment was in an old vacated Hotel, near the river, in company with a crowd of young preachers, and we had to go out and get our meals at different places in the city. The weather was extremely bad; rain, snow, and sleet fell on us. The Conference convened at the appointed time. Bishop Emory presided, much to the satisfaction of the brethren. Business was dispatched by the Bishop, carefully and safely, so that on Sunday the ordinations were attended to, the Bishop preaching at 11 o'clock. I confess I had either looked for too much, set my estimate of the Bishop's preaching abilities too high, or else I was in a bad condition to hear; probably this last; for I was really disappointed, but in looking around I saw a number of the older preachers in tears, viz., E. V. LeVert, R. L. Walker, R. L. Kennon, James H. Mellard, Ebenezer Hearn, and others, so that I decided certainly it is in me, but could not help thinking that if I were up there saying those identical words, using the same gestures and intonations of voice, not a tear would have been shed, their heads would have been hung, perfectly ashamed of me. I was not the only one that entertained such thoughts. Brother James Thompson, an excellent local preacher of the Cedar Creek Circuit, who was at the Conference for ordination, and who heard the Bishop's sermon, told me he had the same thoughts. We both concluded that a position and name had a great deal to do in producing effects by some divines. Bishop Emory was certainly a good divine, a good writer, and an intellectual preacher; but somehow it did not, to my weak capacity of judging, so appear that day. In due time the work of the Conference was closed, and every one ready to leave, and only waiting for the secret roll to be unfolded, and receive their appointed sphere of labor for the next year. The Bishop very gravely approached the stand and announced the appointments.— Quoted in Anson West, *A History of Methodism in Alabama* (Nashville: Methodist Publishing House, 1893), pp. 448–49.

The Methodist Circuit Rider

Much of the success of the Methodist Church was due to the activities of the circuit riders. The circuit rider, who literally rode a circuit which sometimes took him weeks to complete, was a welcome figure on the frontier. He not only held religious services, preached funerals, and married couples, but he also loaned books, carried news, and served as a contact with the outside world.

William Culverhouse described in his annual report to Conference his work as a circuit rider in south Alabama in 1830.

Escambia Mission, December 10, 1830.

Rev. Sir: I have been apprised that my duty as a Missionary requires that I should transmit to you quarterly, information relative to the state of this Mission. In this respect I confess I have been faulty; but I solicit your forbearance, as I have been engaged in a great work, and will now endeavor to give you a succinct and comprehensive view of what has been done throughout the year.

After a pleasant and safe journey from Conference, I arrived on my mission ground in good time, and after a few days' rest set out in order to arrange my appointments: part of them I made on the east, and part on the west side of Escambia, or Conecuh River, in the following order: commencing in Alabama, Butler County—across the Conecuh in said County—down to Montezuma, or Falls of Conecuh, in Covington County and through Conecuh County into Florida, to within twenty-six miles of Pensacola; then returning on the west side by Fort Crawford and Brooklyn across the Sepulgah—on the waters of Pigeon Creek— into Butler County again. This route formed a three weeks' circuit, and contained seventeen appointments; three of them were given me from the Mississippi Conference, two from Pensacola Mission, and one from Pea River Circuit. Within the bounds of my Mission I found one hundred and ten members; I have, during the year, taken on trial sixty-eight, making in all one hundred and seventy-eight members. Recently my Mission has been enlarged, so as to form a four weeks' Circuit, and now extends down to the Escambia Bay.

A Camp-meeting was held for this Mission on 4th to 8th November, at a new Camp-ground, whereon twelve large and commodious tents were built. It is situated on the waters of Conecuh, near Brooklyn. The congregations were good and appeared remarkably attentive to the preaching of the word. Much good was done, and ten were received as probationers among us. Also, we have commenced a church edifice, at the same place, of forty by thirty feet, which we expect will be finished the ensuing winter. There is also a probability of two others being shortly built within the Mission.

Notwithstanding strong prejudices, which existed among some of the people, against Missions and Missionaries, when I first came among them, the major part of them have received me very kindly; and some who would not come to hear me preach in the commencement of the year, now come out, and appear to give great attention to the word. I think there is considerable religious excitement prevailing all round my Mission; and notwithstanding the 'reform' excitement has prevailed very much near our borders, there is nothing of it within the bounds of this Mission; we are all sailors of the old ship, and feel perfectly satisfied with her chart; and while we are passing on the ocean of time we have peace and harmony abounding among us. Dear brother, pray for us, that the Lord may prosper his work in this part of his moral vineyard, to the glory of his great name, and the salvation of these people.—Ibid., pp. 274–75.

The Right Reverend N. H. Cobb was bishop of the Protestant Episcopal Church, Diocese of Alabama, from 1844 to 1861. Extracts from his annual report for 1853–1854 show the nature of his work as bishop and the extent of the Episcopal Church in Alabama. Twenty-four parish churches made reports at the meeting.

In compliance with the Canons, I herewith lay before the Convention of the Diocese, my Annual Report of my official acts during the last year.

May 12th, 13th, 14th, and 15th, 1853.—Attended the Annual Convention of the Diocese, and was much gratified at the general prevalence of peace and harmony, as also with the many evidences of the increasing prosperity of the Diocese. On Whitsunday, I preached in the morning and administered the Holy Communion, assisted by the Rev. Messrs. Hanson and Lee. I also baptised two adults privately. In the afternoon, I baptised an adult and an infant, and confirmed three persons. I was greatly encouraged to see a number of families from different Counties attending the Convention, and manifesting a lively interest in the exercises of the occasion. . . .

July 14.—Read the Burial Service over the body of a colored member of the church.

August 9.—Preached at Mt. Meigs, baptised three adults, confirmed three persons, and administered the Holy Communion.

August 13th.—Preached at the house of Mr. Edward Taylor, to his Negroes, who, neatly dressed, were assembled for public worship. Mr. Taylor manifests a proper Christian solicitude for the spiritual improvement of his servants. And I would remark that I know of no wider field of usefulness for the Church than is presented on the plantations of Alabama. Multitudes of the planters would cheerfully and liberally contribute to the support of Clergy-men, who would preach to the Negroes on their estates. It is very gratifying to witness an increasing sensibility on this subject amongst the planters in the South. I could at this time give employment to a number of Clergymen in this very interesting field, if they could be obtained.

August 17th, 18th, and 19th.—Preached several times in St. Paul's Church, Greensboro, and confirmed twelve persons. I found the Parish in an encouraging condition. In the afternoon of the 19th I went ten miles into the country to confirm a sick young lady.

August 20th.—Visited St. Michael's Church, Marengo county, preached in the new Church, though in an unfinished state. This church will probably be completed in the course of the ensuing summer.

Thirteenth Sunday after Trinity.—Visited Woodville and preached a number of times, and confirmed nine persons, and amongst them Mr. S. R. Wright, late a Presbyterian Clergyman. I have never seen this Parish in a more flourishing condition, notwithstanding heavy losses, both by deaths and removals. I was gratified to find that their Church building will soon be handsomely finished.

August 24th.—St. Bartholemew's Day.—Preached in the morning in St. David's Church, Dallas County, and in the afternoon preached to a congregation of colored persons, and confirmed one colored person. This small, but interesting Parish was at this time vacant, but is now happily supplied by the Rev. R. D. Nevius.

October 2d.—Left home to attend the session of the General Convention in New York. Of this General Convention, I will remark that it was a most interesting one. It was characterised throughout by an unusual degree of unanimity of fraternal love. There seemed to be, in a great degree, the absence of party spirit. . . .

Twenty-sixth Sunday after Trinity.—Visited Eufaula, preached a number of times, baptised three adults and one infant, administered the Holy Communion, assisted by the Rector, and confirmed six persons.

November 25th.—Attended Church in St. John's, Montgomery, and assisted in the services on occasion of Thanksgiving appointed by the Governor.

January 5th, 1854.—Went to St. John's in the Wilderness, but in consequence of detention on the Rail Road, failed to reach the Church in time for my appointment. I regret that this Parish is without a Clergyman. On one of the Plantations in the neighborhood, there is a Chapel and an interesting congregation of colored people.

Second Sunday after Epiphany.—Spent this day in Selma. Preached in St. Paul's Church in the morning, and in the evening, after a Sermon by the Rev. Mr. Cushman, confirmed five persons. I was much gratified to find the Church enlarged and handsomely improved.

January 17th.—Visited Marion, preached in St. Wilfrid's Church, and confirmed eight persons. I found the excellent School, conducted by the indefatigable Rector, in a flourishing condition. I am well persuaded that from this School there will go forth an influence that in time will be felt for the good of the Church throughout the Diocese. It is truly refreshing to the heart of a Christian parent, to witness the reverence and devotion of the body of that School during the worship of the Church. I wish it was in the power of the Rector to accommodate ten times as many as he now instructs, for in that event I am sure we should, in a few years, have a noble band of zealous Clergymen, fitted and trained to do good service in the cause of Christ and his church.

Third Sunday after Epiphany.—Visited Tuskaloosa, spent several days, preached a number of times, baptised an infant and confirmed seven persons, of whom one was colored.

January 27th and 28th.—Visited Butler, the county seat of Choctaw county, preached and confirmed five persons.

Fourth Sunday after Epiphany.—Preached at Pushmataha in the morning and confirmed one person, and in the afternoon preached to an interesting congregation of colored people on the plantation of Mr. Ruffin. On Monday morning preached again at Pushmataha. There is an encouraging field for the Church in this part of Choctaw county.

Purification of the Virgin Mary.—Spent this and the following day at Sumterville, preached three times and confirmed one person. A little band of Churchmen here have fitted up a small but convenient Chapel in which services are held.

Fifth Sunday after Epiphany.—Spent this day and the preceding Saturday in Livingston, preached three times and confirmed five persons.

February 7th.—Visited Eutaw, preached twice, baptised an adult and confirmed five persons. I was glad to learn that there is a Church in progress of erection in St. Mark's Parish, Greene county, in which the Rev. Mr. Smith labors in connection with Eutaw.

Septuagesima Sunday.—Preached twice in St. John's Church, Montgomery.

Sexagesima Sunday.—Visited Huntsville, preached a number of times and confirmed eight persons. . . .

February 28th.—Preached in a small Meeting House, twelve miles from Huntsville, in Madison county, and confirmed one person. In this retired neighborhood a little congregation is forming by the exertions of one of the most devoted daughters of the Church who, with a zeal that I have hardly ever seen equalled, is nobly struggling with difficulties and discouragements that to persons of weaker faith would seem unsurmountable. It is but seldom that my sympathies are so deeply interested as they were in witnessing the spirit and earnestness of that amiable Christian lady, the worthy daughter of a worthy Clergyman.

Ash Wednesday.—Visited Athens, the County town of Limestone county, and preached in the Methodist Church, to an attentive congregation. I would here express my obligations to the Hon. D. Coleman, for the kind hospitality extended to me by himself and his interesting Christian family. I have but seldom made a visit to any family that was more gratifying to my feelings.

First Sunday in Lent.—Visited Florence, preached, baptised three children and confirmed two persons.

In the afternoon of the same day went to Tuscumbia and preached; and again on Monday. During this visit I baptised two adults and confirmed fifteen persons. . . .

March 9th.—Returned to Huntsville, preached and confirmed one person.

March 10th and 11th.—Visited Guntersville, preached a number of times, and confirmed six persons. This is a new and encouraging field occupied by the Missionary, the Rev. Mr. Morris. I was here kindly entertained by Judge Wyatt and his interesting family, who, though members of a different communion, take a lively interest in the services of our faithful Missionary. Judge Wyatt generously offers to give a lot in the town for the erection of a Church.

Second Sunday in Lent.—Went to Bellefonte, preached a number of times and confirmed eight persons.

Fourth Sunday in Lent.—Visited Mobile, and in the morning preached in Christ Church, and confirmed sixteen persons.

Although I found the congregation in a flourishing condition, yet the pleasure of my visit was greatly marred by no longer meeting with my old and beloved friend, the Rev. N. P. Knapp, who had been very recently smitten down by the hand of death in the midst of the years of his usefulness. In the death of Mr. Knapp, not only the congregation of Christ Church, but the Diocese of Alabama, has sustained a heavy loss. He was one of the earliest Clergymen who had settled in the State. He had, in a measure, grown up with the Diocese, and had contributed not a little to the moulding of its character. He was a sound, well balanced Theologian, a thoroughly conservative Churchman, and a most faithful, practical and evangelical Preacher. . . .

In the afternoon of the Fourth Sunday in Lent, I consecrated a new and very neat and beautiful Church, by the name of St. John's. This Church has been erected mainly by the liberality of three individuals, and good cause have they to be gratified with the result of their labors. A large and flourishing congregation has already been gathered by the zealous and indefatigable labors of the Rev. J. H. Ingraham, whose services were fortunately secured by the Vestry of the new Parish, and whom I was much gratified to receive into the Diocese. Although the Church has been in use only a few months, it has been found necessary to enlarge it in order to accommodate the crowds that attend. . . .

Saturday and Sunday before Easter.—Preached in St. Andrew's Church, Prairieville, and confirmed one person. There is here a neat and beautiful Church, which is now nearly completed, and which will be an ornament to the neighborhood. In the afternoon of Sunday, preached in Trinity Church, Demopolis, and catechised the children. On Monday morning, I preached again, and on Tuesday morning preached in St. Andrew's Church, Prairieville. It is with great pleasure I am authorized to state that Mr. James Dubose, of this Parish, has generously determined to give to this Parish and to the Parish of St. David's, Dallas County, respectively, eighty acres of land for the purposes of a Rectory. . . .

Besides the services which I have enumerated in the above report, I may add that on almost every occasion of Confirmation, I have delivered addresses, and that when in Montgomery, I uniformly attended on services of the Church, on Wednesdays and Fridays, and on the saint's days.

The summary of my labors during the past year is as follows:

Baptisms—Adults	14
" Infants	25
Funerals	8
Marriages	3

Confirmations	223
Sermons	130
Ordinations	2
Communions	18

I have thus been enabled, by the good Providence of God, to visit almost every portion of the Diocese in which there is an organized Parish, and although it is with us the day of small things, yet there are sufficient signs of encouragement to cheer us onward to perseverance. As a whole the Diocese is steadily advancing in all the elements of permanent and substantial strength.

I am gratified to inform the Convention that at the last session of the Legislature of Alabama, an Act was passed incorporating the Society for the relief of the Widows and Orphans of deceased Clergymen. The claims of this Society on the sympathies of the Diocese are so obvious and so urgent as to make it unnecessary for me to say a word in their behalf.

The Clerical changes that have taken place in the Diocese are as follows: the Rev. M. F. Maury has been transferred to the Diocese of Kentucky; the Rev. J. H. Morrison and the Rev. R. B. Sutton to the Diocese of Maryland. The Rev. J. H. Ingraham has been received from the Diocese of Mississippi; the Rev. J. B. Ramsdell from that of Indiana. The Rev. Peyton Gallagher is residing in Western New-York. The Rev. S. R. Wright has been ordained, and the Rev. Mr. Leacock, though not as yet canonically transferred to the Diocese, is now in charge of Christ Church, Mobile.—*Journal of the Proceedings of the Twenty-third Annual Convention of the Protestant Episcopal Church of the Diocese of Alabama, held in St. Paul's Church, Carlowville, on the 11th, 12th, and 13th of May, A.D., 1854* (Mobile: Benjamin Jeter & Co., 1854), pp. 19–27.

Camp Meetings

The camp meeting was the most spectacular evidence of the religious bent of Alabamians. While it had its beginning in frontier days when people were scattered, churches were few and preaching was infrequent, it continued even after frontier conditions ended. Camp meetings, in somewhat altered form, have persisted in some sections well into the twentieth century.

A detailed description of a Methodist meeting is given by E. A. Powell.

At these meetings large crowds would gather, the preaching would generally be plain, pointed and powerful, and the effects produced would cause the beholder to almost think that he was witnessing the reenactment of the scenes of the day of Penticost. Could almost hear the cry of the startled multitude; "Men and brethren what shall we do," and then the answer coming as if from one of the sons of thunder, "repent." At these meetings would occur many things which some people would

call extravagant, still looking back now and following the subsequent
life of great numbers of the subjects of these exciting occasions. When
I can remember that I have seen the saloon keeper of long years standing, transferred from the saloon to the Pulpit; the unfortunate inebriate
taken out of the mire of the slough and made a sober man for life.
The man whose habit of profanity had become so closely interwoven
with his every day life that people regarded it as a part of his nature,
at once and forever break off from the habit. Yes: when I can go back
in thought and remember all these and many, very many more, of
similar character, all the results of these if you please extravagant meetings. I am almost ready to say would to God that these days of religious
excitement or if you prefer it extravagance, would return.

Speaking of camp meetings, I remember one place deserving particular notice—"Old Bethlehem." Oh! what are the memories clustering
around thy sacred precincts; how many hundreds have I known to go
there in the 'gaul of bitterness and in the bonds of iniquity'—return
rejoicing in hope, and who have long since left the walks of men, but
leaving behind them a bright evidence that all was well, blessing God
that they ever attended a camp meeting at that place. And then, too,
I remember so many of the old, and elderly men of that day under
whose auspices the meetings were held. In imagination I can see old
father McCraw, James Murry, Mathew Davis, and scores of others
giving their time and influence to the success of the meeting, and all
for the good of others. The preachers—and where are they? There was
Kennon, a Hearn, a Caloway, a Levert, a Weir, a Shanks, and a Murrah
who filled the office of Presiding Elder, all of whom have long since
gone to their reward except Murrah, he is still in the field, blowing
the trumpet, though not in the effective work. . . .

Before leaving the old ground, I must recur to one other camp meeting occasion, 1833; Rev. E. V. Levert was conducting a meeting, at
first the prospect did not seem encouraging. . . . But on Sunday night
a deep interest sprung up, which grew in intensity until the whole
country for miles around was so leavened by its influence, that for
several days the topic of conversation every where was the meetings,
and if you met a neighbor in the road, the first inquiry was the news
from the meetings. . . .

The Cumberland Presbyterians also had a church and camp ground
in the country. They were a good people, many of them would tent
at the Methodists at theirs, so that each meeting would be well supported. Among their preachers were several that ranked deservedly high.
There was Shock, Stevenson, Wilson, Oden, and others. They preached
and labored faithfully; many of them sang almost seraphically. Of the
old side Presbyterians I know but little, they had no church organizations in the country. I only knew a few of their members, who were
very excellent people. Since that day the Campbellite, or Christian
church has grown to considerable proportions and today they have
several churches, and quite a large membership. They were generally a
good people, their preachers are rather fond of debate, and proselyting.

Some of them would transpose the declaration of Paul where he thanked God that he was sent not to Baptise, but to preach the Gospel. At this day the Methodists and Missionary Baptist are the leading denominations in point of numbers. . . .—E. A. Powell, "Fifty-Five Years in West Alabama," *Alabama Historical Quarterly,* vol. 4, pp. 462–64.

Revival Meetings

The revival meeting, like the camp meeting, was a common occurrence on the frontier in the early days.

A pioneer in the revival movement was the Cumberland Presbyterian Church organized in 1810 when it broke away from the Presbyterian Church in Cumberland County, Kentucky. The leaders of the revivalistic movement, being concerned for the vast numbers of pastorless people on the frontier, were ordaining men who did not meet the traditional educational standards of the parent church.

The revival meeting Mrs. Anne Royall described here was being conducted by the Cumberland Presbyterians. Mrs. Royall, who has been previously quoted, was a visitor from Virginia who spent much of five years in the Tennessee Valley during the transition from territory to state. She considered herself a religious person and found some good in most churches, but she had utter contempt for hypocrisy and little patience with ignorance, both of which she saw in the meeting at Moulton.

Moulton, April 30th, 1821

I placed myself in front of the preacher (a great rough looking man) and the congregation sat some on fallen timber, some on benches carried there for the purpose, some sat flat on the ground, and many stood up—about 500 in all. His text was, "He that hath ears to hear, let him hear." The people must have been deaf indeed that could not have heard him. . . . He is one of the Cumberland Presbyterians. They are Calvinists, it is said, but do not deem education a necessary qualification to preach the Gospel. But to the sermon. He began low, but soon bawled to deafening. He spit in his hands, rubbed them against each other, and then would smite them together, till he made the woods ring. The people now began to covault, and dance, and shout, till they fairly drowned the speaker. Many of the people, however, burst out into a laugh. Seeing this, the preacher cried out, pointing to them with his finger, "Now look at them sinners there—You'll see how they will come tumbling down presently.—I'll bring them down." He now redoubled his strength; spit in his hands, and smote them together, till he made the forest resound, and took a fresh start; and sure enough the sinners came tumbling down. The scene that succeeded baffles description. Principally [it was] confined to women and children. The young women had carefully taken out their combs from their hair and laid them and their bonnets in a place of safety as though they were going to set in for a fight, and it was much like a battle. After tumbling on the ground, and kicking sometimes, the old women were employed in keeping their clothes civil, and the young men (never saw an old man go near them) would help them up, and taking them by the hand, by *their* assistance, and their own agility, they would spring nearly a yard from the ground at every jump, one after another, crying out glory, glory, as loud as their strength would admit; others would be singing a lively tune to which they kept time—hundreds might be seen and heard going on in this manner at once. Others, again, exhausted by this jumping, would fall down, and here they lay cross and pile, heads and points, yelling and screaming like the wild beasts in the forests, rolling on the ground, like hogs in a mire—very much like they do at camp meetings in our country, but more shameless; their clothes were the color of dirt; and like those who attended the camp meetings, they were all of the lower class of people. I saw no genteel person among them. . . . I am very sure a half dozen words of common sense, well applied, would convince those infatuated young women that they were acting like fools. In fact, a fool is more rational. Not one of those but would think it a crying sin to dance.

The noise of the preacher was effectually drowned at length, and a universal uproar succeeded louder than ever. Whilst this was going on, I observed an old woman near me, snivelling and turning up the whites of her eyes (she was a widow—all widows, old and young, covaulted) and often applying her handkerchief to her eyes, and throwing herself into contortions, but it would not do, she could not raise the steam.

I pointed to one young woman, with a red scarf, who had tired down several young men, and was still covaulting, and seeing she jumped higher than the rest, I asked who she might be. One of the gentlemen . . . gave such an account of her (men know these things) as would shock a modest ear. "D--m her, she gets converted every meeting she goes to. . . ."

The preacher having spent all his ammunition, made a pause, and then called upon all the sinners to approach and be prayed for. Numbers went forward, all women and children (children of ten years old get religion) and the priest began to pray; when a decent looking man approached the stand, and took a female by the arm, and led her away. As he walked along, the preacher pointed to him and said, "God strike that sinner down!" The man turned around, and in an angry tone said, "God has more sense than to mind such a d--d fool as you are" and resumed his course. . . . The lady was his wife.

Being tired of such an abominable scene, I proposed returning home, and taking a near cut through a slip of woodland, we surprised the red scarf lady in a manner that gave us no favorable opinion of her piety.—*Letters from Alabama* (University: University of Alabama Press, 1969), pp. 205–207.

A Universalist Visits Alabama

Most of the clergy who came into Alabama were of orthodox faith with Baptists, Methodists, Presbyterians, and Episcopalians leading the list. However, there was an occasional non-conformist like the Reverend George Rogers, a Universalist preacher from Pennsylvania (a self-styled heretic), who visited several places in western and central Alabama in the late 1830's.

February 16, [1837]. Arrived a few hours before sunset at the flourishing town of Greensborough; hitched my horse to a post and commenced adventures toward a meeting for the evening and made . . . a most lucky commencement. I accosted the keeper of the first store into which I stepped. "I am a Universalist preacher, sir. Do you know of any room in the place to which I could have access for the purpose of a meeting this evening?" "Yes sir, I know of one if you will accept it. It is pleasant and well situated. I mean the theatre in this town." "I will accept, sir, any place—truth is truth, no matter where communicated—and to whom shall I apply for its use?" "I have control of it, sir, and will engage to have it opened for you." "And lighted, too?" "Yes, sir." I thanked him and forthwith wrote an advertisement which he procured a boy . . . to carry through the town. . . . I next ventured to inquire, "Do you know, sir, of any believer in my doctrine in the place who would be likely to entertain myself and horse over the night?" "I really do not, sir, but if you put up with such fare as I can afford, you will be entirely welcome. . . ."

Well, the theatre was handsomely lighted and . . . the meeting was respectably attended. My stand was on the stage in front of the drop curtain, and never surely stood a speaker there whose voice and manner and attitudes were less adapted for stage effect upon an audience. Happily I had no thrilling horrors to relate "whose lightest word would harrow up the soul, freeze the young blood, and make every particular hair to stand on end, like quills upon the fretful porcupine." Mine was a mild message of gospel mercy, and needed no "stare and start theatric" to give it effect.

Feb. 17. Rode to Marion, Perry county, a remarkably neat county town, possessing several features of a yankee village, all honestly come by for it has been partly built under yankee supervision. Here were my eyes greeted by the first painted meetinghouse spire that I had seen in several hundred miles travel and the first regular market house I had seen since leaving Louisville. . . .

I called upon Mr. L. and I. Upson, who are eastern men, with them I truly felt myself at home and oh how much good it did me to hear myself called Brother Rogers once more! . . . The Upsons are nearly alone in point of religious faith; they have, however, and deservedly, a good share of influence, and will, I think, not be alone long. I delivered three discourses there to rather small and exclusively male audiences. . . .

Feb. 27. I am now at General Brantly's whose wife is one of the most zealous, rejoicing, and practical Universalists I know of. A beam of gladness lighted up her features so soon as I had introduced myself. "I must take your hand," said she, "I didn't know that I should see another gospel preacher." I preached yesterday in what is termed the Shady Grove Meeting house in this neighborhood. A good audience was in attendance, but from two causes the meeting was not agreeable. First, by a sudden change the weather had become cold, and meeting houses in this region in the country are the most comfortless houses imaginable, completely open to the weather on both sides. Second, certain lewd fellows of the baser sort evinced their lack of sense by their lack of decency . . . and afforded a beautiful illustration of that oft repeated orthodox truth that "sinners love Universalism." However, there are several highly respected friends to the cause in this neighborhood who, without doubt, would liberally sustain the stated ministrations of the gospel here. The Shady Grove Meeting house is but nine miles from Selma. . . .

In Selma I found but one professed Universalist, the wife of Dr. Grigsby; it is but feeble praise to say of her that she is well adapted to do the profession honor. Her station in society gives her influence and she needs no prompting in order to use that influence aright. I delivered three discourses in the Presbyterian Church to very attentive audiences. The Presbyterian clergyman attended two evenings. The Methodist minister, I believe, attended all three. . . .

The Universalist church in Montgomery is a neat and tasteful fabric, surmounted with a steeple and bell and furnished with an excellent organ. It was gotten up, however, and entirely supported by about three individuals, two of whom, Majors Wood and Cowles live the one seven and the other four miles out of the town. It might have been foreseen, methinks, that it could not live long under such circumstances. . . .

About sixteen miles from Montgomery across the Coosa River in a neighborhood which bears the name of Mount Olympus there is a little Universalist society which meets for religious worship steadily on the first Sundays in each month. Mr. Atkins resides there and preaches for them on those occasions . . . he was formerly a Methodist and the main support of that church in the same neighborhood. . . .

There is a free colored man who with his family are members of the Mt. Olympus society, the first Universalist person of color I had ever seen, for the African race are in general very ignorant and prone to superstitions. . . .

[At Wetumpka] on the fourth Saturday evening, as I was about dismissing the audience, the Baptist minister arose and reminding me of a declaration I had made in a previous discourse that I could establish the correctness of my views concerning the closing paragraph of the twenty-fifth of Matthew by such evidence as would settle any question in a court of justice, said he would give me one hundred dollars if I would make my declaration good. I told him I accepted his terms and inquired when it would suit him to have it done; he named the next evening and I made the appointment accordingly.

Sunday forenoon I preached in the Episcopalian Church and notwithstanding the other meetings in town, the seats were all filled. In the evening it was crowded to excess. . . . At length on the motion of the Baptist clergyman, we transferred the meeting to his church which was larger. . . . Nothing could exceed the attentive interest with which I was listened to by that large assembly while I attempted to show . . . that the coming of Christ referred to in the twenty-fifth Matthew was an event of past occurance, instead of yet to take place as the popular scholiasts pretend. When I had finished, the Baptist minister succeeded me in an harangue—it was nothing more. . . . I deemed it superflous to occupy more than ten minutes in rejoinder. . . .

I have reason to believe I left many friends and well-wishers in our cause in Wetumpka. . . .—George Rogers, *Memoranda of the Experience, Labor, and Travels of a Universalist Preacher* (Cincinnati, 1845), pp. 213–20.

A Church Trial

In antebellum days the church more than any other institution was the arbiter of morals. Church members were expected to live according to the accepted moral code and to abide by the rules of the church. Church authorites did not hesitate to call transgressors before the church courts to answer for their waywardness. Church minutes are full of cases of lying, stealing, adultery, swearing, and dancing.

The case of the young couple being tried for dancing at their wedding is from the "Proceedings of Concord (Greene County) Presbyterian Church," Ms., Presbyterian Historical Foundation, Montreat, N. C. Tuscaloosa Presbytery, through Rev. Robert Moody Holmes, stated clerk, kindly permitted me to quote the passage below.

Mr. Childs and his lady both members of the church, having participated in the amusements of a dancing party given to them in the village of Havana November 1828 on the occasion of their marriage after a private interview was held with them by the pastor of the church and he having expressed a willingness to meet the session, he accordingly appeared before them this day.

The session after hearing all the circumstances of the case and his confession of sorrow for the offence unanimously Resolved 1st that in yealding to the solicitations of his friends to engage in that amusement he did not maintain that firmness and decision of character which became the professed friends of Christ under such circumstances.

Resolved 2nd that in consideration of the peculiar situation in which Mr. Childs was placed on the above occasion his conduct hitherto as

a church member and the candid declaration he has this day made of
sorrow for the offence, the session do feel themselves bound to extend
to him that forgiveness which we all so often need for ourselves. At
the same time we affectionately admonish Mr. Childs that should he
ever in the Providence of God be placed in like circumstances be more
upon his guard to endeavor to exercise greater firmness of Christian
principle.

Missions and Missionaries

The nineteenth century church in America was a missionary
church, sending its sons and daughters to the far corners of the
earth to carry the Christian gospel. Under the influence of what
is sometimes called the Second Great Awakening, Presbyterian,
Methodist, Baptist, and Congregational churches formed their own
boards of missions or joined in one or two of the great interdenom-
inational boards: The American Board of Commissioners for
Foreign Missions (1810) and the American Home Missionary
Society. While cooperation with such a movement appears praiseworthy, it was one of the questions that led to a split in some of
the churches at a later date.

Generally speaking, churches in Alabama were also missionary-
minded. Here the first official activity of the Methodists and Presbyterians was conducted by missionaries. In spite of frontier conditions and the poverty of the settlers, denominations early began
taking regular offerings for foreign missions which included the
Indians. The very first reference to missions in the annals of the
Alabama Presbyterian Church was a small offering taken at Wilson's Hill (Montevallo) in 1822 for the Chickasaw Indians at Monroe Station in Mississippi. By 1831 all churches in North Alabama
Presbytery took regular offerings for foreign missions. In one
church in southern Alabama, the Negroes had their own missionary
society which contributed $15.00 to send the gospel to their ances-
tral homeland in Africa. This (1839) is the first mention of a
foreign continent in the records of the Presbyterian church in this
state. Rev. William H. McAuley from Sand Ridge Church in
Autauga County became the first (1839) Alabama Presbyterian to
go as a foreign missionary. He served in India for a period of ten
years before his wife's declining health forced him to return to
the United States. Rev. Robert M. Longbridge of Tuscaloosa, who
served as evangelist among the Creeks in Oklahoma for over
twenty years, was only one of several who did so.

Alabama Baptists, after being violently antimission for a period,
surprised the state convention in 1857 by raising $1000.00 for R. W.
Priest who had gone to Africa some years earlier. Mrs. Martha
Foster Crawford, sister of Dr. D. L. Foster and Chancellor John

A. Foster, went from Tuscaloosa to China in 1850 as a Baptist missionary. The missionary activities of this state denomination increased so rapidly that by 1888 it had seventeen missionaries in Cuba alone.

The Alabama Methodist Conference for 1853 was held in Tuscaloosa. On the fourth day of the meeting there was a "Missionary Anniversary" at which the Rev. Thomas O. Summers delivered an address of "thundering sound and learned length," and Dr. Benjamin Jenkins of South Carolina, who had served his church in China, gave an address on the Celestial Empire. At the close of the lecture, the Rev. James S. Belton, who had just been admitted into full connection with the Conference, explained to the audience of ministers his reasons for deciding to devote his life to the China mission. The assembly was so impressed with his desire to "disenthrall the heathen" that they subscribed $300.00 to pay for his passage to India, and one member of the Conference raised over $1000.00 to help pay for a printing press to be sent along with Mr. Belton.

The Methodists seem to have been more active among the Indians within the state than the other churches. In 1821 the South Carolina Conference authorized the creation of two missions among the Creeks in Alabama. The one near Tuckabatchee named McKendree for the bishop was never opened, but Asbury near Fort Mitchell operated until about the time the Creeks were removed from the state. Making civilized Christians out of the "naked savages" took time, but eventually a number did become church members. The school there, which became for all practical purposes a manual labor school, got more results. The Rev. William Capers, Isaac Smith, and Andrew Hammill were the men responsible for Asbury Mission.

While many church people did not consider work with the slaves as missions, they did have a decided interest in it. There were a few all black congregations but many more biracial. Of the all-Negro churches one of the most successful was the Mobile State Street Colored Mission sponsored by the Methodists. In 1855 it had 500 full and 50 probationary members, a good Sunday School, and a brick building on which they had already paid $4000.00 of the $6000.00 cost. The Methodists seem to have been the most active in special work among the slaves. In 1854, for example, Alabama Conference had 35 men with this kind of assignment. However, the vast majority of slaves belonged to the churches with their masters. Baptist, Episcopalian, Methodist, Presbyterian, and possibly other churches accepted Negroes in full membership. They sat in special areas in the gallery (some of which can still be used), at the rear, or to one side, but they were in the same room. They heard the same sermons, sang the same hymns, and were subject to the same rules.

There were a few Negro preachers. One of the best known was Caesar Blackwell, or McLemore, who often accompanied his Baptist minister master on preaching assignments. After the master's death the Alabama Baptist Convention purchased his freedom so that he could spend his time ministering to his people. He preached and baptized at Wetumpka, Mt. Giliad, Montgomery, and other churches in south central Alabama.

One of the most interesting cases involving the church in Alabama, Negroes, and foreign missions is that of Harrison Ellis, a slave of Mr. Robert Cresswell of Eutaw. In January, 1843, the Alabama Synod of the Presbyterian Church began a movement to raise $2500.00 to purchase Ellis, his wife, his son, and daughter to send them to Liberia as missionaries. Money for the purchase was slow coming in, but by August, 1846 it was completed. Ellis was not free but the property of the Synods of Alabama and Mississippi. He was under the jurisdiction of the Tuscaloosa Presbytery after his purchase.

The next step in the foreign mission process was the licensure of Ellis, the former blacksmith. Accursed as the world has been taught to believe the slave system was, let it here be noted that Ellis was about to become a Presbyterian minister and so must needs stand an examination. This covered

> Latin
> Greek
> Natural and Revealed Religion
> Ecclesiastical History
> Church Government

and his own testimony was accepted to the effect that he had read

> Natural Philosophy—Olmsted
> Moral Science—Wayland
> Homoletics—Porter
> Interpretation—Ernest

after which he read a sermon from the text, "And I give unto them eternal life; and they shall never perish, neither shall any man pluck them out of my hand. My father, which gave them me, is greater than all; and no man is able to pluck them out of my Father's hand."—John 10:28–29.

As an advertising element in raising the funds to complete the payments to Mr. Cresswell, Tuscaloosa Presbytery at Bethel Church decided to go over all this ground again at Synod in Wetumpka for the completion of the licensure by ordination, the procedure taking up part of three days. George Howe of Columbia Seminary was present in Synod and was asked to examine Ellis in Hebrew. To the surprise of

Howe—and perhaps many members of Synod—Ellis showed a better knowledge of Hebrew than many of Howe's Columbia graduates.

R. B. Cater, one of the oldest members of Synod, examined him on Theology.

"How is a sinner saved?"

"By grace."

"What do you mean by grace?"

"Something for nothing."

This was but one instance of the originality of his answers which were of more than ordinary interest to the large assembly of the people of Wetumpka who were attracted by the unusual prospect of seeing a Negro slave initiated into the office of the Presbyterian ministry.

To all appearances Ellis at this time was about thirty years of age, of large brain, high forehead, fine physique, and spoke quite deliberately. He had learned his letters by having his master's children draw them with charcoal and also by cutting them from newspapers and pasting them on the walls of his blacksmith shop. Without regular teachers, without any books except as he begged or borrowed them, he had reached his goal almost as soon as those whose facilities were multiplied, all the while delivering his tale of bricks in his calling of blacksmith. When some member of Synod asked him who had helped him, he replied, "Dr. Stillman," upon which reply Stillman claimed that all the aid he had given Ellis would not amount to twelve hours. His ordination sermon was from the text, "This is a faithful saying, and worthy of all acceptation, that Christ Jesus came into the world to save sinners; of whom I am chief"—First Timothy 1:15. It goes without saying that the examination was unanimously sustained, and ordination followed, R. B. White presiding, Robert H. Chapman preaching the sermon, and J. L. Kirkpatrick charging the minister.

Everything was now in readiness for his departure; so according to previous arrangement Charles A. Stillman accompanied him to New Orleans where the family took passage on the schooner, "Eliza Wilkes," January 12, 1847, for Liberia. The date of arrival is given as March 22, indicating that the voyage consumed 69 days.

The next we hear of Ellis is in connection with the progress of the mission to the extent that a Presbytery was formed which is always a joy in the Presbyterian denominational program of expansion. This court was established in 1848 and lived for four years.—James W. Marshall, *Presbyterian Church in Alabama*, vol. 4, pp. 1674–76. Ms. Department of Archives and History, Montgomery.

There were charges of misconduct made against Ellis in Africa which were not proved, and after a suspension he was restored by his fellow missionaries in Africa to the work of the ministry. When the General Assembly decided to create the Presbytery of Africa, attaching it to the Synod of New York, the the names of Ellis, James W. Priest, D. S. Wilson, all Alabamians, were erased

from the rolls of Tuscaloosa Presbytery. After 1869 nothing more
was heard of Ellis.

Churches were not always of one mind about missions, however.
The early Baptist Church in Alabama, for example, was almost
wholly antimission; only gradually did it change its position. In doing so it caused one of several splits within its ranks, the antimission people becoming the Primitive or "Hardshell" Baptists. Doc-
trinally their position was based on belief in ultra predestination.
Believing that each man's fate in eternity was already settled,
they saw no need to waste money and effort in trying to alter God's
will. If a man was "lost," he was "lost," and no amount of Sunday
Schools, theological seminaries, tract societies, and other modern
devices would change it. Mt. Olive Primitive Baptist Church
(Shelby County) recorded its position on such matters.

> . . . This church will not fellowship any church or churches who
> are engaged in supporting any missionary, Bible, tract or Sunday School
> union or advocate state conventions, theological schools, nor any other
> society that has been or may hereafter be formed under the pretents
> [sic] of circulating the Gospel of Christ.—Copy in Shelby County file,
> Department of Archives and History, Montgomery.

The Churches Split

There were other questions on which large numbers disagreed,
"modernism" and slavery heading the list. In spite of (or possibly
because of) the fact that the churches grew rapidly in Alabama,
the three main denominations were rent asunder before 1860: the
Methodist and Baptist over slavery and the Presbyterian over
the Old School-New School issue. The Presbyterian was the first.

THE PRESBYTERIAN U. S. 1837

The Presbyterian Church, U. S. (Southern), resulted from a split
in the parent body in 1837. During the 1830's there were two parties in the church, the Old School, and the New School, which came
to a head-on clash in 1837. Basically the controversy was between
the Conservatives (Old School) and the Liberals (New School). The
issues at stake were the doctrine of original sin, the handling of
benevolences, and, although it is not mentioned in the proceedings,
the institution of slavery. The General Assembly of 1837 had a
majority of Old School men who proceeded to rid the official
body of offending presbyteries and made agreements to make
the boards of the church the only agents of the church. About
five-ninths of the ministers and members became the Presbyterian
Church, U. S., and the other four-ninths (led by the New School
forces) formed the Presbyterian Church, U. S. A.

In the Presbyterian Church, the local Presbyteries must take action on matters affecting the whole church. The resolutions over a period of years on the controversial issues in North Alabama Presbytery are given here to show the development of the controversy.

ACTION OF THE NORTH ALABAMA PRESBYTERY ON THE CONTROVERSIAL ISSUES, 1831–1838
[1831]

Resolved that it be recommended to all churches within our bounds to take up a monthly collection in aid of the funds of the American Board of Commissioners for Foreign Missions.

[April 5, 1832]

The committee appointed to take into consideration the minutes of the Convention in Cincinnati, & the report of the minority, made the following report, viz.

Whereas, the minutes of the convention which met in Cincinnati in 1831 by recommendation of the last Genl. Assembly to consult on Missions, and also the report of the minority of said convention have been sent to this Presbytery with the design that they may express their views on the subject, Resolved that this Presbytery severely regret, that the evils occasioned by the collisions of Assembly's Board and the Board of the American Home Missionary Society from their separate action in the valley of the Mississippi appear not likely to be removed by the measures adopted by that convention.

Resolved that the measures proposed by the minority of the convention to request the next Genl. Assembly to form a Separate board in the west were in the view of this Presbytery made in the spirit of compromise, and would in their opinion be the most probable means of removing the evils, complained of, & producing peace in the church.

Resolved, that although in view of the feelings of a large portion of our church on this subject, a union of the two boards is not now to be expected, yet this presbytery do approve of the organization & rejoice in the operations of the American Home Missionary Society. This report was adopted by the following vote, viz, 9 to 7.

[Sept. 7, 1837, Moulton, Ala.]

Saturday morning, 8½ o'clock.

Presbytery met and was constituted with prayer.

The committee appointed to draft a resolution or resolutions expressive of the views of this presbytery in regard to the doings of the last assembly in reference to the attempted excision of the Synods of Western Reserve, Genessee, Geneva & Utica etc. Reported, which report was accepted, and, is as follows, viz.:

The Committee appointed to draft a resolution or resolutions expressive of the views of this Presbytery in reference to the doings of the last Gen'l Assembly in regard to their attempted excision of the four Synods of Western Reserve, Geneva, Gennessee, and Utica, and also their attempted effort to dissolve the third Presbytery of Philadea— beg leave to present the following report—

Resolved, 1st Th[at] the Presbyteries of our Church being the appointed guardians of its constitution it is at once our duty and privilege as a Presbytery to review the proceedings of the General Assembly and to express our approval or disapproval of any measures adopted by them.

Resolved 2d. that the attempted excision of the four Synods above mentioned is highly unconstitutional. The following reasons are offered in proof of this position.

First, These Synods were regularly constituted by the Gen'l. Assembly whose province it is to form Synods. These Synods were not created by the Plan of Union of 1801, and did not depend for their original existence or continuation upon that plan. Were we to admit the propriety of the act of abrogation, it can do no more than take away the privileges it conferred, among these may be enumerated as most objectionable the provision which admitted a committee man to have a seat in the Presbytery, now the act of abrogation takes away this privilege, and the committee man has no longer a seat—

But how this feature in the plan of union or any other which it contains goes to vitiate the entire structure of Presbyteries & Synods formed by the Assembly itself your committee cannot see.

Secondly, whatever may be the gentle language of the friend of excision, denying that it is excision—it appears to us most manifestly a judicial act of the utmost severity cutting off from the church a very large number of ministers and laity without giving them the opportunity of a hearing. . . .

Resolved 3d. That the Third Presbytery of Philad. has just cause of complaint against the last genl. assembly in their effort to dissolve that Presbytery—The resolution purporting the dissolution of that Presbytery was manifestly unconstitutional because it virtually condemned theirs without accusation or citation—It was an assumption of power not authorized by the Book of Discipline. . . .

Resolved 4. That we do hereby cordially sympathize with the so called ejected Synods and with the third Pres. of Philada. and that we concur in the opinion expressed by a large number of the brethren, that the Presbyteries comprising those Synods together with the Pres. of Philada. should go on to elect commissioners to the next Genl. Assembly as heretofore regarding the action of the last Assembly, in reference to them as entirely unconstitutional—

Preamble & first Resolution unanimously adopted—
Second Resolution adopted
Third & fourth Resolution lost
[Oct. 6, 1838]

The committee to examine the minutes of the Assembly, reported, which report was accepted and the resolution which it contained adopted, and it is as follows—

They recommend to the attention of the Pres. the acts of the Assembly on the State of the Church, pps. 34,35, and would recommend the adoption of the following resolution in regard thereto, viz.—

Resolved that while it is known that there exists a difference of opinion among the members of this Presbytery in regard to the regularity or expediency of some of the acts of the Assemblies of '37 and '38. They do nevertheless hereby declare their cordial adherence to the body which met in the 7th Pres. Church in the city of Philadelphia and continued its session there until its close as being the true & only Gen. Assembly of the Presbyterian Church in the United States of America.

Adopted 9 for
       5 against

W. W. Sweet (ed.), *Religion on the American Frontier: the Presbyterians* (New York: Harper and Bros., 1936), pp. 444–48.

THE BAPTISTS, 1844

For more than a decade the Baptist Convention had been disturbed by the "sinister agencies . . . clandestinely seeking to incite the slaves to resistence. . . ." This Church, like the other Protestant Churches, had wavered in its attitude toward slavery, but by the 1840's had taken what might be called a "hard line." The breach between the Alabama Baptists and their brethren in the free states (and their withdrawal from the Triennial Convention) came in 1844 in Marion; and it was over the query "Is it proper for us in the South to send any money to our brethren at the North for missionary and other benevolent purposes before the subject of slavery be rightfuly understood by both parties?" The answer was "Alabama Resolutions," authored by Dr. Basil Manly, pastor of the Tuscaloosa church.

Whereas, the holding of property in African negro slaves has for some years excited discussion as a question of morals between different portions of the Baptist denomination united in benevolent enterprise, and by a large portion of our brethren is now so imputed to the slaveholders in these Southern and Southwestern states as a sin at once grievous, palpable and disqualifying,

1. *Resolved,* that when one party to a voluntary compact among Christian brethren is not willing to acknowledge the entire social equality with the other as to all privileges and benefits of the union, not even to refrain from impeachment and annoyance, united efforts between such parties, even in the sacred course of Christian benevolence, cease to be agreeable, useful, or proper.

2. *Resolved,* That our duty at this crisis requires of us to demand from the proper authorities in all those bodies to whose funds we have contributed or with whom we have in any way been connected, the distinct explicit avowal that slaveholders are eligible, and entitled equally with non-slaveholders to all the privileges and immunities of their several unions, and especially to receive any agency, mission, or other appointment which may run within of their operations or duties.— Quoted in F. B. Riley, *A Memorial History of the Baptists of Alabama* (Philadelphia: The Judson Press, 1923), p. 82.

Dr. J. B. Jeter was the state delegate to a meeting of the Baptists from eight slaveholding states which met in Augusta, Georgia, that organized the Southern Baptist Convention on May 10, 1845.

THE METHODIST EPISCOPAL CHURCH, SOUTH, 1846

In 1846 the Methodist Episcopal Church, South, went into operation. At that time there were about 32,000 white and 15,000 black members.

The formation of a separate church resulted from a series of events which culminated in the crisis of 1844. Slavery was the central question debated at the General Conference meeting in New York which lasted six weeks. Specifically, the debate centered around the connection of Bishop James O. Andrew of Georgia to slavery. After many reports and heated discussion, a resolution was passed debarring Bishop Andrew (who through marriage had become a slaveholder) from his ecclesiastical office until "this impediment" should be removed. This led to the final break in the church.

A public meeting of the citizens of Russell County, Alabama, was held at Crawford, on June 8. This meeting was convened for political purposes, and passed a preamble and resolutions in accordance with these purposes. The following resolutions, adopted, among the rest, without a dissenting voice, will interest the readers of this paper:

Be it further Resolved, That this meeting has witnessed with intense interest, and painful anxiety, the agitation of the slave question in the General Conference of the Methodist Episcopal Church, now convened in the City of New York. They have seen that a topic, which hitherto has excited the bad passions of man only in the orgies of fanaticism, or in the strife of factions in their unprincipled struggle for political power, has been transferred to the foot of that throne which ought to be sacred to charity, peace, and good will among Brethren of the same Faith. They have beheld with unutterable indignation, the humiliating fact of a Bishop of the State of Georgia, eminent for his piety, learning, ability, and Christian virtues put in effect upon his trial as a culprit, for the alleged sin of marrying a lady possessed of slaves, by which it is insultingly affirmed, that a slaveholder is an unfit Teacher of the Word of God, and must submit, if tolerated as a member of the Church of Christ, to a subordinate station in the Ministry. A discrimination which finds no warrant in the sacred oracles of God, and which involves both insult and outrage to the people of an entire section of this Union.

Be it further Resolved, that if Bishop Andrew should be deposed from his Episcopal functions, we earnestly invoke the clergy of the Methodist Episcopal Church at the South, to take immediate measures for their secession from a Conference which has placed so gross a stigma not only on themselves but on their respective Flocks. An insult which can admit of but one remedy, in the application of which they may be assured of the warm sympathy and unalterable support of the religious congregations of the whole Southern States of every sect and denomination.—Quoted in Anson West, *A History of Methodism in Alabama* (Nashville: Publishing House, Methodist Episcopal Church, South, 1893), pp. 440–43.

In summary, what was the role of the church in antebellum Alabama? It did the obvious things in organizing churches and holding weekly, monthly, or quarterly church services. To reach a wider audience it conducted revivals and camp meetings. It regulated to some extent relations between members of a congregation, between masters and slaves, and between its members and the community. In the records of every denomination there are accounts of trials of members who were "churched" (found guilty and expelled) for one or more of a variety of sins. Often, as in the case of Thomas Gill at Providence Church, the church designated a committee to bring the wayward person to reason or to heal the rift between differing members.

The three leading denominations in the state were vitally interested in providing education for both their ministers and others. To that end they established colleges like Southern University, Howard College, Judson, Tuskeegee Female College, La Grange, and many more, but at the same time did not neglect lower education in a number of academies.

After its initial purpose of preaching the gospel, the most important role of the church was social in nature. The church, more than any other institution in antebellum Alabama, was the center of life. Whether it was at revivals, camp meetings, "regular preaching," or funerals, neighbors visited, farmers exchanged news of crops and politics and were even known to arrange sales, women swapped recipes and home remedies, young people courted, children played, and politicians solicited votes. The church, whether in the rural areas or in urban centers, very often had the largest building in the community, and it was frequently used for lectures, rallies, and meetings of various kinds.

The path of the church was often far from smooth, however. At times denominationalism seemed more important than Christianity with the churches fighting over such doctrines and practices as original sin and free will, the proper form of baptism, church hierarchy, missions, and Sunday Schools. Not only did denominations attack each other, but they also disagreed within their own bodies to such an extent that there was an occasional separation to form a new church. In spite of differences and bickering, however, the church marched on, increasing in both size and influence.

Chapter 8

SCHOOLS IN ANTEBELLUM ALABAMA

There must have been schools in Mobile under the French regime but the earliest school in what is now Alabama that we know anything about (and that is very little) was the one run by John Pierce at Boat Yard on Lake Tensaw in 1799. He had what was known as a "blab" school at which the pupils studied aloud. Here he taught the children of wealthy planters and members of several half-breed families—the Weatherfords, McQueens, Durants, and others. John Pierce with his brother William, however, soon turned to a more profitable business than that of a school keeping, erecting cotton gins and engaging in mercantile enterprises.

Whether there were other schools before 1800 is not certain, and it was not until 1811 when the Mississippi Territory chartered Washington Academy at St. Stephens that official action was taken to establish one. This did not mean, however, that there was no interest in schools. As early as 1805, settlers in Washington County (which still included a large tract in what is now Mississippi) petitioned the House of Representatives of the United States to exchange some sixteen sections of public land, set aside for schools, for a tract of eighty acres "on which the old Spanish Fort, called Fort St. Stephens, and an old priest's house are standing, these buildings now being occupied by the United States trading house for the Choctaws. . . ." This tract was suitable for a town which could support a school. Up to that time the inhabitants had been unable to attract competent teachers to settle among them and, consequently, "their children have scarcely any opportunities" to be instructed at home and they were so remote that sending them elsewhere for that purpose was impractical. Therefore the petitioners asked

246

That one of the courts of the county or district of Washington, be authorized to appoint trustees of schools in each of the several townships which are settled within this county,—to fill vacancies from time to time occasioned by death, resignation or removal out of their townships respectively, and to exercise such a general superintendence over them as may be necessary in order to ensure a faithful discharge of the duties of their trusts.

That the trustees of every township have power to locate within their township for the support of a school within the same, any quantity of vacant land not exceeding 640 acres, and that where so much vacant land cannot be found within their township, they be authorized instead thereof to appropriate for the same purpose, one section in any other township, provided that if trustees have been appointed in such other township, they shall make a previous location for the benefit of such township.

That the trustees of the township in which the aforesaid tract containing about eighty acres, (and which is bounded by the Tombigby river, and the lands of John Chastang, Peter Malone & Edwin Lewis) or the greater part thereof may lie,—be authorized to lay off the same for a town, and to dispose of the lots at public auction, reserving an annual rent on each for the use of the school within such township— to take possession of the public buildings standing on the said tract for the benefit of such school, whenever the President of the United States shall make known to them that the United States have (no) further use for them,—and moreover to locate one (or) more sections (as it may please your honourable house) on the east side of the Tombigby river, (when the indian title shall be extinguished) for the support of such school, which shall be deemed a superior school, for the general advantage of the county of Washington.

That the trustees of the several townships be empowered to divide the lands entrusted to them into such portions as they may deem expedient, and publicly to lease the same from time to time for any term not exceeding (blank) years, that the proceeds thereof be under their direction for the sole use of their respective schools,—and that they be authorized to employ as teachers for their respective townships, persons of respectable character & qualifications.—C. E. Carter, ed., *Territorial Papers* (Washington, Government Printing Office, 1937), vol. 5, pp. 438–40.

Of Washington Academy we know almost nothing beyond the charter and the fact that it was rechartered as St. Stephens Academy in 1818. Of Green Academy, Huntsville, which was chartered by the territorial legislature in 1812 and lasted for fifty years until federal troops burned the building during the Civil War, we know considerably more. It, like Washington Academy, was to be tax exempt, could raise up to $4,000 by public lottery, and was given $500 out of the territorial treasury. A board of trustees (fifteen at the start) had the responsibility for locating the school conducting the lottery, raising other money as needed, and doing whatever was required to get the school underway. Not until 1816 did the legislature actually appropriate the promised $500 and, because of other delays, the buildings were not ready until 1819. It was located on the corner of Lincoln and Williams Street. The exact date the academy started classes seems to be unknown but it had been functioning in temporary quarters before the building was erected. Tuition brought in some money, but welcome additional funds came from the Planters' and Merchants' Bank of Huntsville. In late 1818, the Alabama legislature authorized the bank to increase its capital stock by selling shares to the public. Ninety percent of the profits or excess of a designated sum was to go to support the academy.

For many years it was the only institution for advanced education in north Alabama and consequently many of the area's prominent men were trained there. Among its trustees were some of the best known Alabamians of the period: a later governor, at least one United States senator, several legislators, and business and professional men. After the buildings were destroyed during the Civil War, it was not reopened.

Green Academy seems to have been the only successful school dating from the territorial period. It was both private and public; it depended largely on tuition for support but was chartered by the government, received $500 from the public treasury, and other funds from the public through the bank and the lottery.

In 1819 the new state was given the sixteenth section in each township for schools. This practice dates back to the 1787 Northwest Ordinance and was later applied to all lands in the southwest as well. Furthermore, the framers of the state's first constitution (1819) stated firmly their position on public education by setting aside lands for the support of a state university and for the promotion of the arts, literature, and the sciences.

With what appears to be adequate support in land and a favorable attitude in government one might expect the state to have moved toward a state-wide, public-supported school system within a reasonable time. Unfortunately, such was not the case. Many factors entered into the delay—mismanagement of funds, scattered population, indifference toward public-supported schools—and it was not until 1854 that legislation providing for a school system was passed. Gallant efforts were made to get it in operation but it was only in the infant stages at the outbreak of war in 1861.

This does not mean, however, that Alabama was without schools before that date. There were many of them. We do not know how many elementary or private schools there were but Dr. A. B.

Moore says that more than 250 academies had been chartered by the legislature in the antebellum period. Although lines were not clearly drawn between elementary schools and academies (and academies and colleges, for that matter), an academy was generally expected to give "advanced" instruction. They could compare roughly with the secondary schools of a later date but many of them also gave instruction to beginners. Academies were often, but not always, boarding schools. They were private schools, some being exempt from taxes but none of them receiving other financial aid from the state. These academies were chartered by the state legislature for churches, fraternal organizations, a group of people, a community, or an individual. Many towns had both male and female academies since few schools beyond the lowest "grades" were coeducational. Some towns had several: Talladega, for example, had East Alabama Masonic Female Institute, Talladega Male High School, Southward Select School, and Presbyterian Collegiate Female Institute. Huntsville, Tuscaloosa, Selma, Montgomery, and Mobile were other places that had numerous schools.

Advertisements in the newspapers furnish much information about these antebellum institutions, not only their location but also subjects offered, textbooks, training of faculty, and costs. The public notice given here can be multiplied many times.

SIBLEY ACADEMY,
At Montrose.

This Institution, situated on the East Shore of Mobile Bay, is NOW OPEN for the reception of Pupils of both sexes at any stage of advancement.

The Trustees have secured the services of ANSEL LAMSON, A. B., a graduate of Harvard University, and highly recommended as a competent Teacher in all the branches of a thorough education, as Principal of the Male Department.

Miss Louisa L. Morse, a lady of much experience and established reputation as Teacher, possessing acquirements pecularly adapting her to the position, takes charge of the Female Department.

The Course of Study will be the same as that pursued in our best Seminaries of learning, and it will be the aim in every Department to render instruction both attractive and thorough.

The situation of Montrose offers superior advantages to the students, on account of the salubrity of its atmosphere, its freedom from epidemics, and its convenient distance from Mobile.

It is the design of the Trustees to place the institution upon such a basis as will entitle it to the confidence and patronage of parents and guardians at home and abroad.

For information regarding terms or other particulars, apply to the Principal of either Department, or to

One of the best known and successful academies run by an individual was Professor Henry Tutwiler's Greene Springs School. Tutwiler, the holder of two degrees from the University of Virginia, had been on the faculties of both the University of Alabama and La Grange College before deciding to establish his own academy in 1847. He chose Greene Springs, which had been popular as a resort or "watering place," in Hale (but then Greene) County, not far from the village of Havana, but far enough that the students would have few distractions. The first buildings were the remodeled hotel buildings.

The academy was a success from the beginning. Because there was always a waiting list, Mr. Tutwiler could select his students with care and easily replace any "bad or obstinate" boy he had to send home. A statement in the catalog dated June 29, 1876, when the school was more than a quarter of a century old, helps to explain both its popularity and its success.

'To prepare young men for the business of life, or for the higher classes in our colleges and universities,' was the object proposed at the foundation of the school, and this object has been, and will continue to be, kept steadily in view. There is no division of the whole body of students into classes, but each individual is placed in such classes, in his various studies, as he may be prepared to join with benefit to himself. A prominent place is given to the studies of ancient languages and mathematics as those best calculated to promote sound and thorough intellectual training. * * * At the same time, we have long been impressed with the conviction that our ordinary system of education is defective in not calling the attention of the young, at a sufficiently early age, to an observation of the phenomena around us; thus blunting, instead of stimulating, that curiosity which is a part of our nature. It has been our constant aim, therefore, to interest our students in those sciences which have revolutionized the whole domain of industry, and diffused the comforts and luxuries of life among the great mass of mankind. For this purpose, we have provided apparatus sufficient for illustrating the various branches of natural philosophy and chemistry, and additions are made, from time to time, to enable us to keep pace with the progress of these sciences. Besides having regular classes in these studies, lectures, accompanied by experiments, are delivered frequently to all the students. * * * Ancient geography and history are taught in connection with ancient languages. The mathematical course embraces not only the theory of the branches usually taught, but also the practical applications of trigonometry to heights and distances, field surveys, levelling, navigation, etc., and suitable instruments are provided for this purpose. Instruction is given in modern languages by competent teachers. English compositions are required weekly from all the students, and a portion of Saturday is devoted to this purpose. * * * A library of several thousand well-selected volumes is open, free of charge, to all the students, many of whom are thus induced to employ, in a profitable manner, those spare moments which would otherwise be wasted. Additions of new and valuable books are made several times a year, and all books that have a tendency to corrupt the taste are carefully excluded. There are also libraries belonging to the literary societies of the school to which the members of the societies have free access. * * * The school has been supplied with a fine telescope of high magnifying powers, the gift of an esteemed and generous friend, Joel E. Mathews, Esq., of Selma.—Quoted in Willis G. Clark, *History of Education in Alabama, 1702–1889* (Washington, D. C.: Government Printing Office, 1889), p. 206.

The home life that the Tutwiler family provided made a deep impression on the boys. Mr. Tutwiler, and very likely his wife, spent much time with them and especially on Sundays when he met them informally after breakfast, dinner, and tea.

Greene Springs was coeducational. Its founder believed in giving his daughters (and the daughters of some of his planter friends) as good an education as any man's sons. His daughters, including Julia who later was a leader in many movements in the state, attended classes with the boys, had the same assignments but, probably for practical reasons, had separate study halls. In her later life, Miss Julia Tutwiler said that the contacts she made at her father's school with future judges, legislators, and business leaders were invaluable in getting public measures accomplished.

Greene Springs continued wthout interruption, even during the war years, under the same principal until 1877 when Mr. Tutwiler was ordered to take a year's rest. Born in 1807, he was then past seventy. Operations began again in the fall of 1879 and continued until his death in 1884.

Few educators in Alabama touched more lives more positively than did the admirable Mr. Tutwiler.

Life in an Academy

Sarah Lowe was a student at Huntsville Female College but her diary indicates she was doing preparatory work.

Thursday and Friday
Jan 31st and Feb. 1st, [1862]

The first of these days passed off as usual; nothing happening to distinguish the monotony of school life except new lessons. I was glad when Mrs R. presented me with my Logic today, so now I can commence studying it. I took my music lesson as usual this evening, but I do not think that Mr Laroni was very much pleased with my progress in that abomnible piece, which *he* terms my favorite Ce exercise. Thursday night it began raining and continued until Friday evening, consequently we could not attend the concert given by the girls, nor to school in the day, of which I cannot say I was particularly sorry. Saturday morning I went with cousin Mary to see Miss Millie and Little Ellie Lowe. After dinner I went up town to get some [gruel] and at night to the concert which I enjoyed very much. The music and the company I was in were both very agreeable Sunday was very dull and dreary and as Sister thought I would be sick after my imprudence on the preceeding evening (that of going in thin shoes to the concert) I was deprived of going to church and Sunday School, but had a very agreeable time at home with Richard.

Tuesday Feb. 5th

I can scarcely realize that I have been only a week at school it seems as if it were a month. But lessons were recited better today and I hope that I may continue to improve and make the time at school pass very more swiftly. After school this evening I went in company with some of my friends to the new hotel I like it very much. I believe I would enjoy boarding there for a short while until the novelty wore off and then return home. Our poetry in Logics today was badly learned, I think if there is any such thing as "dog latin" that must be a speciman of it. Miss Sneed gave the same Geography lesson over for tomorrow because the girls neglected to point out the places on the map. I thought the lesson was quite interesting. It treated of winds which by the heat disturbing the equilibrium of the air is divided three classes, i. e. Constant, Periodicals and Variable. And also according to its physical characteristics into cold, hot, moist and Dry.

Wednesday Feb. 6th

The day has been bright and beautiful, not a cloud was seen to destroy its loveliness. I spent the day very pleasantly, at school as usual. We are doing no better Logic. I do not think we would make good lawyers. I went to see Sister Mattie this evening after school and found her a good deal better. Geography was a continuation of the winds. The Eterian winds blow across the medeterian Sea and are caused by the hot winds of the Sahara Desert. Northers are visitent winds from the north which sweep across the prairies of Texas and Mexico, and Variable Winds come from the temperate and polar regions rarily continuing many successive days.

Thursday Feb. 7th

The day has been windy, but that was pleasant. Alice White was at school this morning but went home at dinnertime. She looks right badly. I was very much slighted this evening when I heard of the handsome entertainment that was to be given and I was forgotten or left out. I do not know which. Will my journal show how I have spent the day? Will I not believe I exactly know we arrived at school this morning early enough for prayers, after which I studied and recited alternately the rest of the day until school was out and then took music lesson as usual. Then I went with Kate Lane for Mrs Goode at the hotel and by the time she went through her usual course of primping it was dark and of course when I returned home a scholding awaited me. But this I took with great fortitude. Our Geography lesson of today was short and interesting. The subject or subjects was whirlwinds and Tropical storms or Hurricanes, Typones, Cyclones and Tornadoes.—Manuscript diary in the Department of Archives and History, Montgomery.

There were schools besides academies, of course. Families of means could and did hire tutors. In other places a group of planters joined informally to hire a teacher, construct a simple log building, and thus open a school. Sometimes these are called "old field" schools because of their location in an abandoned clearing. Philip Henry Gosse (1810–1888) had such a one at Pleasant Hill in Dallas County in 1838.

Gosse is one of several outstanding people who have paused briefly in Alabama. He was a naturalist who had spent several years in Newfoundland and Canada. Having failed there as a farmer he went to Philadelphia, seeking some kind of a position. Someone there advised him to seek employment in Alabama and this school is the result. He was in Alabama only seven months before returning to his native England. There he won fame as an author and the founder of marine biology.

Dallas, June 1, 18—

You are aware that my intention in coming south was to open a school. Schools here generally are not private enterprises, as in the old country, but the ordinary mode of procedure is as follows. Some half-dozen planters of influence meet and agree to have their children educated together, each stipulating the number of pupils to be sent, and the proportion of expense to be borne, by himself. These form a board of trustees, who employ a master at a fixed salary, and, though they allow others to send their children at a certain rate, are yet personally responsible for the whole amount in the respective proportions of their stipulated subscriptions. I found no difficulty in obtaining an engagement of this kind, and have undertaken, at a liberal remuneration, the charge of about a dozen "young ideas." My schoolroom is a funny little place, built wholly of round, unhewn logs, notched at the ends to receive each other, and the interstices filled with clay; there is not a window, but, as the clay has become dry, it has dropped or been punched out of many of these crevices, so that there is no want of light and air, and the door, hung on wooden hinges, and furnished with a wooden latch, scarce needs the latter, it remains open by night as well as day. The desks are merely boards, split, not sawn, out of pine logs, unhewn and unplaned, which slope from the walls, and are supported by brackets. The forms are split logs, with four diverging legs from the round side, the upper side being made tolerably straight with the axe. Some wooden pegs, driven into auger holes in the logs, receive hats, &c. A neat little desk, at which I write, and a chair on which I sit, are the only exceptions to the primitive rudeness of all our furniture, and the pupils are, mostly, as rude as the house,—real young hunters, who handle the long rifle with more ease and dexterity than the goose-quill, and who are incomparably more at home in "twisting a rabbit," or "treeing a 'possum," than in conjugating a verb.

The situation of the school is singularly romantic; a space of about a hundred yards square has been cleared in the forest, with the excep-tion of two or three lofty oaks which are left for shade. On every side we are shut in by a dense wall of towering forest trees, rising to the height of a hundred feet or more. Oaks, hickories, and pines of different species extend for miles on every hand, for this little clearing is made two or three miles from any human habitation, with the exception of one house about three quarters of a mile distant. Its loneliness, how-ever, is no objection with me, as it necessarily throws me more into the presence of free and wild nature. At one corner a narrow bridle-path leads out of this "yard," and winds through the sombre forest to the distant high road. A nice spring, cool in the hottest day of summer, rises in another corner, and is protected and accumulated by being inclosed in four sides of a box, over the edges of which the superfluous water escapes, and, running off in a gurgling brook, is lost in the shade of the woods. To this "lodge in the vast wilderness," this "boundless contiguity of shade," I wend my lonely way every morning, rising to an early breakfast, and arriving in time to open school by eight o'clock.— *Letters from Alabama Chiefly Relating to Natural History* (London: Morgan and Chase, 1859), p. 43–44.

John Massey, one of the state's outstanding educators, was born in 1834. He attended the University of Alabama where he earned two degrees and later was awarded an honorary doctorate. Massey held several prominent positions, the longest being the presidency of Alabama Conference Female College at Tuskegee from 1876 to 1909.

The schools he described here were the simple ones of 1852 in his native Choctaw County.

As the spring of 1852 came on I had to stop school and go to work to make a crop. In addition to corn, fodder, potatoes, and other produce, we made a small crop of cotton, which I sent along with a neighbor's load of cotton to Mobile. With part of the proceeds I bought the follow-ing books: Milton's "Paradise Lost," Young's "Night Thoughts," "New-ton on the Prophecies," "Mrs. Herman's Poems," and "Lord Chester-field's Letters to His Son." I selected these books upon the recommenda-tion of my friend Mr. Hayes, who had consulted Rev. Paul F. Stearns about what books I should buy. I read all of these books very atten-tively and thought I understood them. I guess it is a good thing that young people have some conceit, for it would be paralyzing to turn upon them all at once a full knowledge of their verdancy.

MY FIRST ATTEMPT AT TEACHING

In the fall I was induced by Mr. Hayes to teach a little school in the community. When I told him that I doubted my qualifications for teaching, he informed me that Mr. James had spoken to him so favorably of my ability that he was sure that I could teach the school, which would not be composed of any advanced students. He gave me a copy of a contract in Mr. James's handwriting, from which I wrote out some articles of agreement between myself and the patrons and entered upon what was destined to be my profession. . . . I lived at home and for the first month collected the magnificent sum of seven dollars and twenty-five cents! The wonder is that I did not quit the business of teaching forever. . . . The following months I did somewhat better in the way of collections.

Among the pupils of this my first school was Miss Fannie Hayes, the oldest daughter of my good friend Reuben Hayes, a girl of twelve years, a modest, ladylike girl, who set a fine example to the younger students. After the lapse of sixty-two years, I received a letter from her signed, "Mrs. Fannie H. Cochran," in which she said that she was prompted to express her appreciation, before it became too late, of what I had done for her in the long ago. I know that my instruction was immature, my manners those of an unpolished country boy; but if I conducted myself in such a way as to have caused this good woman's respect and gratitude to live through all the wrecks of these sixty-two years, I am deeply grateful. I am sure that our friendship will not end with the few fleeting days that may remain to us here.

In the spring of 1853 I went about three months to Dr. Allen, who had moved to another neighborhood five miles from my mother's. I walked this distance every morning and evening over a very hilly road. During this term I studied elementary geometry and surveying, in addition to some of the studies I had formerly gone over. While the course in surveying was very elementary, I found I had learned enough about the subject to do plain surveying quite accurately when I had occasion to put it into practice. I wish to acknowledge my obligation in this connection to Dr. Allen, who soon passed out of my knowledge.

MY SECOND ATTEMPT AT TEACHING

During the summer and fall 1853 I taught another school in our vicinity. Some of my pupils had been my fellow students under Dr. Graham and Mr. Kimbrough. In this school I had two or three young ladies older than myself. In justice to them I wish to state that their demeanor was excellent and that I never had a school in the course of fifty years' experience that gave me less trouble. This must have been due to the character of the pupils, for it certainly was not due to my native or acquired ability as a disciplinarian. With the proceeds of this school I made my preparation to enter the academy that had recently been established at Pierce's Springs, Mississippi, about eight miles from where we lived. I entered the academy the first of

January, 1854. In order to economize as much as possible, I walked
from home on Monday mornings and returned on Friday evenings.—
John Massey, *Reminiscences* (Nashville: Methodist Publishing House,
1916), pp. 55–57.

What did a pupil study in 1846? John Massey gives an answer.

COURSE OF STUDY

My studies during the first summer session with Mr. James were
spelling, reading, and writing. The spelling book was Webster's blue-
back. The readers were the New York Readers—First, Second, and
Third. They contained excellent selections of prose and poetry. Mr.
James was a good reader himself and paid particular attention to the
reading of his students. I have often wished to see those old readers
again, but have not been able to find a single copy. They seem to
have gone with the past generation of men.

The next summer, 1847, Mr. James taught in a new schoolhouse in
a more central location, about two miles from us. During this session
I began grammar and arithmetic. We used a new series of readers, just
published, by Dr. W. H. McGuffrey, of the University of Virginia. I
was very much interested in grammar and reading and everything moved
on smoothly as far as I was concerned.—Ibid., pp. 48–49.

One day of school as a thirteen year old boy saw it is given here.
John Rayburn was born near Gunter's Landing on December 30,
1838. He says in the preface of his diary that as a young child he
was "very weakly," yet he started to school when he was four.
He made little progress in his studies until he began Latin with
Mr. Nicholson and under his "tuition" his mind began to expand.
John's father required him to keep a diary to improve his writing.
At the end of each day's entry are his father's comments. This
entry is for June 1, 1852.

I arose this morning when the sun was up. I got up about Breakfast
time i et my brecfast and went off for school. When i had got to scool
i ran about a little while then commensed getting my lesson. i learned
my lesson very well to recite to my master, when i had said my lesson
the master called us to spell. i spelt and then retired to my dinner. When
i et my dinner i went Back to school. I played about a little and then
the master rang the Bell for Books. I went and read my lesson in the
History of Alabama and then i got my rule in the arithmetic for the
Ballance of the evening and after recess the master called the arithmetic
class. i recited my rule and that was my studies for the day and after i
spelt in evening i went home and went into my father's office and began
writing the business of the day.

The manuscript diary is in the Department of Archives and History, Montgomery.

Still another, and more advanced, type of school was the one established in Prattville by Daniel Pratt, who founded, owned and operated the industrial complex there. He was a New Englander by birth and brought with him respect for sound learning for which that region had long been famous. He incorporated some of the features of New England schools in his own institution.

Shadrick Mims, writing in 1886, remembered the Prattville school in the antebellum period.

> When I first came to this place there was a school house built by him located on the side of the hill southwest from where the Foundry now stands. This building was complete in all its arrangements, the seats built on the Lancastrian plan, i.e., one above the other with desks complete, leaving a space in front for the teacher and recitations. The school house was situated in a cool sequestered place completely surrounded by a forest growth of young oaks and a cool spring running from the hill. The school was taught by Mr. T. B. Avery, an accomplished scholar and gentleman. I liked his method of teaching on the Induction plan—drawing out the mind and teaching it to be self reliant. It is far preferable to the Lecture plan which teaches the pupil to let others think for them. This house could not with all its fixtures cost less than one thousand dollars. Not only the children of the village, but those from all the surrounding country attended.—Shadrick Mims, "History of Autauga County," *Alabama Historical Quarterly,* vol 8, p. 261.

The manual labor school, which incorporated academic study and physical work at some productive job, was popular in the United States around the 1830's. There were never many in Alabama. The Asbury Mission near Fort Mitchell has already been mentioned; the Presbyterians had one at Marion, incorporated on December 16, 1833, as the Manual Labor Institute of South Alabama, Perry County. Its history is obscure. The Baptists had one for a few years at Greensboro. It is always called the Manual Labor School but it had been christened The Alabama Institute of Literature and Industry. According to Benjamin F. Riley, Alabama Baptists had more interest in this school than they had had in anything up to that time. It was opened in the fall of 1835 on a 335 acre farm (for which they paid $6,390) with fifty students. A year later when the Baptist Convention was told that in the first year the farm had produced 700 bushels of corn and 150 of sweet potatoes, their confidence in the future success of the school was "stiffened," and there was talk of raising a large endowment for it. The primary purpose of the school was to train ministers but the denomination wisely decided to admit other young men who wished to pursue a literary course.

The school failed at Greensboro in 1837, partly because of the financial panic and partly from dissension within the faculty.

Apparently it was moved to Marion the next year although its history is somewhat hazy. An opinion of this school is contained in an interesting letter written in the late summer of 1839. It is reproduced here with the original spelling and punctuation.

Manual Labor Institute
August 20, 1839

Dear Cousin:

I expect you have nearly despared of receiving another epistle from me, but I wanted to surprise you. I can make no apology for not riting, but I think if I am not mistaken I rote to you last, but I won't be positive. I expect you will be a little astonished at my being a student of this institute, but so it is, I am here and I wish I was at home, or at some other institution. I don't think that labor is any advantage to my broken constitution, or at least it appears so at present. I suppose that labor would be an advantage to me in a moderate way, but I think there is too much at this place. I go out very morning and work an hour and a half in the wet dew and when I come back I am wet as if I had been baptized and there is need to change my clothes twice a day and you may rely on it, there is no time for study. I have been sick every since I came to this place. In the first place I was taken with flux, and after that I was taken with fever and ague, and I have just recovered sufficiently to return to my studies. And the rules are very strict. You are not allowed to leave your room after dark unless on very particular business. There was a student come very near being expelled today for leaving his room last night. The fare heretofore has been horrid, but is some better now than it has been heretofore. I have progressed very slowly on account of my health and this is no place to study nohow. I am reading Sallust at present, I expect to commence in the Greek testament and algebra before long. Father speaks of going to Virginia next spring and taken me to the University, but I don't know, he changes very often. I think-by prevailing and teasing him a little he will let me go. [Singuid] will finish his education this session and if he lives will next year lay the foundation of his future happiness in this world of sin, pain and sorrow. And dear cousin, we should remember that our time is not far hence when we shall have to mount the stage of action, and wade through the dark and dismal path of live by ourselves. With those thoughts in our minds, we should endeavor to obtain that understanding which will place us upon a high degree of prosperity which may make useful members of society and honor to our country. In preparing for that event we should cultivate good morals, good manners and after all good character, by which we may pass through the dark and gloomy path of life in peace and happiness. I hope it will not be too long before you answer my letter. Give my regards to Uncle Zeke.

I. B. HOLMAN

Mr. John T. Holman Esq.
Buckingham Courthouse, Va.—Letter in private hands.

Public Education

To say that Alabama's public schools began in 1854 is stating only a part of the truth. To be sure, before that date there had been no state-wide system of schools, no superintendent of education, and no provision for regular financial support, but there was some public money from the sixteenth section lands and there were some few township schools. Furthermore, Mobile had an admirable county-wide system of public schools that helped pave the way for a state system.

It was a vexing problem to know how best to use the sixteenth section land. As early as 1820 the state began a plan of leasing that was amended often thereafter. Some counties were allowed to lease for 99 years or to sell outright their school lands and to invest the money gained from these transactions in bank stock. Only the interest was to be used for operating schools. In this way land was put in a form that would actually benefit the schools. This was the ideal but when the panic of 1837 hit the state, the school funds were lost in the bank failures. Stephen D. Weeks gives a good summary of the intricacies of this period.

In the meantime the State had entered on a new era of prosperity, everybody was speculating and borrowing, and the State bank was making so much money that on January 9, 1836, direct State taxation was abolished and on the State bank was placed the burden of "defraying all the necessary expenses of the government" of the State up to $100,000. The school fund came in for its share of this prosperity, and the law of January 31, 1839, ordered the bank to pay to the schools $150,000 annually; the law of February 3, 1840, increased this to $200,000. These laws concern mainly the administration and use of the sums earned by the sixteenth section funds, and are therefore considered in detail in chapter 5. But it is proper to add here that while the share of the Surplus Revenue of 1836 coming to Alabama and amounting to $669,086.78 had been made a part of the school fund and deposited in the State bank as a part of its capital stock, the sum of $200,000 demanded under the law of February 3, 1840, as interest by the State for all of its school funds, was much more than a fair rate of interest on both the sixteenth section and Surplus Revenue funds would allow, and the difference between the actual interest and the sum required must be regarded as a privilege tax placed on the bank and its branches for the right to do business. It was entirely in accord with the spirit of the times which looked to the State bank for the expenses of goverment. From 1836 to 1842 State taxation was abolished, and the necessary funds for the conduct of public business came out of the profits of the State bank and its branches. The bank's success as a financial institution made possible the acts of 1839 and

1840. But this prosperity did not last. It was found necessary by February 13, 1843, to repeal the act of January 9, 1836, and revive taxation for State purposes; and, since the bank could no longer meet its obligations either to the State or to the school fund, the $200,000 contribution required by the law of February 3, 1840, was also repealed (act of Jan. 21, 1843). It would appear that practically the whole income of the public school fund was cut off by this failure of the bank. What that income was during the next five years is uncertain, but it is certain that it was unimportant. We shall see how the State later provided funds by recognizing the now worthless State bank certificates as a valid claim against itself, thus creating a paper fund.—Willis G. Clark, *History of Education in Alabama, 1702–1889*, p. 28.

The bank funds were still in the process of being straightened out when the act for public schools was passed.

An act of 1823 established two administrative school units in the state, the township and the districts. At the head of each township was a board of three commissioners who had the responsibility to administer the school lands, "establish schools and disperse moneys to them in proportion to the number of students enrolled, and to examine and certify teachers." Each school had three trustees, elected by voters in the districts, who were responsible for erecting school buildings, employing teachers, choosing text books and examining applicants in order to determine who would and who would not pay tuition. The law required that each school make an annual report to the legislature. It is unknown how many such schools there were or how many made their reports. It is known that large sections of Alabama had no schools under this system which lasted with only minor changes until 1854.

Mobile had a working system of schools that proved to be both the incentive and the model for the state. Its county-wide education began in 1826 when the state legislature created a board of school commissioners for Mobile County. These commissioners were given "full power and authority to establish and regulate schools and to devise, put in force, and execute such plans and devices for the increase of knowledge, educating youth, and promoting the cause of learning in said county as to them may appear expedient." The act was amended several times, most often to change the number of commissioners or to expand the sources of revenue.

Barton Academy is the product of this early school system; in the 1970's it is an important landmark in historic Mobile and the headquarters for the Mobile County School Board. It was authorized in 1836 and built with money raised by a public lottery. The erection of the building was due mainly to the efforts of Henry Hitchcock, one of the original commissioners. It was built on land purchased for a nominal fee from Thomas H. Lane and named for Willoughby Barton, an extensive landowner in the area.

Funds for Mobile schools came from the school lands (which the county used more wisely than some), certain fines and penalties, several special taxes and twenty-five per cent of the ordinary taxes. Until 1852, however, the county did not try to have its own schools. Instead, it made grants to parochial and private schools and rented out Barton Academy. Methodist Parish school, for example, received $1,200 in 1851–52 and the Catholic schools a like sum.

The year 1852 was important in the development of public schools. The school issue came to focus in a proposal to sell Barton Academy. From the excitement that the proposal caused one judges that there was more interest in education than some of the discouraged leaders had believed. When the matter was put to public vote, the "no sale" people won by a vote of 2,225 to 244. The decision to keep the building was considered a mandate for public schools. Consequently a committee began work on additional buildings that culminated in the first system of public schools in the state. These schools opened on the first Monday of November 1852 with four hundred children. Within a year the number had exceeded a thousand. Willis G. Clark, lawyer and editor of the Mobile *Daily Advertiser,* is given much of the credit for the final success of the movement, but he was ably supported by other prominent citizens.

It is not surprising that the legislative delegation from Mobile spearheaded the movement for state-wide public schools. A. B. Meek, poet, orator, editor, public official, and in 1854, legislator from Mobile, is often called the "father" of public schools in Alabama since he introduced the bill creating them. These schools also had a lot of "uncles" who supported Meek: the other legislators; Governor John A. Winston; Robert M. Patton, a later governor; and J. L. M. Curry, the executive director of the Peabody Fund for schools in the period after the Civil War.

The Act of 1854, creating the state public schools, provided for a state superintendent of education, elected by the legislature for two years. School money was to be divided among the counties according to the size of the school population. Money in the Educational Fund came from those sixteen sections that still belonged to the schools, small revenues from escheats and taxes on bank stock, insurance companies and railroads, and $100,000 from the state treasury. For the calendar year of 1855, the first year that the schools were in operation, the funds available for public schools amounted to $237,515.39.

The Act of 1854 designated the judge of probate in each county to enumerate the children of school age and do whatever was necessary to provide the state superintendent with his job of initiating schools; these duties were above and beyond his office as probate judge. There were no county superintendents of education. This situation soon proved to be unworkable so by a supplementary act of 1856 the office of county superintendent was created. After that the affairs of the schools were more effectively handled.

The first Alabama superintendent of education was William F. Perry (1823–1901) a native of Jackson County, Georgia, who migrated with his family to Chambers County, Alabama, in 1833. His formal schooling was not extensive but he was well-read. He had been principal of several schools, including the high school at Talladega from 1848 to 1853. Perry was living in Tuskegee where he had just been admitted to the bar when he was elected to the new office in 1854. He was twice reelected.

Perry's report of his first years in office has become a classic in the development of public education in the state.

THE FIRST STATE SUPERINTENDENT OF SCHOOLS IN ALABAMA TELLS OF THE DIFFICULTIES IN LAUNCHING THE SCHOOL SYSTEM IN THAT STATE, 1855

Alabama was the first of the Cotton States, and one of the first of the slave-holding States, to enter upon such an undertaking. The session of the Legislature of 1853-54 found public opinion prepared for definite action. This body contained several men of prominence, who at once gave the movement shape, among them Robert M. Patton, Senator from Lauderdale, Jabez L. M. Curry, of Talladega, and Alexander B. Meek, of Mobile. The committee having the work in hand were aided by the counsels of Dr. Andrew A. Lipscomb, a gentleman of varied accomplishments, then living in Montgomery.

Those who drafted the original school law, as well as those charged with its administration, may justly be said to have embarked upon an uncharted sea.

It is true that highly developed systems of popular education existed in other States. The school systems of New England had been the growth of years, and had recently received a great uplift through the labors of Mr. Horace Mann. Successful systems also existed in several of the North Western States. But there, the population was homogeneous; the school lands were more valuable; and the proceeds of their sales, under the terms of the grant, had been consolidated into general school funds. But no precedents were anywhere to be found which could safely be followed in shaping a system adapted to the social conditions then existing in Alabama.

It is not surprising, therefore, that the first draft of a law thus made without experience to guide, or precedent to follow, should have contained features which required modification; and should have omitted details which had to be supplied, either by the Superintendent in the course of administration, or by subsequent legislation. And still it can be truly said, to the honor of its authors, that the system, in its subsequent development, shaped itself by the outline and framework which the original draft supplied.

It purported to be a law for the establishment of a system of free public schools in the State. To sustain this system, it appropriated one hundred thousand dollars to be paid annually from the treasury, the interest of the sixteenth section fund, which then amounted to about sixty thousand dollars per annum, together with some few other sources of revenue.

It provided for the election of an officer styled the "Superintendent of Education," and clearly defined his duties. The county administration was imposed upon the Judges of Probate, who were required to perform their duties without compensation. The township officers consisted of a board of three trustees. They were charged with duties which called for more than ordinary administrative power. They were to raise means for the erection of school houses when such were needed; to divide the townships into such districts as the situation demanded; to select and employ teachers and supervise the schools; to make settlements and submit annual reports.

The use of the word free in connection with the schools was unfortunate. It created exaggerated expectations, which were doomed to the shock of a sore disappointment.

The weakest feature of the system was in the county administration. The Judges of Probate, not without good reason, regarded the imposition of new and onerous duties upon them without compensation, as a great hardship; and while many of them were faithful and efficient, they could not give the amount of attention that was absolutely essential to the prompt and effective inauguration of an untried system.

The adoption of the township as a school corporation, although under the circumstances a necessity, involved great inconveniences. It complicated the duties of the trustees, who were generally plain unlettered men, and led to neighborhood jealousies and dissensions in reference to the locations of schools. Lines of latitude and longitude pay no respect to the physical features of a country, or to the convenience of the people. Many good neighborhoods, capable of sustaining a single school, were split by township lines, and thrown into two, three, or four different corporations.

THE SUPERINTENDENT

The session of the legislature was approaching its close, when the school law was enacted, and the next day was set for the election of a Superintendent. No one had been spoken of in connection with the office, except Dr. Lipscomb; and it was generally understood that he would be the only candidate.

Gen. J. Tipton Bradford, however, decided to put me in nomination against him, although I was a hundred miles away, and personally unknown to nine-tenths of the members. Gen. Bradford was a man of extensive influence, a remarkable judge of men, and an indefatigable worker. By the aid of a few of my personal friends, including Mr. Curry and Chief Justice W. P. Chilton, of the Supreme Court, whom he used as referees, he had succeeded in securing the pledges of a majority of the members before the two Houses met in joint session for the election. The result, after four ballots, was a startling surprise to all except to the masterly tactician who had brought it about, and was justly a source of sore disappointment and chagrin to the friends and admirers of Dr. Lipscomb.

A few days afterwards, having given bond and taken the oath of office, I was turned into an empty room in the Capitol, oppressed with a sense of the responsibility upon me, and with ominous forebodings of the herculean labor that was before me. I was in my thirty-first year; had little experience in public affairs, and no knowledge of the practical workings of public educational systems.

ORGANIZATION

After setting my office in order, I opened correspondence with the Judges of Probate, asking them to order elections of trustees in the townships and to instruct them, when elected, to ascertain and report the number of youth of school age in their respective townships. It was explained that such reports constituted the only data obtainable for the apportionment of the money set apart for the support of schools; and that under the law, the apportionment must be made before the establishment of schools could be authorized.

All this seemed very simple; and I was ignorant enough to expect that the work could be accomplished in the course of two or three months at farthest. But unexpected difficulties were encountered.

Quite a number of the Judges of Probate paid no attention to my request, and it was not found out until after a great delay. Many of them who earnestly endeavored to do their duty found it difficult to reach the townships. Circulars could not be addressed to townships which had no organization and no legal representative. Notices in the county papers often failed, while in many counties no paper was published. And then, there was the inertia of ignorance, the difficulty of getting masses of uninformed people out of the ruts in which they have been moving for generations.

To the people of more than one-third of the State, the township as a corporation, or as a body politic of any kind, was unknown. The very boundaries had faded from their minds and memories with the disappearance of the marks made on the forest trees by the surveyors who had located them. To reach these large masses of people, induce concerted action in tracing out their long-forgotten boundaries and in organizing themselves into corporations, was a task the difficulty of which no one had anticipated, and which was accomplished at last by dint of hammering.

It is easy to see that the almost fatal weakness was found in the county administration. Duties which would have employed the whole time of officers chosen for the purpose, and paid for their services, were unwisely, and unjustly, imposed upon men who were already busy, and who found it necessary either to neglect the new duties for which they received no compensation or the duties which they were elected and paid to perform.

There can be no question that energetic officers, employed for the purpose and paid for their services, by personal visits to the townships, could, in six or eight weeks, have accomplished a task that had required as many weary months. It is but just to say that no difficulty occurred in the counties whose townships had maintained their school organization.

APPORTIONMENT.

It was late in the Fall before complete returns were received, and the apportionment was begun. In the absence of any specific direction of law, the distribution was made by giving to the townships that had nothing, and adding to those that had little, until the appropriation was exhausted, leaving those whose school revenues exceeded the average thus produced simply to retain what they had.

The appropriation thus distributed yielded a per capita of one dollar and thirty-thee cents. It seemed meager enough, and was a great disappointment to many who persisted in cherishing the illusion, which I had vainly striven to dispel, that there was to be a mammoth system of schools wholly supported by the State.

DIVIDENDS AND INSTRUCTIONS.

A statement was sent to each Judge of Probate showing the amounts to which the townships of his county would be entitled. They were accompanied with circulars of advice and instruction to the trustees in reference to the establishment of schools.

The preparation of these instructions cost me much anxious thought. While such a course seemed to have been contemplated by the law, I felt that it would have a dwarfing effect upon the system, and upon the minds of the people to fall into the habit of employing teachers for only such time as the public money would last; and was anxious, at the beginning, to give such directions to the State appropriation that it would stimulate, rather than suppress, the spirit of self-help in the people. The trustees were therefore advised to authorize teachers whom they approved to raise their own schools by subscription, the patrons being responsible to the teacher for the tuition, at specified rates, of the pupils subscribed, and the trustees engaging to use the money under their control, as far as it would go, in discharging the liability of the patrons.

All this seemed bungling enough; but to my mind it had several advantages; 1st, It would avoid all danger of complaint that the trustees had imposed upon the people a teacher who was not acceptable; 2nd, it put all the parties upon a method of procedure with which they were already familiar; 3rd, it showed them that the State had not proposed to relieve them of all expense and responsibility in the education of their children, but to guide and assist them in the performance of a duty which they could never abdicate.

MOVEMENT

The first of January, 1855, was fixed as the beginning of the school year; and the rude machinery began to move, slowly here, with jar and friction there, but it moved!

The year 1855 was spent in visiting the counties of the State, and in conducting an extremely heavy correspondence. Questions of all shapes and sizes, growing out of every thinkable complication of conditions, came in a continuous stream. At first, some of them were very embarrassing. After a time, however, I became so saturated with the system, in its entirety and in its detail, that my mind reached conclusions with ease and confidence. Of course, I made it understood that my opinions carried with them no judicial authority; but it is, even now, a source of pleasure to remember that no case ever came to my knowledge in which the parties in controversy failed to acquiesce in my decision; and that I was able in numerous instances, to harmonize dissensions and prevent litigation.

In my tour through the State, I found the schools generally in operation and the people pleased and hopeful, especially in those counties which were most benefited by the system; and returned to my office feeling fully assured that the public educational system of Alabama, though still crude and imperfect, had come to stay.

It was a source of much regret, that the statistics, which I was able to collect, of the first year's work of the schools, were not such as could be set forth in tabulated form in my report to the legislature, which met in December, 1855. I, therefore, gave only a brief history of what had been done, and discussed some changes in the school law which were imperatively demanded.

I was very apprehensive that the tardiness with which the machinery has moved off, and the fact that I was unable to make a complete report, would furnish a pretext to the enemies of the system to make an assault either upon it, or upon my administration; but was gratified to find no open manifestation of hostility.

RECONSTRUCTION

The Committees on Education of the Senate and House of Representatives, 1855-56, were gentlemen of broad views, in thorough sympathy with the purposes of the system. The Hon. R. M. Patton, of Lauderdale, and Col. Thomas H. Hobbs, of Limestone, were the Chairmen. The Committees met in joint session, and requested my presence at every meeting. The utmost harmony prevailed, and there was everywhere visible an earnest desire to do the best possible for the interest of public education in the State.

The school law was entirely remodeled and greatly simplified and improved. The creation of the office of County Superintendent was a change of vital importance, and would of itself have marked an epoch in the history of the system.

The appropriation was so increased as to raise the pro-rate to one dollar, fifty cents. The methods of disbursement were also greatly simplified. The amounts declared to be due the various counties, by the State Superintendent, were required to be deposited in the county treasuries to be subject to the drafts of the County Superintendents; and all officers were held to strict accounts for money coming into their hands.

Having been re-elected without opposition, and now assured of efficient County administration, I entered upon my second term of office with renewed confidence and energy. The revised school law with notes and explanations were published in connection with complete book of forms and instructions for all transactions connected with the public schools.

The methods previously recommended for the employment of teachers, and for the disbursement of the public money were continued; and minute directions for the distribution of the money in payment of tuition were given to the teachers, illustrated by an actual example of a settlement made upon assumed data. I was still haunted by the dread of a miserable little system of free public schools supported with inadequate means.

To systematize and facilitate the work of the County Superintendents, an account book was prepared, which, by various rulings and captions in different parts, was adapted to every possible record connected with their office. It was so arranged and spaced, that if properly kept, it would contain a complete history, statistical and financial, of the county schools running through a series of years.

It was with a feeling of inexpressible relief that I saw the great bundles of instructions carted to the post office to be sent to their destination. It was such as a mariner might experience who had been long bound in shallows and quicksands, when he first spreads his sails on an open sea beneath a clear sky.

RESULTS

I felt confident that new life and vigor would be imported to the system; and the results fully equalled my expectations. The County Superintendents entered upon their duties with energy and enthusiasm. Deadlocks were at an end, and jar and friction were fast disappearing. Many new schools were established, and more attention was given to the comfort and convenience of schoolhouses, though much still remained to be done in that direction. Increased interest and larger compensation had a marked tendency to bring into the schools teachers of better qualifications. At the end of the year, full reports were received from all the counties showing most gratifying results of the year's work. . . .

The report of 1857 showed still farther progress on all lines. There was a decided increase in the number of children reported by the trustees, and in the number both of schools and of pupils in attendance. My recollection is, that the number of pupils attending the schools was about one hundred thousand, and there was evidence to believe that the people, stimulated by the aid extended by the State, had expended far more on their schools than they had ever done before.

It will doubtless be observed that the law contained no requirements, either as to the character of the school houses used, or as to the qualifications of the teachers employed. Some would doubtless urge this as a fatal defect of the system; but it was the result of deliberate design. So much was to be done, that it was thought best to attempt but one thing at a time; to begin at the bottom and build up, rather than make a vain attempt to begin at the top and build down. If even moderate requirements had been made and strictly enforced, either as to the qualifications of

teachers, or as to the character of the buildings which they were to occupy, more than half the schools would have disbanded, and the system would have collapsed. The demand of the hour was visible results
in the shape of schools; and it was the part of wisdom to bend every
energy to perfect the external machinery by which that demand could be
met.

But this had now been done. The external machinery of the system
was working without friction. A trial of two years had disclosed no
feature that needed material modification. In the legislative session of
1857-8, no amendment was adopted, or even suggested.—W. F. Perry,
"Genesis of Public Education in Alabama," *Transactions of the Alabama
Historical Society*, vol. 2, pp. 18–27.

Higher Education

The constitution of 1819 provided for a seminary of learning, a
state university. The federal government gave the state more than
46,000 acres of public land scattered throughout several counties
in the state in support of such an institution. However, the
Legislature made it mandatory on the trustees (by an act in 1823)
to invest the income from these lands in the state bank. These
funds of course were lost along with the sixteenth section funds
in the financial debacle following the panic of 1837. Consequently,
the university has never had the income the founding fathers of
the state intended. Gradually much, but not all, of the lands were
sold.

The board of trustees recommended (and the General Assembly
approved) Tuscaloosa for the location of the university. A spot
about one and a half miles from the courthouse on the Huntsville
road was chosen for the campus. The selection was made in 1828,
erection of the buildings begun shortly thereafter, and classes began on April 17, 1831, with a faculty of five and a student body
of fifty-two. Rev. Alva Woods, a Baptist minister who was president of Transylvania University, was elected to head the new state
university. Henry Tutwiler was professor of ancient languages.
Among the students was Alexander B. Meek. A local newspaper
gave an account of the inauguration of President Woods on April
12, 1831. The ceremonies were held in the Episcopal Church.

It was an interesting day to the people of Tuscaloosa and other
citizens of the State who were present. After singing and music from
the organ and by the choir, and an appropriate prayer by the Rev.
A. A. Muller, rector of the church, the president-elect of the University
was addressed by the Hon. Samuel B. Moore, Governor of the State and
president of the board of trustees. The address was neat, brief, sensible, and to the purpose. He concluded by delivering to Dr. Woods the
keys of the University, thereby investing him with the office and all
its rights and privileges.

President Woods then delivered his inaugural address. The leading subject of the discourse was the importance of learning and knowledge to the safety, liberty, prosperity, and moral and religious improvement of man.—*Spirit of the Age,* April 16, 1831, quoted in Clark, *History of Public Education in Alabama,* p. 37.

The minutes of the board of trustees makes interesting, if sometimes gloomy and discouraging, reading. From them we learn much about the salaries of the faculty, the academic offerings, and some of the problems facing the infant university.

SOME EARLY RESOLUTIONS OF THE TRUSTEES OF THE UNIVERSITY OF ALABAMA, 1829–1832

Resolved that the Salary of the Professors first to be appointed in the University of Alabama shall be $1500 per annum, together with such fees for Tuition as may be required by the Board of Trustees, which they retain to themselves the power to fix at a moderate rate, provided however that the compensation to each professor shall not be less than $2000 annually. (January 5, 1829)

Resolved by the Board of Trustees that they will proceed in pursuance of an Act of Assembly to elect a head of the University of Alabama to be styled the President of the University of Alabama (January 7, 1830)

Resolved That the salary of the adjunct Professor to the chair of Chemistry shall be established at one thousand dollars pr. annum. (January 7, 1830)

Resolved, That twenty thousand dollars be appropriated for the purpose of purchasing a Library and Chemical and Philosophical apparatus for the use of the University of Alabama, and that the President of the University be requested to proceed to the Northern States or to Europe for the purpose of purchasing the same as early as possible; and further, that the President of this Board be requested to solicit our Senators and Representatives in Congress to use their best exertions for the passage of a law authorizing the said Library, Chemical and philosophical apparatus if purchased in Europe to be imported free from duties. (January 13, 1830)

Resolved, That the sum of forty & 37½/100 dollars be allowed to James A. Bates for his expenses for candles furnished the Board of Trustees and attending the Board during their present Session as Door Keeper. (January 18, 1830)

Resolved by the President and Trustees of the University of Alabama, that ten thousand dollars of the funds appropriated at the last meeting of this Board for the purchase of a Chemical and Philosophical apparatus, together with a library, be subject to the order and control of Professor John F. Wallis of this University for the purpose of making purchase of a Philosophical and chemical apparatus, and if he shall deem it expedient to do so, he is authorized to visit Europe and remain absent until July next, for the purposes aforesaid—(July 1, 1830)

Be it ordained by the President and Trustees of the University of Alabama, that the President of the University of Alabama shall receive a Salary of three thousand dollars per year payable quarterly.

Be it further ordained, that the salaries of the Professors of said University as heretofore fixed by ordinance of the Board shall be payable quarterly. (November 24, 1830)

Resolved that the board shall be furnished by the Steward of this University to the Students thereof who may choose to board with him at the rate of eighty dollars for the collegiate year.

And that all such Students as may pay for their board shall be required to board with the Steward—(December 20, 1830)

Resolved that the President of this Board be and he is hereby authorized and empowered to employ William McMillian as a librarian to the University until the Faculty shall think proper to change such appointment and that he also be employed in the collection of Specimens of Natural History and shall have power to make him compensation at the rate of two hundred dollars pr. annum for the time he may be employed as such librarian or collector of specimens, and that the President of this Board at any time he may think proper shall have power to dismiss said McMillian from such employment paying him only for the time he may have been employed—(January 2, 1831)

Be it ordained by the Trustees of the University of Alabama that it shall be the duty of the President of the University of Alabama as soon as may be—to make out a list of all such Books as in his opinion may be necessary to form a library for the commencement of instructions in this university, calculated for the use of one hundred students, and forward one of such lists to Mr. David Woodruff of Tuscaloosa, one to Mr. Lowar and Hogan of Philadelphia, one to Mr. C. O. G. Carrill of New-York and to such other booksellers of Philadelphia, Newyork or Boston as he may think proper, and request them to inform him at what price or for what sum they will undertake to furnish the Books contained in the said list, and deliver them safely at the university. . . .

Resolved by the President and Trustees of the University of Alabama, that it shall be the duty of the Secretary of the Board of Trustees, immediately after the adjournment of the present Session to contract for the printing and publishing of one hundred copies of the ordinances and Resolutions of a public and General nature which may have been passed by the Board of Trustees since the close of their annual session in the year 1826—(January 8, 1830)

Resolved that Fifty dollars be allowed William McMillian for services rendered the University in collecting Specimens of Natural History the year 1830—(January 15, 1831)

Resolved by the President and Trustees of the University of Alabama that a Teacher of French, Spanish and other Modern Languages be appointed in this University on a Salary of one thousand dollars, and the Faculty be requested to furnish this Board at their next meeting, the names or name of individuals in their opinion qualified for that office, together with such testimonials as may be in their possession, as to their qualifications. (April 13, 1831)

Resolved by the President and Trustees of the University of Alabama that a Teacher of Elocution and of English literature be appointed on a Salary of one thousand dollars, and that the Faculty be requested to present to this Board at their next meeting, the name or names of individuals in their opinion qualified for that office, together with such testimonials as may be in their possession as to their qualifications. (April 13, 1831)

Be it ordained by the President and Trustees of the University of Alabama that the Teachers of Modern Languages and of Elocution &c. to be appointed by the previous resolutions of this Board during the present term shall be required to perform the duties of Tutors in the other departments under the direction of the President, whenever in his opinion they can be so engaged with advantage to the Institution. (April 14, 1831)

Resolved by the President and Trustees of the University of Alabama that fifteen hundred dollars be and the same is hereby appropriated for the purpose of paying for the Cabinet of Minerals purchased under the authority of the Board by the Faculty of the University from Professor Nuttall. (December 30, 1831)

And be it further ordained that each member of the Faculty shall have under his special care a certain number of Students rooms, which he shall visit every night in the week and also every day in the week with the exception of the day time of Saturday and Sunday—Should any officer be necessarily prevented from attending to this duty, he shall procure some other member of the Faculty to visit the rooms in his place —and should any Student not be found in place, and not give within a sufficient time a satisfactory reason for his absence he shall be reported to the Faculty, and by them to the parent or guardian—and should such absences continue to occur during the hours of study, it shall be the duty of the Faculty after having tried admonition in vain to dismiss such Student from the institution.

And be it further ordained that each member of the Faculty shall as often as once in two months, report to the Faculty all the damages done in the rooms under his care, and the Faculty shall cause the necessary repairs to be made, and the amount to be charged to the authors when known, otherwise to the occupants of rooms. (January 17, 1832)— Compiled from the minutes in the University library. Printed in Edgar W. Knight, ed., *Documentary History of Education in the South Before 1860* (Chapel Hill: University of North Carolina Press, 1952), vol. 3, pp. 235–39.

Dr. Basil Manly (1798–1868), also a Baptist minister, was the second president of the University, serving eighteen years from 1837 to 1855. At his resignation, he returned to his native South Carolina and pastored the church in Charleston. Always interested in higher education, he was one of the founders of the Southern Baptist Theological Seminary which was eventually moved to Louisville, Kentucky. In 1859, he returned to Alabama as pastor

of the First Baptist Church in Montgomery and lived there through
the exciting days of the early Confederacy. In the summer of 1852,
he made the following masterly report to the board of trustees.
It includes a very fine statement on the importance of the liberal
arts to the educated man.

EXTRACTS FROM PRESIDENT BASIL MANLY'S REPORT ON COLLEGIATE EDUCATION TO THE TRUSTEES OF THE UNIVERSITY OF ALABAMA, 1852

University of Alabama
July 20, 1852

At the last annual session of the Trustees of the University of Alabama,
the Board directed enquiry to be made whether any changes in the system of education pursued in the University are necessary and proper, in
order to extend the benefits of the Institution to a greater number of
the citizens of the State. To meet the purposes of the enquiry is the aim
of the following pages.

The University of Alabama was opened, for instruction, April 17,
A.D. 1831. It aimed to establish the four regular college classes, and
the general features of the ordinary college system; yet it freely admitted students to the partial course;—and, among those who were
candidates for a diploma, it allowed of their reciting with different classes
according to their stage of advancement.

The written memorials preserved of the first two years do not distinguish students of the partial and of the regular course; nor without
much labor can we certainly distinguish, out of the aggregate numbers
in each of the first seven years of its existence, those which were new
students in each year. A preparatory school was begun in 1835, and
continued through that year and the next.

The following table exhibits statistics of the years from 1831 to 1837,
inclusive.

Year	No. Students	Par. Course	New Students	Graduates	Prep. sch.
1831	95	0	0	0	0
1832	111	0	0	0	1
1833	93	30	0	6	0
1834	101	37	0	11	0
1835	105	21	0	8	11
1836	157	52	0	10	27
1837	101	39	0	0	0

During the period from 1838 to 1852, inclusive, there was no preparatory school connected with the University; the classes were kept
distinct; students were not admitted to the partial course, at will,—nor
without a special reason calling for such indulgence; and it was the
steady aim of the Faculty to attain an elevated standard of scholarship.
During the last 10 years about 34 per cent of all who had gained ad-
mittance into each class, including partial course students, have been

graduated; and, in the same period about 22 per cent of the students registered have annually withdrawn, on different accounts;—varying from 07 to 33 per cent. Failures to sustain themselves in study have rarely occurred in the mathematical or scientific departments, unless there was also a very low standing, if not a failure, in the classical. Of applicants for admission, since 1842, many have failed to attain the class to which they had aspired, comparatively few applicants have wholly withdrawn, without joining some class.

After the experience of twenty years, the Trustees have seen fit to pause and take a deliberate survey of all questions affecting the prospect of greater and more extended usefulness of the Institution; and it would be wholly unbecoming the age, as well as their own high trusts, to do this with prejudice, or in the spirit of party.

It has been charged on colleges that, while everything is progressive, they [are] immoveable; conservative, indeed, but of knowledge, elsewhere forgotten or useless, opposed to what is intelligible, practical and popular. This is a serious charge, if true. It is admitted, that they do not consider every change an improvement; and that they do not reject or abandon methods because they are old; and that they are more disposed to repair, than to overturn.

If the college system of this country, maintaining a remarkable similarity notwithstanding varieties and changes, were originally the result of intelligent consideration, as is fair to be presumed, this is a becoming spirit. In any well-considered scheme, changes must *grow; and gradually incorporate themselves into the original structure;*—nor should the conceit of superior, or exclusive, wisdom in succeeding generations of managers be suffered to obliterate the labors of predecessors. Every thing we enjoy is, in some degree, inherited. . . .

If the present collegiate system has preserved its main features without radical modifications, for centuries, is it from a stolid aversion to change? or because the inventive generations have found nothing substantially better?

The main features of the collegiate system appear to be, a substratum, required alike of all, formed by the contemporaneous study of the ancient classics, (the Latin and the Greek languages and their literature) and of mathematics; to which a provision is made for adding, with some variety according to circumstances, a knowledge of the sciences successively developed, and of their applications to the useful purposes of life.

Of the importance of mathematics, not only as a means of cultivating a capacity for profound consecutive investigation, for close conclusive reasoning, but also as fundamental to much of our most important knowledge and business, less doubt seems to be entertained, than with respect to the ancient classics—on which the servant assault has been made.

As no satisfactory attainment can be made in this branch of knowledge without much and long-continued labor, the time for the acquisition of dead languages, which are the exclusive repositories of no science, is regarded by some as thrown away,—for all purposes of practical utility.

To this is replied, that these languages are the most finished and re-fined ever spoken or written; that they are fountains of eloquence never surpassed, seldom equalled; that, if it be one of the highest attainments of a man of action and thought, to reason, instruct, convince and persuade, the knowledge of such an instrument as these afford cannot be dispensed with, but gives him a double advantage—that of the mastery of language, and of sharpening his own powers by intercourse with the master-minds of the world. These languages have been deemed indispensable to a thorough education for the last thousand years, in every clime, under all governments, and by every fraternity of learned men. If we should agree to call men learned without them, would the rest of the world think so? Among colleges, there is a republic, a sort of fellowship, of letters; the maintenance of which is of greater im-portance and wider scope than the temporary advantages gained, in numbers of popularity, by trimming or abridging their course to suit in-dividual circumstances. The diplomas of colleges must mean and certify, substantially, the same thing, or they will certify nothing definite and intelligible; and he, that would ascertain the literary qualifications of another, for any purpose, must examine him for himself. And this con-sideration is specially important for us, as Americans—a people isolated and peculiar, who must hold an elevated rank as scholars among the nations of the earth.

So large a part of our own language, especially in the terminology of the learned professions and of the sciences, is derived from the ancient classics, that we cannot be masters of our own language without them. These, too, are the basis of the living tongue, the languages of com-merce and of modern science; in so much that the full mastery of these will be even most economically made through the intervention of the classics.

As mathematics are more difficult, and require a greater vigor and maturity of mind, these languages furnish a needful preparation for them, filling up, with varied practice in the most useful description of training, the sort of intercalary period between elementary studies and the exact sciences. Below a certain period, difficult to fix, because varying with different individuals, the too early prosecution of mathematics and other studies demanding the vigorous and continued exertion of the reasoning powers may operate injuriously, even on those whose ready memory and ardent ambition may bear them successfully through. Precocity is usually followed by a stunted growth;—and the importance of the classics, as an intermediate exercise, has been considered so great that a finished instructor in mathematics has been wont to say that he would inscribe over the door of his recitation room—"Let no one ignorant of the classics enter here."

It is obvious that mathematics, also, are open to objections of this class. The unwilling student, with great force to his own mind, raises the question, "Of what possible use, in the business of life, can these mathematical abstractions be?" In reply, it might be asked, —how can any man, claiming to be liberally educated, imagine a position in life appropriate to such a character, in which he may not need them?

Through this branch of knowledge, in its various applications, it is that all the powers of nature have been brought under man's control. All knowledge, like the bays and inlets of the ocean, is connected and dependent; and the stress of an occasion may, at any time, require us to lean on points of support and to draw on resources, wholly unforeseen. Facts of this kind are of daily occurrence among the education walks and stirring scenes of life. A thorough college training, other things being equal, will enable its possessor, placed in such contingencies, to outstrip his competitors, who have not that training; he will have confidence in his own resources, and feel the consciousness of power:—furnished generally for self-mastery, with elevated tastes and aspirations,—he appears a man, and difficulties and men give way before him. All subjects in Education are instruments, not ends; and their value is to be estimated by their bearing, first and mainly, on education; and through that chiefly on particular portions of college studies have remained to be of direct use in the business of life: but there is something left, the fruit of them, which is of direct use,—acuteness and energy on the one hand, refinement and grace on the other. Could any result be more practical, more directly useful?

The general voice, if consulted, would not be more diverse and inconsistent on any subject, perhaps,—than with respect to the object of education. Some would have every thing of direct utility;—others would train the mind. It would seem but rational to conclude that the first thing is to subdue and train the faculties—first, in the order of time, as well as in importance. The study of languages and mathematics affords an equable culture of the various powers—attention, memory, comparison, abstraction, association, analysis, and the methods of reasoning by induction and analogy. For this purpose, no substitute has been found for them. The exact sciences are but the application of mathematics to a few data derived from the universal experience of mankind; and, therefore, cannot be thought of as substitutes for those studies upon which they so exclusively depend. The natural sciences have been proposed, but are clearly inadequate; many of them are not of a nature to offer such training; a large part of the residue, great and glorious as they are, cannot be understood as sciences, by a mind that has not learned to enquire, discriminate, reflect, and apply itself severely to other subjects; —while some absolutely demand both previous knowledge and training to be studies at all. . . .

The proper object of collegiate education is the knowledge of principles and causes, rather than of facts, which belongs to a specific or professional education. The one is fundamental to the other. If the foundation is broad, deep and substantial, the superstructure whatever its designation, is secure. Professional education, commencing its adventurous career at the point where the college curriculum has completed its functions, can be rendered as specific and definite as we wish, and efficient to some purpose. And here is the true point of divergence. The college suits all alike, affording the substratum which all intellectual pursuits require. To limite its usefulness to what are called learned professions, those of law, medicine, and theology, is but tacitly confessing that other professions are not intellectual, and require no high exercise of the mind. So weak and shallow an imputation this busy age will not even stop to refute or consider; and even its haste and enterprise, so eager for tangible and immediate results, cannot wholly overlook the genial and productive influence of superior preparation in all the active departments of life.

The relative position, to which the sons of Southern planters seem, by their very birth-right, devoted, combines within itself the high and varied functions of law-giver, physician, moralist and judge; and, if the benefit of a liberal culture is peculiarly suitable to any class of men under heaven, it must be to those whose leisure, otherwise a curse, admits, while their responsibilities demand, it. The question is portentous what will Southern youth become if not highly educated?

And even if the theory of education did not prescribe a common training for all those who aspire to a position above that of the mere laborer, other considerations, conjointly, would.

A college is a miniature world; and the commingling of all classes within it, on terms of equality, preparatory to entrance on the actual world, forms the character best. Engaged in the same studies, with couragement; friendships are formed, relations are fixed, and the habit of self-command established;—indispensable attainments all,—which no other situation can so well impart.—The organization of a college, involving great expense in officers and complicated arrangements, is not susceptible of accommodating itself to an extended variety of cases.

If pupils of unequal attainments are thrown together in the same classes, the instructor will be under an invarible tendency to adapt his instruction to the weaker portion; and, if his compensation is made to depend on the numbers attracted and retained under his instruction, the effect will be inevitable. Thus the grade of attainment will be insensibly lowered, to the injury of the better prepared portion, and the detriment of the general interest of learning, without such adaptation or depression in the style and quality of instruction, the association in the same task of parties materially unequal, either retards the advance of the better qualified portion, or inflicts the evil of superficial, confused and unsatisfactory attainments on the less qualified.

If an attempt is made to accommodate the varying attainments and wants of all, by the multiplication of classes or sections, beyond a certain limit this soon runs into an expense and complication which no establishment can bear;—while classes broken into shreds, lose the stimulus of numbers, the excitement of competition—of mind whetting against mind.

To provide for the accommodation of the greatest number of promising subjects, within the means to which each institution is limited is both a duty and privilege of public educators. But a specific accommodation to each would require as many colleges, with all their costly equipments, as there are students; or in a proportion corresponding to the degree in which the accommodation is made specific. It then becomes a question to be settled by expediency and the nature of the case, shall the college adapt itself to the varieties of students? or shall they adapt themselves to the college? To us, it seems to meet the responsibilities of a college, if they can comprehend within their plan the peculiarities of the *greater part* of those come into their sphere,—while they afford to all equal opportunity of access to means of instruction *requisite for all,* and *sufficient for all.* The college having gone so far toward a compromise, then devolves on the minority of the individuals concerned to accomplish the remainder. . . .—Compiled from the minutes in the University library. Printed in Edgar W. Knight, ed., *Documentary History of Education in the South Before 1860* (Chapel Hill: University of North Carolina Press, 1952), vol. 3, pp. 235–39.

Some six years later, the enrollment had dropped to seventy-five which caused one editor great distress.

Well endowed, fortunately located with a corps of able and learned professors, it is a reproach to the State that we do not have pride enough to sustain our own university while the names of hundreds of Alabamians are found in the catalogs of other states. . . .—*The Dallas Gazette,* Dec. 10, 1857.

According to the best available information, the first degree-granting institution in the state was not the University but La-Grange College which opened its doors on January 11, 1830, at Leighton in north Alabama. The Tennessee Conference of the Methodist Church had initiated the project in 1826; in 1829 the commissions who had been appointed to carry "such an institution into operation" met on January 10, 1829, and selected "that beautiful and commanding eminence called Lawrence Hill" as the site for LaGrange College. It opened its doors almost exactly a year later under the presidency of the Rev. Robert Paine who headed the school until 1846 when he was elected a bishop. Nine years later (1855), the college was moved to Florence. Although in a flourishing condition at the outbreak of the war in 1861, the buildings were burned in 1863 and the school was not reopened. In the thirty years of its life, however, it had served the people of the state and the Methodist Church well.

Dr. Marion E. Lazenby, modern historian of the Methodist Church, observes that "no one can accuse the early Methodists of being uninterested in education," and then proceeds to name a long list of schools and colleges that denomination founded or took over: Sims Female Seminary, Tuscaloosa; Tuscaloosa Female College, Tuscaloosa; East Alabama Male College, Auburn; Auburn Female College; Oak Bowery Institute; Bascom Female College; Tuskegee Female College; Talladega Conference Institute; Andrews Institute in DeKalb County; Mallalieu Institute at Kinsey; Downing-Shofner Industrial School at Brewton; Centenary Institute at Summerfield; Athens College; Southern University at Greensboro and many others.

A close rival for the honor of being the first college in Alabama is Spring Hill College, located in the Spring Hill section of Mobile. It is still in operation and therefore can justly claim to be the oldest college in the state.

Founded by Bishop Michael Portier, a native of Lyons, France, in 1830, it began classes in temporary quarters in February of that year but soon moved to the new campus on the Hill. The formal opening was on July 2, 1830. The physical plant consisted of two frame buildings. It was not only one of the first colleges in Alabama, preceding the University by some eight months, but it also was the first permanent Catholic College in the South. Furthermore, unlike many other such institutions, it stayed open during the difficult years of the 1860's. In 1865 it had approximately 300 students. For many years it had classes during the summer months and vacation in the winter, apparently the first to do so. The location of the college on a high hill made it free from the epidemics of yellow fever that ravaged the port city area at intervals and many families sent their sons there for safety. Although a Jesuit institution and planned especially for seminarians, from the beginning it had a mixed student body. The Rt. Rev. Mathias Loras was the first president and the Rev. Francis de S. Gautrelet (1847) was the first Jesuit president.

There seems to be no existing account of the opening of the college but *The Catholic Directory* of 1833 carried a copy of the prospectus published on October 29, 1830.

COLLEGE OF SPRING HILL, ALA.

Under the Direction of Right Rev. Dr. Portier, Bishop of Mobile

The college of Spring Hill is situated on the great mail route, from Washington City to New Orleans, and seven miles west of the City of Mobile. Its elevated situation, overlooking the surrounding country and commanding a distant view of the Bay of Mobile; the happy choice which has been made for its location; the number of Springs and the purity of the water which surround it, together with its other physical advantages, all concur to render it a collegiate residence, not less healthy than agreeable.

The character of the founder, and the constant testimonies of esteem and confidence with which the citizens of Louisiana honored him during the years which he consecrated to the instruction of their youth, are a sufficient guarantee of all that relates to the moral and religious basis of a good education.

Two professors of the English Language, two of the French, two of the Latin and one of the Spanish, a professor of the Mathematics and a Director General of Studies, constitute the Faculty or the Council of the College, under the direction of the Founder—Doctor Portier, or the President, his Vicar General, to whom is also assigned the duties of the Greek Professorship.

It is needless to mention that Geography, Astronomy, History, Rhetoric, Belles Lettres, the elements of Physics and Chemistry, &c. &c. are included in the course of studies.

The College of Spring Hill is designed to be *essentially Classic.* All the students, without exception, will pursue according to their age, progress, and the direction of the Council of Professors, in connection with other branches, the study of the Ancient and Modern Languages. English will be, however, the exclusive language of communication.

Though the regency of the College be Catholic, yet no influence will be exercised upon pupils bred in the principles of other Christian Denominations. Good order, however, will require them to attend the public exercises of morning and evening prayers, and the Divine service of the Sabbath. A rigid *moral* police will be exercised over all.

CONDITIONS:

1. The price for the Scholastic year is fixed at Two Hundred and Sixty Dollars; one half is payable semi-annually in advance.

2. The equivalent for this sum includes the board of the pupils, their washing, mending, lodging, (with the exceptions hereinafter mentioned) tuition, books, stationery and whatever else pertains to their studies.

3. No pupil can leave the College except at the end of each semi-annual term, and in all cases, (sickness excepted) payment for a term once commenced, will invariably be required—and

4. Parents who do not reside in Mobile or New Orleans, will be required to appoint in one or the other of these cities a correspondent, and every correspondent will be held responsible for all dues.

GENERAL REMARKS:

1. The Fine Arts, such as Drawing, Painting, Music, &c., will constitute an extra charge.

2. Pocket money will be confided to the President, who will disburse it according to the internal regulations of the College.

3. Every pupil will furnish himself with a bedstead, mattress, and the necessary bedding, (moscheto bars are entirely unnecessary), a pillow, 2 pairs of sheets—also a wash-bowl and a stand, and also 12 shirts, 6 cravats, 6 napkins; 6 towels, 12 pocket handkerchiefs, 3 summer suits and a suit for winter, consisting of a blue cloth dress coat, a surtout and two pairs of pantaloons, also a silver fork and table spoon.

4. Medical services and Medicines will be at the expense of the parents, unless they commune with the Physician of the College.

5. No pupil will be received whose age *exceeds 12 years* [sic.]—*This regulation admits of no exceptions.*

6. Pupils of bad habits, or who are insubordinate to the regulations of College, after all the means suggested by wisdom and prudence for their reformation have been employed ineffectually, and after their parents or correspondents have been informed of their conduct, will be expelled, and safely re-conducted to their homes.

7. Neither the Director of Studies, nor the Professors are allowed, on any consideration whatever, to inflict corporal, or other severe punishment.

8. Twice during each semestre, or semi-annual term, parents will

receive bulletins containing detailed statements of the conduct and progress of their sons at College.

9. The pupils will be required to speak the French and English Languages each successive, alternate week. The studies as above mentioned, will be pursued in English.

10. The pupils will be required to write to their parents at least once every month, and no such letters will be subject to the inspection of the Faculty or President.

11. The pupils will be permitted to leave the College but once a month, nor then unless they shall have obtained from their respective professor, certificates of good conduct and application; nor even with these unless their parents or correspondents cause them to be accompanied by persons responsible for their good conduct during absence.

This regulation does not, however, deprive pupils of recreation under the surveillance of the Faculty, on the College grounds, which include an area of nearly one mile square, affording a delightful and picturesque landscape with the most agreeable diversified native scenery.

12. No visits will be received at the College except on holidays.

In fine, it is believed that a more healthy locality cannot be found in the Southern States. Many persons, foreigners and entire strangers in the Southern climate, have resided nearly a year under the same roof, not one of whom has experienced the slightest indisposition. The high elevation of Spring Hill, rendering it inaccessible to the fogs of the lowlands; the regular and daily prevalence of invigorating sea breezes during the summer; the clear and serene atmosphere, the excellency of the water, the facilities for bathing; the nature of the soil, wholly incapable of producing noxious exhalations; and in addition to all this, a large, spacious and well ventilated college edifice, surrounded by a great variety of pleasing shade and shrubbery, unite all the advantages which the most scrupulous attention to health can require.—Michael Kenny, *Catholic Culture in Alabama: Centenary Story of Spring Hill College, 1830–1930* (New York: The American Press, 1931) pp. 69–71.

The Baptists, in spite of early low educational standards for their ministers, had become ardent supporters of schools and colleges as the following report for 1852 shows.

EDUCATIONAL ACTIVITIES OF THE BAPTISTS IN
ALABAMA, 1852
Howard College, Marion

The importance of providing for the education of the ministry was felt at an early period by some of the leading members of the Baptist denomination in Alabama, but it was not until 1833 that any decisive measures were adopted by the Baptist for establishing a Seminary of learning. At the session of the State Convention held in August of this year, a special committee, appointed to take into consideration the subject of ministerial education, reported in favor of establishing a "Seminary of Learning on the Manual Labor Plan, for the education of indigent young men called to the ministry." The preliminary steps were immediately taken for carrying into effect the suggestions of this committee.

The Board of Trustees appointed, purchased a farm in the neighborhood of Greensboro. The necessary buildings were erected, and the Institution was opened for the reception of students in January, 1836. The enterprise, however, proved unsuccessful. In little more than a year the exercises were suspended, and pecuniary embarrassments compelled the Convention to dispose of the property. From the proceeds of the sale the debts were paid, and a balance of $1,754 remained on hand. This was held sacred to the object for which it was originally contributed, and subsequently became the basis of the present Theological Fund of Howard College.

Ten years after, the Convention resolved "to establish and endow a College," and in connection with it a Theological department. A Board of Trustees was appointed, and Marion selected as the location. The friends of the new enterprise endeavored to profit by the experience of the past, and took their first steps with much caution. They resolved to contract no pecuniary liabilities beyond their available means, a resolution to which they have always strictly adhered. An act of incorporation was obtained in December, 1841, soon after which a commodious building for a preparatory school, was purchased at a cost of $4,500, and paid for. The funds were contributed entirely by the citizens of Marion. In this building a Classical School was opened in January, 1842.

In November following, the Board of Trustees suggested to the Convention the propriety of commencing the endowment of the Theological department, believing that funds would be more cheerfully contributed for this object than for the literary branch of the proposed institution. This suggestion was received with favor, and in the course of a year $20,000 were raised, a sum sufficient for the permanent endowment of one Professorship. Rev. Jesse Hartwell, D.D., was elected the first Professor of Theology and entered upon his duties January, 1844.

The Board now began to direct their attention to the ultimate object which the Convention had in view, and for which they had been constituted, viz, "to establish and endow a College." The increasing number of students, the demands of both the literary and theological classes, as well as the expectation of the public, called for a more extensive course of instruction, and the four usual College classes were accordingly organized in 1847. The first class, consisting of seven members, graduated in July, 1848. In the mean time a new college edifice was erected at a cost, including lot, of $15,000; apparatus was purchased at an expense of $2,600, and over $20,000 were raised towards the permanent endowment of the College.

Since its organization as a College, the institution has been steadily progressing in means, in the number of students, and in the confidence of the public. The last report of the Board of Trustees shows that the permanent funds now amount to about $60,000, the interest of which is available for current expenses. By the exercise of rigid economy in all expenditures, this and the proceeds of tuition, sustain a faculty of four Professors, a Tutor, and a Preparatory Teacher.

The College edifice is a brick, four stories high, and contains a chapel, laboratory, recitation, and other public rooms, and several dormitories for students. There is no provision for the steward's hall, and the students board, and most of them lodge, in private families, an arrangement which is adopted in preference to the dormitory and commons system.

The future prospects of the College are decidedly encouraging. The denomination which orginated it is rapidly increasing in wealth, in numbers, and intelligence. It is gradually developing its energies, and greater harmony and unanimity prevail in all its counsels and efforts. A spirit—of enlightened benevolence and liberality is becoming general, and there is every reason to hope that the Baptists of Alabama will soon place their College on an independent and liberal foundation.

Instructors.—Rev. H. Tallbird, A.M., President, and Professor of Theology and Moral Sciences; S. S. Sherman, A.M., Professor of Chemistry; A. B. Goodhue, A.M., Professor of Languages; Rev. Russell Holman, A.M., Professor of Mathematics; J. A. Melcher., A.B., Teacher of Preparatory Department.

JUDSON FEMALE INSTITUTE, MARION

This institution was established in January, 1839, under the direction of Rev. Milo P. Jewett. In 1841, an act of incorporation was obtained from the Legislature, granting full power to confer diplomas on pupils formally completing the course of study prescribed by law.

In the autumn of 1843, a tender of the Institute to the Alabama Baptist State Convention was made by its founders and proprietors, and, at the next session of the Convention, in 1843, this transfer was formally consummated. The object of this arrangement was to promote the interests of education at large throughout Alabama, and particularly to concentrate upon the institute the affections of the Baptist denomination. The liberality of the founders in thus relinquishing their right to an exclusive control over the institution, was duly appreciated, and the arrangement has been productive of great good. The value of the property thus placed under the control of the Convention is about $30,000.

The Seminary edifice presents a front of 150 feet, consisting of a main building four stories high, and two wings, each three stories—the main building extending back 100 feet.

The Institute is provided with a library, cabinet of minerals, shells, etc., philosophical apparatus, maps, books of reference, etc. The classes in Chemistry and Natural Philosophy attend the lectures on these subjects in Howard College.

The course of study is comprehensive and thorough, enbracing all the solid and ornamental branches taught in the highest Female Seminaries in the United States. The best professors and teachers are employed in the Music department, and the number of pupils on the piano, harp, guitar, etc., is about one hundred. There are belonging to the Institute one harp, fourteen pianos, and a variety of other instruments.

The Faculty of instruction, government, etc., comprises the Principal, a Professor of Music, three female Music Teachers, four or five instructors in the various solid and ornamental branches, a Governess, a Matron and Nurse, and the Steward and his lady.

The number of pupils for the year ending August 1st, 1852, was one hundred and ninety—embracing young ladies from Alabama, Mississippi, Arkansas, Louisiana, and Texas.

The total annual expenses for board, tuition, books, etc., of a student desiring a diploma, amount to two hundred dollars. The expenses, per annum, of a young lady pursuing only English branches with music on the piano, are $240.

The Judson Female Institute having been conducted with great success and for a longer term of years under the direction of the same Principal, than any other Female Seminary in the Southern States, is regarded as a permanent institution, a Female College, in the highest acceptation of a term. Hence, it attracts students from every part of the South West, and commands the patronage of intelligent parents and guardians, without regard to religious denomination.

The Judson Institute derives its name from the talented and heroic Mrs. Ann H. Judson. It was planted in prayer, and has been watered with tears of many pious parents, who have invoked on it the choicest blessings of heaven. These fervent supplications have not been in vain. Seven distinct seasons of revival of religion have been enjoyed in the institution, and scarcely a single year has passed without witnessing the conversion of some of the pupils. Of the sixty-eight graduates, fifty-two are hopefully pious. Most of the revivals have originated in the ordinary religious instruction imparted in the Institution, or in the labors of faithful, pious teachers. The usual religious exercises are—morning and evening devotions; public worship on the Sabbath; the Sabbath School on Sabbath morning; the Bible classes on Monday morning; the meetings of the Missionary Society on the first Sabbath of every month; and the prayer meetings held by the pious young ladies every Sabbath evening.

It may not be unworthy of notice as one of the prime causes of the prosperity of the institute, that habits of system, order, industry, economy, and punctuality are most rigidly enforced in the arrangements and discipline of the School. A uniform dress, simple and neat, is prescribed, all jewelry, even ear-rings and finger-rings, is prohibited; and every temptation to extravagance is removed.

Faculty—. Rev. Milo P. Jewett, A. M., Principal, and Instructor in Ancient Languages, and in Mental and Moral Science. F. Augustus Wurm, A.M., Professor of Vocal and Instrumental Music. Miss Lucy E. Smith, Instructor in English Branches, Embroidery and Waxwork. Miss Lucina D. Salisbury, Instructor in Modern Languages, Drawing and Painting. Miss Mary A. Griswold, Instructor in English Branches. Miss Jennie A. Morey, Instructor in English Branches, and Presiding Teacher in the General Study Hall. Miss Phebe F. Holman, English Branches.

Miss Sarah E. Smith, Instructor in Music, Piano. Miss Mary Jane Davis, Instructor in Music, Piano. Miss Mary A. Booth, Instructor of Music, Piano and Guitar. Miss Emma M. Conrad, Instructor in the Primary and Preparatory department. Governess, Miss Mary A. Griswold. Librarian, Miss Georgiana Bennett. Steward's Department, Mr. and Mrs. William Hornbuckle. Matron and Nurse, Mrs. Hannah C. Eastman.—*American Baptist Record for 1852* (Philadelphia, 1853) pp. 421–24, quoted in Knight, *A Documentary History of Education,* vol. 4, pp. 394–99.

Dormitory Life

Judson Female Institute is a good example of a school on the border between a secondary school and a college. It soon began offering college work but for many years it had preparatory courses. In fact, in the early days it had three departments: primary, preparatory, and collegiate.

The Institute, or The Judson as it is always called in early Baptist literature, opened its doors January 7, 1839; it is now (1971) the only four year college for women in the state.

Dormitory rules at the school reflect a way of life that was vastly different from the secular, affluent, permissive society of a century and a quarter later.

GOVERNMENT

THE GOVERNMENT is vested in the Principal, aided by his Associates in the Faculty of Instruction. A prompt and cheerful obedience to the laws is always expected; and is enforced by appeals to the reason and to the conscience of the Pupil. This course, sustained by constant reference to the *Word of God,* has been uniformly successful in securing alacrity in the discharge of duty. Should the voice of persuasion remain unheeded, and any young lady continue perverse and obstinate, in spite of kind and faithful admonition, her friends would be requested to withdraw her from the Institution. None are desired as members of this seminary, except such as are happy in observing wise and wholesome regulations.

REPORTS TO PARENTS

MONTHLY REPORTS, showing the scholarship and deportment of the Pupils, are sent to the Parents and Guardians.

CORRESPONDENCE

LETTERS for the Pupils should be directed to the care of the Principal, POST-PAID. All correspondence, except between Pupils and Parents and Guardians, is liable to inspection.

All instructions relative to their Correspondence will be carefully observed.

No Books, Magazines, or Newspapers to be received, without permission of the Principal.

No Boarder shall send any Letter or Package to the Post Office or to any individual of either sex, without permission of the Principal. Nor shall any Boarder receive, either for herself or for any other Pupils, any Letter or Note, Package, or Parcel; any Bouquet of Flowers, any Memento or Token of regard, or any Verbal Communication from any unmarried Gentleman, on penalty of expulsion.

RELIGIOUS TRAINING

Pupils attend church, once at least, on the Sabbath, under the direction of their parents or guardians as to the place of worship. Other religious exercises are attended at the discretion of the Principal, but all sectarian influences are carefully excluded.

With intellectual and physical education, is combined the most careful moral and social culture. The BIBLE is constantly used as the Text Book in Morals, and all the religious training of the pupils is conducted on the broad principles of the Gospel . . . Sentiments of truth and honor, piety and benevolence are sedulously inculcated. All external evil influences are rigidly excluded, and Parents may here safely trust their daughters, assured that they will be strongly though tenderly guarded, in all that is dear to a parent's heart.

ADVANTAGES OF BOARDING AT THE INSTITUTE

Only by boarding in the institute, can the highest advantages of the Institute be realized. Here, young Ladies are always under the inspection of the Governess and Teachers; they have regular hours of study and recreation; habits of order, system, punctuality, neatness and economy, are constantly fostered. They also enjoy an amount of moral and religious culture, which cannot be extended to others less favorably situated. The regularity of their lives; the alternation of sedentary habits with exercise, of hours of study with amusement, the kind and judicious supervision constantly maintained, secures the highest degree of mental vigor and bodily health.

SOCIAL LIFE

THE MANNERS, personal and social HABITS, and the MORALS of the young Ladies are formed under the eyes of the Governess and Teachers, from whom the pupils are never separated.

The Boarders never leave the grounds of the Institute, without special permission of the PRINCIPAL.

They attend no public parties, and receive no visitors, except such as are introduced by Parents or Guardians.

MONTHLY Levies are held, conducted by Committees of the older Pupils, under the supervision of the Governess. These are attended by members of the Board of Trustees and other married gentlemen with their ladies. They are designed to FORM THE MANNERS of the young ladies, and make them practically familiar with the usages of polite society.

SHOPPING

They go to town but once a month, and then all purchases must be approved by the Governess.

They are allowed to spend no more than fifty cents each month from their pocket-money.

No young lady will be allowed to have money in her own hands; all sums intended for her benefit must be deposited with the STEWARD.

No accounts will be opened in town; and no purchases will be made for the Pupils, except under special instructions from the Parent or Guardian.

DRESS

To promote habits of economy and simplicity, a UNIFORM DRESS is prescribed.

For winter, it is a DARK GREEN WORSTED. Of this fabric, each young lady should have three dresses, with three Sacks of the same— one of the sacks to be large and wadded.

For Summer, each Pupil should have two PINK CALICO, two PINK GINGHAM, and two COMMON WHITE DRESSES, with one SWISS MUSLIN. Also, one BROWN LINEN dress. Every dress should be accompanied by a sack of the same material.—Compiled by A. Elizabeth Taylor, *Alabama Historical Quarterly*, vol. 3, pp. 24–49.

Medical College

Dr. Josiah C. Nott, whose report on yellow fever in Mobile is given elsewhere, was active in promoting the idea of a state medical school. The Alabama Medical Association, organized in 1846, supported the campaign and in 1856 the Legislature passed an act authorizing the establishment of such an institution, but without appropriating any money for it. In 1859, however, Dr. Nott opened the school under a private charter and was able to get $50,000 state money to supplement the sum raised by citizens of Mobile.

In a letter (July 15, 1859) from Paris where he had gone to buy the latest materials for a medical museum, he named the members of the Medical College faculty for whose departments he was buying. In addition to himself (surgery and pathology), he named Dr. F. A. Ross, Dr. Gordon (obstetrics) and Dr. G. A. Ketchum, "whose branch covers the whole range of the profession." Dr. Nott was of the opinion that their museum would be "a superb one" which would enable the faculty to give a thorough course of instruction and would be an honor to the state. The school was closed sometime during the Civil War and, occupied by the Freedmen's Bureau in September, 1865, did not reopen.

THE MEDICAL COLLEGE IN MOBILE

We are glad to see that this institution is about to open with such facilities for instruction and with such a faculty as will at once place it among the first class medical schools of the country. Dr. Nott is now in Europe selecting a museum for the college which . . . is to be one of the best, if not the best, in the United States, affording the students very unusual facilities in every department of medical instruction. And no one who is acquainted with the gentlemen who compose the faculty can, for a moment doubt that they do full justice to these ample materials for illustrating their lectures and making them as useful as they are interesting.

We consider the success of this college as a matter of importance to the whole state. At the very lowest estimate, more than $250,000 are annually taken from Alabama by medical students, and spent in enriching other communities—for the most part northern cities. It surely would be better policy, and better economy, to provide means of instruction within our own borders and to allow our own citizens to reap the benefits of this large and progressively increasing sum, so that if any institution of this kind is worthy of "State aid," this is one. It is not merely a Mobile enterprise (though so far, none but citizens of Mobile have assisted it). The State Medical Association, several years ago, formally recommended the establishment of a college and unanimously designated Mobile as the place for it. . . .

It is high time Alabama was acting in this matter. . . .—*Dallas Gazette,* August 19, 1859. Photostat in Josiah C. Nott Papers, Alabama Historical Collections, Medical Center Library, Birmingham.

For a rural state only recently emerging from the frontier stage, Alabama was well supplied with colleges. In addition to the University (established in 1831), it had several colleges: Judson, Howard, La Grange, Spring Hill, and Southern University. Furthermore, there were many collegiate institutes giving some instruction on the college level among the preparatory courses. Also, there was a medical college in Mobile. Dr. A. B. Moore summarizes the school situation in 1860 by saying that there were 61,751 pupils in public schools with 2,038 teachers. There were 206 academies that enrolled 10,778 students. There were 2,120 students enrolled in the seventeen colleges in the state. A bit of simple arithmetic will show that the average school was small. Moreover, buildings were shabby, support inadequate, and instruction uneven. There were many highly educated people in the state, but nevertheless, illiteracy ran high in antebellum Alabama.

Chapter 9

THE WAY THE PEOPLE LIVED

In treating the social pattern, or life style, of the residents of Alabama before 1860 it is essential to remember certain basic facts. The first is that it had changed greatly from territorial days, when almost all the state was raw wilderness, to the outbreak of the Civil War, at which time the population had reached 964,201, and was generally spread widely over the state. Furthermore, it had changed in varying degrees. In Mobile, for instance, where the French had planted their civilization in the eighteenth century, life was more sophisticated than in the sections where the Indians had lived until a much later date. There, pioneer conditions largely determined the way people lived even long after the 1860's. Alabama was an agricultural state and its people depended directly or indirectly on the products of the soil for their living. Mobile's wealth was based on the cotton that went down the Alabama and Tombigbee Rivers. The finest houses in the port city were built by cotton factors. While people in all parts of the state made a living from the land, the returns were uneven. In the river valleys and the Black Belt, the soil was fertile and the profits high. Here the plantation and plantation way of living dominated. In the hill and mountain counties and the section that became known as the "Wiregrass," soil was thin and the returns lower. In these areas the family farm prevailed, depending less on cotton than on a variety of other farm products. All these factors are reflected in the pattern of living—in the social interests, forms of entertainment, and in the way that homes were built.

Alabama homes varied according to the time they were built, the wealth, and taste of the people who lived in them. There were mountain log cabins, modest but comfortable (or uncomfortable) homes, and elegant mansions of the Greek revival style. Some had no yards at all, others a clean-swept patch around them, and still others extensive grounds and beautiful landscaping. There are still many gardens that have antebellum boxwood, cape jasmine, camellias, and magnolias that bear testimony to an early love of beauty.

The Log Cabin

The log cabin was a common denominator in pioneer Alabama. Before 1830, practically every family coming into Alabama built and lived in a simple one-room log cabin, even though some soon replaced them with fine houses. Many people continued to live in such homes, even into the twentieth century, never knowing anything better.

F. L. Olmsted, architect and landscape artist who planned New York's Central Park, made an extensive tour of the South and Southwest in the 1850's. While Olmstead was an ardent anti-slavery man and took a critical view of much he saw, his descriptions are usually honest. He made a trip into north Alabama in the summer of 1853 where he saw varying life styles.

Northern Alabama, June 15th.—I have to-day reached a more distinctly hilly country—somewhat rocky and rugged, but with inviting dells. The soil is sandy and less frequently fertile; cotton-fields are seen only at long intervals, the crops on the small proportion of cultivated land being chiefly corn and oats. I notice also that white men are more commonly at work in the field than negroes, and this as well in the cultivation of cotton as of corn.

The larger number of the dwellings are rude log huts, of only one room, and that unwholesomely crowded. I saw in and about one of them, not more than fifteen feet square, five grown persons, and as many children. Occasionally, however, the monotony of these huts is agreeably varied by neat, white, frame houses. At one such, I dined to-day, and was comfortably entertained. The owner held a number of slaves, but made no cotton. He owned a saw mill, was the postmaster of the neighbourhood, and had been in the Legislature. . . .

I passed the night at the second framed house that I saw during the day, stopping early in order to avail myself of its promise of comfort. It was attractively situated on a hill-top, with a peach orchard near it. The proprietor owned a dozen slaves, and "made cotton," he said, "with other crops." He had some of his neighbours at tea and at breakfast; sociable, kindly people, satisfied with themselves and their circumstances, which I judged from their conversation had been recently improving. One coming in, remarked that he had discharged a white labourer whom he had employed for some time past; the others congratulated him on being "shet" of him; all seemed to have noticed him as a bad, lazy man; he had often been seen lounging in the field, rapping the negroes with his hoe if they didn't work to suit him. "He was about the meanest white man I ever see," said a woman; "he was a heap meaner 'n niggers. I reckon niggers would come somewhere between white folks and such as he." "The first thing I tell a man," said another, "when I hire him, is, 'if there's any whippin' to be done on this place I want to do it myself.' If I saw a man rappin' my niggers with a hoe-handle, as I see him, durned if I wouldn't rap him—the lazy whelp. . . ."

These people were extremely kind; inquiring with the simplest good feeling about my domestic relations and the purpose of my journey. When I left, one of them walked a quarter of a mile to make sure that I went upon the right road. The charge for entertainment, though it was unusually good, was a quarter of a dollar less than I have paid before, which I mention, not as Mr. De Bow would suppose, out of gratitude for the moderation, but as an indication of the habits of the people, showing, as it may, either closer calculation, or that the district grows its own supplies, and can furnish food cheaper than those in which attention is more exclusively given to cotton.

June 17th.—The country continues hilly, and is well populated by farmers, living in log huts, while every mile or two, on the more level and fertile land, there is a larger farm, with ten or twenty negroes at work. A few whites are usually working near them, in the same field, generally ploughing while the negroes hoe.—F. L. Olmsted, *The Cotton Kingdom* (New York: Alfred A. Knopf, 1953), pp. 381–86.

Philip Henry Gosse in 1838 described a homestead in Dallas County where cotton culture was the rule. The Bohannon family with whom he lived was not one of the great planters but it was far from being poor. The fact that a man of his standing would live in such a dwelling was hard for Gosse, and other visitors to similar homes, to believe. Yet, as Gosse pointed out in the following passage, these crude houses had many attractive features.

You ask me whether the farms here are similar to such as you are familiar with. There are some peculiarities about them, and as all are laid out pretty nearly upon the same plan, a description of one will serve, with a little variation, for all. Of course the houses differ in their degrees of comfort and elegance, according to the taste or finances of their proprietors, but in general they are built double; a set of rooms on each side of a wide passage, which is floored and ceiled in common with the rest of the house, but is entirely open at each end, being unfurnished with either gate or door, and forming a thoroughfare for the family through the house. Various kinds of climbing plants and flowers are trained to cluster about either end of these passages, and by their wild and luxuriant beauty take away the sordidness which the rude character of the dwellings might otherwise present. The *Glycine frutescens* with its many stems twisted tight together like a ship's cable, hangs its beautiful bunches of lilac blossoms profusely about, like clusters of grapes; the elegant and graceful Scarlet Cypress-vine with hastate leaves, and long drooping vermilion flowers, shaped like those of a convolvulus; the still more elegant Crimson Cypress-vine whose flowers, shaped like those of the sister species, are of the richest carmine, and whose leaves are cut, even to the mid-rib, into a multitude of long and slender fingers; our own Sweet-brier, the Trumpet Honeysuckle, whose deep scarlet tubes are the twilight resort of the sounding-winged Hawkmoths. These, with other favourite plants, cover the rough logs and shingles with so dense a mass of vegetation and inflorescence, as effectually hide them from view. When the air within the house is close and sultry, almost to suffocation, and the unmerciful rays of the sun, without, glare upon the head beyond endurance, it is a pleasant relief to sit in these halls beneath the shade, where too there is a current of air whenever there is a breath stirring. Here the southern planter loves to sit, or to lie stretched at full length; and here, particularly at the approach of evening, when the sunbeams twinkle obliquely through the transparent foliage, and the cool breeze comes loaded with the fragrance of a thousand flowers, the family may usually be seen, each (ladies as well as gentlemen) in that very elegant position in which an American delights to sit, the chair poised upon the two hind feet, or leaning back against the wall, at an angle of 45°, the feet upon the highest bar, the knees near the chin, the head pressing against the wall, so as now and then to push the chair a few inches from it, the hands (but not of the ladies) engaged in fashioning with a pocket-knife a piece of pine-wood, into some un-couth and fantastic form; the tongue discussing the probability of a war with the "British," and indulging a little national egotism, in an-ticipation of the consequences to follow thereupon, "whipping the British" being of course assumed.

Very many of the houses, even of wealthy and respectable planters, are built of rough and unhewn logs, and to an English taste are destitute of comfort to a surprising degree. There is one about a mile distant, belonging to a very worthy man whom I have often visited, which is of this character. I will try to give you an idea of it. It is a ground-floor house of two rooms. Fancy the walls full of crevices an inch or more in width, some of them running the whole length of the rooms, caused by the warping of the logs, the decay of the bark, or the dropping out of the clay which had been put in to fill up. There is no window in the whole house; in one room there is a square hole about two feet wide, which a shutter professes to close, but as it is made of boards that have never felt either saw or plane, being merely riven by the aid of the broad-axe out of an oak log, you may guess how accurately it fits. A door formed of similar boards, rarely shut, at least from dawn till night, gives light and air to each room, though the crevices of the logs, and those of the roof, would afford ample light when both door and shutter were closed. You will perhaps wonder how a door can possibly be made of boards whose edges have never been made straight by the plane; the fact is, the boards are not laid edge to edge, but the edges lap over each other, as board-fences are sometimes made in England; to speak scientifically, the boards are laterally imbricated.

A bed-room has been added since the original erection; unbarked poles were set in the ground, and these riven boards nailed outside, edge over edge, by the way of clapboard; there is nothing of lathing, or boarding, or papering within, nothing between the lodger and the weather, but these rough, crooked, and uneven boards, through which, of course, the sun plays at bopeep, and the wind and rain also. It forms a lean-to, the roof being continued from that of the house. The lowest tier of logs composing the house, rest on stout blocks about two feet from the ground; beams go across from these logs, on which the floor is laid; the planks are certainly sawed, but they are not pinned to the beams, being moveable at pleasure; and as the distance between the lowest logs and the ground is perfectly open, the wind has full liberty of ingress through the seams of the floor, as well as in every other part.

The roof is of a piece with the rest; no ceiling meets the eye; the gaze goes up beyond the smoke-burnt rafters up to the very shingles; nay, beyond them, for in the bright night the radiance of many a star gleams upon the upturned eye of the recumbent watcher, and during the day many a moving spot of light upon the floor shows the progress which the sun makes towards the west. But it is during the brief, but terrific rainstorms, which often occur in this climate, that one becomes painfully conscious of the permeability of the roof; the floor soon streams; one knows not where to run to escape the thousand and one trickling cascades; and it is amusing to see the inmates, well acquainted with the geography of the house, catching up books, and other damageable articles, and heaping them up in some spot which they know to be canopied by a sound part of the roof.

There is a fireplace at each end of the house, a large open chimney, the fire being on the hearth, which is raised to a level with the floor; the chimney itself is curiously constructed; simply enough however, for the skeleton of it is merely a series of flat slips of wood, laid one upon another in the form of a square, the ends crossing at the corners, where they are slightly pinned together, the square contracting from five feet at the bottom to little more than one at the top. As this framework proceeds, it is plastered within and without with well-beaten clay, to the thickness of two or three inches. This is considered a sufficient protection against the fire; for though, on account of the clay here and there dropping off, the slips of wood often ignite, and holes are burnt through, yet the clay around prevents the fire from spreading, and these holes are regarded with a very exemplary philosophy. I should have observed, however, that at the bottom of the chimney, and more particularly at the fire-back, the clay is increased in thickness to more than a foot. Add to this description a ladder of three steps at each end of the passage, from the ground to the floor, and you have my worthy friend's hospitable mansion.

Now poor and mean houses may be found in every country, but this is but one of the many; it is not inhabited by poor persons, nor is it considered as at all remarkable for discomfort; it is, according to the average, a very decent house. There are some, certainly, much superior; but these are frame-houses, regularly clapboarded, and ceiled, and two, or even three stories high, including the ground-floor. They are mostly of recent erection, and are inhabited by planters of large property; these have comforts and elegancies in them which would do no dishonour to an English gentleman.

The house in which I am residing stands in the middle of a large yard, formed partly by a fence of rails and posts, and partly by the offices and out-buildings, such as the pantry, kitchen, spinning-house, dairy, &c.; these are distinct buildings, formed of logs, and always more or less distant from the house. Two or three of the negro-houses are likewise usually placed in the yard, that hands may be called on at any moment if needed, the general range of huts being out of sight and hearing of the house. Little black children, stark naked, from a few weeks old to six or seven years, at which age they go out into the field, play, or grovel about the yard, or lie stretched in the glaring sunbeams, the elder ones professedly taking care of the younger or more helpless. Here of course they are early inured, by kicks and cuffs, to bear the severe inflictions of the lash, &c., which await them in after life. The pigs and fowls entertain very little respect for the Negro children, with whom there is a perpetual squabbling; and what with the scolding of the youngsters, the squealing of the pigs, the cackling of the guinea-fowls, the gobbling of the turkeys, and the quacking of the Muscovy ducks, the yard does not lack noise. Of these last there is always a troop of all ages and sizes; it is the only duck *patronised;* the "English duck," as our common species is called, being kept only as a curiosity. The greater size of the former, approaching to that of the goose, is a recommendation, but it is far inferior in beauty, and, in my opinion, in flavour, to the common kind.—Philip Henry Gosse, *Letters from Alabama* (London: Morgan and Chase, 1959), pp. 151–52, 157–58.

While most Alabamians continued to live in simple houses, mansions were being erected in increasing numbers. Built sometimes in towns but more often on plantations, they reflect the growing wealth and sophistication of Alabamians. Few houses that could be called mansions were built before 1820 and most of them were put up after 1840. They were concentrated along rivers and in towns (often also on rivers) like Mobile, Montgomery, Selma, Greensboro, Huntsville, Tuskegee, Eufaula, and others. Ralph Hammond in 1951 wrote that there were over two thousand of them still standing.

Classical architecture, also called Greek revival, popularized in America more by Thomas Jefferson than any other individual, was not confined to the South. But it was especially popular there because it met the needs of the region. With its central hall, large rooms, high ceilings, and columned porches or verandas, this style of architecture provided a maximum of relief from summer heat. It provided ample room for big families—and frequent guests— and was easily enlarged by the addition of wings. How much the popularity of classical literature among southerners influenced their choice of building plans is debatable but the "Greek temple" was spectacular and stylish, two characteristics a planter would consider when he had made enough money to build a fine house. The goals of the mansion builders, according to Hammond, were:

> unadorned beauty, lasting dignity, boldness toned with grandeur, quality of line and form and grace, magnificence of conception, and a profound goodness and permanence of construction. It was an era in which man strove for beauty in much the same manner as did the ancient Greeks . . . ; an era in which the Alabama builder borrowed much from his Greek predecessor and proceeded then to add his own inspiration and ideas which thus provided buildings that suited his needs, his luxuries, his desires.—Ralph Hammond, *Ante-Bellum Mansions of Alabama* (New York: Architectural Book Publishing Co., 1951), p. 17.

Of the many elegant homes in Alabama that could be used as examples, Anna M. Gaye Fry's description of the Joel Mathews home at Cahaba is given here.

> Two miles south of Cahaba, immediately on the banks of the Alabama River, was the home of Mr. Joel Mathews, one of the most beautifully improved places in the South. The house was of brick built in the old English style with an open court in front and a broad gallery entirely across the southern portion. It was in a grove of large forest trees extending to the banks of the river. On the east and west in front of the house were extensive grounds with broad walks and circular carriage drives bordered on each side with trimmed hedges of Yopon and Pyracanthia, surrounding large beds and mounds rioting in myriads of beautiful flowers. Roses, japonicas, cape jasmine, spirea, snowballs, hyacienths, tulips, sweet shrubs, jonquils, and violets gave forth their rich perfume, and the mocking bird sang perpetually from the bowers of honeysuckle and wisteria, heavy and purple with blossom in spring. . . . apricots, nectarines, and figs of many varieties grew luxuriantly and bore abundantly. On the north side of the house was the garden through which was the entrance to the family burial ground, with its handsome monuments, beautiful shrubbery, and even rarer flowers than the yard contained. A short distance from the house on the south side was the luxurious bath house with an immense cemented pool through which flowed a constant and continuous stream of gushing water from the artesian well. South of the residence was the plantation with its broad acres, its church, its ball room and comfortable log house, occupied by hundreds of slaves, devoted to their master and his family. This was an ideal Southern home, the embodiment of cordial and princely hospitality with its well trained servants, magnificent library and every surrounding for comfort, ease, and luxury and a home that was noted far and wide for the kindness and cultivation, the refinement and liberality of its owners.—*Memories of Old Cahaba* (privately printed, 1905), pp. 53–54.

Alabama mansions were sometimes built by architects from abroad, more of them by residents of the state. William Nichols did in "a smaller degree" for the University of Alabama what Jefferson had done for the University in Virginia. He was architect for both the president's mansion on the Tuscaloosa campus and the Gorgas home. Two other well-known architects were Stephen Decatur Button who built the state capitol in Montgomery and George Steele who planned many of the fine homes in Huntsville. On the other hand, Nathan Bryan Whitfield was his own architect and builder. With only a book of instructions and the labor of the slaves whom he trained himself, he built Gaineswood, his beautiful home at Demopolis. Doubtless, most Alabamians followed the the same method, even if the results were somewhat less spectacular.

Men and Manners

While many residents of the state were described as having elegant, genteel or charming manners, visitors especially foreigners, found most Americans in the interior, including Alabamians, crude and ill-mannered. James S. Buckingham, English author and world traveler, was making a four-year tour of America when he visited Alabama in the 1830's.

In the course of our way up the Alabama we had abundant occasion to observe the disagreeable peculiarities by which the manners of the middle classes in America are distinguished from those of the same classes in England. Among the gentlemen, scarcely one took off his hat on entering the cabin, but nearly all sat with their hats on, during every part of the day, except at meals; and chewing and spitting was nearly universal, brass boxes being placed in rows along the floor of the cabin, to save the carpet from defilement. At meals, considerable etiquette is manifested in waiting for the ladies, who are always placed at the head of the table; the gentlemen stand behind their chairs, and no one presumes to seat himself, however long he may be kept waiting, until the ladies appear, to take their seats first. In leaving the table, however, no such punctiliousness is observed; . . . every person rises as soon as he has finished, which is frequently in ten minutes or less, retiring from the table chewing his last mouthful as he goes, and then hastens to the forepart of the vessel, to light his cigar, the common accompaniment of every meal.

At the meal, all persons convey their food to the mouth on the point of the knife, which practice, from its universality, attracts no notice except from a stranger. Silver forks are rarely seen, except at the best private tables; and the steel ones used have rarely more than two prongs. The knife has a very broad blade, and expanded round point, to take up a good knifeful of the food in use, and convey it to the mouth; and both knives and forks are set in large, rough, and uncouth handles of buck-horn, so irregular in shape, that it is difficult for any but a practised hand to hold and manage them pleasantly. The principal dishes are taken off the table, and carved or hacked on a sideboard by the negro stewards, who load the plates with so great a quantity of everything asked for, and so bury the whole in gravies or sauces, that it requires a very strong appetite to conquer the repugnance which it creates. No delicacy is observed in the mode of carving, serving, or helping the guests; and the gentlemen are all too busily occupied in despatching their own portion, to take this duty out of the servants' hands. Puddings are usually handed round in small white saucers, instead of plates, with a spoon in each, and nothing is refused. Every one seems to think it is a duty to accept and be thankful for whatever is set before him, and appears to exercise no more power of rejection or refusal, than children at school.

At breakfast and at supper—for so the evening meal at seven o'clock is usually called—coffee is more frequently used than tea; and of tea, green is almost the only kind seen. Both are made at a sidetable by the negroes, and handed round to the guests as they are seated. High and large cups of thick white earthenware are chiefly used; and though originally furnished with handles, three out of four will have had their handles knocked off; but neither this, nor cracks, though sufficient to make both cups and saucers leaky, is deemed disqualification for service; so that there are generally more broken vessels than whole ones on the table. . . .

In other matters, also, there is a great dissimilarity in the manners of the English and the Americans. In England, for instance, no person, even in the humblest ranks of life, would venture to approach a table where a gentleman was writing, to look over his papers, or take up his books for examination, without permission. But here I had been so frequently subject to the former, that I felt obliged to give up writing anywhere but in my own bedroom, and even there I was not always safe from intrusion; while as to the latter, persons in the rank of merchants and bankers would seat themselves at the table, take up any of the books which you might be using for perusal or reference, cut them open, read them, and sometimes even take them off to their own cabins, to read through, without asking permission, or seeming to think this at all necessary. On one occasion, when I said to a gentleman who was thus walking off with a volume which he had taken from under my very elbow—"I beg your pardon, Sir, but that is private, and does not belong to the ship, as perhaps you suppose," he coolly replied—"Oh, never mind, I only want to read it; and when I have done with it, you shall have it again."

In mentioning all these traits of manners, I must at the same time, in justice, observe, that however disagreeable they may be to English persons, chiefly because they differ from what they are accustomed to witness in similar classes of society at home, it is not fair to consider them as acts either of vulgarity or rudeness. . . . From this I think the Americans are more free than the people of any nation I have ever travelled in. They are almost uniformly decorous, civil, obliging, willing to yield in any matter for the accommodation of others, quiet, orderly, and inoffensive; and neither at the hotels, nor in the steamboats, or on railroads, is the ear so often offended as it is in England, by oaths, vociferations, quarrels, complaints, bickerings among equals, and abuse of inferiors.—James S. Buckingham, *Slave States in America* (London, 1842), vol. 1, quoted in Walter B. Posey, ed., *Alabama in the 1830's* (Birmingham, Ala.: Birmingham Southern College, 1938), pp. 43–44.

Harriet Martineau, also an English writer, came to America in 1834 in quest of health. She spent about two weeks in and around Montgomery the following year. She was decidedly opposed to slavery and bitterly critical of much she saw. Nevertheless she found southern hospitality delightful and the bountiful table most welcome.

It was now the middle of April. In the kitchen garden the peas were ripening, and the strawberries turning red, though the spring of 1835 was very backward. We had salads, young asparagus, and radishes.

The following may be considered a pretty fair account of the provision for a planter's table, at this season; and, except with regard to vegetables, I believe it does not vary much throughout the year. Breakfast at seven; hot wheat bread, generally sour; corn bread, biscuits, waffles, hominy, dozens of eggs, broiled ham, beef-steak or broiled fowl, tea and coffee. Lunch at eleven; cake and wine, or liqueur. Dinner at two; now and then soup (not good,) always roast turkey and ham; a boiled fowl here, a tongue there; a small piece of nondescript meat, which generally turns out to be pork disguised; hominy, rice, hot corn-bread, sweet potatoes; potatoes mashed with spice, very hot; salad and radishes, and an extraordinary variety of pickles. Of these, you are asked to eat everything with everything else. If you have turkey and ham on your plate, you are requested to add tongue, pork, hominy, and pickles. Then succeed pies of apple, squash, and pumpkin; custard, and a variety of preserves as extraordinary as the preceding pickles: pineapple, peach, limes, ginger, guava jelly, cocoa-nut, and every sort of plums. These are almost all from the West-Indies. Dispersed about the table are shell almonds, raisins, hickory, and other nuts; and, to crown the whole, large blocks of ice-cream. Champagne is abundant, and cider frequent. Ale and porter may now and then be seen; but claret is the most common drink. During dinner a slave stands at a corner of the table, keeping off the flies by waving a large bunch of peacock's feathers fastened into a handle,—an ampler fan than those of our grandmothers.

Supper takes place at six, or seven. Sometimes the family sits around the table; but more commonly the tray is handed round, with plates which must be held in the lap. Then follow tea and coffee, waffles, biscuits, sliced ham or hung-beef, and sweet cake. Last of all, is the offer of cake and wine at nine or ten.—Harriet Martineau, *Society in America* (London, 1837), vol. 1, pp. 295–305, *passim,* quoted in Posey, *Alabama in the 1830's,* p. 35.

Another visitor, Anne Royall, found generous hospitality in the home of Colonel Leroy Pope in Huntsville (1826). Pope was among the wealthiest men of the state and lived in "princely style."

> His house is separated from Huntsville by a deep ravine and from an eminence overlooks the town from the west; and on the east lies his beautiful plantation on a level with the house. . . . If I admired the exterior, I was amazed at the taste and elegance displayed in every part of the interior; massy plate, cut glass, china ware, sofas and mahogany furniture of the newest fashion decorated the inside.—Anne Royall, *Sketches of History, Life and Manners in the United States* (New Haven: Privately printed, 1826), p. 14.

To those who were unacquainted with the wealth of the new country, "the superb style" of the inhabitants would appear "incredible."

Weddings and Other Occasions

In the early days and even much later in the "backwoods" where life was hard and daily tasks left little time for fun, work and play were often combined. House-raisings, log-rollings, corn shucking for the men, and quilting bees for the women were opportunities to socialize and work simultaneously. After the work was done, the host family provided ample, if rough, food and drink for the guests. There were "play parties" for those who objected to the music of the fiddle, square dances, and shooting and "wrastlin'" matches. The man of the greatest physical strength and the most accurate aim was held in high esteem.

For the more sophisticated, balls, races, house parties, cruises on the river, vacations at various springs or "watering places," were parts of their social life. For all people, of whatever economic level or background, the wedding was an important event. In the early days, it often had to be deferred until the circuit rider came; in later times it could be planned at the convenience of the bride and groom.

Surprisingly, there are few detailed descriptions of weddings in Alabama. Dr. Hardy Vickers Wooten lived in Lowndesboro during his adult years but the wedding of his brother-in-law's niece took place in Georgia in 1829. Many other Alabamians came from Georgia and it seems safe to assume that wedding customs would be little changed by crossing a state line.

> It was fashionable in those days for all who held any official station at a wedding to wear white pantaloons, and I had none. . . . At length the wedding day came around. I was all embarrassment and drunk with anticipation. Many girls were in attendance for sometime before, assisting in the preparation. . . . On the wedding day after dinner time

I repaired to my room and fixed out to go and escort the bridegroom to his "lovely fair." After I had "rigged out", I called in my mother who pronounced all right and then gave me a charge how to proceed in the duties of my office. I memorized it all as well as I could and put out. I found the young man dressing out, his other attendant with him. Soon a goodly company was collected to accompany him. Just about starting time, there came a good rain to lay the dust, this however somewhat disconcerted the party as it was thought that it would prevent many from going and it was desirable to have a jolly company. The rain stopping, we all mounted, the groom and his attendant in front abreast. . . . We rode on, now and then falling in with others until we came nearly in sight of the house. When we stopped to "fix up" here, a consultation arose as to gait we should move in our approach. It was soon decided that a gallop was decidedly the most graceful and comely. So we arranged ourselves and charged up. Here indeed was a scene. During my short absence a large concourse of people had assembled. The men of riper years were in groups about the yard talking over their farming business; the young beaux were strolling about in burning impatience for the company to mix; while a few white heads were sitting in the big room around the fire, talking of "old times." The ladies, many of them, were seated around the room in prim array, the younger ones looking out at the windows, while many had not passed thru the dressing room and were yet there. The whole of the exterior yard fence was covered with boys. The road was full of gigs, barouches, carriages, etc., and the surrounding grove was literally clogged with horses, while just in front of the gate stood some well-greased kinky heads to take the horses of the groom's party.

Now the bustle commenced. The boys commenced scrambling for more conspicious places, and consequently falling off the fence; the men pushed forward in solid crowds, while the women, rather modest to run out, crowded to the windows as if to try who could stand pressing best. The window of the dressing room presented quite a ludicrous spectacle. Many naked neck and shoulders were to be seen, squeezed out with as much eagerness as if there had been a groom arriving for each and all of them. Indeed, everything was literally on tiptoe at our approach. We alighted and pressed our way thro the crowds to the house. . . . All of us but my fellow attendant were entirely new hands. The chairs were so arranged that each one must set by his girl, and though I had been raised among women, this was the first time I had ever seated myself by one. I, however, looked as wise and easy as I could. . . . The ceremony past off and supper came on. All set up to the table . . . and we, the attendants handed round and about the eatables except bread and coffee, tea, etc. . . . I passed through the supper scene with only a few little blunders . . . spilling part of my cargo now and then and only once hitting a lady's forehead with the edge of a plate. . . . After supper a play commenced as fashion run. The plays were various but every one had some kisses in it. I dodged these as long as I could, but finally being hemmed, I was compelled to kiss a girl, a thing I had never done, but I performed with astonishing grace, and from the moment, fell deadly in love with her tho she was one whom I had before always disliked. . . . Many went home, but some who lived too far stayed all night, and all the bedrooms being crowded with women and children they had to sit up. . . . Morning came, the men took a drink, the ladies walked in the garden and all were soon refreshed. About ten o'clock we all prepared ourselves and rode to the bridegroom's mothers where we had a sumptious "infare." That is a feast of eating and drinking in further celebration of the marriage. . . . Now it was the fashion for the bride to sit at one end of the table and the groom at the other, and the attendants also to take their respective ends. So I took my stand at the brides right hand. Now the rub came! My first job was to carve a fowl. This I had never done only at home. . . . So I commenced with a trembling hand and a dull knife, two very awkward instruments. Now it was fashionable to have sundry trimmings, and dressing stored around the fowl on the margins of the dish and, after I had nearly exhausted my patience in dividing a joint, I made a desperate effort, the fowl slipped and displaced divers eggs, etc., into the snow lap of the blushing bride. She however drew her handkerchief over them and passed it off very well, tho I could not afterward well recollect what happened about that time. . . .

With this and a few more blunders the infair passed off and towards night all the company put off for home, I among the rest.—Diary, Ms., Department of Archives and History, Montgomery. Dr. Wooten writes this "diary" late in life and it should properly be called a memoir of reminiscences.

While the following is not actually a description of a wedding, it is a unique record of one.

The State of Alabama, Dallas Co. To any licensed minister of the gospel, judge of the circuit or county court or justice of the peace of said county, you are hereby authorized to celebrate the rites of marriage between Mr. John Chesnut and Miss Elizabeth G. Craig and join them together in the holy bonds of matrimony and for so doing this shall be your sufficient warrant—Given under my hand at office the 19th day of January 1841—Sanford Blann, clerk.

> I rode through wet and stormy weather
> To join these loving folks together
> And notwithstanding mud and weather
> John Chesnut married Bob Craig's daughter
> So, Mr. Clerk, you'll please record it
> In this same style in which I word it,
> That I pronounced them man and wife
> Thus to remain throughout their life.
> Let no man interfere betwixed 'em,
> And let them stay just as I fixed 'em
> And whether it be for woe or weal
> This I certify under hand and seal

The twentieth day of this first moon,
Eighteen hundred and forty-one.

WILL E. BIRD, Judge
Marriage Records, 1818–1845, Dallas County, pp. 186–87.

"Horseplay," tricks played on a bride and groom, is not entirely gone but it is neither as rough or systematic as it was a century and a half ago. The serenade or shivaree was a "surprise" to the young couple on their wedding night. When lights were out and the house quiet (few went away on a honeymoon trip), friends, cronies of single days, and neighbors assembled with all kinds of noise-makers and, at a signal, made as much din as possible. It became customary for the newlyweds to have refreshments for the crowd which would not go away until they were served. While most such events were done in good fun, they could be rough with unpleasant consequences as the one at St. Stephens in 1813 or 1814.

To enable you to form some idea of the character and morals of the people of St. Stephens, I will relate a circumstance that occurred there shortly after I received the appointment of magistrate. There resided on a lot adjoining my own a maiden Lady the name of Whiting (all the way from Yankee Land) who was address'd by an old widower in the neighborhood, and after being woo'd for some time consented to his leading her to the hymenial altar—On one Sunday afternoon the marriage was solomnized in the presence of some two or three particular favorites only, the lady from extreme youth (being bashful, one might infer) objecting to many persons being present—Those few favorites *only* being invited, was taken in high dudgeon by the slighted ones—a meeting was called and it was resolved that they would revenge themselves in a signal manner on the offenders, and they unanimously agreed to give them *one grand serenade.* The sounding of the tocsin, at the commencement of night fall, was to be the signal for the assembling at the Bank house, (which was agreed on as the place of rendezvous) with instruments of music of every description—The time having arrived, and the signal, they poured from all quarters, bringing with them every thing that could be imagined, from which a sound could be extracted—viz drums & fifes, Clarionets, tamborines, triangles, violins, French horns, bugles, old tin pans, bells and in fact, some came rolling up old barrells, and hauling up old carts, on counting noses, it was ascertained that there were some absentees—Press gangs were sent out with instructions to seize every male person they could find, and bring them forthwith to headquarters—In one of those expeditions, my old and valued friend, Major Smoot was caught whom they bore off with great self-congratulation, to the scene of the day . . . The line of procession was then formed, and marching orders issued & in a short time all was in motion—It will be much easier to imagine, than to describe what ensued—Never was there such scene exhibited, before, or since in St. St.—To cap the climax of absurdity—such a *dust* as was kicked up (literally) Such music!! Such sounding of horns, bugles, trumpets, drums, fifes, & violins—Such hideous yells, and rattling of old barrels & carts never were heard before, I am sure in any community— It seemed as if Old Scratch had unchained at least one thousand of his Imps.

The avow'd object of all this, was to honor the newly married couple, who at that time snugly ensconsed in each others arms, dreaming of no such honors its being a Sabbath evening, they took it for granted, of course, that the sanctity of the day would not be inviolated—there impressions however, were badly founded, for the inhabitants of St. Stephens, at that Sabbath I believe, however, they were perhaps more the Sanctity of the Sabbath I believe, however, they were perhaps more righteous at that time, in the place, than were in Sodom when the angels descended from Heaven to send off righteous Lot, that he might escape the shower of fire & brimstone, about to be poured out on that doom'd City.

The serenade having been completed, they marched on and halted immediately in front of my door, where they commenced a species of extravagance & folly which was at most without parallel—It was the most perfect scene of boisterous revelry and reminded me more than any thing else I had ever witnessed to those midnight orgeries, once celebrated in honor of Bacchus.

The actors in this scene having set at defiance all law, with human and divine merited, in my opinion, not only the most pointed reprehension, but the infliction of all the punishment that the Statute of the Ter. would warrent, accordingly, on the succeeding morning I commenced issuing warrents against all those who had been engaged in the affair— and the whole of that week was occupied in trying the delinquents *most* of whom were fined, the evidences in *some* cases not being sufficiently clear to convict the persons arraigned.

The fines collected amounted to about $45, exclusive of Constables fees which amounted to 10 or 15 more, my own fees I would not suffer to be exacted in any instance.—Letter from General Patrick May, Greensboro, to A. J. Pickett, in 1846. Pickett Papers, Department of Archives and History, Montgomery.

The funeral was an event that brought large numbers of people together. Only recently someone remarked that if it were not for the specific cause that a funeral is held he would enjoy it because he saw people there whom he saw at no other times. This feeling of fellowship and the desire to pay respect to the dead help to explain why southern people go to funerals as they do.

In pioneer days simple burials seem to have been the rule and the delayed funeral (if there was a funeral as such) became common. When the weather was bad and roads impassable, the family would have a burial and wait for the good weather and roads of summer and the presence of a preacher (possibly the circuit rider) to have the funeral "preached." Dr. A. B. Moore says that on such occasions the audience listened with great interest—and curiosity —to see how the preacher interpreted the life of the departed. They expected to hear whether he was enjoying the "bliss of heaven" or the "torments of hell," and this was especially true if some mystery surrounded the departed during his life. Under normal circumstances, of course, death, funeral, and burial would take place within a few days.

For prominent people and especially public figures, the funeral oration became customary. The man honored to deliver it left out little; he would recount the state of public affairs, the public services and the virtues of the departed, and the circumstances under which he died. One such person thus eulogized was Zebulon Montgomery Pike Inge of Mobile who fell at the battle of Palo Alto, May 9, 1846, during the Mexican War. Rev. William T. Hamilton was the orator at the services "over the remains" at the Government Street Presbyterian Church in Mobile. Inge died of nine wounds, each one described. He was thirty-two years of age.

He who had passed unscathed through the arduous service of the Florida war, was cut down in the very second action that awaited him, on the opening of the campaign against Mexico. He fell, literally covered with wounds, while leading in a charge of unexampled daring. The nearest parallel to this exploit was Napoleon's passage of the bridge of Lodi. But not until his own artillery had dismounted and rendered utterly useless the guns of the enemy that *had* commanded the bridge, did Napoleon put himself at the head of his column, to lead in that celebrated passage. Inge and his fearless superior Captain May, waited only until the enemy's battery was discharged, and then, with an impetuous onset, while the enemy were reloading, they rushed up to the mouths of these reloaded guns, and, by their daring rapidity of movement in attack, took possession of the batteries, before there had been time again to fire! 'Twas a splendid act, boldly planned and nobly executed. 'Twas the first decided defeat of the Mexicans, yielding safety to Gen. Taylor at the time, and furnishing a happy omen of the brilliant achievements that have since followed. Inge fell in the discharge of his duty, covered with glory, regretted by his companions in arms, and honored by a grateful country.—Whatever laurels may yet be reaped by America's sons in the Mexican war, those laurels will be found to have sprung from the graves of Ringgold, Brown, and Inge, and to have been nourished by the hearts' blood of this brave, this noble trio. *Tears, then, for the gallant dead, and honor to their memory!*— INGE is a name that will henceforth be dear to Alabama, and *honored* wherever a true American is found. . . .

Here, then, on the third day from his landing at Point Isabel, Lieut. Inge put himself at the head of his company of dragoons, led his column, in perfect order, and at full gallop, in face of a well served battery, to the very mouths of the bristling cannon, and, boldly leaping over guns and gunners both, he fell in the arms of victory, and in the performance of a heroic act, unparalleled in modern times. Nobly did he discharge his duty! We, who here surround the ashes of the gallant dead, may love our country fervently, and may be willing to make many sacrifices for her, but HE has done more. *He offered on the altar of patriotism,* his ALL,—*his honor,—his dearest and his best affections.* He freely yielded up his *life* to the service of his country, and he has left to the guardianship of that country, a youthful widow to be cherished, an aged mother to be honored, and a *name* to be held in grateful remembrance, hallowed by the purity and fervor of his patriotism,—a *name* to be recorded on the pages of history, a *name* to be emblazoned on the pillar of fame, a *name* already engraven deep and indelible on the hearts of his countrymen!

Alabama will open her bosom to give a resting place to these sacred ashes of her lamented son.

Alabamians will raise o'er his resting place a monument that shall point out to after ages the spot where repose the mortal remains of the beloved Inge; that shall record his name, his bravery, and his patriotic end; that shall serve to stimulate posterity to honor his memory and to imitate his virtues. But the best, the most enduring monument of Lieut. Inge will be found in the grateful recollections of his countrymen, to whom the name of *Inge,* as of Ringgold and Brown, will be henceforth and ever dear.

Peace, then, to the ashes of as gallant a hero as ever faced a foe! . . . .

Tall in person, and of commanding appearance, Lieut. Inge was a fine scholar, a polished gentleman, and an accomplished soldier: perfectly an enthusiast in his profession, as was also the noble Ringgold. Trained to military exercises from his early youth, Lieutenant Inge is said to have been one of the best horsemen in the service, and equalled by few, and excelled by none, as a swordsman.

Irreproachable in his morals, amiable of disposition, and singularly modest and unassuming, he was held in high esteem among his brother officers, was generally popular in the army, and greatly beloved in the wide circle of his acquaintance; for Lieut. Inge had the rare faculty of gaining friends, securing their warm attachment and their profound respect, and of retaining their friendship.—Address delivered at the Government Street Church Presbyterian, Mobile, Thursday Morning January 28, 1847 over the Remains of Zebulon Montgomery Pike Inge. . . . Pamphlet (Mobile: Dale and Thomapson, 1847) Department of Archives and History, Montgomery, pp. 10, 12, 13.

As had already been indicated, the church was central to much that Alabamians did together. The funeral is a good example and the baptismal service even better. Baptism was a part of the creed of the Episcopal, Methodist, and Presbyterian churches but since they used sprinkling it was not a spectacular ceremony. A "babtizin' " by the Baptists was a community event; not only did the Baptists attend, but also members of other faiths or of no faiths at all. Immersion required a body of water and the ceremony was held, usually on a Sunday afternoon, on a river or creek, a pond or, in Huntsville, at the Big Spring.

In the sixties the spring was already famous. From time immemorial the pool below it had served the same purpose for the negroes about as did the River Jordan for the earlier Christians, and a baptism at the Big Spring, both impressive and ludicrous, was a sight never to be forgotten. The negroes came down the hill, marching with solemn steps to weird strains of their own composing, until they reached the edge of the stream that forms below the spring. Here the eager candidates for immersion were led into the water, when, doused for a moment, they would come up again shrieking shrilly a fervent Hallelujah! As a rule, two companions were stationed near to seize the person of the baptised one as it rose, lest in a paroxysm of religious fevour he should harm himself or others. As the baptisms, always numerous, continued, the ardour of the crowd of participants and onlookers was sure to augment, until a maniacal mingling of voices followed, that verged toward pandemonium. The ceremony was as strange and blood-curdling as any rite that might be imagined in the interior of the Dark Continent.— Virginia Clay-Clopton, *A Belle of the Fifties* (New York: Doubleday, Page and Company, 1905) pp. 162–63.

Visiting Celebrities

Important visitors were often the occasions for a series of social events. Among the prominent people who came this way were Sam Houston, former President James K. Polk, and the aging General Lafayette who passed through Alabama on his way to New Orleans. The account of the Lafayette tour was recorded by Auguste Levasseur, who was much more interested in the Indians than anything else and often digressed with incidents regarding them.

GENERAL LAFAYETTE

It was on the banks of the Chattahoochee that we met with the first assemblage of Indians in honour of the general. A great number of women and children were to be seen in the woods on the opposite bank, who uttered cries of joy on perceiving us. The warriors descended the side of a hill at a little distance, and hastened to do that part of the shore at which we were to disembark. . . . At the moment the general prepared to step on shore, some of the most athletic seized the small carriage we had with us and insisted the general should seat himself in it, not willing . . . that their father should step on the wet ground. The general was thus carried in a kind of palanquin a certain distance from the shore when the Indian . . . approached him and [made a welcoming speech.] After the chief had finished his speech, the other

Indians all advanced and placed their right arm on that of the general in token a friendship. They would not permit him to leave the carriage, but dragging it along, they slowly ascended the hill . . . on which one of their largest villages was situated. . . .

When we arrived at the brow of the hill, we perceived the glitter of helmets and swords; troops were drawn up in line along the road. These were not Indians; they were civilized men sent by the state of Alabama to escort the general. [They spent two nights at Line Creek, on the border of the Indian lands where they were entertained by the natives in various ways but the narrator was especially interested in a ball play which he described in detail.]

We quitted Line Creek on the 3rd of April, and the same day General Lafayette was received at Montgomery by the inhabitants of that village and by the Governor of the state of Alabama, who came from Cahawba with all his staff and a great concourse of citizens who had assembled from great distances to accompany him. We passed the next day at Montgomery and left it on the night of the 4th and 5th after a ball. . . .

At two o'clock in the morning we embarked on the Alabama on board the steamboat "Anderson," which had been richly and commodiously prepared for the general and provided with a band of musicians sent from New Orleans. All the ladies of Montgomery accompanied us on board where we took leave of them; and at the moment the reports of the artillery announced our departure, immense fires were lighted on the shore. Our voyage as far as the Tombigbee was delicious. It is difficult to imagine anything more romantic than the elevated, gravelly and, oftentimes, wooded shores of the Alabama. . . . We stopped one day at Cahawba where the officers of the government of the state of Alabama had, in concert with the citizens, prepared entertainments for General Lafayette, as remarkable for their elegance and good taste, as touching by their cordiality and the feelings of which they were the expression. Among the guests with whom we sat down to dinner we found some countrymen whom political events had driven from France. . . . They now lived in a small town they had founded in Alabama to which they had given the name Gallopolis [Demopolis]. I would judge they were not in a state of great prosperity. I believe their European prejudices and their inexperience in commerce and agriculture will prevent them from being formidable rivals of the Americans for a length of time.

From Cahawba we descended the river to Claiborne, a small fort on the Alabama. The general was induced by the intreaties of the inhabitants to remain a few hours, which were passed in the midst of the most touching demonstrations of friendships. . . .

Finally we arrived on the 7th of April in Mobile Bay, at the bottom of which is situated a city of the same name. . . .

The arrival of the steamboat in the bay was announced by discharges of artillery from Fort Conde; and when we reached the wharf at Mobile, the general found the committee of the corporation and all the population assembled to receive him. He was conducted to the center of the town under a triumphal arch, the four corners of which were adorned with the flags of Mexico, the republics of South America and Greece. In the center was that of the United States. Here he was complimented by Mr. Garrow in the name of the city and in presence of the municipal body. He was then led to an immense hall, expressly constructed for his reception. He there found all the ladies, to whom he was presented by the governor, after which Mr. Webb addressed him in the name of the state. . . .

In returning his thanks to the orator and the citizens of Alabama, the general took a rapid survey of the struggles for liberty in which he had borne so important a part and concluded by expressing his deep conviction of the necessity of the closest and most intimate union among the states.

The inhabitants of Mobile, hoping the general would pass some days with them, had made great preparations for entertainments to him, but the most part were rendered useless. Limited in his time, he was obliged to yield to the solicitations of the deputation from New Orleans, who pressed him to depart the next morning. Nevertheless, he accepted a public dinner, a ball and a masonic celebration, after which he went on board the vessel . . . to obtain a few hours of that repose which a day filled with so many pleasant emotions had rendered absolutely necessary.—Auguste Levasseur, *Lafayette in America in 1824 and 1825, or, Journal of a Voyage to the United States* (Philadelphia, 1829), vol. 2, pp. 75 ff.

Hunting and Other Activities

The proximity of the forest made it inevitable that much of the sport of early Alabamians should be connected with the outdoors. Hunting, whether for a bee tree, wild hogs, deer, or possum, was a favorite form of recreation, at least for the men. Marksmanship was of a high order, of course.

Philip Gosse, the English schoolmaster in Dallas County in the 1830's, described many hunting trips in his *Letters from Alabama*.

In the comparative solitude of these vast forests, the clearings are small compared with the immensity of the untouched wilds; the dwellings few and remote from each other; many of the occupations, and especially the amusements, which belong to the crowded inhabitants of Europe are here unknown. The wild animals are more familiar to man than his fellows; the planter often passes days, or even weeks, without seeing a human face except those of his own family and his overseer; his Negroes he scarcely considers as human; they are but "goods and chattels." Self-defence, and the natural craving for excitement, compel him to be a hunter; it is the appropriate occupation of a new, grand, luxuriant, wild country like this, and one which seems natural to man, to judge from the eagerness and zest with which every one engages in it when he has the opportunity. The long rifle is familiar to every hand; skill in the use of it is the highest accomplishment which a southern gentleman glories in; even the children acquire an astonishing expertness in handling this deadly weapon at a very early age.

But skill as a marksman is not estimated by quite the same standard as in the old country. Pre-eminence in any art must bear a certain relation to the average attainment; and where this is universally high, distinction can be won only by something very exalted. Hence, when the young men meet together to display their skill, curious tests are employed, which remind one of the days of old English archery, when splitting the peeled wand at a hundred paces, and such like, were the boast of the greenwood bowman. Some of these practices I had read of, but here I find them in frequent use. "Driving the nail" is one of these; a stout nail is hammered into a post about half way up to the head; the riflemen then stand at an immense distance, and fire at the nail; the object is to hit the nail so truly on the head with the ball as to drive it home. To hit it at all on one side, so as to cause it to bend or swerve, is failure; missing it altogether is out of the question.

Another feat is "threading the needle." An auger-hole is pierced through the centre of an upright board; the orifice is just large enough to allow the ball to pass without touching; and it is expected to pass without touching. A third is still more exciting—"snuffing the candle." It is performed in the night, and the darkness of the scene adds a wildness to the amusement that greatly enhances its interest. A calm night is chosen; half-a-dozen ends of tallow-candle and a box of matches are taken out into the field, whither the uproarious party of stalwart youths repair. One of them takes his station by the mark; a stick is thrust perpendicularly in the ground, on the top of which a bit of candle is fixed either in a socket, or by means of a few drops of grease. A plank is set up behind the candle, to receive the balls, which are all carefully picked out after the sport is over, being much too valuable to be wasted. The marker now lights the candle, which glimmers like a feeble star, but just visible at the spot where the expectant party are standing. Each one carefully loads his rifle; some mark the barrel with a line of chalk to aid the sight in the darkness; others neglect this, and seem to know the position of the "pea" by instinct. There is a sharp short crack, and a line of fire; a little cloud of smoke rises perpendicularly upwards; an unmerciful shout of derision hails the unlucky marksman, for the candle is still twinkling dimly and redly as before. Another confidently succeeds; the light is suddenly extinguished; his ball has cut it off just below the flame. This won't do; the test of skill is to snuff the candle, without putting it out.

A third now steps up; it is my friend Jones, the overseer on the plantation where I am residing; he is a crack shot, and we all expect something superb now. The marker has replaced the lighted candle; it is allowed to burn a few minutes until the wick has become long. The dimness of the light at length announces its readiness, and the marker cries "Fire!" A moment's breathless silence follows the flash and the report; a change was seen to pass upon the distant gleam, and the dull red light has suddenly become white and sparkling. "Right good!" cries the marker; the ball has passed through the centre of the flame and "snuffed the candle," and whoops and shouts of applause ring through the field, and echo from the surrounding forest. This extraordinary feat is usually performed two or three times in every contest of skill.

A common exploit is "barking off" a squirrel. My worthy friend Major Vanner, the other day, at my request, performed this. A couple of fox-squirrels were playing far up on a towering beech in the yard, little suspecting what was coming "for the benefit of science." My friend went in, and brought out his trusty rifle; waited a moment for one of the little frisky gentlemen to be rightly placed, for it is needful to the feat that the squirrel should be clinging to the bark of the tree. The first shot was a failure; the squirrel fell dead indeed, but it was pierced with the ball, which was not the object. Perhaps the creature had moved a little at the instant, or perhaps the planter had been too carelessly confident; however, his mettle was up, and he took care that the second should be all right. The ball struck the trunk of the tree just beneath the belly of the animal, driving off a piece of the bark as large as one's hand, and with it the squirrel, without a wound or a ruffled hair, but killed by the concussion.

The Wild Hog occasionally varies the hunter's amusement and affords good sport. I have before alluded to these sylvan swine, runaways from domestication, of course, or the offspring of such, but yet absolutely wild in habits, possessing all the acuteness of senses, all the perfection of resources, that distinguish a savage animal.

They are generally of a brindled foxy colour, or black; as long as they are unmarked they are free game, and are hunted in the usual manner with avidity. The pork of the wild hog has little fat, but there is a peculiar game flavour, which is altogether lacking in the flesh of a denizen of the sty. A tame hog would have scarcely a minute's lease of life if put to his speed before a pack of hounds, but these wild ones manage to lead the dogs a gallant chase and even to baffle them.

One Christmas-day, a party of some twenty horsemen, with sixteen or eighteen couple of hounds, met at a known cover to try for a fox. For a time they beat the bush, a capital jungle, but found no trail. At length one dog gave tongue in the covert, and a good run of half an hour followed, without a fault, though not a glimpse of Reynard had yet been seen. One of the party then gave the view halloo, shouting, "A black fox! A black fox!" Another invisible run for nearly an hour longer, up beside a "branch," or rivulet, brought the company to the thicket near the spring-head, whence issued a long grunt. On the coming up of the hounds, out bolted a black pig, making off with unabated speed for another thicket. A shout of laughter and acclamation hailed the development of the game, and all agreed that the gallant swine should be spared to run again. The reluctant hounds were accordingly whipped off.

As I pass through the oak woods on my morning walk to the school, I frequently see the lairs of the forest swine. These consist of fallen leaves, brought together into heaps as large as the diameter of a waggon-wheel, and nearly a yard high, and in these cool mornings I often see them reeking with steam, the luxurious rogues having up-started but a moment before, probably disturbed by the sound of my approaching footsteps. The people tell me, what indeed I should certainly infer from the appearance of the smoking beds, that the boar and sow sleep side by side in these cosy nests, and surely none could be devised, in the circumstances, softer, drier, or warmer.

Aug. 15th.

I was out last night 'Possum-hunting, and snatch an early hour this morning to describe to you the important affair, amusing enough, certainly, if not very profitable. For several days past, the "niggers," on bringing in the daily cart-load of water-melons for house-consumption, have been loud in complaints of the robberies committed by the " 'Possums;" and though it would be perfectly competent for these sable gentlemen to impute to Mr. Possum their own delinquencies, the value of a water-melon is scarcely a sufficient inducement even for a Negro to lie and thieve, seeing that he has abundantly more than he can de-vour in his own patch, and those, in all probability, finer and better grown than "mas'r's." The report was therefore received with all due credit, and an expedition against the 'Possums was resolved on as soon as the *vis inertioe* could be overcome. . . .

As soon as field-work was done, and supper swallowed, preparations commenced. The overseer blew his horn to call such of the hands as were within hearing, out of whom some half-a-dozen were selected, nothing loth; for Sambo likes the wild excitement of a hunt, especially by night, as well as his betters, and enters into it with as much zeal and zest. One or two were set to saddle the horses, others to collect the dogs of the establishment, and others to search up axes for felling trees, knives for clearing away tangled briers in the woods, and a few other small implements, while another was sent into the swamp to procure a dozen pine-knots for torches. Meanwhile the overseer was busy with lead, ladle, and bullet-mould, at the smithy fire, casting ball for the rifles. These preliminaries disposed of an hour or more; there was no hurry, for it would have been useless to go out until night was well commenced, as it was desirable to allow the depredators full time to issue from their retreats, and begin their nocturnal business in the melon-patches.

About half-past nine, then, we set out, a goodly and picturesque calval-cade. There was, first, my worthy host, Major Kendrick, a stout sun-burnt fellow of six feet two, as erect as a sundial, grizzled a little with the labours of some sixty years in the back woods of Georgia, but still hale and strong, with as keen an eye for a wild-cat or a 'coon as the stalwart nephews by his side. His attire would be deemed peculiar with you, though here it is the approved thing. A Panama hat made of the leaves of the palmetto, split fine, low in the crown, and very broad in the flap; a "hunting shirt," or frock, of pink-striped gingham, open all down the front, but girded with a belt of the same; the neck, which is wide and open, is bordered with a frill, which lies upon the shoulders; loose trowsers, of no describable colour, pattern, or material; short cotton socks, and stout half-boots, of domestic manufacture. Such is the costume of our "king of men," and all the rest of us approach as near to it as we may. . . .

It was a lovely night. The sky, almost cloudless, had a depth of tint that was rather purple than blue; and the moon, near the full, was already approaching the zenith. A gentle breeze, warm and balmy, breathed in the summits of the trees, and wafted to us the delicate perfumes from leaf, flower, and fruit, from gum and balsam, with which the night air is commonly loaded. Bright as was the night, however, it was thought requisite to have artificial light, especially as we should have to explore some tall woods, whose gloomy recesses the moon's beams were quite insufficient to illuminate. The knots of the pitch-pine answer admirably for torches, being full of resin, and maintaining a brilliant flame for an hour or more. The glare of broad red light which these flambeaux cast on the leafy walls along which we rode, and the beautiful effect produced on the surrounding shrubs and intervening trees, when the torch bearers passed through some narrow belt of wood, or explored some little groves, was highly novel and picturesque; the flames, seen through the chequering leaves, played and twinkled, and ever and anon frightened a troop of little birds from their roost, and illuminated their plumage as they fluttered by.

At length we reached the melon-patch, and having dismounted and tied our horses to the hanging twigs of the roadside trees, we crossed the rail-fence to beat the ground on foot. It was a large field, entirely covered with melons, the long stems of which trailed over the soft earth, concealing it with the coarse foliage and the great yellow flowers of the plant; while the fruit, of all sizes, lay about in boundless profusion, from the berry just formed, to the fully matured and already rotten-ripe melon, as large as a butter-firkin. Abundant evidences were visible of the depredations of our game, for numbers of fine ripe melons lay about with large cavities scooped out of them, some showing by their freshness and cleanness that they had been only just attacked, while others were partially dried and discoloured by the burning sun. Moths of various species were collected around the wounded fruit, some of them (which I should have prized for my cabinet, if I had had time and means to capture and bring them home) inert and bloated with the juices which they had been sucking; others fluttering by scores around, or attracted by the light to dance round the torches.

The party had dispersed. I accompanied the planter to the edge of a wood at one side of the patch, while the young men took up similar stations at some distance. The object was to intercept the vermin in their retreat, as, on being alarmed from their repast, they at once make for their fastnesses in the lofty trees. A Negro with his pine-knot, stood at each station, illuminating the hoary trunks of the great trees.

Meanwhile the other servants were scouring the field with the dogs, shouting and making as much noise as possible. Again the twinkling lights looked beautiful, and the sound of the negroes' sonorous voices, raised in prolonged shouts with musical cadences, and now and then a

snatch of a rattling song, the favourite burden being how a "big racoon"
was seen—

"— — —a sittin' on a rail,"

fell very pleasantly on the ear. Occasionally the barking of the curs
gave token that game was started; and, presently, the approach of the
sound towards us was followed by what looked to be a white cat
scampering towards the very chestnut-tree before us, closely pursued
by one of the mongrel curs. My friend's fatal rifle turned the creature
over as soon as seen; but the very next instant another appeared, and
scrambling up the fissured trunk, made good its retreat among the
branches. . . .

It seemed a hopeless case; but young Zachariah, vexed at being done
by a 'coon, continued to peer up into the tree, hoping that he might get
another glance of the animal. Familiar with the habits of the wild
denizens of the woods, the youth directed his patient searching gaze
to the bases of the great boughs, well knowing that in the fork of one
of these the wily creature would seek shelter. At last, he saw against
the light of the moon, what seemed the head of the Racoon projecting
from one of the greater forks, and steadily watching it, distinctly saw
it move. The fatal ball instantly sped, and down came the creature,
heavily plumping on the ground. . . .

The torches were extinguished, and we sauntered slowly home, my
friend the planter amusing me by relating a favorite legend to the
glory of one Major Scott, who seems in these parts to be the very
"Magnus Apollo" of rifle-shooting. It was to this effect:—An old he-
raccoon had made himself somewhat notorious by his depredations in
the poultry-yards, and by his successful stratagems to evade punishment. His favorite fastness was in the topmost boughs of a very lofty
sycamore, beyond rifle-reach. One day, a certain Colonel Sharp, who
vaunted his skill as a rifleman rather strongly, went out expressly to
bring down this same Raccoon. The wily rouge, from his impregnable
retreat, hearing footsteps, calls out, "Who's there?" "It's I, Colonel
Sharp, the smartest shot in all creation, and I'm come out for you." "Oh,
ho!" says 'coon, and, laughing immoderately, begins to play all sorts of
pranks, jumping on the boughs, and wagging his tail from side to side, as
the unsuccessful shots followed in rapid succession. At length, other
footsteps were heard; "Who now?" "It's Major Scott, a lookin' out for
'coons." "O Major! don't waste your powder, I give in; I'm a gone
'coon!" And down he came, and surrendered at discretion.

The Opossum which had been worried by the curs, was not by any
means dead when we reached the house, and I had an opportunity of
witnessing the curious dissimulation which has made the name of this
animal proverbial. Though, if left alone for a few moments, the attention of the by-standers apparently diverted from it, it would get on its
legs and begin to creep slyly away; yet no sooner was an eye turned
towards it, than it would crouch up, lie along motionless, with all its
limbs supple, as if just dead; nor would any kicks, cuffs, or handlings
avail to produce the least token of life, not the opening of an eyelid,
or the moving of a foot. There it was, dead, evidently, you would say,

if you had not detected it the moment before in the act of stealing off. The initiated, however, can tell a real dead 'Possum from one that is shamming, and the overseer directed my attention to the last joints of the tail. This, during life, is prehensile, used to catch and hold the twigs like a fifth hand; and even in the hypocritical state in which I saw it, the coil of the tail-tip was maintained, whereas in absolute death this would be relaxed permanently. The propriety of correct classification was impressed on me during my examination. I inadvertently spoke of it as "a singular creature;" but creature, or rather "critter," is much too honourable a term for such an animal, being appropriated to cattle. The overseer promptly corrected my mistake. "A 'Possum, Sir, is not a critter, but a varmint."

An hour or two's sport was the only object of the expedition, the game being all consigned to the blackies. The flesh of both Opossum and Racoon is scarcely ever eaten by the whites, and never in summer; and though the fur of the latter is of some value, it was not of sufficient importance to be retained.—Gosse, *Letters from Alabama,* pp. 130–31, 226–27, 270–71.

Christmas was a big event in the year. The Negroes were given several days free from work and special treats. The season was a time of much partying. In Dallas County the boys had fireworks which included rockets, roman candles, wherligigs and all had feasts. A menu from Selma shows that at one Christmas dinner (1858) the family had "barbecued meats of all kinds, roast fowl of all descriptions, boiled and baked hams, oysters, salads, cakes, jellies, fruits, champagne, etc., etc." (*Dallas Gazette,* December 31, 1858).

Maria Lide wrote her sister about the Fourth of July celebration in Dallas County.

The citizens of Carlowville celebrated the fourth of this month; and it was really a very pleasant day. Col. Dawson delivered the oration in the baptist church which was a well written piece and would have sounded well from a more fluent speaker, but he delivered it very badly indeed. . . . Mr. McIver read the Declaration of Independence and Mr. Lee prayed. Lizzy myself and a few of the young ladies sat in the galery opposite the pulpit, and sang "Hail Columbia" "The Star Spangled Banner" and "America" very suitable pieces but very badly sung. I was so much mortified at our performance that it curtailed my enjoyment somewhat. After the oration was over we all repaired to the grove between the two academies, where there was a very long table spread with all kinds of nice things very neatly arranged; but we had no Ice cream or lemonade; the ice was ordered but the boat got aground and staid until the ice melted and the lemons were spoiled. After we had dined, some musicians from Cahawba, entertained us with some delightful vocal and instrumental music. They had two violins and a flute. We staid until five oclock, when we all dispersed, some quietly to our homes, while others still disposed to frolic, repaired to the Female Academy and danced until sundown, and then went to Mr. Bernard Reynolds house, and danced until 12 oclock at night.—Maria Lide to Hannah L. Coker, July 15, 1845, Fletcher M. Green, ed., *Lides Go South and West* (Columbia: University of South Carolina Press, 1952), p. 36.

The Masonic Lodge which seems to have had a wide following had a celebration in Greensboro.

The ceremonies of the day took place at the Methodist Church, and were highly interesting in their character. The Address for the occasion —after an appropriate prayer from Dr. R. G. Hamill, and Music by the Amateur Band—was delivered by the Rev. C. C. Calloway, of the Methodist E. Church; and was listened to with much attention by the large audience in attendance.

The leading subject of the Address, was the principles and objects of masonry, rather than its antiquity.

After the close of the Address, and some additional performances by the Amateur Band, an Installation of Officers took place,—which, as the day was most oppressively warm, we did not remain to witness.

At the close of the ceremony of Installing Officers, a brief Address was delivered by James D. Webb, Esqr.

The ceremonies of the day were closed by a Public Party in the evening, which was very well attended, and which proved, no doubt, decidedly pleasant to those present—notwithstanding the melting hot weather.

The Supper for the occasion was prepared by the Ladies of the Presbyterian Church, and was, as those acquainted with the good taste of the ladies engaged in getting it up would naturally expect, an elegant affair.—*Alabama Beacon* (Greensboro), June 30, 1854.

There were other amusements, of course, some of them made by the people themselves but others provided by outsiders. There was an occasional circus like the Peoples' Circus that performed in Montgomery in April 1851. An occasional lecturer improved the minds of the people who lived in the larger towns. When the English traveler, James S. Buckingham, spoke in Mobile in the 1830's on Egypt, he had good audiences averaging about five hundred. He noted that he attended a public dinner observing an anniversary of the Hibernian Society and "had the opportunity of seeing all the fashion and beauty (and there was much to admire in both) at a very brilliant concert given by Madame Caradori Allan. . . ." There were also plays given by a few local groups (Montgomery had one) and touring companies. The first professional troupe played Huntsville in the winter of 1818–19, while Alabama was still a territory.

N. M. Ludlow, actor and manager for thirty-eight years, who with his group of actors toured the south and the Mississippi valley for many years, records his first visit to the north Alabama metropolis of some 1200 people.

Our commencement at Huntsville was with considerable misgivings of success. First, because the town was very limited in point of population; and, secondly, because there did not appear much expression of a desire to witness theatricals. Both of these apprehensions disappeared, however, as we came to understand that the wealthiest and best informed classes, those from whom we really obtained our principal support, resided not generally within the town limits, but from two to five miles around in the adjacent country, being mostly planters, and men of wealth and leisure. These would frequently come to town in their carriages and bring their families to witness our performances; and they soon began to consider theatrical amusements necessary to their pleasure. As our company was so very small, and half of it entire novices, we were much troubled to find pieces we could place before the public with any probability of affording satisfaction; but, with some skill in managing on our part, and a large share of indulgence on the part of our auditors, we succeeded, I believe, in meeting their expectations.

The opening play was Tobin's comedy, in five acts, called the "Honeymoon," but cut down by me to three acts, and performed under the title of the "Duke's Marriage;" the first time, I imagine, it was ever played under that name. The whole piece was not badly played, except that Mr. Flanagan made the Spanish count an Irish count. Our opening farce was Sam Foote's "Liar."

We were not able to procure musicians enough to form even a quartette band, so had to rely upon one instrument, a piano, played by an Irishman named Thomas, who gave marches and waltzes during the intervals of the entertainments. The price of admission was $1 for each person, adult or child, to which no one objected; by this rule every seat was made to "tell," and we were not much annoyed with crying children.

Now I will desire of my readers to bear in mind that this was the *first company of professional actors that ever performed in Alabama, throughout the whole Territory or State.*

We performed in Huntsville about ten weeks, giving entertainments only three nights of each week,—Mondays, Wednesdays, and Saturdays. We could not, with our novices, get pieces ready oftener; and even then had to make many "repeats." Our season may be said to have been a success, inasmuch as we gave pretty general satisfaction; and though we made little or no money, we did not leave the town in debt, or fail to pay our company their weekly salaries. We made many pleasant acquaintances, who seemed anxious to have us return at some future day.—N. M. Ludlow, *Dramatic Life As I Found It* (St. Louis, Mo.: G. I. Jones and Company, 1880), pp. 173–74.

In the following years Ludlow played Tuscaloosa, Cahaba, Montgomery, and Mobile, where a theatre was built in 1824–25. He used American plays, some European popular works and, when he had a skilled cast, a Shakespearean tragedy. In Mobile especially, he and his wife were accepted in society and shared many social events with the élite.

Life also had its temptations. A German lecturer in Mobile in 1825–26 was surprised to find a number of gambling houses there run by Frenchmen. Each of them paid a thousand dollars in taxes annually to the city. They seemed to be popular places.

I was told that respectable merchants were in the habit of going there to have an eye over their clerks, and also to observe what mechanics, or other small tradesmen, played there, to stop giving credit to such as haunted the resorts of these gentry. I was taken to two of these gambling houses . . . to see how they were conducted. In one of them were two roulette tables in two separate rooms. In the other . . . one roulette and one pharo table. There was betted here silver and paper, but not more than twenty dollars bank notes and most of them did not bet more than a dollar at a time. . . . Several of the better sort appeared to be country people who had brought their corn and cotton to markets and only played off their profits. . . . We found rather low company collected in both houses.—Karl Bernhard, *Travels Through North America* (Philadelphia: Carey, Lea, and Carey, 1828), vol. 2, pp. 50–51.

There was a surprising number of springs throughout the state. Enterprising businessmen had turned many of them into resorts where families could vacation to escape the "sickly season" of summer that prevailed in the lowlands. The Athens *Herald,* June 13, 1856, carried the advertisement for such a one.

VALHERMOSO
WHITE SULPHER SPRINGS
MORGAN COUNTY, ALABAMA

This celebrated watering place formerly kept by J. Wallace Manning & Co. has been put in repair and will be opened to visitors on the 1st of July, 1856. The different mineral waters and their efficacy in curing rheumatism, dyspepsia, and diseases of the skin are too well known to require further notice here, and the water of the new spring has also proved highly beneficial in several instances. The rooms have been fitted up with entire new furniture, beds and bedding; a vineyard and pleasure grounds have been laid off and a stable and carriage house put up. For the young and gay a succession of amusements will be provided and fine hunting and fishing grounds can be found in the immediate vicinity of the springs. A hack will run from Huntsville to the Springs on Mondays, Wednesdays, and Fridays, and a conveyance will be sent to Bowers Landing (3 miles) for those coming by the boats.

RATES OF CHARGES

Board by the day		$1.25
" " " week		7.00
" " " two weeks		6.00

Children according to age. Servants half price.

J. J. Giers & Co.

I state with pleasure that by the use of the waters at the White Sulpher Springs last season I was entirely cured of a very severe attack of rheumatism which had paralized my arm and that another member of my family was restored to health at the same place.

Wm. Matkin

For most Alabamians life was simple. They seldom, if ever, saw a play, witnessed the breathtaking acts of a circus, or spent a summer at a "watering place." They stayed at home, attended revival meetings, visited neighbors and created their own good times. John Massey, who has been quoted earlier on schools, described the daily routine of the people in Choctaw County in the 1840's and 1850's.

We lived the simple rural life. We raised everything in the way of provisions at home. Cows furnished milk and butter, and beef occasionally. Hogs supplied bacon and lard, and spareribs and backbones at "hog-killing time". Sheep furnished mutton chops and wool for our winter clothing. Bees produced the honey for sweetening and wax for candles. The poultry yard supplied eggs and chickens for frying and chicken pies. Deer furnished venison frequently. Wild turkeys, partridges, squirrels, and opossums were easily procured for variety in the way of meats. Yams, Spanish, red and white (called "nigger killers") potatoes were grown in abundance and put up in banks for winter use. Turnips, coleworts (called "collards"), onions, white peas and beans were the standard vegetables.

Often our meal was ground on a hand mill made of two rocks about sixteen or eighteen inches in diameter, the lower one fixed stationary in a section of a large hollow tree, the upper one made to turn on a pivot and with a hole in the middle about three inches in diameter, into which the corn was placed by the handful as it was ground out of the mill. The upper rock was turned by a staff sharpened to a point at the lower end and placed in a small hole in the edge of the rock and made to work loosely in a hole some five or six feet above, which held the staff stationary at the top. By means of this staff the rock was turned, and the meal came out through an opening adjusted with a spout into a vessel below. This grinding by hand was hard work and was one of the ocupations of my boyhood.

There were two water mills in the country, one about six miles from us and the other about eight. Another of my occupations was "going to mill" an occupation that could not entirely be appropriated by Henry Clay, "the mill boy of the slashes." A bushel and a half or two bushels of corn were put into a long sack, divided into two equal parts, and placed upon a horse. I rode upon the sack to mill even when I was so small that the miller had to take the sack from the horse when I reached the mill. I had to "take my turn". If there were few ahead of me, I could get my corn ground and return home early; but if there were many ahead, I would sometimes be in the night getting home. One of the diversions while waiting for my corn to be ground was swimming in the mill pond. I have remained in the pond for hours, until my back would be so blistered in the sun that my mother would have to grease it with cream.

Our clothing was all made out of homespun cloth. This was carded, spun, woven, cut out, and made at home. Many a night I have read and studied by a "lightwood" fire while mother cared the rolls and spun the thread which was to go into the loom after it was dyed in copperas (reddish yellow), indigo (blue), walnut bark (dark brown), or sumac berries (dark red). I never had a store-bought garment until I was quite a large boy. I remember the first pair of shoes I ever had, made by my father, who was the shoe maker, cooper, and blacksmith for the household. Whiles we had plenty of all the necessaries of life, we had little money. I do not think I ever saw, all told, ten dollars in money until I was twelve or fourteen years old.

There were no such things as matches in that early time. In the winter, when we had large fires made of oak and hickory wood, it was easy to keep fire through the night by banking the coals with ashes; but in the summertime we used flint and steel to strike the fire with and plunk (called "Spunk") for tinder to catch and kindle the sparks into flame. Sometimes we took a very small quantity of powder and a wad of cotton and struck the flint and steel over it, the flash of powder igniting with the cotton, which was kindled into a flame. With this flame fat lightwood splinters were lighted.

Games

Our games were simple compared with the highly developed games of the present day. They served well, however, for sport and athletic exercise. We played "cat", "town ball", and "bull pen"—all of which had some rules. We also wrestled, jumped and ran foot races. I was very fond of this last form of sport, because I could excel in it. I never did like to engage in anything in which I could not be among the first. I met only one man, a Mr. McKithern, who could excell me in a regular foot race. There was in the neighborhood an Indian by the name of Tom who taught me one thing in the matter of foot-racing in which I could surpass all competitors I ever met. In this it was: Lying on my back, with my head, my hands, and my heels on the ground, my competitor standing even with my head, at the signal, "One, two, three" we sprang forth and ran. Such control had I over my muscular system and so well practiced was I in this feat that I could leap forth at one bound and get even with, if not ahead of, my rival.

Drinking and Fighting

In those early days I never heard of such a thing as prohibition. Everyone made as much whisky and wine as he chose, sold as much as there was demand for, gave away a good deal, and drank to his satisfaction. Some people kept spirits (usually whisky or brandy) on their sideboards all the time. Visitors could always take a drink if they desired. Whiskey was nearly always used at "log rollings" and "house raisings". It was thought to be necessary to give vim and spirit in heavy work. It was not a very common thing to see men get drunk and helpless from intoxication, but it was very common to see them become excited and boisterous and quarrelsome. Fightings and killings were sometimes the result, especially on election days. In these fights the men very rarely used guns; and I do not think they carried pistols, as a rule. They generally fought fairly with their fists; and whenever a man was down and cried out, "enough! Take him off!" It was considered dishonorable to hit him another lick. They did some-times, however, fight with pocket knives. We had more fights then than we have now, but fewer killings; for the "pistol-toting" habit, so far as I knew, was not then in vogue. If pistols were used at all, it was on duelling occasions.—John Massey, *Reminiscences* (Nashville: Methodist Publishing Co., 1916), pp. 22–23, 29–30.

The Reverend F. L. Cherry described an equally simple life about the same time across the state in Russell and Lee Counties.

Hog-killing day, in order to be a success, must be a cold day—not a "bitter cold day", for such days are known only to be improvident,— but a bracing, cold day. And such was the day in question. The hogs had all been successfully slaughtered, scalded, dressed, gambreled, hung eviserated, hauled up to the smoke house, dissected, ready for salting the next morning and the air was fragrant with sage and savory "yarbs", prophetic of sausage and spare rib. The "big tub", full of nicely prepared-well-here I pause and acknowledge my utter inability, even with the assistance of the best living English lexicographer in the country, to find a word in the language nice enough to convey a correct idea of what was in that "big tub" . . . .

All things were ready, and about mid-eve two of the "girls of the period" sat out to invite the "company" to the old-time party to be given at night. The "plough-critters" were all out in the pasture, consequently there was nothing to be found on the place fit to ride on such an errand. But off they started afoot, and the first "invite" was at the house of a neighbor who had a blind horse "as gentle as a cat," and as nobody was at home to invite, they extended their invitation to old Dobbin to go the rounds with them. Of course, this invitation did not consist in consulting Dobbin's wishes or inclination on the subject, or anybody else's except their own as to that matter, but purloining a bridle, with-out even consulting Dobbin's master, and a meal-bag for a saddle, they mounted, one before and one behind, and away they went, as merry a brace of mischief loving little spirits as ever played a prank of "big bud", or any other "bud".

Dobbin, being blind, had to be carefully guided, or he was prone to lead into a kind of mischief not very highly relished by the young ladies. The path led by the hog-pen, and, in an unguarded moment Dobbin, feeling his way as best he could, passed "under the gallows" . . . "Look out!" cried Sprite No. 1, as she "ducked" her head down low on Dobbin's mane and passed under safely.

But Sprite No. 2, who was "riding behind"—a fashion more in vogue in those days than riding bare-back—was not so fortunate, and failing to "duck" in time, the "gallows" took her about the neck. Fortunately, the belles of those days did not require so much gold chain, and ornaments of that sort, to set off their personal attractions to advantage —nature having supplied all deficiencies in perfect development of true beauty—or there might have been execution without the aid of a hangman; nor were there any knots on the gallows, nor was it fashionable to wear their hair quite so long as in the days of the "Kings of Israel", or the "role" of Absolem might have been played, with only two spectators, and one of them a blind one. As it was, Sprite No. 2 lost her temper and gained a tumble on the ground, garnished with a few scratches on shoulder, neck and arms, just missing a large barrel of water in which the hogs had been scalded. Sprite No. 1 made the grand old forest ring and moss-covered rocks on the banks of Chewacla mock each other in echoes of wild, weird music-laughter, which the granddaughter of today would be glad to imitate. Notwithstanding this mishap, the guests were invited and the party assembled in due time. Parties of days of "lang syne" in a Christian community were a "feast of reason and a flow of soul", which combined all the elements of true social enjoyment without the introduction of demoralizing agencies which has embittered society. Tricks and pranks could be indulged in without the risk of abuse, because the wise and prudent Christian parent knew how, and had the moral courage to check extravagance, without checking the pleasure and enjoyment of the hour. Nevertheless, it must be acknowledged that their vigilance and prudencial policy was taxed to their extreme tension on occasions, where "pa" and "ma", forgetting they were "old folks" would join in the general hilarity on the explosion of some wild and apparently heartless prank.

On the occasion referred to, the guests had enjoyed the hour to their heart's content and all had retired, except a few who had been prevailed on to "stay all night" at the hospitable and roomy old log farm house. At the hour of retirement, two of the boys, who are of the grandpas of today, had retired to their comfortable room and prepared for bed. Then the mischief-loving girls, who are of the grandmas of to-day, began to wait for the explosion of a plot which they had laid for the special benefit of these same boys. These same mischief-loving girls had visited that "big tub" which was full of nicely prepared—your help again, Dr. Mc., please— and having extracted therefrom four or five of the same, tieing a thread securely around one end of each, which were about six feet in length, and with a quill, inflated them with air so as to resemble a certain reptile of creation, to come in contact with either dead or alive, day or night, well-clad or otherwise, is not supposed to be promotive of agreeable sensations, to say the least of it, and having turned down the cover at the foot of the boy's bed, placed these deftly prepared artificials in for proper position, re-arranged the cover and waited in pa and ma's room for them. And the developments came. The play opened with a screech, which a steam engine of today might envy; a howl, which would put the combined chorus of a pack of prairie wolves to the blush, and a kick, which sent the bedclothes flying to the ceiling like mammoth flakes of snow. One of the boys in his mad effort to free himself, became entangled among the artificials which seemed to crawl around his legs, arms and body, and in an ecstacy of fright, leaped from the bed and began to circule the room as rapidly as impeding chairs and tables would possibly permit, screaming at every leap: Snakes! Snakes!! Snakes!!! And those mischievous girls? When the curtain fell it was found that they had actually laughed themselves so helplessly weak that they had to be tenderly helped to bed and storatives applied.—"History of Opelika," *Alabama Historical Quarterly,* vol. 15, pp. 229–31.

Everyday Life

How did an average housewife spend her day? Probably no better record has been kept in Alabama than that of Mrs. Sarah R. Espy who lived in the eastern part of the state.

October 20th—Put in quilt for Olivia.

October 21st—Spent day in quilting. Some Hog drovers spent the night here.

November 2nd—Preparing a web of cloth for the loom. Write to Thomas. I would like to know this evening where Columbus is [He had gone to Texas.]

November 5th—Went to Yellow Creek. Mr. Flood preached on election and did his subject credit I thought—

November 7th—Cousin James and Robert Espy came this morning and commenced to recover our house, this with its noise and litter makes a disagreeable affair.

November 8th—Mrs. and Miss Echols spend the afternoon with us. Loaned Miss E. a piece of my painting which she wished to copy.

November 15th—Still cold, we received this morning, by the boat of yesterday our winter shoes also some cloth.

November 21st—Pleasant weather, commenced making calico dresses, also pants for Mr. E.

November 22nd—Mr. E. brought us a fine cheese from Dublin.

November 26th—Newspapers are filled with the abolition riot at Harper's Ferry. A great excitement prevails. . . . May the northern assassins be put down with their free Negro allies.

December 7th—This has been a busy day. We slaughtered 15 hogs, large ones. It is my birthday and I sit this evening by a cheerful fire, recording the fact—44 have I seen and as I look back over the road. . . .

December 8th—Mr. E. has had a time of it today with his frozen meat . . . I dried up 22 gallons of lard. . . .

December 10th—. . . . finished our sausage, made up and put to press cheese souse, we begin to feel like we are nearly through a disagreeable job.

December 19th—. . . . . . put in a quilt—also cut a vest for Mr. Brewer.

December 24th—Christmas Eve, yet all seems quiet, a few guns have been fired, how different from the time of my earliest recollection! Nothing hardly could be heard but the thunder of artillery.

December 31st—. . . . the last day of the old year. Where shall we all be this time next year.

February 2, 1860—I moulded our year's allowance of candles.

February 17th—Cloudy—planted "onions sets"—beet seed.

February 20th—Ice this morning, yet I see the yellow jonquils are in bloom; mother's favorite flower, which she more than 50 years ago brought with her from N. C. A tin peddler staid with us tonight.

March 28th—I wrote to Columbus and warped a web for counterpane.

April 9th—I sowed butter and other beans.

April 12th—I commenced weaving today.

April 14th . . . . . . Exchanged fowls with Mrs. Hail.

April 22nd—. . . . . the garden looks like an Eden, with its wealth of early roses and jonquils and pinks. The kitchen garden is splendid.

May 1st—Olivia went with large party maying on the mountain and to the falls.

May 12th—. . . . . .trimmed the girls bonnets.

May 15th—. . . . . . everything is now growing finely and the place is gay with roses. The multifloro, crimson and blush roses are in their prime, the white lillies are also beginning to open.

May 24th—The "Pennington" is now coming up the river and she blows in earnest too, she is evidently expecting passengers at Dublin.—Ms., Department of Archives and History, Montgomery, quoted in Minnie Claire Boyd, *Alabama in the Fifties,* pp. 116–18.

Sickness and Health

Sickness was a constant threat to people everywhere a century ago. To the people of Alabama there was, in addition to the ills that all mankind was heir to, the threat of irregular but deadly epidemics of yellow fever and the annual recurrences of malaria. It was a rare family indeed that escaped the summer without chills and fever. Physicians were generally using "the bark" (quinine) for malaria but they were ignorant of its causes. They knew almost nothing about the treatment of "yellow jack" but did recognize that it always started in Mobile and spread up the rivers.

Medical science may have known nothing about germs and viruses, and physicians worked without laboratories; yet in spite of little understanding about the causes of disease, they learned to deal with the disease itself and, as in the case of yellow fever, even anticipated the real cause of it.

Modern medicine was in its infancy, but Alabama seems to have been blest with a goodly number of physicians, many of them well-trained and a few even famous. In 1821 Mrs. Anne Royall found a surprising number of young doctors in the Tennessee River towns. In characteristic exaggeration she said every town was "flooded" with them.

> They are strung along the roads like so many blacksmiths shops. You can neither walk nor ride, but you have a physician on each side, one in front, and one in rear. There are seven in Florence—seven more went away from want of room. . . . I left thirteen doctors in Courtland, a much smaller place. One hundred passed through the latter, [going] south unable to get in. . . . Almost every practicing doctor has three or four students.—Anne Royall, *Letters from Alabama,* (University, Ala.: University of Alabama Press, 1969), pp. 230–31.

The first physicians in the region made fortunes; others followed, hoping to do as well.

Physicians were numerous elsewhere in the state. The Alabama Medical Association (organized in 1847) reported in 1852 that Mobile had forty regular practitioners plus several others, including three "general quacks" whom the medical profession did not recognize. Perry County had twenty-seven physicians with diplomas, two with licenses and four Thomsonions who apparently treated everything with steam baths. Most other counties had fewer.

Alabama's medical college was not established until the very end of the antebellum period and, consequently, physicians had to be trained elsewhere. Some "read medicine" as apprentices under an established doctor, others trained in private medical schools like Grafenberg Medical Institute at Dadeville. Still others, an estimated 250 annually, sought professional education out of the state. The schools that seemed to have attracted the greatest number were the Georgia Medical College, Charleston Medical College, Tulane, Medical College of Nashville, Memphis Medical College, and Jefferson College in Philadelphia. In the class of 1851 at Tulane, fourteen of the thirty-seven graduates were Alabamians.

Undoubtedly most of these men served their patients to the best of their medical knowledge but their reputations seldom extended far beyond their communities. A few, however, won nationwide fame. Dr. H. V. Wooten, whose account of a wedding appears earlier in this chapter, was called from his Lowndesboro practice to the chair of the Theory and Practice of Medicine in Memphis Medical College. Even better known were Dr. J. Marion Sims, and Dr. J. C. Nott.

MALARIA

Dr. Sims, "the woman's surgeon," was a native of the Lancaster district of South Carolina. After graduating from South Carolina College and Jefferson Medical College, he set up practice at Mt. Meigs, Montgomery County, in the fall of 1835. He later lived in and around Montgomery until 1852 when he went to New York. Pioneering in several fields, he was the first in the South to treat successfully strabismus and clubfoot. It was in the diseases of women, however, that he did his most famous work. After he went to New York he was instrumental in getting Women's Hospital established, and was for many years its surgeon-in-chief.

The following passage comes from Dr. Sims' autobiography and gives a vivid, but typical, description of the ravages of malaria.

During June and July I was sent for in every direction to see sick people, and there was sickness enough in all conscience. The whole country was down with malarial fever. There were not enough well people to wait on the sick ones, and so it was that in private families people suffered for the want of medical attendance and the want of nursing, and Death seemed to me to walk in the wake of the doctors. I have never known such a mortality as there was at that time. I had never had a day's sickness in my life, and never thought that I could be sick. On the 4th day of September I went to the plantation of Mr. John Ashurst. The Ashurst family had taken me up as a doctor . . . and through their influence I had plenty to do.

On the 4th of September I went to John Ashurst's, who had a white house two miles from the village of Mount Meigs, where there were twenty or thirty sick Negroes. I went from cabin to cabin, prescribing for them, and I felt very tired from the day's work. About twelve o'clock in the day, when I had made my rounds, I felt a little shiver run down my back. I made my way to the overseer's house, and soon I had a heavier chill, and half an hour later a raging fever with delirium. The fever passed off, moderately, toward night, and I was then barely able to mount my horse, and ride slowly back to Mount Meigs, where I went to bed. The next day Dr. Lucas came to see me; he was exceedingly kind to me and prompt in coming, although he was worked to death, going day and night, with more to do than he could possibly do well. When he came in, he examined me very minutely. Looking around, he saw a little mulatto girl, Anarcha, in the room, and he said, "Bring me a string, and a little cotton, and a bowl; I am going to draw a little blood from the doctor."

I said, "My dear, good doctor, you are not going to bleed me, are you?"

He said, "Yes, sir, old fellow, I'm going to bleed you."

I said, "Doctor, do you think I will die to-night, or before tomorrow, if you don't bleed me?"

He replied, "No, by God! you won't die before to-morrow if I do not bleed you."

"Then, doctor," I said, "you will excuse me if I am not bled to-night."

"Well," he said, "that is just as you please; but you ought to be bled. I had an idea that you were a d— —d contrary fellow, and now I know it."

If I had been bled I should never have got well nor been here to tell you this story. I was very ill; the fever raged, and I didn't know how to arrest its progress by the treatment with quinine. This was before the days of quininism, and fevers were allowed to take their course. Patients were bled, purged, administered tartar emetic, and given fever-mixtures every two hours during the twenty-four; the patients were salivated, and the patients died, some of them sooner than others. Those who were bled and purged the strongest died the quickest. I got worse day by day. At last the fourteenth day came, and the fever still continued. By that time there were no doctors to be had. Often I was three days without seeing a doctor. I had no nurse; poor Mrs. Judkins was down sick; one son was expected to die in the same house, and all the servants were sick. A little Negro girl would sleep in the room with me, and hand me a drink of water occasionally. But I had no treatment, and nothing to arrest the progress of the disease or of the fever. On the fourteenth day of my illness a young Englishman, living in Montgomery, a druggist, named Thomas B. Coster, having been out on a collecting excursion, happened to arrive in Mount Meigs about sundown. He stopped at the village hotel kept by Colonel Freeney. While at supper he said to Mrs. Freeney, "You have a young doctor living here, a nice young fellow, whom I know very well. Last June I was in the Creek Nation with him. He was in Captain Ashurst's company. He is from South Carolina. Can you tell me about him?"

"Yes," said she, "I can tell you all about him. He is a nice young fellow, and we all think a great deal of him, and we are all fond of him; and he has made friends with everybody. But he isn't going to be with us long; he is going to die to-night, they tell me."

"What? Is that possible?" he said. "Where does he live? Where is he? I must go to see him."

"Right up the street, about one hundred yards," Mrs. Freeney said.

So he came up to see me at once. I was an emaciated skeleton, in the last agonies, and with little or no pulse, and a cold, clammy sweat. My pulse had not been felt below the elbow for some time; but my mind was perfectly clear. He said, "Doctor, what are you taking? Who is attending you?" I said, "I haven't seen a doctor for three or four days."

"But," he said "are you taking nothing? Don't they give you any brandy? Don't they give you any quinine? Have you no nurse?"

"No," I said, "I have no nurse, for there are not well people enough to wait on the sick. Poor Mrs. Judkins is sick in the next room; her son is going to die, and there is nobody to wait on the well people or the sick ones. I feel that I am dying; I think that I shall die to-night."

"Who is to sit up with you?" he asked. When I told him that I expected nobody, he continued, "Then I will sit up with you, and see you through the night."

I turned over and wept like a child to see such kindness, which was perfectly disinterested. All that I remember was that, during the night, a soft hand like a woman's would be placed back of my head, and his tender voice, saying, "Drink, doctor; take this drink; drink just this; it is only a little brandy;" and very soon again the brandy would be poured down me, and then again the same voice would say, "Here, doctor, I have some quinine that I travel with, and I am going to give you some on my own responsibility." I swallowed some of the most nauseous doses that night, but I felt that the hand of a ministering angel had been tending me.

The next morning he left me. He bade me not despair; that many a man had recovered from a prostration as severe as mine, and he hoped that I would get well. That was the turning-point in my disease. The reaction was brought about by the administering of the proper remedies in the hand of my friend Mr. Coster. The pulse returned, and although he could feel it when he went away that morning, and said he hoped that I would get well, still he has told me many a time that he never expected to see me alive, or lay his eyes on me again. My recovery was very, very slow indeed.

Alabama never saw so sickly a season as that. Scarcely a single family escaped, and the whole country was left in mourning. One poor fellow, living across the way from us, who had moved there only six months before from Georgia, lost his wife and two children and the only Negro that he had. When he went to bury his wife there was no one to help him, or that was well enough to follow her coffin, but himself and two or three Negroes that officiated at the grave. That year's sickness was a great lesson to me. I learned much from observation and from experience, and especially how much mortality followed the practice of the doctors. I became exceedingly conservative; I never bled, and gave as little medicine as possible. But it was not long before the practice of the country was completely revolutionized. The writings of Fearne and Erskine, in Alabama, were the first to throw light upon the proper method of treating malaria and malarial fevers. Until their day, the doctors were in the habit of bleeding and physicking people until the fever disappeared, and then giving them quinine, a grain or two, three times a day. But Fearne and Erskine and others preached the doctrine of giving it without any regard to preliminary treatment, giving it always in the beginning, if possible, and giving it in sufficient doses to affect the system at once.—J. Marion Sims, *The Story of My Life* (New York: D. Appleton & Co., 1884), pp. 171–75.

YELLOW FEVER

Yellow fever was probably the most dreaded plague in our early history. Mobile was always the hardest hit but at times the disease spread into the interior. Not knowing its true origin, people fled before "Yellow Jack" like it was the scourge of God. Only those who could not escape stayed behind in the port city.

However, the disease varied in intensity. For example, the outbreak in 1847 had been mild with only 68 deaths out of a reported 600-700 cases but the epidemic of 1853, here reported by Dr. Josiah C. Nott, was severe. Of the hundreds of cases, the dead from yellow fever (from August 1 to November 1, 1853)—those who were buried in Mobile cemeteries—numbered 1331. Mobile at the time had an estimated population of 25,000.

Dr. Nott is one of the best known physicians who ever lived in Alabama. A native of Columbia, South Carolina, and a graduate of the University of Pennsylvania, he settled in Mobile in 1833. In addition to his reputation as a surgeon and the founder of the Medical College in Mobile, Dr. Nott's fame rests firmly on two other items. He was interested in anthropology and wrote (in collaboration with George R. Glidden) two well-known works, *Types of Mankind* and *The Indigenous Races of the Earth* in which he upheld the unitary origin of the human race at a time when the polyphyletic theory was generally accepted. Also, before the Civil War he advanced the "insect hypothesis," suggesting that the mosquito was the villain in spreading yellow fever.

Dr. Nott reported the 1853 epidemic in Mobile.

The first cases of yellow fever which occurred in Mobile, it is commonly conceded on all hands, were imported from New Orleans on board the barque *Miltiades*. . . .

The *Miltiades* sailed from Portland, Maine, to New Orleans, where she lost several of her crew from yellow fever; from thence she came to Mobile Bay and anchored below Dog River Bar . . . on the 11th July; and on the 13th, Peter Johnson, on of the crew, was sent to our Marine Hospital . . . where he died of the black vomit. . . .

On the 14th, three days after the arrival of the vessel, the stevedores went on board to load her with cotton for Liverpool. One of them, John Johnson, was taken down with yellow fever on the 19th or 20th, and was brought to town on the steamer Daniel Pratt, and placed in the "Sailor's Home," where he died with the black vomit on the 25th. On the 25th four others were brought up from vessel sick on the same steamer. . . . [There were six or eight cases from same ship and

others on other ships from New Orleans.] . . . The first case I can
trace among our citizens who had no communication with the *Miltiades,*
was Mr. McDowell, a patient of Dr. Levert; he slept at Hollywood, a
watering place on the opposite side of the Bay, and came to town
every day on the steamer *Junior;* he sickened on the 31st of July and
recovered.

A few days after this, rumor was busily at work and cases were talked
of in distant parts of the town. . . . On the 18th I made a memorandum
in my notebook to the effect that up to that date, from the best information, there had been in the town about 30 cases. I inquired
among the physicians as to their dates and localities and could trace no
connection between the cases; they seem to have been sown broadcast
over a mile square. I kept as was my custom, the range of the
thermometer, the winds and rain, from the 1st of May until frost, and
could see nothing in the season to account for disease. . . . Yet I
predicted, a month before its appearance, with great confidence, that
we should have a terrible epidemic in Mobile. . . . I expected unusual
virulence because this had been its character everywhere it had gone,
and I shall be greatly deceived if the same disease does not attack cities
on the Atlantic next season. . . . The germ is sleeping, not dead. . . .

[The epidemic spread to Spring Hill, and Citronelle.]

In reasoning from analogy, the "insect hypothesis" of Sir Henry Holland, explains best the habits of certain epidemic diseases and it is the
part of true philosophy to abandon such theories as the old malarial
one, which is in accordance with no known laws, and to explore in a
direction towards which rational hypothesis points. . . . By what various
means the poison of insects . . . might be communicated through the air
or directly to individuals, we know not. . . .—"The Report of the
Yellow Fever Epidemic to the Sanitary Commission of New Orleans."
Typescript in the Alabama Historical Collection, Medical Center Library,
Birmingham.

Dr. Wooten may have been correct when he said the great majority of people in Lowndes County were attended by a physician
at the time of their death. But for every family that summoned a
medical man in case of illness there were dozens of others who did
their own doctoring. Therefore, most family cookbooks, diaries,
daybooks, and journals contain recipes for home remedies and
directions for treating various ailments. Many medicines were
brewed from various barks, roots, and leaves. Cherry bark, rhu-
barb, elder blossoms, butterfly weed, dill seed, and sassafras appear
in many different recipes. Calomel, quinine, and laudanum were
used in many combinations. The number of cures is almost endless
but the following from only three sources will be sufficient.

CURES

Burns or Scalds.
1 table spoonful of Honey—1 Do. Mutton suet, or Tallow—work

it well together & add as much good rum as will bring it to the consistence of Salve. Wash the part with castile soap & warm water twice a day, and lay on a plaister (*sic*) of the above—Or mix about an equal quantity of Lout oil and Lime water, shake it well together and it will make a soap or linament, anoint the part with it. This is also good on inflammation of the Eye—

Ointment for Tetters or Rheumatism.

Take a handful of the root of Bearsfoot split fine, and the same quantity of the herb, Saint John wort—add water enough to cover it in a pot, Boil it to a Strong decoction—Then strain it and return the liquor into a clean pot, and add one pint of Neatsfoot Oil—Simmer out all the water—set it off the fire & when cooled a few minutes add four table spoonsful of Spirits of Turpentine, and shake it well together. When bottled Anoint the part once a day & rub it well in—

Recipe for Tetter and Scald-Head.

Put one pound of bark of the root of prickly-ash, one pound of the bark of dogwood, and one-quarter pound of the root of walnut, into three gallons of water. Boil to one gallon; strain this, and boil it to one quart. Wash the affected part with Castile soap, and apply the mixture once a day.—Weymouth T. Jordan, ed., "Martin Marshall's Book: Homemade Medicines," *Alabama Historical Quarterly,* vol. 3, pp. 118–19.

A Cure for the asthma

Burn half a sheet of paper in a room where the patient is that has been soaked in strong salt petre water.

A Cure for a burn

Take 4 ounces of allum and put it in a quart of hot water in which dip a cotton cloth and apply to the burn and when it becomes dry replace it by another.

A Cure for Gangreen

Boil the bark of live oak and thicken it with pounded charcoal and corn meal of which make a poultice and apply to the place.

A Cure for spleen

Put one handful of burdock in a quart of spirits of which drink frequently. Say three times a day.

A Cure for a Cough

⅔ of an oz phial of antimonial wine ½ pint molasses one gill good vinegar 60 drops laudanum of which take one table spoon full on going to bed.

For a Cough

One tablespoonful of new tar one do of ground ginger one teaspoon full of sulphur worked in brown sugar and made into pills of which take one pill morning noon & night.—L. B. Moseley's Account and Farm Record 1833–1857, Ms. in private hands.

The Weather and Other Natural Events

For any people as close to nature as the people of rural Alabama, weather and other natural phenomena are of great interest and importance. This is understandable because farming people are often dependent on the whims of the weather, whether good or bad, for the success or failure of their crops. It is not surprising, therefore, that the actions of the elements make news.

STARS FELL ON ALABAMA

Stars fell on Alabama on the night of November 12-13, 1833. The event has become a landmark in state history. Huntsville "was the scene of great commotion, particularly among the blacks who were praying and shouting, thinking the day of judgment had come." There was temporarily "a great revival among the Christians" of whatever color who interpreted the falling stars as signs of approaching doom. At Fayette Court House a group of carousing young men took alarm and "went rushing to the house of the Methodist preacher . . . and roused him up and had him offer prayer," but next day each was joking about how bad the others had been scared.—Of the many possible newspaper accounts, the one from the Florence *Gazette,* November 16, 1833, is given here.

> We were called up at five o'clock on Wednesday morning to witness a remarkable phenomenon of "falling stars or meteors."
> The night of the 12th was clear, cool, and extremely beautiful; the stars shone with uncommon brilliancy. Some of these luminous bodies were seen occassionally darting along the firmament, as they are often known to do of a clear evening. About three o'clock a citizen perceived the most extraordinary appearance of meteors and awakened his neighbors to behold the wonders of the night. Thousands of luminous meteors were shooting across the firmament in every direction; their course was from the center of the concave toward the horizon, and then they seemed to burst as if by explosion. The scene was as magnificent as it was wonderful. To the eye it appeared to be in reality a "falling" of the stars; as we heard one describe the scene, "it rained stars." There was very little wind and no trace of clouds to be seen. The meteors succeeded each other in quick succession until the dawn of day, presenting a scene of nocturnal grandeur. . . .

HURRICANES

Tropical storms are no strangers to Alabama. From the early days of Spanish and French exploration, hurricanes have driven ships ashore, changed channels, closed harbors, and destroyed uncounted numbers of buildings. The custom of giving storms names is of recent origin so the storm that Madam Octavia Le Vert described has to be called merely the Mobile hurricane of 1851.

Mobile has been visited by the most terrific Hurricane of this Century. It began on Tuesday 24th of August. During the night it increased to a Gale. On Wednesday, it continued increasing in violence until nine o'clock at night, when a slight abatement was visible. At eleven the Hurricane came on. Oh! the horrors,—the terrors of that night no words can shadow forth. There was neither Thunder or Lightning but the rain poured in endless torrents. The wind had the sound of Cannon and struck the house, with the force of its Balls. Then would come a wail— like myriads of human voices in their Death Agony—Shrieks as tho' the Dead were bursting their Graves—Tremblings of the solid earth. Ah! my soul went up in fervent prayer, for those hapless creatures, whom I felt were at those terrible moments yielding up their lives. There was a frightful wildness in the Tempest, which told me Death was riding on the dark wings of the Hurricane.

No sleep came to my eyes, & by the window I watched for the coming day. Ah! how terror multiplies Time! The night seemed endless, the minutes dragged on as tho' they were hours. At last came the Daylight and I thanked the Good God, I was permitted to look upon it once more. The black heavy clouds, gradually rolled up, as the light came on, and revealed the unchecked horrors of the Tempest. Great trees were up rooted as tho' they were Spring flowers. Houses were un-roofed, and one Square below us, rushed in the mad billowy waves of the Gulf, bearing on their tide, every variety of merchandise, which their fury had torn from the various stores, all Front, Commerce & Water, the three business streets of the town. Never did I behold such a scene of Desolation & Ruin. It was a sight to remember forever! The sky had an inky darkness, unrevealed by one gleam of Lightening. It was like a grand Funeral Pall over those who had perished in the Tempest—Tender Children were swept from their Parents' arms, and old Age, struggled with the waters e'er the sweet cup of Life, was exhausted. Strong men battled with the Flood nobly e'er they perished and young women were engulfed like the Autumn Leaves, in the mud seething Waters. At mid Day the Hurricane abated and the waves, as they wearied with the Devastation they had wrought, quietly retired to their usual channels. Then did the Merchants perceive the immensity of their losses! Thousands and hundreds of thousands, even unto millions of Dollars were destroyed by the flood. All descriptions of provision—All kinds of fine Fabrics—of beautiful Jewelry—of gorgeous Carpetings were the one mass of terrible ruin. The Wharfs all gone, their places supplied by thousands of trees, torn from their native soil, and wildly dashed upon the shore. The hopes of years—the labour of months in a few short hours all gone, all despair where "Expectation yester night sat smiling."—Diary, *Alabama Historical Quarterly,* vol. 3, pp. 51–52.

This, in brief, is the way Alabamians lived in the antebellum period. There was some social stratification but all life was too near the frontier for class lines to be rigid. Any energetic—and lucky—young man could rise in the social, economic, and political scale. This was a vigorous, almost flamboyant, period in which the chief concern was the conquest of the wilderness. Whatever else people did along the way made life interesting and rich, but did not change their goal. There were contrasts between things as they were in 1819 and the way they had become by 1860. There also were contrasts between the life style of the affluent and cultured planters and merchants and the illiterate poor mountain white, and between them and the vast number of comfortable independent farmers. In some sections people were still pioneers, living in conditions little different from what they were in territorial days. In marked contrast, there were many centers of culture and learning, where the leading residents came from some of the best families of Virginia and South Carolina. Places like Tuscaloosa, Huntsville, Greensboro, Selma, Eufaula, Montgomery and Mobile had elegant homes, good schools, a sophisticated social life, and wealth. But in spite of differences, the various life styles fit together, in much the same way that a "crazy" quilt did, to make a harmonious, recognizable whole society.

Chapter 10

POLITICS BEFORE 1860

To treat in a single chapter a half century of politics in a state where politics was of vital importance is a staggering task. Alabamians have always been interested in politics, not only political hopefuls themselves but also school boys and girls, housewives, plantation overseers, and others. The newspaper was the most popular form of current literature; most of these publications had an avowed party attachment. Writing on political subjects whether in news, editorials, or letters to the editor, took up a big portion of the space in each issue. Some of these papers were mere hack work but others were outstanding publications. The best seem to have been published in Mobile, Montgomery, Tuscaloosa, and in the north Alabama towns of Huntsville and Florence. Public debate, rallies, and conventions were often the most exciting form of entertainment available. People by the hundreds, men and women, black and white, attended these. In an age when oratory was a fine art, Alabama had its outstanding speakers. William L. Yancey, Henry Hilliard, Dixon H. Lewis and William R. King stood out among their peers. Alabamians had ample opportunity to be well-informed on the public issues of the day.

If one can judge correctly from the newspapers and the published proceedings of the legislature, the questions that attracted the most attention and occupied the most time were national issues: tariff, money, internal improvements, Indians, Texas, the Mexican War, California, presidential campaigns and, of course, slavery and abolition. Nevertheless, some issues that engrossed Alabamians were local. Candidates ran for office in heated campaigns, officers administered their duties, and judges held court. They struggled over matters of finance, the Indians, slavery, the bank, schools, the location of the capital and other matters that often reached no further than the bounds of the state.

Campaigns and Elections

Alabamians voted under liberal election laws. The Constitution of 1819 provided for universal white manhood suffrage. There were no property qualifications for voting or holding office as there were in many states. Elections and the campaigns that preceded them were often exciting and there are many accounts of them.

E. A. Powell was a mere youth when he witnessed his first election.

I come now to the first general election I ever attended. It was in 1832. There was a Senatorial election for the District, composed of the counties of Fayette, Pickens and Marion. Fayette was the centre county and had no candidate in the field. Pickens county brought out Col. Rufus K. Anderson, while Marion marched under the banner of James Moore. It was conceded that each candidate would come into Fayette county with nearly a solid vote from his own county, and the strength of the counties being nearly equal, of course Fayette became the pivotal county, and was consequently the battle ground in the contest. I have since witnessed many exciting elections—but never one of the same magnitude, that produced more. The excitement extended to the boys in the country, and every one from ten years old and upwards arrayed himself on one side or the other of what they conceived the great contest. "Hurrah! for Anderson!"—"Hurrah! for Moore!" was heard in almost every crowd of boys for several weeks before the election. Fayette county divided almost equally between them,—giving Anderson eighteen majority. This of course threw the parties back to their respective counties. Anderson received a few more votes in Marion than Moore did in Pickens,—winning the race by about "a length"—one hundred and twenty eight in the contest. I was an Anderson boy, but long before I grew to manhood I became satisfied that Moore ought to have been elected. . . .

I have said this was the first general election I ever attended. I saw one thing at the election which should be noticed: In a dry-goods store there was improvised, outside the regular counters, a board reaching clear across the room. On that board was ranged along in regular order, fine decanters filled with Whiskey, Brandy, Wine, Rum, etc.,—each handsomely labeled, "Col. James K. Anderson,"—"Major James Moore,"—and so on through the entire list of candidates. Some of the voters were very liberal. They did as they said Charles Crowley did at the Camp Meeting on Sunday: it is said he ate all around the encampment. —These voters drank all around the board.—E. A. Powell, "Fifty-Five Years in West Alabama," *Alabama Historical Quarterly*, vol. 4, pp. 469–70.

Women did not have the vote until well in the twentieth century but this did not keep them from being interested in public affairs and from accompanying their husbands in their political activities. The story told by Mrs. Clement C. Clay, Jr. about her husband's campaign is a good case in point. The Clays were a prominent north Alabama family. Clement C. Clay, Jr., the son of a former governor, was running for Congress when this incident occurred but he held many other offices, including United States Senator. After the formation of the Confederacy, he served in many capacities and, toward the end of the war, he went on an important, but fruitless, mission to Canada.

Mrs. Clay wrote:

. . . The most conspicuous man on that memorable north-bound train, Congressman W. R. W. Cobb, who called himself the "maker of Senators," and whom people called the most successful vote-puller in the State of Alabama. Mr. Cobb resorted to all sorts of tricks to catch the popular votes, such as the rattling of tinware and crockery—he had introduced bills to secure indigent whites from a seizure for debt that would engulf all their possessions, and in them had minutely defined all articles that were to be thus exempt, nor scorning to enumerate the smallest items of the kitchen—, and he delighted in the singing of homely songs composed for stump purposes. One of these which he was wont to introduce at the end of a speech, and which always seemed to be especially his own, was called "The Homestead Bill." Of this remarkable composition there were a score of verses, at least, that covered every possible possession which the heart of the poor man might crave, ranging from land and mules to household furniture. The song began,

"Uncle Sam is rich enough to give us all a farm!" and Mr. Cobb would sing it in stentorian tones, winking, as he did so, to first one and then another of his admiring listeners, and punctuating his phrases by chewing, with great gusto, a piece of onion and the coarsest of corn "pone." These evidences of his democracy gave huge delight to the masses, though it aroused in me, a young wife, great indignation, that, in the exigencies of a public career my husband should be compelled to enter a contest with such a man. To me it was the meeting of a Damascus blade and a meat-axe, and in my soul I resented it.

In 1849 this stump-favorite had defeated the brilliant Jere Clemens, then a candidate for Congress, but immediately thereafter Mr. Clemens was named for the higher office of U. S. Senator and elected. In 1853 an exactly similar conjunction of circumstances resulted in the election of Mr. Clay. I accompanied my husband during the canvass in which he was defeated, and thereby became, though altogether innocently, the one obstacle to Mr. Cobb's usually unanimous election.

It happened that during the campaign Mr. Clay and I stopped at a little hostelry, that lay in the very centre of one of Mr. Cobbs strongest counties. It was little more than a flower-embowered cottage, kept by

"Aunt Hannah," a kindly soul, whose greatest treasure was a fresh-faced, pretty daughter, then entering her "teens." I returned to our room after a short absence, just in time to see this village beauty before my mirror, arrayed in all the glory of a beautiful and picturesque hat which I had left upon the bed during my absence. It was a lovely thing of the period, which I had but recently brought back from the North, having purchased it while en route for Doctor Wesselhoeft's Hydropathic Institute in Brattleboro, Vermont.

The little rustic girl of Alabama looked very winsome and blossomy in the pretty gew-gaw, and I asked her impulsively if she liked it. Her confusion was sufficient answer, and I promptly presented it to her, on condition that she would give me her sunbonnet in return.

The exchange was quickly made, and when Mr. Clay and I departed I wore a pea-green cambric bonnet, lined with pink and stiffened with pasteboard slats. I little dreamed that this exchange of millinery, so unpremeditated, and certainly uncalculating, was a political master-stroke; but, so it proved. It undermined Mr. Cobb's Gibraltar; for at the election that followed, the vote in that county was practically solid for Mr. Clay, where formerly Mr. Cobb had swept it clean.

When, upon the train en route for the capital in the winter of '53, Senator Fitzpatrick insisted upon presenting the erstwhile triumphant politician, I took the long, flat-like hand he offered me with no accentuated cordiality; my reserve, however, seemed not to disturb Mr. Cobb's proverbial complacency.

"I've got a crow to pick with you, Mrs. Clay," he began, "for that pink bonnet trick at old Aunt Hannah's!"

"And I have a buzzard to pick with you!" I responded promptly, "for defeating my husband!"

"You ought to feel obliged to me," retorted the Congressman, continuing "For I made your husband a Senator!"

"Well," I rejoined, "I'll promise not to repeat the bonnet business, if you'll give me your word never again to sing against my husband! That's unfair, for you know he can't sing!" which, amid the laughter of our fellow-passengers, Mr. Cobb promised.—Mrs. Clement C. Clay, Jr., *A Belle of the Fifties* (New York: Doubleday, Page and Co., 1905), pp. 21–23.

Williamson R. W. Cobb, Clay's opponent in this sketch, was elected to Congress in 1853 and served his district (his home was in Jackson County) in Washington until secession in 1861. William Garrett, long the Secretary of State for Alabama, gives a description of Cobb that supports Mrs. Clay's.

Mr. Cobb was a tall, long-armed man of some intelligence and more shrewdness, and well-versed in the school of the demagogue. This was his principal stock in political trade, and it paid him well. He never let an opportunity pass to secure a vote and the mailbags and postoffice were his channels of communication. . . . Every section of his districts that wanted a mail route and any neighborhood that needed a post office was sure to be served by the influence of Mr. Cobb. In his speeches before the people he was apt to play upon their prejudices or poverty and always presented himself as the especial friend of the poor man. . . . —William Garrett, *Reminiscences of Public Men in Alabama* (Atlanta: Plantation Publishing Company's Press, 1872), pp. 396–97.

Cobb, who had once been a peddler of clocks among the rural people of north Alabama, electioneered constantly. He was "a remarkable and successful man."

The Party Structure

Antebellum Alabama had a vigorous two-party system. Even in the territorial period (the so-called Era of Good Feeling) when people were supposed to be too busy conquering a wilderness, "united by mutual difficulties and vicissitudes . . . and stress of life in a new country," to be concerned about such matters, there were two distinct political factions. The most powerful was the "Georgia Machine," the other was without a name but led by men of Virginia and the Carolinas.

The strength of the "Georgia Machine" was due to the influence of Secretary of the Treasury William H. Crawford of Georgia. He had real estate interests in the country to the west and also handled patronage for the Monroe administration. He was responsible for the appointment of his friend and neighbor William Wyatt Bibb to the governor's post in the Alabama Territory. Leroy Pope and his son-in-law, John W. Walker, from the same part of Georgia as Crawford, were early settlers in Huntsville. Walker was president of the Constitutional Convention in 1819 and one of the new state's United States senators. Charles Tait, who had represented Georgia in the Senate along with Bibb, deeming it unwise to force his election to the Senate from Alabama, settled for a district judgeship in south Alabama. Bolling Hall, another Georgian, became a large planter and leading politician in the Montgomery area. The officers in the bank, land office, and most other appointive positions Crawford filled. For a time it looked as if the Crawford-Georgia power might be perpetual.

The Carolina-Virginia faction considered themselves representatives of the plain people, not the aristocratic planters who made up the majority of their opponents. Their leader was Israel Pickens, a former North Carolinian, whose election to the governorship in 1823 is credited with breaking the "strangle hold" of the Georgians.

After the election of 1824, politics in the state took on a different hue to be intensified by the passage of the "Tariff of Abominations" in 1828. Andrew Jackson was by far the favorite national hero.

The way his inauguration was greeted in one north Alabama town is typical of the day in most parts of the state.

FOURTH OF MARCH

Yesterday commenced an era long to be remembered in our country. A new administration was organized—General Jackson is now President of the United States; and the evening of his inauguration was no doubt marked by various demonstrations of joy throughout the country. Our little village contributed its "mites" to the general joy. Nearly all the houses on the Square (the Court House in particular) were handsomely illuminated—all done without previous arrangement or concert—had it been generally known that an illumination was intended, it would have been much more general. The evening passed off peaceably.—*The Athenian* (Athens) March 5, 1829.

But Jackson's popularity and the Democratic party's power did not go unchallenged. The followers of Henry Clay of Kentucky, calling themselves successively Young Republicans, National Republicans and finally Whigs, organized to oppose Old Hickory. This opposition is the most positive and unqualified thing that can be said about them. They differed among themselves on almost everything else. Generally they stood for nationalism rather than states' rights, tariff rather than free trade, big plantations rather than small farms, and upper class rather than plain people. Any number of exceptions can be found in any one of these (and other) categories. A large number of able editors were Whig in politics. The greatest strength of the party lay in the Black Belt and the cotton counties of the Tennessee valley. The day of the Whigs was from 1832 to 1852. Their acknowledged leader was Henry W. Hilliard, college professor, minister, lawyer, public official and orator *par excellence*.

The Compromise of 1850 in Congress was responsible for a drastic party realignment in the state. The formal organization of the Union Party took place in Montgomery on January 19, 1851. A majority of the delegates were from the Black Belt. The convention passed resolutions supporting the Compromise and denying the right of secession. This pro-compromise stand was taken as a challenge to the opponents of the measure who shortly thereafter (February 10, 1851) organized the Southern Rights Party. Beginning nearly two years earlier, John C. Calhoun had urged such an organization but it took the Compromise to spur Alabamians into action. William L. Yancey, J. J. Seibels, editor of the Montgomery *Advertiser*, John A. Elmore, former Governor A. P. Bagby, S. F. Rice, all residents of the Montgomery area (and all former South Carolinians), were among the leaders of the Southern Rights Party.

During the decade before 1861 the state heard more and more from them.

The appearance of these two new parties in the state complicated the political situation and threatened the balance between the Democrats and the Whigs. Consequently, the Democrats called a convention to meet on January 8, 1852, with two purposes in mind: getting control of the Legislature and electing the United States senator. Similar efforts to revitalize the Whig party were less than successful. Many of its leaders had already broken with the national party, feeling that it was too strongly abolitionist. Furthermore, they had become the majority in the Union Party and some of the leaders opposed any return to the old party. In 1852, they were divided on candidates and two of the party leaders, Alexander White of Talladega and James Abercrombie of Montgomery, both of whom had been elected to Congress as Union Whigs, refused to attend the party's convention. The party was almost dead.

Before the Whig's final gasp, however, Henry W. Hilliard for the Whigs and William L. Yancey for the State's Rights Democrats engaged in one of the best chronicled campaigns in Alabama history, the congressional race of 1852. It is almost forgotten that the actual candidates were John Cochran (Democrat and secessionist from Eufaula) and James Abercrombie (Whig and unionist from Montgomery) and not Yancey and Hilliard. Inevitably, however, it became a contest between the two political giants.

There is a strong element of truth in Dr. A. B. Moore's statement that Alabama's history of the 1850's is the biography of William Lowndes Yancey. Yancey dominated the political scene like no one before him. Born in Georgia, educated there, and in New York where he went with his minister-step-father, and at Williams College in Massachusetts, he returned south to study and practice law. In 1836 he left Greenville, South Carolina, and migrated to Dallas County, Alabama, where he edited the Cahawba *Democrat* and engaged in planting. Three years later Yancey moved to Wetumpka (then in Coosa County) and entered politics as a Jacksonian Democrat. In 1841 he ran successfully for the state legislature; in 1844 he was sent to the United States House of Representatives and again in 1846. Thereafter he did not seek national office, choosing instead to use his considerable talents in the fight to stop what Alabamians interpreted as encroachments on Southern rights. In Wetumpka Yancey edited the *Argus* which served as a mouthpiece for the states' rights extremists. Later he practiced law in Montgomery. Often a delegate to party conventions, he led the walk-out at the Charleston Convention in 1860 and had great weight in

subsequent events in Baltimore. It was Yancey who drafted the
Alabama Ordinance of Secession and had more influence than any-
one else in leading the state out of the Union. His chief rival in
Alabama politics wrote of him:

> Mr. Yancey was in every way an extraordinary man. Of great intellect,
> high culture, commanding presence, great magnetism, and powerful in
> debate, especially before the people, he belonged to that class of states-
> men who held extreme Southern views of the government, known by
> the popular phrase "fire-eaters". He believed with Mr. Calhoun that the
> powers of the general government should be limited, and insisted that
> the States were sovereign, united under a league, rather than forming
> a part of the government, whose authority, under the provisions of the
> Constitution, covered them. I regarded him as the most powerful ad-
> vocate of the Southern-rights doctrine to be found in the whole country;
> and in his appeals to the people, when he stood before them on the
> platform, he was thought by many to be irresistible.—Henry W. Hilliard,
> *Politics and Pen Pictures* (New York: G. P. Putnam's Sons, 1892), p.
> 255.

Important as he was, Yancey did not dominate the period as exclusively as Dr. Moore implies. Henry W. Hilliard also stood out
in these years of strong personalities and stirring events. Hilliard,
a native of North Carolina, came to Alabama in 1831 to take a
professorship at the newly created university in Tuscaloosa. After
three years there, he resigned to practice law in Montgomery. He
served many times in the legislature and after 1845 was in Congress. Of him William Garrett said, "He was a Whig of the State's
Rights School, ardently devoted to the interests of the South, yet
in his patriotism embracing the whole country. But few men could
charm an audience by the gracefulness of manner, ease and beauty
of delivery, and the rich imagery of conception more than Mr. Hilliard. . . ."

In the 1852 election, Hilliard had agreed to take the stump for
Cochran on the condition that he would not meet anyone in public
debate. Nevertheless, Yancey challenged him and the following
events, here described by Hilliard, took place.

> One of the leading papers stated that I must not be permitted to speak
> to the people of the district without meeting some one to reply to me;
> that there was one gentleman whom I had never yet met, who would take
> the field against me; that Hon. William L. Yancey, who had, like my-
> self, declined a re-election to Congress, would meet me at my appoint-
> ments throughout the district.
>   My first appointment was at Union Springs, forty-five miles east of
> Montgomery, an interesting town in the midst of a beautiful country
> where wealthy planters resided. When I reached the place I found an

immense concourse of people assembled. There was no railroad connecting the place with Mountgomery at that time, but a number of ladies were present, who took the greatest interest in such discussions at that time. My friends had erected a platform for public speaking which they supposed would be occupied by me alone. Some short time before the hour arrived when I should address the people, several of my friends came to me and stated that Mr. Yancey was on the ground and proposed to meet me in debate. After some conversation, I said to them that I was reluctant to engage in a public discussion, but that as Mr. Yancey seemed determined to draw me into it I should not avoid it. I authorized them to arrange the terms of discussion with Mr. Yanceys friends, reserving to myself the right on that occasion to make the closing speech. The scene presented to my view as I ascended the platform was one of extraordinary interest. Mr Yancey, who had already taken his place, advanced and extended his hand, and we greeted each other cordially. It was a bright summer day, the sun shone with splendor upon a beautiful landscape, and large numbers of carriages were drawn up near the stand, while the improvised seats were filled with the people. The chairmen, one chosen from each of the parties, presided, and the discussion opened.

Mr. Yancey's speech expressed in strong terms his views of the state of the country; he believed that the South should be represented in Congress by men ready to defend its interests to the last extremity; he did not believe that the compromise measures would be generally accepted as a settlement of the slavery question; that they did not deal justly with the South, and that they were vehemently opposed by the leading men of the North. He denounced compromises, and insisted that the people of the South should be ready at all times to vindicate their rights and withdraw from the Union if further aggressions should be made by the government. He spoke for more than an hour with animation, but not with the vigor that I had expected from him.

When I rose to reply I was received by my friends with enthusiasm, and I spoke for an hour and a half upon the state of the country, insisting that the recent adjustment of the slavery question might be regarded as satisfactory; that the South had lost nothing by the settlement, and that our true policy was to assert our rights vigorously within the Union, resisting any encroachment that might be made. Statesmanship of a high order under our government consisted in recognizing the authority of the general government to the full extent of its constitutional powers, and by asserting our rights under its protection rather than by restorting to menaces and proclaiming our purpose to subvert the Union. I stated that I was loyal to the South and at the same time a friend of the Union, which spread the aegis of its powerful protection over the country.

Holding opinions directly in opposition to those of Mr. Yancey, and being in sympathy with the great Whig party, I met Mr. Yancey from time to time in a regular series of debates covering my congressional district, which was very large, extending from the Alabama River to the Chattahoochee, and down to the Florida line. The series of debates which had just been opened continued for some weeks; we were followed from place to place by a large concourse of gentlemen deeply interested in politics, who never swerved from their attention to our discussions until the end of the canvass.

These debates became so heated that when we reached Eufaula it was thought prudent to make arrangements for us to address the people from different platforms. Mr. Yancey, attended by his friends, spoke at one place, and I, by a large body of gentlemen who supported me, from another.

After this, proceeding to the counties below Eufaula, we met as before, some explanations having been made by mutual friends.

The great question at issue between Mr. Yancey and myself was the policy of inflaming the people of the South in opposition to the measures of the general government affecting our institutions. He insisted that our only safety was to be found in restraining the action of the general government within limits which left little power to accomplish any great result affecting the interests of the South.

I contended that the true policy of the South was to uphold the authority of the general government within the limits prescribed by the Constitution, and at the same time to protect the interests of the Southern people by a vigorous resistance in Congress to anything like encroachment upon our rights.

Mr. Yancey, impatient under opposition, chafed occasionally under my statement of the ruinous tendency of the policy which he advocated. He had voted for the bill organizing the Territory of Oregon, which contained a clause excluding slavery; before the passage of the bill he had voted to strike out this anti-slavery clause, but when it was embodied in the bill he voted for the measure. When, therefore, in the presence of great bodies of the people, he arraigned the Whig party for its opinions and denounced their policy as hostile to the South, I thought it proper at length to say it seemed to me that the gentleman himself should be more tolerant in his judgment of his political opponents; that while I did not doubt the gentleman's loyalty to the South, he had himself conceded the authority of Congress to exclude slavery from a territory of the Union by voting for a measure forbidding its introduction. This roused Mr. Yancey to an extreme degree, it put him on the defensive, it made it necessary that he should explain the circumstances under which he had voted for the Oregon Bill, believing that it was important to organize that remote territory by an act of our government.

On one occasion when we were about to open our debate at an important point I was met a mile or two from the place by a large body of gentlemen mounted on horseback, who acted as an escort up to the place where the discussion was to take place. Before the debate opened Mr. Yancey and I were seated in pleasant conversation, when he said to me: "Mr. Hilliard, shall we have a friendly debate to-day?" I replied: "Mr. Yancey, I must mention your vote on the Oregon question; I cannot overlook it to-day."

The result of this canvass was the full vindication of my views on the relation of the South to the general government. The elections that followed this protracted debate showed a decided ascendancy for the

Whig party. From the commencement of the discussions between Mr.
Yancey and myself the two candidates for Congress stood aside, and
were never present, but the genleman brought out by the Whig party
was elected.—Ibid., pp. 251–55.

Political songs gave color to this campaign. In 1928 an ex-slave
remembered one that began

> Now turn out for our native land
> And raise the standard high;
> For Cochran leads a gallant band
> To glorious victory.
> The South he'll give those peaceful joys
> Our Fathers thought were meet;
> "Southern Rights" forever, boys,
> For Cochran can't be beat.

—Quoted in Lewy Dorman, *Party Politics in Alabama from 1850
Through 1860* (Montgomery: The Alabama Department of Archives
and History, 1935), p. 57.

The Know-Nothing Party was the last party to appear on the
political horizon before 1860. The battles of the 1830's and 1840's
between the Whigs and the Democrats were the usual kind; few
considered the strife more than the normal rivalry between parties.
With the coming of the American or Know-Nothing party, however, the Alabama public, if one can judge from the press, became
genuinely alarmed. The star of the party rose rapidly in 1854–55,
ran a slate of offices in the 1855 election, and just as rapidly waned.
J. L. M. Curry who ran against the Know-Nothings remembered
them vividly.

It was a secret political organization with degrees or orders of membership and a ritual of initiation. Strong oaths were administered to persons
admitted. The party suddenly became very popular, lodges were organized in nearly every neighborhood, village, town, and city in the
United States. . . . The leading object was to cultivate an intense
Americanism, and exclude aliens from suffrage, and Roman Catholics
from office. Nearly all the Whigs, and many of the Democrats were
beguiled into the party. . . . Excitement ran high in Alabama. I was
from the beginning to the end inflexibly opposed to the secret party
and its principles. . . . Only July 3, 1855, I was by a county convention unanimously nominated for the legislative house of representatives.
. . . Having apparently no option, I accepted the nomination; and from
that day until the election on the first Monday in August I traveled and
spoke everyday, except Sunday. The Know-Nothings never doubted
of success; and I had to meet in debate Lewis E. Parsons, a knightly
antagonist, one of the ablest lawyers in the state, a thorough gentleman,

afterwards governor by presidential appointment, and Hon. Thomas B. Woodward, who had been a member of the nullification convention in South Carolina. . . . The crowds were large and the debates warm and excited. Several times I spoke in face of threats of personal violence. Having obtained one of the little "yellow books" . . . containing the oaths and ritual, I used them unsparingly. I rode on horseback to our various appointments and never more enjoyed intellectual encounters. My whole ticket was elected.—Edwin A. Alderman and Armistead C. Gordon, *J.L.M. Curry* (New York: The Macmillan Co., 1911), pp. 108–110.

It is difficult to explain the phenomenal growth of the Know Nothings. Just how many of them there were is hard to say, but some 30,000 persons voted for George D. Shortridge, the Know-Nothing gubernatorial candidate, in 1855. As they stated in their platform, they were opposed to Roman Catholics and immigrants who, as it happened, were often one and the same. Alabama had few of the former besides the French in Mobile and only a scattering of foreign born. The census of 1860 says only slightly more than 12,000 residents of the state were born abroad, and most of them lived in Mobile County. Why then, the sudden movement to the new party?

There seems to be little doubt that some Alabamians, like Americans elsewhere, were genuinely disturbed with the growing number of newcomers not in the Anglo-Saxon, Protestant tradition. In the 1855 contest, Shortridge pointed out that the foreign population in many areas held the balance of power and both parties were vying for their votes. The "American ballot-box was at the mercy of whatever whim might at the time prevail amongst the ever floating and unorganized foreign masses. . . ." He said:

> Already we are called on by societies, composed of foreigners, for a new Constitution. . . . The liberty that is here restrained by law and regulated by courts of justice is not such liberty as is now audaciously demanded by the escaped jailbirds of the old countries; they must have a shelter for felons. . . . They demand liberty to rob, to equalize property, to confiscate and divide among themselves the hard earnings of the more thrifty of our citizens.—Quoted in William R. Smith, *Reminiscences of a Long Life* (Washington: William R. Smith, Sr., 1889), vol. 1, p. 255.

The last item in their platform was "purity of the ballot box and the enforcement of law and order."

In explaining the rush to the Know-Nothing standard, the student probably finds a more applicable reason in local political conditions. Many of the Know-Nothings in this state had been Whigs who after their party's virtual demise between 1852 and 1855 had no political home and they could not bring themselves to join the Democrats. There was also the practical issue of state aid to railroads. John A. Winston, the Democrat candidate for governor, was opposed to it. Shortridge favored it, a position that would gain him support in the Mobile, Selma, and Montgomery areas. If the party could capture these groups along with the states righters and slave owners, there was some chance of victory.

Shortridge is one of the host of public figures whose actual accomplishments never fulfilled their ambitions nor probably ever used all their considerable talents. Born in Mt. Sterling, Kentucky, son of Eli Shortridge whose brilliant career as a lawyer was cut short by "conviviality [that] ripened into habit," he grew up in Tuscaloosa and was a member of the first class that entered the University of Alabama. He graduated in 1833 along with A. B. Meek and several others whose careers are closely associated with the state's public affairs. Of these

> George D. Shortridge was the one of the most pronounced ambition. He made no scruple of expressing his designs, and affected no concealment of his lofty aspirations.—Ibid., p. 249.

He was a great admirer of Henry Clay, John C. Calhoun, Daniel Webster and Thomas Hart Benton and

> seemed already [as a student] to have set himself vigorously to work to climb up to the lofty castle of renoun which they had erected, with intent to make himself a familiar habitant therein.—Ibid., p. 250.

He studied law, "pushed his fortunes with practical energy" and shortly found himself "fairly afloat under bright auspices." After he moved to Montgomery, he "got himself mixed up in monetary affairs" as a director of the branch bank there. He seems to have extricated himself successfully for he was elected a circuit judge and served for ten years in that capacity. He also was mayor at one time. Just what prompted him to carry the standard for the new party is not known but after his defeat he withdrew from public life, serving again only in the secession convention. His wife was Elizabeth King, daughter of Edmund King of Montevallo and sister of William M. King, a classmate of his at the University. He lived for many years in Montevallo and at his death in 1870 was buried in the King family cemetery which is now encompassed by the University of Montevallo campus.

In their campaigns, the Know-Nothings had much to say about the evil forces that threatened the ballot box. Probably because of this, the editor of the Camden *Republic* used the following heading. He, too, had fears.

GOD SAVE THE BALLOT-BOX IN ALABAMA

The above is rather a startling heading to an article in this republican land, and in this hitherto free-voting State of Alabama—but, nevertheless, it is an appropriate one. The time has come when republican men—especially those who desire to see the freedom of the ballot box maintained—must buckle on their armor and not only exert their own strength, but look to an overruling providence for assistance in this dark day of dark-lantern parties.

What has led me to these remarks, is the secret instructions which have been conveyed to the Know Nothing Councils throughout this State from the Grand State Council recently held at Montgomery. I have obtained a copy of those sent to this county, which are the same as those sent throughout the State. They are as follows:

"Each member is at liberty to acknowledge his membership, and to assist, advocate, defend, and define its principles.

"It is required that the President of each Council shall hold meetings as often as it is convenient; once a week, at least, if possible.

"That at the first meeting of each Council, a vigilance committee of twenty shall be appointed,

"1st. To find out such persons as are friendly to the principles we advocate, and have them presented for membership.

"2d. To see that all members register their names in their proper Councils.

"3d. To make out complete lists of the total inside and outside vote, and the names of such voters, embraced within the limits of their respective Councils.

"4th. To attend to the polls on the day of election, and to see to it, that none but legal votes are given.

"5th. To see to it, that every member of the order and friend of it, comes forward and votes.

"6th. To use their best endeavors to calm all excitements, and use all proper means to influence the outside vote.

"By order of the State President.

"Attest, LEWIS A MIDDLETON,

"Secretary"

I can now understand why the declaration or asseveration made a few days ago by a Know Nothing and since by others, should have been made; viz: "that all things were now fixed in this county, and that the vote could not be altered between now and the August election."

You will see by reference to the 3d count in the instructions—that the complete inside and outside vote within the limits of each Council is to be ascertained, and a list made out of the names of the voters. You will see also by the 2d count, that all members are required to register their names in ther proper Councils. Thus, a full knowledge is obtained of the vote to be given on the first Monday in August next—provided that there is no bolting. Against this contingency, see 5th count. This vigilant committee of twenty is "to see to it every member of the order, and friend of it comes forward and votes."

Thus the votes are fixed unchangeable in the opinion of some of these Know-Nothings in this county. And why? Because twenty men at each box have been organized into a committee of surveillance and espionage—whose duty is to make members of the Know Nothing order, and those friendly to it, vote the Know Nothing ticket, whether they will or not. Failing to coerce their members into the support of their candidates, they are at least to be prevented from voting at all. All the terrors of the Secret Inquisition are to be held up in vivid colors before their eyes. They are to be told that they took an obligation "to support in all political matters, for all political offices, members of this (Know Nothing) order." This failing, they are to be reminded still farther of an obligation which they took, and of the terrors which are to pursue them. They are to be told, that they bound themselves, under oath, "under the no less penalty than that of being expelled from the order, and of having their names posted and circulated throughout the United States as perjurers, and as traitors to their God and their country—as being unfit to be employed, entrusted, countenanced, or supported in any business transaction—as persons totally unworthy of the confidence of all good men and as those at whom the finger of scorn should ever be pointed," if they voted otherwise than as the order dictated.

These twenty at each box are to do all this, and more. They are not only to compel their members to vote the Know Nothing ticket, if they can; but they are to prevent, by force, their voting otherwise. Hence the appointment of this strong force of twenty. Hence the belief on the part of some that the Know Nothing vote of this county is now fixed. But this is not all. The timid of the anti-Know Nothing party are to be prevented from voting. These twenty are to be supported, if necessary, by other members of the order who may be present; and anti Americans, as they term us who are not favorable to the order, are to be disfranchised, as far as they can effect such an object by obstacles and force thrown in the way of voters. This was the course pursued at the late elections in New Orleans, at Cincinnati, and at Louisville.

I am sorry, Mr. Editor, that you have not room (as you inform me) for a brief account of the proceedings at those elections—those proceedings of riot, bloodshed, murder, and destruction of ballot boxes—and democratic ballot boxes at that,—by the Know Nothings, or the self-styled American party.

But if I can't do this, I can at least appeal to the free people of Wilcox to buckle on their armor, and, invoking the great God of battles to their assistance—to go forth to the battle on the first Monday of August next, in defiance of all secret Inquisitions, and in defiance of all committees of twenty at each box, appointed to intimidate and control the voters at the same.

Well may we exclaim—to what a pass in political matters have we come, when twenty men in secret are appointed to watch and control the votes of freemen! The people are no longer able to exercise their rights as freemen—but must have twenty OATH-BOUND MEN, to guide, to guard, and to direct them; or in the language of the 5th count in the instructions, to see to it that every member of the order, and

friend of it, comes forward and votes! And votes how? Why for this
Know Nothing party.—They are no longer free, but they have been sold
"like sheep in the shambles," and are to be governed and directed by this
committee of twenty at each box! well may we say, when this is the
case, "God save the ballot box in Alabama." A. FREEMAN.—Quoted in
The Alabama Beacon (Greensboro), July 27, 1855.

After the defeat at the polls, the party died out as rapidly as it
had risen.

The Bank

Of the many domestic issues, one of the most perplexing was the
state bank. Banking is essentially an economic matter, yet economics
and politics were inextricably entwined in the banking system of
early Alabama.

The Constitution of 1819 provided for a state bank, which was
in operation by 1823. Opened at Cahaba, it was moved to Tuscaloosa when the capital was relocated there in 1826. It was managed
by a president and board of trustees, appointed annually by the
state legislature. The state bank was involved in politics from the
beginning and was frequently an issue (if not the principal one)
in state elections.

The state banking system began on the eve of "flush" times in
the state when there was almost endless demand for credit with
which to purchase lands and slaves. People were willing to mortgage
their future in order to get the paper money the banks issued.
Under such "boom" times the banks loaned more money than their
capital stock justified but nevertheless seemed to prosper. For a
brief period Alabamians held to the erroneous notion that income
from the bank would be great enough to abolish all taxes!

The panic of 1837 brought a sad reckoning. Money from school
lands which had been used as capital was lost. There was evidence
of mismanagement, fraud, and extravagance. Consequently, banking reform became the chief issue in the election of 1841 when
Benjamin Fitzpatrick was elected governor. Although the reforming governor never got the kind of action he wanted, the legislature
did appoint John A. Campbell of Mobile as chairman of the committee on banks. He recommended several pieces of legislation designed to prevent further mismanagement.

Professor A. B. Moore summarizes the bank situation by saying:

While it is impossible to get precise information about the affairs of
the banks, the investigations of Campbell's committee and other agencies
showed that enormous sums were owed the banks, and a very high
percentage of the debts were not recoverable. A legislative committee
in 1838 estimated the 'bad debts' at $100,000, and by 1841 it was said

to be more than $3,500,000. A joint legislative committee reported January 9, 1843, that out of a total debt of $16,392,873.77, bad debts amounted to $5,501,493.16, and $2,048,244.81 more were doubtful. . . .—A. B. Moore, *History of Alabama,* p. 232.

The bank was made even more complicated by the fact that each branch bank had its own board of directors and was not subject to the regulations and decisions of the directors of the parent bank. Since all directors were chosen by the legislature, there was much room for "politicking" when the time of appointment came. William Garrett who was at the capitol as a clerk many years before he became secretary of state in 1840 described the contest for places on the various boards.

As the time for electing the several boards approached, (the heel of the session,) candidates for bank directors began to arrive in great numbers. The charters allowed fourteen to each of the banks, making three score and ten, in the aggregate, to the State Bank and its four branches, and more than thrice that number were in attendance as candidates, thronging the capitol and besieging the rooms of members, and furnishing at the restaurants oyster suppers and other entertainments to secure votes. An anecdote illustrating this is given here. A member (Mr. Sullivan, of Perry,) died, and the House, in respect to his memory, resolved that the members wear the usual badge of mourning (crape on the left arm for thirty days). This was a mark by which members were known, and was especially noticed by the candidates for the bank directorships who had not the advantage of extensive personal acquaintance. It so happened that E. Herndon, of Benton county, in one of his trading excursions, came to Tuskaloosa about this time. He liked attention, was social in his feelings, and sharp and observant of the best means to accomplish his ends. Seeing the magic influence of crape on the arm in the attention it received, especially in the articles of good cigars, liquors, and oysters, he at once assumed the character of a member, by wearing the badge, and soon found himself the recipient of many civilities, and being that way inclined, he made a good thing of it.—*Reminiscences,* pp. 42–43.

The panic of 1837 caused financial distress all over the nation. Alabama was probably no harder hit than other states, but the attending problems were grave nevertheless. Banks everywhere suspended specie payments in the spring of 1837.

Merchants, manufacturers, planters, and all occupations requiring money to prosecute them to advantage, were swept overboard, or greatly staggered by the storm. Few escaped. In Alabama the pressure was so decided that Gov. Clay called the Legistlature together in extra session, in May, to devise some measure of relief to the people. Then it was that a loan of $5,000,000 on State bonds was authorized, to be divided among the State Bank and Branches, and the amount to be issued in bank notes for circulation. Those persons who were most in danger from judgments and executions were preferred in discounts, on their executing the proper securities to the Bank. . . .

At this juncture of affairs—caused by the former expansion of Bank credits, and the consequent ease in the currency, followed by the curtailment which was more or less increased by the withdrawal of the Government deposits from the Bank of the United States, and the issuing of the specie circular of President Jackson, in 1836, requiring all payments for the public lands to be made in coin—it was the fortune of the Hon. Arthur P. Bagby to be elected Governor of Alabama. When he was installed in office, on the 21st day of November, 1837, he found the State, and all classes of the people, laboring under the depression caused by the financial difficulties which prevailed.—Ibid., pp. 201–203.

The country slowly recovered but the affairs of the bank continued to defy solution. In late 1845, Governor Joshua L. Martin gave a comprehensive survey of the problem.

Executive Department,
Tuskaloosa, December 16, 1845.
Gentlemen of the Senate and House of Representatives:

In entering upon the discharge of my official duties, I feel called upon by recent events to communicate to you my views upon the various subjects connected with the affairs of our State Bank and Branches; and with the indebtedness of the State—subjects which have for some time past occupied the attention of our constituents, and which have recently become so important in their view as to engross all others. To these subjects I shall confine myself in this communication.

From the reports of the several legislative committees whose duty it has been, from time to time, to inquire into the condition of our State Bank and Branches, it appears, that for the last seven years, these institutions have suffered one unbroken series of losses; resulting in the disastrous condition in which they were found at the last session of the General Assembly. The causes which have brought about these continuous and heavy losses, are readily discovered by a recurrence to the history of their management; the whole tenor which proves, beyond doubt, that less regard has been had to the interests of the Banks than the convenience and accommodation of their debtors.

By the report made to the Legislature at the session of eighteen hundred and thirty-seven and eight, it is shown that the indebtedness of [to] the State Bank and Branches amounted at that time to more than twenty millions of dollars; of which but little more than one hundred thousand dollars were considered bad; and but little more than five hundred thousand dollars doubtful. The first act of the Legislature, changing the usual course of business in those Banks, was passed a short time before, at the called session in June, eighteen hundred and thirty-seven. This act extended the time of payment of the debts then due; dividing them into three annual installments; the first, of twenty-five per cent.; the other two of thirty-seven and a half per cent. each. And it authorized further loans, payable in like installments.

At the session of eighteen hundred and forty and forty-one, a report was made to the Legislature, by which it appears, that under the influence of the act referred to, commonly known as the relief or extension law of eighteen hundred and thirty-seven, the bad debt had increased to more than three and one half millions of dollars; while the doubtful debt had swelled to an amount exceeding one million and a half of dollars. And in this report is introduced a new item denominated "unknown debt," amounting then to more than one million and a quarter of dollars. Thus is shown a deterioration of the debts due to the Banks, by which losses have been incurred, to be estimated at not less than one million and a quarter of dollars annually, during the three years immediately preceding this report.

At the session of the Legislature of eighteen hundred and thirty-nine and forty, another act was passed (approved the third of February, eighteen hundred and forty) by which it was required that, "not more than twenty per cent." of the several debts due the Banks should be demanded, per annum. Under the operation of this act, connected with that above referred to, as shown by a report of a committee, at the last session of the General Assembly, the good debts were reduced to six mililon, nine hundred and ninety-three thousand, nine hundred and sixty-five dollars, and thirty-six cents—($6,993,965.36.) The doubtful debt to four hundred and eighty-four thousand, one hundred and thirty-two dollars and forty-six cents—($484,132.46.) While the bad debt had reached the enormous sum of six millions, two hundred and ninety-two thousand, five hundred and ninety-nine dollars and seventy cents— ($6,292,599.70.) Each of the laws here referred to required that the President and Directors of the several Banks should demand further security, if by them deemed necessary, as a condition precedent to the extension. How far this provision was regarded, may be judged of by the results.

This cursory glance at the history of the legislation, and management of our Banks, must clearly show that the extension laws, and the manner of their execution, were the principal causes of the immense losses sustained by these institutions. A more minute examination would but fortify this conclusion. As however, it is important to know the causes of the evils, simply with a view to avoid them in future, I shall not pursue this inquiry further. We find our Banks at the last session of the Legislature in the situation mentioned. We have no reason to believe that they are in a better condition now. The mischief is done, and it is the part of wisdom to make the best that we can of our present condition. To do this, we should adopt such measures as may promise to collect the largest amount of the entire indebtedness to the Banks with the least expense, and at the same time bring their affairs to the most speedy adjustment and conclusion, compatible with that important object.

At the session of eighteen hundred and forty-two and three of the General Assembly, acts were passed repealing the charters of the four

Branch Banks, so far as to deprive them of banking powers, and putting them in liquidation. On the first day of January last, the charter of the State Bank expired by its own limitation. None of its banking powers have been renewed, but by an act of the last session of the General Assembly it was put in liquidation. By the same act, the officers of the State Bank and of each of the Branches were made to consist of a President and two Directors, a Cashier, and two clerks; and one additional clerk in the Branch at Mobile.

The impolicy of keeping up five banking establishments, with five presidents, ten Directors, five Cashiers, eleven clerks, and other agents, attorneys and servants, engaged upon salaries and pay—with a variety of other sources of expense, which might be mentioned—swelling the actual expenditure of the State Bank and all its Branches to a sum not very far short of the expense of our State Government, is too obvious to require argument; looking alone to its disregard of a proper economy. When to this is added the utter inefficiency of the system for the attainment of the great object in view—collecting and securing the debts, and winding up the concerns of the Banks in the most speedy possible manner—a reform of the system becomes an imperious duty. Without a change, judging the future by the past, we have but little ground to hope that this complicated business will be brought to a beneficial and satisfactory close in any reasonable time.

With these views, and others which will suggest themselves to you, I respectfully recommend to your consideration the propriety of dispensing with all the officers of the State Bank; and of each of the Branches. And I recommend that provision be made for the appointment of one agent to remain at each of the Branches, with authority to receive payment from the debtors, giving proper receipts and acquittances, and to do such other ministerial acts as may be necessary and expedient for him to do in furthering collections, but with no other powers. I further recommend that provision be made for the appointment of three Commissioners, in the mode now prescribed for the appointment of Directors, with such salaries as will command the best qualifications for the purpose to be found anywhere in the State, who shall reside at the State Bank, and devote their entire time and attention to the important object of securing and collecting the whole Bank debt, with full power and authority to appoint all necessary attorneys, clerks and agents; to transfer the books and papers of the Branch Banks to the State Bank—except the evidences of debt running to maturity—to dispose of the real and personal property of the State Bank and Branches, and when necessary and proper, looking alone to the interest of the State, to compromise and compound debts that may at any time be considered doubtful or bad: thus concentrating the whole business at the State Bank. I further recommend that these Commissioners be empowered to pay the interest, as it may become due, upon the State debt, and to extinguish the debt as fast as they may be able, from their collections and funds, under such rules and regulations as you, in your wisdom, may prescribe, giving to them ample powers for all these purposes, at the same time securing the State against its abuse by proper restrictions and sureties.

By this system it is obvious that after the payment of such salaries as are contemplated, and every other expense incident to it, a vast amount of the present annual expenditure would be saved. None, I think, can doubt its superior efficiency. With suitable Commissioners, I am induced to believe but few years would be required to bring the whole of the affairs of our Banks to a final close; at least to enable our citizens to understand what ought to be known to all, but what is now known to none, the true pecuniary condition of the State.

By an act passed at the last session of the General Assembly, the debtors of the State Bank and Branches were required to pay, by the first of June last, one-third part of their respective debts, with interest. And it was provided, that, upon a compliance with these terms, the remaining two-thirds should stand over until the first of June next. It was generally understood that a further provision would be made at the present session, in favor of those who complied, extending one-half of the balance due for twelve months longer, upon the payment of the other half, by that day, with interest. The reports of committees touching this subject, clearly indicated this to be the policy which would be adopted. Under this expectation, it is believed, many of the Bank debtors complied with the requisition of the law, with some inconvenience and sacrifice. I respectfully recommend that this expectation be met by the enactment of a law for that purpose, with proper guards and provisions. The first day of June may not be the most suitable day for the required payment. It may be proper to appoint another day somewhat more distant. This, however, in my opinion, should be the limit. No other extension should be conceded; nor should this apply to any other debtors than the class here specially referred to.

It will be seen to be indispensable, as already intimated, that some steps be taken at your present session, to provide for the payment of the interest of the State debt as it may hereafter become due. The plighted faith of the State requires it. Having no other known available effects than the assets of our Banks, it will be necessary, in prescribing for collections, to keep this object steadily in view. You will have before you the means of ascertaining the amount collected, under the late act on this subject and the consequent reduction of the circulation of the State Bank and Branches. You will also be able, from the documents before you, to form an estimate of the amount of circulation yet remaining out. A very large portion of the interest to be provided for being that which accrues on our foreign debt of $9,215,255.55, amounting annually to the sum of $471,907.80, is payable in New York, New Orleans, and in England, in par funds. The necessity of requiring collection of an amount which, together with the taxes, will absorb the circulation of the State Bank and Branches, and furnish an additional sum in sound funds, sufficient to pay the interest thus to become payable, must be clear to all. For it will hardly be contended that the notes of those Banks, after being returned to the State, either in payment of taxes, or in payment of debts due the Banks, can legitimately be put again in circulation; the powers of the Banks which issued them for this purpose having terminated. If, however, there be any one who suppose it can be done with the sanction of law, the destructive policy of throwing our Bank notes into the market by the State, to be sold for such funds as will, from time to time, be demanded of us, would utterly forbid it. Instead of relieving the country of the depreciated currency—one of the great purposes of winding up the Banks—such a policy would not only keep up the supply, but increase its depreciation. The losses to the State would be enormous. The fact being known, through the country, as it certainly would be, that the State relies upon the sales of the State Bank notes as the means of raising money to pay the interest accruing from time to time, we would find ourselves in the hands of brokers and shavers, compelled to submit to such terms as their cupidity might dictate. Very few rounds of the circle—receiving our notes at par, and selling them at such a discount as would be demanded—would result in the exhaustion of the remaining assets of our Banks, to pay the interest only, leaving the principal debt, in all its magnitude, bearing heavily upon us, swelling with still further interest. This suicidal policy, I trust, will not be adopted, even as a temporary measure. It involves the same principles which have too long prevailed in the management of our Banks, favoring the Bank debtors at the expense of the taxpayers of the State.

It is believed that the amount, now in suit against those who refused to accept the provisions of the act of the last session of the General Assembly, in regard to Bank debts, added to one-half of the debt extended in virtue of that act, and the sum to be raised, will relieve the pressing necessities of the State. The propriety and importance of prosecuting these suits, and enforcing collections, when all the circumstances are properly considered, must be obvious. The reasonableness of the terms proposed by the act is perceived, when we remember that most of these debts were contracted more than seven years ago, for money lent; and for which indulgence had been given from time to time, to that period. By that act, they were required to pay one-third only, of the amount due; a sum which was imperatively demanded by the necessities of the State, to meet her own liabilities. Punctuality on the part of our debtors, in meeting all reasonable demands upon them, is now all-important to the State; for upon this may depend the preservation of our faith and credit. If these debtors are put upon an equal footing with those who paid as required, the precedent will encourage a disregard of our demands; and punctuality will cease to be a virtue. A controlling reason is found in the consideration, that less than the proposed collection will not place beyond contingency, our ability to meet the demands of the State. And we are bound in justice to the great body of our constituents, who are without fault, and who have received no benefit from the Banks, to save the honor of the State from peril; even if it requires some sacrifice by those who have been so long in the enjoyment of Bank accommodations.

The time has arrived when we should cease to dally with this subject; when, by a firm adherence to the enactments of the Legislature, and a faithful execution of them, it should be made manifest that they are intended to effect the object indicated by their provisions. Bank debtors should understand that the laws are intended to operate equally upon all; not to spend their force upon one portion, who regard them; then to be changed and modified to suit the convenience of other portions, who treat them with neglect.

There is an obvious propriety in extending to agents entrusted with the duty of making collections, every aid in our power, to facilitate their efforts. And while no one can be less inclined to do unnecessary injury, either in feeling or interest, to our debtors, than I am, I can not doubt, that in ascertaining the course proper to be pursued, it is our duty to consult the interest of the State, untrammeled by any unreasonable apprehension as to the effect which it may have upon them. The aid of our citizens should be invoked. They are directly interested in this great subject, being responsible for any deficiency, in the form of taxes to discharge our State liability. With this view, I submit to your consideration the propriety of publishing in such form and manner as may cause it to reach our citizens generally, a list of the names of the bad, doubtful and unknown debtors; with the amount due from them respectively. The people of the State have the right, at any rate, like all other creditors, to know who their debtors are. And I entertain no doubt that our collecting agents would acquire much assistance from information, which this means would cause to be communicated. Those debtors could have no cause to complain. They are in default. They have no right to withhold from the State any of their effects. And if any are withheld, every means should be essayed to discover and apply them.

In connection with this subject, I submit to your consideration the propriety of causing a rigid scrutiny in the conduct of the officers, attorneys and agents, under whose management the astounding losses to our Banks have accrued, holding them to strict accountability. Such an inquiry seems to be called for, as well for the purpose of enforcing justice from delinquents, as to relieve those who have been faithful from unmerited imputation. For our constituents justly consider it difficult to perceive how the affairs of our Banks have been brought to their present condition, without great and culpable mismanagement in their officers, attorneys, and agents. When these things shall have been done; when all shall have been collected that can be collected; when the burden shall have been made as light as it can be made; our patriotic citizens will not shrink from it. Though it be heavy and bear hard upon them, they will not falter under it. They will pay whatever may be necessary to sustain the plighted faith and honor of the State. They will march forward with their treasure, as heretofore they have done, not only with that, but with their blood also, to preserve untarnished our fair escutcheon. On our course now, theirs may depend hereafter. I hope, therefore, I may not be considered too importunate, when, in the name of everything dear to us, I commend this subject to your most deliberate consideration.—Quoted in Ibid., pp. 417–21.

The charter of the bank expired in 1845 and was not renewed.

One of the obvious results of the panic and banking crisis was the loss of population to new regions in the west. "Gone to Texas"

was not just a joke but a reality. It is estimated that Monroe
County alone lost 1500 residents, most of them moving to the
recently independent Republic of Texas. One observer noted that
Alabamians were faced with the alternative "of high taxes to pay
the interest on money so improvidently borrowed from England
or to suffer the disgrace of repudiation. . . ." The planters to whom
much of the borrowed money had been loaned had "nearly all
of them moved off and settled beyond the Mississippi." The pes-
simistic commentator described the problems created by the loans.

> First, our Legislature negotiates a loan; then borrows to pay the in-
> terest of it; then discovers after some years that five out of the sixteen
> millions lent to us have evaporated. Our democrats then stigmatise those
> who vote for direct taxes to redeem their pledges as "the high taxation
> men." Possibly the capital and interest may eventually be made good,
> but there is some risk at least of a suspension of payment. At this moment
> the state is selling land forfeited by those to whom portions of the bor-
> rowed money were lent on mortgage, but the value of property thus
> forced into the market is greatly depreciated.—An unidentified resident
> of Claiborne, quoted in Sir Charles Lyell, A Second Visit to the United
> States (London: J. Murray, 1849), vol. 2, pp. 60–63.

To its credit, Alabama did not repudiate her debt, but the work
of settling the matter took Francis L. Lyon of Marengo County
until 1858. He had been commissioned to do whatever was necessary "to ascertain the assets, credits, and debts of the banks, collecting the outstanding claims and the disposition of their physical
property."
Writing in 1846, Sir Charles Lyell was

> stuck with the warning here conveyed against lending money to a new
> and half-formed community where everything is fluctuating and on the
> move—a State from which the Indians are only just retreating and
> where few whites ever continue to reside three years in one place—
> where thousands are going with their negroes to Louisiana, Texas, or
> Arkansas—where even the County Court houses and State Capitol are
> on the move, . . . for example, the seat of Legislature [is] about to be
> transferred from Tuscaloosa to Montgomery. In the midst of such in-
> stability, a feeling of nationality, or State pride, cannot easily be fostered.
> Nevertheless, the resources, both mineral and agricultural, of so vast a
> territory as Alabama, a fifth larger in area than the whole of England
> proper, may enable them with moderate economy to overcome all their
> difficulties.—Ibid., p. 63.

The Capital

The location of the capital was a question of prime political importance. The choice of Cahaba in Dallas County in 1819 was a

signal victory for Governor W. W. Bibb and the south Alabama forces, but the victory had its price. Those favoring some other site, north or west, did not give up the fight to move it. At first, the legislature approved a mere $10,000 to erect temporary quarters for the government; six years later it voted to remove these quarters to Tuscaloosa. The decision was made after a Seat of Government Committee, headed by Levin Powell of Tuscaloosa, had studied the location of Cahaba.

> They [the committee] have ascertained that Cahawba is on a low situation, and liable to be inundated by the waters of both the Cahawba and Alabama rivers. The inundation of a part of the town occurs almost annually; and at times it has been impracticable to reach the State House without a conveyance by water. It has been ascertained that during the last session of the legislature every street leading from the country into the town was overflowed to the depth of several feet. . . .—William H. Brantley, *Three Capitals* (privately printed, 1947), p. 167.

Health conditions in the summer months were so bad that the Supreme Court would not meet there and that the inhabitants, being unwilling to risk their health, were in the habit of migrating "to some situation which promises better health." Residents of Dallas County to this day discredit stories about the depth of the floods, but the capital was moved to the western Alabama town where it remained until a new movement forced the legislators to choose Montgomery.

The capital was changed by constitutional amendment. It was attached as a rider to the act that replaced annual sessions of the legislature with biennial sessions and thus became law in January 1846. On January 28, the legislature met in joint session to choose a new site for the capital. Passing over Tuscaloosa, Wetumpka, Marion, Selma, Statesville, and Mobile, they chose Montgomery on the sixteenth ballot. Tuscaloosa residents bitterly resented the removal by use of the rider, considering it to be unfair and underhanded.

One of the reasons for the selection of Montgomery was the promise of the business men there to build a capitol building at no expense to the state. This they did and the building was near enough finished that the official records were moved in 1847. This was the building that burned on December 14, 1849, the thirtieth anniversary of statehood.

> The two Houses had been in session a month and two days, and were industriously engaged in the dispatch of business, which promised an early termination of the session, when an event occurred, which in the disorder and the derangement produced, and the introduction of new

questions, extended the session nearly one month longer. I allude to the burning of the State Capitol on the 14th day of December.

About fifteen minutes after one o'clock in the afternoon, when both Houses were in session, it was discovered that the Capitol was on fire over the Representative Hall—the volume of smoke issuing with rapid increase. Gen Frazier, of the Senate, upon the first intimation of such a thing, hurried to the upper story, and into the room leading, by a trapdoor, to the top, to see what discoveries could be made; but was met at the door by a dense volume of smoke, which arrested his progress.

The Senate adjourned hastily; but the House broke up its sitting without the formality of an adjournment—such was the panic and confusion that suddenly seized upon the members. The fire extended rapidly from the south end of the building against a pretty stiff northern breeze, and in three hours, that superb, elegant structure—a monument of the liberality of the citizens of Montgomery, and the pride of the State—was in ruins; nothing left but portions of the blackened walls.

The combined efforts of the members and citizens, with the heads of departments, saved the public property upon the basement and second floor. The State Library on the third floor could not be entered without peril. After the archives of his office were saved, the writer conducted a number of gentlemen to that apartment, to assist in throwing the contents out of the windows; but the heat was so great and increasing, that they could not remain, and the large collection of public documents, lawbooks, manuscript Journals of the General Assembly, historical works, maps of the several States, and valuable papers, with a variety of publications presented to the State in exchange for similar courtesies, and other volumes constituting a fine collection for public use—were all destroyed.

The archives and papers of the Executive, of the Secretary of State, the Treasurer and Comptroller, of the Supreme Court, and of the Senate and House of Representatives, including all belonging to the public offices in the Capitol, that were saved, were secured in rooms procured for the purpose in the city, until the House should determine the location of the different offices.—Garrett, *Reminiscences of Public Men,* pp. 517–18.

There was talk of moving the capital elsewhere after the fire but nothing came of it and the present capitol was erected shortly. Reuben Chapman (1847–1849) and Henry W. Collier (1849–1853) were governors during the early days of the government in Montgomery.

Alabama did not lead the nation in many reforms but nevertheless it had considerable interest in improving the lot of prisoners and the insane. William Garrett records the early action on a state prison.

STATE PRISON

At this session [1838] several important measures were adopted; among them, the establishment of a penitentiary. This measure had been strongly urged by Gov. McVay, in his annual and only message in 1837;

but the recommendation was not then acted upon. The fact that the adjoining States of Tennessee and Georgia had adopted the policy, had a good deal of weight with the majority. But the bill encountered strong opposition in both Houses, and passed the House of Representatives by a vote of 48 to 36, and in the Senate by an easy majority. The bill provided that the site of the institution should be determined by a majority of the two Houses; who should, also, elect three commissioners to compile for the consideration of the Legislature, a penal code adapted to the change. Wetumpka, Montevallo, Centerville, and Marion were placed in nomination for the site, and, on the first ballot, Wetumpka was elected. Messrs. William Hogan, Malcolm Smith, and A. M. McWhorter building commissioners, etc. The three Judges of the Supreme Court, Collier, Goldthwaite, and Ormond, to prepare a penal code.

This action of the Legislature was an onward step in the march of jurisprudence, and in keeping with the spirit of the age. Mankind had already begun to exhibit those new traits of character in cunning, dishonesty, and villainy, which, in every age, attend progress and development of the productive ability of a people, and especially so in this age. The expansion of paper money and credit had opened a new era, and developed new features of character requiring a different form of punishment, and with greater certainty, which, more than anything else, deters men from the commission of crime. Under the trials of veteran offenders, and the rigid technicalities of the law, with the old punishments of hanging, branding, cropping, whipping, and the pillory, but few men in this day, whatever the enormity of the crime, could be brought to punishment. Public opinion, in its progress, has kept such modes of penal justice in the back ground, as the relics of a barbarous age. It is proper to say that the Hon. B. F. Porter was the author of the measure establishing a State prison and penitentiary in Alabama. Subsequently his efforts in the Legislature went to the extent of proposing to abolish capital punishment altogether, and substituting therefor solitary imprisonment for life.—*Reminiscences of Public Men,* pp. 67–68.

It would be a long time, however, before the state would be willing to appropriate sufficient funds for the prison. Operation of the institution, therefore, went to the highest bidder and in 1846 it was leased to John G. Graham and Company of Coosa County for $500.

To Dr. Peter Bryce, a native of South Carolina, goes the credit for founding the state hospital for the insane. But before 1860 when he opened the doors of the new institution in Tuscaloosa, much preliminary work had to be done. Miss Dorothea L. Dix, pioneer in the humane treatment of the insane, did much to stir up interest in the matter when she visited Montgomery in 1849. Miss Dix, a Bostonian, was on tour of the United States in an effort to get states to establish public-supported insane hospitals. As is shown by the following account, she was welcome in the Alabama capitol.

MEMORIAL OF MISS DIX

The well known and highly respected philanthropist, Miss D. L. Dix, of New York, visited Montgomery during the session, and presented a memorial to each branch of the General Assembly for the establishment of a hospital for the insane. The memorial was referred to a select committee. In the Senate—

Mr. Stewart, from the Select Committee to whom was referred the memorial of Miss D. L. Dix on the subject of the establishment of a hospital for the insane, reported as follows:

That they are very much gratified in having the opportunity, by reason of the valuable information communicated to them by Miss Dix, to present to this body the means of performing a duty so long neglected and so sadly delayed. It is a stranger who, having nobly devoted her life to the succor of the afflicted, now pleads their cause before us, and from no other motives than the pure dictates of Christian charity and benevolence. She admonishes us, and we must admit it as a lamentable fact, that the State of Alabama, one of Heaven's most favored social communities, whose population claim to be recognized as a Christian and civilized people, alive and adequate to all the purposes of self-government, has existed as a sovereign State for thirty years, and yet she has wholly omitted and neglected to perform one of the first of her moral, social, and religious duties—that pleasing duty of charity to the afflicted.

Your Committee believe they would fall far below the standard of the people themselves now, when all the requisite information is laid before them, showing them the means necessary to be adopted, by a person so well skilled from experience to furnish it, with all the details necessary to create, organize, and conduct such an institution with sucess —if they failed to act at once, and to do, in the name of the people of Alabama, this act of charity and Christian duty.

They have there fore directed me to report

A bill to be entitled "An act to establish a State hospital for insane persons in Alabama," and of which they recommend the passage by this body.

GEORGE N. STEWART, Chairman

On motion of Mr. Ware, the bill was laid upon the table, and 133 copies ordered to be printed.

In the House of Representatives—

Mr. R. H. Smith, from the Select Committee to whom was referred the memorial of Miss D. L. Dix, on the subject of a State hospital for the protection and cure of the insane, reported:

That the Committee think no statement or argument can be necessary on the importance of such an institution; no extraordinary appeals are required to elicit our sympathies in behalf of affliction. Increasing legislation throughout the civilized world for the protection and relief of the unfortunate of every class, speaks the tendency of the age too plainly to require comment. The census of 1840 informs us that there were then three hundred and fifty-seven persons within our State idiotic and insane. When it is remembered that the computation was mere incidental duty to ascertaining the population, it will appear that the number must have been much larger, especially as the lunatics from Alabama in the hospitals of other States were probably not included.

We are advised by the touching memorial of Miss Dix, whose philanthropic life has been largely devoted to ascertaining and ameliorating the condition of this unfortunate class, that, according to the lowest estimate, there are not fewer than seven hundred idiots, epileptics and insane within our State. Observation teaches how deplorable and distressing must be the condition of such out of an asylum. All testimony coincides in acknowledging the restorative and ameliorating effects of treatment in one.

The Committee, impressed with the importance of such an institution, have never felt the force of an objection to its present establishment on the ground of expenditure. The necessity for prudence and economy in the present exigencies of the State is sensibly appreciated, but the Committee think the object to be accomplished rises above the objection. A comparison of the property and taxes of Alabama with the property and taxes of some of the most flourishing States of the Union, will leave us little cause to complain that we are heavily burdened.

But your committee do not think the establishment of an asylum will be considered as an ordinary act of appropriation, to be made or withheld on strict rules of economy. They look upon the protection of our afflicted people as the duty of the State, as high, as obligatory, as that of securing to her citizens the enjoyment of liberty and estate.

The Committee instruct me to report the following bill to establish a State hospital for insane persons in Alabama.

Said bill was read and ordered to a second reading.

Miss Dix was present in the Legislature when the bill was taken up and discussed. It would no doubt have passed at the session of 1849, but for the burning of the Capitol. At the next session, however, it was passed, and the institution located at Tuskaloosa, where it has received the fostering care of Drs. Searcy and Guild, of that city, and of Dr. Mabry, of Dallas, who have taken much interest in it.—Garrett, *Reminiscences of Public Men,* pp. 520–22.

This was her second visit to Alabama; she had been in Tuscaloosa some three or four years earlier on a similar mission and had made several acquaintances who respected her as a well-informed person. While in the state:

She visited the Penitentiary of Alabama, and turned things about, pointing out many defects, and suggesting improvements. She furnished the first library to that institution which it ever had . . . . Her efforts were untiring. She seemed to feel that she had an important mission to perform and had no time to lose.—Ibid., p. 522.

Everywhere she went she was regarded with profound respect as the "John Howard of America."

There were other domestic issues, of course, which demanded solutions. The public affairs, however, that received the most news-paper publicity and even official action were not purely local but national or at least regional in their origin. The old South has been accused of withdrawing from the mainstream of national events. Be that as it may, the reading public had ample opportunity to know the issues that faced the nation. Furthermore, generally speaking while public opinion on the various questions can be identified, there was a vigorous difference of views on most of them. Not until the 1850's waned did it become inadvisable to take an opposing position. The exception to this rule was, of course, abolition which few people had openly espoused for several decades.

When South Carolina nullified the tariff in 1832 and threatened secession, Alabama was sympathetic but turned a deaf ear to the overtures for action. John Coffee from north Alabama assured President Andrew Jackson that the state was "sound on the nullifi-cation doctrine" and the state legislature by simple resolution re-fused to give support to South Carolina.

Texas and the Mexican War

Alabamians were vitally interested in the Texas question. The territory was near, many Alabamians had removed there in the 1830's and several had shed their blood for Texas independence. William B. Travis, commander of the small band of Americans that went down at the Alamo, was reared in Conecuh County, Alabama. It was generally accepted that eventually Texas would become a part of the United States but Alabamians believed that no overt action should be taken to annex it until it became a recog-nized, self balanced, and independent state. As a slave state, Ala-bama had an interest in developing that area because it, at least the eastern portion, was geographically suited for the plantation system. Eventually this could be added as a slave state which would help to keep the political balance in the national govern-ment. Following the election of James K. Polk on an expansionist platform and three days before he took office, Congress annexed Texas by joint resolution, March 1, 1845. The stage was set for the war that followed.

In comparison to the conflict of 1861–1865, the Mexican War of 1845–1848 gets little attention, much less than it deserves, judging from the consequences. Whether the war was "unprovoked," "un-necessary," or whatever, the fact remains that by the Treaty of Guadalupe Hidalgo the United States acquired a vast amount of new territory, commonly called the "Mexican Cession," including

California. Alabamians supported this war, responding promptly
to reports of conditions in the Rio Grande valley which required
further American troops. Governor Joshua L. Martin issued a
proclamation on May 10, 1846, which concluded.

> Therefore, it is earnestly recommended to the citizen soldiery of this
> state at once to organize themselves into volunteer companies . . . and
> report themselves as ready in the event of a formal requisition [for
> troops], to engage in the defense of their country . . . .—Macon *Banner*
> (Macon, Clarke County), May 23, 1846.

The governor pledged that this state would defray all expenses that
would be necessary for such volunteer units.

From his position within the state government, William Garrett
was as well informed about the inner workings of the state in this
period as any man. His account of Alabama's participation in the
war is given here.

> Since the last session of the General Assembly a war has been de-
> clared to exist between the United States and the Republic of Mexico,
> and requisitions have been made by the President upon Alabama for
> troops for its prosecution. The first requisition was made in May, 1846,
> for "one regiment of volunteer Infantry or Riflemen," to serve for the
> term of twelve months. This force was supplied in June of the same
> year. In a short time thereafter I was requested by the War Department
> to raise five companies of the same description of troops to be held in
> readiness to enter the service of the United States when called for. This
> request was complied with, and duly reported; the troops, however, have
> not been called for by the Government. . . .
>
> The excitement that prevailed at that time throughout the country
> was such as to induce a large number of volunteer companies to proceed
> to the city of Mobile without my order, where they were received and
> mustered into the service of the United States by the order of General
> Gaines, to serve for the term of six months. One regiment was organized,
> and elected their field officers; and six additional companies were re-
> ceived as a part of a second regiment. I had no farther connection
> with this procedure than to commission the officers. Entertaining fears
> that the course of General Gaines in regard to these troops might not
> meet the sanction of the President, and feeling anxious that our patriotic
> citizens thus engaged should not be disappointed, apprehending too, that
> injurious consequences would follow their discharge, in future efforts
> to raise a volunteer force in this State, I addressed a communication to
> the Secretary of War, urging their acceptance—describing the high
> quality of the troops, and the patriotic motives by which they were gov-
> erned—adverting also the consequences which would probably follow
> their rejection.
>
> Before the reply of the Secretary of War reached me, I received
> a communication from that Department, which rendered it necessary

that I should disband this force, which I proceeded to do without delay, as it was clear from this communication that the troops could not be received. Having proceeded without authority of law, there was no provision for paying those troops, which rendered their condition extremely unpleasant. In order to relieve them as far as possible, I caused the discharge of each man to be so framed as to embody all the facts which might be necessary to secure the benefit of such provision as should thereafter be made by Congress for their compensation, for I did not doubt but that provision would be made. With these, I was enabled to relieve them from embarrassment, and to afford the means of conveyance for each to the neighborhood of his home. My expectations were soon after realized in regard to the action of Congress in the premises. Provision was made for the compensation of these troops, and the whole matter was adjusted to the satisfaction of all concerned, as I have been informed.

Four companies of the regiment mentioned, under the command of Lieutenant-Colonel Raford, had embarked for Point Isabel, before the receipt of the communication referred to. Fearing that aid might become necessary to them, I dispatched Maj. Sanford, of General Smith's staff, to make such provision for them as might be required. I am happy to be able to say, however, that no difficulty was encountered by them requiring the assistance contemplated. These companies were sent back by the Government to Mobile, where they were discharged, and returned home. The important aid afforded me in the management of this difficult and painful subject by Gen. Walter Smith, and his staff, entitle them to my gratitude and thanks.

Early in May last, a further requisition was made by the President on this State for troops to the extent of one company of mounted volunteers, and five companies, or one battalion, of infantry, to serve during the war with Mexico. This call was made known to our citizens by a proclamation dated on the 6th day of May, 1847, in which they were requested to respond to it promptly. In a very short time thereafter, the company of mounted volunteers was furnished. I was not so fortunate in regard to the infantry requested. Having failed to obtain a single company, on the 30th day of September last I published a second proclamation, in which I urged upon our citizens the importance of supplying the force called for by our country. I ascertained in a short time that unless the necessary expenses to be incurred in raising and subsisting the troops were provided for, no effort which I could make would be successful. In consequence of which, and in order to preserve the honor and standing of the State, which I felt to be deeply involved in the success of my efforts, on the 14th of October last, I published an address to the people, in which I undertook to provide for the expenses mentioned, with the funds of the State. The result of this course has been the accomplishment of the great object sought.

The five companies of infantry called for have been tendered me, and accepted, two of which have been mustered into the service of the United States, and the other three are en route to Mobile, the place of rendezvous for muster. The expenditures which have been made, so far as they have been certified to me, have been paid out of the contingent fund, which will be reported to you by the Comptroller. I have endeavored to observe throughout proper economy in the application of this fund to the object mentioned. My instructions to the agents who have disbursed the funds have been to require proper vouchers for the claims certified for payment, which I presume have been strictly observed. I entertain no doubt, from the past course of Congress on like occasions, that, upon proper application, the amount expended, or most of it, will be refunded. And I submit to you the propriety of making such application.

I made the expenditures mentioned, under a full knowledge that my power to do so was of questionable character—and that my course involved great responsibility. I could not have been induced to pursue such a course upon an ordinary occasion. I trust, however, that I shall never see a time when I will hesitate to maintain the honor of the State at any hazard. I have acted in good faith, for the best interest of the State, in view of the emergency presented, and I submit my procedure on this subject, with confidence, to the Representatives of the people.— Garrett, *Reminiscences,* pp. 461–63.

The war over, volunteers flocked home to Mobile from their various Mexican stations, pale, diseased, and dying in the port city at the rate of 35 a week.

The war not only provided battlefield training for officers who would fight on opposite sides in the Civil War, but it also produced a number of political hopefuls for the presidential election of 1848. The Democrats nominated Lewis Cass of Michigan as their standard bearer; the Whigs by-passed Henry Clay and nominated General Zachary Taylor whose political fortunes rose perceptibly after the battle of Buena Vista. The campaign produced the usual speculation and activity over the state. In Camden, for instance,

Political meetings are held night after night, by both Democrats and Taylorites; the Whigs too speak occasionally. Last Friday evening a Taylor meeting was held at the Courthouse; Mr. Childers was the principal speaker. Mr. Langston of the *Advertiser* was silent . . . [he] can't quite go the "whole hog" for Taylor and Fillmore.—*Southern Recorder* (Camden), July 19, 1848.

The new territory acquired by the Treaty of Guadalupe Hidalgo was for the most part south of the Missouri Compromise line and might be expected to be opened to slavery. The proslavery forces were counting heavily on California to reinforce their dwindling strength in Congress. Every student of American history knows that California chose to come into the union as a free state and Congress, in attempting to settle some of the pressing problems facing the nation, passed the Compromise of 1850.

For months California overshadowed all other news in state papers, some reserving the middle of the front page in each issue for the latest news about it. Opinions on it varied, of course, as is shown by a summary found in the *Alabama Journal* (Montgomery) for October 3, 1850.

CALIFORNIA—OPINIONS OF THE DEMOCRATIC PRESS OF ALABAMA

The Greensboro Beacon, an agricultural (formally democratic) paper, in an article on the admission of California, says:

But, whilst we view the whole proceedings as informal, and without a precedent in the history of our government to justify them, and think the Congress should have promptly rejected her application for admission as a State, and organized a territorial government for her— yet, in view of the fact—and a very important one we consider it— that the leading opponents of this measure in the Senate, and some of them among the ablest men of the country, and the truest friends of the South, concede the point that Congress has the power, without any violation of the Constitution, to ratify and confirm what had been done by the people of California—thus yielding up the constitutional question involved—the action of Congress in the premises cannot, of course, now be resisted on the ground of its having been in violation of the constitution—Col. King, in a speech he delivered on the compromise bill, stated distinctly, that he and the Southern Senators generally, who were acting with him in opposition to the admission of California, based their objection to her admission chiefly on the ground of the extent of her boundaries. All other questions, he said, would be waived by himself and his Southern friends, provided the Southern limits of California could be restricted to 36:30. But in this objection, there is no constitutional question involved, but merely one of expediency; for, if California could have been constitutionally admitted into the Union, by merely restricting her boundaries, then it certainly cannot be contended that she has been unconstitutionally admitted. And if there has been no violation of the constitution in her admission, upon what ground can the South resist her admission? None that appears to us at all tenable.

We have seen no Journal which seemed to feel greater joy than the Florence Gazette, one of the leading Democratic Journals of North America. Hear him:

"We are too happy this week to write editorial. All we can say is, that the compromise bills have passed—the Union is saved, and the Rhettites and disunionists are numbered among the things that were. If we were not the big dog among the Sons of Temperance, we should unquestionably take a spree. Friends, rejoice with exceeding great joy."

The Tuscaloosa Observer, another prominent and leading organ of the Democratic party of this State, remarks:

"California is admitted as a State, the Texas bill, the New Mexico and

Utah bills, without the Wilmot proviso, have become laws before this time. While we deeply deplore the admission of California with her enormous limits, and could have wished that other counsels on this matter could have prevailed, we wish it distinctly understood, that we are not among those who would dissolve the Union on that account. The whole matter of admitting California we believe to be internal, to say the least, and was unwisely hastened by executive interference—But other States have been admitted without passing through the preparatory steps, and though we think both Congress and the last administration are highly to blame, the one for improper interference, the other for not reducing her limits, we repeat it, that we are not in favor of a dissolution of the Union for this reason alone.

"We are firm believers in the resolutions of '98 and '99—and guided by them, we do not think this action of Congress so "dangerous" in its tendency as to call upon the South for the "extreme physic" of secession. The remedy of State interposition, according to Mr. Madison, is only to be invoked by the States on 'occasions deeply and essentially affecting the vital principles of their political system.' Acting, then, upon the principles thus laid down, we are not in favor of a separation of the Union because California is admitted. Though its admission may be illegal and unconstitutional, still it is not in our opinion sufficient cause for destroying the Confederacy.

"The Texas bills as we understand it, if acceptable to her, should unhesitatingly be accepted by the Southern people. For the surrender to the United States of a portion of her territory in the North western part of the State—which though large, is yet but a small portion of her vast domain—she is to receive $10,000,000, to be paid to her by the United States.—This is not only highly beneficial to Texas, but will tend greatly to strengthen the South and her institutions. Texas, it will be remembered, has never ceded her public lands to the United States, but reserved them as fund to pay off the debt created when she was a separate government. She, for a surrender of but a small portion of her territory, receives enough to discharge her public debt, and will retain for her own use the bulk of her vast domain. This will put her in a condition which will invite emigration from every part of the country— the extent and fertility of her soil—the cheapness of her lands—the exemption from high taxes, will form inducements to settlers, such as no new State has ever held out, and we may speedily look to see the State divided into several new slave States. In this view, we regard the Texas bill as a decided benefit to the South—and look upon it as the future means of strengthening our institutions.

"Upon the whole, we are glad the troublesome question is settled, and we shall rejoice if it be the means of restoring harmony to a distracted country."

The Mobile Register, also, if we understood it, does not consider the admission of California any just ground for revolutionary measures.

There are other democratic papers in the State which hold the same views, which we have not the space to quote. We allude to this to correct the impression attempted to be produced by some, that ultraism and disunion are denounced only by whigs. The great body of the democrats of the State are Unionists.

When the various measures later included in the Compromise of 1850 were pending in Congress, delegates from Alabama met in Nashville (March 1850) with other Southern representatives to see what could be done to protect their rights. John A. Campbell of Mobile led the delegates favoring compromise. Senator William R. King, always a Union man, strongly supported Henry Clay's compromise.

"The great body" of Democrats in the state may have been unionists who could accept compromise with good grace, but there were many Southern rights people who were not so agreeable. Some of these were disgruntled delegates to the Nashville meeting; others, like William L. Yancey who had not attended it but who felt that the time had come to "call the hand" of the federal government. Many believed secession was the only answer. Two neighboring states, Georgia and Mississippi, held secession conventions over the crisis, but Alabama did not.

There was, however, considerable Southern rights feelings and many meetings, similar to the one in Henry County, were held throughout the state.

SOUTHERN MEETING IN HENRY COUNTY

A mass meeting of the citizens of Henry County was held at Abbeville on the 25th day of July, 1850, in accordance with the arrangements of a previous meeting, held on the 1st inst., to take into consideration the action of the Nashville Convention and to ascertain completely the sentiments of the people of Henry as to the great crisis which threatens the loss of her dearest Constiutional rights and most sacred honor.

A large concourse of citizens assembled, numbering, as estimated by many, at near 3,000 persons. Many persons from the surrounding counties and from Georgia attended, thereby evincing the great interest felt elsewhere in the great struggle for constitutional rights. The assemblage was called to order, and GEORGE W. WILLIAMS, Esq. and Gen. A. J. MCALLISTER were elected to preside over the deliberations of the meeting. Messrs. JAMES PYNES, W. H. WOOD, JOSEPH LAWRENCE and Maj. H. E. CHITTY, were designated as Vice Presidents, and DANIEL McCRIMMON and JAMES A. CLENDINEN, Esqs. appointed Secretaries.

On motion, a Committee of 21 gentlemen, to wit: John W. Harper chairman, A. McAllister, J. A. Clendinen, Sidney A. Smith, E. W. Teague, Joseph Watson, Robert Kennedy, John A. Wood, W. T. Kirkland, T. Y. Smith, J. Bennett, S. B. Watson, T. Battle, J. B. Appling, J. Murphy, L. Bird, J. Wood, W. Stewart, C. Oats, T. Chambers and J. Wilcoxon, were appointed to draft and report resolutions for adoption.

At the meeting of the committee two of the above named gentlemen, viz: Sidney A. Smith and Maj. John B. Appling, were released, by request, from acting on said committee; there were also two others absent. The residue of the committee unanimously reported, through the chairman, J. W. Harper, Esq., the following preamble and resolutions:

PREAMBLE AND RESOLUTIONS:

We the people of Henry county, in Convention assembled pursuant to public notice, in view of the perilous condition of the country, and the threatened destruction of the equality of the Southern States in our Federal Union, do hereby publish and declare— — —

1. That we approve, endorse, and ratify, the resolutions and address adopted by the Southern Convention, recently assembled in the city of Nashville.

2. That the bill now pending before the Senate of the United States, known as the "Clay Compromise Bill", and recommended as an adjustment of the great questions now dividing the Northern and Southern sections of the Union, is wholly unworthy the name of a Compromise bill, and ought to receive the unanimous opposition of the people of the entire Southern States.

3. That the people of the Southern States are entitled, with the people of all the other States, to an equal participation in the territories of California and New Mexico, acquired by the common blood and treasure of the whole country, and that to acquiesce in such legislation by the Congress of the United States as would deprive us of such equality, would be to submit to the dictation of a fanatical and dominant majority, unworthy of our common ancestry and disgraceful to us and to our posterity.

4. That out of love and veneration for that Union which was ordained and established by the patriots of the revolution, and to preserve and perpetuate it to our children as a glorious inheritance of freemen, and forasmuch as the South has acquiesced for a long series of years in such division, we will consent to a division of the common territory of the Union by an extension of the Missouri Compromise Line of 36 degrees 30 minutes, North latitude, to the Pacific Ocean, with a clear recognition of the right of the Southern people to migrate with and enjoy their property of every description south of that line, and that our constitutional right of equality in the public domain, or a division of the same as here indicated, we never should, we never can, we never will surrender.

5. That attempts now being made in New Mexico to rob our sister State of Texas of her soil and jurisdiction east of the Rio Grande are insurrectionary and rebellious on the part of the people of that country, and if sustained by the authority of the Federal Government should meet the firm resistance, not only of Texas, but of all the Southern States which have with Texas a common interest and common destiny.

6. That our Senators in Congress be requested and our Representatives instructed to advocate the ultimatum laid down in the above resolutions.

7. That we cordially repond to the call made by our fellow-citizens of

Eufaula for a District Convention as assemble at Clayton on the first
Monday in September, to fill up our delegation of the Southern Conven-
tion which will re-assemble at Nashville, and that Maj. H. E. Chitty, H.
F. Owens, J. Bennett, S. A. Smith, J. Murphy, C. Oats, A. C. Gordon,
J. B. Appling, John W. Harper, J. A. Clendinen, J. Pynes and Wm. H.
Wood, be appointed as delegates to represent the county of Henry in
said District Convention.

Eloquent, patriotic, and truly "soul stirring" speeches were delivered
by George W. Williams, Esq. of Henry. Col. J. J. Seibels of Montgomery,
Col's. P. T. Sayre, J. G. Shorter and James L. Pugh, Esq. of Eufaula.

On motion the reported resolutions were unanimously adopted by the
meeting.

On motion of Col. A. McAllister it was ordered that a copy of the
proceedings of this meeting be sent the several papers of the district with
a request to publish.

A large and well arranged Barbecue was prepared for the occasion
and all passed off in the most felicitous manner.

A motion to adjourn was made and acceeded to, and the large assemblage, the largest ever before assembled in Henry county, dispersed
peaceably and quietly.

> Daniel McCrimmon,
> James A. Clendinen, Sec'ys.
>
> GEORGE W. WILLIAMS, Prest's.
> ALEX. J. MCALLISTER
>
> —*Alabama Journal* (Montgomery) August 6, 1850.

The unionists were equally active, holding meetings in all parts
of the state. In fact, if one can judge by the press, sentiment was
about equally divided. The meeting in Montgomery is similar to
dozens of others.

THE UNION MEETING ON SATURDAY—There was a glorious turnout
of the friends of the Union at the barbecue on Saturday, and their determination to adhere to it while it could be maintained with honor,
enthusiastic and unanimous. The assemblage was much larger than we
had anticipated owing to the season. The low river, dusty state of the
roads, change in the time of the arrival of the cars, etc. may have kept
back many; still, there was an immense gathering, and the demonstration was as decided as could be wished. The assemblage, during the
meeting, was accurately counted at different times, and the number found
ranging from one thousand to thirteen hundred, including upwards of
two hundred ladies. Owing to the pressure of business at this time,
comparatively few of our citizens were enabled to participate, and the
mass of the meeting was composed of gentlemen from the surrounding
country, the planters and bone and sinew of the land. We observed upon
the stand and elsewhere gentlemen venerable in years, of large experience, eminent in patriotism, and the holders of the largest interest in
slave property of any in the community. Gentlemen of all parties long
separated by party differences, cordially met on the platform of their

country, for the South and the Union, hallowed by the blood and remembrances of their patriot ancestry.

Men of all parties—men of the earliest and deepest interest in the soil, true and long tried in their devotion to the rights of the South, met to express, in one unanimous voice, their deliberate and firm conviction that the issue of secession, now before the public, on account of the late compromise acts of Congress, was in no wise demanded, either on the score of justice, policy, or the honor of the South. The action of the meeting—the resolutions—speak for themselves, in the true spirit— freely declaring the prevailing sentiment of the people in reference to the present circumstances of the country, and providing for the future. While they show a patriotic love for the common Union and the common glory of our country, they evince the firm determination to resist all unconstitutional aggressions and infractions of the existing compromise.

These are not merely resolutions on paper, like many got up for effect by a few politicians, but the voice of the people, and will be sternly adhered to. The support of the Union, the glorious work of our republican fathers and the noblest fabric of republicanism that the world has ever seen, and the constitution, while it remains intact, is their duty as patriots, and will be manfully adhered to in true fealty and devotion. An infraction of its provisions and invasion of their rights as equals in the Union, will be met with like determination by such means as the emergency demands. We mention this that none may misunderstand or misrepresent the objects and action of the meeting. The resolutions, as we before remarked, speak for themselves. They are such as we opine every patriot can unite on. . . .

After dinner, the meeting was again addressed by the old patriotic veteran, James Abercrombie, of Russel, who had arrived by the 2 o'clock cars, and by Mr. Baker, Esq., of Russel, and F. S. Jackson, Esq., of Montgomery, in speeches able, eloquent and adapted to the occasion, and to which we will recur on a future occasion, as the necessity of going to press compels us to cut short our notice. . . .— *Ibid.*, November 19, 1850.

The Compromise became the campaign issue of the congressional election of 1851 in which the name of William L. Yancey was placed in nomination.

THE SECESSION CANDIDATE—We learn that the Secession Convention of this District in session on Monday at Clayton, nominated unanimously W. L. Yancey, Esq., as their candidate for Congress. He is a gallant leader, and we are glad from various reasons which we will briefly express that they have made this nomination. First because it is time for the peace of the South and the union of the South, that the issue, a real issue, a manly, fair issue, an issue which will test public opinion, should be made. If the Compromise acts are of such an oppressive and disastrous nature as to require secession, it is time the South was about it—if not, then this ruinous agitation, which so distracts, weakens and paralyzes the South, should cease. Under Mr. Yancey, the issue will be made fairly, honestly, and with none of the disreputable equivocating and vascillating which has so marked the course of many of those who have so long styled themselves resistance and Southern Rights men. Mr. Y. sees no ground to stand on between secession and the Georgia platform. We must either acquiesce in the Compromise acts, or go to work and break them up by resistance. All other talk is idle; on this no argument is necessary.—Ibid., May 3, 1851.

The editor of the *Alabama Journal* was glad Mr. Yancey was the candidate because the issues would be clear-cut with no "childish humbuggery." He would neither deny his opinions nor shirk his responsibilities and he had the boldness to say what he thought. If the secession movement failed, he said, it would not be for "the want of a gallant and able leader." Yancey declined the nomination. As it proved, his talents were more effective on the state and regional level than in the halls of Congress. More people were willing to compromise in 1850–51 than they were ten years later.

In the early 1850's a remarkable number of voices were raised in behalf of moderation. When interest in the Kansas-Nebraska Act was keen, N. R. King, editor of the Montevallo *Herald* supported it, not because it made either territory slave or free, but because it offered a democratic method of settling the issue. The bill . . .

wishes to leave to the *people* of the respective territories whether slavery shall exist within their limits, ... to take it from Congress to those more immediately interested in it. There cannot be one single constitutional objection to this and its adoption will tend more to the preservation of the Union than anything else.—Montevallo *Herald,* March 3, 1854.

Slavery had agitated Congress for too long, he said, and it could not be too soon removed. It had been the "cause of more strife, sectional feeling, and vituperation" than all the political differences "human flesh had been heir to" and he thought Senator Stephen A. Douglas deserved the warmest thanks of the Southern people for introducing the measure.

But in spite of the seeming optimism and the continuing prosperity in the cotton states, there were festering sores on the body politic. The loss of California upset the balance between the slave and free states in the Senate; the failure of governmental authorities to enforce the fugitive slave act and the concerted efforts of citizens in some Northern states to thwart their efforts to do so convinced Southerners that they were losing in the Compromise; the growing boldness of the abolitionists in imposing their views on the South had pushed Southerners, including Alabamians, into a defensive position; *Uncle Tom's Cabin,* although few copies reached the South, was considered to contain a lie on every page; the Wilmot Proviso had failed to pass in 1846 but the same spirit to limit by Congressional action expansion of slavery into new territory lived on. Leaders like Yancey were gloomy or defiant by turns at what they considered the dwindling influence of the slave states in the affairs of the nation. They seemed to overlook the fact that Alabama's William R. King was elected vice-president of the United States in 1852, that John A. Campbell was a justice of the Supreme Court, that Alabama Congressmen and other Southerners held respected places in national affairs, and that every president had been either a Southerner or a strong sympathizer of the Southern position. Whatever the facts, Alabamians, both politicians and laymen, devoted more attention to the dual questions of slavery and the rights of the states. In an attempt to force the issue, politicians adopted a statement of principles which they later presented to the Democratic nominating convention in Charleston. It was the work of Yancey and contained basically the same ideas that he had formulated in 1848 in reference to the Wilmot Proviso.

PLATFORM OF THE ALABAMA DEMOCRACY
Adopted at Montgomery, January, 1860

1. *Resolved* by the Democracy of the State of Alabama, in Convention assembled, That holding all issues and principles upon which they have heretofore affiliated and acted with the National Democratic party to be inferior in dignity and importance to the great question of slavery, they content themselves with a general re-affirmance of the Cincinnati Platform as to such issues, and also endorse said platform as to slavery, together with the following resolutions:

2. *Resolved further,* That we re-affirm so much of the first resolution of the Platform adopted in Convention by the Democracy of this State, on the 8th of January, 1856, as relates to the subject of slavery, to wit: "The unqualified right of the people of the slaveholding States to the protection of their property in the States, in the Territories, and in the wilderness in which Territorial Governments are as yet unorganized.

3. *Resolved further,* That in order to meet and clear away all obstacles to a full enjoyment of this right in the Territories, we re-affirm the principle of the 9th resolution of the Platform adopted in Convention by the Democracy of this State on the 14th of February, 1848, to wit: "That it is the duty of the General Government, by all proper legislation, to secure an entry into those Territories to all citizens of the United States, together with their property of every description, and that the same should remain protected by the United States while the Territories are under its authority.

4. *Resolved further,* That the Constitution of the United States is a compact between sovereign and co-equal States, united upon the basis of perfect equality of rights and privileges.

5. *Resolved further,* That the Territories of the United States are common property, in which the States have equal rights, and to which the citizens of every State may rightfully emigrate with their slaves or other property, recognized as such in any of the States of the Union, or by the Constitution of the United States.

6. *Resolved further,* That the Congress of the United States has no power to abolish slavery in the Territories, or to prohibit its introduction into any of them.

7. *Resolved further,* That the Territorial Legislatures, created by the legislation of Congress, have no power to abolish slavery, or to prohibit the introduction of the same, or to impair, by unfriendly legislation, the security and full enjoyment of the same within the Territories; and such constitutional power certainly does not belong to the people of the Territories in any capacity, before, in the exercise of a lawful authority, they form a Constitution preparatory to admission as a State into the Union; and their action in the exercise of such lawful authority certainly cannot operate or take effect before their actual admission as a State into the Union.

8. *Resolved further,* That the principles enunciated by Chief Justice Taney, in his opinion in the Dred Scott case, deny to the Territorial Legislature the power to destroy or impair, by any legislation whatever, the right of property in slaves, and maintain it to be the duty of Federal Government, in ALL of its departments, to protect the rights of the owner of such property in the Territories; and the principles so declared are hereby asserted to be the rights of the South, and the South should maintain them.

9. *Resolved further,* That we hold all of the foregoing propositions to contain CARDINAL PRINCIPLES—true in themselves, and just and proper, and necessary for the safety of all that is dear to us, and we do hereby instruct our Delegates to the Charleston Convention to present them for the calm consideration and approval of that body— from whose justice and patriotism we anticipate their adoption.

10. *Resolved further,* That our Delegates to the Charleston Convention are hereby expressly instructed to insist that said Convention shall adopt a platform of principles, recognising distinctly the rights of the South as asserted in the foregoing resolutions; and if the said National Convention shall refuse to adopt, in substance, the propositions embraced in the preceding resolutions, prior to nominating candidates, our Delegates to said Convention are hereby positively instructed to withdraw therefrom.

11. *Resolved further,* That our Delegates to the Charleston Convention shall cast one vote of Alabama as a unit, and a majority of our Delegates shall determine how the vote of this State shall be given.

12. *Resolved further,* That an Executive Committee, to consist of one from each Congressional district, be appointed, whose duty it shall be, in the event that our Delegates withdraw from the Charleston Convention in obedience to the 10th resolution, to call a Convention of the Democracy of Alabama, to meet at an early day to consider what is

best to be done.—In D. L. Dumond, *Southern Editorials on Secession* (New York: Century Co., 1931), pp. 517–18.

When the Charleston Convention refused to adopt the platform, Yancey led the withdrawal of the Alabama delegates, killing any chances the Democrats had for unity and, in effect, assuring the election of the Republican candidate, Abraham Lincoln.

On February 24, 1860, the legislature passed an act making it the duty of Governor A. B. Moore to call a convention if the Republican nominee were elected. The election of delegates to this was held on December 24. With this secession convention the period of the Old South in Alabama ended.

By way of summary, in the forty years between statehood and secession, Alabama had gone through several political stages. Early exhibiting as many Western as Southern characteristics, it was strongly nationalist in point of view, supporting Andrew Jackson in most issues except the matter of the Creek Indian lands in the state. After the Mexican War with its resulting problems, the tendency was to take a states' rights position.

The state had a vigorous two-party system which did not let the monolithic trend go unchallenged. There was a vocal opposition which, although it may have been somewhat muted in the early days of the war, never died out entirely.

Just as the nation was plagued by sectionalism, so was the state. Each party had its greatest strength in a particular part of the state, the Whigs, for example, in the Black Belt and the cotton counties of the Tennessee Valley. The Democrats had their greatest voting strength among the small farmers of the hill counties. This rivalry, usually designated as north-south rivalry, was evident in matters of the location of the capital, internal improvements, basis of voting, many domestic issues, and eventually secession.

Chapter 11

THE WAR—1861–1865

Buckets of ink have been consumed in the search for an accurate and acceptable name for the conflict of 1861–1865. Among the people thus engaged, the most militant group supports the "War Between the States," because its members maintain that the Confederate States of America was an independent government and the war was between two nations. Others prefer "Lincoln's War," while still others think that the "War for Southern Independence" is the most accurate. Most historians and laymen, however, have accepted the term "Civil War" for a number of reasons. Some historians point out that it was a term widely used during the war and that Jefferson Davis himself used it. Others base their preference on Lincoln's plan of Reconstruction which was simple because he believed the revolted states had never been out of the union, an opinion upheld by the Supreme Court in the case of Texas *vs* White (1869). For most people the question of nomenclature is largely academic and they find the "Civil War" an easy and short term.

Regardless of what one prefers to call it, the fact remains that the war was and still is a focal point in American history. For many Alabamians "the war" is still the conflict of 1861–1865. To some the history of the war is the history of the state. In such an attitude there is danger of giving the war a place in our history larger than it deserves. Nevertheless, the war was a traumatic experience for the whole nation and especially for the defeated Confederacy.

This is not the place to explore fully the causes of the war. However, it seems appropriate to point out that most Alabamians who favored secession (and some who did not) felt that the rights of the state within the union were being violated with increasing frequency so that there was no longer any security under the federal Constitution. There were many variations of this theme but all of them indicated that the place of the state in the union as they understood it was being jeopardized. Alabamians read with growing apprehension what they regarded as inflammatory statements made by leading figures in the free states that boded ill for Alabama and the other slave states. They were shocked by events such as John Brown's raid and could not comprehend how anti-slavery people could consider Brown a hero.

It was in this state of mind that the legislature meeting in 1859–60 passed resolutions directing the governor to call a convention if the up-coming presidential election turned out as they feared it would.

> Whereas, anti-slavery agitation persistently continued in the non-slaveholding states of this Union, for more than a third of a century, marked at every stage of its progress by contempt for the obligations of law and the sanctity of compacts, evincing a deadly hostility to the rights and institutions of the Southern people, and a settled purpose to effect their overthrow even by the subversion of the constitution, and at the hazard of violence and bloodshed; and whereas, a sectioned party calling itself Republican . . . has acquired the ascendency in nearly every Northern State, and hopes by success in the approaching Presidential election to seize the Government itself. . . .—*Acts of the Seventh Biennial Session of the General Assembly of Alabama, 1859–60,* (Montgomery: Shorter and Reid, 1860), pp. 685–86.

In this view, a Republican victory would "pervert" the whole machinery of government, and the Alabama assembly felt they were honor bound to provide the means by which they might escape "such peril and dishonor" and "devise new securities" for perpetuating the blessings of liberty to themselves and posterity. Therefore, they passed a resolution saying that, if a Republican president was elected, "it shall be the duty of the Governor to issue a Proclamation, calling upon the qualified voters" to hold an election, not more than forty days after the federal election to choose delegates to a convention "to consider, determine, and do whatever in the opinion of the said convention, the rights, interests, and honor of the State of Alabama requires to be done for their protection."

Lincoln, of course, was elected, but without the help of Alabama. John Breckenridge, candidate for the Southern Democrats, carried the state but John Bell and Stephen A. Douglas each polled a considerable vote.

By mid-October Governor A. B. Moore was certain of a Republican victory and began making inquiries when he should call the convention, forty days after the election or after the official electoral count. It was the opinion of Edward Courtney Bullock of Barbour County (a member of the so-called "Eufaula Regency" which

ardently and consistently supported secession) that the election
for delegates should be held before the end of the year because
the shorter the interval between the popular election and the
election of convention delegates the less time the "resistance men"
would have to organize. Showing that there were others who likewise anticipated the need for action, Bullock reported that

> There are several companies in this section of the State organized
> for months past, and clamoring for arms but unable to obtain them. I
> know how impossible it is . . . to please every body and do not doubt
> that there is some satisfactory reason for the delay . . . .—E. C. Bullock
> to Governor A. B. Moore, October 22, 1860, "A. B. Moore Cor-
> respondence Relating to Secession," *Alabama Historical Quarterly,* vol.
> 23 (Spring 1961), p. 5.

Bullock was correct in his prediction that the "resistance men"
would oppose a hastily called election. Septimus D. Cabiness of
Huntsville was fully convinced that little of a constructive nature
could be done since so much disharmony existed in the state. In
spite of all the talk of the will of the majority, he did not believe
that more people would vote for Breckenridge in the Tennessee
Valley than in Jackson County, and probably Morgan. The people
in north Alabama were well aware that the leaders of the opposition party (the Democrats) were leading their followers into a
belief that "the only remedy is the right of revolution on the part,
not of the state, but the people of the state." Success alone would
exempt them from a "traitor's doom." People in his part of the
state were asking that if the state could secede from the Union,
a county might also secede from the state. This might well happen
if the south Alabama counties carried the state out of the Union.
If the states' rights party got control of the convention, Cabiness
believed it would result "not only in no good, but in the deep and
bitter humiliation of that party" and bring down on them more
federal control. But all the hot heads were not in the secession
party.

> Many of our own party are as mad and almost inconsiderate as those
> of the opposition and I fear that in adopting the course which I have
> suggested . . . will encounter the earnest and perhaps bitter opposition
> of some of your more "precipitate" friends.—S. D. Cabiness to Governor
> A. B. Moore, Huntsville, October 29, 1860, ibid., p. 9.

On December 6, Governor Moore issued the proclamation for
election of delegates to be held on Christmas Eve, December 24,
1860. The vote for these delegates was sectional, south Alabama

(mostly in the Black Belt) electing delegates who favored immediate secession and the hill counties choosing men who became known as "cooperationists." Men in the latter group agreed that the new president had not yet done anything to alienate the South and therefore the state should adopt a "wait and see" policy. Probably the direction of the convention was determined when William M. Brooks of Perry, a Black Belt county, was chosen as president over Robert Jemison of Tuscaloosa by a vote of 54 to 46, north Alabama voting for Jemison and central and south Alabama for Brooks. The vote would change little during the whole convention.

The convention was filled with able men, many of them former Whigs, whose names were associated with public affairs in the state: Thomas H. Watts, John T. Morgan, David P. Lewis, Jeremiah Clemens and, of course, William L. Yancey who may have been the only "agitator" in the body but he was a host in himself. He had stumped the state, urging the choice of immediate secession delegates and he dominated the convention when it met.

EXTRACT FROM THE ADDRESS OF WILLIAM L. YANCEY IN THE SECESSION CONVENTION OF ALABAMA, JANUARY 11, 1861

Some have been disposed to think that this is a movement of the politicians, and not of the people. This is a great error. Who, on a calm review of the past, and reflection upon what is daily occurring, can reasonably suppose that the people of South Carolina, Georgia, Florida, Alabama, Mississippi, and Louisiana who have already elected conventions favorable to dissolution, and the people of Arkansas, Tennessee, North Carolina and Virginia were contemplating an assembling in their several conventions, have been mere puppets in the hands of politicians? Who can for a moment thus deliberately determine that all these people, in these various States, who are so attached to their government, have so little intelligence that they can be thus blindly driven into revolution, without cause, by designing and evil minded men, against the remonstrances of conservative men? No, sir! This is a great popular movement, based upon a widespread, deep-seated conviction that the forms of government have fallen into the hands of a sectional majority, determined to use them for the destruction of the rights of the people of the South. This mighty flood-tide has been flowing from the popular heart for years. You, gentlemen of the minority, have not been able to repress it.

We of the majority have not been able to add a particle to its momentum. We are each and all driven forward upon this irresistible tide. The rod that has smitten the rock from which this flood flows, has not been in Southern hands. The rod has been Northern and sectional aggression and wrong, and that flood-tide has grown stronger and stronger as days and years have passed away, in proportion as the people have lost all hope of a constitutional and satisfactory solution of these vexed questions.—William R. Smith, *History and Debates of the Convention of Alabama* (Montgomery: 1861), pp. 113–14.

Whether Yancey represented only a minority as his opposition charged or the majority as he maintained, he did more than any other individual to take the state out of the Union.

The secession convention met on January 7; on the eleventh the delegates voted 61 to 39 for secession.

The State of Alabama

At a convention of the People of the State of Alabama, begun and holden at Montgomery on the seventh day of January in the year of our Lord, one thousand eight hundred and sixty-one, and continued to the twelfth day of February in the same year.

AN ORDINANCE

To dissolve the Union between the State of Alabama and other states united under the compact styled "The Constitution of the United States."

Whereas, the election of Abraham Lincoln and Hannibal Hamlin to the offices of President and Vice President of the United States of America, by a sectional party avowedly hostile to the domestic institutions and to the peace and security of the people of the State of Alabama, preceded by many and dangerous infractions of the Constitution of the United States by many of the states and people of the northern section, is a political wrong of so insulting and menacing a character as to justify the people of the State of Alabama in the adoption of prompt and decided measures for their future peace and security; therefore,

Be it declared and ordained by the people of the State of Alabama in convention assembled, That the State of Alabama now withdraws and is hereby withdrawn from the Union known as "the United States of America" and henceforth ceases to be one of the said United States and is, and of right ought to be, a Sovereign and Independent State.

Section 2. *Be it further declared and ordained* by the people of the State of Alabama in Convention Assembled, That all the powers over the Territory of said State, and over the people thereof, heretofore delegated to the Government of the United States of America, be and they are hereby withdrawn from said Government, and are hereby resumed and vested in the people of the State of Alabama.

And as it is the desire and purpose of the people of Alabama to meet the slaveholding States of the South, who may approve such purpose, in order to frame a provisional as well as permanent Government upon the principles of the Constitution of the United States,

Be it resolved by the people of Alabama in Convention assembled, That the people of the States of Delaware, [and other slaveholding states which are named] be and are hereby invited to meet the people of the State of Alabama by their delegates, in Convention, on the fourth day of February, A. D. 1861, at the city of Montgomery, in the State of Alabama, for the purpose of consulting with each other as to the most effectual mode of securing concerted and harmonious action in whatever measures may be deemed most desirable for our common peace and security.

And be it further resolved, That the President of this Convention be, and he is hereby, instructed to transmit forthwith a copy of the foregoing preamble, Ordinance, and Resolutions to the Governors of the several States named in said resolutions. WILLIAM M. BROOKS, President of the Convention.—*Ordinances and Constitution of the State of Alabama* (Montgomery 1861), pp. 3–4.

As the 61 to 39 vote indicated there was considerable opposition. Jeremiah Clemens made a minority report in opposition to secession, proposing a meeting of representatives from all the slave-holding states in Nashville to consider the wrongs done them and suggest remedies—within the union if possible. They were asking for specific things.

1. A faithful execution of the Fugitive Slave Law, and a repeal of all State laws calculated to impair its efficiency.
2. A more stringent and explicit provision for the surrender of criminals charged with offences against the laws of one State and escaping into another.
3. A guarantee that slavery shall not be abolished in the District of Columbia, or any other place over which Congress has exclusive jurisdiction.
4. A guarantee that inter-state slave trade shall not be interfered with.
5. Protection to slavery in the Territories, while they are Territories and a guarantee that when they ask for admission as states they shall be admitted into the Union with or without slavery as their constitutions may prescribe.
6. The right of transit through free States with slave property.
7. The foregoing clauses to be irrepealable by amendments to the constitution.—*Journal of the Convention of 1861* (1861), pp. 38–39.

These proposals were voted down with little debate.

An eye-witness to the stirring events in Montgomery, January 10–11, 1861, was Dr. W. H. Mitchell, pastor of the Florence Presbyterian Church and a friend of several leaders in the convention. At one time, he was pastor to William L. Yancey in Wetumpka and knew him intimately. Dr. Mitchell found the capital "in a perfect whirl of excitement," with military companies in uniform on their way to Pensacola to take the fort, and much speculation about what was going on in the secret sessions of the convention. There was "considerable apprehension," he wrote, "lest the North Alabama delegation should secede from the convention." He did not believe it would and, since he was a strong Southern rights man, he sincerely hoped not. On the evening of January 11, he wrote his wife a full account of the events of the day.

> Republic of Alabama!
> January 11, 1861

My dear Wife:

I have spent a most fatiguing day. From ten o'clock until four I have been standing in anxious expectation in the Hall of the Capitol awaiting the birth of our Republic. The excitement was most intense—all crowding around the door of the Hall of Representatives where the Convention was in Secret Session, in anxious expectation of its opening. About two o'clock the door keeper gave orders to several persons to take up the new State flag which was accordingly done and the flag was held in a horizontal position towards the floor. The door was then closed again much to our chagrin; and nearly half an hour elapsed when it was opened amid the most deafening cheers. The scene that followed was perfectly thrilling. The galleries were crowded with ladies and gentlemen. The flag was calmly unfurled and held out so as to display its beauty. Then followed the most deafening cheers and peals of applause, amid which the great Alabamian [Yancey] dressed in homespun arose and said, Mr. President & Gentlemen of the Convention on behalf of the ladies of Montgomery I present this Flag of the State of Alabama: to say it is presented by ladies who are beautiful would be but the least part of their praise! for beauty is the least desirable of woman's perfections. This is presented by the noble-hearted, pure and patriotic women of Montgomery, on whose cheeks the dews of regret (for the departure of sons & brothers who have gone to fight their Country's battles) have not yet dried. On one side of this flag is painted the goddess of liberty with a sword drawn to defend her rights; above her is the motto "Liberty Now & For Ever" and at one side the single star of Alabama. On the other field is a cotton plant to indicate the source of our material wealth, and beneath it is a rattle snake coiled to manifest our determination to defend our rights. It is coiled, because ours is not an aggressive position; and above is the motto "Noli me tangere" ("Touch me not"). The rattle snake is peaceable & harmless until disturbed; but death to the individual who assaults it. Such is our position. We make no war on others, but woe betide the power which essays to crush our liberties. We present this flag then to wave over the Capitol of our new Republic, with its glorious motto—"Liberty Now & For Ever". Then again followed peal after peal of applause.

The flag being accepted, that gentleman from Tuscaloosa known as little Billy Smith got up and made a beautiful speech stating that he envied not the man who had unmingled emotions of exultation at the consumation which had just occurred. That when he saw that flag unfurled his mind recurred to the old Stars and Stripes which had been unfurled on sea & land; and which had led us on to battle and to victory; beneath which even the British Lion cowered. He had tears of regret for the past but he had joyful emotion in view of the present; and much as he regretted the necessity of the separation, now that the Single Star was unfurled he would always be found the advocate of Alabama's rights and "liberty now & for Ever. . . ."

Bells were ringing—cannons firing a steam boat whistling. Take it altogether it was one of the most stirring-enthusiastic & thrilling scenes I ever witnessed. It is going dark and I must close. I am going to tea to Dr. Petrie's. Goodbye. May the Lord bless you and the children.

Ever yr devotedly attentive husband
W. H. MITCHELL

Before adjourning the convention, President Brooks said

If any of you hold to such a fatal opinion [that Alabama would again link herself with the Northern states], let me intreat you, as you value the blessings of equality and freedom, dismiss it at once. There is not, cannot be, any security or peace for us in a reconstructed government of old material . . . . The people of Alabama are now independent; sink or swim, live or die, they will continue to be free, sovereign, and independent . . . .—Quoted in Joseph Hodgson, *The Cradle of the Confederacy* (Mobile: Register Printing Office, 1876), p. 527.

Alabama left the United States on January 11, 1861 and joined the Confederate States on March 13 when it ratified the new constitution. In these two intervening months, what was taking place? The newspapers furnish the best answer to the question. Editors and citizens writing to the papers make frequent use of the terms "republic" and "free state," yet there is little evidence that the average citizen thought the political situation had changed much. To be sure, the secession convention continued to meet, severing the remaining ties with the federal government and the non-slave holding states. The legislature met in January and passed, or at least introduced, bills on a great many routine matters—for the relief of certain individuals, for prohibiting the sale of intoxicants within a given distance from specified towns, for granting a small number of divorces and for many other things. It set railroad rates, legalized the suspension of certain banks and discussed expelling all free Negroes from the state. In this period the papers carried accounts of several brutal murders, repeated cases of arson, and at least one near-lynching of an abolitionist in Hayneville. The University cadets presented a "fine and soldierly appearance" when they were reviewed by Governor Watts in Montgomery. This was a campaign year and already candidates were beginning to announce. If they appeared less confident than at earlier dates, this is easily attributed to the unsettled political situation.

Just to leave the union was not enough; the state must be put in readiness for possible trouble.

AN ORDINANCE

To provide for the Military Defense of the State of Alabama.

Sec. 1. *Be it ordained* by the people of Alabama in convention assembled, That the Governor be and is hereby authorized and empowered, in the event of a declaration of war against the State of Alabama, or of an actual invasion of its territory, or of imminent danger of such invasion, to cause to be enlisted, and to call into actual service a number of troops, not exceeding one thousand non-commissioned officers, musicians and privates, to be enlisted for a term of three years, unless sooner discharged. . . .

Sec. 5. *Be it further ordained,* That whenever the public shall demand it from any of the aforementioned causes, in addition to the aforesaid number of troops, the Governor shall be . . . empowered to accept the services of any number of volunteers who shall associate and offer themselves for the service, either as artillery, cavalry or infantry and the volunteers so accepted shall have power in the first instance to elect their own company officers. . . .—Ibid., p. 9.

The convention also passed an ordinance that would clarify the position of civil laws.

AN ORDINANCE

To preserve the Laws of Alabama, and such Offices, Rights, and Remedies as are consistent with the Ordinance of Secession and with other ordinances adopted by this Convention.

Sec. 1. *Be it ordained* by the people of Alabama in Convention assembled, That no law enacted by the authority of the State of Alabama in force on the eleventh day of January A. D. 1861, and consistent with the Constitution of this state, and not inconsistent with the ordinances of this Convention, is affected by the ordinance known as the Ordinance of Secession, adopted on said day and entitled "an Ordinance to dissolve the union. . . ."

Sec. 2. No office, civil or military, created by this State, or under authority of its laws, in force on the eleventh of January, 1861, and no officer lawfully exercising the powers or duties of such office, is affected by said Ordinance of Secession, except the offices of the members of the House of Representatives and of the Senators of the Congress of the United States of America, and these are abrogated.

Sec. 3. No offence against the laws of this State, committed before or since the adoption of the said Ordinance of Secession is affected by said ordinance; and no offender against said law is relieved or discharged from the consequences of such offences by said ordinance. . . .

Sec. 6. No right, title, franchise, easement, license, or privilege given, granted, or conferred to, or upon, any person or body corporate, under and by authority of the laws of this State . . . is affected by the said ordinance. . . .—Ibid., pp. 28–29.

Secession brought forth various emotions and revealed hidden talent. Myra Mirtle, a native of Claiborne, was moved to write a long narrative poem to be sung to the tune of the *Star Spangled Banner*. Taking each seceding state in turn, the author wrote this stanza about Alabama:

> Another star rises—a sister in light—
> She rises and night her rays is dispelled.
> Oh, tis Alabama, so steady and bright,
> And ere her an omen of tyranny quelled!
> The star of the state where cotton fields glow
> In the light of the sun, like a mantle of snow,
> The Cotton Plant treasure! Oh, long may it wave
> O'er the land of the free and the home of the brave.
>   —*Southern Messenger* (Greenville), February 20, 1861.

At the suggestion of South Carolina and on the invitation of Alabama, the Confederate Convention met in Montgomery on February 4 to form a new government. It performed three important functions: it drew up and adopted a constitution remarkably like the federal Constitution but clarifying the ambiguous passages about such matters as slavery, internal improvements, and tariff; acting as an electoral body, it chose Jefferson Davis of Mississippi, an acknowledged moderate, and Alexander H. Stephens of Georgia, a unionist, as president and vice-president of the Confederate States of America; having done these things, it turned itself into a provisional congress to function until an election could be held. The delegates also chose Montgomery as the temporary capital only until the government moved to Richmond. There were many protests about this last decision, mostly because the Virginia capitol was only about one hundred miles from Washington and therefore more exposed to the dangers of invasion than Montgomery would have been.

Jefferson Davis was at Brierfield, his Mississippi plantation, when the delegation from Montgomery went to notify him of his election. A week later, on February 16, he arrived in the new capital. Newsmen from many parts of the nation were present to witness his inaugural. The Charleston *Mercury,* February 19, 1861, carried the following account of Davis' arrival.

MONTGOMERY, February 16.—President Davis' trip from Jackson, Mississippi, to Montgomery, was one continuous ovation. He made no less than twenty-five speeches upon the route, returning thanks for complimentary greetings from crowds of ladies and gentlemen. There were military demonstrations, salutes of cannon, &c., at the various depots.

The Committee of Reception, appointed by the Southern Congress, and also the Committee appointed by the Montgomery authorities, met President Davis about 80 miles from the city and formally welcomed him. Two fine companies from Columbus, Ga., formed an escort to Opelika. The *cortege* reached Montgomery Friday night at ten o'clock. Salvos of artillery greeted his approach, and a very large crowd assembled at the depot, hailing his appearance with tremendous cheering. President Davis, returning thanks, said that he was proud to receive the congratulations and hospitality of the people of Alabama. He briefly reviewed the present position of the South. The time for compromise, he said, had passed, and our only hope was in a determined maintenance of our position, and to make all who oppose us smell Southern powder and feel Southern steel. If coercion should be persisted in, he had no doubt as to the result. We would maintain our right to self-government at all hazards. We ask nothing, want nothing, and will have no complications. If other States should desire to join our Confederation, they can freely come on our terms. Our separation from the old Union is complete. NO COMPROMISE; NO RECONSTRUCTION CAN BE NOW ENTERTAINED. (Tremendous applause.)

A large crowd awaited the President's arrival at the Exchange Hotel. The ladies were equally enthusiastic with the gentlemen. At a quarter before eleven, in response to enthusiastic calls, he appeared on the balcony and said:

Fellow Citizens and Brethren of the Confederate States of America— for now we are brethren, not in name, merely, but in fact—men of one flesh, one bone, one interest, one purpose, and of identity of domestic institutions. We have henceforth, I trust, a prospect of living together in peace, with our institutions a subject of protection and not of defamation. It may be that our career will be ushered in, in the midst of storms —it may be that as this morning opened with clouds, mist and rain, we shall have to encounter inconveniences at the beginning; but as the sun rose, lifted the mist, dispersed the clouds, and left a pure sunlight, Heaven so will prosper the Southern Confederacy, and carry us safe from sea to the safe harbor of constitutional liberty. (Applause) Thus we shall have nothing to fear at home, because at home we shall have homogeneity. We have nothing to fear abroad, because, if war should come—if we must again baptise in blood the principles for which our fathers bled in the Revolution, we shall show that we are not degenerate sons, but will redeem the pledges they gave to preserve the sacred rights transmitted us, and show that Southern valor still shines as brightly as in the days of '76—in 1812, and in every other conflict.

I was informed by friends that your kindness only required that I should appear before you, fatigued, as I am, by travel—hoarse and unable to speak at length—and I came out merely to assure you of my gratitude for these manifestations of good will. I come with diffidence and distrust to discharge the great duties devolved on me by the kindness and confidence of the Congress of the Confederate States. I thank you, friends, for the kind manifestations of favor and approbation you exhibit on this occasion. Throughout my entire progress to this city

I have received the same flattering demonstrations of generous support. I did not regard them as personal to myself, but tendered to me as an humble representative of the principles and policy of the Confederate States. I will devote to the duties of the high office to which I have been called all I have of heart, of head and of hand.

If, in the progress of events, it shall become necessary, and my services shall be needed in another position—if, to be plain, necessity shall require that I shall again enter the ranks as a soldier, I hope you will welcome me there.

Now, friends, again thanking you for this manifestation of your approbation, allow me to bid you good night.—Quoted in Dunbar Rowland, *Jefferson Davis, Constitutionalist* (Jackson, Mississippi: State Department of Archives and History, 1923), pp. 47–48.

Inauguration of President Davis

Jefferson Davis became the president of the Confederate States of America at the Alabama capital on February 18, 1861. The following account of the inauguration as one man saw it, with comments on the informal nature of the new government and on Montgomery, were written by Thomas C. DeLeon who resigned his clerkship in Washington at the break with the union and went to Montgomery.

All Montgomery had flocked to Capitol Hill in holiday attire; bells rang and cannon boomed, and the throng—including all members of the government—stood bareheaded as the fair Virginian threw that flag to the breeze. Then a poet-priest—who later added the sword to the quill—spoke a solemn benediction on the people, their flag and their cause; and a shout went up from every throat that told they meant to honor and strive for it; if need be, to die for it. What was the meaning of the pact, then and there made, had been told by a hundred battlefields, from Texas to Gettysburg, from Santa Rosa to Belmont, ere the star of the South set forever, and her remnant of warriors sadly draped that "conquered banner . . . ."

Little ceremony, or form, hedged the incubating government; and perfect simplicity marked every detail about Mr. Davis. His office, for the moment, was one of the parlors of the hotel. Members of the Cabinet and high officials came in and out without ceremony, to ask questions and receive very brief replies; or for whispered consultation with the President's private secretary, whose desk was in the same room. Casual visitors were simply announced by an usher, and were received whenever business did not prevent. Mr. Davis' manner was unvarying in its quiet and courtesy, drawing out all that one had to tell, and indicating by brief answer, or criticism, that he had extracted the pith from it. At that moment he was the very idol of the people; the grand embodiment to them of their grand cause; and they gave him their hands unquestioning, to applaud any move soever he might make. And equally unthinking as this popular manifestation of early hero-worship, was the clamor that

later floated into Richmond on every wind, blaming the government—
and especially its head—for every untoward detail of the facile descent
to destruction.—Thomas C. DeLeon, *Four Years in Rebel Capitols*
(Mobile: The Gossip Printing Co., 1890), pp. 23, 25–26.

There were other witnesses to these stirring events besides reporters like DeLeon. Mrs. Jefferson F. Jackson, a native of Boston
but in 1861 a resident of Montgomery, wrote her sister Mary about
her part in the ceremonies.

> Yesterday was the greatest day in the annals of Montgomery. . . .
> Yesterday was bright and pleasant and a very large crowd of people
> assembled at the Capitol and on the streets to see the procession and
> attend the inaugural exercises . . . .
> I was one of the mass of people in front of the Portico. The balconies
> and every front window were filled with ladies who went *early* . . . .
> My share of the interesting occasion was to furnish a most beautiful
> wreath of japonicas and hyacinths and small spring magnolias—also
> a large bunch of flowers for the vice president . . . .—"A Contemporary
> Account of the Inauguration of Jefferson Davis," February 19, 1861,
> edited by Virginia K. Jones, *Alabama Historical Quarterly,* vol. 23,
> pp. 273–74.

Montgomery continued to be the center of the Confederacy for
the following two months. On May 21 the capital was officially
moved to Richmond but the president and many of the department
heads had already gone. The Alabama city lost not only population
but the excitement of official life and consequently settled into its
role as capital of a state somewhat removed from the hub of activity. Nevertheless, much important work went on there.

Joining the Army

When war came (and even before, in some instances) companies
of volunteers were formed in all parts of the state. The men elected
their own officers, more on their popularity than military skill,
and went off to war together, often staying in the same unit the
whole time. The troops departed in high spirits, expecting to end
the war shortly—if indeed it was not over before they reached a
battlefield. Their leave-taking was lighthearted, making it appear
much like an excursion. Kate Cumming, who became the most
famous Confederate nurse, was in her home city of Mobile when
she saw a company leaving by train for Virginia. She observed:

> At that time I thought, like many others, that they were going more
> on a frolic than anything else, as we could not think it possible that
> the north really meant to try and subjugate us . . . .—Kate Cumming,

The Journal of a Confederate Nurse, edited by Richard B. Harwell
(Baton Rouge: Louisiana State University Press, 1959), p. 25.

Most outfits were named, like the North Sumter Rifles to which
young William Fulton belonged, for the place the men lived, or for
the leader, like Cobb's Brigade. Some units had high-sounding
names like the Emerald Guards and Mobile Humphries Dragoons.
The story of Fulton's departure is typical of hundreds of others
in the early days of the war.

I reached home [from college] and found the war spirit aflame on
every hand. Nothing else [was] thought of or talked about. People
seemed desperate and many were anxious for it to commence, seeming
to prefer the actual thing to the suspense that hung over the hearts of
all. In the spring of 1861 a company was organized at Gainesville,
Alabama, composed of young men and boys from Warsaw, Alabama,
and the vicinity of Gainesville. It was named "North Sumter Rifles."
Sob Vandegraaf was elected captain, Jas. Winston, 1st, Husted, 2nd and
Wade Ritter, 3rd, lieutenants. The company procured tents and went
into camp in an old field a few miles northwest of Gainesville. Two
cadets from the University at Tuscaloosa came over and took charge
to perfect us in manual and drill. . . . We were here for some two
months probably, and the girls of the surrounding country . . . would
visit us daily. These were the happy days of our camp life. Free from
every care with only a few drill hours daily to bother us, with the pretty
girls calling on us everyday, of course we enjoyed it. After becoming
quite efficient in our drill work, and war having been declared by the
firing on Fort Sumter in S. C., April 12, 1861, orders were received
from Richmond, Va., . . . to take the train . . . for Manassas. The long
expected had happened, but it produced great excitement among us and
our friends. It was exactly what we wanted and expected and many of
us . . . were afraid it would end before we got there. Yet the idea of
separation from dear and loved ones cast a damper over our exuberant
spirits. . . . The company was paraded in full equipment in front of
Col. McMahon's big hotel, "The American," in Gainesville, each member armed with guns picked up at home, mostly old squirrel guns. Our
banner was a beautiful silk one, with a strutting gamecock worked in
the center, the gift of Miss Lucy Reavis, the talented daughter of Judge
Reavis. This was a memorable scene. About ninety young men, the pick
and flower of the county, standing there in line with merry laughter
and jest on their lips, all light-hearted, about to bid adieu to friends,
relatives, and boyhood associations and all that rendered life happy. . . .
Our captain called us to attention and after putting us through the
manual for the benefit . . . of the spectators, and going through a certain
amount of ceremony, the command to "break ranks" was given and
everyone was at liberty to go at will until recalled. We understood it
to mean that we were to speak the farewell word to loved ones. . . .
Soon the company was called to "attention," the line reformed, and

we started on our first march from Gainesville, Alabama, to Scooba, Mississippi, where we were to take the M. & O. train for Virginia. As we started through the street from the American hotel, Private Hill was blowing his fife at the head of the column to the tune, "The Girl I Left Behind Me," while Ned Fargo and Pat Murphy kept time with their drums. Our hearts were light that day and beat in sympathy with the tune. . . . All along the route jests and jibes were the order of the day, and it was more like going to a picnic than to war.—William Frierson Fulton, *Family Record and War Reminiscences* (no place, no date), vol. 2, pp. 39–41.

Many outfits of these volunteers, finding no action, returned home as the Greenville Guards did.

This noble band of patriot soldiers returned to their homes on Saturday last, and were received with warm and hearty greetings from their numerous friends. Though they have returned and have resumed the pursuit of their daily business avocations, they have not forgotten and will not forget, their duty to their beloved country, but will hold themselves in readiness to march to the field of action whenever the tocsin of war shall be sounded by Lincoln and his fanatic horde.—*Southern Messenger* (Greenville), February 20, 1861.

War Comes to Alabama

Although on January 4 Governor Moore had ordered state troops to seize Forts Morgan and Gaines at the mouth of Mobile Bay and the federal arsenal at Mt. Vernon, the state had no early military activity on her own soil. This does not mean that her forces were idle. There were Alabama troops at the Battle of Bull Run and nearly every major battle thereafter. At Bull Run the Fifth Alabama under Col. J. J. Seibels of Montgomery were part of General Beauregard's army. The Fourth Alabama under General Bee lost about a third of its 750 men in this battle. Dr. Josiah Nott, the founder of the medical college in Mobile, was in the medical corps at Bull Run and he was to serve for four years on the medical staff of General Braxton Bragg. At Shiloh, on the Mississippi-Tennessee border, was fought the first great battle of the west, April 6 to April 11, 1862. Alabama troops were there, some seven regiments of them, over 6,000 men both infantry and cavalry. Thousands of them were in Virginia, Kentucky and Georgia, wherever the need was.

War came to the northern part of the state. Following the fall of Forts Donelson and Henry (on the Tennessee and Cumberland Rivers) Brigadier-General O. M. Mitchell marched into Huntsville, occupying it on April 11, 1862. At the same time Athens was burned by Colonel John Basil Turchin, a Russian-born soldier of fortune. These were the first land forces in Alabama but gunboats had gone up the Tennessee River as far as Florence during February. As long as the war lasted, the Tennessee Valley was the scene of frequent skirmishes, raids, and passing of troops.

General Mitchell reported his activities on the day he entered Huntsville.

> Sir: After a forced march of incredible difficulty, leaving Fayetteville yesterday at 12 M., my advanced guard, consisting of Turchin's brigade, Kennett's cavalry, and Simonson's battery, entered Huntsville this morning at 6 o'clock.
>
> The city was taken completely by surprise, no one having considered the march practicable at this time. We have captured about 200 prisoners, 15 locomotives, a large amount of passenger, box and platform cars, the telegraphic apparatus and offices, and two Southern mails. We have at length succeeded in cutting the great artery of railway intercommunication between the Southern states.—*Official Records of the War of Rebellion* (Washington: U. S. Printing Office, 1880–1898), 1st Series, vol. 10, pp. 641–42.

Confederate Major-General E. Kirby Smith made his official report on the event.

> Knoxville, Tenn., April 13, 1862
>
> MAJOR: On the 11th General Mitchel, with a Federal force, well ascertained to be about 8,000, with four batteries, entered Huntsville, capturing twenty-one engines and three trains of cars. They came from Murfreesborough via Shelbyville and Fayetteville, and were followed by two additional regiments, making a force between 8,000 and 10,000 strong. Pushing their trains on beyond Stevenson, they destroyed the bridge over Widdem's Creek, 4 miles west of Bridgeport, and secured their flank against any movement by rail from Chattanooga. I have two regiments at Bridgeport and two at Chattanooga, under the command of General Leadbetter; one of the latter, the Forty-third Georgia, is awaiting the arrival of arms from Richmond.
>
> General Maxey, with three regiments and a battalion, passed through Huntsville the day previous to its occupation by the enemy. The three armed regiments between Bridgeport and Chattanooga were to have completed the re-enforcements intended for General Beauregard. My own command not being large enough for offensive movements, and feeling that on the fate of the army at Corinth hung the fate of East Tennessee, I felt justified in ordering this force to General Beauregard even before being called upon by him for re-enforcements.
>
> General Beauregard telegraphs that six regiments from Pemberton's command are en route for Chattanooga. He suggests a movement from that point, taking the enemy in reverse at Huntsville. I could add four regiments, making a force of between 5,000 and 6,000 effective men, but the destruction of the road west from Bridgeport renders the opera-

tion of artillery on that line now impracticable. A demonstration of 5,000 infantry toward Huntsville might alarm Mitchel, but no decisive results could be reasonably anticipated. The advance of a force from Kingston by Sparta or Nashville is the strategic move, offering the greatest results and the most practicable in operation. I so telegraphed General Beauregard, notifying him of the destruction of the bridges on the Memphis road, and giving him an opportunity to countermand the order to the South Carolina regiments and to direct them to reinforce him by (the) Montgomery and the Mobile and Ohio road.

The Eufaula Artillery, which was ordered here with its battery, is still without guns. The pieces, with ammunition, should be sent from Richmond as soon as practicable.—Ibid., p. 641.

Mrs. W. D. Chadick kept a diary of the war in Huntsville from April 11, 1862, until April 1865. She was the wife of the Reverend W. D. Chadick, a Cumberland Presbyterian minister who became known as the fighting parson. He was away from home for long periods of time and one of the purposes of the diary was to keep a record for him.

A DIARY BY MRS. W. D. CHADICK

(April 11, 1862.) On the morning of April 11, General Mitchell's division (Federalists) took possession of Huntsville. There was no opposition, there being only a few wounded and sick Confederate soldiers in the town.

They entered at daybreak, first taking possession of the railroad and some 15 engines. The southern train was just coming in, having on board 159 Confederate soldiers, some wounded, going to their homes, and others, who had been on furlough, rejoining their regiments.

The train endeavored to make its escape, but was fired into by two cannons. One of the firemen was seriously wounded. All aboard were taken prisoners. The well soldiers were confined in the depot house, and the wounded remained in the cars.

The telegraph office and postoffice were next seized. Many wounded soldiers quartered in town and many prominent citizens and refugees made their escape during the day. Among them was the secretary of war, Pope Walker, the Hon. John Bell and others. There was a great deal of excitement and consternation among the citizens, as it had not been generally believed that the enemy would come here.

About 7 o'clock, in company with Mrs. Bradford, Mrs. Mayhew, Mrs. Francis, Mrs. Powers, Mrs. Tony and other ladies from the college, we waited on Gen. Mitchell to ask permission to visit our wounded soldiers he had taken on the cars. We were ushered into his august presence in the parlor of the hotel at the depot. He received us politely, remarking that he was always glad to see the ladies, provided they "did not rail at him as they had done at Fayetteville."

The object of the visit then was stated to him by Mrs. Bradford, when, instead of a direct reply, he went on to speak of the very great surprise he had given us that morning, and expressing great surprise on his part that we had no reception prepared for him! I had it in my heart to let him know "that we had one grand reception prepared for him at Corinth," but considering that "discretion was the better part of valor," kept silent.

He went on to enumerate the towns he had taken in his route, saying that he did not know how much farther south he should go. He expressed surprise that we had so few provisions here (all our government stores had been removed), and said that we should be compelled to call on the North for help. He also said he blushed to speak of some Southern ladies who had taunted his soldiers with our late victory at Corinth, all of which was very magnanimous on the part of a great general going forth "conquering and to conquer," especially where he had no armed force to oppose him.

He, however, gave us permission to visit our wounded and do what we could for them. We found them still on the cars in a very uncomfortable position, and many of them suffering dreadfully, and having no nourishment in two days!

Among them we found three Confederate officers—Major McDonald and Capts. Means and Byrd, who by their gentlemanly bearing, refinement and severe wounds, received in the Battle of Corinth, enlisted our deepest sympathies and interest. We also visited the well prisoners in the depot house and found them suffering for something to eat.

In the evening, we returned to them with milk, wine, soups and a great quantity of provisions—enough for all. Some of the Federal officers informed us that their wagon trains would not be in for two days (so forced had been their march), and that they would have to tax the citizens for food for their own men.

Through Dr. Thumesd, we obtained permission to move our wounded to the hospitals. Mrs. Harris and myself, accompanied by Mr. Brown (Methodist minister), were deputized to set the house and beds in order, while Mrs. Bradford and some others remained behind to superintend their removal. Everything was soon arranged and, before night, they were all on comfortable beds, and their wounds dressed. They declared that they were the sweetest beds they ever lay down upon—poor fellows! One of them was wounded in nine places and was perfectly helpless. Miss Clapham and Miss Danils from the college went around and washed all their faces and hands which they declared was another luxury.

(Saturday, April 12.) Truly our town is full of the enemy. There is a sentinel at every corner. Everybody keeps the front door locked, and I make it a point to answer the bell myself, not permitting children or servants to open it.

They have been searching the houses today for arms. We have not been molested. Servants are giving information of all the arms and soldiers who have been concealed.

Visited the wounded prisoners. One poor fellow had his hand amputated today. His name is Gregory. Promised him a shirt tomorrow. Found three or four others suffering immensely from their wounds, the Federal surgeons having neglected to dress them. Went for Dr. Sheffey to attend to them. Gave the major a bouquet and promised him some butter.

(April 13.) Visited the well prisoners at the depot. Our visit seemed to delight and cheer them very much. Many of them asked us to write their wives and friends, and gave some of their valuables into our keeping. As yet, they have no food, only what we carry them. The wounded officers were removed this evening to the college. One of the prisoners at the depot (Duncan of Louisiana) gave me a little tea bell as a keepsake.

Had a conversation with a Federal officer, Capt. Doughty, in the course of which he remarked that the "Western men who form Mitchell's division are fighting for the right of secession, and whenever we become convinced that the slavery question is involved, we shall lay down our arms and go home."

(April 14.) Some arrests have been made today of prominent Secessionists. Among those were Matt Steele, but they have been released.

Visited the hospital, and was mortified to find that many of our wounded men had taken the oath and were going home. Expressed our mortification and disappointment in the presence of the Federals, and exhorted the others never to do likewise. Those who had not taken the oath said they would die first. The prisoners at the depot refused nearly to a man thus to disgrace themselves, and the ladies openly commended them for it. Some of them have made their escape. . . .—
Alabama Historical Quarterly, vol. 10, pp. 199–202, 226–27; 286–88.

Moore Diary of Tuscumbia

J. B. Moore, a lawyer in Tuscumbia, kept a diary of events in his Colbert County home at the same time Mrs. Chadick was keeping hers in Huntsville. It is as interesting in many respects and, in contrast to the latter which ends with Lee's surrender, extends into the Reconstruction era. It is also more critical of his fellow north Alabama residents, especially those erstwhile secessionists who were nowhere to be found when the enemy approached. He says emphatically that he was no Union man, only a moderate.

Saturday, February 22, 1862
Went to town, could hear no news. Our government has taken possession of telegraph lines. This day our permanent government goes into operation and we hear that the French government has acknowledged our independence, though I do not believe it. If so, upon the heels of so many reverses, it would again restore confidence. Some are now doubting our ability to contend with the north—are refusing confederate money, which of itself implies a doubt of our ultimate success. There is without doubt though a good deal of recovery from the panic caused by the fall of Donaldson. Several are trying to raise companies for the war—major Robertson has suspended the La Grange military school and proposes to raise a regiment—Our Government has called for 12

regiments—Miss. for 10, Tenn. and Ark. have called out the whole militia, the Governors proposing to take the field. There breathes a determination throughout the preparations of the South to achieve our independence or die. Already they are ringing the vows of Patrick Henry "It is too late to retire from the contest if we would; there is no retreat but in chains and slavery." Already troops are being thrown into Tenn. to support Johnson in a pitch battle near Nashville. But there is one thing cannot but strike the close observers of passing events. When Alabama seceded, this county voted 1100 majority against it—the secessionists polled about 350. They were at that time rempant-for a fight wanted the contest to come. Swore that 1 Southern man could whip 5 Northern ones—now where are they? For this county, I can speak. Some of them are packing up preparing to run off and leave the poor and moderate men to do the fighting. W. L. B. Cooper and Norman fixing to run off instead of shouldering their gun and facing like men the contest they invited; they are fixing to shirk the issue, instead by their example attempting to restore confidence; they are adding to the panic. The same I learn is true of John E. Morris and R. W. Walker of Lauderdale. Now do they expect the poor people are fools, not to draw their own conclusion from their action. Do they suppose the poor men of these counties have forgotten their promises that there will be "no war" at the time they were hastening the state into the attitude of rebellion. That when the contest came if in the course of events, it did arise (which they affirmed it would not) they would be the first to shoulder their guns and fight. My opinion is they are about played out. Let them go.

The worst of it is they leave the rest of us in a deadly contest in persuing which we had not the slightest agency—and at a time when retreat and submission leads us seems to me to certain destruction. If it is true, the north, when they possess themselves of Southern soil, they offer the alternatives to the citizens of an oath to support Lincoln's Govn't or confiscation of property. About a time when another government is in full operation over us. Then well may it be said submission is destruction. Probably this is only one step and the first one in the list of Southern degradation. What is the 2nd step—Why they swear you first to support Lincoln's Govn't against all of its enemies. Don't you see it at once places you in antagonistic relation to the Southern Confederacy. The next request will be to take up arms and help drive the Southern army off of Southern soil. It seems to me there would be no escape from it. Would not the legitimate results claiming protection of Lincoln's government bind in an indissoluble oath to support it, even if it dragged us to the battle field, against Southern friends and Southern armies?

April 19, 1862

The operation of secession in this valley . . . presents the most curious illustration of the versatility of the human mind—the weakness of some southern characters, that ever was seen, heard or read of. Our secession friends here first told us there would be no war. They found at least that there was no truth in this prediction. They then told us, *when the*

time came, each one of them would shoulder his *shotgun* and meet the invaders and fight until death for every inch of the soil of Alabama. Some of them cursed the slow approach of the Northern soldiers and so full of fight were some of them that they went in squads, some to Richmond, some to Nashville, some to Columbus, Ky., to go into the Army for the fight as they said, but soon they were seen returning with the excuse they could not get in. Now anyone would have supposed that when an enemy approached this valley, an army of men, standing as a wall, bristling with *shot guns,* old flint rock rifles and every conceivable weapon would have been found to resist the approach. Now what spectacle presents itself today. When the northern soldiers landed at Decatur, every one — — warriors took to their heels, and have concealed themselves wherever their friends let them and any can't find them. Nine-tenths of the men have left, overseers of Negroes and sometimes leaving the helpless, defenceless families of females without protection.
April 30, 1862
. . . Heard some of the raids of the Federals and depredations upon private property. It must be that the worst part of the army were sent down in this valley. They took from widow ladies silver plates and watches, meal, broke open all houses that were closed and robbed them of their contents. Some large planters, they left without meat entirely. At Dr. Houston's they even destroyed his medicine and carried away his library and would have destroyed his house and furniture but for the interposition of the negroes on the place (the Dr. and family were absent. . . .).

Their visit here has done two things, it dispelled the illusion some were laboring under that they would respect private property, and taught us what we may expect at their hands, in the event of our subjugation. They talk freely of seizing upon our lands, liberating the slaves and confiscating our other property—and secondly, their visit here has to a great extent demoralized the Negroes, especially near where they camped. They made the ignorant blacks believe they had come to free them, equalized themselves with the negro, called them brothers, rigidly and scrupulously respected the right of the negroes to the property they claimed as theirs. The negroes were delighted with them and since they left enough can be seen to convince anyone that the Federal army, the Negroes and the white Southern people cannot inhabit the same country. . . .
August 14 (Thurs.) 1862
. . . Tonight about the hour of midnight, Sarah, our nurse, came to where Ella and I were sleeping and whispered to us that the yard was full of Federal soldiers. I awoke and sure enough they were all around the house at every window where they got stationed, they knocked at the front door. I told Sarah to open the door and light the candle. She did so—they enquired for me. I dressed and went to the door. The leader, Major Quackenbush, commander of the 14 Michigan, spoke and said he had come to see Mr. Moore, I told him I was the gentleman and to be seated. He apparently had 25 or 30 soldiers with him. He said that he had come to ask me a few questions, which if I answered

to his satisfaction he would leave me undisturbed. If not, it would be his duty to arrest and carry me to Tus(cumbia). He went on to state that he had been informed I had within the last few days been seen with a sword on drilling a squad of men with the view of joining the Southern army. I denied the accusation, told him it was false, that I knew nothing of any company's being drilled, had taken no part in the way, but had been staying at home attending to my own business.

He asked me how old I was. I answered over 30. He said I was too old to tell him an untruth, but that he had pretty strong evidence against me. I told the major I was not a fighting man, but to produce the witness and I would cut his ears off. That no man could stand before me and say I had been drilling a company. He asked me if I was willing to take the oath of allegiance to the U. S. I answered I was not. My reasons were just such as the conservative Northern journals were urging, viz. That the Southern Confederacy was a defacto government. That the citizens within its bounds by virtue of its existence owed it allegiance. That the war should not be levied against them but against the armies in the field. He seemed to think there was some reason for my objections, at least he did not urge me to take one or the other. He asked me if I was willing the house should be searched for arms. I told the major it was a very unreasonable hour to search a house. He remarked he did not propose to search it. I told him at a proper time he was at liberty to search the house for arms. He asked me if I had arms. I told him I had a shot gun and remarked that the constitution which he said he was fighting for guaranteed me arms in self defense. He said so it did and that he expected me to have shot guns and revolvers, that he had them himself, but he was hunting for muskets, etc. Was I sure there was no musket under the house. I told him I was sure, unless it has been put there tonight of which I had no knowledge or agency. He conversed for some time and said he did not come to disturb anything and that he was sorry to have disturbed me at such an hour, that he would call or send out to me soon again and should expect to find me at home. I told the major not to send but to come himself and that I should be very apt to be at home. That I had had every opportunity before the Federal army come to run off from home if I had been so disposed. That I was not. Asked me how much cotton we had on hand. I told him Mrs. Pearsall [his wife's mother] had some 16 or 18 bales. That we had a pretty good crop growing. He thought that was a pretty good evidence of what he termed loyalty. He bid me good night and called his men and left. They behaved civilly while here and took nothing but a few old hens they found in the coop.

[He was at a loss to know why he had been visited thus.]

. . . I from the first opposed secession as being no remedy for the evils with which the South was threatened by Lincoln's election. I still maintained that he ought to be permitted to take his seat and if he violated the Constitution then I was for hurling him from his seat and I believe the conservative north and south would aid in doing so. But the holiday patriots in the South were determined upon secession. For occupying my position I was denounced as a union man, a Lincolnite, and it is a pretty good rule to judge other communities by the one in which you live—where are the strait out secession men in the valley now (?). Those men that were were anxious to bring on the fight wanted some of them, as they said to go to the Potomack to get in a fight. These men are now at home crouching at the feet of the conquers, instead of shouldering their muskets and going off to fight as they swore they would do or even fighting when the Federal soldiers came to their doors. They are crouching down to them, trading, trafficking and drinking with them.

. . . I am sometimes disposed to believe that the secessionists are not in earnest. Are they lying to the people or did they commence it to speculate upon human life.—Typescript in Alabama Department of Archives and History, original owned by Miss Earnestine Deavouers of Laurel, Mississippi.

Unlike Virginia and Kentucky where there was almost constant fighting in some form for four years, Alabama was spared many of the horrors of war. There was never a major land battle fought within its borders and the naval battle of Mobile Bay came near the end of hostilities. Residents in many sections of the state never saw a Yankee soldier; others had only a brief encounter with the enemy as they rode through, headed for some distant destination. However, war came to Alabama in many places and in many ways. From a military point of view, raids did the most harm.

Straight's Raid, 1863

In April 1863 Colonel A. D. Straight of the federal army made the first extended raid across the state. Starting at Eastport in Colbert County with 2,000 picked troops, he led a daring raid across the mountainous region of Alabama. His destination was Rome, Georgia, to seize Confederate supplies and to cut railroad lines between Atlanta and Chattanooga. His movements were followed closely by Confederate cavalrymen under General Nathan Bedford Forrest. Never having sufficient force to risk an attack, Forrest harassed the enemy at every step. Finally, the federal forces (1,466 men) surrendered to Forrest only to find that he had only about 600 men with him. During this raid, John H. Wisdom rode sixty-seven miles in seven hours riding time to warn Rome that the Yankees were coming and Emma Sansom, a girl of only fifteen, became more than a local heroine by showing Forrest's men a crossing over Black Creek after the bridge had been burned.

A Union officer, Lieutenant H. C. Roach, who was with Straight, as aide-de-camp, wrote this account of the raid. It should be remembered he was being pursued by Forrest's band of unknown numbers.

This day's march brought us to the base of a range of hills, known as the Sand Mountains. Here it was determined to bivouac for the night. . . . Up to this time we had made slow progress in the direction of the grand object of the expedition, merely marching in that course with our foot soldiers, while our mounted force was engaged, day and night, scouring the country in every direction in search of horses and mules; and now that sufficient number had been obtained, we were ready to push forward on the following morning with dispatch and rapidity.

On the morning of April thirtieth, 1863, the sun shone out bright and beautiful, as spring day's sun ever beamed; and from the smouldering camp fires of the previous night the mild blue smoke ascended in graceful curves, and mingled with the gray mist slumbering on the mountain tops above. . . . Scarcely was the column in motion when our rear was attacked by the enemy's advance; sharp skirmishing continued for some time between our rear guard and one of General Roddy's regiments.

It was Colonel Streight's intention to avoid, if possible, a general engagement, as the prosecution of our expedition towards its intended destination was of vastly more importance than a victory in this locality could possibly be to our cause. But the enemy pressing us closely, and bringing up his artillery, throwing shot and shell into our column, a battle was the only alternative; we therefore, soon as a favorable position was obtained, halted and dismounted, and after concealing our animals in a deep ravine in our rear, formed in line of battle for the coming conflict. . . . The hour for action has come, and the battle of Day's Gap soon commences. . . . The cannonading is heavy, and the rattle of musketry is sharp, especially on our left. The enemy fights well, for they are principally General Forrest's trained veterans. A loud and prolonged shout now bursts on the ear. It comes from the Third Ohio and Eightieth Illinois, who have charged and taken the enemy's battery. The enemy feel the loss of their guns and their line wavers! Cheer after cheer bursts from our brave boys, for the enemy are giving way! They are already running in the utmost disorder and confusion. Our gallant soldiers still pursue, making the ground quake and the rebels tremble. The rout is complete and the field is ours. But the victory is won by the sacrifice of some of the best and bravest blood in our heroic little brigade.

Those are proud moments for the soldier, when he stands victorious on the bloody field, and sees the columns of the enemy in full retreat before him.

In this fight the enemy received such a severe chastisement that he would not have dared to pursue us further, had he not been reinforced by a large brigade of Forrest's troops, which, unfortunately for us, came to their assistance while his routed and demoralized masses were fleeing from the scene of their late inglorious defeat. . . . After leaving Day's Gap, we proceeded several miles without any evidence of the enemy being in pursuit, but about four o'clock in the evening our rear was again attacked, and as we did not want to lose time by halting to give battle, if it could possibly be avoided, the column was kept in motion, skirmishing fighting going on, however, all the time between Captain Smith's two companies of cavalry and the enemy's advance. Captain Smith, with his little handful of men, kept the enemy at bay for more than two hours. But they were now pressing us so closely that Colonel Streight resolved to halt his command, and again give them battle. In a short time the bloody strife was raging with all the fury of brave and determined men. Charge after charge, made by the enemy, was met and repulsed by our brave boys, who drove back with terrible destruction each successive effort, to dislodge them from the admirable position selected for our line of defense.

This engagement raged with greater desperation for some time than the preceding action in the morning. The report of fire-arms was terrific; the flashes from musketry and artillery lighting up the hills on all sides, rendering the scene, although of death and carnage, one of the grandest sublimity. It was now about ten o'clock, yet by the light of the full moon, which looked calmly down on the bloody scene, we were able to discover that the enemy had begun to waver and fall back, unable to contend longer against the terrible fire our men were pouring with fearful destruction into their ranks. In a short time all was quiet, and the still air of night, that but a few moments before resounded with the roar of artillery and musketry, was only broken by the lonely notes of the whip-poor-will, as they came from his secluded spot in the surrounding forest. And the Provisional Brigade was victorious on two bloody fields in one day. . . . The enemy in this action had their whole force engaged, yet, by the skillful maneuvering of our little brigade, we met and repulsed them at every point. To this, and the bravery and determination of our men, we alone can ascribe our success in meeting and driving back discomfitted numbers, so much our superior, and having at their command several heavy field pieces. Our artillery consisted of two small mountain howitzers, and the two pieces taken from Forrest in the morning; for the latter we had but a small quantity of ammunition, the caissons being nearly empty when captured; they were, therefore, soon of no service, and were ordered by the Colonel to be spiked, and the carriages cut down. . . . Colonel Streight, anticipating an advance of Forrest's forces, soon as it was known to them that we were moving, directed Colonel Hathaway, with his regiment, (Seventy-Third Indiana) to lay concealed in the heavy timber nearby, for the purpose of ambushing them in case of an immediate advance. But a few moments elapsed before the enemy's column was discovered approaching; and soon their advance battalion came up unsuspectingly within forty yards of our concealed regiment, which at that instant poured a full volley of musketry into their ranks, sending them back, pell mell, in the greatest consternation and disorder, with the full conviction, no doubt, that every tree for miles around conceals a Yankee soldier with a musket charged to the muzzle. But relying on the advantage of being in their own country, consequently acquainted with every road and by-path, also conscious of their superior numbers, they soon rallied, and attacked us again about two o'clock in the morning, when Colonel Streight again resolved to ambush them;

which proved so successful, and gave them such a taste of Yankee courage and skill, that we had no further annoyance until about eleven o'clock
next day, when our pickets were attacked just as we were leaving
Blountsville, where we had halted to feed our animals and refresh the
exhausted and fatigued men, who had not had a moment's rest for
two days and nights. . . . On the morning of May 2nd we crossed Black
Creek, near Gadsden, Alabama, on a fine wooden bridge, which was
afterwards burned by our rear guard. This, it was thought, would delay
Forrest's forces long enough to enable us to reach Rome, Georgia, before he could again overtake us, as the stream was very deep and seemed
to be unfordable. But among a lot of prisoners captured by us in the
morning, and paroled, was a young man by the name of Sansom who,
soon as set at liberty, made his way direct to the pursuing force of
General Forrest, and piloted that officer and his command to a ford
where the whole force soon crossed and started again in pursuit of our
brigade. From this incident the rebels manufactured the following bit of
romance: "General Forrest had been pursuing the enemy all day, and
was close upon their heels, when the pursuit was effectually checked by
the destruction by the enemy of a bridge over a deep creek, which, for
the time, separated pursuer and pursued. The country was exceedingly
wild and rugged, and the banks of the creek too steep for passage on
horseback. General Forrest rode up to a modest little farm house on
the road side, and seeing a young maiden standing upon the little stoop
in front of the dwelling, he accosted her, and inquired if there was any
ford or passage for his men across the creek above or below the destroyed bridge. The young girl proceeded to direct him, with animated
gesture, and cheeks flushed with excitement, and almost brethless in
her eagerness to aid the noble cause of the gallant Confederate General.
It was a scene for a painter. The Southern girl, her cheeks glowing and
her bright eyes flashing, while her mother, attracted by the colloquy,
stood holding the door, and gazing upon the cavalcade over her venerable
spectacles, the cavalry chieftain resting his legs carelessly over the
saddle-pommel, his staff drawn up around him, and his weather-worn
veterans scattered in groups about the road, and some of them actually
nodding in their saddles from excessive fatigue. After some further inquiry, General Forrest asked the young lady if she would not mount
behind him and show him the way to the ford. She hesitated, and turned
to her mother an inquiring look. The mother, with a delicacy becoming
a prudent parent, rather seemed to object to her going with the soldiers.

"Mother," she said, "I am not afraid to trust myself with as brave a
man as General Forrest."

"But, my dear, folks will talk about you."

"Let them talk," responded the heroic girl, "I must go."

And with that she lightly sprang upon the roots of a fallen tree, Forrest
drew his mettled charger near her, she grasped the hero fearlessly about
the waist and sprung up behind him, and away they went over brake
and bramble, through the glade and on towards the ford. The route was
a difficult one, even for as experienced a rider as Forrest, but his fair
young companion and guide held her seat like an experienced horse-

woman, and without the slightest evidence of fear. At length they drew near to the ford. Upon the high ridge above, the quick eye of Forrest descried the Yankee sharpshooters, dodging from tree to tree, and pretty soon an angry minnie whistled by his ear.

" 'What was that, General Forrest?' asked the maiden.

" 'Bullets,' he replied; 'are you afraid?'

"She replied in the negative, and they proceeded on. At length it became necessary, from the density of the undergrowth and snags, to dismount, and Forrest hitched his horse, and the girl preceded him, lead-ing the way herself—remarking that the Yankees would not fire upon her, and they might fire if he went first. To this Forrest objected, not wishing to screen himself behind the brave girl; and, taking the lead himself, the two proceeded on to the ford under the fire of the Yankee rear guard. Having discovered the route he returned, brought up his axemen and cleared out a road, and safely crossed his whole column.

"Upon taking leave of his fair young guide, the General asked if there was anything he might do for her in return for her invaluable services. She told him that the Yankees on ahead had her brother prisoner, and if General Forrest would only release him she should be more than repaid. The General took out his watch, and examined it. It was just five minutes to eleven. 'To-Morrow,' he said, 'at five minutes to eleven o'clock, your brother shall be returned to you.' And so the sequel proved. Streight, with his whole command, was captured at ten the next morning. Young Sansom was released, and dispatched on the fleetest horse in the command to return to his heroic sister, whose cour-age and presence of mind had contributed so much to the success of one of the most remarkable cavalry pursuits and captures known in the world's history."

The true version of this story is, as near as possible, as follows: whenever we captured any prisoners, they were immediately paroled, and not taken along with the command any distance; especially not forty or fifty miles, as this rebel romance would indicate. And the young Con-federate soldier, Sansom was with General Forrest when our command surrendered, and notwithstanding his solemn oath not to aid or comfort in any manner whatever the enemies of the United States, was fully armed and equipped, and boasted that it was the bullet shot from his gun that killed the noble Hathaway.

Soon after crossing Black Creek, we passed through the town of Gadsden, where we destroyed a quantity of rebel stores, and captured some prisoners. We then proceeded on to Blunt's plantation, where we halted for the purpose of giving the men an opportunity of preparing a hasty meal for themselves and to feed their animals. But the anticipated pleasure of a cup of steaming coffee, which the Union soldier considers one of his indispensables, was soon dispelled by the report of musketry in the direction of our picket line. The command was immediately given to prepare for action, and almost instantly every man in the Provisional Brigade seized his gun, and was marching out bravely and defiantly to engage once more the vastly superior force of the enemy, with whom we had contended successfully for three days, and had completely routed and defeated in two regular pitched battles. Colonel Hathaway, with his regiment, was directed to the front and center, to support our two howitzers, which were doing such fearful execution in the ranks of the enemy, that they seemed to have resolved to capture them if possible, regardless of the cost in blood. Their efforts, however, were fruitless, for although nearly every gunner and man connected with the two pieces was either killed or wounded, Colonel Hathaway so determinedly maintained his position that the enemy recoiled in the greatest confusion, our men pouring a perfect hail of lead into his retreating columns. This action lasted for nearly three hours, the enemy charging our lines from right to left repeatedly, but was as often repulsed, with severe loss, by our gallant regiments. When the sun set on that tranquil evening, sinking slowly down behind the forest, unstirred by the least breath of wind, the sharp and bloody struggle was decided. The enemy was retreating badly hurt; his dead men and horses strewing their line of retreat. . . . Affairs are now rapidly approaching a crisis; every one felt that the next twenty-four hours would decide the fate of our expedition. We were now within sixty miles of Rome, the point at which we designed crossing the Coosa river. . . .—*The Prisoner of War and How Treated* (Indianapolis: Railroad City Publishing House, 1865), quoted in Robert Selph Henry, *As They Saw Forrest* (Jackson, Tennessee: McCoward-Mercer Press, 1956), pp. 225–33.

When Straight's forces surrendered, they were sent to Libby Prison in Richmond. Officer Roach and about one hundred others escaped on February 9, 1864, through a tunnel they had dug. Roach says that Colonel Straight being "somewhat inclined to corpulency, *stuck fast,* and was compelled to back out and divest himself of coat, vest, and shirt, when he was able to *squeeze* through, pulling the garments aforesaid through with a string after him."

Emma Sansom's own story of the incident, written in 1899, differs somewhat from the Roach account.

We were at home on the morning of May 2, 1863, when about eight or nine o'clock a company of men wearing blue uniforms and riding mules and horses galloped past the house and went on towards the bridge. Pretty soon a great crowd of them came along, and some of them stopped at the gate and asked us to bring them some water. Sister and I each took a bucket of water and gave it to them at the gate. One of them asked me where my father was. I told him he was dead. He asked me if I had any brothers. I told him I had "six." He asked me where they were, and I said they were in the Confederate Army. "Do they think the South will whip?" "They do." "What do you think about it?" "I think God is on our side and we will win." "You do? Well, if you had seen us whip Colonel Roddey the other day and run him across the Tennessee River, you would have thought God was on the side of the best artillery." By this time some of them began to dismount, and we went into the house. They came in and began to search for fire-arms and men's saddles. They did not find anything but a side-saddle, and one of them cut the skirts off that. Just then some one from the road said, in a loud tone: "You men bring a chunk of fire with you, and get out of that house." The men got the fire in the kitchen and started out, and an officer put a guard around the house, saying: "This guard is for your protection." They all soon hurried down to the bridge, and in a few minutes we saw the smoke rising and knew they were burning the bridge. As our fence extended up to the railing of the bridge, mother said: "Come with me and we will pull our rails away, so they will not be destroyed." As we got to the top of the hill we saw the rails were already piled on the bridge and were on fire, and the Yankees were in line on the other side guarding it. We turned back towards the house, and had not gone but a few steps before we saw a Yankee coming at full speed, and behind were some more men on horses. I heard them shout, "Halt! and surrender!" The man stopped, threw up his hand, and handed over his gun. The officer to whom the soldier surrendered said: "Ladies, do not be alarmed, I am General Forrest; I and my men will protect you from harm." He inquired: "Where are the Yankees?" Mother said: "They have set the bridge on fire and are standing in line on the other side, and if you go down that hill they will kill the last one of you." By this time our men had come up, and some went out in the field, and both sides commenced shooting. We ran to the house, and I got there ahead of all. General Forrest dashed up to the gate and said to me: "Can you tell me where I can get across that creek?" I told him there was an unsafe bridge two miles farther down the stream, but that I knew of a trail about two hundred yards above the bridge on our farm, where our cows used to cross in low water, and I believed he could get his men over there, and that if he would have my saddle put on a horse I would show him the way. He said: "There is no time to saddle a horse; get up here behind me." As he said this he rode close to the bank on the side of the road, and I jumped up behind him.

Just as we started off mother came up about out of breath and gasped out: "Emma, what do you mean?" General Forrest said: "She is going to show me a ford where I can get my men over in time to catch those Yankees before they get to Rome. Don't be uneasy; I will bring her back safe." We rode out into a field through which ran a branch or small ravine and along which there was a thick undergrowth that protected us for a while from being seen by the Yankees at the bridge or on the other side of the creek. This branch emptied into the creek just above the ford. When we got close to the creek, I said: "General Forrest, I think we had better get off the horse, as we are now where we may be seen." We both got down and crept through the bushes, and when we were right at the ford I happened to be in front. He stepped quickly between me and the Yankees, saying: "I am glad to have you for a pilot, but I am not going to make breastworks of you."

The cannon and the other guns were firing fast by this time, as I pointed out to him where to go into the water and out on the other bank, and then we went back towards the house. He asked me my name, and asked me to give him a lock of my hair. The cannon-balls were screaming over us so loud that we were told to leave and hide in some place out of danger, which we did. Soon all the firing stopped, and I started back home. On the way I met General Forrest again, and he told me that he had written a note for me and left it on the bureau. He asked me again for a lock of my hair, and as we went into the house he said: "One of my bravest men has been killed, and he is laid out in the house. His name is Robert Turner. I want you to see that he is buried in some graveyard near here." He then told me good-bye and got on his horse, and he and his men rode away and left us all alone. My sister and I sat up all night watching over the dead soldier, who had lost his life fighting for our rights, in which we were over-powered but never conquered. General Forrest and his men endeared themselves to us forever.—Emma Sansom, "A True Statement of the Incident," John Allan Wyeth, *Life of Lieutenant-General Nathan B. Forrest* (New York: Harper and Brothers, 1899), pp. 210–12.

Rousseau's Raid on the Railroad

Major-General Lovell H. Rousseau believed that with a force of 3,000 he could reach and destroy the vital industrial complex at Selma and then by swinging east his troops could tear up sections of the West Point and Montgomery Railroad. After considering all the circumstances, however, his superior officer, General William T. Sherman, ordered him to concentrate on the railroad. This was in July, 1864; thus Selma was spared for another nine months.

Starting from Decatur he went by Blountsville to west of Opelika where he destroyed sections of track and then swung northeast to the Atlanta vicinity.

A correspondent along with Rousseau reported that the work the expedition was sent out to accomplish had been done. They had marched over three hundred miles in nine days, destroyed over thirty miles of railroad track, depots, water tanks, turntables, one locomotive and other railroad equipment and supplies—and struck terror "into the heart of rebeldom."

One of the small towns hit by Rousseau's forces was Auburn. On September 15 following, Confederate Captain Thomas H. Francis reported to Brigadier-General T. A. Shoup, Army of Tennessee, what took place there during the raid.

On 18th July the Yankee raid, under Rousseau, passed through the town, burning depots and warehouses containing Government property, and railroad from Notasulga to Opelika. As before stated, I took command but two days previous and had no provost guard or force of any sort with which to defend the post. In the emergency I got a few convalescents from the Texas hospital and such of the militia as could be collected, amounting in all to about eighteen men, mounting them on horses impressed from the neighboring citizens. I also telegraphed to Columbus for arms or re-enforcements, but received neither. With this little force, armed with shotguns, I proceeded to reconnoiter the enemy, and skirmished with him, keeping him out of the town for about twenty hours; but finding his force to be about 2,500 men, I ordered my command to disperse and seek safety separately. The raid entered town about 2 p.m., [Monday] and left next morning, 19th July. During this occupation the negroes owned by citizens in the town and surrounding country broke into stores and carried off everything movable. There were no white persons present while this was going on, and consequently the negroes carrying off plunder could not be subsequently identified. I have since made every effort to recover stolen property, but so far with but little success.

The following-named officers have their offices at this post: Surg. L. A. Bryan, Texas hospital; Capt. A. G. Durkee, post and hospital quartermaster; Maj. W. H. C. Price, superintendent Niter and Mining District No. 10, and Maj. J. Shelby Williams conscription officer for Congressional District No. 7. The first two mentioned report to me at this office; the last two report to their immediate superior officers. There is also a board of surgeons for examining conscripts, but they form part of the Conscript Bureau and do not report here. The Texas hospital, in charge of Surg. L. A. Bryan, makes a daily morning report to this office. . . . From September 1 to 15 . . . average remaining in hospital was 380. . . .—Ibid., pp. 973–74.

The East Alabama Male Institute, closed for instruction during the war, was used as the hospital to care for the wounded. Major Price reported that of his supplies of munitions the enemy stole 27 barrels of potash and burned 12,000 pounds of lead, but that he was able to save some of the nitre and office papers which he moved out into the country.

Wilson's Raid

The greatest raid on Alabama soil was the one conducted by federal Major-General James Harrison Wilson in March and April 1865. General Wilson was a graduate of West Point and a career officer, who had done effective fighting in the Army of the Potomac before he was transferred to the west. After battles at Franklin and Nashville in late 1864, he went into winter quarters at Gravelly Springs in Lauderdale County, Alabama. There he spent the following months drilling his cavalry until it was one of the best fighting units in the whole war. Leaving from his quarters on March 22 with 13,500 cavalry, he marched southeastward, dividing his men at Elyton, Jefferson County. Part of them he sent under General John T. Croxton to Tuscaloosa where they destroyed the University which reportedly was training Confederate officers. Wilson led his own forces south through Montevallo and Shelby Springs, where he destroyed the iron works, and Plantersville on his way to Selma. Just south of Montevallo and at Plantersville, Forrest engaged Wilson in "delaying action" but was unable to stop him. Wilson found Selma defended by 2,500 cavalry and about the same number of militia manning the fortifications that completely surrounded the city. In the action that followed, Selma fell on April 2, 1865.

Wilson's raid and especially the battle around Selma is as well documented with contemporary accounts as any action within the state during the entire war. Only three, the official report of Wilson, one by a Confederate private, John Milton Hubbard who was with Forrest, and one by a resident of Selma will be used here.

General Wilson filed this report on April 4 from Selma.

My corps took this place by assault late on evening of the 2d. We have captured 20 field guns, 2,000 prisoners, besides over 2,000 in hospitals, and large quantity of military stores of all kinds. Large arsenals and foundaries with their machinery are in my possession intact. I shall burn them today, with everything useful to enemy. I have already destroyed iron-works north of here, eight or ten in all, and very extensive. . . . The place is strongly fortified with two continuous lines of parapets and redoubts, the outer one with a continuous stockade on the glacis extending from river above to river below city. They were defended by four brigades of cavalry and all the first and second class militia of this section, from 6,000 to 9,000 men.—*Official Record of the War of the Rebellion,* vol. 49, pt. 2, p. 217.

As he made his report, Wilson was undecided where he would move next, whether to the west to meet Forrest who had escaped his clutches in the dark or to Montgomery. Circumstances sent him to the latter.

Private Hubbard saw the campaign from the Confederate point of view.

As we entered the extensive piney woods section east of Tuskaloosa, we were critically near the right flank of the enemy, pushing on towards Selma. Croxton's Federal Brigade had been detached to destroy the Confederate supplies at Tuskaloosa and burn the university. It so happened that this brigade dropped into the road between the rear of Jackson's Cavalry and the front of his artillery and wagon train. If the Federals had continued to move west, they inevitably would have captured the trains. They turned east to follow the cavalry, and Jackson being apprised of this made the proper disposition to fall upon them in camp in the early morning. In the meantime, Croxton had changed his mind and had turned again to march, as luck would have it, by another road to Tuskaloosa, without knowing that he had our trains so nearly within his grasp. As it was, Jackson ran on his rear company in camp and captured men, horses, and ambulances. Croxton fled north with his command, crossed the Warrior forty miles above, turned south and reached Tuskaloosa, where he carried out his orders. This was the 3rd day of April, and he was now so far separated from his chief that he did not join him at Macon, Ga., till the 20th of May. When Jackson turned to pursue Croxton, unfortunately another detachment under one of the Fighting McCooks, took possession of the bridge over the Cahawba, where Forrest, with his escort, had already crossed, and where we were expected to cross. They boldly came to the west side and put themselves across our path at the village of Scottsville. That night the woods seemed to be full of them. Some of our men, getting out to do the usual little "buttermilk foraging" met some Yanks at a farm house where Johnny Reb thought he had the exclusive privilege. There was a tacit consent to a truce while they shared such good things as the farmer had to contribute. The next morning, April 2nd, Bell's Brigade of Jackson's Division collided with a part of McCook's men and rapidly pushed them back to Centerville. They completely blocked our way by burning the bridge over the Cahawba. It was now impossible for Jackson to join Forrest on the road from Montevallo to Selma, where with Roddy's Cavalry and Crossland's small brigade of Kentuckians, he and escort were fighting to the death to hold Wilson in check till the Confederate divisions could be concentrated and hurled against those of the Federals in one grand conflict. The Federals, having intercepted certain dispatches of Forrest and Jackson, knew just how to subvert their plans. Wilson, seeing that there was now no chance for Jackson to fall upon his rear, according to the original plan of Forrest, pushed his forces with all his energy in the direction of Selma. Forrest, being reinforced by some militia and two hundred picked men of Armstrong's Brigade of Chalmers' Division, on the first day of April, did some of the fiercest fighting of the war, much of it hand to hand. At Bogler's creek near Plantersville, it was at close quarters with two thousand against nine thousand, but the Confederates had the advantage of position. The Federal advance was a regiment of veteran cavalry who charged with drawn sabers. The Confederates received them at first with rifles and closed in with six-shooters, most of the men having two each. The Confederates being forced back by a flank movement, there was a bloody running fight for several miles. From the desperate characters of the fighting here, it might be inferred that the great contest, planned to take place along these lines, would have been terrific, if Forrest, Jackson, Chalmers and Roddy could have joined their forces.

If all the forces named had been concentrated, as Forrest had intended, somewhere between Montevallo and Selma, Ala., would have been fought the cavalry battle of the ages. Who is not glad the whole plan miscarried?

When the Confederates were crowded into Selma the next day, their lines were so attenuated that the Federals, with overwhelming numbers, assailed the works and carried them, though with very heavy loss. Night was coming on as the contest ended and the streets were filled with Federals and Confederates in the greatest possible confusion. This enabled Forrest and Armstrong, with hundreds of their men, to find an opening through which they rode out and escaped in the darkness. In doing this, Forrest cut down his thirtieth man in the war, which closed his fighting career.—quoted in Henry, *As They Saw Forrest,* pp. 214–16.

John Hardy, from whose book *Selma: Her Institutions and Her Men* the following passage is taken, was a native of the Selma area and the former editor of the *Alabama State Sentinel,* a strong pro-Union, anti-secession paper. Since he was hostile to the Confederacy, it is certain he did not over-estimate the damage done by the federal forces. He says that the city daily expected Wilson to arrive for ten days before he did.

There were a large number of bomb-proof officers and stragglers in the city, upon whom little reliance could be placed. But on Saturday it was determined that the place should be defended. Everybody who could walk was called upon to go to the breast-works, with whatever arms could be procured. Squads of armed men were traversing the streets, and examining various buildings for soldiers to go to the breast-works, sparing nothing that wore pantaloons, and by Sunday, 12 o'clock, there were collected in the ditches, around the city, about four thousand persons, not more than two thousand of them reliable, to meet a force of nine thousand of the flower of the Federal army, and equipped in a manner unexampled in the history of ancient or modern armies. Gen. Dick Taylor left the city as fast as a steam engine could carry him, about 12 o'clock Sunday, leaving the command of the city divided between Gens. Forrest, [D. W.] Adams and [Frank C.] Armstrong, and as the latter had the control of really the only force in the fight, was gallant enough to meet the invaders at the point of the first attack, on the Summerfield road, and Long's division felt the result. A large number of the women and children had been sent out of the city. A number of the quartermasters, too, had gone with their supplies, mostly to Meridian. The assault was made, and no one who comprehended affairs could doubt the result. The Federal forces, with the flush of victory, entered the city in the hour of night, and terrible scenes of plunder and outrages were witnessed in every direction.

At the breast-works, the Confederates fought with all the vigor their arms and experience allowed.

About 10 o'clock Sunday night, the first house set on fire was the three story brick building on the corner of Water and Broad streets, the third story of which had been used by the Confederates for a year or so, as a guard house for Union men and skulkers from the Confederate service. It was said this house was set on fire by a man by the name Gibson, who had been imprisoned in it. From this house others along Broad street took fire, and were consumed. Next day the Arsenal, the Naval Foundry, and all the places of manufacture were set on fire by an order from General [E. F.] Winslow, Commander of the post, in charge. The fire continued to rage until about Tuesday night [April 4] by which time the city was nearly destroyed. During this time there was scarcely a house in the city, either private or public, but what had been sacked by the Federal soldiers. The small contents of private stores were most wantonly destroyed, and by Friday morning there was but little of any kind of property left in the place. The 2,700 prisoners, comprising almost every man in the city, were huddled together in a large stockade just north of the Selma and Meridian railroad track, on the east of the Range Line road, near where the Matthews cotton factory now stands. This stockade was built and had been used by the Confederates. In this pen, in which a dry place scarcely large enough for a man to lay down could not be found, were the prisoners kept until Saturday morning, when they were all paroled and allowed to go wherever they pleased or could. On the 6th of April Gen. Wilson met Gen. Forrest at Cahaba, for the purpose of arranging for an exchange of prisoners, but no definite arrangment was effected. On the 9th, Wilson's forces commenced evacuating the place by crossing the river on pontoons, and by the 10th his entire force had succeeded in crossing the river. Thousands of negroes had flocked to the Federal camps, of all ages and sex, and after crossing the river four regiments were organized out of the able bodied black men in and around the Federal camps. To these regiments proper officers were assigned, and those unable to bear arms were driven from the camps. Gen. Wilson, in speaking of these regiments said, "that in addition to *subsisting themselves upon the country,* they would march thirty-five miles in a day, and frequently forty. About four hundred wounded Federal soldiers were left behind in Selma, all huddled together in the different stories of the present hardware store of John K. Goodwin.

One scene of utter ruin was presented. The commons around the city were almost covered with dead and crippled animals, and the people without means to move them. A meeting of the few citizens of the place was held, and all went to work, and in a few days all the dead animals had been hauled and thrown into the river, and subsistence was collected up from the spoils and wastes of provisions, thus enabling the people to get a scanty living.

Many scenes of outrage were perpetrated upon private persons. Col. P. J. Weaver, who it was said had a large amount of gold and silver in his house, was called upon on Sunday night by a gang of about twenty-five soldiers, and his money or his life demanded. The old man refused to give up his money. As they were preparing a rope around the old man's neck, his faithful body servant, Jack, whispered to one of the crowd that he knew where the money was, and if they would not hang "Mass Phill," and go with him, he would show them the money. They did not take time to take the rope from Col. Weaver's neck, but all hastened to follow Jack, who led them to the West Selma graveyard, and pointed out the spot where he said the money was buried, *ten feet* under the ground. While spades and shovels made the dirt fly, Jack made good his escape, through the darkness of the night. It is unnecessary to say no money was found . . . .

It is due to both Gen. Wilson and Gen. E. F. Winslow, to say that in no instance, after Sunday night, when they were applied to for protection to person and private property, but that protection was readily given and by Tuesday evening almost every private family in the city had a soldier or soldiers stationed on the premises.

Taking into consideration the severity of the battle and the overwhelming members of the Federal forces, the small loss of the Confederates was remarkable. Of the 4,000 persons in the battle, there were not more than twenty Confederates killed and scarcely as many wounded, . . . With the fall of Selma and the evacuation of Richmond, Va., on the same day, Sunday, 2d of April, 1865, did the Confederacy fall.— John Hardy, *Selma: Her Institutions and Her Men* (Selma, Ala.: Times Book and Job Office, 1879), pp. 51–53.

Selma was a strategic point for several reasons but especially because the Confederacy had there the biggest concentration of ordnance works in the deep South. It was considered second only to Tredegar Iron Works near Richmond, Virginia, in the amount and quality of its munitions. The naval yards there had cast considerable cannon and had built the C.S.S. *Tennessee,* an ironclad that featured in the battle of Mobile Bay. The variety and extent— and the destruction—of the government operations are indicated in the report made by Brigadier-General Edward F. Winslow, a native of Maine to whom the assignment was given to destroy "everything which could be of benefit to the enemy."

The following is a partial list, which was not made complete, as in many cases the whole property could not be destroyed in the limited time allowed:

1. Selma Arsenal—Consisting of twenty-four buildings, containing an immense amount of war material and machinery for manufacturing the same. Very little of the machinery had been removed, although much of it was packed and ready for shipment to Macon and Columbus, Georgia. Among other articles here destroyed were fifteen siege guns and ten heavy carriages, ten field pieces, with sixty field carriages, ten caissons, sixty-thousand rounds artillery ammunition, one million rounds of small arms ammunition, three million feet of lumber, ten thousand bushels coal, three hundred barrels resin, and three large engines and boilers.

2. Government Naval Foundry—Consisting of five large buildings, containing three fine engines, thirteen boilers, twenty-nine siege guns, unfinished, and all the machinery necessary to manufacture on a large scale naval and siege guns.

3. Selma Iron Works—Consisting of five buildings, with five large engines and furnaces, and complete machinery.

4. Pierces Foundry, Nos. 1 and 2—Each of these contained an engine, extensive machinery, and a large lot of tools.

5. Nitre Works—These works consist of eighteen buildings, five furnaces, sixteen leaches, and ninety banks.

6. Powder Mills and Magazine—Consisting of seven buildings, six thousand rounds of artillery ammunition, and seventy thousand rounds

small arms ammunition, together with fourteen thousand pounds powder.

7. Washington Works—Small iron works, with one engine.

8. Tennessee Iron Works—Containing two engines.

9. Phelan and McBride's Machine Shop, with two engines.

10. Horse Shoe Manufactory—Containing one engine; about eight thousand pounds of horse shoes from this establishment were used by our army.

11. Selma Shovel Factory—This factory contained one steam engine, eight forges, and complete machinery for manufacturing shovels, railroad spikes, and iron axle-trees for army wagons.

12. On the Alabama and Mississippi Railroad—One roundhouse, one stationary engine, and much standing machinery, together with twenty box and two passenger cars.

13. On the Tennessee Railroad—One roundhouse, with machinery, five locomotives, one machine, nineteen box and fifty platform cars.

14. In the Fortifications—one thirty-pound, four ten-pound guns, eleven field pieces, ten caissons, two forges, and five hundred rounds of fixed ammunition. . . .—*Rebellion Record* (1868), Vol. II, pp. 701–702.

Winslow said positively that only public buildings were ordered destroyed. The private buildings were burned by accident or because drunken Federal soldiers disobeyed specific orders not to pillage private dwellings or molest the citizens. The destruction was unbelievable; one reporter said it was the most totally destroyed place he had ever seen.

Instead of making a stand against Wilson's forces as they moved east, the authorities in Montgomery simply evacuated the city and surrendered without a fight on April 12, 1865. As it has been pointed out, the date was exactly four years from the order to fire on Fort Sumter, an order which originated in Montgomery. The war had made a full cycle. Governor Thomas H. Watts had left the city for Union Springs with the intention of establishing the capital at Eufaula, and the city fathers had ordered the burning of 97,000 bales of cotton so that it would not fall into the hands of the enemy. The city surrendered without a struggle and was not destroyed like Selma but it did not escape all damage. Most of the troops were marched through the city without incident; the isolated cases of robbery were done by stragglers. The buildings destroyed were those of a public nature which could be used for war purposes, e.g., the depots of the two railroads, Janney's Foundry, Bibb Rolling Mill, and the Nitre Works. Four steamers on the Alabama River were burned. The editor of the Montgomery *Advertiser* attributed the minimum of looting to the absence of liquor. The Confederates had taken the precaution to see that barrels containing whiskey were emptied before the Yankees got there.

Four days after the surrender of Montgomery, a part of General Wilson's forces met the Confederates at Girard for what proved to be the last military engagement on Alabama soil. This was April 16, 1865. General Robert E. Lee had already surrendered his troops in Virginia so the fighting was over.

Naval Battle of Mobile Bay

One of the purposes of Wilson's raid on Selma was to divert Confederate attention from Mobile which did not fall after the Confederate defeat in the Bay in August 1864. The battle is considered one of the most important naval engagements of the war. In number of ships involved and scope of operation, it outranks the battle between the *Monitor* and the *Merrimac* in Hampton Roads.

The first two passages are the orders of Admiral David G. Farragut, a native Tennessean, for the federal ships, and the report of Confederate Franklin Buchanan, a native of Baltimore.

GENERAL ORDERS   U. S. FLAGSHIP HARTFORD,
No. 10.   Off Mobile Bay, July 12, 1864

Strip your vessels and prepare for the conflict. Send down all your superfluous spars and rigging. Trice up or remove the whiskers. Put up the splinter nets on the starboard side, and barricade the wheel and steersmen with sails and hammocks. Lay chains or sand bags on the deck over the machinery, to resist a plunging fire. Hang the sheet chains over the side, or make any other arrangement for security that your ingenuity may suggest. Land your starboard boats or lower and tow them on the port side, and lower the port boats down to the water's edge. Place a leadsman and the pilot in the port quarter boat, or the one most convenient to the commander.

The vessels will run past the forts in couples, lashed side by side, as hereinafter designated. The flagship will lead and steer from Sand Island N. by E. by compass, until abreast of Fort Morgan; then N. W. half N. until past the Middle Ground; then N. by W., and the others, as designated in the drawing, will follow in due order until ordered to anchor; but the bow and quarter line must be preserved to give the chase guns a fair range, and each vessel must be kept astern of the broadside of the next ahead; each vessel will keep a very little on the starboard quarter of his next ahead, and when abreast of the fort, will keep directly astern, and as we pass the fort will take the same distance on the port quarter of the next ahead, to enable the stern guns to fire clear of the next vessel astern.

It will be the object of the admiral to get as close to the fort as possible before opening fire. The ships, however, will open fire the moment the enemy opens upon us, with their chase and other guns, as fast as they can be brought to bear. Use short fuzes for the shell and shrapnel, and as soon as within 300 or 400 yards give them grape. It is understood that heretofore we have fired too high, but with grapeshot it is necessary to elevate a little above the object, as grape will dribble from the muzzle of the gun.

If one or more of the vessels be disabled, their partners must carry them through, if possible; but if they can not then the next astern must render the required assistance; but as the admiral contemplates moving with the flood tide, it will only require sufficient power to keep the crippled vessels in the channel.

Vessels that can must place guns upon the poop and topgallant forecastle and in the tops on the starboard side. Should the enemy fire grape, they will remove the men from the topgallant forecastle and poop to the guns below until out of grape range.

The howitzers must keep up a constant fire from the time they can reach with shrapnel until out of its range.—*Official Records of the Union and Confederate Navies in the War of the Rebellion* (Washington: United States Printing Office, 1906), Series 1, Vol. 21, pp. 397–98.

It was in the engagement in Mobile Bay that Admiral Farragut, when told that the water was full of torpedoes, exploded with his now famous "Damn the torpedoes. Full speed ahead!"

Admiral Buchanan reported from Pensacola where he was taken as a prisoner.

U. S. NAVAL HOSPITAL
Pensacola, August 25, 1864

Sir: I have the honor to inform you that the enemy's fleet under Admiral Farragut, consisting of fourteen steamers and four monitors, passed Fort Morgan on the 5th instant, about 6:30 a.m., in the following order and stood into Mobile Bay: The four monitors—*Tecumseh* and *Manhattan,* each carrying two XV-inch guns, the *Winnebago* and *Chickasaw,* each carrying four XI-inch guns—in a single line ahead about a half a mile from the fort; the fourteen steamers—*Brooklyn,* of twenty-six; *Octorara,* ten; *Hartford,* twenty-eight; *Metacomet,* ten; *Richmond,* twenty-four; *Port Royal,* eight; *Lackawanna,* fourteen; *Seminole,* nine; *Oneida,* ten; and *Galena,* fourteen guns—in double line ahead, each two lashed together. The side-wheel steamers offshore, all about 4 miles from the monitors, carrying in all 199 guns and 2,700 men. When they were discovered standing into the channel, signal was made to the Mobile squadron under my command, consisting of the wooden gunboats *Morgan* and *Gaines,* each carrying six guns, and the *Selma,* four, to follow my motions in the ram *Tennessee,* of six guns, in all 22 guns and 470 men. All were soon underway and stood toward the enemy in a line abreast. As the *Tennessee* approached the fleet, when opposite the fort, we opened our battery at short range upon the leading ship, the admiral's flagship *Hartford,* and made the attempt to run into her, but owing to her superior speed our attempt was frustrated. We then stood toward the next heavy ship, the *Brooklyn,* with the same view. She also avoided us by her superior speed. During this time the gunboats were also closely engaged with the enemy. All our guns were used to the greatest advantage, and we succeeded in seriously damaging many of the enemy's vessels. The *Selma* and *Gaines,* under Lieutenants Commanding P. U. Murphy and J. W. Bennett, fought gallantly, and I am gratified to hear from officers of the enemy's fleet that their fire was very destructive. The *Gaines* was fought until she was found to be in a sinking condition, when she was run on shore near Fort Morgan. Lieutenant Commanding Murphy was closely engaged with the *Metacomet,* assisted by the *Morgan,* Commander Harrison, who, during the conflict, deserted him, when, upon the approach of another large steamer, the *Selma* surrendered. I refer you to the report of Lieutenant Commanding Murphey for the particulars of his action. He lost two promising officers, Lieutenant Comstock and Master's Mate Murray, and a number of his men were killed and wounded, and he was also wounded severely in the wrist. Commander Harrison will no doubt report to the Department his reason for leaving the *Selma* in that contest with the enemy; as the *Morgan* was uninjured his conduct is severely commended on by the officers of the enemy's fleet, much to the injury of that officer and the Navy.

Soon after the gunboats were dispersed by the overwhelming superiority of force, and the enemy's fleet had anchored about 4 miles above Fort Morgan, we stood for them again in the *Tennessee,* and renewed the attack with the hope of sinking some of them with our prow. Again were we foiled by their superior speed in avoiding us. The engagement with the whole fleet soon became general at very close quarters and last about an hour, and notwithstanding the serious injury inflicted upon many of their vessels by our guns, we could not sink them. Frequently during the contest we were surrounded by the enemy and all our guns were in action almost at the same moment. Some of their heaviest vessels ran into us under full steam with the view of sinking us. One vessel, the *Monongahela,* had been prepared as a ram and was very formidable; she struck us with great force, injuring us but little. Her prow and stem were knocked off and the vessel so much injured as to make it necessary to dock her. Several of the other vessels of the fleet were found to require extensive repairs. I enclose to you a copy of a drawing of the *Brooklyn,* made by one of her officers after the action, and an officer of the *Hartford* informed me that she was more seriously injured than the *Brooklyn.* I mention these facts to prove that the guns of the *Tennessee* were not idle during this unequal contest. For other details of the action and injuries sustained by the *Tennessee,* I refer you to the report of Commander J. D. Johnston, which has my approval. After I was carried below, unfortunately wounded, I had to be governed by the reports of that valuable officer as to the condition of the ship, and the necessity and time of her surrender, and when he represented to me her utterly hopeless condition to continue the fight with injury to the enemy, and suggested her surrender, I directed him to do the best he could, and when he could no longer damage the enemy, to do so. It affords me much pleasure to state that the officers and men cheerfully fought their guns to the best of their abilities and gave strong evidence by their promptness in executing orders of their willingness to continue the contest as long as they could stand to their guns, notwithstanding the fatigue they had undergone for several hours, and it was only under the circumstances as presented by Captain Johnston that she was surrendered to the fleet about 10 a. m., as painful as it was to do so. I seriously felt the want of experienced officers during the action. All were young and inexperienced and many had but little familiarity with naval duties, having been appointed from civil life within the year. The reports of Commander Harrison, of the *Morgan,* and Lieutenant Commanding Bennett, of the *Gaines,* you have no doubt received from those officers.

I enclose the report of Fleet Surgeon D. B. Conrad, to whom I am much indebted for his skill, promptness, and attention to the wounded. By permission of Admiral Farragut, he accompanied the wounded of the *Tennessee* and *Selma* to this hospital and is assisted by Assistant Surgeons Booth and Bowles, of the *Selma* and *Tennessee,* all under charge of Fleet Surgeon Palmer, U. S. Navy, from whom we have received all the attention and consideration we could desire or expect.

The crews and many officers of the *Tennessee* and *Selma* have been sent to New Orleans; Commander J. D. Johnston, Lieutenant Commanding P. U. Murphey, and Lieutenant W. L. Bradford and A. D. Wharton, Second Assistant Engineer J. C. O'Connell, and myself are to be sent North. Master's Mates W. S. Forrest and R. M. Carter, who are with me acting as my aids, not having any midshipmen, are permitted to accompany me; they are valuable young officers, zealous in the discharge of their duties, and both have served in the Army, where they received honorable wounds; their services are valuable to me.

I am happy to inform you that my wound is improving and sincerely hope our exchange will be effected, and that I will soon again be on duty. Enclosed is a list of the officers of the *Tennessee* who were in action.

I am, respectfully, your obedient servant,

FRANKLIN BUCHANAN,
Admiral.

Hon. S. R. Mallory,
Secretary of the Navy.

N. B. —September 17. Since writing the above I have seen the report of Admiral Farragut, a portion of which is incorrect. Captain Johnston did not deliver my sword on board the *Hartford.* After the surrender of the *Tennessee,* Captain Giraud, the officer who was sent on board to take charge of her, said to me that he was directed by Admiral Farragut to ask for my sword, which was brought from the cabin and delivered to him by one of my aids.—Ibid. pp. 576–78.

The battle of Mobile Bay was not unexpected. New Orleans fell to the federals in mid-summer of 1862 and Pensacola shortly thereafter, leaving Mobile the only major port on the Gulf in the hands of the Confederates. To be sure, the coast had been blockaded since the spring of 1861 and there were usually some ships off shore to remind residents of the fact. An occasional blockade runner made it into port; at other times they were not so fortunate. The *Ivanhoe* was among the unlucky ones. Lt. Robert Tarlton wrote his future bride, Miss Sallie B. Lightfoot, who was living on a plantation near Eutaw, that since his last letter to her

We have had something of a little misunderstanding with our Yankee friends about an English steamer the "Ivanhoe", which ran a ground last Thurs. night trying to run the blockade. She lies about a mile east of the fort within a few yards of shore. The guns of the enemy awakened us about midnight. . . . After an hour of impatient waiting among the blood thirst mosquitoes, we were dismissed to our quarters. Shortly there after, I received a summons from Major Gee to go with my company to defend a stranded vessel. A march of half an hour brought us to the vessel, a light beautiful steamer just over from England on her first trip and loaded with government stores. . . . Sure enough, as soon as it was light the Yankee gun boats bore down toward us. Five gun boats, a sloop of war and a small craft steamed up, and arranging themselves in a semi-circular line about 3½ mi. from the fort [Morgan] and 2½ from the Ivanhoe poured in a hot fire of shot and shell, heavy and light, round and cylindrical. They kept this up all morning. June 5, 1864.—*Mobile: 1861–1865,* edited by Sidney Adair Smith and C. Carter Smith, Jr. (Privately printed, 1964), pp. 29–30.

After heavy fighting around Blakely and Spanish Fort at the same time Wilson was in Selma, Mobile surrendered. Captain Evans wrote an exultant letter to his folks in Ohio about the last days of the port city.

Mobile is ours! Tuesday noon [April 12] . . . we steered for Dog River Bay on the opposite side. . . . By 10 a.m. the fog cleared away and our leading man-of-war, approaching the batteries, fired a few rounds but received no reply; so the whole fleet of gun-boats and transports moved rapidly to the landing. The Johnnys were all gone but a citizen came down to the wharf bearing a white flag. . . Thus in the capture of the last strong-hold of treason, ended our campaign against Mobile.— Evans to family, Whistler Station, April 15, 1865, Ibid., p. 41.

And in Tuscumbia, J. B. Moore whose comments on secession have been given earlier, recorded in his diary for April:

Well, Mobile is taken with several thousand prisoners. This gives the Federals complete possession of all South Alabama. I wonder if Gov. Watts and the rabid secessionists of South Alabama can now see the handwriting on the wall. Gen. Wilson has taken Tuscaloosa, Selma and other places, has a large cavalry force under him and is living at his ease in South Alabama. Now I wonder how they feel. They ought to give these fellows hell. They are the ones who carried this state out of the union. North Alabama voted overwhelmingly against it and for three years she has suffered the most terrible the mind can conceive of. While in South Alabama they have been speculating upon our misfortunes— and calling us terms. Now I wonder what they think.

Away from the Firing Line

Although much of the state was spared the destruction of pitched battles, all parts of it were hurt in other ways. It was a rare family that had no one involved in the war in some capacity.

The Congress of the Confederate States passed its first conscription act on April 16, 1862, some eleven months before the United States Congress passed a similar measure. The act was amended many times, changing the age limit and the classes of men exempted from military service. In the early days of the war, the Confederacy had relied on volunteers and, as is well known, government officials were overwhelmed by numbers they could neither supply nor use. Many of these units returned home without seeing action and, in some instances, before the war actually started. Furthermore, believing the war would be brief, most of these early patriots had signed up for short periods of service. There was also a growing feeling among the small farmer class that the conflict was "a rich man's war and a poor man's fight" since they held few offices in the army and were ineligible for exemptions from duty. It was to solve some of these manpower problems that congress enacted the conscript law. It was still possible to volunteer before being drafted and many did so, some to escape the odium of being called a "conscript" and others to collect the $50 bounty money. There was always friction between the Confederate and state authorities regarding the enforcement of the law. This and other problems of recruiting is the subject of a letter from James Phelan to Jefferson Davis.

Why is it the conscript acts are so inefficiently enforced? So far as I could learn in the course of my travels, conscription is a mere farce. Two months had elapsed since the enemy evacuated Northern Alabama and yet no enrolling officer had been there. Crowds of men subject to duty are everywhere—on cars, boats, in the streets, stores, &c.; but the subject of their conscription seems not to have entered their heads. The enrolling officers, now as important as President, so far as I see or hear, are young men utterly unfit for that sacred, stern duty, whom nobody fears, for whom nobody cares, and who exercise their discretions as to exemptions with unblushing partiality and indifference. I believe the enforcement of the act in this State and Alabama, where I have been, to be an utter failure. Instead of being, as it ought to be, a measure that saved the country, it threatens to be the cause of its subjugation. It arrested all volunteering, &c., and assumed by force the augmentation of the army, and now failing to do so our "last end is worse than the first." I had a talk with Governor Shorter, of Alabama, upon the subject. He gives an account of the correspondence between Mr. Randolph and himself, which left the matter in confusion, and he admits the enforcement of the act in Alabama is a humbug and farce. Surely the most stern, sober, substantial men should be selected for enrolling officers. If not enforced, as they ought to be, with iron and unrelenting firmness, our cause is lost. You cannot imagine the open, bold, unblushing attempts to avoid getting in and to keep out of the army. All shame has fled and no subterfuge is pretended, but a reckless confession of an unwillingness to go or to remain. All that gave attractive coloring to the soldier's life has now faded into "cold, gray shadow" with nine tenths of the army, and if permitted, in my opinion, would dissolve tomorrow, heedless of the future. Let an iron band be welded around it; for the pressure, take my word for it, is nearly overwhelming. There are many plausible reasons for this desire to get away which I need not detail. A rigorous enforcement of the conscription would tend to allay this spirit of discontent. Reorganize the whole system, and let popular attention be started and attracted by the prominent, rich, and influential men being swept into the ranks.

Never did a law meet with more universal odium than the exemption of slave-owners. Its injustice, gross injustice, is denounced even by men whose position enables them to take advantage of its privileges. Its influence upon the poor is most calamitous, and has awakened a spirit and elicited a discussion of which we may safely predict the most unfortunate results. I believe such a provision to be unnecessary, inexpedient, and unjust. I labored to defeat it and predicted the consequences of its enactment. It has aroused a spirit of rebellion in some places, I am informed, and bodies of men have banded together to resist; whilst in the army it is said it only needs some daring man to raise the standard to develop a revolt. As I opposed the provision violently, predicted the consequences, and believe they have occurred, I hope you will satisfy yourself of the truth with reference to the recommendations of your message. I shall offer a bill to repeal it the first day of the session.

I am satisfied that the whole policy of admitting substitutes is wrong. The reasons I need not detail. Let me, however, suggest one. In case of large pay it causes a certain class of men to seek exemption on their own account, straining to reach beyond the age, to be regarded as mechanics, &c. Again, it causes men who are liable to be ever on the search to find some man to take their place, and therefore never become imbued with the spirit of the soldier nor buckle on the harness for regular duty. A bill nearly abolishing the whole system did pass the Senate but was lost in the House by having been foolishly and unconstitutionally linked with another measure. I shall offer to abolish it *in toto,* and wish you could give it the benefit of your recommendation.—Phelan to Davis,

December 9, 1862, *Official Records of the Rebellion,* Vol. 17, p. 790.

In the spirit of "state rights," Alabama also passed a conscription law which applied to state troops (militia) not part of the Confederate army. There was a long list of exemptions as the following act specifically states.

No. 2.]   AN ACT

Declaring who shall be exempt from Militia duty in this State.

SECTION 1. *Be it enacted by the Senate and House of Repsentatives of the State of Alabama in General Assembly convened,* That the following persons and no others, except persons over the age of forty-five years, shall be exempt from service in the militia of this State, to-wit; County treasurers, all physicians who have been in regular practice seven years immediately preceding the approval of this act, provided that any time such physician shall have been in the Confederate States or State military service shall be considered as embraced in the time of said practice, if such physician was a practicing physician when he entered such service; all ministers of the gospel who are now engaged in the regular discharge of their duties as such; all persons who are actually engaged in teaching school and have followed as a profession the calling of teacher for three years next preceding the passage of this act, provided that any time that any such person shall be in the Confederate or State military service shall be considered as embraced in the time if such person was a teacher when he entered such service; also, one blacksmith in each beat, unless there is a negro smith working for the public in said beat, or some man not liable to conscription, provided that said blacksmith has been engaged as such for two years; the city police and members of chartered fire companies of the cities of Mobile, Montgomery and Selma, not exceeding the present number, provided the foreman of said companies shall make affadavit that the places of the persons so exempt cannot be supplied with negroes, and the names of the persons so exempt shall be published three times in the newspaper having the largest circulation in the place where said fire company is located; the officers of the Penitentiary of Alabama; the general administrators of counties who have actually been in office and service five years immediately preceding the approval of this act; necessary financial or produce agents of the Confederate States, so long as they are required by the Confederate government to continue the business of such agency; necessary millers, the Governor shall determine who are necessary millers, if appeal is taken to him; the necessary superintendents, conductors, master machinists and engine drivers of all railroads actually running; the necessary pilots, captains, mates, clerks and engineers of all steam boats plying the waters of this State, while actually serving on such boats; the cashier, discount clerk and deposit clerk of each bank in this State in actual operation; all overseers who are, or shall be exempted or detailed under acts of the Confederate Congress so long as they may be exempted or detailed as such; one owner and one machinist of all brass and iron foundries; and such others persons as the Governor shall specially exempt, and no exemption in any case can be made except for State or public purposes; *Provided, however,* that all persons thus exempted shall be enumerated and subject to service in the first class or county reserves.

SEC. 2. *Be it further enacted,* That any person who makes as much as ten bushels of salt per day on his individual account, or on account of a company or partnership in which he is concerned, who shall in good faith sell whenever he can do so for Confederate or State treasury notes, the salt he makes or causes to be made, in quantities called for by purchasers at a price not exceeding fifteen dollars per bushel, shall be exempt for service in either class; and any person engaged or concerned in any way or to any extent in making salt, who or any of whose associates in making salt shall sell or exchange, or permit to be sold or exchanged, for anything whatever, salt, exceeding fifteen dollars per bushel, shall be subject to enumeration and service in the second class, whether he be under or over forty-five years of age, or a citizen of this State or not: *Provided,* but one person making salt for a company shall be exempt under this act.

Approved August 29, 1863.—Printed in *Alabama Historical Quarterly,* vol. 23, pp. 245–47.

This conflict of interest would never be resolved and proved to be one of the contributing factors in final collapse of the Confederacy.

Union Sentiment

All romantic tales to the contrary, Alabama was not wholly united in the cause of the Confederacy. An element in the war that loyal Alabamians often choose to ignore is the high rate of desertion. There were deserters from every county, Dr. Bessie Martin tells us in her book, *Desertion of Alabama Troops from the Confederacy,* but most of them from the hill counties of the north and the wiregrass section in the southeast, the same areas that had opposed secession. How many there were is impossible to say, but the Army of Northern Virginia reported that for the whole period of the war a little over 1,800 (6 percent of the aggregate) deserted not to return. Dr. Martin estimates that the total is between 10,000 and 20,000 and feels that the larger number is more nearly correct. Union sentiment was only one factor; genuine concern over the welfare of their families was the principal reason large numbers went home.

Most of the so-called Loyalists or Tories who opposed the Confederacy or actively supported the Union lived in the hill counties south of the Tennessee River with Walker, Morgan, Marion, Fayette, Franklin, Winston, and Blount furnishing the most recruits to the First Alabama Cavalry, U.S.A. This region had few slaves, produced little cotton and had voted against immediate secession in 1861. They had little to gain from a Confederate victory. There were few men of wealth among them, and according to contemporary accounts, the Union recruits were ignorant and poor. And many of them were fiercely loyal to the United States as is attested by the note written by one of them.

> I was Bornd and Raised in the Union and I expect to dy with a union principal in me I will dy before I will take an oath to support the Southerun Confedersa when ever lincoln dues eny thing contrary to the Constitution I am redy and willing to help put him away from their so I ad him no more.—Quoted in Hugh Bailey, "Disloyalty in Early Confederate Alabama," *Journal of Southern History*, vol. 23, p. 577.

The presence of a large disaffected group was recognized early in the war when Robert P. Blount reported to Confederate Secretary of War Judah P. Benjamin what he found in Greene County.

> SIR: Since addressing you a few days ago I have been credibly informed that another company of Union men are secretly organizing, and have elected their officers, in adjoining county to the one where the 300 are encamped I wrote you about, which it is supposed are intended to act in concert with them. They are avowed Union men, and have never declared what their intentions were. The superintendent of the military institution at Tuscaloosa in inclined to believe their intentions are to secure the prisoners at Tuscaloosa. I have the promise of one field piece and can get another and half the State Cadets, if necessary, to disperse them, if it is your order to do so. I am having their movements closely watched, and will keep you advised of them if you think it necessary. I am satisfied something serious is intended from all I can gather. The Governor does not feel authorized to issue orders to me, as we are intended for the Confederacy, but is willing for half the Cadets to act with me. I would be pleased to have an order to co-operate with any other troops that might be ordered there.—Blount to Benjamin, January 19, 1872, dateline, Camp Newbern, Green County, *Official Records of the War of the Rebellion*, vol. 7, p. 840.

There is no accurate record of how many union sympathizers there were. The *Compendium of the War of the Rebellion* lists only 2,678 white men who actually enlisted in the United States Army. How many more who formed irregular units like that in Greene County or fought and harassed the Confederates individually will never be known, but as more than one officer said, the "woods were thick with them." Brigadier-General Grenville M. Dodge, later famous as the leading spirit in the Union Pacific Railroad, who commanded the First Alabama Cavalry, wrote Adjutant-General T. S. Bowers that

The rebel conscription is driving into our lines a large number of Union men, who furnished substitutes, and men who have always stood by us and keep out of the rebel army by taking to the mountains. They desire to go into our service, and prominent men among them think they can raise a regiment. Can you authorize me to enlist them, and have a regiment to be known as the Second Alabama Cavalry? I raised and officered the First Alabama Cavalry at Corinth, now 800 strong, and I have no doubt I can raise another. These men flock to my lines from this fact.—*Official Records. . . .* vol. 21, part I, p. 256.

Major-General W. S. Rosecrans also wrote of the number of Alabamians joining the Union forces

We have organized and mustered into service, under authority already received, several companies of loyal Alabamians, for twelve-months' service. Since the occupation of this country and East Tennessee, men are fast organizing and applying to be mustered—some for one year, some for three. I request permission to organize regiments instead of companies from the States through which we pass, and to accept the companies for such time—not less than one year—as they may elect, and that arrangements be made to commission the officers.—Rosecrans to Col. E. D. Townsend, September 11, 1863. *Ibid.,* vol. 23, part 2, p. 11.

The action that took place in the Alabama hills is a classic example of internecine warfare. W. Stanley Hoole, a recent scholar of the Unionists in the state described their depredations on their Confederate neighbors.

Forming themselves into bands of so-called "Destroying Angels" or "Prowling Brigades," they occasionally swept down out of their piney-wood strongholds to raid their more fortunate neighbors in the valleys. Not infrequently, they burned cotton, gin-houses, jails, county court records, public buildings, and dwellings, willy-nilly "confiscating" food and other properties as they went. By their depredations thousands of Confederate sympathizers were driven from their homes—some to be stripped and whipped by the marauding guerillas and not a few to be murdered or raped. Even to the Union conquerors. . . , the Tories were sometimes "as vicious as copperheads."—W. Stanley Hoole, *Alabama Tories: The First Alabama Cavalry, U.S.A., 1862–1865* (Tuscaloosa, Ala.: Confederate Publishing Company, 1960), p. 6.

All the violence was not perpetrated by the Tories; the Confederates could and did mete out some of the same treatment. General Dodge complained of what was taking place in the hill counties.

CAPTAIN: I have the honor to submit a statement of a few of the outrages committed upon citizens of Alabama by the Confederate troops.

While all their leaders, from the President down, are boasting of their carrying on this war in accordance with the laws that govern nations in such cases, and are charging upon our troops all kinds of depredations and outrages, I think a few simple facts must put them to the blush, and make those parties and our press and people who are seconding the efforts of Davis to cast stigma upon us ashamed of the work they are doing. I will merely state what I know to be true. Abe Canade and Mr. Mitchell were hung two weeks ago for being Union men. They lived on the Hackelborough Settlement, Marion County, Alabama. Mr. Hallwork and daughter, of same county, were both shot for the same cause; the latter instantly killed. The former is yet alive, but will probably die. Peter Lewis and three of his neighbors were hunted down by one hundred bloodhounds and captured. The houses of Messrs. Palmer, Welsly, Williams, the three Wrightmens, and some thirty others were burned over their heads, the women and children turned out of doors, and the community notified that if they allowed them to go into other houses, or fed or harbored them in any manner, that they would be served the same. Mr. Peterson, living at the head of Bull Mountain, was shot, &c. I am now feeding some one hundred of these families, who, with their women and children, some gray-haired old men, and even cripples on crutches, were driven out and made their way here, through the woods and byways, without food or shelter—all done for the simple reason they were Union men, or that they had brothers or relations in our army. The statements of these people are almost beyond belief, did we not have the evidence before us. I am informed by them that there are hundreds of loyal men and women in the woods of Alabama, waiting for an opportunity to escape.—Dodge to Captain R. M. Sawyer, January 24, 1863, *Official Records. . . .*, vol. 23, part 2, p. 11.

On the political side, they held mass meetings and a group in Winston County passed resolutions that for all practical purposes made it the "Free State of Winston." After the war, this section showed its defiance to the rest of the state by remaining Republican in politics when the rest turned solidly Democratic.

Castle Morgan

Alabama had a military prison at Cahaba, named Castle Morgan, probably for John Hunt Morgan, famous as a "Rebel Raider." Just when it was built is not known but it was in active use in 1862. Jesse Hawes, later a prominent physician, was a Union prisoner there. His description is the most we know about it.

The prison had been an old cotton and corn shed—the property of Colonel Samuel Hill—located but a rod or two from the banks of the Alabama River. . . .
The walls of the structure were about fourteen feet high, thick and strong. A roof at one time had covered all portions of it, but the warring elements had stripped half of the roof away and had corroded in-

numerable holes through the remainder. It had been so long unused, that there was no incentive to repair the damage done by the years of rain and wind and sun. So poor were the accommodations it offered to its inmates, that as late as March, 1864, the Confederate Surgeon, R. M. Whitfield, who was in charge of the prison, in making his monthly report to the Medical Director, P. B. Scott, M. D., at Demopolis, used the following language: "I have the honor to transmit to you with this my monthly report. When you know the sanitary condition of the prison you cannot be surprised at the large number of cases reported. A brick wall covered by a leaky roof, with sixteen hundred feet of open space in its centre, four open windows, and the earth for the floor, constitutes the prison. . . ."

In the early part of 1864, in February or March, five or six large multiple bunks were placed in the prison. These, by most of our men, were called not bunks, but "roosts," as they presented to their occupants about the same comforts that chicken roosts would give. Each roost consisted of four or five tiers of rough boards placed one above the other, with spaces between each tier of about thirty inches. The upright timbers of the roosts were four inches square, ten feet long, and separated from each other about seven feet. These upright pieces were fastened to each other by cross-pieces, and upon this framework were laid the rough boards upon which the men were to sleep. There was neither straw nor bedding of any kind. In the report of Dr. Whitfield, quoted from above, he states that through the winter of 1863 and 1864 the prisoners would average about two blankets to each five men, but through the following winter this estimate would be excessive. Upon each roost, packed like sardines in a box, could be stowed away from sixty to eighty men, according to the height and length of the roost. During the summer of 1864 there were added to the number of the roosts enough to make them nine in all, and capable of furnishing lying-down room to about six hundred persons. During the winter of 1864 and 1865 the remaining twenty-five hundred made their beds upon the ground. . . .

While the water-supply of Castle Morgan was fairly abundant, since it came from an artesian well of the town a few blocks away from the prison, it was, unfortunately, warm, of a sweetish taste, and impregnated with a sulphur gas (sulphuretted hydrogen), strongly suggestive of eggs "too ripe."

To many of the inmates the water was nauseating and cathartic; if, however, we could have been assured of its purity the objections to it would have been fewer. Doubtless, the majority of those who drank it attributed all bad tastes to the mineral with which it was known to be impregnated, but from the report of Confederate Surgeon Whitfield, mentioned above, I quote the following: "The supply of water for drinking, cooking, and bathing, as well as for washing, is conveyed from an artesian well along an open street gutter for two hundred yards, thence under the street into the prison. In its course it is subjected to the washings of the hands, feet, faces, and heads of soldiers, citizens, and negroes; in it are rinsed buckets, tubs, and spittoons of groceries, offices, and hospitals; in it can be found the filth from hogs, dogs, cows, and horses, and filth of all kinds from the street and other sources."

Further on in his report Surgeon Whitfield takes occasion to complain of the inefficiency of the quartermasters at Cahaba, in the following language: "The two quartermasters at this post, with only the prison and one small hospital to supply, have failed to be equal to the task of having this prison supplied with good and sufficient wood, water, and bunks, and putting it in a condition in which it would be moderately comfortable, clean, and healthy. It is only useless to remark that I have made repeated complaints . . . to have these defects remedied. . . ."

The water entered the prison through a covered trough, or pipe, passing under the west wall near its centre. This trough was covered within the prison until it reached nearly the centre, where a ditch a foot deep, two or three feet wide, and twenty or thirty feet in length, was excavated. Sunk in the ditch were two barrels, placed on their ends, separated from each other by a few feet, with the upper ends open; water remained in the ditch at all times a foot in depth and in the barrels was deeper. . . .

The waste water from the inside of the prison passed in an open box beneath the seat of the water-closet, and served as a vehicle to carry away the fecal dregs. The open box extended only a foot or two beyond the walls of the privy, then its contents passed in an open ditch directly to the river. At the point where the ditch passed through the stockade, instead of planks or split logs placed close together, as in all other parts of the stockade, there were placed vertically small spruce or pine saplings, only three or four inches in diameter, of the same height as the remainder of the stockade, and separated from each other by a space of a few inches. This arrangement of the saplings assisted several persons in escaping over the stockade during the months of our confinement. It was possible to climb the saplings, but it was almost if not wholly impossible to climb over the stockade at any other point. The walls and floor of the water-closet were planks two inches thick, placed close together at the time it was built, but shrunken by drying, so that cracks a half inch wide existed between the planks.—Jesse Hawes, M. D., *Cahaba: A Story of A Captive Boy in Blue* (New York: Burr Printing Company, 1888), pp. 12–21, passim.

When the writer first saw the "castle" on July 26, 1864, it had about three hundred men in it, many of them picked up at "innumerable skirmishes and small engagements." Hawes escaped without too much difficulty—one suspects from his story the guards were glad to have him go—and made his way to Vicksburg where he joined other Union troops.

At Home

It was the non-military effects of the war that hurt everyone, if not more acutely, at least more constantly. The blockade created shortages in medicines like morphine and quinine, in necessities like pins, needles and salt, and in luxuries like silks, bonnets and spices. Since the South was an agricultural region, accustomed to buying its manufactured articles in the North or abroad, after the war began, when an article broke or wore out, there was no way to get a replacement. One of the most interesting phases of the war is the ingenuity with which Southerners found substitutes and made ersatz products for the familiar items no longer available.

More for convenience than anything else, the selections illustrating this phase of the war in Alabama came from one source, a journal kept by a very intelligent young woman, a teacher who stayed on her job during the war, Parthenia Hague.

Bicarbonate of soda, which had been in use for raising bread before the war, became "a thing of the past" soon after the blackade began; but it was not long ere some one found out that the ashes of corncobs possessed the alkaline property essential for raising dough. Whenever "soda" was needed, corn was shelled, care being taken to select all the red cobs, as they were thought to contain more carbonate of soda than white cobs. When the cobs were burned in a clean swept place, the ashes were gathered up and placed in a jar or jug, and so many measures of water were poured in, according to the quantity of ashes. When needed for bread-making, a teaspoonful or tablespoonful of the alkali was used to the measure of flour or meal required.

One of our most difficult tasks was to find a good substitute for coffee. This palatable drink, if not a real necessary of life, is almost indispensable to the enjoyment of a good meal, and some Southerners took it three times a day. Coffee soon rose to thirty dollars per pound; from that it went to sixty and seventy dollars per pound. Good workmen received thirty dollars per day; so it took two days' hard labor to buy one pound of coffee, and scarcely any could be had even at that fabulous price. . . . Others saved a few handfuls of coffee, and used it on very important occasions, and then only as an extract, so to speak, for flavoring substitutes for coffee.

There were those who planted long rows of the okra plant on the borders of their cotton or corn fields, and cultivated this with the corn and cotton. The seeds of this, when mature, and nicely browned, came nearer in flavor to the real coffee than any other substitute I now remember. Yam potatoes used to be peeled, sliced thin, cut into small squares, dried, and then parched brown; they were thought to be next best to okra for coffee. Browned wheat, meal and burnt corn made passable beverages; even meal-bran was browned and used for coffee if other substitutes were not obtainable.

We had several substitutes for tea which were equally as palatable, and, I fancy, more wholesome, than much that is now sold for tea. Prominent among these substitutes were raspberry leaves. Many during the blockade planted and cultivated the raspberry-vine all around their garden palings, as much for tea as the berries for jam or pies; these leaves were considered the best substitute for tea. The leaves of the blackberry bush, huckleberry leaves, and the leaves of the holly-tree when dried in the shade, also made a palatable tea. Persimmons dried served for dates.

Each household made its own starch, some of the bran of wheat flour. Green corn and sweet potatoes were grated in order to make starch. This process was very simple. The grated substance was placed to soak in a large tub of water; when it had passed through the process of fermentation and had risen to the surface, the grated matter was all skimmed off, the water holding the starch in solution was passed through a sieve, and then through a thin cloth to free altogether from any foreign substance.

The woods, as well as being the great storehouse for all our dye-stuffs, were also our drug stores. The berries of the dogwood-tree were taken for quinine, as they contained the alkaloid properties of cinchona and Peruvian bark. A soothing and efficacious cordial for dysentery and similar ailments was made from blackberry roots; but ripe persimmons, when made into a cordial, were thought to be far superior to blackberry roots. An extract of the barks of the wild cherry, dogwood, poplar, and wahoo trees was used for chills and agues. For coughs and all lung diseases a syrup made with the leaves and roots of the mullein plant, globe flower, and wild-cherry tree bark was thought to be infalliable. Of course the castor-bean plant was gathered in the wild state in the forest, for making castor oil.

Many also cultivated a few rows of poppies in their garden to make opium, from which our laudanum was created; and this at times was very needful. The manner of extracting opium from poppies was of necessity crude, in our hedged-around situation. It was, indeed, simple in the extreme. The heads or bulbs of the poppies were plucked when ripe, the capsules pierced with a large-sized sewing-needle, and the bulbs placed in some small vessel (a cup or saucer would answer) for the opium gum to exude and to become inspissated by evaporation. The soporific influence of this drug was not excelled by that of the imported article.

When the blockade had inclosed the South, our planters set about in earnest to grow wheat, rye, rice, oats, corn, peas, pumpkins, and ground peas. The chufa, a thing I had never heard of before, now came to the front, and was soon generally cultivated, along with the ground pea, as our position necessitated the production of cheap food for swine. The chufa was easily cultivated, and on fresh sandy or porous soil produced large crops. Every available spot was planted with the chufa, ground peas, and peas. Even in orchards the interstices between the fruit-trees were filled with these nutritious ground nuts. I remember an orchard near where I taught school, planted with chufas. The tubers were dropped about every two feet, in furrows three feet apart. They seemed like great bunches of grass, which spread until the interval between the plants was one mass of green foliage and roots from furrow to furrow. The owners of that orchard said the feed for their poultry had cost them nothing that season, as the whole brood of fowls lived among the chufas from the time they left the perch in the morning till they were called to be housed for the night, and that never before had poultry been so well fitted for the table, never before had the flesh been so white or so well flavored.

Ground peas were rarely grown before the war, and were generally called "goobers." I do not remember that I knew them by any other name; so one day in school hours, when one of the little scholars called to me that "Hetty's got my pindars," I was somewhat mystified as to what a "pindar" was, and when I called the little girl to fetch the pindars to me, she laid two or three goobers in my hand. They were to be seen on all sides, branching out in all directions, in patches large and small. Many planters in giving their corn and cotton the "laying-by" plowing, as it was called, would plant in the middle furrows ground peas, chufas, and cuttings from the sweet potato vines, which required very slight additional labor in harvesting the crops; and by the time the crops had all been gathered in and frost appeared, the tubers were well matured, and were great helps in fattening pork thereby enabling the planter to preserve more corn for the use of the government.

Beside growing the ground pea for help in fattening pork, a good supply was housed for seed and the use of the family. I have pleasant recollections of the many winters evenings when we would have the great oven brought into the sitting-room, placed on the hearth, with glowing red coals underneath, filled with white sand, in which we parched the pindars nice and brown. Or perhaps the oven would be filled partly with our home-made syrup, with raw ground peas hulled and dropped into the boiling syrup. Properly cooked, what nice peanut candy that made! Oil from the peanuts was also expressed for lamps and other uses during war times. In fine, peanuts, ground peas, goobers, and pindars, all one species, though known by all these names, played an important part during the blockade.

. . . Hundreds during the war resorted to such devices for freeing their grain of chaff; yet flour was very scarce, although the South put forth her best energies to cultivate wheat. After delivering the government tithe, and sharing with our home ones, the crop rarely lasted till another harvest. It was quite amusing to hear the neighbors as they met in social gatherings, or perhaps when separating from service at church, press their friends to come and see them, or come and have dinner, "For we have got a barrel of flour." It was even more amusing to have friends sit at the dining-table, and, when a waiter of brown, warm biscuits was passed round, to see them feign ignorance of what they were.

Bolted meal, when obtainable, made a very good substitute for flour, though millers said it injured their bolting-cloth to sift the corn meal through it; yet nearly every household, in sending its grist to be ground, would order a portion of the meal to be bolted for use as flour. Such bolted meal, when sifted through a thin muslin cloth and mixed up with scalding water to make it more viscid and adhesive, was as easily moulded into pie crust with the aid of the rolling-pin as the pure flour. Nice muffins and waffles were made of bolted meal, and we also made a very nice cake of the same and our home-made brown sugar.

All the moist and marshy places in the fields that had hitherto been thought fit for naught as to the growing of farm products, were utilized for rice and sugar-cane patches, and were found to yield plentifully. Some people, not having dank or moist spots suitable for rice on their farms, planted rice on the uplands, and were surprised to find they had an average yield with those who had planted the moist spots; and thus it has come about that even now in the South rice is planted on the uplands. Some few rude rice mills were hastily put up for stripping the coarse brown husks from the rice, but as they were distant from most of the planters in our settlement, wooden mortars had to be temporarily improvised. A tree of proper size would be cut down; from the stock a length suitable would be cut or sawed; a cavity would be hollowed with an adze in the centre of the block endwise. For the want of better polishing tools the cavity would be made smooth by burning with fire. The charred surface was then scraped off and made even, the hollow cleared free of all coal dust, and the pestle, made, perhaps, from a bough of the same tree, completed the primitive rice mill. Rough rice pounded in such a mortar and winnowed by the wind was clean and white. The only objection to it was that it was more splintered than if it had gone through a better mill.

Mills had also to be erected for grinding sugar-cane and the sorghum-cane, as some sorghum was raised in southern Alabama. In our settlement only the "green" and "ribbon" cane were grown, which, like the cereals, were never cultivated before the war.

Our shoes, particularly those of women and children, were made of cloth, or knit. Some one had learned to knit slippers, and it was not long before most of the women of our settlement had a pair of slippers on the knitting needles. They were knit of our homespun thread, either cotton or wool, which was, for slippers, generally dyed a dark brown, gray, or black. When taken off the needles, the slippers or shoes were lined with cloth of suitable texture. The upper edges were bound with strips of cloth, of color to blend with the hue of the knit work. A rosette was formed of some stray bits of ribbon, or scraps of fine bits of merino or silk, and placed on the uppers of the slippers; then they were ready for the soles.

We explored the seldom-visited attic and lumber-room, and overhauled the contents of old trunks, boxes, and scrap-bags for pieces of cashmere, merino, broadcloth, or other heavy fine twilled goods, to make our Sunday shoes, as we could not afford to wear shoes of such fine stuff every day; home-woven jeans and heavy, plain cloth had to answer for everyday wear. When one was so fortunate as to get a bolt of osnaburgs, scraps of that made excellent shoes when colored. What is now called the "baseball shoe" always reminds me of our war-time colored osnaburgs, but ours did not have straps of leather like those which cross the baseball-shoe. Our slippers and shoes which were made of fine bits of cloth, cost us a good deal of labor in binding and stitching with colors and thread to blend with the material used, before they were sent to the shoemaker to have them soled.

Sometimes we put on the soles ourselves by taking wornout shoes, whose soles were thought sufficiently strong to carry another pair of uppers, ripping the soles off, placing them in warm water to make them more pliable and to make it easier to pick out all the old stitches, and then in the same perforations stitching our knit slippers or cloth-made shoes. We also had to cut out soles for shoes from our home-tanned leather, with the sole of an old shoe as our pattern, and with an awl perforate the sole for sewing on the upper. I was often surprised at the dexterity with which we could join soles and uppers together, the shoe being reversed during the stitching, and when finished turned right side out again; and I smile even now when I remember how we used to hold our self-made shoes at arm's length and say, as they were inspected: "What is the blockade to us, so far as shoes are concerned, when we can not only knit the uppers, but cut the soles and stitch them on? Each woman and girl her own shoemaker; away with bought shoes; we want none of them!" But alas, we really knew not how fickle a few months would prove that we were.—Parthenia Hague, *A Blockaded Family: Life in Southern Alabama During the Civil War* (New York: Houghton-Mifflin, 1888), pp. 16–103, passim.

The tasks of creating these substitutes, running a household, and managing a farm or plantation generally fell to the women-folk. There was a provision in the conscription law for the exemption of one white man, whether master or overseer, for each plantation having a slave work force of more than twenty. There are, however, many instances of such households without a grown man there and, of course, the majority of families had few or no slaves at all and the men would not be exempt. In such cases, the women did the best they could to keep things going.

Mrs. Mariah Hindsman Cotton, who lived in the Mt. Olive community, Coosa County, was typical of myriads of simple but plucky women who kept their homes going while their menfolk were away at war. She with her seven children (all under twelve) was left to run the farm with the help of a hired slave.

Alabama Coosa Count August the 21 1862
my dear husband I now seat my self to rite you a few to let you hear from me and the children the children is all well at time and as for my self I am not atall sick but I trouble all most to death about you and our little cricket death it all most breaks my hart to think that you are gone so farr off from me and the children but I can only hope that the time is coming when you will get home to us all again I hope thes few lines may find you well everything is doing very well you stock is all doing very well so far I hant much of importen to rite to you for I cant hear of eny thing but war all the time they say tha are fixing for a big battle at richmond again I want you to rite to me weth you gon fether

of than you were before or not and rite to me all about how you far
wether you get annuf to eat or not I hear of some not getting anuf to
eat I so uneasy about you not getting anuf to eat so I want to no. . . .
you par sed he think that I will make a mity good crop of corne ther
is a heep of complant about sarrow crop I dont no what will become of
us all crop is sarrow and worms is eaten up the grass and ther is some on
the fodder I dont no whether tha will hurt the fodder or not you brouther
William and the rest of the conscript men started from around hear the
19 of this thear is a tauke of thear taken of them hier than thirty five but
I hope that wont take no more. wever do you want me to sell any of
you weet for seed or not you rite to me about what to do about it you
muct rite mea all the good advice you can for I need advice you no I
receive a letter from you a Monday it is now thursday it was date the
third of this I was glad to fom you I was sorrow to hear that you and asa
was not well I so uneasy about you I dont what to do I wood this hold
world if you was at home with me so I cood no when you sick or well
you sed that you wood bee uneasy till you heard that the children was
all well of the measels tha are all well of them now sweet and Jinny
has no had than yet I dont think tha will have them now so you must
not uneasy you self about the measells now sinch I commence this
letter nancy com up hear with a letter that she got today from asa it was
date 11 and it sed that you was in the horsepitol sick you dont no how
bad I felt to hear of you being in a horsepitol sick Oh that I ony cood
bee ther to wate on you I will bee so uneasy till hear from you I cant
rest but I hope you are better by this time and I hope by the time you get
this letter you will bee well Mr. Lessley got a letter William Legsley
that was date the 19 it sed you was sick he sed tha had sent the sick to
Atlanta and so I don't no wat to do about sending this letter and so I
did not send it I nevery was as uneasy in my life nuth mor at present but
remain your affecttion wife until death Mariah Cotton.—Lucille Griffith,
ed., *Yours Till Death: The Civil War Letters of John Weaver Cotton*
(University, Alabama: The University of Alabama Press, 1951), pp.
16–17.

It was the women who had the responsibility of securing the
family valuables when the enemy approached. Miss Lena Lockhart's
grandmother at Thomaston hid her jewelry under squash hills
when she knew Wilson's raiders were near. Ella Storrs Christian
remembered how her family hid their valuables in Perry County,
not far from Uniontown.

There now began to be a feeling of disaffection among some of the
negroes (not those we inherited), so as we were afraid they might be
tempted, or threatened into telling the raiders where the things were
concealed we had to pack our valuables at night, after the servants had
left the house, and the children were asleep. You can form no idea of
what a job this was. We packed all of my jewelry in a wooden box,
put the spoons and forks in glass jars, and wrapped the large heavy

pieces in cloth, and tying them altogether, wrapped the bundle in oil cloth. This I now see was a great mistake, as your father was not strong enough to dig as large a hole, as was necessary to properly conceal a bundle of this size. It would have been better to have several small bundles hidden in different places. He first buried it in the shelter of the carriage house, I, watching and listening to see that he was not spied on. But the next morning we found that the place could easily be seen, so while the house servants were at breakfast he dug the bundle up, and brought it to me, and hid it in the big wardrobe until night. Your father then went off alone and buried it, but next he thought of a better hiding place, so that night the bundle went traveling again. Just as he finished digging the hole he felt sure he heard the sound of someone breathing, but the night was so intensely dark the he could not see anyone and the bundle came home again. It made several other trips, but for various reasons was always brought back to the house. I positively grew to hate the sight of that bundle, and felt that I would cheerfully give it to the first Yankee who came. At last your father decided to leave it in the house until the Yankees were reported much nearer.—Ella Storrs Christian, "The Days That Are No More," *Alabama Historical Quarterly,* vol. 15, p. 128.

As it developed, women provided much of the care for the sick and wounded. This role of nurse to the family was a familiar one. The authorities only reluctantly used their services in hospitals. The Confederate government was slow in setting up a medical service. To care for the sick and wounded in the meantime, the state authorized hospitals to be set up close to the fields of action. Governor John Gill Shorter appointed Arthur F. Hopkins of Mobile to be superintendent of the Alabama hospitals. His wife, Juliet Opie Hopkins, was his able assistant and did much of the work. The state appropriated large sums for hospital work but the bulk of the supplies came from donations. Ladies in every part of the state formed soldiers' aid societies to knit socks, roll bandages, and pack boxes for Mrs. Hopkins. The letter from Cahaba is typical of scores of others.

Cahaba, Dallas Co. Ala.
Oct. 8, 1861

Mrs. Arthur F. Hopkins,
My dear Madam,
 The ladies of the Military Aid Society of this place, desiring to contribute toward the relief of the sick and wounded of the Alabama Hospital under your care, have instructed me to forward to you the Enclosed check for fifty four dollars, from the Bank of Selma, on W. B. Isaacs & Co. of Richmond, payable to your order.
 We also shipped, yesterday to you, via Montgomery, a box of supplies for the same purpose, an imperfect list of which I enclose—these were contributed by ourselves and the citizens, generally, and we trust that you

will find them useful among the numerous recipients of your motherly care and attention.

We have been mindful of your noble efforts for the alleviation of the sufferings of our sick and wounded soldiers in Virginia, from the beginning of the War, and rejoiced to see that your plans were duly appreciated on a more enlarged scale, of your hospital.

With great respect   Mrs. John D. F. Williams
I am very truly yours   Sec. M. Aid Society.

List of articles contained in box, shipped to Ala. Hospital, Richmond from Military Aid Society of Cahaba Dallas Co., Ala.

44 bottles Brandy	1 ” Tomato Catsup
1 ” ” Peach Brandy	1 ” Pepper Sauce
2 ” ” Cordial	6 Pillow Ticks
2 Muscadine Wine	4 ” Cases
3 ” Sherry ”	12 Sheets
1 ” Whiskey	57 prs of drawers
2 ” Bay Rum	50 Shirts
2 ” Cologne	1 Jar Brandy Peaches
6 ” Ginger Wine	1 Jar Peach Marmalade
2 ” Capers	2 ” Plum Jelly
1 ” Grape Jelly	3 Cans Lobster
1 ” Pickled Peaches	2 Cans Fruit
1 ” Pickled Onions	4 doz. and more of Gelatine
1 ” Sweet pickles	2 lbs Sage
1 ” ” Cabbage Pickles	6 lbs Tapioca
1 Bot. Cucumber Catsup	6 ” Castile Soap
1 ” Mustard	1-⅓ doz. Towels

—Mrs. A. F. Hopkins' Papers, State Department of Archives and History, Montgomery.

At the beginning of the war the only women with any training in nursing were the Sisters of Charity. This religious order had two hospitals in Mobile and founded a third in Montgomery, all of which were used as army hospitals. Many prominent women volunteered their nursing skills and some actually performed dedicated service. The best-known of the nurses from Alabama was Scottish-born, Mobile-reared Kate Cumming. Miss Cumming was a lady and had to overcome strong family objection before she began her wartime career. Beginning in April 1862, she spent most of her time with the troops in north Mississippi, eastern Tennessee, and northwestern Georgia, wherever a battle raged and battle casualties needed her services, until the end of May 1865.

The End

At the end of her long and detailed journal, Kate Cumming wrote some final thoughts about the meaning of the war.

This year has developed the fall of the South. Time has revealed the utter loss of all our hopes. A change must pass over every political and social idea, custom, and relation. The consummation makes the year just passed ever memorable in our annals. In it gathers all the interest of the bloody tragedy; from it begins a new era, midst poverty, tears, and sad memories of the past. O, may we learn the lesson all of this is designed to teach: that all things sublunary are transient and fleeting, and lift our souls to that which is alone ever-during and immutable— God and eternity! And forgetting the past, save in the lessons which it teaches, let us . . . redeem the time, live humbly, and trust God for future good. . . .—Harwell, ed., *Kate*. . . , p. 307.

Other Alabamians, when realizing the war was over, recorded less lofty thoughts. Mrs. Chadick in Huntsville said "came home heartsick and thoroughly disgusted with everything." J. B. Moore who had been disgruntled all along was glad to have it over. "Well, slavery is at an end. Let it go. . . . The most disgraceful war ever inaugurated and the most causeless. In fact, commenced for no real injury whatever." Many disillusioned service men doubtless agreed with the young soldier who declared, "I'll be damned if I ever love a country again!"

The war had ground to a halt and what had Alabama contributed to its progress? In addition to having provided the first capital, she had furnished two cabinet officers: Leroy Pope Walker of Huntsville, the first Secretary of War and Thomas H. Watts, Attorney General from April to August 1862. Josiah Gorgas, a career army man who married the daughter of Governor John Gayle, resigned his commission and became the hard-working Chief of Ordnance for the Confederacy. The various establishments in Selma had produced much of the hardware for the war, including some ironclads. There had been 63 infantry regiments, "from 12 to 15" regiments of cavalry and at least 18 batteries of artillery in the Confederate service. Also there were an estimated 3,000 Alabamians in the Union army. Of those who served in the Confederate army, it is impossible to say how many men were involved, because records were imperfectly kept or since lost; estimates run from 75,000 to 100,000. Out of a total white population of just over half a million, this is a large percentage and so is the estimated list of casualties which varies from 25,000 to 70,000.

This had been a very personal war, touching thousands whose lives heretofore had been lived simply and close to home. There had been cowards and deserters, to be sure, but the majority had given their best which had proved to be not enough. Their cause was lost and they were faced with the necessity of building a new world for themselves.

Chapter 12

RECONSTRUCTION, 1865–1874

The Confederacy had lost the war. Southerners had begun with high hopes and extravagant (as it proved) confidence. They had met news of early reverses in battle with utter disbelief. Four years after the bombardment of Fort Sumter, their armies were shattered and defeated. General Lee had surrendered at Appomattox, and other commanders had done likewise elsewhere. What had gone wrong? Students of the period have pinned the blame on many different causes, but from the vantage point of a century later certain factors begin to emerge more clearly. As in all complicated matters, there is no one simple answer.

There are still a few "unreconstructed rebels" who insist that the Confederacy was overwhelmed by sheer weight of numbers. There is a current story about an old soldier, who having just seen the battle of Atlanta in the movie, *Gone with the Wind*, was asked what he thought of it. His reply was that if he had had that many men, he could have licked the whole blank, blank lot of them! The South was outnumbered in manpower, to be sure, but total enlistments (Union 1,556,678; Confederacy 1,082,119) do not show any outstanding superiority in the North's military strength. Considering the requirements of offensive warfare and invasion, the maintenance of long lines of communications, the Union's numerical advantage was less than these figures would indicate. But, on the other hand, these statistics give no indication of the percentage of the total population in relation to the armed services. The population of the North was in round numbers 22,000,000; of the South 9,500,000, of whom 3,500,000 were slaves, leaving 6,000,000 from which to draw the total fighting forces. This means that one out of every six whites was in uniform. In some communities there were almost no able bodied men left; by the last months of the war there were almost no reserves on which to draw. Is this the reason the South lost the war?

After examining the various theories of Confederate defeat, Dr. Malcolm C. McMillan concludes that all of them indicate that the war was lost on the homefront, not on the battlefield. He names as supporting evidence:

> . . . the weakening effect of states' rights when some centralization was needed to win the war; the blockade and dislocation of the southern economy because of lack of manpower, both of which resulted in shortages; the failure to win foreign aid; the complete breakdown of finance and taxation; the collapse of transportation facilities; the lack of industry or the one-sided agricultural economy of the South; and the incompetency of President Davis, or Congress, or various Southern leaders.—Malcolm C. McMillan, *The Alabama Confederate Reader* (University, Ala.: University of Alabama Press, 1963), p. 321.

The Role of Women

The irony of this conclusion is that some of the most valiant deeds of the war had been performed on the homefront by women who had their first opportunity to serve in a sphere wider than their homes and immediate neighborhoods. H. E. Sterkx in a recent book about Alabama women in this period says:

> Rich and poor alike were caught up in a conflict that they regarded as much their war as did the men who fought the battles and managed the affairs of government. Their thoughts and actions demonstrated this beyond contest. Many took an inconspicuous but definite hand in promoting secession and in building the new nation. As willing participants in the struggle for independence a heretofore homebound population helped in raising armies, formed auxiliaries in behalf of the war effort, and labored incessantly in caring for sick and wounded soldiers. The less inhibited and better educated struck out against apparent injustices in a way few would dare consider undertaking during less troublesome times. They also performed men's work, experienced severe economic privations with a minimum of complaint, and took time out to provide consolation and amusement for their beloved warriors. Scores experienced the brunt of invasion with all its accompanying horrors and destruction and finally, like the men, became weary of war, lost faith in the Confederacy, and gave up.—H. E. Sterkx, *Partners in Rebellion: Alabama Women in the Civil War* (Rutherford, N. J.: Fairleigh Dickinson University Press, 1970), p. 200.

Yet, in spite of such heroic endeavors and competence, the war did little to free women from their traditional place in society. The only new occupation opened to them was school teaching. A few participated in temperance societies, church activities, and the

Grange, but most of them had to wait until after the turn of the century before their voices would be heard so clearly again.

The Role of the Enlisted Man

Americans in general have tended to emphasize the role of the officers in war, overlooking that of the men who represent the vast majority of the fighting forces. Even though some of them were ignorant, some cowardly, and some little given to following orders, the majority of them exhibited praiseworthy qualities of bravery and resourcefulness. As Bell Irvin Wiley pointed out in his presidential address to the Southern Historical Association in 1955, the war gave the privates and other enlisted men their first opportunity to exhibit their personal qualities, and he found them admirable; for them it was a time of greatness. One of the men he quotes is John Weaver Cotton of Coosa who wrote his wife Mariah about his homesickness.

> I want to come home bad as any body can . . . but I shant run away . . . I don't want it throwed up to my children after I am dead and gone that I was a deserter . . . I don't want to do anything if I no it will leave a stain on my posterity hereafter—*Yours Till Death*, p. 65.

Unlike the women who sank back into their accustomed role, these plain men took on a new importance in the economic and political life of the post-war period.

The Role of the Freedmen

The Negroes, of course, were the ones whose life was changed the most. We know relatively little about what they thought about the war at the time. We do know that there was no apparent widespread unrest among them until near the end of hostilities. When a federal army moved into an area, there were wholesale "desertions" among the plantation blacks, but until that happened, life went on much the same. There is evidence that most of them knew even before the Emancipation Proclamation that their future was at stake. Nevertheless, many of them were active contributors to the Southern cause. They worked to produce the food that the government was urging the people to grow instead of cotton; they protected the women and children left at home; at times they were accomplices in hiding the family valuables; there are instances of a faithful servant diverting the attention of the enemy to the advantage of his master; many went to battle with their masters to look after them. In later months, they were impressed to do manual work such as digging trenches; and there was a definite plan to draft them into the army which did not materialize because the war ended.

One of the few pieces of evidence of impressment of slaves that has come to light is the following letter:

Centerville, Bibb Cty., Alabama Nov. 17, 1864

Mr. J. H. Green

Sir you are hereby notified to furnish one (1) able bodied hand for 12 months, said hand will be hired or impressed at your option by the government "to increase the efficience of the army by the employment of slaves in certain capacities." You will receive $15.00 per month, rations and clothing furnished by the government or $25.00 per month rations only furnished by the government. You will deliver me said hand with 4 days rations at Centerville, Bibb Cty.—Ala. on the first day of Dec./64 when you will be [   ] therefore.

L. E. Starr
Agt. Impressment Bibb Cty. Alabama
—Privately owned, xerox copy furnished by Miss Ann Hamilton.

Adjustment to Freedom

When Cato was 101 years old, he still remembered the end of the war and how he was set free in Wilcox County, near Pineapple.

Massa Cal come back, and he was all wore out and ragged. He soon called all the niggers to the front yard and says, "Mens and womens, you are today as free as I am. You are free to do as you like, 'cause the damned Yankees done 'creed you are. They ain't a nigger on my place what was born here or ever lived here who can't stay here and work and eat to the end of his days, as long as this old place will raise peas and goobers. Go if you wants, and stay if you wants." Some of the niggers stayed and some went, and some what had run away to the North come back. They always called, real humble-like, at the back gate to Missy Angela, and she always fixed it up with Massa Cal they could have a place.—B. S. Botkin, ed., *Lay My Burden Down: A Folk History of Slavery* (Chicago: University of Chicago Press, 1945), pp. 87–88.

The true picture of the Negroes' reaction to freedom is difficult to draw because the written records are by whites, former masters, army officers, and personnel with organizations like the Freedmen's Bureau. From these, however, it appears that, in their simplicity, these former slaves believed freedom meant freedom from work and the opportunity to go wherever they pleased. They flocked to the army encampments, expecting the same care they received on the plantation. They came in such numbers that the authorities simply could not handle them. Health conditions were so bad in the hastily erected tent villages that uncounted numbers became ill. Some followed the army when it moved; others drifted to towns where a few eventually found jobs; still others returned to their former homes. The tenant farming system would eventually be the solution to the large number of rootless freedmen.

Mrs. V. V. Clayton, whose delightful account of plantation days before the war has been used earlier, wrote the following account of one of their former servants and his adjustment to freedom.

After Emancipation, Lewis remained with us many years. His home was only a short distance from our home. He cultivated a farm successfully, and soon had acquired not only the neccessaries of life, but some luxuries. He had a pair of nice horses, a buggy and wagon, and other things, and lived well; but he had never known freedom entirely without Mars' Henry's supervision. One day he came to the conclusion that he would move away and enjoy freedom to its fullest extent. He came to see Mr. Clayton in the fall to say something about it. He seemed embarrassed when Mr. Clayton addressed him: "Lewis, what it is you want?" "Well, Mars' Henry, I want to move away and feel entirely free and see what I can do by mysef. You has been kind to me and I has done well, but I want to go anyhow." Mr. Clayton said, "Very well, Lewis, that is all right, move when you please; but when you leave, nail up the door of your house and leave it until you want to come back. No one will go into it."

Lewis and his brother, Ned, rented a farm some miles beyond Clayton, moved, and we heard no more of them until the next fall, when Lewis made his appearance, very much dejected. Mr. Clayton said, "How are you, Lewis? How are you getting on?" "Bad, Mars' Henry. I have come to ask ef I cen go into my house again."

Lewis and Ned had hired hands, gotten a merchant to furnish them, and lost almost everything they had started out with. Lewis moved back, and has been loth to leave the Claytons since, and is now with us, an old man. . . .—Clayton, *Black and White under the Old Regime* (Milwaukee, Wis.: The Young Churchmen Co., 1899), p. 172.

Freedmen's Bureau

Churches and private organizations attempted a variety of aid programs, often of an educational nature, for the freedmen, but the one governmental agency designed to assist them to adjust to their new status was the Bureau of Refugees, Freedmen, and Abandoned Lands.

The Bureau was created by act of Congress on March 3, 1865. General O. O. Howard was named its head. He moved with remarkable speed and had operations underway before the end of May. Brigadier-General Wager Swayne, assistant commissioner for

Alabama, arrived in Montgomery on July 26 and undertook his job with vigor. He had the responsibility for the some 430,000 former slaves in the state who had become wards of the Bureau on May 4 when General Richard Taylor surrendered the last of the Confederate troops east of the Mississippi River to General Edward R. S. Canby at Citronelle, in Mobile County. Before General Swayne's arrival what official assistance had been given was through the efforts of T. W. Conway, assistant for Louisiana whose efforts were confined chiefly to the southern part of the state, and of his counterpart in Tennessee in the northern counties. Their work had been chiefly in the form of relief, often furnished by the army.

Alabama could have had a much worse commissioner than Wager Swayne. Walter L. Fleming who, having grown up during the bitter days following the war, found little praiseworthy in Reconstruction, but said that under Swayne's charge, the Bureau was probably the "least harmful" of all in the South. He had been born in Ohio, the son of Noah H. Swayne, a successful lawyer and justice of the federal Supreme Court. The elder Swayne was a native Virginian, but his Quaker views on slavery caused him to go west to Ohio. The son, after graduating from Yale and the Cincinnati Law School, became a partner with his father. At the outbreak of the war, he volunteered for the army and rose in the ranks to become a major-general. He was in the battle of Atlanta and in the fighting in northwest Georgia around Dalton. When the federal troops moved north, he saw action in the Carolinas and lost his right leg in the battle at River's Bridge, South Carolina. An efficient regimental commander, he was awarded the medal of honor for bravery. In the Carolina campaign he had attracted the attention of General O. O. Howard who appointed him to the position in Alabama.

The Bureau in Alabama had five departments: Department of Abandoned and Confiscated Lands, Department of Records (Labor, Schools, and Supplies), Department of Finance, the Medical Department, and the Bounty Department. The State was divided into five geographical districts with headquarters at Mobile, Selma, Montgomery, Troy, and Demopolis. The twelve northern counties were under the jurisdiction of General Clinton B. Fisk, assistant commissioner for Tennessee. Most of the men in charge of these districts were members of the Veteran Reserve Corps.

The purposes of the Bureau were admirable and although many leading citizens heartily disliked its presence in their midst, the Bureau received a relatively small amount of criticism until after radical congressional Reconstruction took over the state. After that time the Bureau and the Union League, a political organization to educate and propagandize the blacks into the Republican party, tended to merge. Officers of the two were often the same people, and the Bureau ceased to be little more than another political agency. Swayne was removed from office in January, 1868.

When Swayne arrived in Alabama, he was pleasantly surprised to be received with little hostility. Nevertheless, his task was staggering. He found whites fearful of the future and the blacks confused as to the meaning of their new freedom. He had few guidelines, but following the principles laid down by General Howard, he selected those applicable which he could use in his own situation. These were:

> . . . to introduce practicable systems of compensated labor, removing the prejudices of the planter against employing their former slaves and the belief of the freedmen that they could live without labor; to provide the destitute, aged, and sick in cooperation with the northern aid societies, while compelling the able-bodied to labor for their own support; to afford facilities to the aid societies and state authorities for the maintenance of schools for refugees until a system of free schools could be supported by the local authorities; to protect loyal refugees and to assist them in returning to their homes; and to adjudicate differences arising between Negroes and between Negroes and whites where there was an interruption of civil law or where the Negroes' rights to justice were disregarded.—Elizabeth Bethel, "The Freedmen's Bureau in Alabama," *Journal of Southern History,* vol. 14 (February 1948), pp. 50–51.

The Bureau assumed many of the duties which the planters had formerly performed for the blacks.

Swayne believed that the Bureau's task was to "mold existing institutions" that were permanent rather than to replace them with "a temporary antagonism of military power." Consequently, he cooperated with the civil authorities where he could. Nevertheless, he found that since the courts were closed to the freedmen and being unwilling to establish special courts administered by non-residents of the state, he designated the judges and magistrates then holding office to serve as agents of the Bureau for the administration of justice. He made it clear that they had no other powers in the Bureau and also that if they refused to accept such an assignment, they would be removed from office and replaced by someone who would. And this was done. For example, Mayor Stough of Mobile who persisted in his "determination not to admit negro evidence against white persons," resigned and John Forsythe, who "took a more practical view of the question," was appointed to the office. Governor Parsons assured compliance with Swayne's order by issuing a proclamation for all judges to abide by it.

Among the many activities of the Bureau one of the most appreciated in the early days was that of securing and distributing provisions of food supplies. From June, 1865, to September, 1866, the Freedmen's Bureau issued 2,522,907 rations to white refugees and 1,128,740 to freedmen. As time went on, however, the number of refugees seeking food decreased sharply.

It was not long before the Bureau was charged with withholding rations until just before an election and then trading bacon for ballots, Republican ones. Just before one election excessive amounts of bacon were being distributed in all parts of the state. M. G. Candee, for example, issued in Wilcox and Monroe Counties 24,902 pounds, and Holland Thompson and J. C. Hendrix in Montgomery issued for several communities 14,151. Talladega County alone received 7,500 pounds. Reports such as the one made by deputy United States Marshall Perrin, prompted an investigation:

I issued the bacon for Monroe County. Previous to doing so, a report was circulated among the negroes that in order for them to obtain bacon they would have to vote the straight Republican ticket: and if they received bacon, and afterwards refused or neglected to vote the said Republican ticket, they would forfeit their rights in law. As I was a candidate for the Legislature upon said ticket, I did not consider it necessary to correct this report. . . . It was extensively circulated through Monroe, Conecuh, Clark, and Wilcox Counties that a barbecue would be held at Monroeville on election day, and that all negroes who would attend and vote the Republican ticket would receive bacon enough to last them a year. This induced many to come from adjoining counties to Monroeville and vote on said day. The barbecue was held and largely attended. . . . At least five hundred illegal votes were cast there for the Republican ticket.—Fleming, ed. *Documentary History of Reconstruction,* vol. 2, p. 84, quoting House Report #262, Forty-third Congress, 1299.

The Bureau engaged in many other activities. It established and operated hospitals for the freedmen; in 1866 there were six of these but only three in 1869. They opened two Freedmen's Savings Banks (a project which had the special interest of General Howard), in Mobile and Montgomery. It sponsored several settlements for landless and rootless blacks and supervised the making of labor contracts.

Beginning in 1869, the assets of the Bureau were liquidated, and after 1870 no more money was appropriated for it. In the five years of its existence, it had spent $645,213.42. Elizabeth Bethel says the funds were carefully accounted for. This does not mean that there was no fraud at the local level nor that the Bureau always acted fairly. It had its greatest success in the fields of relief and educational work. When the Negroes were given the suffrage and whites disfranchized, many of the Bureau officials became civil officials and, as has been noted earlier, officers in the Union League, a purely political organization. Fleming concedes that Swayne was a "man of common sense, a soldier and a gentleman" who honestly desired to do what was best for all—the Negro first—but that the system was corrupt and doomed from the beginning. It is debatable whether it had any lasting success, but its initial motives were admirable.

Readjustment to the New Order

The Reconstruction period made harsh demands of everyone and the ones who probably suffered most severely were the returning soldiers. They had been defeated on the battlefield, their cause was lost, and their pride was humiliated. They returned to homes ravaged by war or damaged by four years of neglect. Their labor was gone, and their money worthless. Those who had the most had lost the most. In spite of all this, the majority who wrote down their feelings expressed a willingness to forget the past, accept the realities of defeat, and become active citizens of the United States again. Such was the attitude of John Massey, educator and clergyman.

THE OATH OF ALLEGIANCE

After the surrender I was not molested by the officers of the United States government. In November 1865, I went voluntarily to Lieutenant Schrann, the officer in charge of Choctaw County, and took the oath of allegiance to the United States. I took this oath in good faith and have always considered it as binding as if nothing had happened from January 11, 1861, to November, 1865.

When Alabama seceded, I believe that she was the only body politic to which I owed allegiance. When the Confederacy was formed and Alabama became a part of it, my allegiance went to that government also. But when Alabama had, by the terms of the surrender, accepted these results of the war—namely, that the Confederacy was extinct, that secession was dead—and when she had by vote declared her purpose to remain in the Union, I considered that I was under obligation to declare my allegiance to the government of the United States, if I intended in live under it and claim its protection.—John Massey, *Reminiscences* (Nashville: Publishing House of the M. E. Church, South, 1916), p. 221.

Several newspapers throughout the state took the editorial position that can be summed up in the words of the Eufaula *Daily News*. "Let us accept the fact that we are part and parcel of the United States government . . . ." The Montgomery *Daily Advertiser* carried an editorial elaborating on this theme.

THE DUTY OF THE HOUR

Whatever of bitterness has been engendered in the hearts and minds of the people during the last four years, good policy now dictates that it be cast aside . . . . The great leaders who are at liberty have set the example of laboring earnestly, not only to secure a livelihood, but to reconcile the people to a hearty support of the existing order of things. July 25, 1865.

In stressing the acceptance of things as they were, it just must not be overlooked that men everywhere in the South were surrounded by physical and emotional results of the war. They could not help contrasting present conditions with those before the war.

It is scarcely possible to exaggerate the effects of the late desolating war. Where five years ago every thing wore the cheerful aspects of affluence and refinement, where happiness and prosperity abounded, where were apparent domestic and social amenities such as can scarcely be found in any other portion of men's earthly heritage, there is now desolation, poverty, sorrow and suffering; fields are lying waste and unfenced that were then teeming with rich abundance; heaps of ashes and naked chimneys now mark the sites of thousands of splendid dwellings; hopeless misery and helpless despair now brood in sullen silence where but recently princely hospitality and every social and domestic virtue were found in their most attractive forms. In fact, in almost every part of the South the march of hostile armies, the deadly carnage of fiercely contested battles, and all the horrors and devastations of ruthless war may be traced in ruins, blood, and new-made graves.—A. Greene, "The Political Crisis," *De Bow's Review,* I (May, 1866), p. 468.

Nevertheless, many, if not most, men in Alabama were willing to accept the "new order." The new order, while it required great economic and social adjustments on the part of both whites and freedmen, proved to be decidedly political.

Politics of Reconstruction

The course of National Reconstruction following the Civil War is so familiar to students of history that only the barest outline is needed here. Lincoln's plan of Reconstruction was based on the simple theory that the states had never been out of the Union and the sooner they were back in their proper relation the better. He asked only that the states agree to emancipation and, when ten percent of the 1860 voters agreed, they could hold elections and begin a normal political life again. Before peace was three days old, Lincoln was dead, but Andrew Johnson tried to carry out the same program with only minor changes. Both presidents believed Reconstruction was an executive matter. Alabama accepted his plan and began to rebuild her state government in preparation for re-admission to the Union. The summer of 1865 was crucial.

The troops surrendered in mid-April and Governor T. H. Watts was arrested by the Federal authorities on May 1, 1865. From that date until June 21 when a provisional governor was appointed, there seems to have been virtually no state and local government. Where troops were concentrated, the generals attempted some kind of authority, but that was about all. That the state did not experi-ence extreme anarchy or a bloodbath may be attributed to the facts that the blacks were busy celebrating their new-found free-dom and the whites were too stunned and exhausted from their recent experiences. There were many acts of violence but apparent-ly most of them were committed by troops stationed in various centers, bands of ruffians claiming to be soldiers, or men bent on plunder.

Lewis E. Parsons, a lawyer from Talladega, was President Andrew Johnson's choice for provisional governor. He was ap-pointed on June 21, 1865, to serve until a civilian government could be elected; he was in office six months. Parsons had lived in Talla-dega since 1840, but he was a native of New York state. In politics he was a former Whig (as were many of the post-war leaders in Alabama); he had opposed secession, but once it was an accom-plished fact, he served in the state legislature as he had done before the war.

An Alabamian who knew him described him as a "remarkable man."

He was in the prime of life, of imposing stature, handsome countenance and a fluent speaker . . . . In early manhood he came to the village of Talladega to practice law and rapidly rose to the front of the bar, where Rice, Morgan, Heflin, White, Bowie and other distinguished [jurists?] there challenged his powers. He built, perhaps, the most imposing residence of the settlement . . . .

Parsons was the leading Whig or Union stump speaker of his part of the state. Yancy pronounced him to be the ablest of all Union de-baters . . . .—John Witherspoon DuBose, *Alabama's Tragic Decade, 1865–1874* (Birmingham, Alabama: Webb Book Company, 1940), pp. 38–39.

Governor Parsons was the only government official in office; there was no state legislature. There had been a move to hold a meeting of the old one as soon as possible, but a presidential proclamation forbade it. Parsons was required to do several things: register those who would take an oath of loyalty to the United States (56,825 did on August 31), hold an election for delegates to a convention for drafting a new constitution (September) which would embody a declaration that secession was null and void, a repudiation of the state's war debt, and the abolition of slavery.

The oath was not difficult for men of good will to take. It read:

I _____ of the County of _____, State of Alabama, do solemnly swear, in the presence of Almighty God, that I will hence forth faithfully support, protect and defend the Constitution of the United States and the union of the States there under; and that I will, in like manner, abide by and faithfully support all laws and proclamations which have been made during the existing rebellion with reference to the emancipation of slaves; So help me God.

Subscribed and sworn before me, this 1st day of December A. D. 1865.

—Form used by W. D. King, the great-grandfather of Jimmie and Lida Wood, students at Alabama College.

There were special categories, however, who had to apply directly to the president for amnesty: leading officials in the Confederate and state governments, high ranking officers in the army and navy, and men who had property worth $20,000 or more. The petition of the Reverend Basil Manly shows the kind of information given in such cases.

To His Excellency, Andrew Johnson, President of the U. S.

The petition of B. Manly, aged sixty-seven, a minister of the Gospel, & for the last few years a planter, respectfully showeth,

That he was in favor of the separation of the slave-holding states from the General Government in 1861; and that, in 1862, he subscribed sixty (60) bales of cotton to the confederate government; but that he never held or sought a political office under the same, nor under the state in which he resides;—

That he accepts the pacification which has been attained; that he has taken the oath appended to the proclamation of amnesty by the President, of May 29th. 1865 (which oath he requests may be taken as part of this petition), and that he expects to spend the residue of his days in a quiet and peaceable manner.

He further states that he has six children, two of whom are daughters, and residing in Virginia and South Carolina. Of the sons, the two eldest are ministers of the Gospel & pastors, and have remained with their charges respectively, during the whole of the late hostilities. The two younger sons have been in the confederate service,—one as a machinist in the Ordnance department; the other as a captain in the 59th, regiment of Ala. Vols; and that both have now taken the oath required of them.

He further states that he is in possession of property, almost wholly in lands, of which the estimated value may possibly extend as high as twenty thousand (20,000) dollars;—in any estimate, however, your petitioner desires the benefit of the President's amnesty; and, as in duty bound, your petitioner will ever pray, &c.

I put this petition into the hands of James H. Fitts, Esq. who is to present it to the President. I have at the same time, taken an oath to defend the Constitution & union of the states, and to support the proclamations in regard to slavery issued during the war. I have answered certain interrogations propounded by order of Gov. Parsons.—All done Aug. 3, 1865.—Printed in *Alabama Review,* vol. 5, pp. 144–45.

Governor Parsons had a difficult time because government (as well as society) was in a chaotic condition, and he received his share of criticism. The Montgomery *Daily Advertiser,* however, often found reasons to praise him and reported favorably on many of his activities. On July 22 it said,

. . . Gov. Parsons evidently intends to administer justice with that fearless impartiality, moderation and consistency which has characterized his past life. We think Alabama fortunate in having appointed over her at this critical juncture a gentleman of his enlarged views, cultivated intellect and thorough identity with the State.

The *Advertiser* also approved of the gestures of good will being made by the freedmen in the city.

Dinner to Gov. Parsons and Gen. Smith. On Saturday the colored brethren of the Methodist Benevolent Society served an elegant dinner in the southern suburbs of the city in honor of Gov. Parsons and Maj. Gen. Smith. These honored personages were escorted out by the Alabama Fire Company #2, consisting of negro gentry, and the splendid band of the 8th Iowa. Brig. Gen. Swayne, Col. Buckley, the mayor of the city, and others were in attendance. After dinner, Gov. Parsons, Gen. Smith and Gen. Swayne were called on to speak, and improved the occasion by giving the blacks some wholesome advice. We observed no claims to equality put forth by the negroes, who seemed only proud to have it in their power to pay their respects to their superiors. Perfect order was observed throughout, and we hope much good may result from a better understanding between the authorities and freedmen. August 1, 1865.

On July 20, 1865, Parsons called for an election to be held on August 31. The one hundred delegates thus chosen were to meet on September 12 to carry out the president's Reconstruction plan. As Malcolm McMillan points out in *Constitutional Development in Alabama* (p. 92), this was a convention of old men, forty-five of them over fifty. Among them were two former governors, one United States senator, one former representative, one minister to Belgium, twenty-nine lawyers, and over forty planters and farmers. The membership was divided between the anti-Confederates and the anti-secessionists who were often moderates. Former Governor

Benjamin Fitzpatrick of Wetumpka, who had opposed secession in 1861, was elected president of the convention.

J. B. Moore, a lawyer from Tuscumbia, was a delegate. Some of his pungent comments about the convention are in his diary.

17 Sept, 1865

"The convention is a body of very moderate men, in point of ability— but few of real ability—a good many chuckle heads so far as I can judge them.

18 Sept, 1865

Coleman spoke on the ordinance abolishing slavery—opposed it—In favor of just doing nothing and let the supreme court determine the question.

22 Sept, 1865

In convention—Langdon, Cooper, Drake and Winston made speeches in favor of the abolition of slavery and White in support of his amendment which was voted down and we passed the former ordinance prohibiting slavery by a unanimous vote except 3—White, Clemmins and Crawford voting against it.—Diary, typescript, Department of Archives and History, Montgomery.

The Eufaula *Daily News* carried full accounts of the activities of the convention.

ALABAMA
STATE CONVENTION
MONTGOMERY: SEPT. 15, 1865

Call of the Counties.

Mr. Sanford introduced an ordinance to reduce the size of counties from 900 to 400 square miles; which, on motion of Mr. Rather, was amended by striking out "400" and inserting "600", and ordered to a second reading on to morrow.

Mr. Cooper, of Cherokee, offered a resolution that all ordinances, resolutions, &c., presented for the action of this Convention, be read on three separate days before the same shall be adopted, provided that the rule may be suspended by a vote of the majority of the delegates present; which was laid over until to-morrow.

Mr. Moore, of Franklin, an ordinance providing for taking parole testimony in the settlement of contracts made since the 11th day of January 1861; ordered to a second reading on to-morrow.

Mr. Webb, an ordinance ratifying all laws passed by the Legislature since January 11th, 1861, which have not been repealed, and which are not inconsistent with the Constitution and laws of the United States, except those relating to the issuance of State treasury notes in payments of taxes due the State; which was referred to second special committee under resolutions of Mr. Mudd.

Mr. Dox, of Madison, introduced the following resolutions, which were, on his motion, laid over until to-morrow:

Whereas, The object for which this Convention was assembled, was that such measures might be adopted as should be deemed necessary to restore the State of Alabama to its proper relations to the Government of the United States, and this object being accomplished, the duty of this Convention at its present session will have been performed.

Therefore be it resolved, That it will not be expedient for the Convention, and its present session, to consider or act upon any propositions changing the Constitution of the State of Alabama as it existed prior to the 11th of January, 1861, excepting by the adoption of the following:

1. An ordinance providing for the adoption of the repeal of the ordinance of secession passed 11th of January, 1861, and other ordinances consequent upon said ordinance of secession.

2. An ordinance acknowledging the abolition of slavery in this State by the military power of the United States and prohibiting its future restoration in this State.

3. An ordinance providing security and protection for the large class of persons (lately slaves) who, by being suddenly emancipated, have been left helpless and dependent upon this State.

4. An ordinance ratifying and affirming the proper qualifications, all laws enacted in this State subsequent to the 11th of January, 1861, and all judicial decisions and decrees by courts of equity made since the said 11th of January, 1861, in all cases where such laws, judgments and decrees are not incompatible with the Constitution of the U. States, the Constitution and laws of the State of Alabama, as they existed prior to the 11th day of January, 1861, and the ordinances to be adopted by this Convention.

And whereas, it may seem proper to the people of this State in view of the exigencies of their new and untried relations to alter and amend their State Constitution in other particulars than are indicated by the foregoing resolutions, it is therefore,

Resolved, That when this Convention adjourns it will do so to meet again upon the call of the President thereof, who is hereby empowered to convene this body, at such time as in his judgment shall be deemed proper by a due regard to the welfare of the State.

By Mr. Rather—An ordinance providing that in computing the time necessary to create the bar of the statute of limitations and non-claims the time elapsing between the 11th day of Jan, 1861, and the passage of this ordinance, shall not be estimated. Referred to second special committee.

By Mr. Mudd, of Jefferson—An ordinance to amend section 12 of the declaration of rights in the constitution of this State.

Be it ordained, &C., That section 12 of the declaration of rights in the constitution of this State be amended by inserting the following proviso: Provided, That the legislature in cases of petty larceny, assault and battery, affray, unlawful assembly, vagrancy, and other misdemeanors, may dispense with the grand Jury, and may authorize such prosecutions before Justices of the Peace, or such other inferior courts as may hereafter be established by the Legislature, and the proceedings in such cases shall be regulated by law. Referred to the committee on amendments to the constitution.

By Mr. Overall—An ordinance to legalize decrees of divorce granted by the Chancery Courts of this State since Jan. 11th, 1861. Read twice and referred to second special committte.

Mr. Cooper, of Wilcox, introduced a resolution authorizing the President of the convention to appoint a committee of 11 (one member from each judicial circuit) to transcribe the Constitution, as the same may be amended by this Convention; and providing that the committee shall have authority to employ a clerk. Adopted.

Mr. Clark, of the special committee appointed to employ two short hand reporters to report verbatim the proceedings of this Convention, reported that the committee had employed Messrs. Burnham and Bartlett, at the rate of $15 each per day. The report of the committee was concurred with.

Mr. Cooper, of Cherokee, Chairman of Committee on Propositions and Grievances, reported that the Committee had under consideration the memorial of L. M. Stiff, formerly Receiver of Public Moneys of the Coosa Land District, asking to be reimbursed in the sum of $1500 gold, which amount (in Government funds) was in his hands when the State seceded, and was in pursuance of a law of the first Convention paid to the State Treasurer; that the Committee believed the claim a just one, but recommended that the matter be laid over for future legislation.

Mr. Long, from the same Committee, presented the following minority report:

The minority of the committee to whom was referred the application of Mr. Stiff for relief on account of paying over as receiver of money belonging to the United States from the sale of land in the Coosa land district, in compliance with an Ordinance of the State Convention of 1861, approved March 29th, 1861, beg leave to submit the following report:

We consider the ordinance of secession passed 11th January, 1861, illegal and void, and as a consequence, all indebtedness of the State incurred by reason of secession, to aid and encourage the same, as void; that the applicant has no higher claim for relief than the holder of the bonds or State treasury notes issued since the 11th of January, 1861; that the State is as much bound, legally and morally, to pension and relieve the destitute families of soldiers who were forced by the action of Alabama into the service of the so-called Confederate States as it is to pay claims of this character.

B. M. LONG, C. J. BEASON.

When the convention ended, Moore summed up its accomplishments and his part in it.

30 Sept, 1865
(Convention ended). I think the convention has placed the state in a

condition to resume her relations with the Governor. We men all swore
before we went there to forever prohibit slavery and we did so. This was
the main thing that caused the call of the convention.

My constituents made me promise to touch the constitution just as
lightly as possible. So as to place us in a position to get in harmony
with the Federal Government and consequently I was bound by my
promise to vote against some things in the Convention that my judgment approved. (One was extending jurisdiction of J. P's to $100.00
suits). In mixing with the members of the convention I soon found
that they were determined not to submit the Convention to the people,
as amended for ratification. Having lived under the Constitution of
Alabama since 1819 the people had [prospered as] a people never did.
I was unwilling to force any change in that instrument upon them without their consent at the ballot box. The people have the right to be
consulted. That they have a right to say what change they desire.
[There] were radicals in the convention in favor of tearing the Constitution to pieces and building a new one. My constituents were opposed
to this and under my promise to them, I opposed any change, but that
which I deemed necessary to get us back in the union.

President Johnson had not required that Negro suffrage be one
of the prerequisites for return to the Union, but he had hoped that
the convention would make provision for the better educated
leaders to vote. It did not.

The voters went to the polls on November 6 to choose a governor,
a legislature, six representatives to Congress, and other publicly
elected officers.

Sergeant Mathew Woodruff, a twenty-one year old Missourian in
the federal army stationed at Pascagoula, Mississippi, was in Mobile when the election was held.

There was a general election held throughout the State of Ala. yesterday to send Representatives to Congress and returns are not in yet . . . .
I think it went off verry peaceable considering. heard of several drunken
rows which are verry common on election days, & to tell the truth, most
any day in a southern city like Mobile . . . . Politicans of either side
can not say that the election in Mobile was controled by Yankee
Bayonets . . . . if they have not elected *Loyal* candidates, their
Treachery is confirmed by their own Voice as well as deeds . . . .—
Mathew Woodruff, *A Union Soldier in the Land of the Vanquished,*
F. N. Boney, ed. (University, Alabama: University of Alabama Press,
1969), pp. 58–59.

There were three candidates for governor: Robert M. Patton of
Lauderdale County, M. J. Bulger of Tallapoosa, and William R.
Smith of Tuscaloosa. Patton ran ahead, polling 21,442 votes. The
representatives elected to Congress were C. C. Langdon, George C.
Freeman, Cullen A. Battle, Joseph W. Taylor, Burwell T. Pope, and

Thomas J. Foster. All of these were former Whigs except Battle and most of them had opposed secession, although they aided the Confederacy after its formation. When the legislature met, it chose Lewis E. Parsons and George S. Houston to the United States senate. The state had complied with the president's requests. It had sent its elected officials to Washington, and it was hoped that shortly all would be settled and the state could return to normal. Alabamians, and other southerners, however, had not anticipated the strong opposition to executive Reconstruction and to the president personally.

There was in Congress a vigorous Radical Republican element which believed that presidential Reconstruction was based on a false theory, that it was too lenient, and, what seems to have been even more important, that it prevented the radicals from carrying out their own purposes. Consequently, they refused to seat the Alabama delegation in Congress. The state, therefore, was without representation until after it adopted the 1868 constitution and complied with other requirements of Congress. Congress did recognize the state legislature and the inauguration of Patton on December 13.

When Congress refused to seat the delegation from Alabama, the state legislature passed the following resolution, expressing its disapproval:

Resolved by the Senate and House of Representatives of the State of Alabama, in General Assembly convened, That the people of Alabama, and their representatives here assembled, cordially approve the policy by Andrew Johnson, President of the United States, in the reorganization of the Union. We accept the result of the late contest, and do not desire to renew what has been so conclusively determined: nor do we mean to permit any one subject to our control to attempt its renewal, or to violate any of our obligations to the United States Government. We mean to cooperate in the wise, firm, and just policy adopted by the President, with all the energy and power we can devote to that object.

2. That the above declaration expresses the sentiments and purposes of our people, and we denounce the efforts of those who represent our views and intentions to be different, as cruel and criminal assaults on our character and our interests. It is one of the misfortunes of our present political condition that we have among us persons whose interests are temporarily promoted by such false representations; but we rely on the intelligence and integrity of those who wield the power of the United States Government for our safeguard against such malign influences.

3. That involuntary servitude, except for crime, is abolished, and ought not to be reestablished, and that the negro race among us should be treated with justice, humanity and good faith, and every means that the wisdom of the Legislature can devise should be used to make them useful and intelligent members of society.

4. That Alabama will not voluntarily consent to change the adjustment
of political power, as fixed by the Constitution of the United States, and
to constrain her to do so in her present prostrate and helpless condition,
with no voice in the councils of the nation, would be an unjustifiable
breach of faith. . . .—*Acts of Alabama, 1865–66*, p. 606. The date was
February 22, 1866.

However much Alabamians disliked its action, Congress had the
power to refuse seating the delegates from this and the other
Southern states and used it.

Civil government came almost to a halt. Governor Patton was
not removed from office, but most authority was exercised by the
military authorities. Within a month after General Lee's surrender, federal troops were placed in several central locations in
Alabama. In some places they actually broke up or superseded
county and local governments (and in others merely imposed restraints). The troops were supposed to retire after the creation
of the provisional government, but Walter L. Fleming says that
they did not do so; they continued instead to interfere with civil
government. Professor Fleming suggested that part of the chaotic
political conditions in the former Confederate states resulted from
the titanic struggle going on between President Johnson and Congress over Reconstruction. Had there been a mutually accepted
policy in Washington, there would have been less confusion in
Alabama.

The organization of the military government imposed on the
South shifted many times between 1865 and 1868 when Radical
Reconstruction went into effect. At the end of the war, Alabama
was put in the Military Division of Tennessee under General George
H. Thomas. General C. R. Woods commanded the Department of
Alabama with headquarters in Mobile. After other shifts in or-
ganization that made little change in the state, General Wager
Swayne was put in charge of the Alabama sub-division of the
District of the Chattahoochee. This was on August 6, 1866. This
would stand until the reorganization following the passage of the
Reconstruction Acts in March, 1867. At that time, Alabama was
put in the Third Military District along with Florida and Georgia.
General John Pope was commander for the district (and lived in
Montgomery much of the time), and Swayne kept his post in
Alabama. Pope, although he had praise for Alabamians, was often
criticized for the literalness with which he interpreted the law.
Both Pope and Swayne were relieved of their offices on December
28, 1867. Generals George D. Meade and Julian Hayden, who took
their places, were the military officers until after the adoption of
the Constitution of 1868.

On July 21, 1868, the state's elected representatives were finally seated in Congress. This marked the end of the military regime but did not return the government to the former political leaders. Until the election of 1874, carpetbaggers, scalawags, and Negroes would control the political power. Three more elected governors served as heads of state. After Swayne's brief term as military governor in 1868, and the registration of voters under the Constitution of 1868, William H. Smith, a native Georgian and a resident of Randolph County was elected governor. His administration quickly ratified the Fourteenth and Fifteenth Admendments.

Under the Constitution of 1868 the governor served only two terms; so 1870 was another election year. Smith sought reelection, but Robert B. Lindsay, a Democrat, ran against him and won. However, Smith refused to vacate and for two weeks the state had two governors. The courts decided Lindsay was the rightful governor. Lindsay, a native of Scotland, lived in Tuscumbia where he practiced law. He, too, had opposed secession but had supported the Confederate cause. Lindsay's two years were stormy, dominated by party politics, but Auburn University, and the cities of Gadsden and Birmingham had their beginnings during this time.

David P. Lewis (1872–1874) was the last of the carpetbag governors. A native of Virginia, Lewis had lived successively in Madison and Lawrence counties. He, like his predecessors, had opposed secession but later was a member of the Confederate congress. His administration was highlighted by a squabble over the legislature. Determined to send only Republicans to the Senate, he "formed a fraudulent legislature" of his own in competition with the duly elected body. President Grant intervened in Alabama affairs at this point and upheld the Lewis courthouse legislature.

While the former leaders who had hopes of an early return to normal times were dismayed at the passage of the Reconstruction Acts of 1867, their public utterances were tempered with moderation. At a public meeting in Mobile, the following resolutions were adopted:

Resolved, Without expressing any opinion as to the [Reconstruction Acts]
. . . we hereby manifest our gratification at the spirit of moderation which the major-general [Pope] commanding the Third District brings to the discharge of the responsible duties and to the exercise of the great powers committed to him; and that we feel called upon to meet him in a like spirit and hereby to express to him our purpose to throw no obstacle in the path of his official duties, but that in all that tends to a genuine desire for the restoration of the Union under the Constitution . . . we pledge ourselves to a most earnest and cordial cooperation. . . .

We recommend to all who are qualified to register and vote under the provision of the law, to do so as early as convenient after the opportunity is offered for that purpose, and to scrupulously abstain from any act which might be construed into a disposition to hinder or disturb any other person in discharge of any duty or the exercise of any privilege conferred by law. . . .

We find nothing in the changed political condition of the white and black races in the South that ought to disturb the harmonious relations between them; that we are ready to accord to the latter every right and privilege to which they are entitled under the laws of the land; that we sincerely desire their prosperity and their improvement in all the moral and intellectual qualities that are necessary to make them useful members of society; that we are their friends, both from gratitude for their fidelity in the past—in war as well as peace—and because our interests in the future are inseparably connected with their well-being.— *The Mail* (Montgomery), April 21, 1867.

At the first political convention held after the war, the delegates, mostly former Whigs, adopted a platform given here in an abbreviated form. These men called themselves the Conservatives, a name they would keep until "Democrat" had lost some of its association with secession and rebellion.

THE CONSERVATIVE MEN OF THE STATE OF ALABAMA . . . adopt, as an expression of their views, the following resolutions of the Conservative men of the State of Pennsylvania, adopted at a recent convention in that State:
1. The Constitution of the United States is binding upon every inhabitant of all ranks, sexes, colors, ages, and conditions, and it is the duty of each and every one, without exception, or modification under any circumstances, to adhere to, protect, and defend the same.
2. In all conflict of powers under that instrument the supreme judiciary power is the only arbiter. . . .
3. The Union of the States is decided by the war and accepted by the Southern people to be perpetual. . . .
4. Congress is not the Federal Government, nor is the President, nor the Supreme Court. The Federal Government is that frame of civil polity established by the Constitution consisting of all three, each supreme in his own limits, and each entitled, equally with the others, to the loyal obedience of every inhabitant of all the states.
5. By the Constitution and under the fundamental law the Federal Government . . . and of which Congress itself is the creature, representation in Congress and the electoral colleges is a right, fundamental and indestructible in its nature, and abiding in every State; being a duty as well as right pertaining to the people of every State, and the denial of which is the destruction of the Federal Government.

The Conservative men of Alabama adopt, as a further expression of their opinions and purposes, the following:
6. Each State under the Constitution has the exclusive right to prescribe the qualifications of its own electors.

7. . . . It is our earnest aim and purpose to cultivate relations of friendship, harmony, and peace between the two races . . . to deal justly with the blacks . . . to instruct and aid in instructing them in a proper understanding of all their duties to themselves, to society, and to the country—and we denounce as treacherous and base all attempt by bad men to engender or encourage antagonism between the two races.

8. . . . We are inhabitants of a common country, sharers and sufferers of a common destiny—and we will do all in our power to instruct and elevate the colored race in its moral, social and political responsibilities.

9. . . . While we have much charity for the colored man, and feel inclined to look indulgently and tolerantly on his prejudice of race, inculcated and encouraged as they have been by recent events, and by insidious counsel of bad men, we appeal to him by the common interest of a common country, to place his trust in those he knows to be honorable, and to deal cautiously with strangers who bear no evidence that they were honored where they are better known.—*Annual Cyclopedia* (1867), p. 28, quoted in Fleming, *Documentary History of Reconstruction,* vol. 1, p. 422.

Not all resolutions, platforms, and statements of principles were drawn up by whites. The blacks had become an articulate group as the following passage shows. It is not known who was responsible for the statement or the meeting in Mobile that prompted it. Few freedmen had the ability to write such a document. There was in the port city, however, a number of rather remarkable Negro, or mulatto, men of good education. Of the 2,690 free blacks in Alabama in 1860, Mobile had 817. Ovide Gregory, a free Negro born of free parents, owned and operated a cigar stand in Mobile. He spoke several languages and had traveled widely in Mexico, Latin America, and much of the United States. He was a delegate to the 1867 Constitutional Convention. Another leader among the blacks was John Carroway who was born a slave in North Carolina, was set free, went North, and became a tailor, but when white tailors objected to his competition, he went to sea. After the war in which he had seen action in the 54th Massachusetts Division, he went to Mobile which he had visited while at sea. There he became an active member of the Republican Party and the assistant editor of the Negro Mobile *Nationalist.* He, too, was a delegate to the 1867 convention. He may well be the author of the colored convention's resolutions.

Because this is one of the first public statements by Negroes themselves, it is given in its entirety.

ADDRESS OF ALABAMA COLORED CONVENTION, 1867

As THERE SEEMS to be considerable difference of opinion concerning the "legal rights of the colored man," it will not be amiss to say that we claim exactly *the same rights, privileges and immunities as are en-*

joyed by white men—we ask nothing more and will be content with nothing less. *All legal* distinctions between the races are now abolished. The word white is stricken from our laws, and every privilege which white men were formerly permitted to enjoy, merely because they were white men, now that word is stricken out, we are entitled to on the ground that we are men. *Color can no longer be pleaded for the purpose of curtailing privileges, and every public right, privilege and immunity is enjoyable by every individual member of the public.*—This is the touchstone that determines all these points. So long as a park or a street is a *public* park or street the entire public has the right to use it; so long as a car or a steamboat is a public conveyance, it must carry all who come to it, and serve all alike who pay alike. The law no longer knows white nor black, but simply men, and consequently we are entitled to ride in public conveyances, hold office, sit on juries and do everything else which we have in the past been prevented from doing solely on the ground of our color. . . .

We have said that we intend to claim all our rights, and we submit to our white friends that it is the height of folly on their part to withhold them any longer. One-half of the voters in Alabama are black men, and in a few months there is to be an entire reorganization of the State government. The new officers—legislative, executive and judicial—will owe their election largely, if not mainly to the colored people, and every one must see clearly that the voters will then be certain to require and the officers to compel a cessation of all illegal discriminations. The question which every man now illegally discriminating against us has to decide is, whether it is politic to insist upon gratifying prejudices during a few dull months, with the certainty by so doing, of incurring the lasting displeasure of one-half of the voting population of the State. We can stand it if they can, but we assure them that they are being watched closely, and that their conduct will be remembered when we have power.

There are some good people who are always preaching patience and procrastination. They would have us wait a few months, years, or generations, until the whites voluntarily give us our rights, but we do not intend to wait one day longer than we are absolutely compelled to. Look at our demands, and then at theirs. We ask of them simply that they surrender unreasonable and unreasoning prejudice; that they cease imitating dog in the manger; that they consent to allow others as well as themselves to prosper and be happy. But they would have us pay for what we do not get; tramp through the broiling sun or pelting rain, or stand upon a platform, while empty seats mockingly invite us to rest our wearied limbs; our sick must suffer or submit to indignity; we must put up with inconvenience of every kind; and the virtuous aspirations of our children must be continually checked by the knowledge that no matter how upright their conduct, they will be looked on as less worthy of respect than the lowest wretch on earth who wears a white skin. We ask you—only while in public, however—to surrender your prejudices, —nothing but prejudices; and you ask us to sacrifice our personal comfort, health, pecuniary interests, self-respect, and the future prospects of our children. The men who make such requests must suppose us devoid of spirit and of brains, but they will find themselves mistaken. Solemnly and distinctly, we again say to you, men of Alabama, that we will not submit voluntarily to such infamous discrimination, and if you will insist upon tramping on the rights and outraging the feelings of those who are so soon to pass judgment upon you, then upon your own heads will rest the responsibility for the effect of your course.

All over the state of Alabama—all over the South indeed—the colored people have with singular unanimity, arrayed themselves under the Republican banner, upon the Republican platform, and it is confidently predicted that nine-tenths of them will vote the Republican ticket. Do you ask, why is this? We answer, because:

1. The Republican Party opposed and prohibited the extension of slavery.
2. It repealed the fugitive slave law.
3. It abolished slavery in the District of Columbia.
4. It abolished slavery in the rebellious states.
5. It abolished slavery throughout the rest of the Union.
6. It put down rebellion against the Union.
7. It passed the Freedmen's Bureau Bill and the Civil Rights Bill.
8. It enfranchised the colored people of the District of Columbia.
9. It enfranchised the colored people of the nine territories.
10. It enfranchised the colored people of the ten rebel states.
11. It provided for the formation of new constitutions and state governments in those ten states.
12. It passed new homestead laws, enabling the poor to obtain land.

In short, it has gone on, step by step, doing first one thing for us and then another, and it now proposes to enfranchise our people all over the Union. It is the only party which has ever attempted to extend our privileges, and as it has in the past always been trying to do this, it is but natural that we should trust it for the future.

While this has been the course of the Republican Party, the opposition has unitedly opposed every one of these measures, and it also now opposes the enfranchisement of our people in the North. Everywhere it has been against us in the past, and the great majority of its voters hate us as cordially now as ever before. It is sometimes alleged that the Republicans of the North have not been actuated by love for us in what they have done, and therefore that we should not join them; we answer that even if that were true they certainly never professed to hate us and the opposition party has always been denouncing the "d—n nigger and abolitionist" with equal fervor. When we had no votes to give, the opposition placed us and the Republicans in the same boat, and now we reckon we'll stay in it. It may be and probably is true that some men acting with the Republican Party have cared nothing for the principles of that party; but it is also certainly true that ninety-nine-hundredths of all those who were conscientiously in favor of our rights were and are in the Republican Party, and that the great mass of those who hated, slandered and abused us were and are in the opposition party.

The memories of the opposition must be short indeed, to have for-gotten their language of the past twenty years but we have *not* forgotten it.

But, say some of the members of the opposition party, "We intend to turn over a new leaf, and will hereafter give you all your rights." Perhaps they would, but we prefer not to put the new wine of political equality into the old bottles of "sectional animosity" and "caste feeling." We are somewhat fearful that those who have always opposed the extensions of rights are not sincere in their professions. . . .

Another fact should be borne in mind. While a few conservatives are making guarded promises to us the masses of that party are cursing us, and doing all they can to "make the d—d niggers stay in their place." If we were, therefore, to join that party, it would be simply as servants, and not as equals. Some leaders, who needed our votes might treat us decently, but the great majority would expect us to stay at home until election day, and then vote as our employers dictated. This we respect-fully decline doing. It seems to us safest to have as little as possible to do with those members of the community who delight to abuse us, and they are nearly, if not quite, all to be found in the ranks of the opposition party. . . .

It cannot be disguised, however, that many men calling themselves conservatives are disposed to use unfair means to carry their points. The press of Mobile, and other parts of the State, contain numerous threats that those colored people who do not vote as their employers command, will be discharged; that the property-holders will combine, import white laborers, and discharge their colored hands, etc. Numerous instances have come to our knowledge of persons who have already been discharged because they attended Republican meetings, and great numbers more have been threatened. "Vote as we command, or starve," is the argument these men propose to make [use] of, and with it they expect to succeed.

In this expectation they will be mistaken, and we warn them before it is prosecuted any further, that their game is a dangerous one for themselves. The property which they hold was nearly all earned by the sweat of our brows—not theirs. It has been forfeited to the Government by the treason of its owners, and is liable to be confiscated whenever the Republican Party demands it. The great majority of that party is now opposed to confiscation, but if the owners of property use the power which it gives them to make political slaves of the poor, a cry will go up to Congress which will make the party a unit for confiscation.

Conservatives of Alabama, do you propose to rush upon certain de-struction? Are you mad, that you threaten to pursue a policy which could only result in causing thousands of men to cry out to their leaders, "Our wives and little ones are starving because we stood by you; be-cause we would not be slaves!" When the nation abolished slavery, you used your local governments to neutralize and defeat its action, and the nation answered by abolishing your governments and enfranchising us. If you now use your property to neutralize or defeat this, its last act, it will answer by taking away the property you are only allowed to retain through its unparalleled mercy and which you have proved yourselves so unworthy of retaining. . . .

So complete, indeed, will be our victory, that our opponents will become disheartened unless they can divide us. This is the great danger which we have to guard against. The most effectual method of preserving our unity will be for us to always act together—never to hold separate political meetings or caucuses. It may take some time for us to get to pulling together well, but perseverance and honest endeavor will overcome all obstacles. In nominations for office we expect that there will be no discriminations on account of color by either wing, but that the most capable and honest men will always be put in nomination. We understand full well that our people are too deficient in education to be generally qualified to fill the higher offices, but when qualified men are found, they must not be rejected for being black.

This lack of education, which is the consequence of our long servitude, and which so diminishes our powers for good, should not be allowed to characterize our children when they come upon the stage of action, and we therefore earnestly call upon every member of the Republican Party to demand the establishment of a thorough system of common schools throughout the State. It will benefit every citizen of the State, and, indeed, of the Union, for the well-being of each enures to the advantage of all. In a Republic, education is especially necessary, as the ignorant are always liable to be led astray by the arts of the demagogue.

With education secured to all; with the old and helpless properly cared for; with justice everywhere impartially administered, Alabama will commence a career of which she will have just cause to be proud. We shall all be prosperous and happy. The sad memories of the past will be forgotten amid the joys of the present and the prospect of the future.—*Daily State Sentinel* (Montgomery), May 21, 1867.

The Constitutional Convention, 1867

The Reconstruction Acts of March, 1867, stated that only those who could take the "iron-clad" oath that they had never willingly aided the late rebellion in any way were eligible to vote. William R. Smith of Randolph County, a former Alabama legislator who had defected to the Union side in 1863, was put in charge of registration. Federal officers were the enrolling personnel. Negroes, of course, were expected to register and also those whites who could. There was a difference of opinion among the latter group as to whether they should register or not. Some argued that the best way was to boycott registration, while others urged all who could should register, vote, and cooperate with the Radicals as the only means of saving the state from further chaos. Before election day (October 1–5, 1867), 104,518 Negroes and 61,295 whites had registered. A majority of the total number (but less than a third of the whites) voted for a constitutional convention which met in Montgomery the following November 5.

Of the one hundred delegates all but two were Republicans. The exceptions were James Hart Howard of Crenshaw and G. J. Dykes of Cherokee. There were eighteen Negroes among the delegates, thirteen from the Black Belt, three from the Tennessee Valley, and two from Mobile. According to the *Daily State Sentinel,* November 16, 1867, the delegates classified themselves occupationally as: 16 lawyers, 9 physicians, 46 planters, 4 carpenters, 2 teachers, 3 manufacturers, and many others as artisans in many fields. There were at least 10 preachers, a number of them attached to the Freedmen's Bureau.

Malcolm C. McMillan, the undisputed authority on constitutional development in Alabama quotes the New York *Herald,* November 29, 1867, as having the best contemporary analysis of the convention.

I have been at some pains to discover as nearly as possible the amount of property represented by the delegates. . . . Three-fourths of the delegates are men possessed of scarcely any property, and in many cases of no property at all. The Negroes are with one exception penniless, some of them having worked, prior to their election as delegates to the convention at eight dollars a day and mileage, as field hands on cotton plantations at ten dollars a month. The one exception, Gregory, was a free Negro before the war, and has made some money by keeping a cigar store in Mobile.

[The Carpetbaggers] . . . who have settled in the State subsequent to the close of the rebellion . . . are for the most part almost impecunious. The few hundred dollars they had when they came down here they have sunk in buying small parcels of land or in merchandising, and very few of them have increased their substance since, having, like the rest of the inhabitants of the State, prospered well, if in these days of ruin and poverty, they have never wanted for food and clothing. Twelve of this class of men are Bureau agents, but these of course are comparatively rich. Four of them are mechanics working for day wages, while a good many are earning a livelihood in a very mysterious manner by doing nothing at all. . . .

[The Scalawags] . . . consist either of Alabamians, most of whom come from the northern part of the State, or of men from the other Southern States, who have settled here prior to the war. In this class may be included . . . the moderates and rational delegates, all men of any property or social standing in the convention. Certainly all the lawyers, with one or two exceptions, to be found in the convention come from this section of it. Some of these . . . were men of very large fortune before the war, and are still of considerable means, but most of them if they were ever rich have been ruined by the rebellion, and now find themselves destitute of any ready money, or of any prospect of raising any, except by selling their land at something between sixty cents and three or four dollars an acre; while some have never been anything more important financially than small farmers in such of the counties as were too sterile to afford a profitable field of employment for slave labor. From an estimate, which I have made up with some care, I find that there are not thirty men in the convention who are accounted by the people of the counties in which they reside as possessed of more than one thousand dollars; that there are not thirteen who are worth five thousand, and that there are not seven who are worth over ten thousand. The rest are believed to be worth—nothing.

In social standard the convention ranks at about the same standard of value. Montgomery before the war, and even during the war—for it escaped almost entirely the devastation inflicted upon other cities in the South—was the most fashionable city in the State; and yet here nearly all the delegates are unknown, even their names being strange and unfamiliar. . . . Two of them . . . have been recognized as ex-bushwhackers, who deserted first the rebel and then the Union army, and finally carried on war on their own private account, and for their own personal advantage and benefit. . . . There may be exceptions, but it is undoubtedly the case that all the men who are reputed to be worthless, alike in pecuniary standing and reputation, cling to the more violent and extreme wing . . . while the men of considerable standing in the State . . . form the non-proscriptive and temperate party in the convention. . . .

Having thus given, as truthfully as possible, and without any, even the slightest, political bias, the social complexion of the convention, I shall proceed to sketch out its political lineaments. First, of course, comes the colored brigade, numbering some sixteen wooly headed delegates. These are all directly under the control of the White leaders. Two of them are influenced by the moderate men, and the remaining fourteen implicitly follow the lead of the "extreme and violent" party chieftains. They are, without any exception, simply automats, to be put in motion, not by their own volition, but by the will of the sentient beings. . . . The Whites in the convention may be divided politically into three classes, which are very nearly of equal strength. There are extreme men, moderate men, and men who fluctuate to whichever side seems to be the strongest and most successful in the State. The extreme men consist of the Bureau officials, all of whom are, of course, interested in preserving the existing system of things, and from a dozen to twenty men, who seem impelled by some inscrutable law of their nature, or because they can only attain to any prominence by their extravagance, to be reckless, violent fanatics. These are headed by Bingham and Griffin. . . . It is remarkable that the Negroes are wholly under the control of this class of men, who have probably gained their support and favor because they have been more lavish and profuse in the promises of future favors than the other side. The moderate men as I have mentioned before, consist nearly entirely of all the men of standing, property, and good fame in the convention. The men who stand between the two factions have heretofore acted with the extreme men, and have rivaled Bingham himself in the wild fervor of their proscriptive harangues.—Quoted in Malcolm C. McMillan, *Constitutional Development in Alabama, 1798–1901*, pp. 115–16.

The three previous Alabama constitutions had been ratified by convention, not by referendum. The Reconstruction Act of 1867 required that the new document be submitted to the vote of the people and this course was followed. On February 1–5, 1868, the people went to the polls, 70,812 voting for the constitution and 1,005 against it. The whites had stayed away from the polls in great numbers, and the total lacked 8,114 of being a majority of the registered voters. After much acrimonious debate in the state and in Congress, a special act admitted Alabama (along with four other southern states) into the Union as soon as the newly elected legislature ratified the Fourteenth Amendment. The best argument for the admission of the state was that a majority of those voting had favored the new constitution. Even overlooking the alleged fraud and irregularities in the elections, the document was ratified only by special act which gave rise to the theory still held by a few Alabamians that the Constitution of 1868 really never legally existed. Nevertheless, it is the one under which Alabamians lived until 1875.

The Constitution of 1868

There is little doubt that the proposed constitution aroused the bitterest resentment and engendered the most acrimonious debate in the history of government in the state. Whatever outsiders may have thought about the uniformity in the "bogus convention," there were differences of opinion within the convention itself. Outside, the former Confederates may have been disfranchised, but they were not silenced, and a surprising number of the articulate ones seem to have had access to a newspaper. In fact, newspapers became the chief organs of political debate. The Selma *Times and Messenger,* a conservative paper, said editorially essentially what many like papers were saying.

> Convened under the reconstruction acts by a bare majority of the registered voters; composed (we speak deliberately and advisedly) in good part of negroes who had never read and could not read the constitution of the United States, or the constitution of any one of the states, deserters from the Confederate service, thieves, defaulters, Bureau men —without residence, and mere adventurers without acquaintance or domicile in the State, the convention went beyond the requirements of the reconstruction acts . . . among other things in proclaiming the equality of the races, in providing for mixed schools sustained at public expense and particularly in exacting a test oath of electors which no honest white man from the North or South can or will take.—February 2, 1868, quoted in ibid., pp. 157–58.

The conservative press throughout the state attacked with vehemence certain provisions of the constitution: Negro suffrage, provisions for integration on common carriers or in the public schools, proscription of whites (an estimated forty thousand), no prohibition against interracial marriages and many others. The effect of the Radical constitution in the state, said the Montgomery *Mail* (December 7, 1867), was to give political control to the Negroes, surrender municipal government to them, to establish public schools where white and black children would sit side by side, to permit no white man to vote unless he swore never to change the basis of suffrage, and to establish a militia system in which one-tenth of the population would rule over the other nine-tenths. The reaction of a housewife to the constitutional convention is given in her "Journal" by Sally Randle Perry.

> The Mongrel crew who lately assembled in convention in Montgomery have adjourned after having used every effort to fasten the vilent indignity upon our unhappy state. Verily much has been done to strengthen the loyalty of our people. We are indeed fallen when thieves and adventurers from the North, former slaves, are allowed to disgrace the halls of our state house. Oh justice! Where is thy sword? Liberty is dead. She breathed her last on Southern soil when Gen. Lee surrendered his sword trusting to the honor of a yankee's plighted word. I sadly [credit] the life blood of the Southern braves will again flow like water ere she again rises phoenix like from the ashes.
>
> After the havoc of War these northern vultures still hover over the fair lands of the South to prey upon a helpless people—A political war of races has been begun—the first gun was fired by Mr. Keiffer at Montgomery. "Oh God where will it all end?"—Ms., Department of Archives and History, Montgomery.

Since only a small number of blacks could read, the Republican leaders made their most effective appeals to the public at rallies, many of which they held in the areas where the Negro population was the heaviest. There was, however, a Radical press. The Mobile *Nationalist* (whose assistant editor was a mulatto) was among them. The purpose of the constitution, the editor advised, was to gain for Negroes the same rights and privileges any other citizen had. Much depended on its ratification.

> The white people of the State have a great deal depending on the result of the pending election but the interest of the colored voter in it is of transcending importance. The citizenship of the white is not in any way dependent upon the ratification or rejection of the constitution, but that of the colored man is to be decided by the votes now being cast.
>
> Adopt the constitution and the colored man is and will always be an enfranchized citizen of the State of Alabama. . . .
>
> Ratify the constitution and secure the power to protect yourselves through all coming time, and spend at least one day in inducing others

to do the same. Will you do it? Or, in other words, are you men—or still slaves?—Mobile *Nationalist,* February 6, 1868, quoted in ibid., p. 163.

Republican John Hardy, whose account of the destruction of Selma has been given earlier, gave his reasons for voting for the constitution.

> Do you want Alabama again in the Union? Vote for the Constitution!
> Do you want a loyal good government, to protect life, liberty and property? Vote for the Constitution!
> Do you want the return of peace, order, and prosperity? Vote for the Constitution!
> Do you want the railroads built and manufactories erected? Vote for the Constitution!
> Do you want your children educated? Vote for the Constitution!
> Do you want time on your old ante-war and war debts? Vote for the Constitution!
> Do you want the speedy development of all the resources of the state? Vote for the Constitution!
> Do you want capital to come into the State and money in freer circulation? Vote for the Constitution!
> Do you want immigrants to buy your land and cultivate the soil properly? Vote for the Constitution!—*Daily State Sentinel* (Montgomery), January 30, 1868.

In spite of all the efforts of the Republicans, they failed to get a sufficient vote. Governor Robert M. Patton, in an open letter to the public, explained why.

> There were two important causes which operated to defeat the Constitution at the late election in this State. One was found in the obnoxious features of the Constitution itself; and the other was the objectionable character of many of the men who were to go into office under it. If the Convention which framed the Constitution had gone no farther than the plain requirements of the Reconstruction Acts of Congress, the Constitution would probably have been ratified. But instead of doing this, a test oath was established for voters which is generally regarded by our people as contrary to the spirit of Republican institutions, and which few people in any State can approve.
> Again: the Constitution provides for a system of public schools which will cost far more money than the entire revenue of the State has heretofore been. There was a wide spread belief that under the practical operations of that system, negro children alone would derive any benefit from it. This point was much debated in the Convention; some contending that white children, in order to obtain the advantages of public schools must attend them in common, and upon a perfect equality with negroes. In order to remove all doubt upon this point, a proposition was introduced in the Convention to have separate schools

for whites and blacks. The proposition was distinctly voted down. Another proposition was offered to prohibit the intermarriage of whites and blacks. This too, was voted down, and hence, so far as the sense of the Convention is concerned, it positively refused to recognize any distinction between whites, and blacks in public schools; and likewise declined to prohibit the amalgamation of the races. The white people of the State very naturally look upon all this as indicating a determination to establish, not only legal, but perfect social equality between the whites and blacks. An ordinance was adopted by the Convention (which is irrepealable by the Legislature,) providing a militia system on a large, expensive and dangerous scale. In practical effect, it would be a regular army, almost as numerous, both as to rank and file, as the United States Army was before the war. No facts or arguments are necessary to show that this army, in the present peculiar condition of the country, would be mainly composed of negroes.

Nearly all the persons elected to office in the States are new comers, and strangers to our people. With the peoples' wishes and interests, they are wholly unacquainted. In a large number of the counties, the negroes preponderate largely over the whites. Where such is the case, these strangers, having the ear of the unintelligent freedmen, had a complete monopoly of the offices, the whites being utterly powerless. Many negroes were elected to office, a considerable number of which, it is true, are of little value to the incumbents, as the compensation is but trifling; although they are of considerable importance to the people. These are such offices as Constables, Justices of the Peace, and County Commissioners. I know of several cases where the negroes elected do not know a letter in the book. In one county, all three of the Commissioners are negroes, all of whom are of the character mentioned. State Solicitors have been chosen in some counties who are not only unlicensed lawyers, but who are wholly uneducated.

I forbear to speak of the obnoxious character of many strangers among us, who have been chosen to prominent offices, so far as their characters have been developed in this State. To do so, I should be compelled to employ epithets for which I have no taste. And yet nothing but the very plainest and strongest language could be truthfully employed. It is sufficient to say that in a large number of cases there is a lamentable want of all those qualities which inspire the confidence or secure the respect of good citizens.—*Shelby County Guide* (Columbiana), April 30, 1868.

With all the objectionable features its critics found in it, this constitution had several features that were more in keeping with the forthcoming modern industrial age than any of its predecessors. Two of these were the articles on education and industry.

ARTICLE XI
EDUCATION

SECTION 1. The common schools, and other educational institutions of the State, shall be under the management of a Board of Education, consisting of a Superintendent of Public Instruction and two members from each Congressional District.

The Governor of the State shall be *ex officio,* a member of the Board, but shall have no vote in its proceedings.

SEC. 2. The Superintendent of Public Instruction shall be President of the Board of Education, and have the casting vote in case of a tie; he shall have the supervision of the public schools of the State, and perform such other duties as may be imposed upon him by the board and the laws of the State. He shall be elected in the same manner and for the same term as the Governor of the State, and receive such salary as may be fixed by law. An office shall be assigned him in the capitol of the State.

SEC. 3. The members of the Board shall hold office for a term of four years, and until their successors shall be elected and qualified. After the first election under the Constitution, the Board shall be divided into two equal classes, so that each class shall consist of one member from each District. The seats of the first class shall be vacated at the expiration of two years from the day of election, so that one-half may be chosen biennially.

SEC. 4. The members of the Board of Education, except the Superintendent, shall be elected by the qualified electors of the Congressional Districts in which they are chosen, at the same time and in the same manner as the members of Congress.

SEC. 5. The Board of Education shall exercise full legislative powers in reference to the public educational institutions of the State, and its acts, when approved by the governor, or when re-enacted by two-thirds of the Board, in case of his disapproval, shall have the force and effect of law, unless repealed by the General Assembly.

SEC. 6. It shall be the duty of the Board to establish, throughout the State, in each township or other school-district which it may have created, one or more schools, at which all the children of the State between the ages of five and twenty-one years may attend free of charge.

SEC. 7. No rule or law affecting the general interest of education shall be made by the board without the concurrence of a majority of its members. The style of all acts of the Board shall be, "Be it enacted by the Board of Education of the State of Alabama."

SEC. 8. The Board of Education shall be a body politic and corporate, by the name and style of "The Board of Education of the State of Alabama." Said Board shall also be a Board of Regents of the State University, and when sitting as a Board of Regents of the University shall have power to appoint the president and the faculties thereof. The President of the University shall be, *ex officio,* a member of the board of regents, but shall have no vote in its proceedings.

SEC. 9. The Board of Education shall meet annually at the seat of government at the same time as the General Assembly, but no session shall continue longer than twenty days, nor shall more than one session be held in the same year, unless authorized by the Governor. The members shall receive the same mileage and daily pay as the members of the General Assembly.

SEC. 10. The proceeds of all lands that have been or may be granted by the United States to the State for educational purposes; of the swamp-lands; and all lands or other property given by individuals or appropriated by the State for like purposes; and of all estates of deceased persons who have died without leaving a will or heir; and all moneys which may be paid as an equivalent for exemption from military duty, shall be and remain a perpetual fund, which may be increased but not diminished, and the interest and income of which, together with the rents of all such lands as may remain unsold, and such other means as the General Assembly may provide, shall be inviolably appropriated to educational purposes, and to no other purpose whatever.

SEC. 11. In addition to the amount accruing from the above sources, one-fifth of the aggregate annual revenue of the State shall be devoted exclusively to the maintenance of public schools.

SEC. 12. The general assembly may give power to the authorities of the school-districts to levy a poll-tax on the inhabitants of the district in aid of the general school-fund and for no other purpose.

SEC. 13. The General Assembly shall levy a specific annual tax upon all railroad, navigation, banking, and insurance corporations, and upon all insurance and foreign bank and exchange agencies, and upon the profits of foreign bank bills issued in this State by any corporation, partnership or persons, which shall be exclusively devoted to the maintenance of public schools.

SEC. 14. The General Assembly shall, as soon as practicable, provide for the establishment of an agricultural college, and shall appropriate the two hundred and forty thousand acres of land donated to this state for the support of such a college, by the act of Congress, passed July 2, 1862, or the money or scrip, as the case may be, arising from the sale of said land, or any lands which may hereafter be granted or appropriated for such purpose, for the support and maintenance of such college, or schools, and may make the same a branch of the University of Alabama for instruction in agriculture, in the mechanic arts, and the natural sciences connected therewith, and place the same under the supervision of the regents of the university.

ARTICLE XII
INDUSTRIAL RESOURCES

SECTION 1. A Bureau of Industrial Resources shall be established, to be under the management of a Commissioner, who shall be elected at the first general election, and shall hold his office for the term of four years.

SEC. 2. The Commissioner of Industrial Resources shall collect and condense statistical information concerning the productive industries of the State; and shall make, or cause to be made, a careful, accurate, and thorough report upon the agriculture and geology of the State, and annually report such additions as the progress of scientific development and extended explorations may require. He shall, from time to time, disseminate among the people of the State such knowledge as he may deem important, concerning improved machinery and production, and for the promotion of their agricultural, manufacturing, and mining interests; and shall send out to the people of the United States and foreign countries such reports concerning the industrial resources of Alabama as may best make known the advantages offered by the State to emigrants; and shall perform such other duties as the General Assembly may require.

SEC. 3. It shall be the duty of the General Assembly, at the first session after the adoption of this Constitution, to pass such laws and regulations as may be necessary for the government and protection of this bureau, and also to fix and provide for the compensation of the commissioner.

SEC. 4. This bureau shall be located, and the commissioner shall reside at the capital of the State, and he shall annually make a written or printed report to the Governor of the State, to be laid before the General Assembly at each session.

SEC. 5. In case of the death, removal, or resignation of the commissioner, the Governor, with the approval of the Senate, shall have power to appoint a commissioner for the unexpired term.—*The Federal and State Constitutions, Colonial Charters, and Other Organic Laws* (Washington: Government Printing Office, 1909), vol. 1, pp. 148–51.

The article on education provided for a highly centralized system and bestowed extensive legislative powers to the state Board of Education, making it equal with the General Assembly in educational matters. It also provided ample funds for running public schools.

Carpetbag Government

It is next to impossible to get a dispassionate picture of government under the carpetbaggers. Life was turned upside down; often it was chaotic. Since few whites could take the "iron-clad" oath, only men from out of state and the inexperienced local residents were left to vote and hold office. Negro voting was new. J. B. Moore noted in his diary on April 1, 1867:

> They had an election at Tuscumbia for mayor and alderman and for the first time so far as I know in the state Negroes voted. 53 negro votes were polled and nearly all for Sloss, an ex-Confederate major for mayor.

It was not until later in the year, after Smith had enrolled those not disfranchised, that any large number of them went to the polls. They not only voted, they also held office from the local level to the legislature.

THE LEGISLATURE

This body assembled at Montgomery on Monday last. The attendance was not full on the first day, but sufficient were present to form a quorum. There are 26 negroes in the House, and one in the Senate.

The county of Lowndes, where the election was declared null, in consequence of the ballots being stolen, is mis-represented by one C. W. Buckly, of Massachusetts, who was admitted to a seat by the action of the House. The Constitutional Amendment was adopted Monday evening by a vote of 69 to 3 in the House, and 26 in the Senate.

The next business in order will be the election of two U. S. Senators; Spencer, Warner and Humphries are the prominent candidates.—*Shelby County Guide* (Columbiana), July 16, 1868.

Little good has been said about the actions of the carpetbag governments. One of the chief criticisms was its extravagance and resulting high taxes. Fleming quotes the following figures to show how, even in the face of depreciated property values, the taxes rose phenomenally.

	Census Valuation	State Tax	County Tax	Town Tax
1860	$432,198,762	$ 530,107	$ 309,474	$ 11,590
1870	156,770,387	1,477,414	1,122,471	403,937

—Walter L. Fleming, *Civil War and Reconstruction in Alabama* (New York: Columbia University Press, 1905), p. 574.

The governor's salary was doubled; circuit judges who had been paid a total of $13,500.00 before the war now cost the state $36,000.00; stationery for the executive departments rose from $1,200.00 per year to $12,708.77. Only in 1868 did the state collect as much as it spent; in other years the deficit was filled by the sale of bonds. Finances were haphazard, and the state teetered on the brink of bankruptcy. In 1874 a commission appointed to "ascertain and adjust" the public debt found it to be approximately $30,037,563. Interest on it amounted to over $2,000,000 annually, twice as much as the yearly income. To liquidate this staggering debt explains in large part the extreme frugality of the "Bourbon" period after 1874.

There were waste and countless frauds, but a big portion of the increased budgets was spent on two items that deserve commendation, schools and railroads. A. B. Moore says that the total cost of government in 1866–67 was $676,476.54 of which $413,849.97 was spent on schools. Weeks, however, offers statistics to show that more money was appropriated than spent for schools. He does not indicate to what the difference was diverted.

Year	Money Appropriated	Money Received	Diverted
1869–1870	$500,407	$306,872	$187,872
1870–1871	581,389	320,480	260,908
1871–1872	604,978	166,303	438,675
1872–1873	522,810	68,313	454,496
1873–1874	474,346		474,346

—Stephen B. Weeks, *History of Public School Education in Alabama* (Washington: Government Printing Office, 1915), p. 104.

Since railroads will be taken up in a later chapter, only the total obligations of the state for lines constructed are given here. Dr. A. B. Moore says it amounted to about $17,000,000. The mileage by 1883 was about twice what it was in 1860.

Some of the frauds of elections were recounted by Samuel A. Hale from New Hampshire who became dissillusioned with manipulations of the freedmen's vote and the political situation in general. He later became a Democrat.

> Their election was the most ridiculous farce ever held. I wish you could have seen the poor ignorant blacks giving in their "bits of paper," as they called their printed ballots, when they knew no more of the names on them, who they were, what they were, than you did at the same time in your far-off home. . . . In all the elections ever held in the United States, there has not been so much fraud committed as there was in this one (1867). The negroes think they have been greatly wronged because they have not been paid for voting. Of the three delegates sent from this county, two were white and one was black. The two whites were strangers here. . . . One of them, called Rolfe, is said to be a vagrant from the State of New York, where it is said he has a wife and family living, whom he has not seen in four or five years. . . . He had been here some three or four months prior to his election as a delegate, sometimes working as a carriage trimmer, sometimes drinking whisky and making drunken exhibitions of himself upon our streets. . . . Of the other white delegate, called Yordy; . . . I had never heard of him until the day of his nomination. Neither of them ought ever to have been thought of for the responsible station to which they were elected. Nor would they have been thought of had the nomination of delegates been left to the white Union party of the county. It did not, however, suit the purposes of the military power that now so insolently tramples upon the people of this State to leave the nomination of the delegates to the Union party. Emissaries were sent here by military officers, who are now themselves candidates for election and the nomination of these men forced upon us. Unfortunately for us poor proscribed members of the Union party, these military men have too much influence with our ignorant black population. . . . It places every interest of the State at the disposal of the negroes. Every office, from governor to constable, from the chief justice of the supreme court to the magistrate of a county beat, is made elective and placed at the disposal of the blacks not one in five hundred of whom can either read or write, and who know no more of what they are doing, when they vote, than would a hog or mule know, if those brutes had the privilege of voting. . . . The reckless and unprincipled adventurers who have come among us from the Northern States and affiliated with the blacks, . . . assemble the negroes in large numbers, in convenient places, or meet them in the

Union Leagues, and address them in inflammatory speeches, upon the treatment they received from their masters while they were slaves, and they warn them against their former masters, telling them that the only friends they have in the South, are the men of the northern army who came here and fought for their liberation from slavery. . . . First, we have Tobias Lane, as nominee for the probate judgeship of this county. Lane is a stranger here, from Ohio, . . . is altogether ignorant of our laws; and it is not pretended, even by his friends, that he is qualified for the office. He has been put in nomination over the present incumbent, a long-tried and worthy member of the Union party, but who had the misfortune to have been a slaveholder. The second is Yordy, . . . [who] claims to have been a captain in the Federal Army; hence the secret of his nomination for the senate from this county. The candidates for the lower house of assembly are one white and two black men. The white man, when last seen here in this town, was an inmate of our county jail. . . . No one knows who he is or where he came from. Then we have two brothers of the name of Cecil, from Ohio; the one for sheriff and the other for treasurer of the county. The would-be treasurer is now engaged in partnership with a negro in the retail grocery business here —in vulgar parlance, keeping a negro doggery. . . . Another stranger, of whom I never heard before, is in nomination for the office of tax-assessor. For the important offices of commissioners of revenue and roads, we have one white man, of whom I never heard before, and three negroes. I have been thus particular in the mention of these candidates, not only on account of their being entire strangers among us, and of the way in which their nomination was effected, but more particularly for the purpose of calling your attention to the following facts in connection with the election at which these delegates are to be chosen. Lane and Rolfe are candidates for the two most important offices in the county—probate judge and tax-collector. They are also members of the board of registration, and, by virtue of their office, managers of the election. . . . Was it ever before heard of, that candidates for office in a popular election were not only the managers of the election, in which they were to be chosen, but were also clothed with the power of determining who shall and who shall not vote in their election?—*Ku Klux Report, Alabama Testimony,* p. 1832, quoted in Walter L. Fleming, ed., *Documentary History of Reconstruction* (Cleveland, Ohio: The Arthur H. Clark Co., 1906), vol. 1, pp. 44–46.

There was no law compelling a man to vote in his precinct, and there were repeated stories of the blacks being rounded up and marched to the polls to the beat of a drum and handed their ballots there.

This practice presented a challenge to some of the young "bucks" in west Alabama who took great delight in beating the carpetbaggers at their own game.

The Republicans always tried to mass the Negroes at one or two places in the county so they could control them. There were quite a lot of Negroes in Gordo precinct and we boys decided we would make all of them vote the Democratic ticket and this is the way we decided on and which acted to our satisfaction.

I had built a gin house on a creek about a quarter (mile) from my house and had put down a good floor in it and had never sawed out the places for the bands to go through, so the floor was solid and smooth. I told some of the Negroes that if they would let me fix their tickets for them in the coming election I would give them a big dance and candy pulling and they could have all the fun they wanted. I told them I would furnish ten gallons of molasses and five pounds of good tobacco for the frolic and the way I would manage so no Negro that voted the Republican ticket could come in I would give each one that let me fix his ticket a ticket to the dance and candy pulling and if I caught one there without a ticket I would bat him off the place. It so turned out that I voted every Negro in Gordo beat and by so doing we elected our man we wanted for tax assessor.

This kind of maneuvering sounds strange these days but back then any Negro that was twenty one or looked like he might be that age could vote and they could be bought as easy as some white men are to-day and nearly as cheap and their voting depended largely on what they thought they could get out of it. This frolic mentioned here was fully enjoyed by quite a mass of Negroes and they felt good knowing they had voted to suit the best people in the neighborhood. Such a frolic as that would be a great show to the young people today and would be the best picture show by odds for these darkies sure enjoyed it and entered into it with all the vim they had in them and such an old fashion candy pulling one never sees any more. . . . It made some of my Radical brethren pretty mad when they found I played a trick on them and voted every Negro in the country.—John L. Hunnicutt, *Reconstruction in West Alabama* (Tuscaloosa, Alabama: Confederate Publishing Co., 1959), pp. 44–45.

Some of the trials of a scalawag county leader are seen in a letter from Pickens County, Alabama. B. C. Thomas, who had run a blacksmith shop in Carrollton before the war, replaced Z. L. Nabers, a sound lawyer and well qualified by study and experience for the office, as probate judge a few months after this letter was written.

Honorable Thaddeus Stevens:
Dear Sir:

As you well know, we have no Representative in your Honorable body, we take the responsibility of addressing you. At I understand the Constitution, it promises us protection of Life, Liberty, and the pursuits of happiness. We are destitute of all these. When I say we are the Union Republican Party, (Equal rights and universal suffrage). We cannot vote without alsorts threats to intimidate—a perfect Rule of terror as was in sixty-four. Our courts are mocks, all of the offices are full Rebels. Freed men are shot with impunity, all go off as Justified

Homicide. A grate many disappear misteriously, dround or disposed otherwise. We have some five hundred Republicans white men. Only sixty-seven voted in the last election of the constitution, from the fear of being ill treated by the Rebs. I talked to them, and find this to be so. We rote for trupes. None come and in counties where they ware doin good. Either put us under strict military Rule or turn us lose and give us a rite to defend ourselves.

I will make some suggestions. Be certain to Impeach Jonson and Receive Alabama in the Union, and thene the worke is finished. And give us some good military officer to stay with us until we are properly organized. You need not fier Alabama. She is Republican by at least forty thousand.

Our post offices stocked against us, fild with Rebs. We have no chance to write in safety to you. This may reach you, but I am doubtful.

I cold write pages of in Relation to matters and things. As I expect you have been informed by more suitible writers than I, I will desist, and worey you no further. These are facts and true statements and worthy of Consideration, altho pend in an awkward manner.

The salvation of our Gloryous union, depends on the Impeachment of A. Jonson, President of the United States.

I will Recommend myself by saying that I am President of what is cauld the union League of America, at Carrollton. Our strength is six hundred. That is why I say the country is Republican by Eight hundred majority for our president in the next election. . . .

I will bring this to a close by saying we have confidence in your untiring ability and skill, and will expect Some Relief. I (am) a native of Alabama, and love her name, also, the star spangled Banner.

My leter is badly Rote. Excuse me, this is my first attempt to address you Honor. My name Represents Eighteen hundred voters, in my official capacity.

Your most Ob't sv't

B. C. THOMAS, PRESIDENT of U. L. A,
Carrollton, Alabama.

—March 15, 1868, quoted in James F. Clanahan, *The History of Pickens County, Alabama, 1540–1920* (Carrollton, Alabama: Clanahan Publications, 1964), pp. 169–70.

That government under the carpetbaggers went to extremes cannot be denied; that it was unpopular with the whites who had been disfranchised is also indisputable. The extent of the first is hard to determine, but its excesses led to an equally extreme movement, the Klan.

The Ku Klux Klan

The Ku Klux movement is the term used to designate the opposition to the excesses of Reconstruction. Organizations in different localities had different names, but the purposes were much the same. Some of the local organizations were purely protective and intended only to check what they looked upon as Negro excesses; others acted as regulators of morals; and still others sought to rid the community of corrupt officers.

Governor R. B. Lindsay, Democrat, who was elected in 1870, said the Klan was formed to stop the excesses of the Union League.

> The origin, as it is generally understood, the prime moving cause of the existence of the Ku-Klux, was the result of Union Leagues. Union Leagues were organized in every little hamlet and town throughout North Alabama, composed principally of colored men, with a sprinkling of whites. Those Union Leagues were supposed . . . to have not only a political object, but to a certain extent an object of crime; that they were banded together for the purpose of committing depredations upon the whites. . . . During the process of reconstruction there were no courts in the State of Alabama, either competent or active in the administration of the laws. Everything to a certain extent was chaotic, every man and every part of society were entirely at sea. And this band of Ku-Klux was said to have been organized to counteract the objects and acts of the Union Leagues, and to punish crime where the laws failed to administer justice. . . . Unfortunately, under the reconstruction measures in Alabama, we had placed in power a great many incompetent officers, men who were not capable of discharging the functions either of judge or prosecuting attorney; men who were totally unfit either by their moral or their mental character to administer the laws.—Quoted in Fleming, *Documentary History of Reconstruction,* vol. 2, p. 331.

General James H. Clanton, a "white supremacy" advocate, spoke of conditions that brought forth such a movement.

> There is not a respectable white woman in the Negro Belt of Alabama who will trust herself hardly outside of her house without some protector. . . .
> So far as our State government is concerned, we are in the hands of campfollowers, horse-holders, cooks, bottle-washers, and thieves. . . . We have passed out from the hands of the brave soldiers who overcame us, and turned to the tender mercies of squaws for torture. . . . I see negro police—great black fellors—leading white girls around the streets of Montgomery, and locking them up in jail.—Ibid., pp. 331–32.

The Republican state superintendent of education, 1870–72, was Virginia-born Joseph H. Speed, a Hampton-Sydney graduate, college professor, and Confederate army officer. Now advocating "universal amnesty and universal suffrage," he took a more level headed look at the origins of the Klan than some others.

> Great bitterness was engendered among the white people by the disfranchisement of their representative men; and I think that that bitterness was greater toward the negro after his enfranchisement than it

would have been if there had been no disfranchisement of the whites. I think that this was the commencement of the trouble. The beginning of bitterness in our country was the disfranchisement of the whites; and out of that grew, in a great measure, their opposition to this movement of reconstruction. This, coupled with negro suffrage, was the origin of the difficulty. The white people in our country, though they may accept what is known as the "new departure," are at heart unalterably opposed, in my opinion, to negro suffrage.—Ibid., p. 332.

S. F. Rice, another Republican, saw the resentment and frustrations of the whites as causing the movement.

I think it is caused by this long continued indulgence of the passions, accompanied by a conviction that the southern people are the most grossly wronged and outraged people on the face of the earth. This is the honest belief of the white people generally. It is this feeling, doubtless, that makes them so bitter, especially towards a man like myself. I was a nullifier; a States-rights man out and out. I entertained extreme Southern views until I became a republican.—Ibid.

Notices of meetings and warnings to the public, such as the following, frequently appeared on handbills and in newspapers.

BLINKEYED CAVE, NO. XXX
DARK MOON! BLOODY HOUR!
FOURTH MOON!
K K K DIVISION XXX
CHIEF'S DECREE
I salute. Brothers are preparing! The hours are growing Auspicious! The X deed must be avenged! Avenged! Avenged!!! Be firm, Steadfast, true! Fear not; truth must prevail, justice shall be meeted out! Honor fears not, truth and justice triumphs!
SILENCE! WATCH!! DUTY!!!
BY ORDER G. G. C., D XXX
—Quoted in Clanahan, *History of Pickens County,* p. 231.

John L. Hunnicutt, whose recollections vividly portray the turbulent conditions of affairs in Pickens County, shows some of the roles the Klan played.

There is no doubt the effect of the Ku Klux Klan was the salvation of our country under the trying condition through which we passed for it made men out of many who would have been clogs to the wheel of prosperity. I want to mention one party in particular for he was a frequent visitor of the saloon in those days and when he would go home he would most always be under the influence of whiskey and it seemed to be his ambition to whip his wife if anything crossed him.

He married a widow ladys daughter and these people were once in good financial condition before the negroes were set free.

The good old lady thought by staying with her daughter her presence would make the man less brutal, but he came home one Saturday night full as usual and because his wife did not have a good warm supper for him he got some switches and proceeded to wear her out. Her mother commenced to intercede for her daughter and the brute grabbed her and gave her a sound thrashing.

The Klan ordered a bunch of us boys to call on this party so in a few nights we called on this man and told him the people were getting tired of his actions and we had come to show him how whipping felt and to get down on his knees and pull off that shirt and one of the boys took his halter rein and he sure did warm him good and proper. His wife and his mother in law both got down on their knees and begged for him. We told them we were very sorry but their pleadings had no effect on him and we would have to go ahead with our beating. Finally he said gentlemen if you will stop I will promise I will never take another drink of whiskey and will never speak a cross word to these women, but will go to work and make them a good living.—John L. Hunnicutt, *Reconstruction in West Alabama,* William Stanley Hoole, ed. (Tuscaloosa, Alabama; Confederate Publishing Company, 1959), pp. 104–105.

In central Alabama also the Klan was busy.

About a week ago Saturday night the Ku Klux came into town to regulate matters. They were here from eleven p.m. to three o'clock A.m.—five hundred in all. They shot one very bad negro, putting six balls through his head. Many heard the noise, but did not know what was going on. They also hung three or four negroes nearly dead, and whipped others severely in order to make them tell them about their nightly meetings, and what their object was in holding the same; also, as to who their leaders were. They made a clean breast of the whole matter, telling everything. The strongest thing about these Ku Klux was that they did not hesitate to unmask themselves when asked to do so; and out of the whole party none were identified.—Every one who saw them says their horses were more beautiful than, and far superior to, any in the country round about. They spoke but little but always to a purpose. They went to several stores and knocked; the doors were opened at once. They then called for rope, and at each place a coil was rolled out to them. They cut it in suitable length to hang a man with. No one asked for money and they offered none. They did not disturb any one else, nor did they take any thing except some few Enfield rifles which were found in possession of some very bad negroes.—They called on the revenue officer and passed a few remarks with him. What transpired is not known, but it has made a great improvement in his conversation. The visitants advent has been productive of much good and benefit to the community, though all regret such steps should have to be resorted to, every one says "give us peace," and really I believe them to be truly sincere.—*Shelby County Guide* (Columbiana), December 3, 1868.

A favorite antic of the klansmen was to pretend they were returned from the dead. A former slave in Sumter County remembered a visit from them.

Seems like there wa'n't no trouble 'mongst the whites and blacks till after the war. Some white mens come down from the North and mess up with the niggers. I was a mighty little shaver, but I 'members one night after supper, my daddy and mammy and us childrens was setting under a big tree by our cabin in the quarters, when all at oncet, lickety split, here come galloping down the road what look like a whole army of ghostes. Must have been 'bout a hundred, and they was men riding hosses with the men and hosses both robed in white.

Cap'n, them mens look like they been ten feet high and they hosses big as elephants. They didn't bother nobody at the quarters, but the leader of the crowd ride right in the front gate and up to the big dug well back of our cabin and holler to my daddy: "Come here, nigger!" Ho-oh! Course we scared. Yes, sir, look like our time done come.

My daddy went over to where he setting on his hoss at the well. Then he say: "Nigger, git a bucket and draw me some cool water." Daddy got a bucket, fill it up and hand it to him. Cap'n, would you believe it? That man just lift that bucket to his mouth and never stop till it empty. Did he have 'nough? He just smack his mouth and call for more. Just like that, he didn't stop till he drunk three buckets full. Then he just wipe his mouth and say: "Lordy, that sure was good. It was the first drink of water I's had since I was killed at the battle of Shiloh."

Was we good? Cap'n, from then on there wasn't a nigger dare stick his head out the door for a week. But next day we find out they was Ku Kluxes, and they found the body of a white man hanging to a post oak over by Grand Prairie. His name was Billings, and he come from the North. He been over round Livingston messing up the niggers, telling 'em they had been promised forty acres and a mule and they ought to go 'head and take 'em from the white folks.—E. A. Botkin, ed., *Lay My Burden Down* (Chicago: University of Chicago Press, 1945), pp. 262–63.

The atrocities of the Klan came to the attention of General Meade in the spring of 1868. He tried to suppress it with troops but without success. The state legislature outlawed it by official act later that year.

THE KLANS OUTLAWED
Anti-Kuklux Statute

WHEREAS, there is in the possession of this General Assembly ample and undoubted evidence of a secret organization in many parts of this State, of men who, under the cover of masks and other grotesque disguises, armed with knives, revolvers and other deadly weapons, do issue from the places of their rendezvous, in bands of greater or less number, on foot or mounted on horses, in like manner disguised, generally in the late hours of the night, to commit violence and outrages upon peaceable and law-abiding citizens, robbing and murdering them upon the highway, and entering their houses, tearing them from their homes, and the embrace of their families, and with violent threats and insults, inflicting on them the most cruel and inhuman treatment; and whereas, this organization has become a widespread and alarming evil in the commonwealth, disturbing the public peace, ruining the happiness and prosperity of the people, and in many places overriding the civil authorities, defying all law and justice, or evading detection by the darkness of night, and with their hideous costumes therefore

Section 1. *BE IT ENACTED* . . . That any person appearing away from his home by night or by day, in company with others, or alone, wearing a mask, or disguised in other costume, or both, shall be held guilty of a high crime and misdemeanor, and on conviction shall be fined in the sum of one hundred dollars and be imprisoned in the county jail not less than six months nor more than one year, at the discretion of the court having jurisdiction of the same.

Section 2. . . . Any such (disguised) person . . . shall be held guilty of a felony, and his disguise shall be sufficient evidence of his evil intent and of his guilt, and on conviction shall be fined one thousand dollars, and be imprisoned in the penitentiary not less than five years nor more than twenty years at the discretion of the court trying the same; and any one who may shoot, or in any way kill or wound such person, while under the cover of such disguise, and while in the act of committing, or attempting or otherwise to commit such violence or trespass, shall not be held guilty before the law of any offense against such person or the State, or be made to suffer any penalty for such act.

Sec. 3. . . . If any person or persons so disguised, or without disguise, shall unlawfully and with force, demolish, pull down, or set fire to, or destroy any church, or chapel, or meeting house, for religious worship, or school house, or other building used or intended for educational purposes, shall be guilty of a felony, and upon conviction, shall be imprisoned in the penitentiary not less than ten or more than twenty years, at the discretion of the court having jurisdiction of the same.

Sec. 6. . . . (If) any magistrate, to whom any complaint is made, or designated in section five of this act, or any sheriff or other officer, shall refuse or neglect to perform the duty required of such magistrate or officer, by this act, shall, on conviction, thereby forfeit his office, and shall be fined the sum of five hundred dollars.—*Acts of Alabama, 1868,* p. 444, quoted in Fleming, *Documentary History,* vol. 2, pp. 375–76.

Still, acts either by the Klan or, as its members maintained, violent men using their disguises, continued and the local radical authorities were helpless. Congress came to their rescue with the Ku Klux Act of April 20, 1871, which gave the president authority to declare the Southern states in rebellion and to suspend the writ of habeas corpus after a proclamation outlawing insurrection, domestic violence, unlawful combinations, and similar crimes. On May 3, 1871, President Grant issued a proclamation calling attention to the law, stating that when necessary he would not hesitate "to exhaust the powers" invested in him. The failure of local governments to protect all citizens would make it necessary for the national government to interfere.

Fleming, no friend of Radical Reconstruction, says that "to justify the passage of the Enforcement Acts and to obtain material for campaign use the next year," Congress voted to investigate conditions in the Southern states. From June to August 1871 the committee took testimony in Washington and then a subcommittee visited Alabama (and other states) where it held sessions in Huntsville, Demopolis, Montgomery, Livingston, and Columbus, Mississippi, for West Alabama. This testimony fills hundreds of pages and stresses the violence being done to Negroes. The case of Smith Watley of Coosa County is typical of scores of others.

Montgomery, Alabama October 17, 1871
SMITH WATLEY (colored) sworn and examined.
By the Chairman:
Question. State to the committee where you are living at this time.
Answer. I stay here at Montgomery. I have been here about four months, but go to my family back and forth and for my crop.
Question. Where did you formerly live?
Answer. I lived in Coosa County, twenty miles above Wetumpka, at the twentieth mile-post.
Question. How long had you lived there before the 6th of June last?
Answer. About two years; part of the time twelve miles above the place I am living now, above Allen Thomas's place, two miles this side of Nixburg, on the old plank road.
Question. What business were you employed in on the 6th of June last, in Coosa County?
Answer. Farming.
Question. On whose land?
Answer. Allen Thomas's. I rented from Allen Thomas.
Question. Proceed and state to the committee what violence was done to your person on or about the 6th of June last.
Answer. Well, I went to Nixburg that evening after it got done raining. It was Friday, in the evening, I went to Nixburg. My wife told me to go and get a good pair of shoes. I went by Alex Smith's, about a mile from my house, and he asked me what did I give Allen Thomas for that mule I was riding, and I said, "One hundred and fifty dollars, Christmas." He said, "Smith, that's a good trade you made, this time." He says, "Who carried that wagon away from your house, this evening?" I told him one of Mr. Thomas's black men, that I wanted to buy the wagon of; I wanted to buy one but the black man bought the wagon. Alex. Smith asked me about it. The next thing he says, "You know a man in the day-time, but in the night you don't know him. It was about sundown, and I went on to Nixburg. I said to my wife, "Caroline, what do you reckon all them men are gathering at Nixburg for?" She says,

"I don't know. I expect they are up to some meanness. You had better take my son and lay out tonight." I said, "I won't do it;" just so. That is the answer I gave her.

Question. Did you notice many men gather at Nixburg?

Answer. I told her about it. I said, "What do you reckon Mr. Bowen looked at me so under his hat—so ugly for?" She says, "There's some rascally trick after you by the white folks, and you take my son and lay out to-night." I says, "You have got a good pair of shoes, and don't want me to sleep with you to-night." I said that just for devilment. She looked at the shoes and put them on. She was going to her daughter's, and that night she said, "You had better go out to-night." I said, "No." She laid down before I did, and in about two hours, or three hours, as near as I could tell to-day, they came in.

Question. Who did?

Answer. The Ku-Klux. They struck my dogs, and she jumped, and said, "La, Smith here's the school teacher, Olliver; here is the Ku-Klux." I said, "Hush." Olliver is the school teacher. I says, "Hush, he'll kill you. I know who it is, too. If they got in here, they will kill you." She gets up and puts on her clothes and walks across the house, and takes my by the left hand and pulls me out of bed. I was slow getting out. I went to the window and I saw twelve men in the yard. I says, "I can't whip all these men." She says, "Don't open the door." They were hauling at the door. I went to the door; she kept hold of it, and says, "Don't open it; don't open it." I says, "I must open it. Don't you hear them?" He says, "Open in there; I don't walk: all my men flew from hell!; I am bound to see you to-night." I said, "I had better open the door." She says, "No, don't open it." I says to her, "Open it." He says, "Open the door." She says, "No, don't open it." He says, "we come here; we didn't ride; we didn't walk; our men flew from hell, and are bound to see you to-night." She hung to me, and I threw her away, and opened the door, and Olliver gathered me on the right arm, and Doctor Mc-Clernand on this other arm, and Joe Leonard catched me in the breast, and the next man, I don't know who he was; and after he turned me loose, Joe Leonard had a rock and struck me on the head, but he didn't knock me down; they were holding me up. They took me out. They made me strip off my shirt and led me outside of the door. Then they set in and whipped me. These all went to whipping me right off, all six at once. I took notice and counted the men. Then, after Olliver was done whipping, Joe Leonard took the whip out of his hand and whipped me, and that made seven men. Then my wife went to the horses, to see who they were as well as she could, and she saw two colored men. She said one was Pomp Moore, and the other was Aleck Temples. They were not disguised, she said. I couldn't get there. She said Joe Thomas blowed a whistle, and made them stop whipping me at the time they were whipping me.

Question. What happened after that?

Answer. After that she says, and her son says the same thing, and swears, and her daughter-in-law swears she saw them. I didn't see them, because, at the same time they whipped me, they had my brother-in-law, and laid him right down by me.

Question. What was his name?

Answer. Jesse Watson.

Question. Was he staying in your house that night?

Answer. Yes, sir; he was not in in my house, but in a room between him and me.

Question. Did you see him whipped?

Answer. No; they just stripped him right beside me.

Question. What did they do to him?

Answer. Nothing but just stripped him. They made him strip. This Foster Anderson was one of the men that went to help me hunt for my wife, and instead of that she was around the horses, and I couldn't find her. There was so many around me I couldn't find her. She run off to see about the horses, and see where they was. Jack, my step-son, says Mr. Bowen was one of the men.

Question. Did you count the men that came to your house that night?

Answer. Yes sir; I counted sixteen men in my yard. I almost knowed the height of the men when they went from me. I knew them all almost.

Question. Had they any disguises on?

Answer. Yes sir.

Question. Describe to the committee the kind of disguise they wore.

Answer. As near as I could get at them, they had crowns going up from their heads like a crown, and they had gowns going down like a cloak or a sheet. They were not sheets, but gowns; they had sleeves and cuffs to them, and all. I noticed them.

Question. Did they have anything before their faces?

Answer. Olliver's came off. They had the crowns coming down over, and the mouth and noses and eyes, and at the time he was whipping me his came loose, and Joe had to take his place.

Question. So you could see Olliver's face?

Answer. Yes, sir; and so I could swear to him so hard. It came loose.

Question. Did they come there on horseback?

Answer. Yes sir. I went to where they tied the horses next morning.

Question. Were the horses in disguise?

Answer. Yes sir; they had white sheets. She said that; I didn't see them. She got close enough to see what they had on, but she was afraid to go closer. John North said the horses was covered with sheets.

Question. How many licks did they hit you?

Answer. I can't tell; they whipped me so long, and so many whipped me, I can't tell. They laid me down right outside of the steps at my door and whipped me; and they took me and my brother-in-law outside on the grass there, and whipped me some out there. But they didn't hit him a lick.

Question. How long were they there?

Answer. It was an hour before day when they left my house, as near as I could tell, because I never laid down any more, because they abused my back. They took my shirt off.

Question. What did they say they whipped you for?

Answer. They said it was because I had said the Ku-Klux ought to be dead; but I said a man that burned up a church ought to be dead, or any one that took a man out of his house and whipped him ought to be dead.—*Report of the Joint Select Committee to Inquire into the Condition of Affairs in the Late Insurrectionary States* (Washington: Government Printing Office, 1872), vol. 3, pp. 1004–1005.

Some Alabamians found the Reconstruction period so unbearable that they sought a new life in a foreign country. While some went to Central America, the majority of those who left accepted the offer of welcome extended by the Brazilian government. Excerpts from the diary of Dr. John Washington Keyes, a dentist from Montgomery, portray the strong feeling against carpetbag rule.

THE TRIP TO BRAZIL

Apr. 6th 8½ p.m. [1867]. Left Mobile on the steamer Debleon. Capt. Kirk—Mitchell, clerk—whose boat I commend to all who desire to travel on a good boat and deal with true gentlemen. Every attention and accommodation was shown—expected or desired.

Adieus are sad to say and when in this instance they are to many true and tried friends, whom I never expect to see again, the only way is to say them quickly and be gone.

There are many I am rejoiced it is so—whom I have no desire to see again, because having trusted them implicitly they deceived me—others who taking advantage of the circumstances—and my forebearance defrauded me, but among these it is a consolation to me that I cannot remember one who did his duty to his country in her hour of need. Not one who did not have his price and put money in his pocket, even tho the dependants of these who were enduring the trials and hardships of the camp suffered. I do not think that these would not have been moved by kindly impulses—and relieved in part the destitution that might have been brot to their doors—but that the love of gain served to induce them to follow a course which they knew was wrong in the abstract and practised by many moved of necessity bring their country to the condition it did.

To all of these so called Confederates I trust I have bid an eternal adieu. Before the war there were few men I would not trust—since the war I have found the rule reversed. And what pains me most and urges my departure is that the number worthy of confidence grows less every day.

To the good and true I've left behind my hand is ever extended and my pocket open to assist and aid so far as I may do so with justice to myself. Many of these I will cherish in my heart so long as it pulsates.

Montgomery and loved friends—Goodbye!

Saturday—soft bread, Oatmeal porridge, coffee. Soup, fresh meat, potatoes, hard bread. Hard bread, butter and tea.

Sunday—Soup, salt pork, plum pudding, potatoes, hard bread, apple sauce, hard bread, butter and tea.

April 16 on board Marmion

At a quarter past ten on the morning of the 16th we cast loose and commenced our voyage towards Brazil. We were to have started at 8 o'clock but a thief got on board and we were delayed some time by his hunt for this baggage, etc. Without incident, we reached the mouth of the River and at 6 o'clock crossed the bar. I never saw the sea smoother and the sky clearer.

Good Friday. 19th

I went on deck early this morning, washed off the soil of the U. S. put on clean clothes and thot I had bid adieu to my native land—but alas we are cruelly reminded of the Puritan and his abominations by having cod fish for dinner. Our bill of fare says coffee for breakfast but even here we are punished. Our Yankee friends—ship owners—may have thot there was a pleasant reminiscence for Confederates in corn meal and rye coffee or that it would be more acceptable to the stomach or that we could not beat the pure article—but I suspect none of these charitable possibilities was the cause.—Diary, Alice Keyes Scott Collection, University of Alabama.

The Church and Reconstruction

Before the war, slaves had belonged to the same churches as their masters. After the war, they carried their independence into their religious life, establishing their own churches. The major denominations had a positive interest in the Negro and the establishment of black churches brought forth comments from them. As is seen in official statements by three churches, there were mixed feelings about the wisdom of this movement. The first given here was by the Baptists.

The special Committee, to whom was referred the Report of the Committee on the Religious Instruction of the Colored People, together with instructions on the subject of their report, beg leave to submit the following:

1. *Resolved,* That the Churches of Christ having no legitimate connection with the State, should remain unchanged by the results of political revolutions, except in so far as these may open up new fields of usefulness, or as furnishing inducements for renewed and increased Christian effort.

2. That the changed political status of our late slaves does not necessitate any change in their relation to our churches; and while we recognize their right to withdraw from our churches and form organizations of their own, we nevertheless believe that their highest good will be subserved by their maintaining their present relation to those who know them, who love them, and who will labor for the promotion of their welfare.

3. That the condition of our colored population appeals very strongly to the sympathy of every Christian heart, and demands, at the hands of all who love the Saviour, renewed exertions for their moral and re-

ligious improvement; and to this end we would recommend the establishment of Sunday Schools, the providing for them the preached gospel, and the adoption of all practical appliances which will tend to ameliorate their condition, and induce them to become sharers in a common salvation.—*Minutes of the Alabama Baptist State Convention,* November 1865, quoted in Fleming, *Documentary History,* vol. 2, 245.

The Presbyterians seem to have accepted the realities of the situation.

For many years past . . . we have been enabled to report a marked and deepening interest in the instruction of the colored people. Indeed such instruction was felt by ministers and churches, to be a part alike of ministerial duty and Christian obligation, which might not be neglected. And year after year, our hearts have rejoiced to hear of the signal success attending the labors of our Southern ministry in this direction. And while it is our painful duty to acknowledge, that the distractions incident to the sudden change recently made in their social status, produced a marked falling off in their attendance upon the preaching of our ministry,—such as, for a time, to awaken serious apprehensions, that the door of usefulness was closed to them; yet, there are evidences of returning confidence in our teachings, which afford encouragement to continue our labors for that people. We, therefore, urge our ministers not to be discouraged, but to redouble their efforts for usefulness in this field of labor.—*Minutes of the Synod of Alabama,* October 1865, quoted in ibid., vol. 2, p. 245.

The Methodists recognized the importance of their continuing interest.

1. *Resolved,* that the change in the social and domestic relations of our colored membership does not necessarily demand any change in their church relations.

2. *Resolved,* That we cherish an unabated interest in their spiritual welfare, and are in no wise disposed to withdraw from our oversight and sympathy in this particular.

3. *Resolved,* That we urge upon our ministry and membership the duty of increased attention to the religious instruction and improvement of our colored population, as the best means of fitting them for the duties and responsibilities of their new position.—Montgomery *Advertiser,* November 11, 1865, quoted in ibid., vol. 2, p. 246.

Rev. I. T. Tichenor was a Baptist minister in Montgomery in the decade before the war. He helped train a number of blacks to be voluntary missionaries among their own people. The colored part of the First Baptist Church there, some six hundred of them, had their own pastor, deacons, held their own conferences, disciplined their own members, and otherwise ran their own church affairs.

This experience no doubt eased the transition to all-black churches during reconstruction. Tichenor wrote:

> When a separation of the two bodies was deemed desirable it was done by the colored brethren in conference assembled, passing a resolution couched in the kindliest terms, suggesting the wisdom of the division, and asking the concurrence of the white church in such action. The white church cordially approved the movement, and the two bodies united in erecting a suitable house of worship for the colored brethren. Until it was finished they continued to occupy jointly with the white brethren their house of worship as they had done previous to this action. The new house was paid for in large measure by the white members of the church and individuals in the community. As soon as it was completed the colored church moved into it with its organization all perfected, their pastor, Board of Deacons, committees of all sorts, and the whole machinery of church life went into action without a jar. Similar things occurred in all the States of the South.—I. T. Tichenor, *Work of the Southern Baptists Among the Negroes* (pamphlet), quoted in Fleming, *Documentary History,* vol. 2, pp. 247–48.

A Summary

Much of the writing about the Reconstruction period has been done by men like Walter L. Fleming who they themselves or their families had experienced the upheavals of the post-war years. Probably none of them, however, summarizes the prevading gloom with more flourish than Dr. A. B. Moore.

> In 1873 the people of Alabama were groping in Stygian darkness. They were in a death grapple with the carpetbaggers and colored men for the control of the State. They were in the fathomless debts of bankruptcy; the State debt alone having advanced from about $7,000,000 in 1867 to $32,000,000. Crops had generally been poor since the surrender, and taxes were too heavy to be borne . . . . Thousands of farmers were unable to pay their taxes and their farms were sold by the state at public outcry. One copy of the *Southern Republican* in 1871 carried twenty-one and one-half columns of advertisements of land sales in the four counties of Marengo, Greene, Perry, and Choctaw. . . . Public buildings everywhere were placarded with notices of land sales. Thousands of farms that were not sold for taxes were sold under mortgages . . . . Since the surrender children had grown into young manhood or womanhood unable to read or write. As a crowning stroke of adversity, the panic of 1873 swept across the state, the rivers flooded large areas of crops, and several towns were scourged by yellow fever.—A. B. Moore, *History of Alabama* (University, Alabama: University Supply Store, 1934), pp. 499–500.

One is tempted to say with the prophet, "All is lost! All is lost!"

But life was not all gloomy, nor did people live in a constant

crisis atmosphere. Many succeeded in living normal lives, surrounded by perhaps no greater hardships than were common
throughout much of the country. Editors in Alabama not only
printed news, they also made jokes about their fellow beings,
saving some of their most pungent jibes for the Radicals. A choice
one was an assignment to "parse Radical." Parsing was a favorite
school exercise of the nineteenth century in which the student
described a word grammatically. The answer was:

> A Radical is a compound unconstitutional noun, black in person,
> declining in number, African gender, and desperate case, governed by
> niggers; and according to the Puritan rule, one ignoramous governs
> another.—Quoted by Robert Partin, "Alabama Newspaper Humor
> during Reconstruction," *Alabama Review,* vol. 17, p. 245.

General John Pope, commander of the Third Military District, had
given what has been described as a pompous remark about his
headquarters being in the saddle. To which the Montgomery *Daily
Mail,* February 10, 1867, replied with this verse:

> Pope his "Headquarters" in saddle places, Where other mortals their
> quarters plant, sir. Pray tell me what deduction from this case is? Why
> this is logics clear and easy answer. If Pope has brains by jove he's got
> 'em Where every other mortal has his bottom.—Ibid., p. 249.

A great many planters were ruined by the war or high taxes and
lack of labor during the Reconstruction period. On the other hand,
there were some who were making money. Take the case of Ellic
Davidson, no carpetbagger, in Marengo County.

> Ellic Davidson continues to increase in worldly goods more than any
> man I ever knew. He made last year in a few bales of 600—591 I
> believe. He bought $17,000 worth of Weaver's land early last spring
> for which he paid cash down and in November last he bought the
> Price plantation for which he paid $28,000 cash . . . . He has 100
> mules plowing every day that is fair, and is about buying 14 more. I
> believe he is the wealthiest man in Marengo County except one . . . .
> He is running five large plantations this year.—P. H. Pitts to Lieutenant-
> Governor Edward Hawthorne Moren (Centreville), January 18, 1870,
> Moren Letters, 1870–1874, Ms., Alabama State Archives, Montgomery.

The small white farmer was one of the gainers during the
period. Robert Somers, making an extensive tour of the former
Confederate states in 1871, found much of the farming in north
Alabama being done by the small white farmer.

> The hilly districts have long been occupied by a poor white population,
> who have always produced more or less cotton. But the high value to

which cotton was raised by the war, and the "labor difficulty" of the large plantations have inspired them with new hope, life, and industry. . . . —Robert Somers, *The Southern States Since the War* (New York: Macmillan, 1871), p. 117.

The struggles were not all between radical Republicans and conservative Democrats, and equal righters versus white supremacists. The isssues were more complex than that, and the picture not completely negative. In spite of tragic consequences, there were forces at work that eventually led to improved conditions. Considerable progress was made in education, often through cooperation between native whites and Bureau officials. Under the Constitution of 1868 public education for the first time had ample financial support and promised equal opportunities for all children, although, unfortunately, actual accomplishments fell below hopes and expectations. The carpetbag government, using the resources provided by the Morrill Act, established Alabama Polytechnic Institute at Auburn.

There was once again considerable interest in railroad building, even if critics saw in the expansion of lines collusion between politicians and railroad promoters. The legislature created several new counties: Baker (later changed to Chilton), Bullock, Clay, Cleburne, Elmore, Etowah, Hale, and Lee. It abolished and then later reestablished Colbert and Lamar. Furthermore, the embryonic mining interests of the antebellum period revived, and cities like Birmingham and Gadsden were founded.

What Alabama lacked, many leaders were saying, was a stable government by which they meant a conservative government under white control.

Chapter 13

POLITICS FROM 1874 TO 1900

On November 24, 1874, George Smith Houston was inaugurated governor of Alabama, restoring Democratic, white, home government. The event dramatically ended in this state the period of Reconstruction and began an era historians are wont to call "Bourbon democracy."

For nine years the state had endured Reconstruction government of various kinds and degrees. Why had it virtually come to an end? While the answer is neither easy nor simple, there are a few recognizable reasons. The Republican party, stimulated in part by the reforming element under Horace Greeley, was frankly embarrassed by the corruption and scandals of the Grant administration. Consequently, there were some changes in their program in the South. Quite a number of the Radicals had already left the state, leaving the leadership to local Republicans. The panic of 1873 gave the nation new worries and caused a curtailment of funds that had been supporting the forces of Radical Reconstruction. There were also divisions and rivalry in the Alabama leadership.

Furthermore, the freedmen seem to have lost some of their interest in politics. Disillusioned when promises of benefits such as the "forty acres and a mule" were not forthcoming, they turned to other activities. They remained in the Republican party, but their interest waned and it was not difficult for whites to dissuade them from voting, often through the use of threats and violence.

The issue of the 1874 election was openly race and "white supremacy." The whites, determined to regain political control, used every means at hand to do so. Intimidation of black voters was one but there were more ostensibly legal methods. In May 1872, Congress passed an amnesty act which removed the civil disabilities from all but about five hundred ex-Confederates. Therefore, most whites could and did register to vote.

The issues of the campaign had strong emotional appeal. It was a white man's movement, and its leaders were bent on wresting power from the carpetbaggers. Writing in behalf of a local Democratic candidate,B. Morris of Eufaula spoke of the pride his fellow-countians had in General Alpheus Baker. After an upright boyhood and an honorable four years in the Confederate army, he had been a stalwart against local corruption by the Radicals.

> Since the war no intimidation or seduction could swerve him from fidelity to the cause of the whiteman, which after all is what is called the "lost cause" but which in my judgment is now to be won!—Morris to Edward H. Moren, July 14, 1874, Moren Letters, 1870–74, Ms., Alabama State Archives, Montgomery.

Newspaper editors in south Alabama made dramatic appeals to the voters in the northern "white" counties.

> South Alabama raises her manacled hands in mute appeal to the mountain counties. The chains on the wrists of her sons and the midnight shrieks of her women sound continually in their ears. She lifts up her eyes being tormented and begs piteously for relief from bondage. Is there a white man in north Alabama so lost to all his finer feelings of human nature as to slight her appeal?—Montgomery *Advertiser,* November 1, 1874.

It is doubtful if any abolitionist ever made a more dramatic appeal for his cause than this editor for the release from the bondage of Radical government.

The Democrats were well organized for the 1874 campaign. All over the state, county organizations adopted a platform which seems to have originated in Pike County.

Pike County Platform, 1874.

> *Whereas* the republican party of Alabama, for years past, has distinctly made and tendered to the people of this State an open, square issue of race; and
>
> *Whereas* the tendencies of the doctrines, teaching and practices of said party, as more recently illustrated and evidenced by the passage by the United States Senate of what is known as the civil-rights bill, are to the effect that the negro, by reason of his emancipation, is elevated to, and ought of right to enjoy, social as well as political equality; and
>
> *Whereas* the white people of the South have sedulously endeavored to prevent the issue of race, and in various ways sought to escape and avoid the said issue, well knowing the direful consequences that would follow it; and
>
> *Whereas* the white people of the South have hitherto forborne, and

hoped to escape the consequences thus hurled defiantly into their faces by the poor negroes, at the instance of the thieving crew known as carpet-baggers, and the more contemptible and infamous gang known as scalawags, who, in full view of this issue, have, for the sake of plunder, power, and spoils, sided with the aforesaid deluded negroes regardless of the hateful and direful consequences to ensue from the passage of said odious civil-rights bill, which is the culmination of all radical diabolism.

Therefore, we respectfully suggest to our county convention for consideration the following resolutions:

Resolved, That we, the people of Troy beat, for the protection of our dearest and most sacred interests, our homes, our honor, the purity and integrity of our race, and to conserve the peace and tranquility of the country, accept the issue of race thus defiantly tendered and forced upon us, notwithstanding our determinations and repeated efforts to avoid it; and further

Resolved, That nothing is left to the white man's party but social ostracism of all those who act, sympathize or side with the negro party, or who support or advocate the odious, unjust, and unreasonable measure known as the civil rights bill; and that from henceforth we will hold all such persons as enemies of our race, and we will not in the future have intercourse with them in any of the social relations of life.

These are the sentiments of the democrats and conservatives of Pike County, with their fifteen hundred white majority.—Printed in Walter L. Fleming, *Documentary History of Reconstruction* (Cleveland, Ohio: The A. H. Clark Co., 1906–1907), vol. 2, pp. 388–89.

W. L. Bragg, chairman of the state Executive Committee for the Democratic party, wrote former Lieutenant Governor Edward H. Moren about the campaign.

We have got "a running start" on the Radicals and we are keeping it up in every part of the state. Mass meetings, speeches, and barbecues are the order of the day in north Alabama. East and south Alabama are also very much stirred. The speakers write me that the people insist on a prolongation of the longest harangues—such is the intense feeling among them. The spirit of our people is roused to the highest pitch that will admit of control—the Negroes sink down before it as if stricken with awe—and the white men who have been using the Negroes show by their conduct that they feel Othello's occupation is gone.—W. L. Bragg to Edward H. Moren, August 11, 1874, Moren Letters, 1870–74, Ms., Alabama State Archives.

The white Democrats were not the only ones active in the campaign. In August the Radical state convention met in Montgomery and on the afternoon of the first day passed a number of resolutions on platform. A. H. Curtis, a black, presided.

1. The Republican part of Alabama in state convention assembled again declares its unshaken confidence in and its unalterable devotion to the great principles of human liberty which called it into existence, viz. the civil and political equality of all men without distinction of race or color.
2. In the practical application of these principles we have neither claimed nor desired the social equality of different races or of individuals of the same race. . . .
3. We have not made a race issue in the past, neither do we now make or tender such an issue. What we demand for one man we demand for all men. . . .
4. The race issue now tendered by the Democracy of Alabama is but the outcropping, and is the natural sequence, of the ambitious spirit which led a peaceful people into war with their government in 1861. . . .
—*Advertiser and Mail* (Montgomery), August 23, 1874.

There was a full turnout in the "white counties" which made it possible to elect Houston over the incumbent David P. Lewis by a majority of 13,190. For days after the election, state papers carried full accounts of successes or failures at the polls. The Democrat papers, of course, were exultant.

LIMESTONE COUNTY
Our election passed off quietly yesterday. The Democracy are elected triumphantly, state, county and all by a majority ranging from 250 to 300.

MACON COUNTY
Our people did all they could but were absolutely overwhelmed. In no county were such strenuous efforts made by the Rads as this. . . For a while yesterday we were led to believe that the negroes would not assemble here in force but a little later they came marching into town from every direction in military style, under command of captains and were marched to polls and literally *made* to vote the straight radical ticket. . . .

JUBILEE IN HUNTSVILLE
Our people had a grand jollification tonight over the recent Democratic victories. . . . Madison County elects entire Democratic ticket for county officers and legislature.—Ibid., November 6, 1874.

George S. Houston's inauguration was a time of extravagant rejoicing.

THE HEARTS OF THE PEOPLE MADE GLAD
The wildest demonstrations of delight ever known in Alabama were witnessed this morning. At 8:00 o'clock the streets were crowded and by 10:00 o'clock the sidewalks were packed with rejoicing people, old and young alike participating. . . .—Ibid., November 24, 1874.

After the ceremony in the morning, there was a barbecue dinner at noon, a dress parade later and grand ball and reception at night. It was a great occasion.

Governor Houston

The new governor in a sense had been a compromise candidate but he suited most elements in the Democratic and Conservative party, and the Republicans had little with which to fight him. Houston was born in Tennessee but moved to Lauderdale County with his parents in 1821 when he was ten. Later he lived in Athens. Young Houston read law in Florence and then attended law school in Harrodsburg, Kentucky, and was later admitted to the bar in Alabama in 1831. He had a long and distinguished public career behind him. After being in the state house of representatives from 1832 to 1849, he served in the national house of representatives from 1850 to 1861. It fell to his lot to hand to the Speaker of the House the formal notice that the Alabama delegation was withdrawing from Congress. In 1860 politics he was a Douglas-Democrat and opposed secession as long as he saw a glimmer of hope that the Union might be saved, but once the final break was made, he supported the Confederacy. In 1865, he and Lewis E. Parsons, the provisional governor, were the U. S. senators whom Congress refused to seat. Some of his contemporaries joined the ranks of the Republicans as the best way they saw to salvage the state. Houston continued to be a Democrat but fighting the Radicals became secondary to his law practice and his railroad interests. In short, he could be classed as a loyal but moderate representative of the party.

While a Democrat governor and legislature had been elected, there was some apprehension as to whether Congress, still dominated by Radical Republicans, would allow the new government to stand. The Republicans in the state, not surprisingly, challenged the election but their attempts to get a full investigation came to nothing. As some editors noted, there was a strong possibility that such a probe would reveal as many Republican irregularities as Democratic. When Congress adjourned March 1875 without taking any action against the state, Democrats breathed more easily; evidently the crisis had passed. They could now proceed with plans for a new constitution to replace the one of 1868.

Constitution of 1875

Among the Democrats now in control of the state government there was growing sentiment for a new constitution or extensive amendments to the old one of 1868. It is not surprising that the Republicans saw little necessity for any changes. At the first meeting of the legislature, Governor Houston appointed a committee to report on the advisability of a convention. Peter Hamilton from Mobile was chairman. This committee recommended, and the governor approved, that a convention be held

> to aid in adjusting the state debt, abolish the cumbersome Board of Education, make reforms in the judiciary, forbid state aid to railroads and other corporations, abolish unnecessary constitutional offices created by the radicals and to write a constitution that would make possible economy in government.—*Report of the Joint Committee in Regard to Amendment of the Constitution,* p. 15, quoted in Malcolm C. Mc-Millan, *Constitutional Development in Alabama* (Chapel Hill: University of North Carolina Press, 1955), p. 177.

The people went to the polls on August 3, 1875, to express their wishes about having the convention and at the same time to elect delegates to it. They approved the convention by a vote of 77,763 to 59,928, a majority of 17,835. It was noted that some 63,000 fewer votes were cast at this time than in the crucial 1874 election. Eighty Democrats, twelve Republicans and seven "Independents" were chosen as delegates. The last two groups came from the Black Belt; four of them were Negroes. Sam Rice from Talladega led the Republican forces.

The convention met on the first Monday in September 1875. Leroy Pope Walker from Huntsville, former Speaker of the Alabama House of Representatives, delegate to the Charleston and Richmond conventions in 1860, and the first Secretary of War under Jefferson Davis, was chosen president of the convention. Of the members more than half were lawyers; planters, farmers, editors, preachers, physicians and merchants making up the remainder. It was a middle-aged convention in contrast to the 1865 convention which was made up of many old men. However, among the delegates there were seven who had attended the secession convention and two the 1865 convention but not one from the convention of 1867. The list of leaders of the Democrats sounds like the roll of prominent Alabamians for the next quarter of a century: William Garrett, Francis S. Lyon, William Swearingen Mudd, William Calvin Oates, James L. Pugh, Samuel F. Rice, William J. Samford and many others.

In spite of what appeared to be widespread interest in changing the constitution, Lieutenant Governor Robert F. Ligon of Tuskegee wrote his good friend and predecessor, Edward H. Moren, that he felt the public was apathetic about the forthcoming election.

> I do not know what can be done to arouse our white people. The negroes will vote against it and a larger vote will be cast in the black belt than

there was for the call. If our friends in the white counties do not put themselves to some trouble in getting out voters, I fear the consequences. No objection can be offered against the new constitution. Suffice to say, what the white people want the Radicals and Negroes do not want.— Ligon to E. H. Moren, October 21, 1875, Moren Letters, 1875–79.

On November 16, 1875, the voters of Alabama went to the polls and ratified the proposed constitution by 85,662 to 29,217. This would be the frame of government until 1901.

In summarizing the work of the convention and at the same time describing the constitution, Malcolm McMillan says:

The Conservatives had abolished the Board of Education; forbidden state, county, or city aid to corporations, placed limits on state, county, and city taxation; provided for economy and retrenchment in government; abolished the registration oath; re-apportioned representation in the legislature; made radical changes in impeachment trials; written pre–1868 residence requirements for legislative, executive, and judicial officials into the constitution; abolished "unnecessary offices," limited biennial sessions of the legislature to fifty days; placed prohibitions in the constitution against local and special legislation; moved the state election from November to August; and provided for segregation of the races in the school system.—Malcolm C. McMillan, *Constitutional Development in Alabama*, p. 209.

Bourbon Democracy

The government of Alabama from 1874 to 1901 is generally called "Bourbon democracy." The term comes from a story of doubtful authenticity about Charles X (a Bourbon) who is reputed to have said that the French revolution had meant nothing to him, and that he expected life in 1824 in France to be the same as it had been under the old regime. Following this analogy, Alabama "Bourbon democracy" would be the same political system as before the Civil War and the leaders would be the same or have the same principles.

In spite of the abolition of several radical features in the old constitution, the new one of 1875 was no throwback to antebellum days. It did not abolish universal manhood suffrage nor popular election of the executive and judicial officers. While it reflected the experiences of the Reconstruction years, it did not attempt to disfranchise the Negro. The leaders of the new era were more often former Whigs than life-long Democrats.

In his inaugural address, Governor Houston gave what was in effect the program of the "Bourbons": restore credit, cut expenses, correct abuses in government, preserve state's rights, develop mining, advance manufacturing, invite immigration and capital into the state and encourage education for children. If some of these goals conflicted, frugality would in the main win. In an effort to ease the tensions and smooth over differences, he ended his address with a quotation from Abraham Lincoln: "With malice towards none and charity to all. . . ."

Government became conservative and frugal. It cut expenses (often by eliminating unnecessary offices such as the lieutenant governor), lowered taxes, reduced salaries, but encouraged railroads and industry.

The "Solid" Democratic Party

The successors of Houston in the governor's chair were: Rufus W. Cobb of Shelby County, Edward A. O'Neal of Lauderdale, Thomas Seay of Hale, Thomas G. Jones of Montgomery, William C. Oates of Henry and Joseph F. Johnston of Jefferson. Each of them served two terms. They were ex-Confederates and gave the state twenty-five years of frugal, limited government. They were, as Professor A. B. Moore says, "conservative men who gloried rather in the faithful discharge of their duties than in the introduction of innovations." Former Governor Thomas G. Jones, in a lively tilt with former Governor Braxton B. Comer, engaged in some colorful oratory about these men.

O'Neal, incorruptible, chivalrous, high-minded, winning immortal glory in the Wilderness—Seay, too young to have conspicuous rank, but braving with a frail body the trials of war, pure and stainless and loved in all his afterlife—Samford, sturdily bearing a musket in his teens, faithful to the end, living in peace a life that made his name a household word for truth and honor and all things for which good men strive—Oates, who stood conspicuous for honesty and courage, and linked Alabama's fame with his own at Little Round Top and Snodgrass Hill, and gave an arm in defense of Richmond—one by one, after illustrious service to the state, have gone to their last sleep. . . .—Thomas G. Jones, "The 1890–92 Campaigns for Governor of Alabama," *Alabama Historical Quarterly,* vol. 20, pp. 658–59.

Historians have given these leaders credit for maintaining the solid Democratic South.

For many years the dominant party was called the Democratic and Conservative party; it was made up of bonafide Democrats and former Whigs who had little in common until they joined to fight Radical Republicans. William Garrett, a public official whose observations had been quoted often, in writing from his Coosa County home about the forthcoming 1872 election, spoke of the origin of this hybrid party.

From being Whigs "died in the wool" many of our people have become democrats for the sake of cooperation with the soft appellation "con-

servative" added to kind of sugar coat the pill.—Garrett to Lieutenant
Governor E. H. Moren, May 14, 1872, Moren Letters, Ms., Alabama
State Archives.

The solid political front was more difficult to maintain than appears from the fact that it controlled the state for the next half
century. The only continuous opposition came from the Republicans. At times they were strong enough to put up a slate of
candidates and other times made no attempt to do so. They were
strong enough, however, to elect occasional county officials and
send William F. Aldrich of Montevallo to Congress on three different occasions. As will be shown later in this chapter, his election
was conceded only after a congressional recount. During national
Republican administrations, local leaders dispensed patronage, a
fact which led to a split in the ranks, the Negroes complaining
they were never considered. In April 1889, two Republican conventions were held in Birmingham, one for whites and the other for
blacks. The white convention, made up of carefully selected in-
dustrially-minded men, stated that its purpose was to "advance
the interests of the Republican party and enlist in its upbuilding
the new men and forces now developing the material interests of
the state." The Negroes, complaining bitterly that they were being
ignored in the distribution of patronage, threatened to leave the
party unless given more consideration. Thereafter, for all practical
purposes, Alabama had two Republican parties, one for each race.

The "Greenback splurge," Dr. A. B. Moore says, "was the only
ripple" on the "placid sea of state politics." While the facts do not
support his statement, it is true that the Greenback party gave
political leaders their biggest scare before the Populist revolt of the
1890's. On the national level this party was chiefly interested in a
liberalized money policy; in Alabama its members were chiefly dis-
contented Democrats who could not bring themselves to join
the Republicans but felt the necessity of allying themselves with
a national party. The Huntsville *Democrat* for May 26, 1880,
sneeringly denounced the opponents of the Democrats as "Radical-
Greenback-Independent-Everythingarian-Nothingarian-Hybrid." In
the 1878 election they backed two congressional candidates and
elected William M. Lowe of the eighth district. In 1880, they presented a ticket and although their candidate for governor, the Rev.
J. M. Pickens of Lawrence County, polled only 42,363 votes to
Governor Rufus W. Cobb's 134,908, they did send five representatives to the legislature in Montgomery. In 1882, they made an
even better showing by electing twenty-two members to the
legislature. With the death of Lowe in 1882, however, the strongest

leadership was gone and within two years the party was practically dead.

The Democrat party was composed of men of widely separated views whch led to considerable in-fighting. Democrats often failed to agree on pressing issues such as the public debt, industry, immigration, railroads, and education. There continued to be jealousy between the Black Belt where the white leaders controlled a large black vote, and the white counties. Furthermore, there was frequent discontent with the leadership. One member of the party admitted the Democrats had been honest and economical but complained that the affairs of the government had been conducted

> . . . without order, system, plan, design, or purpose; without method, or checks, or safeguards other than the personal integrity of the several heads of departments and the clerks therein.—R. K. Boyd to Robert McKee, February 26, 1883, McKee Papers, Ms., Alabama State Archives, quoted in Allen J. Going, *Bourbon Democracy in Alabama, 1874–1890* (University, Alabama: University of Alabama Press, 1951), p. 44.

Newspapers of the rising industrial centers found fault with the "old fogies" and the "bald-heads" whom they accused of harboring prejudices against them.

These differences festered but did not erupt on any large scale until farmer discontent led to the Populist revolt in the early 1890's. Until then (and soon thereafter) the one element that held the factions together was the fear of a Republican and therefore Negro victory. This spectre of government by the same people who had run the state during the days of Reconstruction kept most whites within the ranks of the party.

The Populist party was the most serious threat to one-party control and Reuben F. Kolb, Commissioner of Agriculture, Alliance man, and gubernatorial candidate, was the one man who gave any real challenge to the Democrats.

Farmers' Alliance

The Farmers' Alliance originated in Texas in the 1870's; the first Alabama branch was organized at Beach Grove, Madison County, by A. T. Jacobson, an organizer from Texas. The local officers were installed in March 1887. Other alliances soon followed in Limestone, Marshall, and Jackson, and other counties so that a state organization was perfected before the end of the year. The Reverend S. M. Adams, mentioned in the accompanying article, was the second president of the State Alliance.

On the surface the Alliance was just another farmers' organization, born of hard times, low prices, railroad discrimination, and high interest. It started as a farmers' club but before long it had allied itself with other working groups. The specific mission of the Alliance was "to stand between the producer and to eliminate the middleman, improve home life, promote education, build factories, and procure needed legislation." In carrying out the last purpose it became involved in politics, almost from the beginning.

Reuben F. Kolb, one of the leaders in the Alliance movement, was appointed Commissioner of Agriculture in 1887. By utilizing the advantages of his political position, he became the outstanding agricultural leader of the state. As a part of his job, he held farmers' institutes all over the state, often doing the lecturing himself. Kolb was politically ambitious and was a leading candidate for governor in 1890, in 1892, and again in 1894.

The Alliance grew rapidly as the following news item shows.

Alabama awaits developments. The present strength of the alliance in Alabama is about 75,000 members. About 200 sub-alliances, with an average of 20 members each, have been organized since the Ocala convention, but the state was fully organized before that time. Much depends on the action of the old parties, in the meantime, whether or not independent political action will be taken in 1892. Should no concessions be made, the sentiment for a new party will be very great, and so strong as to carry the state I believe. Of course, as an organization, no action will be had, but as individuals, educated along the same line, they will generally act together, and they will be felt.

J. P. OLIVER,
Secretary Alabama F. A. and I. U., Dadeville, Ala.
—Attalla *Vigil,* June 25, 1891.

AN ALLIANCE MEETING

This meeting was held at Mount Pinson.

The Baptist church, a capacious building so imbedded in the shade of a grove—at whose base a perennial brook rushes over rocky bed—was filled, seats and aisles, steps and windows, and the logs on the ground without occupied promptly, as the meeting opened at 10 a.m.

Mr. John Murphy, a prominent local alliance man, was the general floor manager, so to speak, and therefore all details worked smoothly. Commissioner Kolb was on hand to explain the object of the meeting. He read the act of the legislature providing for the farmers' institutes.

Prof. J. S. Newman, special lecturer, then arose and delivered a most instructive address on "Practical Agriculture." Why should Jones' valley not supply Birmingham and all the suburbs with market products now brought from points hundreds of miles distant? At this very time farmers of the valley should be engaged with the preparations for fall and winter crops. Winter crops in this mild climate, when rain is abundant, are most profitable. He mentioned specially the Irish potato crop, which should now be put into the ground. Let the tubers sprout in the cellar, as he explained, and by pursuing his system and methods three crops on the same land would be the return. He enumerated about all the articles of commerce to be found in the stalls of the city market, reminding the farmers that the labor which produced them and the land which produced them must derive a profit, and that the farmers of Jones' valley need not fear if they would enter the field of competition. The vice-president of the alliance is a brainy man, a massive man, and talks fluently and wisely.

President Adams was then introduced by Commissioner Kolb. He is one of the victims of newspaper cuts. I had never seen his face before in life, and therefore had formed a very inadequate idea of his appearance. He is cool and dignified in manner and is a good talker. He spoke on "The Relation of Alliance to a Complete Education for a Farmer." The value of general education to a farmer was elucidated in forcible style. To stimulate the minds of farmers to appreciate the intellectual standing of their avocation was the thought of the legislature when the farmers' institute was provided for as a feature of the commissioner's office. As to political questions, they were inseparable from a progressive society. Farmers were sovereigns in this free land. Political economy was a recognized principle upon which the people must be instructed in order to qualify them to maintain a sound monetary system in government, safe tax laws, etc. Industry alone did not make a successful farmer. He must have that culture which would prepare his mind to seize opportunity, as a soldier does on the field or the sailor on the storm-tossed waves. To illustrate: The educated farmer will study the signs of the times in the market reports. He will not be caught by the false cry, "over-production." Especially should southern farmers be prepared to turn the limitless variety of their climate to the production of crops that will pay.

Mr. Adams touched upon the taxation of the country. He referred to Colonel Milner as authority, saying farmers' property is shingled with mortgages, while their debt is enormous. The cry goes out from theorists to the farmer, "buy for cash." But where is the money? The interest on the debt consumes the cash on hand.

John T. Morgan, said the president of the Alabama alliance, stood up in the senate of the United States arguing for the loan of the credit of the people of this republic to a foreign corporation to the amount of $100,000,000, but when a measure comes up to distribute the lawful money of the republic among the farmers—lo, and behold, that measure becomes unconstitutional! The alliance measure of monetary reform has so stirred up the people that Milner, Carnegie and others everywhere are flooding the papers with lengthy and profound discussions on monetary reform. Coming down to close quarters with opponents of the alliance, President Adams said:

"I stated at Brundidge the other day that Senator Morgan had denounced the sub-treasury as a fraud. I did not hear him do this, still,

I was sincere, for I got my information from the *Age-Herald* and other reliable papers of the state. Mr. Morgan denies it. He says he did not call the alliance a 'humbug.' I have not yet read his letter. I will not vote for John T. Morgan for re-election to the senate of the United States. (Applause.) I will not vote for anybody who favors corporation interest as opposed to the people. I will vote for no man who persistently opposes the best interests of the southern people. The fossils of the senate have kept the south in possession of 'the constitution' while the very same men have been busy providing the north with the money."

The Farmers' alliance had come to the front to demand justice to the farmers of the land. There never was so generous a combination of determined men. They found a vacuum, but instead of laying down immovable propositions and dogmas they invited the universal public to put forward better plans for remedying universally recognized evils than they had done.

Here Mr. Adams closed his able address, which is given here only in part, amidst great applause and demonstration of approval.

The hour of dinner having arrived, a recess of one and one half hours was taken, during which time a bountiful dinner was spread in the shady grove, where all were invited to come forward and help themselves. The abundance and delicious quality of the dinner was fully up to the high standard of the farmers of Hagoods X Roads community. The crowd did full justice to the occasion.

After dinner, Commissioner Kolb introduced Rev. T. M. Barbour of Tuskaloosa county, president of the Sixth district alliance. His subject was "Cultivation of Crops," which he handled in a very able and practical manner, giving numerous hints of incalculable value to every farmer present. Farmers should diversify their products, raise less cotton and more Bermuda grass, should sell more and buy less, raise all they need of everything. Progressive and intensive farming is what we need. Raise a variety of products which can be converted into money. We farmers should assist one another by telling each other how we succeeded, and in this way we all become interested and begin thinking for ourselves. I am merely giving you my experience in the limited time allowed me. Instead of two days in Jefferson county we should have as many months every year for a farmers' institute. It would then do more good. The state should appropriate more money for this purpose. Three thousand dollars is all that is now given and the farmers pay every cent of this. You farmers of this section have great advantages. Birmingham is legally your market. You ought to make that 70,000 people pay you a handsome sum every month in the year. You ought to feed them and make them pay well for your food, fruits and vegetables. But they now buy too much from elsewhere. Potatoes, which these valleys can grow, they buy from Tennessee and Kentucky. When you go to town to take a load of wood always take along also for sale some butter, eggs, chickens, milk, fruit, potatoes, etc. Just pile up the things. It will all bring in the aggregate a nice sum of money. We alliance people are going to bring the state to our way of thinking. We will change things so as to give the farmer an even pull with other occupations. We will remedy these evils peaceably if we can, forcibly if we must. We whipped in the fight with the cotton bagging men because we determined to do it, and our women would go to spinning and weaving cotton bagging if necessary. So we are determined in the political reforms needed, they are bound to come. We whipped the jute trust and we can whip the demagogues of the land also. You farmers are "Lord's of Creation," and why should you ask any one to trust you, or make you advances. Pay cash for what you get. Why should you go and bow down to those in less favored callings and pray for credit. You ought to put the price on your articles. Your products are yours and God intended that you should price them, but the price is fixed in Liverpool or New York. Combinations and trusts have done this. The laws of our land make it possible for corporations to reverse nature's laws. You should unite and combine against these great monopolies.

Mr. Barbour returned to practical farming by saying the pea is the salvation of our country, just as clover is of the middle states. The pea produces the costly and necessary nitrogen. If you do not raise your own nitrogen you must buy it, which no farmer can afford to do.

The farmers showed great interest in Mr. Barbour's address, and not a few were much benefitted thereby.

The next speaker was Prof. John M. Davis of Fayette Court House, Ala., subject, "Agricultural Economy." Professor Davis was a member of the last legislature and is a gentleman of great force and eloquence in speech. It would be an injustice to attempt to reproduce his address. He said: "This farmers' movement is a great thing for everybody; it is but following the dictates of nature. Action is one of nature's laws. If the winds did blow no one could cross a swamp; the poison which rises from the mud is a deadly poison until it is by atmospheric movement swept away. So the farmers' movement intends to purify whatever it touches. It is a grand and necessary movement. Why should not the farmers of Alabama be prosperous and happy? I have traveled over many and beautiful climes, but never have these eyes beheld a fairer land than that in this lovely valley between Birmingham and Mount Pinson. Alabama! Fair Alabama! How beautiful are thy tabernacles! What can we compare to thee! Farmers must be active, up and doing, or they will be left in the race. They must be patriotic and bless the glorious land of Washington and Lee. The star spangled banner! long may it wave over the homes of freemen and the heads of the brave. The money is all accumulating in the hands of a few. New York has almost entirely cut off Mobile and New Orleans from the cotton trade as well as other products. Sub-treasury is a broad term. It means something better. We have not decided as to details yet. Some raise the cry, "Over production" the great evil. They say you are lazy and do not work enough, still you produce too much. Who can reconcile these two ideas? Professor Davis illustrated his ideas clearly by many sidesplitting anecdotes which added much to the amusement of the occasion. When Professor Davis had completed his address Capt. R. F. Kolb came forward amidst the cheers of the audience and announced that he would say a few words on commercial fertilizers. He explained that the ob-

ject of the department of agriculture of Alabama is practical advantages
to the farmers and how they are protected from worthless fertilizers
cast off from other states where stringent laws and rigid examinations
and enforced. A certain editor of an evening paper in Birmingham recently stated that the citizens of Birmingham and Alabama were paying the expenses of this institute. This is absolutely false, and shows
inexcusable ignorance. An editor of any paper in Alabama should be
better informed. The farmers pay every cent of the expense of this institute. It is supported by the tax on fertilizers. This same learned (?)
gentleman says I ought to be in the penitentiary because of small errors
in the financial movement of my office during the years I held it. I will
get to the penitentiary about as soon as that editor will get to heaven;
both are impossible.

The time being almost all consumed Captain Kolb omitted the main
part of his address. He called for Senator John T. Milner, who was
present, and requested that he come forward and address the meeting
in a few words. The senator responded briefly by saying that the alliance had already accomplished great good. It has caused the people to
take up this great financial question and discuss it. In the main I agree
with you, Mr. Adams and Captain Kolb; something must be done.
Our money system is wrong. I have offered a remedy better than the
sub-treasury. Try my plan, study it. It is the proper substitute for the
sub-treasury. Too much of our money goes north. I agree with nearly
all that has been said here today by Mr. Adams. We may differ in some
of the details of the necessary reform.

Captain Kolb then came forward and dismissed the meeting at 4:30
p.m. He renewed his vows to the alliance and the democratic party. He
is an alliance democrat and can never be driven out of the democratic
party.—Birmingham *Age–Herald,* August 26, 1891.

The Populists

The Populist party grew out of hard times and dissatisfaction
with the men in power; it was based on the belief that the state (the
government) had a role to play in the economy.

The convention of the party in 1896 met in Montgomery.

THE STATE CONVENTION
THE PEOPLE'S PARTY MEETS IN HARMONY

A. T. Goodwin Heads the Ticket
They adopt a Platform—nominate a ticket—and have a general good
time all-around. Everybody happy but the Democrats.

The People's Party State Convention met at the McDonald Opera
House in the city of Montgomery, Tuesday morning at 11:30 o'clock.
Chairman G. B. Deans of the State Executive Committee called the
convention to order. Frank Baltzell was called as temporary chairman

and K. S. Woodruff and Warren S. Reese, Jr. were made temporary secretaries. Prayer was offered by Mr. Hearne.

A committee on credentials was named as follows. Judge Zell Gaston, J. B. Townsend, A. J. Hearne, A. P. Longstreet, M. W. Whatley, J. R. Maxwell, W. M. Coleman, C. H. Cooper and R. F. Kolb.

A committee on permanent organization and order of business was appointed as follows: P. G. Bowman, D. B. Anderson of Clarke, T. H. Brown of Pike, Judge W. C. Robinson of Lee, J. W. Pitts, Shelby, J. T. Cason, Coosa, R. H. Seymour, Sumter, J. W. Whorton, Cherokee and J. J. Turrentine of Limestone.

On motion convention adjourned till 2 o'clock.

Afternoon Session

Convention called to order at 2 P.M. Judge Gaston of the committee on credentials reported that no contests were filed and mentioned Wilcox as the only county not represented.

P. G. Bowman of the committee on permanent organization reported recommending that the temporary officers be made permanent. Report adopted by a vote of 272 to 179.

A committee of nine was appointed by the chair to confer with the Republicans as follows: E. Chapman, R. A. Lee, R. E. Lindsey, J. W. Pitts, J. A. Lancaster, S. A. Hobson, S. G. Watson, T. M. George, P. G. Bowman.

After the committee on conference had retired, a committee on platform and resolutions was as follows: G. C. Sibley, A. C. Townsend, J. F. Tate, J. D. Staples, S. M. Dinkins, J. R. Maxwell, W. M. Coleman, J. J. Turrentine, and Joseph Parsons.

While the committees were out, chairman Taubeneck of the National Committee addressed the convention. He spoke briefly indulging in compliments to the convention and stating that the object of his visit here was to meet the leaders and candidates in Alabama and to find out what assistance the National Committee could do in August. "We will not spare time nor financial assistance to help win the victory for our party in Alabama. . . ."

The committee which went out to confer with the Republicans filed in about this time—6 o'clock—and chairman Bowman announced that the Moseley wing would endorse the Populite ticket and make no demand, but had suggested that Mr. James Jackson of Colbert might be put in for Attorney General, he being a Republican free silverite.

Mr. Bowman further said that the other wing, the Vaughn crowd, had not permanently organized and therefore it would be well to wait and have a conference with them later. "It is probable they will all endorse our ticket straight out but at the same time the matter is of serious moment; we want to win this time and hold the victory and the Republicans can help us."

Judge Morris of Dale now moved to suspend the rules and proceed to the nomination for Governor. This was carried unanimously and the Goodwyn enthusiasm broke loose all in a thunder clap.

W. M. Coleman placed the name of Hon. A. T. Goodwyn of Elmore in nomination and in quick succession it was seconded with speeches by Ellis of Elmore, Dr. Day of Morgan, Judge Hobson Leslie of Bullock, Kelly of Choctaw and Capt. Reuben F. Kolb.

The nominee was brought in by a committee and made a five minute's speech of acceptance. The convention adjourned at 7 o'clock until 8.

Night Session

When the convention reassembled again at 8 o'clock the district delegation proceeded to the nomination of state delegates to the National Convention of the Peoples Party at St. Louis. . . .

Mr. Joseph Parsons of the committee on platform reported, and the platform reported, after amendment, was adopted unanimously.

The Platform

The People's Party of the State of Alabama in convention assembled recognizing the supremacy of political liberty over all the questions that can come before the people of the State for solution at the general State election, to take place on the 3rd day of August 1896, reaffirm our allegiance to the cardinal principles of Populism as follows:

First—we demand a free ballot and a fair count.

Second—we demand the free, unlimited and independent coinage of silver and gold at the ratio of 16 to 1 and the abolition of national banks, the expansion of the currency to meet the needs of the people and the demands of commerce, free from the control of corporate influences, and we condemn the issue of interest bearing bonds in time of peace.

Third—we demand that miners and other like corporate labor be paid in lawful money of the United States semi-monthly.

Fourth—we favor a tariff for revenue, so adjusted as to protect as far as practicable the farmers and the labor in our shops, mines, factories, and mills, and their products against foreign pauper labor.

Next came a lot of resolutions which passed unanimously:

Resolved, That it is the sense of this convention that our representatives in Congress be and are hereby requested to use their best endeavors to secure appropriations by the Federal Government to open the Warrior River to navigation from the coal fields to the Gulf of Mexico.

Resolved, That our county appointing boards are hereby requested to give to the political opposition a competent inspector at every polling place in their respective counties.

And we further request the inspector so appointed to give a competent clerk and fixer at each polling place to said political opposition.

The convention proceeded to nominate all the State officers except Secretary of State and Attorney General . . . and then adjourned till 9 a.m. Wednesday.

Wednesday Morning Session

Convention met at 9 a.m. and was called to order by the chairman.

Committee to confer with Republicans reported that the McKinley Republicans had remained in session all night and that they had nominated J. A. Grimmett Secretary of State and W. H. Smith for Attorney General.

Several of the Moseley wing of the Republicans who were present joined in the request that the two gentlemen named by the McKinley convention be endorsed by the convention. . . .—*People's Advocate* (Columbiana), May 7, 1896.

The official platform was more elaborate than had been discussed at the convention.

PEOPLES PARTY PLATFORM STATE OF ALABAMA
1. 1st WE DEMAND A FREE BALLOT AND A FAIR COUNT.
2. 2nd WE DEMAND THE FREE, UNLIMITED AND INDEPENDENT COINAGE OF SILVER AND GOLD AT THE RATIO OF 16-1, AND THE ABOLITION OF NATIONAL BANKS: THE EXPANSION OF THE CURRENCY TO MEET THE NEEDS OF THE PEOPLE AND THE DEMANDS OF COMMERCE, FREE FROM THE CONTROL OF CORPORATE INFLUENCES AND WE CONDEMN THE ISSUE OF INTEREST BEARING BONDS IN TIMES OF PEACE.
3. 3rd WE DEMAND THAT MINERS AND OTHER LIKE CORPORATE LABOR BE PAID IN LAWFUL MONEY SEMIMONTHLY.
4. 4th WE FAVOR A TARIFF FOR REVENUE SO ADJUSTED AS TO PROTECT, SO FAR AS PRACTICABLE, THE FARMERS, AND THE LABOR IN OUR SHOPS, MINES, FACTORIES AND MILLS AND THEIR PRODUCTS AGAINST FOREIGN PAUPER LABOR, PROVIDED THAT THE REVENUE RECEIVED ON IMPORTS DOES NOT EXCEED THE NECESSARY EXPENSES OF THE GOVERNMENT ECONOMICALLY ADMINISTERED.
5. 5th WE FAVOR THE REMOVAL OF THE CONVICTS FROM THE MINES OF THIS STATE.
6. 6th WE FAVOR THE IMPROVEMENT AND EXTENSION OF THE PUBLIC SCHOOL SYSTEM AS FAR AS THE FINANCIAL CONDITION OF THE STATE WILL ADMIT UNDER EXISTING CONDITIONS.—*Weekly Tribune* (Birmingham), July 9, 1896.

Contested Election

Alabama politics was enlivened at intervals by campaigns that ended in contested elections. Many of these, ten of them between 1875 and 1891, were races for the national House of Representatives. Most of them, as in the case of Aldrich vs. Robbins, resulted from efforts of the Republicans to oust the Democrats. And as in this case, they sometimes won. Since testimony in these cases was given under oath, it is more reliable than news in a partisan press, but it is often damning to the party in power which was accustomed to being praised for honesty, uprightness, and morality. There are innumerable cases in which votes were counted by the election officials to suit their needs. There were instances in which more votes were cast for the favored candidate than voters existed in the whole precinct.

In the 1894 contest in the Fourth Congressional district, William F. Aldrich, Republican, engineer and promoter of the coal mining interests around Montevallo, challenged the election of Democrat Gaston A. Robbins, Selma lawyer. This became one of the best known of such cases and revealed much—too much, some Democrats feared—about election practices. Only a few short passages are given here.

NOTICE OF CONTEST

ALDRICH, ALA., December 8, 1894

Hon. GASTON A. ROBBINS.

Sir; I beg to inform you that I shall contest, before the Fifty-fourth Congress of the United States of America, your right to a seat in that body as a Representative of the Fourth Congressional district of the State of Alabama.

I deny that at the election held on the 6th day of November, 1894, being the only election held to fill said office, you were elected by the qualified electors of the Fourth Congressional district of the State of Alabama to represent them in the said Fifty-fourth Congress of the United States of America.

I, in fact, received a majority of the legal votes cast in said election in the said Fourth Congressional district of Alabama, and would have received a certificate of election from the governor of Alabama, instead of your having received the same, but for the wrongs and frauds hereinafter designated.

FIRST.

(1) That in the county of Dallas, in said district, on said day and year, and at the election aforesaid, there was fraud and other improper conduct on the part of managers, clerks, and other officers of election, to such an extent that at the voting precinct No. 2, in said county, commonly called Summerfield, you were allowed and credited with 160 votes and myself with 2 votes, when in truth and in fact only 31 votes were polled altogether in said precinct at said election.

Of the 31 votes actually cast I claim and charge that I received many more than the 2 allowed me.

At precinct No. 3 in said county, at said election, you were allowed and credited with 130 votes and myself with 9 votes, when in truth and in fact only 14 votes altogether were cast at said election.

At precinct No. 5, in said county, commonly called Harrell's, there were actually cast 13 votes, and you were credited with and allowed all of said 13 votes. I claim and charge that I received a large part of said 13 votes.

In precinct No. 7, in said county, commonly called Martin's, there were actually cast at said election only 60 votes, and you are credited with and allowed 503 votes. Of the said 503 votes allowed you at least 443 votes were never in fact cast, and of the 60 votes actually cast I claim and charge that I received a large number thereof, though I was not allowed or credited with any votes at this beat.

At precinct No. 8, in said county, commonly called Orrville, at said election there were actually cast 35 votes. You were credited with and allowed 368 votes and myself 1 vote. Of the said 368 votes allowed you at least 333 were in fact never cast, and of the votes actually cast at said beat in said election I claim and charge that I actually received a large number thereof.

At precinct No. 9, in said county, commonly called Lexington, there were in fact only 35 votes cast at said election, and you were credited with and allowed 250 votes and myself only 1 vote. Of the 250 votes allowed you at least 215 were never in fact cast and of the 35 votes actually cast I claim and charge that I actually received a large number thereof.

SECOND

I charge that the board whose duty it is to appoint inspectors of election in the county of Dallas are all of the same political faction as yourself, and in this election, they were your friends, allies, and partisans, and were acting in your interest and for the purpose of securing your election; and that they did appoint for each of the various beats in said county two shrewd and capable inspectors of the same political faction as yourself, and that said inspectors were strong partisans and allies of yourself; and that, for the purpose of preventing a fair election, and, in order that the returns might show your election, the said inspectors did appoint clerks and fixers of ballots solely from members of your political faction, in fact, generally from the most partisan and biased members thereof; and that the said inspectors refused to allow clerks and fixers from the opposite political faction; and, in consequence thereof, the returns of said election were manipulated in your interest without the possibility of my being able to know or verify the exact number of votes cast for you and for me respectively, so far as the said officials were concerned.

THIRD

I charge that at and before said election in the various beats of said county of Dallas, particularly in said beat No. 36, known as Selma, or city beat, your friends and partisans sought in every way within their power to prevent legal electors from exercising their free choice in voting, and, to such end, used intimidation and threats, and attempted bribery in the most whole and shameless fashion; that the polls on said election day were surrounded by deputy sheriffs who threatened to arrest, and otherwise intimidated and browbeat electors, and thus prevented many from voting who would otherwise have voted for me at said election; that said deputy sheriffs were your friends and partisans, and numbers of them were appointed and acted for the purpose of preventing a full, free, and fair election, all of which was done in your interest.

FOURTH

I charge that the officers in charge of the registration of electors in said county of Dallas were all members of the political faction to which you belong, and were your political friends and partisans, and that they manipulated the registration of electors for said election in the interest of your candidacy, and that said registration lists of registered electors, when made, were kept secret from me and from all members of the political party or faction to which I belong, while you or members of your political party or faction were allowed the use thereof.

I charge that there were not, in fact, registered in the county of Dallas more than 1,800 electors, and, believing that the registration of electors and the lists containing the names of registered electors should be public so as to enable a full and free investigation before the day of election, I earnestly besought the officers in charge of the said registration and of said lists to allow me to inspect the said lists, but they persistently refused or evaded the request. I charge that the said registration lists contained a vast number of names of men who are not legal electors in the said county of Dallas, and that said lists contain the names of a large number of men who did not, in fact, register for said election, but who would otherwise be legal electors, and that said names were fraudulently put upon said lists by said officers with the purpose and intent to cover up the fraud committed in piling up your fictitious and fraudulent majority in the said county of Dallas.

FIFTH

I charge that the inspectors and other election officers who held said election in the said various precincts of the said county of Dallas were not sworn according to law, and the said election in said county of Dallas is therefore null and void. I charge that various electors who voted in said election in said county of Dallas did not present their registration certificates of registration, as provided by law, and permitted electors to vote in violation of law.

From many of said precincts and polling places more votes were returned and credited to you than there were legal electors living in said precincts, and from numerous precincts in said county more votes were returned and credited to you than there were citizens in said precincts who had in fact registered as required by law; the said election in the said various precincts was not held according to law.

At the meeting of the canvassing board in the city of Selma, in the said Dallas County, on Saturday, the 10th day of November, 1894, I protested against the crediting to you of the votes as returned from the various precincts of said county of Dallas, and objected to said votes being counted; and I offered to show the fraud and illegality permeating the said election in the said Dallas County; but the said board, who were all your partisans and friends, refused to heed my protest and objection, and refused to hear said evidence.

SIXTH

The said election, held as aforesaid on the 6th day of November, 1894, for representative in the Fifty-fourth Congress from the Fourth Congressional district of Alabama, was so honeycombed with fraud and corruption from the beginning of the registration of electors until the announcement of the result by the secretary of state that the said election in the said Dallas County is entirely invalid, and in calculating

the result of the said election in the Fourth Congressional district the
votes in said Dallas County should not be counted.

There were similar and equally extensive charges about the election
in Calhoun, Talladega, Chilton, Shelby and other counties in the
Fourth District.

Robbins' reply, of course, was a denial of the charges. He summarized the total votes cast.

> First. I deny that an election held on the 6th day of November, 1894,
> in the Fourth Congressional district of Alabama for a member of
> Congress from the Fourth Congressional district of Alabama in the
> Fifty-fourth Congress of the United States of America, you received a
> majority of the votes of the duly qualified electors of said district for
> said office. I claim that at said election in said district there were cast
> by the duly qualified electors of said district in all 17,250 votes. Of
> this number there were cast for me 10,494 votes and for you 6,756
> votes, giving me a majority of the legally cast votes 3,738. Said votes
> were divided by counties in said district as follows: In Calhoun County
> I received 1,838, you received 1,481; in Chilton County I received 320,
> you received 785 votes; in Cleburne County I received 562, you re-
> ceived 677 votes; and in Dallas County I received 5,464 votes, and
> you received 72 votes; in Shelby County I received 920 votes, and you
> 1,631 votes; and in Talladega County I received 1,390 votes, and you
> 2,110 votes, by the duly qualified electors of said counties respectively.
> I deny that there were any wrongs or frauds whereby you were de-
> frauded out of any majority of said votes.—*Contested Election Case
> of William F. Aldrich v. Gaston A. Robbins from the Fourth Congres-
> sional District in the State of Alabama* (Washington: Government Print-
> ing Office, 1895), *passim*.

Much of the evidence gathered for both sides during the congressional hearings came from interviews with local people. Dr. John
A. McKinnon, Selma physician, was registrar of vital statistics
and county health officer. He testified he knew precinct 36, Selma,
well.

> Q. You have there in your hand a poll list containing the names of
> persons who are said to have voted in the City precinct, No. 36, on the
> 6th day of November, 1894, for the election of a Congressman from
> the Fourth Congressional district of Alabama. Have you made a care-
> ful examination of the poll list?—A. I have.
> Q. How many names do you find recorded upon that poll list?—A.
> Two thousand and twenty-one names.
> Q. Now, Doctor, please, in your own way, make a statement to the
> commissioner with reference to the inspection that you have made of
> this poll list, and what you have ascertained by that inspection relative
> to the names recorded therein. I mean, I want you to state to the

commissioner whether or not the 2,021 names recorded on that poll list are the names of resident citizens and qualified electors in this, the City precinct, No. 36 of Dallas County, Ala.—A. From No. 1 down to No. 221, J. L. Schweitzer, which is the last name that I recognize, there are named 190 people that I know.

Q. Do you recognize those 190 people as qualified electors in this the City precinct, No. 36?—A. Yes, sir; they are men of 21 years of age. Then, from No. 221 I do not recognize any more names on poll list until I get down to 1234, J. H. Nunnelly.

Q. Well, are the persons named from 221 to 1234, in your judgment, resident citizens and qualified electors in this the city precinct, No. 36?—A. No, sir; they are not.

Q. Would it be within the bounds of possibility for that many men whose names are recorded in this poll list, beginning at No. 221 and going down to No. 1234—would it be possible, I say, for that many persons, whose names are recorded there, to be resident citizens and qualified electors in this, the City precinct, No. 36, and you not know them?—A. I do not think so.

Q. Are you not positive now that such a thing could not be?—A. I feel so.

Q. Did you ever hear of those names before this poll list was shown to you?—A. I never did.

Q. I mean as their being citizens of this, the City precinct, No. 36?—A. No, sir; I never did.

Q. Well, what else have you ascertained about that poll list?—A. I know nearly all the the people named from No. 1234 to 1722, B. B. Ballard, but there are a few names between those numbers that I do not recognize. I recognize nearly all of them as resident citizens and qualified electors of this, the City precinct No. 36. Then, from No. 1722 down to No. 2019 I do not recognize any of them as people that I know in this, the City precinct, No. 36.

Q. In your best judgment are the persons named from No. 1722 to No. 2019 citizens of this the City precinct?—A. I do not think that they are citizens of this precinct. If they were, I would be sure to know them.

Q. Would it be possible for those names recorded on that poll list from No. 1722 down to No. 2019 to be the names of resident citizens or qualified electors in this the City precinct, No. 36, of Dallas County, without your knowing it?—A. I think not, sir.

Q. Well, Doctor, what about the other names on that poll list?—A. From No. 2019 to 2021, which are the three last names, I recognized as citizens of this town.

Q. Do you know the last three persons named on that poll list; that is, Mr. W. L. Wood, J. H. Crocheron, and .... Lumpkins?—A. Yes, sir; they live here.

Q. Has the population of this precinct, No. 36, appreciably increased since the census of 1890?—A. I think not, sir.

Q. What, in your best judgment, has been the increase, if any, in the population of precinct No. 36 since the census of 1890?—A. I could not say exactly. I should have to base that, you understand, entirely on the census of the preceding ten years. There was an increase of 100 in the ten years before that in the incorporate limits of this precinct No. 36.

Q. There was only an increase of 100 in the population of city precinct No. 36 from 1880 to 1890?—A. Yes, sir; according to the census.

Q. Doctor, you have been living here continuously from 1890, haven't you?—A. Yes, sir.

Q. I will ask you, from your personal acquaintance with the people here, to state whether you have had during that time, from 1890 to the present time, any appreciable increase in the population of this precinct No. 36.—A. We have not.

Q. Well, now, I will ask you, Doctor, to state what the relative strength of the colored population of this precinct No. 36 bears to the white population.—A. There were about 1,000 more negroes than white people in this precinct according to the census of 1890.

Q. In your judgment, has that ratio been kept up from 1890 up to the present time?—A. I suppose so, but of course I could not say positively.

Q. Are you positive, from what you know of the community here, that the colored people from 1890 to the present time have increased equally as strong numerically as the white people in this precinct?—A. I think so, but I have to be governed entirely by the census in this. The last census shows, I think, 1,000 more colored people than white people in this town.

Q. You are satisfied that there has not been any perceptible change in the population since 1890 in this precinct?—A. I do not think that there has been any particular variation in its population within the last five years. . . .—Ibid.

During the cross-examination Dr. McKinnon told extensively about the political complexion of Dallas County.

Q. Doctor, you are a Republican in politics, are you not?—A. Yes, sir.

Q. You have been so since 1865, have you not?—A. Yes, sir.

Q. How many white Republicans are there in this city?—A. I do not know of any except Judge Craig, Mr. Huckerford, Mr. Stout, who works in the railroad office; Mr. Smith, who works in the shop, and myself. That is what those gentlemen informed me. That is my information on this subject.

Q. Those five are the only white Republicans in this city that you can recall?—A. Yes, sir; just now.

Q. You said just now, Doctor, that the colored man is a natural Republican?—A. That is my observation.

Q. Please tell us why you make that statement?—A. Well, he was allied originally with the Republican party; that is, since his freedom.

Q. What brought about this alliance?—A. The Republican party, in my judgment, set him free, and he naturally had an attachment for the party that set him free.

Q. In your judgment, then, Doctor, the same thing that operates to make the black man a Republican operates to make a white man a Democrat in this country, does it not?—A. The last national election shows that all white men are not Democrats in this country.

Q. If all white men are not Democrats in this country, why have you been able to name only five white Republicans in this city, since you are a man of such large acquaintance?—A. My acquaintance is not so extensive except with my home people.

Q. In answer to Mr. Bowman's question as to whether or not your acquaintance, by reason of your profession and by reason of the official place that you have held, is extensive, didn't you reply in the affirmative?—A. Yes, sir; in the city of Selma.

Q. When you said that the returns of the last election don't show that all white men are Democrats, you didn't refer to the city of Selma, did you?—A. I have no recollection. Do you mean in answer to that question?

Q. You didn't mean then, when you answered that question in that way, to refer to the city of Selma?—A. No, sir; I had no reference to the city of Selma at all. Your question being a broad question, I just answered it accordingly.

Q. Then substantially all the white men in this precinct and in this county are Democrats, are they?—A. Yes, sir; with few exceptions.

Q. You do not know as many as 20 white men in this county who are not Democrats, do you?—A. I do not know. I have not counted them up.

Q. I asked you if you know as many as 20?—A. I do not know. It would take some time to count them up.

Q. Doctor, all of your direct testimony in this case has been on the hypothesis that the city of Selma, within its corporate limits, and the City precinct, No. 36, are one and the same thing, has it not?—A. I have never known any difference.

Q. Your testimony has been predicated on that idea, has it?—A. I have never known any difference between the two.

Q. Has your testimony been predicated on that idea?—A. My idea is that the city of Selma and beat No. 36 are one and the same.

Q. If you had known that they were not the same, then your testimony would not have been as it has been with reference to the population and voters in City precinct, No. 36, would it?—A. Of course not; but I have to be governed entirely by the census of the United States, and I gave my answer according to it.

Q. You remember, Doctor, that a number of years ago the corporate limits of the municipality of the city of Selma were contracted, don't you?—A. Yes, sir.

Q. Supposing that City precinct, No. 36, is constituted by what was formerly the corporate limits of the city of Selma before that contraction, how many additional population would it let into Selma?—A. Do you mean taking in Valley Creek beat territory?

Q. I mean the corporate limits as they used to be. I am not talking about Valley Creek beat. Do you know what the city limits used to be before this contraction?—A. I have heard that the line went to the fair grounds and went across .... street, and went down to Beach Creek, and that is past Valley Creek beat, or rather it is part of Valley Creek beat. That is not part of precinct No. 36, as I understood it, but the map of Selma shows where the city of Selma is. It is marked on the map, and if you will bring me one here I will show you the present boundaries of the city of Selma.

Q. I know where the present boundaries of the city of Selma are.—A. I don't know anything about the city of Selma except—.

Q. You don't know, Doctor, where the boundary lines of the city of Selma are?—A. Not according to definition.

Q. Now, I will ask you this question: If the boundary lines of City precinct, No. 36, are coextensive with what used to be the corporation limits of the city of Selma, would not the City precinct, No. 36, be much larger in point of population than the municipality of Selma?—A. Yes, sir.

Q. Now, if that territory and those persons who were excluded from the municipality of Selma by the contraction are included in City precinct, No. 36, then the population and voting capacity of City precinct No. 36, would be much larger than you have testified it would be; would it not, Doctor?—A. Yes, sir.

Q. How much larger, Doctor, in your opinion?—A. I can not say; it is a thing about which I have never thought.

Q. About how much?—A. I don't know exactly.

Q. Considerably larger, though?—A. Yes, sir; a good deal larger.

Q. From the lines that you spoke about as constituting the old city limits to the present city limits, in your judgment, how many people live in that area?—A. There must be two or three thousand.

Redirect examination:

Q. Are not the persons in that area just referred to in Mr. Wood's last question principally negroes?—A. Yes, sir.

Q. Is not a large proportion of them negroes?—A. Yes, sir.

Q. Are 90 per cent of them negroes?—A. Probably so.

—Ibid.

As a result of the investigation, the committee reduced Robbins' Dallas County vote from 5,452 to 568 and proportionately in other counties and declared Aldrich the winner. This is the first of three times Aldrich successfully contested a congressional election. His case belies the oft-quoted statement that there were no Republicans from Alabama in Congress after Reconstruction days until the 1960's.

Reuben F. Kolb

The leading alliance man—and eventual Populist—was Reuben F. Kolb, a native and life-long resident of Eufaula. Kolb, like most of his contemporaries, was a Democrat but after he failed to get the gubernatorial nomination of his party in 1890, he became an independent and organized his own party, the Jeffersonian Democrats. The official Populist party organization was formed in Clay County by J. H. Manning who seems to have had little to do with Kolb but the Jeffersonian Democrats to all intents and purposes were also Populists. In later years, Kolb returned to the Democratic fold, apparently forgiven. While he was fighting the established Democrats, he was the biggest single threat they had.

Kolb had an impeccable background. Born into a planter family, educated at the University of North Carolina and already a planter when the war broke out, he joined the Confederate army, organizing his own Kolb's Battery. In the army he was characteristically active and won commendation from his officers. At the end of the war, he returned to his cotton plantation. With cotton selling at 17.9 cents per pound, he made money; by 1878 the price was down to 8.59 cents, too low for any profit. Unlike some of his contemporaries who turned to pursuits other than farming, Kolb chose to diversify the products of his plantation and became the leading state advocate of scientific agriculture. His most successful venture in this field was the development of a watermelon for the market, Kolb's Gem. He shipped large amounts of the seed all over the country. In 1887, Governor Thomas Seay appointed him Commissioner of Agriculture. He ran this office with energy and imagination, organizing farmer's institutes all over the state and devising a plan of advertising state products with the use of a display-car called "Alabama on wheels" which he exhibited in many places.

His work with farmers' groups led him naturally into the Alliance in which he played a leading role. He was exceedingly popular with the farmers who referred to him as their "Patrick Henry." Early in life he showed inclinations toward politics (he had been the youngest member of the secession convention) and in 1890 decided to throw his hat into the governor's ring. A. B. Moore says he was backed by northern Republicans, thinking he would be the means of overthrowing the Democrat party. United States Senator, John Tyler Morgan, wrote his friend Robert McKee in Selma his thoughts on the Kolb candidacy.

Since the infamous Know-Nothing adventure, no man *credited as a Democrat,* has attempted, in secret, to create and run a *machine* in the democratic party of Alabama for the purpose of turning its power into unworthy hands, until Kolb came forward.

He employed Knights of Labor, and all that, Republicans and their allies,—the greenbackers—and all that, to serve a great, generous, honest, and noble party, a dirty, mean, low, sneaking machine trick!

Knowing this, you complain that Denson did that, openly, which Kolb did with the aid of these mercenaries, in secret. And now, he is to be awarded with a seat in the Senate! Please put me down for Pugh in that race. . . .—Morgan to McKee, June 5, 1890, McKee Papers, Ms., Alabama State Archives.

Kolb to him was a "selfish and reckless schemer." The Democratic forces concentrated on Thomas Goode Jones of Jefferson County as their candidate; he was elected at the August 4 election.

As was customary, Jones ran for a second two-year term. Kolb also was a candidate in 1892. By this time he had organized the Jeffersonian Democrats. An account of the two party convention is from a central Alabama Populist paper.

TWO CONVENTIONS

Last Wednesday was a memorable day in the history of Alabama politics. Two conventions met at Montgomery, one in the capitol and one in the opera house. One was claimed to be the regular organized Democracy and the other the Jeffersonian Democracy. In one was seen the same class of men who have been attending state conventions for the last twenty-five years. In the other were men, a large number of whom had never attended a state convention before. In the one were lawyers, politicians, the merchants, and office seekers, with soft hands, fair faces, and upon their person fine apparel. In the other were the horny-handed tillers of the soil, with rough hands, sunbrowned faces, and upon their persons the plain garb of the farmer. In the one were the consumers. In the other the producers of wealth. In the one were the men who sow not neither do they reap. . . . In the other were the men who sow and reap and who for the last twenty-five years have been filling up the coffers of the rich—taking little interest in politics except to vote at the August election, but a change has come over the spirit of their dreams and they see that unless the management of the government is taken from the machine bosses and self-constituted leaders, that the result will be that we have a few millionaires and a million paupers in the state of Alabama. And consequently they have laid down the shovel and the hoe, the plow stands still in the furrow, and the sun burned sons of toil are found in convention assembled. What does this mean? It means the death knell of political bossism in Alabama. It means that the machine can no longer make nominations that the people will support. It means a return to first principles and the establishment of state government of the people, by the people and for the people. It means that the nefarious banking system, which for the last thirty years has been sucking the life blood of the nation must go. It means . . . (they) intend to press the demands for reform forward and vote for them whenever they can find an opportunity. The men nominated at the opera house convention in Montgomery are, each and every one in favor of these demands and the battle from now to August will be fought straight from the shoulder. . . .—*People's Advocate* (Columbiana), June 16, 1892.

Kolb had decided before the Democratic party convention that he would run on an independent ticket if necessary. It was necessary because Jones was renominated and won in one of the bitterest races in state history. His majority was a mere 11,435 votes. A modern student of this period, Sheldon Hackney, is of the opinion that if the election had been honestly conducted, Kolb would have won.

In 1894, Kolb ran for governor again, this time against William C. Oates and lost again. After the two previous defeats, Kolb and his supporters accepted the decision at the polls; this time they persisted in the belief that he had been elected and only counted out. By right, they said, he was the real governor.

William C. Oates became governor on December 1, 1894, although there had been dark hints that he might not be allowed to do so. Instead of giving much coverage to that event, the Populist papers gave in considerable detail the "inauguration of Governor Kolb." One of these was published in Columbiana.

> On December 1, Captain R. F. Kolb was sworn in as the governor of Alabama. He did not come up Dexter Avenue escorted by the military, but he came [on foot] like Thomas Jefferson when he took the oath as President of the United States. A large concourse of people witnessed the ceremonies. He and the others on the state ticket . . . took the oath of office in Justice Powell's office. They then proceeded to the Capitol and Governor Jones refused to allow Capt. Kolb to make his inaugural address inside the Capitol grounds so they repaired just outside where he delivered [it].—*People's Advocate* (Columbiana), December 6, 1894.

In his address he reviewed the reasons why he felt he had been elected but did not call for any extralegal action: he ended it with

> I advise moderation. I am not here to advise unlawful procedures. Let us be peaceable and justice and right will reign in Alabama.—Ibid.

Editorially, the same issue of the paper warned that

> The inauguration of William C. Oates on December 1 is the last peaceable inauguration of a man counted in by ballot box stuffers. . . . The honest, intelligent, and patriotic citizens of Alabama have set the seal of condemnation on ballot box thieves and their beneficiaries; the old guard who have heretofore voted dead negroes and pointer dogs to overturn the votes honestly cast by white men in white counties in north Alabama had better pack their "duds" and move to greener pastures. . . .—Ibid.

For a time, Kolb kept up the fiction of being governor of the state but after the executive committee of the Populist party met in February 1895 he abandoned all pretense in the matter for the sake of law and order.

There may have been crookedness in the election as the Kolb followers charged, but the voting strength of the Populists was waning sharply. In 1894, they cast 83,394 against Oates' 109,160, almost 50,000 fewer votes than two years before, most of the drop being in the white counties where the Populists had their greatest strength. In the 1896 gubernatorial contest (in which Kolb was not a candidate) the Populists (now fused with the Republicans) carried only eleven counties and Democrat Joseph F. Johnston easily won. With the return of better economic conditions, and disillusionment with fusion, the party died away and Kolb spent most of his time on agricultural reform. And thus passed the severest test the Democratic establishment had for half a century. While it had few positive results to show for its opposition, it did pave the way for an era of progressivism.

Debt Adjustment

The problem of the public debt faced every administration. During the Reconstruction era that state debts had risen phenomenally. At the outbreak of the war, it was listed at $3,445,000. Since in 1865 the state was forced to repudiate the war debt, it may be assumed that the public debt remaining was essentially the same it was four years earlier. The state sold bonds to pay running expenses even before the Radicals came into power. Afterwards the bonded indebtedness increased so that it was over $10,000,000 when the Democrats took over in 1874. The largest part of the public debt, however, resulted from the state policy of underwriting railroad construction and granting funds to certain lines, usually on a second mortgage. Estimates vary as to the total amount, but the state had endorsed upwards of $19,000,000 railroad bonds. The Debt Commission of 1876 recognized $8,847,000 of this as the responsibility of the state.

Using the figures accepted by the Debt Commission, the state debt was as follows:

Bonded debt for state purposes	$6,766,800	
Obligations and certificates	1,040,000	
Trust funds for education	2,810,670	
Total direct debt for state purposes		$10,617,470
Miscellaneous contingent debt (questionable bonds, claims of the South and North Railroad, etc.)		
Straight bonds issued to railroads	2,300,000	
Straight bonds exchanged for endorsed railroad bonds under 1873 act	1,156,000	

Endorsed railroad bonds   8,847,000
Total liability on account of railroads   12,303,000
Total debt exclusive of interest $25,363,563
—Allen J. Going, *Bourbon Democracy in Alabama, 1874–1890* (University, Alabama: University of Alabama Press, 1951), p. 65.

This sum did not include $4,654,000 of unpaid interests.

The Debt Commission made many adjustments and lowered the debt to a manageable $10,000,000. This adjustment, needless to say, failed to please a great many people.

Default of Treasurer Vincent

The generally frugal administrations of the "Bourbon" governors were marred by the activities of State Treasurer Isaac H. Vincent. Usually state treasurers served only two successive terms and when Vincent was elected for a third term as "Honest Ike," Governor Edward A. O'Neal refused to approve his bond. When a legislative committee made the usual examination of his books, Vincent suddenly left. The investigation revealed that at least $250,000 of state funds were missing.

Vincent was returned from Texas, tried, and sentenced to ten years in the penitentiary, a term that the court believed would cover his natural life. Because of his bad health, he was pardoned toward the end of his term of imprisonment by Governor Thomas G. Jones in 1893. The following is an editorial opposing his pardon.

NO PARDON FOR IKE

The case of our whilom State Treasurer has again come up for trial. He was well and duly tried and found guilty before a jury of his fellow-citizens under solemn oath. He went to the penitentiary because he could not go elsewhere and render justice to the laws—the people—of the great state of Alabama. It was remarked, at that time, that the term was sufficiently short, if not altogether out of proportion to the enormity of his crime. The tide has turned. He has, by his able and pathetic appeals to the public, from the Governor to the humblest of his friends, invoked sympathy and called for assistance. He has succeeded in awakening quite a good degree of interest upon the part of many good citizens. An effort has been and is still being made for his pardon at the Governor's hands. This, we think, ought to be considered well before done. True, we all sympathize, but sympathy is not law—is not justice. The veriest rascal in the land has his sympathizers—his friends—those who deplore his fate. Sympathy alone will serve as but a poor guide. It would empty to-day the penitentiary, jails, and set aside our criminal courts—city, state and national. Let the law have its due course and be glorified. This is due to both the innocent and the guilty—the law-abiding and the lawless—citizen. This is the only sure way of having our statutes obeyed. We cannot make fish of one and fowl of another citizen. There are other men in the state prison to-day who are just as deserving as is Ike Vincent. He did, with culture, refinement and deliberation, what they did in lack of all these. He is all the more blameworthy. What if he shall die in the state prison? Shall we not send any man there? That is where such reasoning ends. Any man sent there may die; therefore, send no man. "It will be bad to die in the penitentiary." True; but it was bad to take Alabama's money. Bad to die in the penitentiary; true, but that is not the question. The question is the satisfaction of the law's demands. It demands these years at Vincent's hands, and he ought to give them, if he die in the attempt. If he die, he will not by any means be the first one. If he were some poor devil, so-called, there would not be such hue and cry for his release. The law, in its excellence, knows no difference. Let him alone. It will do the whole land good. There is not that exactness in these things that should be observed. We are not for granting the pardon and hope the Governor will not extend his clemency.—*Attalla Vigil,* May 28, 1891.

Railroad Legislation

The attitude of the Democrats toward railroads in the 1870's and 1880's was a "mixture of sentiment for encouragement and support with demands to control unjust practices and monopolistic policies." At the end of the war, there was a great need for more and better transportation. Lack of adequate transportation during the war had made it difficult, and at times impossible, to get men and supplies where they were needed. The war had taken a heavy toll from the existing lines. Straight's raid, for example, had destroyed several miles of the road around Opelika. With the war over, politicians and business leaders turned to the state for rebuilding these lines and constructing new ones.

After 1874, the Bourbons found it popular to blame the Republicans for the large debt that the state had incurred. In all fairness it should be pointed out that the practice of endorsing the railroad bonds began before Radical Reconstruction was initiated and the Democrats continued the practice under Democrat Governor Robert B. Lindsay, 1870–1872.

Railroad mileage increased rapidly, especially after the Democrats took over. In 1860, there had been less than a thousand miles of railroads in the state. By 1885, there were 2,226; five years later, 3,422; and in 1895, 3,665 and in 1900, 4,197 miles. Many of the new lines were built to serve the mineral districts in north central Alabama. Many leading politicians had railroad interests. Robert M. Patton, for example, was president of the North and South Railroad and Thomas G. Jones was chief attorney for the Louisville and Nashville in Alabama.

There was mounting criticism of the railroads in Alabama as

there was all over the nation. Rates and fear of out-of-state control seem to have been the basis of most complaints but some men like W. L. Bragg were apprehensive over the monopoly each road had in its area. The Grange, the Alliance, and, to a degree, the Populists advocated some kind of controls over the activities of the roads. The first step was the creation of a Railroad Commission (1881), a three-man board with little more than advisory power. When Governor Rufus Cobb signed it into law, it was described as "mild as a May morning and as harmless as a dove."

Proposals to strengthen the commission met with opposition from the railroads. W. L. Bragg, president of the commission, wrote the following explanatory article.

> . . . The history of this proposed legislation in brief is this: The 28th section of the present Railroad Commission law of Alabama requires the Commissioners . . . to submit such recommendations for further legislation upon the subject of railroads as they deem necessary or advisable for the interests of the State. In obedience to this requirement of the statute the Railroad Commissioners made these recommendations.
>
> The opposition to this proposed legislation was speedily seen in the assemblage of a railroad lobby more numerous and active than any than ever has been seen about the city of Montgomery since. The railroad companies by fraud and bribery were procuring the endorsement of the State to their bonds, and also the bonds of the State in their aid from the carpet bag legislature in the years 1868–69 and 1870. This railroad lobby swarmed around the hotels of Montgomery at night and around the capitol by day. It prepared petitions in Montgomery against this legislation and sent them up and down the railroad lines of the state, procuring the signatures of the merchants generally at country towns along their lines and also petitions signed by a large number of merchants of Montgomery, Selma, Mobile, Birmingham, and Eufaula.
>
> The object of these petitions thus obtained was to produce upon the legislature the impression that the people generally were opposed to such legislation.
>
> The only object of this proposed legislation is to clothe the Railroad Commission of Alabama with power to make reasonable and just rates for the railroad companies in this state instead of merely recommending them; to prevent and correct "unjust discrimination" . . . "extortion" . . . "conspiracies" on the part of railroad companies to evade the laws of the State upon the subject of fair and equal rates to all the people, and to require the railroad laws to furnish fair and equal rates and transportation facilities and accommodations to the people for a just and reasonable compensation. . . .—Montgomery *Advertiser,* December 21, 1884.

THE CONVICT LEASE SYSTEM

The State of Alabama leased its convicts to private industry. This policy was in common with other Southern states and in keeping with the "Bourbon" purpose of operating an inexpensive government. By leasing convicts the state not only saved itself the cost of maintaining prisoners; it also collected fees from the companies to whom the convicts were leased. The credit side of the system is discussed by Governor Joseph F. Johnston in his annual message. Within a few years the system became a burning political issue and was finally abolished in 1928.

EXTRACT FROM GOVERNORS MESSAGE
Convict Lease System

The lease contract with the Tennessee Coal, Iron and Railroad Company expires with the year 1897. The state receives from this source about $11,000 per month which cannot yet be dispensed with. I sanctioned the policy adopted by the inspectors of transferring to Speigner's and the Walls and to hire to saw mill companies and on farms all of the convicts who are unable to work in the mines, or whose health would be greatly impaired by continuing them therein, and this policy should be continued and the number of convicts leased or hired out each year, be greatly diminished as employment elsewhere can be provided for them without loss to the State. This is the only way in which the lease system can be terminated consistently with the interests of the State. That system is less objectionable than in any other State where it prevails because our law makes an inspector follow the convict wherever he goes, on the farm, at the mills, or into the mines and to see that he is properly fed, clothed and not misused or abused. Every month the inspectors visit the mines and reclassify to prevent any of the convicts from being over tasked. It is this close inspection which makes our lease system the best kind extant. . . .

The total amount of receipts of the department from all sources for the two years was $423,874.42

288,066.11 The total amount of disbursement
$135,808.31 Net profit to the state
—*People's Advocate* (Columbiana), November 19, 1896.

The Democrats by 1900 had dropped the "and conservative party" as a part of their name but had kept the principle. They had done most of what they proposed to do when they regained control of the state; they had cut expenses, lowered taxes, reduced the state debt, attracted industry to the state, increased railroad mileage and, above all, managed to stay in office in spite of Republican efforts, Populist assaults, fusion of opposing factions, and dissension within their own ranks. It had been a government favoring the upper classes; only toward the end of the period when Kolb courted the small farmers in the white counties did these "horny-handed sons of the soil," as orators like to call them, count for much on the political scene.

Government in this period had been provided by the state's own leaders and the white citizens generally liked it, especially in comparison with the former government which had been imposed by outsiders. If some of the glamor of the period has faded under later scrutiny, it must be remembered that these Bourbons considered themselves keepers of the public welfare, and also that this was a period of low public morality all over the nation.

There was a movement, begun before the constitution of 1875 was five years old, to replace it but it was not until 1901 that this took place. The desire to disfranchise the Negroes (as Mississippi had done in 1890) seems to have been the dominant reason for change.

Chapter 14

SOCIAL LIFE AFTER THE WAR

The war left a pall of gloom over the South and for years life generally was hard. Families who were once affluent were often now in straitened circumstances. For most people the post-war period meant less wealth, fewer servants (although some former slaves returned to their old masters to work for low wages), and more restrictions on their way of living and entertaining. Life was altered but social life adapted to new conditions. There was a revival of some of the old festivals and customs soon after the war. The tournament was one of them.

The Tournament

The tournament, although originating in earlier times, was still popular and may help to explain why the nineteenth century South has been described as "medieval." It did indeed attempt to recreate a time when knights were bold and ladies were waiting to be rescued. The tournament was an athletic contest in which "knights" on horseback, racing at full speed, attempted to thrust a spear through a ring hanging from a tree limb. The winner had the right to name the queen of the event which lasted all day. It was a social event of importance in the old plantation regions. One of the first to be held after the war was apparently staged in Tuscaloosa in December 1870.

The Tournament . . . come off yesterday afternoon on the beautiful plaza in front of the Methodist College grounds. Thirteen knights contended for the prize which, after a long contest, resulted in three draws between Mr. Hardin Cochrane and Mr. Ed. Warren. The prize was, at last, awarded to Mr. Cochrane.

The victorious knight, bearing a beautiful wreath on the point of his lance, and accompanied by all the knights, approached and crowned as Queen of Love and Beauty, Miss Mary Gooch of this city. The whole city was out in force and enjoyed the sport keenly. Let us have more pleasant things of the same kind. They serve to cheer the gloom of life and add to its length by the pleasure they bring with them.—Tuscaloosa *Observer,* December 10, 1870.

Three years later, there was a much more elaborate tournament.

The young men of this city gave a handsome entertainment, in the way of a tournament, on last Monday evening, the 23rd instant. A goodly crowd of ladies and gentlemen assembled to witness the exercises which came off on the spacious campus in front of the Tuscaloosa Female College. The following Knights entered the lists:
 1. Knight of "Dolly Varden", J. Shep Beale
 2. Knight of "Red Cross", E. Rush King
 3. Knight of "Big Sandy Cyclops", Alec. Miller
 4. Knight of "Big Sandy", Sam Phifer
 5. Knight of "Lancaster", Alf Battle
 6. Knight of "Red Rover", M. Pumphry
 7. Knight of "Coeur DeLeon", Patton Kennedy
 8. Knight of "Golden Cross", Thomas Jones
 9. Knight of "Night Before Last", Easby Smith
10. Knight of "Ivanhoe", M. Allston
11. Knight of "Red and Black Bume", Willie Battle

The Knight of "Dolly Varden", Mr. J. Shep Beale, having won the first prize, crowned Miss Beaulah Wood "Queen of Love and Beauty." The Knight of "Big Sandy Cyclops", Mr. Alec Miller, and the Knight of the "Red Cross", Mr. Rush King, took the second and third prizes, and crowned Miss Sallie Thomas and Miss Julia Blocker, the first and second maids of Honor. The ceremonies, from commencement to close, were beautiful, tasteful, and interesting. A splendid Tournament Ball, given by the Knights, at the hospitable residence of Mrs. M. K. Jones, closed the festivities of the occasion. It was altogether a very charming affair.
—Tuscaloosa *Times,* September 25, 1873.

Mardi Gras

Early in the French colonial period, the inhabitants of Mobile had begun an annual celebration that was to become the ancestor of the modern Mardi Gras. It was not until 1831, however, that it took on its present form. Although there is little record of it, the custom was suspended during the war but revived by one Joe Cain in 1866. Cain is credited with several of the mystic societies that now play a vital role in the Mardi Gras.

The festivities, which end on the midnight before Lent, have a different theme each year. In 1891, it was the Waverly novels.

THE ORDER OF MYTHS
Celebrate their Twenty-Fourth Anniversary Scenes from the Waverly
Novels The Beauties of English Literature
Presented to the Gaze of Admiring Thousands

Last night the Order of Myths celebrated their twenty-fourth anniversary by a grand street parade. On this occasion the Myths endeavored to counteract the pernicious influences of the yellow-back literature, and by illustrating the words of a standard author, sought to impress upon the minds of the younger portion of the community the beauties of English literature. With this end in view they chose for portrayal scenes from the Waverly novels, the subject being illustrated on nine floats, and the incidents being chosen mounted with faithful fidelity to the descriptions given by the greatest of English novelists; and being mostly from the historical novels of Scott, the majority of the floats were ablaze with the pomp and insignia of royalty. The brush of the artist had done its work well, and the applause which greeted the parade as it passed through the streets was merited compliment to the skill of the designer and the brush of the artist.

Headed by a platoon of police and brass band the parade moved through the streets, first in order being

Float I—The Society Emblem
This was the familiar broken shaft of fluted marble, and about the base of which Folly, this year impersonated by a lovely and graceful female, played pranks upon the grim spectre, Death, who bore the scythe and hour glass, gruesome insignia of his rank.

Float II—Gathering of the Clans
From the novel *Waverly* the incident portrayed on this float was selected. From the rocky eminence in the Highlands of Scotland waved the banner of the Pretender to the throne of England, and to his standard the chiefs of the Scottish clans were rallying, ready to do battle in order to establish the claims of their leader. The float bore the Pretender, Waverly, a courtier, and eight Scottish chiefs.

Float III—Knighting of Walter Raleigh
From *Kenilworth* the incident of Raleigh's elevation to the peerage was illustrated on this float. Double columns of marble arising from a base of scarlet and gold, supported a cornice of white marble underneath which was the throne chair, with golden frame upholstered in richest scarlet, from which Queen Elizabeth had just risen to perform the ceremony. Kneeling in front of the throne was Raleigh, awaiting the honor which the Duchess of Rutland's suggestion had given the queen wished opportunity to confer upon him. As witness of the ceremony there were the Earl of Leicester, Sir Richard Varney, who had been previously knighted, the Earl of Essex, Amy Robsard, Lord Oxford, and a page in attendance upon her majesty.

Float IV—The Death of Brian de Bois-Guilbert
The scene of this float is laid about the exterior of the preceptory of Templestowe, the incident depicted being taken from *Ivanhoe*. Rebecca, the Jewess, had been tried for witchcraft, and condemned to the stake

by Lucas Beaumanoir, grand master of the Templars, for her seeming witchery of Bois-Guilbert, one of the Templars who became infatuated by her beauty and endeavored to persuade her to flee the country with him. As a last resort Rebecca threw down the gage, her silken glove, and demanded a champion. Bois-Guilbert, has been assigned to defend the judgment of the grand masters of the Templar in mortal combat. Ivanhoe appeared in the lists, championed Rebecca's cause, but, suffering from wounds . . . is unhorsed. Suddenly Bois-Guilbert reeled and fell from his horse. . . . Ivanhoe sprang quickly to his feet, placed his foot on the breast of the fallen foe, and commanded him to yield or die. The grand master acknowledged Bois-Guilbert vanquished. . . .

Float V—Vision of Lady Forester

The incident here depicted was taken from *Aunt Margaret's Mirror.* . . .

In front of the float was a polished mirror, swinging on two upright supports. Before this mirror, attended by Damiolli, stood Lady Forester, with her friend, Lady Bothwell. The rear of the float revealed the nave of the church, completely surrounded by rose-hued clouds. The lanset windows of the nave were seen in the background, while in front of the altar . . . stood a bishop ready to perform the marriage ceremony. Just outside the chancel rail stood Sir Philip Forester and his bride, attended by two noblemen.

Float VI—The White Lady and Halbert-Glendenning

The incident so beautifully depicted on this float was taken from the *Monastery;* and represented Halbert-Glendenning in search of the mysterious books so loved by the Lady of Avenel. . . .

Only two characters were to be seen on this float—Halbert-Glendenning and the White Lady. . . .

Float VII—Escape of Queen Marry from the Castle of Lochleven

Upon this float was depicted in realistic manner the familiar story of the escape of the unfortunate Queen Mary. . . . The frowning towers of an ancient castle adorned by the rear of the float, the stone walls of which were lapped by the waters of the lake. The front portion of the float was occupied by a boat in the act of leaving the castle entrance bearing Queen Mary and her faithful followers, Catherine Seyton, Henry Seyton, Douglas and Roland. . . . Sir Robert Melville, Lord Lindsay, and Lord Ruthven watched the escape which they were powerless to prevent, from the parapet of the castle. The story of the escape is told in *The Abbot.*

Float VIII—Meeting of the Begum and Tippoo Saib

The scene illustrated on this float represented the royal gardens during the reception of the Begum by the prince. (*The Surgeon's Daughter.*) In the foreground of the float is the royal camel, richly caparisoned, from which the prince had dismounted. Nearby stood the Begum, attended by her general, Middle-mas. . . . In the centre of the platform was the musnud, or state cushion of the prince, composed of crimson velvet, bordered with heavy gold bullion fringe. Upon this cushion sat Tippo Tib, while near him was the Nawaub and three Indian courtiers.

Float IX—Mount St. George

The story of the discovery of the despoiler of the royal standard of King Richard by the hound, Rosival, on Mount St. George was told on this float. . . .

In the front of the float was the affrighted Conrade, as he beheld the faithful dog, with wide open mouth, in the act of springing upon him. In the background was depicted the rendezvous of Mount St. George where King Richard, attended by Queen Berengaria, took up his position where the whole camp was passing in review. . . .

Float X—Reception of Count Robert of Alexius

Count Robert of the Head of the Crusaders had pitched his camp without the walls of Constantinople and was tendered an audience by the Emperor, Alexius Comnenus. This float was gotten up with due regard to all the pomp and circumstances of royalty. . . .

THE BALL

At half past eight o'clock the doors of Temperance Hall were thrown open to the admission of the guests of the society, and an hour later, when the members arrayed in magnificent and costly costumes, reached the hall, they found it crowded almost to suffocation with ladies and gentlemen in evening dress. To afford greater space for their guests in street costume a temporary balcony was erected around the sides of the hall. . . . After making a detour of the hall, the ball was opened with a waltz, in which only members of the society and their fair partners participated. When this concluded, civilians and myths alike mingled in the dance. . . . and then the ball went on in one continued round of pleasure until the hour of midnight when the shrill whistle resounded through the hall, bidding the myths depart to the secret recesses of their den. . . .—Mobile *Daily Register,* February 11, 1891.

The Wedding

By the end of the century, the church wedding was beginning to be popular. In earlier times fashionable weddings were at the home of the bride and others were at the preacher's residence or before a civil official. The wedding of Miss Louella Teague of Columbiana to Dr. T. G. Nelson of Harpersville in the fall of 1895 was an event of importance. The editor reporting it evidently approved of the match.

This wedding was one of the prettiest we ever had the pleasure of attending. All during Thursday a happy, busy crowd of young ladies, assisted by two or three young men, were engaged in decorating the church, and ere they finished it was enchanting to behold. They did not confine themselves to styles of past years, but originated new and tasty designs that displayed their genius in this line.

The ceremony was announced to take place at 8 o'clock, and by that hour the church was crowded to its full seating capacity with

the friends and well-wishers of the popular couple to be wedded. . . .
At exactly 8 o'clock Miss Myrtle Swain took her seat at the organ
and began the wedding march. Two pretty flower girls, Allie Nelson
and Florence Spencer, led the way, opening the gate made of evergreens
at the end of the aisle at the side of the altar. Following came the bride
and the groom. Miss Louella looked beautiful dressed in white silk,
trimmed with lace and passementerle, silk tulle veil and natural flowers.
She was the perfection of beauty, style, and neatness. Dr. Nelson looked
particularly handsome being dressed in most becoming style. As they
marched slowly down the aisle, they absorbed the entire attention of
the large audience and as they took their position in front of the altar,
the numerous tapers arranged about the pulpit, shedding their delicate
light upon them, and standing 'neath an arch of evergreens and flowers,
the scene was both impressive and beautiful. Rev. B. F. Giles performed
the ceremony in a short but appropriate manner, closing with a brief
prayer.

Again the sweet strains of the organ were heard, and the recently
united couple marched out through the opposite aisle by which they
came.—*The Chronicle* (Columbiana), October 3, 1896.

The bride and groom and a large number of their friends "repaired" to the residence of Mrs. Laura Armstrong where they were
"tendered a handsome reception." Refreshments consisted of "ice
cream, cake, fruits, candies, nuts, etc." The happy couple immediately moved into a recently built dwelling in Harpersville and the
editor wished them "all the happiness possible in this world, and
perfect bliss in the world to come."

Christmas

From colonial times Christmas has been the most important holiday in the South, eclipsing July 4 and Thanksgiving. The following
article describes the holiday festivities in Montevallo in 1867.

. . . On Christmas Eve there was a general gathering of both old and
young to the Female Institute where the young ladies of the school
had arranged a Gift Tree upon which presents were placed, not only
for the school children, but for many of the citizens. . . .

Christmas night by special invitation we repaired to the Methodist
Church where we witnessed one of the most beautiful sights it has ever
been our lot to enjoy. Just inside the altar, raised upon a large stand,
was a holly tree filled with glistening leaves and bunches of red berries,
the top reached the ceiling of the church. Hundreds of various colored
tapers threw a clear brilliant light over the tree while a double row of
tapers illuminated the stand upon which the tree was placed. The altar
was beautifully decorated with wreaths of everygreens and lit up with
tapers. On the branches of the tree was hung every conceivable . . .

variety of article from a small ornamented portemonie to large pieces of silver plate. It was a sight *grande, magnifique*. Our observations were interrupted by the entrance of the Sunday School procession. Immediately the organ was opened and the children sang, with spirit and understanding, a glorious Christmas anthem after which a short but expressive prayer was uttered by the minister. Then commenced the excitement of the distribution of the presents and . . . no child was forgotten. But each one went home well satisfied with his share of the spoils of their never-to-be-forgotten Christmas Tree. Several prizes were received for good lessons, good behavior and punctual attendance. What an encouragement was this exhibition of love and good will to the noble cause of Sabbath Schools. . . .

We did not attend many of the social parties, tea-drinkings, and dances that followed each other in lively succession, but one invitation more we received. . . . It was to a Leap Year party, the young ladies being the prime movers, of course. Mr. and Mrs. R. kindly consented for the young ladies to have the party at their residence and . . . prepared for them an elegant supper, consisting of every good thing that could be thought of: rare tropical fruits and mixtures and combinations of single sweets. . . . The party was a complete success. The ladies all looked so pretty and interesting it would do injustice to all to distinguish anyone. The gentlemen were as modest and well-behaved as it was expected they would be on such an occasion and two or three of them, we learn, to whom the question was popped by their fair gallants prudently referred them to mamma and papa.

Thus ended the Christmas holidays in Montevallo. . . .—*Shelby County Guide* (Columbiana), January 21, 1868.

Most social contacts were informal. Barbecues were a part of the summer entertainment in most communities. There were brass band concerts, hayrides, lawn parties, candy pullings, benefit programs and many other kinds of recreation. But by far the most popular form was visiting, indulged in by all classes of society.

Miss Fannie Crenshaw, a teenager from Marion, kept a diary of her visit with relatives near Marion Junction.

June 11, 1892. At Uncle Clarences. I came down here June 9th and am having the loveliest time imaginable. Aunt Dorcas has no cook. She and Aunt Lou cook, Mary and I wash the dishes. Aunt Dorcas intends getting a cook Monday and how Tubbie and I will rejoice to see Monday come.

Mary and I had a hard time getting some letters off today to some boys which was strictly against Aunt's and Uncle's wishes. They do not know it and we intend they shall not until after we have married.

A Mrs. Craig, Miss Fannie Clark, and Miss Mable Lowry called this afternoon, three of the *loveliest* creatures I ever saw, especially Mrs. Craig.

June 18, 1892. Another day has dawned, bright and fair. We were enjoying very much lounging around in our wrappers, when Aunt D. told us that two ladies were coming. Consequently we had to arise and dress. After dinner I undressed and took my usual afternoon nap, after which I got up and dressed. Aunt Lou, Mary and I went to walk with Miss Fannie and Mrs. Gibson. We did not walk far for we saw a cloud coming up and knew it would rain so we bid Miss F and Mrs. G goodbye, and came back home. We had not been in the house half an hour when it commenced to rain. Aunt D. made some cake. Uncle C. and the boys went to the river this afternoon and came back in the hardest rain. After supper Mary and I washed the dishes as usual, then *thinking* we were sleepy, we retired to our room, but after the light was extinguished it was in vain we tried to sleep. So lighting the lamp once again, we had a picnic reading letters, talking, and laughing until Aunt Lou came in after which we had more fun than ever. Well, dear old diary, I will say goodbye until another day.

June 20, 1892. . . . I packed my satchel this afternoon to go home tomorrow. I received a letter from Mama and one from Lem this morning. Lem says it seems as though I was going to spend the summer down here. I would if I thought there was any chance of seeing Euguene two or three times a week. . . .—Ms. diary, courtesy of the late Mrs. J. R. Sheppard, Marion Junction.

Miss Carrie Day wrote her father about the fashionable times and people of Gainesville. Miss Revis was the young lady who designed the Confederate flag the Sumter boys took to war with them. "Parson" Stillman was the Presbyterian minister for whom Stillman College is named.

Gainesville, [Alabama]
April 6, 1868

Dear Papa,

Thinking perhaps you would like to know how I am getting along amid "the fashionable throng" of Gainesville, I will endeavor to pen a laconic missive to you this beautiful afternoon in order to give you a few details. To begin, I'm having a gay time, I have made a great [many] acquaintances and some very good friends. I like the people of Gainesville much better than I anticipated for they are quite sociable indeed. Nearly all the "fashionables" have been round to see us, even "Miss Revis." Don't you think we ought to feel honored? for she does not visit many families living here. Papa, the ladies of G— have been invited by the Capt. of the boat "Clara" to take a pleasure trip up river as far as Columbus, Miss. Now, don't you imagine we will have a splendid time? Hassie & myself have had a "special invitation." All the young men will take a lady with them and Mr. Woodruff is my gallant. I think I will enjoy it finely, particularly the nice dinner. The boat will remain in Columbus about four hours, just long enough for the party to take a full view of the city.

Papa, I have been to church several times since I have been here. The preacher for the Methodist Church is Mr. Thomas who preached in Meridian last year. I have attended the Presbyterian church several times and heard *some* splendid sermons delivered by Parson Stillman. Did you have Yula baptized during Quarterly meeting? . . .

How are you getting along with your crop? Are you going to plant much cotton? Though I suppose not since your hands are so limited. How is the garden? Have you had any vegetables yet? We have had lettuce, mustard, and radishes, have been having lettuce sometime. We have fish very often. Bill O. brought one a few days since that weighed 16 lbs. "sixteen pounds", and I tell you we had a sumptuous time eating fish.

Papa, as I have been writing a good deal I feel tired, I will close this badly written letter by begging you to write soon to

Your daughter with affection,
Carrie

—Ms. letter loaned by the late Mrs. B. A. Jenkins, Emelle, Alabama.

The home, the church and, during campaign years, the court house were the centers of many activities of a social nature and the occasion depended on many things, some of them associated with the war and its consequences. One of these was the practice of decorating the graves of the war dead.

Memorial Day

Memorial Day observance could be as simple as the one in Montgomery or as elaborate as the one in Tuscaloosa thirteen years later.

LADIES AND THE 26TH OF APRIL

It becomes our pleasing duty today to record the touching act of the devotion of the ladies of Montgomery to the lamented dead who lie asleep within the limits of our city cemetery. On yesterday, they gathered in numbers, according to previous appointment, at the cemetery, re-touched and redecorated the grave of every soldier therein interred, planted and strewed them with flowers and performed such offices as their fancies suggested or seemed necessary.—Montgomery *Advertiser,* April 27, 1866.

. . . .

The intelligent people of the Druid City, ever obedient to the prompt-ings of patriotism and gratitude, have kept up this beautiful and appropriate custom for many years; and we rejoice to be able to say that the interest of the people in the exercises of Memorial Day this year was unabated, and that the ceremonies of the occasion were unusually interesting, touching, and impressive. At 4 o'clock P.M. last Saturday, near the Presbyterian Church, the efficient marshall, Col. A. C. Hargrove, formed the procession in the following order:

Silver Cornet Band
Chaplin and Orator
Alabama Corps of Cadets
Students of the Female Colleges
Students of Other schools in the city
Citizens on Foot
Citizens in Carriages

The procession then moved to the cemetery and entered it, the band playing the "Dead March" the soldiers' sad requiem, and the corps of cadets marching with arms reversed and with slow and solemn tread. On arriving at the orator's stand within the cemetery, prayer was offered by Rev. Dr. C. A. Stillman, pastor of the Presbyterian Church. Col. Hargrove then introduced the orator of the day, Rev. O. F. Gregory, pastor of the Baptist Church of this city.

To say that this oration was chaste and polished in sentiment and eloquently delivered, would not be more than its just meed of praise. It sparkled with gems of thought and jewels of rhetoric, breathed throughout an exalted spirit of affection and praise for our departed braves, and altogether reflected much credit upon the speaker who, himself, at the tender age of sixteen, donned the gray and followed in the gallant lead of the chivalrous Hampton.

The oration was followed by Miss Carrie Lewis, daughter of Hon. B. B. Lewis. Although Miss Lewis is as yet scarcely beyond the threshold of her teens, her recitation was animated, forcible, and impressive, and showed that she has inherited in no small degree the thrilling eloquence of her father. The Corps of Cadets, under tht command of Col. McCorvey, then fired three volleys in splendid time and style. Finally, loving hands adorned with beautiful flowers the last resting places of the gallant dead, and the ceremonies of Memorial Day of '79 were at an end.

"The gallant dead," aye, and though it is hard for us to realize it, our principles for which those noble men fought, are also dead, and our cause, for which they freely gave their blood and treasure, is dead. But our hopes are not dead. There is life in the land yet. Let us remember that.—Tuscaloosa *Gazette,* May 1, 1879.

Talladega's Torchlight Procession and Grand Jollification

There had been public rejoicing in many places when the Democrats carried the state in 1874, thereby "redeeming" it from the carpetbaggers. Talladega County was an exception to the rule; it did not rid itself of Radical Republicans until 1876 and then only by a majority of 382. This was the occasion for a celebration that seemed to have eclipsed earlier ones. The exuberant editor of the local paper began his editorial on the election thus:

Talladega Happy!
Talladega Joyous!
Talladega Free!
Talladega Jubilant!
Talladega Smiles!
Talladega Laughs!
Talladega Feels Good Generally!
Talladega Feels Like Talladega once again!
—*Reporter and Watchtower* (Talladega), August 9, 1876.

A week later the same newspaper carried a somewhat tempered, but still joyous, account of the celebration.

Bonfires, illuminations, torchlight processions, transparencies, music and speaking were the order of the evening. Every precinct was represented, and some of them by hundreds. The delegation from Chinnabee came in a procession, six wagons filled with men, several carriages and buggies and about one hundred on horseback, making quite a display. Matt Murphy, the leader of the Chinnabee "Mountain Boys" was dressed in Indian costume, and wearing the champions belt, which Chinnabee had won from Eastaboga on the late election.

A handsome banner prepared by the ladies was presented by Mr. Shep Groce to the Chinnabee delegation. Mr. M. S. Curry received the banner, and responded in a manly speech. Dr. J. H. Johnson, marshal of the occasion, formed the torchlight procession on the west side of the square, and with banners, bells, transparencies, trumpets and music made quite a display as they moved up Court street across Battle to Coffee, and up Coffee street to Second Alley, thence to North and down North to Square. Ladies lined the balconies and filled the windows. Speeches were made in the following order: M. H. Cruikshank, G. K. Miller, Hon. Jno. T. Heflin, F. W. Bowden, Graves Renfroe, Dr. Wm. Taylor, Wm. Baker, Thos. Henderson, F. Dillon, R. J. Conningham, John Ware, Esq., and others. Accompanying the Chinnabee delegation were 30 colored men who were bearing banners and who had voted the Democratic ticket.

Tradition lingers fondly over the countless incidents and accidents of this glorious night for Talladega, recalling with especial zest the untoward fate of one of those oratorical gentlemen who spoke in the list put down by the local paper as the "And others." A stand had been erected on the northeast side of the courthouse, the torches had flickered, flared and many had become extinguished as the small hours began to arrive. Our Democratic speaker was filled with enthusiasm and corn whiskey, and the light was too dim for him to read his manuscript, whereupon a bibulous, but still enthusiastic Democrat volunteered to hold a candle for him. The local Demosthenes proceeded to howl from a written page about "ty-reeny and uppression, libbe-ty and the Lost Caws," at the top of his voice while his drunken friend wobbled about with his lighted candle, frequently setting the orator's whiskers afire, and plastering his Prince Albert coat with tallow from cupalo to foundation stone, all without in the least stopping the flow of eloquence from the lips of one of our "favorite sons." It was a mad orgy for staid Talladega, which village, at that time trembled at its temerity in imbibing a glass of lemonade spiked with wine at a church supper.. . . .—Ibid., August 16, 1876.

Baseball

One pleasant and admirable outgrowth of the Civil War was the great American game, baseball. Jehu Wellington Vandiver described its origins in Talladega.

Base ball was first seen by the Talladega youth when the Yankee garrison was stationed at Talladega in 1865, several teams of the various companies occasionally crossing bats. Town ball, and cat still held sway among the school boys until in the early months of 1870 when a club was formed at the Peabody school. The Peabody school club, after various local games, finally became the Highland City club, under this name acquiring some reputation. The first game of this team played away from home was played at Oxford on April 27th, 1872, against the Oxford Club, the score being 114 runs in favor of the Highland City club as against 14 runs of the Oxford club. . . . After this game Henry Grady, writing in the Rome Commercial in the fine spirit of true sport ever characteristic of him, has this to say of the game:

"Talladega, and her people. How nine little men marched up the hill, and then marched down again. There was a pretty good crowd of us and at about 3 o'clock at night we reached Talladega, a little town on the Selma road where the original inventors of base ball live. One or two citizens met us at the depot, and apologized for the base ball club not being there as they were practicing by moon light on their grounds for the next day's game. We strolled up to the 'H. I. Criswell House' where we found the immortal Criswell sleeping on his counter, his lovely form wrapped in the drapery of a Home Sewing Machine circular. He was waked, we bedded, and dreampt of the morrow. (This dreaming of the morrow was what ruined us.) The next morning we paraded the streets when Bayard whispered down the line, 'Boys let us try and not look proud; it will hurt the feelings of this little village and even when we beat the game don't let us make a fuss about it just lets take the ball quietly, and give three cheers for the defeated club (poor fellows) and go home.'

"But we couldn't help it, we felt so grand that we took on a stock of pride that last till the end of the eighth inning. At that juncture we ate eleven thousand 'humble pies.'

"The game opened lively, Rome ran ahead. 'We've got a soft thing boys, sung out our captain,' so we had, too soft to keep in this hot weather. It spoiled on our hands about the fourth inning and from that time until the end of the game we caught the loftiest Hallelujah that ever fell to the lot of nine poor mortals. In short (excuse these) they licked us. We are going to lick them as soon as we can. In my opinion this will be in about 20,000 years, but with patience we will get through this brief interval. At the close of the game an unpleasant impression prevailed through our club that we had caught the wrong sow by the ear, in fact several sows by several ears. To Messrs. Blackburn, Butler, Vandiver, Knox, Bowman, McLin, Johnson, Woodward and Thornton, our successful opponents, we would say that the Knights never wore laurels more gracefully than they and men were never whipped in an honester fight, and on an honester field, than were the late lamented Pastimes of Rome."—"Pioneer Talladega," *Alabama Historical Quarterly,* vol. 16, pp. 202–203.

Old Soldiers' reunions became very common.

REUNION COMPANY F., NINTH ALABAMA

Company F., Ninth Alabama Regiment under Capt. T. H. Hobbs was enlisted at Athens, Alabama, June 6, 1861. It served in the Army of Northern Virginia. It left Athens with 104 men, rank and file, and subsequently enrolled 155 men, thirty-five of whom are known to be living now.

At the invitation of Mr. T. Maclin Hobbs, eldest son of Capt. Hobbs . . . sixteen battle scarred veterans some of whom had not seen each other since the war, met at Pettusville Springs, Limestone County . . . October 21, 1896, and spent a very pleasant day, recounting their old experiences and reviving hallowed memories. After a sumptious dinner, prepared by the host, the veterans listened to eloquent and pathetic talks from comrades Asce Moore, Robert Culps, S. M. Clay and Mr. Hobbs. Comrades were present from Birmingham, Pulaski and other points.

An organization was perfected and hereafter the company will hold its reunion annually at Athens . . . until none are left to answer at roll call.—Henry J. Fusch, *The Confederate Veteran* (Elkmont, Ala.: 1896), vol. 6, p. 400.

Outdoor and Church Activities

Outdoor festivities and church affairs have always been popular in the South. The following account, much abbreviated here, comes from the Marion *Commonwealth,* May 27, 1869. According to one speaker, this picnic was an annual event, dating back thirty years. The language sounds stilted to the modern ear but it was the nineteenth century polite form.

THE SUNDAY SCHOOL PIC-NIC

The prodigal hospitality of the high-souled sons and daughters of the South was abundantly illustrated by the officers and pupils of the Selma Sunday Schools in the Pic-Nic given by them at Weaver's Grove last Thursday. It was the universal criticism of all those present on that festive occasion that never before had such an abundance and such systematic order distinguished a party of that character. The consequence was that . . . all united in one general ascription of praise to those who had arranged and controlled the program of the day.

The . . . visitors from the Marion Schools, consisting of a little more than one-half the aggregate membership thereof, arrived at Selma about 10½ o'clock. [The Selma Schools acknowledged the compliment of the visit and stood while the long line of Marion people filed by.] Then forming in the rear of the Marion Schools, the whole light-hearted throng "moved in loving accord" to the scene of the coming festivities. Here a large and commodious stage, embowered in flower-begemmed garlands and festoons of evergreen, and bearing on its fairy-like front the genial word "Welcome", and long lines of yet un-furnished tables, gave us to understand that the pleasures of the coming day were to be mental and spiritual as well as corporeal in their character. Nor was our understanding at all disappointed. After the various schools composing the procession had approached by head of column to the front in close order, a beautiful prayer by Rev. Mr. Bounds, followed by a song of welcome from the Schools of Selma and a responsive greeting from those of Marion, initiated the enjoyments of the "day and the hour." At this point Sumter Lea, Esq., not many years ago one of the most popular and gifted of our younger citizens, was introduced to the audience and welcomed the Marion visitors in the following brief, but eloquent, address.

"To the Sabbath Schools of Marion:
It is my pleasing duty, delegated by the Sabbath Schools of Selma, to extend to you on this joyous festive day, our anniversary union, our most cordial greetings and hearty welcome. . . ."

. . . .

After the applause had echoed these words of welcome had subsided, Mr. John George Apsey, of Marion—well known to every Fourth Alabamian, and well beloved by every man, himself honest enough to love an honest manly heart—responded to Mr. Lea's welcome. . . .

". . . Again, officers, teachers and scholars of the Selma Sabbath Schools, we thank you for our greeting; and may we hope that when all earthly things are over, this pleasant gathering in your city may be renewed in that upper and more glorious city whose gates are of pearl, and whose walls are of precious stones—that Heavenly City—the city of our King."

George not only acquitted himself well—he did more. He achieved distinction in that single effort. . . .

Mr. N. D. Cross, Superintendent of Ceremonies, then came forward, and after saying that the greetings thus far extended had been but general in their character and but partially satisfactory in result, dismissed the organizations in order, as he expressed it, that those greetings might be given personally, specially, and as from friend to friend.

For a short time confusion . . . seemed reigning monarch . . . but ere many minutes had elapsed, friend struck hand with friend, kinsmen with kinsmen, sweetheart with lover (perhaps) and "all went merry as a marriage bell."

. . . .

The dinner was a feast. Everything usual on such occasions and more—everything that heart could ask or the inner man require—everything, in short, that the hospitality of Selma could suggest as either necessary or luxurious, was epitomized in that dinner. Some faint idea of its bountiful character may be derived from that fact that the two thousand mouths thereby failed to make any very perceptible diminution of its bulk. . . .

After dinner the amusements of the occasion were resumed—to be broken only by roll of the drum that announced to those of Marion the hour of their departure. . . . At the appointed time, the gay procession, under charge of the energetic and accomplished marshal of the day, Capt. C. W. Lovelace, returned to the train and in short order the precious freight was being rapidly whirled homeward behind the flower-garlanded engine express. At 6½ P.M., safe and sound . . . the happy throng dispersed from the depot at Marion to their several abodes. . . .

In behalf of the Marion Sunday Schools we conclude this notice by tendering the thanks of all (1) to Capt. Lovelace for the order, system, care and attention . . . on this occasion and (2) to the officers (especially the engineers) in charge of the trains for the very considerate care . . . to and from Selma. On these last a heavy responsibility, involving the safety of near a thousand souls was laid and right nobly did they meet the requirements of the trust. . . . Few, perhaps, knew how near at one time [an] accident was at hand. In Mr. Crenshaw's field (near Hamburg) some fiend had placed a large billet of wood upon the track and a little further on a heavy junk bottle. But Jere Munn was at the engine and his circumspection prevented a casualty, and frustrated the designs of the scamp who clogged the track. . . .

ALL-DAY MEETING

In rural Alabama the church has always played an important part. Widely separated, the people have found at church on Sunday a companionship lacking during the week. Each summer there were special occasions such as the revival or "protracted meeting" which went on for a week or longer. Usually such an event would be begun (or ended) with an "all-day-meeting." Booker T. Washington describes a Negro "Big Day," but white people had (and still have in rural areas) similar days at their churches. "Dinner on the ground and preaching all day" is the way such events are often described.

In Macon County, Alabama, . . . the colored people have a kind of church-service that they call an "all-day meeting." The ideal season for such meetings is about the middle of May. The church-house I have in mind is located about ten miles from town. To get the most out of the "all-day meeting" one should make an early start, say eight o'clock. During the drive one drinks in the fresh fragrance of forest and wild flowers. The church building is located near a stream of water, not far from a large, cool spring and in the midst of a grove or primitive forest. Here the colored people begin to come together by nine or ten o'clock in the morning. Some of them walk; most of them drive. A large number come in buggies, but many use the more primitive wagons or carts, drawn by mules, horses or oxen. In these conveyances a whole family . . . make the journey together. All bring baskets of food, for the "all-day meeting" is a kind of Sunday picnic or festival. Preaching, preceded by much singing, begins at about eleven o'clock. If the building is not large enough, the services are held out under the trees. Sometimes there is but one sermon; sometimes there are two or three sermons, if visiting ministers are present. The sermon over, there is more plantation singing. A collection is taken—sometimes two collections—then comes recess for dinner and recreation.

Sometimes I have seen at these "all-day meetings" as many as three thousand people present. No one goes away hungry. Large baskets, filled with the most tempting spring chicken or fresh pork, fresh vegetables, and all kinds of pies and cakes are then opened. The people scatter in groups. Sheets or tablecloths are spread on the grass under a tree near the stream. Here old acquaintances are renewed; relatives meet members of the family whom they have not seen for months. Strangers, visitors, everyone must be invited by some one else to dinner. Kneeling on the fresh grass or on broken branches of trees surrounding the food, dinner is eaten. The animals are fed and watered and then at about three o'clock there is another sermon or two, with plenty of singing thrown in; then another collection, or perhaps two. . . . At about five o'clock the benediction is pronounced and the thousands quietly scatter to their homes with many goodbys and well-wishes. . . .—Booker T. Washington, *My Larger Education* (New York: Doubleday, Page, 1911), pp. 32–34.

LADIES' MISSIONARY SOCIETY

Woman's organizations, which play a large part in the modern church, were late in developing in Alabama. There seem to have been few before the Civil War. By the 1880's, however, they were widespread and flourishing. The following minutes of the Ladies' Missionary and Benevolent Society of Prosperity Associate Reformed Presbyterian Church (Dallas County) gives an idea of the society's activities. The meetings lasted all day. This society was especially interested in a mission in Mexico, quilting, and an occasional entertainment (usually a supper or ice cream supper) for the young people.

The Ladies Missionary and Benevolent Society met according to adjournment at Rev. J. A. Lowery's, November 29, 1894, the day being changed from Saturday (the regular day) to Thursday on account of having services at church on that day.

The Society was opened by the president's reading the 112 Psalm, after which the Lord's Prayer was recited in concert.

Roll was called, 19 members present. Dues collected and some money taken in on work.

The minutes of last meeting read and adopted.

The Treasurer was instructed to pay over $20.00 to Mr. Lowery as a supplement to his salary and also to settle a bill for coffee used that day.

The congregation was canvassed by the Society at a previous meeting to raise money to present our pastor with a bill of groceries. A neat little sum was realized.

The gift was presented by Mr. J. J. Moore in a very impressive manner. Numerous other gifts were made by different members of the congregation and some came from members of other congregations.

The day was pleasantly spent and is one that will be long remembered by Prosperity congregation and pastor.

The pastor addressed the society and congregation in his whole soul way, after which he closed the day with a soul stirring prayer.

KATE A. NEAL, Sec.

—The old ledger containing the minutes from 1888 to 1896 was borrowed by Mr. & Mrs. Harvey Fleming from Mrs. Fleming's great aunt, Mrs. J. R. Sheppard of Marion Junction who kindly permitted me to use it.

STATE OF RELIGION IN BETHESDA CHURCH, 1873.

The session of Bethesda Church respectfully report to Presbytery that we have enjoyed the regular preaching of the word by our pastor elect, Rev. M. C. Hutton, with the exception of a short interval during the summer. Our congregations have been in the main large and remarkably attentive to the word spoken. Some attending who have not done so for months past.

The weekly prayer meeting has been kept up and an increasing interest shown by larger and more regular attendance of those within reach.

The Bible class having been changed from monthly to weekly recitations exhibits decided interest in the study of God's word.

The Sabbath School has been kept up with a fair average attendance. Recently, however, there has been a falling off on the part of some whose parents belong to other denominations to attend their own Sabbath Schools.

The Union and Child's Scripture question book is in use with regular study of the Shorter Catechism on the part of those of our own children and youth. The school is opened by singing, reading the word of God, with short exhortation and prayer, closing with singing and prayer.

The collections enjoyed by the Assembly have been taken up, but we see no perceptible growth in the grace of giving upon the part of our people. But we are hoping for better things in this respect.

The week embracing the 3rd Sabbath of September we had protracted services day and night: our minister being assisted by Rev. C. M. Hutton and Rev. Jas. Summerville. God favored his word. We have been refreshed from his presence. In answer to our prayers His spirit has been poured out upon us. We have rarely ever seen such deep and pervading religious interest as seems now to exist in our community. Members of other churches uniting with us were also refreshed. As the result of these and preliminary services nine were united with us upon a profession of faith in Christ and four by certificate. We hope and expect others to take this step in a short time: while some will join other churches than our own. Thanks be unto our God for His unspeakable gift and the riches of His grace.

By order of Session. Closed with prayer.

S. F. NUNNELLEE, Clerk

—Bethesda Session Book, pp. 107–109, Ms., Presbyterian Historical Foundation, Montreat, N. C. by permission of Tuscaloosa Presbytery.

Most activites of a social nature were mere continuations of similar ones in the past. However, there seems to have been a new development in organized entertainment. Organizations are as old as time but Alabama had more clubs and associations after the Civil War than before. These ranged in purpose from the purely social to the intellectual and cultural.

Southwestern Musical Convention

Alabama is not widely known for its music but in addition to brass bands it has had groups interested in singing. Some, probably most, of these were interested in church music such as the one in Clarke County. The preamble of their constitution read:

We, the Vocalists of Southwestern Alabama, in the pursuance of certain resolutions entered into in the year 1870, declaring it to be the duty of the Southwestern Alabama Vocalists to organize themselves into a body whereby they will be enabled to protect the purity of Sacred Music from the invasion of immoral men, as well as those who are incompetent to discharge the duties which devolve upon a Teacher of Sacred Music; therefore, our object in forming such an association as an Association of Musicians is for the purpose of renovating, improving, and systematizing our Southern Church Music.

It is certainly an evident fact that Sacred Music is essential to the prosperity of every Church, and is not only important for the influence it exerts over the existence of churches, but it is the medium through which the purifying influences of God's regenerating Grace may, does, and has passed to the human heart—hence we have no hesitancy in saying that Sacred Music had a Divine origin; and . . . it must be one among the highest of human attainments, and is worthy of our best efforts for its advancement.—Quoted in T. H. Ball, *A Glance into the Great South-East or Clarke County, Alabama, and Its Surroundings, from 1540 to 1877* (Tuscaloosa, Alabama: Willo Publishing Company, 1962), p. 610. This book was first published in 1879.

Debating and study clubs with a strong literary bent and often with romantic Greek names sprang up in many places. To begin with, both men and women participated in them but eventually women would dominate the club life in the state with men confining their interests to lodges and, in the twentieth century, service organizations.

The Erosophic Literary Society was organized on Friday, October 13, 1894, at Elizabeth Seminary, Jasper. Miss Elizabeth Maude Haley, later Mrs. J. Alex Moore of Montevallo, was the convener. The program of January 18, 1895, is a good example of the kind of study it did.

> The E.L.S. met at the usual hour, the president presiding. When the secretary called the roll, the members answered with quotations from Poe and Lee. The secretary read the minutes of the previous meeting. The critic read her report. Miss Duffee then read an interesting essay on the life of Lee. Annabel Lee was recited with much force by Miss Rosamond. We then had the debate, the speakers for the aff[irmative] being Miss Maude Shields and Miss McGuire and the one for neg[ative] being Miss Johnnie Bee Shields. The question was: "Resolved that the poet has done more for his country than has the warrior." The president rendered his decision in favor of the neg[ative]. The Life of Poe was then read by Mr. Gamble. We then had "The Holidays in Jasper" by Mr. Foster Gamble. Miss Amy Rosamond read "The News of the Year," which we all enjoyed and by which we were all benefitted. The program ended with a song, "Way Down Upon the Swanee River" in which the society was invited to join. There being no further business, the society adjourned.—Photocopy of manuscript minutes, Carmichael Library, University of Montevallo.

Alabama Federation of Women's Clubs

Women's clubs were numerous enough that on April 17, 1895, representatives from nine organizations met in Birmingham to form the Alabama Federation of Women's Clubs. These nine literary clubs, organized for "self-culture and self-expression," were: Highland Book Club, Cadmean Circle, Clionian Club, Pollock-Stevens Alumnae Association, Hippocrenean Literary Society, Pierian Society, all of Birmingham; No Name Club, Montgomery; Progressive Culture Club, Decatur; and the Thursday Literary Circle, Selma. Three of the Birmingham clubs, Pollock-Stevens Alumnae, Hippocrenean and Pierian Societies, were made up of students and soon dropped out but the remaining ones were joined by other adult groups. Miss Mary LaFayette Robbins of the Thursday Literary Circle of Selma was the guiding spirit that brought about the central organization.

Their initial purpose may have been for "self-culture and self-expression," but it was not long before the clubs, separately and jointly, were engaged in a variety of service projects. In 1968 Mildred White Wells looked back on an imposing list:

> Boys' Reformatory, Child Welfare laws, Compulsory Education, Penal Reform, Health Education, Alabama College [the library and scholarships], Girls' Training School, Literacy, Highway Beautification.— Mildred White Wells, *History of the Alabama Federation of Women's Clubs* (Montgomery, Ala.: Paragon Press, 1968), vol. 2, p. 2.

Chautauqua

The Chautauqua came to Alabama in the 1890's, some twenty years after the movement was started in New York state in 1874. One of.the founders was Bishop John H. Vincent, "who first saw the light under the genial skies of Alabama" at Tuscaloosa. Dr. John Massey said he had never known a man who "manifested more concern for the cultivation of deep personal piety, for the right kind of family government, and the proper training of children than Bishop Vincent." The purpose of the Chautauqua was adult or continuing education of a wholesome nature. In the days before easy communication, small towns had almost their only chance to see and hear professional plays, lectures, and concerts during the week or two of Chautauqua programs in the summer.

In 1894, a group of the "intelligentsia" organized the Alabama Chautauqua Association. The first year performances were given in a tent at Shelby Springs. Difficulties in reaching the place on just one railroad caused the board of trustees to consider finding a permanent home elsewhere. A Talladega group bid successfully for it. From 1895 for many years the Chautauqua was a major intellectual treat in the state. To show the scope of the programs, we give here the one for July 5–21, 1899.

> July 5, 8 p.m.—Grand concert by Arion Ladies' Quartette of Chicago. Dr. W. L. Davidson, the superintendent of six Chautauquas, says this is the finest ladies' quartette in America.
>
> July 6, afternoon—An hour with Louis Spencer Daniel, the Tennessee orator, humorist, impersonator. . . .
>
> July 6, evening—Second concert of the Arions.
>
> July 7, afternoon—Last appearance of Daniel. Evening—Last concert of Arions.
>
> Saturday, July 8—Old Fashioned Competitive Singing from Sacred

Harp, four classes competing for prize. Afternoon—Fred W. Truman, the Chicago actor, impersonating twenty characters in Dickens' "Cricket on the Hearth." Evening.—Adrian Plate, the New York Wizard and wonderworker.

July 10—Adrian Plate in Legerademania, presenting Parisian novelties in the afternoon. At 8 p.m. Mr. Egerton R. Young of Toronto, lecturer on "Missionary Life Among the Indians." Dr. Young has a worldwide reputation as an author, hunter, and missionary. . . .

July 11, 4:30 p.m.—Fred W. Truman's impersonation of "Oliver Twist." Evening—Lecture by Dr. Egerton R. Young, "Romantic Life in the Land of the Auroras."

Wednesday, July 12, 4 p.m.—An hour of song, philosophy and fun with T. Elmore Lucey, the author, funny man and singer. Evening— Goodbye lecture of Dr. Egerton Young, "By Canoe and Dog-Train."

Thursday, July 13, 4 p.m.—T. Elmore Lucey in entertainment, "The Scrap Basket." Evening—Rosani, the wonderful equilibrist and juggler in balancing feats and illusions.

Friday, July 14, 4 p.m.—Last appearance of Rosani, the wizard in puzzling poising. Evening—John F. Dillon, the New York entertainer, in songs and stories.

Saturday, July 15, 11 a.m.—Fiddlers' contest. Evening—John F. Dillon in laughing songs and after dinner stories.

Monday, July 17, 4 p.m.—R. H. Mohr, the lightning crayon king and ventriloquist. Evening—John Temple Graves in new lecture.

Tuesday, July 18, 4 p.m.—Mohr, in electric sketches with crayon, and oddities. Evening—Second lecture by John Temple Graves.

Wednesday, July 10, 11 a.m.—College oratorical contest between State University, Auburn, Howard and Southern University. Question: "Resolved, That the United States should not have acquired the Philippines." State University and Howard have the affirmative. Evening—Entertainment by D. L. Leftwich, the baritone singer and humorist.

Thursday, July 20, 4 p.m.—Concert by the Kentucky Colonels Male Quartet. Evening—Lecture by Hon. J. Thomas Heflin of Alabama.

Friday, July 21, 4 p.m.—Concert by Kentucky Colonels. 5 p.m.—Lecture by Honr. A. W. Cozart of Georgia, "The Dignity of Ignorance." Evening—Farewell concerts by the bands and quartettes at 8, [At] 9 p.m. Lecture by Hon. A. W. Cozart, "A Fusillade of Facts and Fun." 10:30—"Home Sweet Home."

—*The Chronicle* (Columbiana), June 1, 1899.

The management offered a week's tickets for $1.75, which meant, as the publicity emphasized, the price of each event was only 7 cents. With many recreational resources available—mineral springs, mountain climbing, wheeling, lawn tennis, and fishing—Talladega was the ideal spot for a delightful summer vacation for the tired worker.

Within white society a new city class developed; its wealth and social position based on industry, mining, banking, merchandising or railroading, and not on planting. While the proud old families were still respected, especially in small towns and rural communities, they found that they had to make the transition to a new era (which usually meant making money in some way) or sink into oblivion. Men like B. B. Comer, Reuben F. Kolb, Thomas G. Jones and others, at home in the old era, made places for themselves in the new industrial world. In rural sections, the planter often became a merchant also and dominated the economic life of the community. The Populist movement gave the white small farmers their first political importance but, generally speaking, classes went their own way with little contact between them.

Birmingham was the fastest growing industrial city and naturally was the center of the new urban society. The most publicized social event there was the "Calico Ball," given when the young city was recovering from the cholera epidemic of 1873.

THE CALICO BALL

On the night of December 31, 1873, Charles Linn, a prominent pioneer of Birmingham, issued invitations to "A Calico Ball," which was intended to celebrate the passing of the cholera and the opening of the new building of the National Bank of Birmingham, of which he was president.

This ball was the first big social event since the cholera epidemic which swept the city like wild-fire and sent hundreds from their homes fleeing from the disease. This event brought the citizenship together again for an evening of dancing and pleasure such as was enjoyed in those days.

The scene of the ball was the second floor of the Bank Building, just completed on the spot where the Brown-Marx Building now stands.

Upon written invitations, the guests, probably five hundred, assembled about nine p. m., on the last night of 1873 to dance the old year out and the new year in. They were greeted at the head of the stairs by the host and his family and given a cordial welcome.

Promptly on the stroke of 9 a band from Montgomery, led by Mr. DeJarnette, which had come to Birmingham especially for this event, began playing the strains of a lively march and the host, taking the lead in the grand march, brought all the dancers to the floor. The figures which were danced were the Virginia reel, lancers, cotillion, Spanish dance, as well as the later popular round dance.

The young ladies wore attractive calico evening dresses, some with trains of various hues and trimmings, some donning the shepherd checks patterns trimmed in solid colors, others black with ermine trimmings and some wore "imported gowns" from Montgomery.

Miss Sallie Harrison (now Mrs. R. H. Pearson) was awarded the prize for the prettiest dress, looking most attractive in a "Montgomery Model."

The gallant escorts wore full dress suits of calico. Mr. Linn was conspicuous among them in his brown and tan calico suit with large buttons.

Several piano selections were rendered by one of the accomplished daughters of the host, Miss Lizzie Linn (the late Mrs. T. H. Molton).

Refreshments, consisted of sandwiches and coffee, and were served on the first floor after which the guests again assembled in the ball room for the midnight hour, when, on the stroke of 12, all stopped dancing and stood to observe the passing of '73 and the dawn of '74, marked by the lifting from view a panel revealing the figures 1873 and dropping into view a panel with the large figures of 1874, just on the twelfth stroke of the clock. This was one of the many original ideas of Mr. Linn. The ball continued until 2:30 a. m.—*Early Days in Birmingham* (Birmingham, Alabama: Birmingham Publishing Co., 1937), pp. 99–100.

With industrialization and subsequent organized unions, labor activities and Labor Day, first observed in 1882 and made a legal holiday in 1894, took on new importance. In Birmingham the local union officials announced plans for the forthcoming celebration.

GRAND LABOR HOLIDAY
PARTIAL LIST OF THE ANNUAL ATHLETIC GAMES, SPORTS AND PRIZES AT THE FREE LIBRARY PICNIC WHICH WILL ECLIPSE ALL FORMER EFFORTS!

The most extensive preparations are being made in all the larger cities throughout the country to surpass all previous demonstrations on next Labor Day. From New York, Boston, Philadelphia, Cleveland, Cincinnati, St. Louis, and other centers of organized Labor, comes intelligence of extraordinary arrangements for the very fullest representation in the annual parade. Following the grand demonstration in the streets of Birmingham on the morning of the national Labor holiday, Monday, September 5, will come the Free Library Picnic in the grounds of the capacious and beautiful Lakeview park, annual contests in the following athletic games and sports and brief synopsis of awards will be a prominent feature:

SPORTS AND GAMES

Scratch race—Drinking cup, Gresham & Sawyer.

Handicap—Pair gent's patent leather oxfords, Hann.

Obstacle race—Pair of shoes by Saint Pierre, quart of Baker rye by Hugh McGeever, box of Little Chief cigars by B. B. Hayes.

Prettiest baby under 12 months—One dozen best cabinet photos by the LABOR ADVOCATE.

Running jump—Pair of suspenders by J. Blach & Sons., one day's board at the Metropolitan hotel by E. Lesser.

Standing jump—Box of enamel paint by T. L. McGowan.

Sack race—Bottle fine whisky by Joe Frank.

Egg & spoon race for girls—Bottle of bay rum by J. W. Hughes, powder puff box by Wythington & Lynch.

Potatoe race for girls—Standard novel by John B. Roden.

Old man's race—Shirt by M. Weil.

Fat man's race—Half dozen pair of socks by Louis Saks, one dozen lemonettes by Houppert & Worcester.

Old man's jump—Necktie by Baltimore Clothing Co., box of Little Chief cigars by B. B. Hayes.

Pinioned race for rooster—Beautiful photo frame by J. W. O'Neill, The Fair.

One-legged race—Half dozen pair of socks by Simpson Bros.

Diving in tub for money—Silver dollar by Secretary Commercial club.

Blindfold wheel barrow race—Watch charm by Rosentihl Bros.

Race to bell—Silk umbrella by Anderson & Clapp

Girl's handicap—Fine fan by Caheen Bros. & Co.

Climbing greasy pole—Silk muffler by Sel Mavens.

Three-legged race—Box insect powder by Birmingham Drug & Chemical Co.

Trundle race for boys—Book by Smith & Montgomery, box by E. Bloch.

Swimming race—Neglige shirt by the Trade Palace.

Diving competition for length—Inch dial 24-hour clock by Harry Mercer.

Diving competition for time—Bottle of sarsparilla by B'ham Drug Co.

Putting the stone—Pipe by Fowlkes & Myatt.

Throwing the hammer—Coffee pot by Sinclair Bennie.

Running hop, step and jump—Pair of fine shoes by Ala. Mercantile Co.

Standing hop, step and jump—Bottle of perfume by Norton Drug Co.

All fours race—Ham by John Fox & Sons.

High Jumping—Silk handkerchief by Fire Store.

Long single running jump—Box candy by Kay Candy & Co., bottle of choice wine by D. L. Brennan.

Tug of war—Rogers pocket knife by May & Thomas, two kegs of beer by the Philip Schillenger Brewing Co., box of fine hand made cigars by John Ward, box of fine blue label cigars by E. Tully.

Most popular young lady—Handsome fan by Loveman, Joseph & Loeb, bottle of choice wine by F. Gallagher.

Best lady waltzer—Pair ladies' evening slippers by J. L. Chalifoux, jewelry receptacle by Parisian Store.

Best gentleman waltzer—Pair patent leather shoes by Pearson & Wyatt, box fine blue label cigars by Solomon & Levi.—*The Labor Advocate* (Birmingham), August 26, 1893.

Alabamians found pleasure in living. The form their enjoyment took may have ranged from a fat man's race at a Labor Day parade to a "tournament" with "knights" on horseback. There were some things that appealed to everyone and others in which class distinctions were still evident and would remain so until wealth, popular education, the automobile, and commercial entertainment of the next century would tend to blot them out.

Chapter 15

EDUCATION AFTER THE WAR

Progress in education in the post-war period was not outstanding. In 1854 Alabama had passed legislation necessary to establish public schools but had accomplished little more than laying the ground rules before the outbreak of the war. During the hostilities, many existing schools had to be closed and all education suffered. In spite of what appeared at the time to be a promising start under Reconstruction, public schools made disappointing gains. This state of affairs resulted from a number of factors: the "wanton extravagances" of carpetbag government; the hard economic philosophy of the Bourbon leaders; the general disinterest in public education; and the policy of maintaining a dual system of schools.

Of school conditions in the late years of the war we have only fragmentary reports. On March 1, 1865, John B. Taylor, state superintendent of education, informed Governor Thomas H. Watts that only fifteen of the thirty-seven counties had made reports on their public schools for the previous year. However, in Dallas County, some semblance of an orderly system had remained. Taylor, in acknowledging the report of Dallas County superintendent W. H. Huston, wrote:

> I am much gratified to learn from your letter of the 8th inst. that the absorbing and engrossing interest of the times and the perilous condition of the country have not retarded the educational interests of the populous and wealthy county which you represent, and that parents evince an "enthusiastic interest in the education of their children." Of a truth "carpe diem" should be the motto of our people at this time, for "we know not what a day may bring forth," nor how soon present advantages may pass away before the invasion of a ruthless foe. . . .—
> John B. Taylor to W. H. Huston, March 11, 1865, Stephen B. Weeks,

History of Public School of Education in Alabama (Washington: Government Printing Office, 1915), p. 81.

Superintendent Taylor expressed the hope that the Congress of the Confederacy would adopt some plan by which disabled service men could be used as teachers.

That there are any records at all was due to Taylor's foresight in carting them away prior to the approach of the Northern armies.

Taylor was in office until April 1, 1866; he was followed by John B. Ryan, who held the position until November 30, 1867. His successor, M. A. Chisholm, was in office less than a year, being removed on July 23, 1868, when Radical Reconstruction began. Dr. N. B. Cloud, who had long been an advocate of agricultural reform and editor of a leading Southern magazine and now a Republican, was head of public instruction from 1868 until 1870. His report for 1869 is the fullest we have for the four preceding years.

> I found that the previous government under the administration of Gov. Patton failed to pay the public-school money apportioned for the school year 1866 to quite a number of the counties of this state. It also failed to pay the public-school money apportioned for the school year 1867 to a much larger number of the counties. Some of the county superintendents received the public-school moneys thus apportioned for the years 1866 and 1867, either in part or in whole, as our books show; but others received none whatever notwithstanding public schools were taught. There seems to be no satisfactory reason to be had from any source explaining why it was that some of the counties received their apportionment . . . while others did not obtain any portion thereof.— Quoted in ibid., p. 84.

The Reconstruction constitution of 1868 (adopted in December, 1867) made public education the duty of the state and created a state Board of Education that had more power than any similar body in the state's history. It was given authority

> . . . to exercise full legislative powers in reference to the public educational institutions of the State, and its acts, when approved by the governor, or when reenacted by two-thirds of the board in case of his disapproval, shall have the force and effect of law, unless repealed by the general assembly.—Ibid., p. 87.

It was the duty of this board to establish in every township or school district at least one school which all children between the ages of five and twenty-one might attend free. The revenues to support these schools came from the old educational fund (made up chiefly of money from the sale of school lands), "one-fifth of the aggregate annual income of the State," poll taxes on all males from 20 to 45 years of age, and taxes leveled on railroads, navigation, banks, insurance companies, and many other companies and agencies.

Dr. Cloud's term of office coincided with the first years of carpetbag government and many of his acts reflected the problems of the times. He wisely decided that Negro schools should have a just share of the sixteenth section school funds; he engaged in a struggle with the Mobile County school authorities over control of their schools (which antedated the state school system and had remained independent of the state superintendent) ; he increased the number of schools for both blacks and whites; he established several normal schools (or at least those offering normal training in connection with existing institutions) ; he quarreled with the Conservatives over the text books, which he attempted to use in the public schools; and he spent $502,156.19 for schools in the last year of his term of office, an average of $1.39 per student. Dr. Cloud may have had the educational interests of Alabama at heart, but he was guilty of haphazard use of money. The governor declared his reports were not only unsatisfactory but revealed "a most shameful and reprehensible state of things."

Dr. Cloud's successor was Joseph Hodgson, a Conservative, who found many irregularities in the handling of school funds—funds unaccounted for and warrants unpaid. Hodgson reduced the administrative costs and during his two years raised the per school capita from $1.33 to $1.36. Hodgson was followed by J. H. Speed, the last man to serve as state superintendent before the restoration of white, home rule. Probably the most outstanding head of the educational system in the whole period was John M. McKleroy who went into office along with Governor George S. Houston and the other Democrat-Conservatives.

The economy-minded politicians were reluctant to spend money on schools, but during the first year McKleroy was able to raise the expenditures on white students to $3.09 per school term of 90 days and $3.79 on the Negroes for a term of 83 days, more than doubling the previous amounts. McKleroy apparently made these gains by careful handling of the funds at the state level and through the dedicated services of the county superintendents of education who were paid on the average $436.96 for the year. Their salary was a mere pittance, yet they gave the schools a multitude of services. Their duties were:

> To have a general superintendence of all free public schools in his
> county; to see that schools are established in each township, and for
> each race, according to law; to visit each school at least once a year;

to note the course and method of instruction, and the branches taught in each; the manner in which teachers discharge their duties and keep their records; the text books used; and examine into the condition of the school buildings, and all other school property; to see that no sectarian religious views be taught in any free public school; to examine all persons applying for license to teach in the public schools, and to grant certificates to such as he may find qualified; to supervise the contracts made by trustees with teachers, and see that the law is in all respects complied with, and to approve or disapprove such contracts, as the law, and the justice and equity of each case may require; to receive, hold and disburse the school fund according to law, and keep proper records of the same; to look after the 16th section lands of his county, see which are sold or not, and to see that those not sold are leased properly, and to protect all against trespasses; to take charge of any money, funds, or property of any kind raised in his county, by county taxation, or which may accrue to the county for educational purposes by gift, bequest, devise, endowment, or otherwise, and see to the proper disposition of the same; to appoint trustees in cases of vacancy, to remove incompetent ones, to see that all perform the duties required of them, and to perform the duties of trustees himself in those townships where no suitable persons will act as trustees; to organize and hold annually one or more teachers' institutes in his county, and to attend the same, and encourage all teachers and school officers and friends of public education in his county, to do the same; to look after the collection of the poll tax, and see that all that is collected is paid over to the school fund of his county, to apportion the same and make report thereof to the Superintendent of Public Instruction; to have the enumeration of persons within the school age in his county, taken at the times prescribed by law and to consolidate the reports and make a return of the same to Superintendent of Public Instruction; to see that a sufficient number of school houses are provided for each township, and to urge and encourage patrons and trustees to give their attention and their means to erection of such, and to furnish them properly; to hear and decide all appeals from the actions of the boards of trustees, and settle disputes between trustees, teachers, and patrons, &c.; to keep an accurate account with each township and race in his county; to notify trustees of the apportionment to their townships respectively, and see that no schools are opened until such apportionment is made, and notice given; to account quarterly with the Superintendent of Public Instruction for all school money received and disbursed by him; to make to the Superintendent of Public Instruction all such financial, statistical, and narrative reports, annually and quarterly, as may be required of him; to keep informed as to the school laws, and to instruct teachers, trustees, and patrons as to their duties respectively, and to give to all persons interested such information as they may desire, respecting the school system; and to be the general medium of communication between this department and the school districts and officers of his county, besides many other direct and incidental duties.—*Report of John M. McKleroy, Superintendent of Public*

Instruction for the Year Ending September 30th, 1875 (Montgomery, Ala.: W. W. Screws, State Printer, 1875), pp. 17–18.

McKleroy's report, which appears to be the most complete to that date, indicated funds were inadequate for the maintenance of a good school system and that outside the cities the school buildings were few and of "an inferior kind." There were three normal schools in operation. Florence has the distinction of being the first (1872) of the normals to survive. The normal at Marion for Negroes was later moved to Montgomery and became Alabama State College (eventually, university) for Negroes.

The Peabody Fund

Superintendent McKleroy reported that the financial situation, admittedly dark, was brightened somewhat by the "generous and judicious appropriations made by the Trustees of the Peabody Education Fund in aid to our public schools," which received from $4,300 to $10,000 per year from this fund from 1868 to 1876.

The Peabody Fund played an important role in public education in the South in the post-war years. It was established by George Peabody, a native of Massachusetts who had reversed the western movement by going to England where he made a fortune in shipping. In 1866 he gave a gift of $2,100,000 which he increased to $3,500,000 in 1869. It was to be used exclusively for schools in the destitute areas of the South. George Peabody College for Teachers at Nashville is the best known product of the fund, but it helped establish or maintain schools in many places and for both races and financed teachers' institutes throughout the state. It did not make donations to colleges, academies, or private, sectarian, or charity schools; the amounts were determined by the daily average attendance. Just as soon as a school system could take care of its needs, it was the policy to cut off funds and apply them to new and needier places.

The first agent of the fund was Dr. Barnas Sears, a graduate of Brown University and later its president. In 1875 he answered McKleroy's request for information about the sum Alabama could expect.

> . . . we aid most those who help themselves most. If the people do little, we do little; if they do nothing, we do nothing . . . .
>
> I can not specify any amount for Alabama just now; first, because I do not yet know definitely what that State and others will attempt this year; and, secondly, because I do not yet know what our income will be . . . . If your schools come fully up to the work as it is done in other states, we may go as far as eight or ten thousand dollars . . . .— Sears to McKleroy, August 2, 1875, ibid., p. 33.

AMOUNTS APPORTIONED TO PUBLIC SCHOOLS IN ALABAMA, FROM THE "PEABODY EDUCATION FUND."

LOCATION	1868	1869	1870	1871	1872	1873	1874	1875	1876
Birmingham	$.....	$.....	$.....	$.....	$.....	$.....	$ 1,000.00	$ 700.00	$ 700.00
Columbiana		200.00	200.00	200.00			200.00		
County Line		300.00							
Girard		1,000.00	600.00	600.00					
Greensboro	400.00	1,000.00	1,000.00		2,000.00		1,000.00		
Huntsville			1,000.00	1,000.00	1,000.00	1,000.00	1,000.00	1,000.00	1,000.00
LaFayette			550.00						
Mobile	2,000.00			2,000.00	2,000.00	2,000.00	2,000.00		
Montgomery		1,500.00		1,500.00	1,500.00	1,500.00	2,000.00	1,500.00	2,000.00
Opelika		1,000.00			1,000.00	1,000.00	1,000.00		
Roanoke									300.00
Selma	2,000.00	2,000.00	2,000.00	2,000.00	1,500.00	1,500.00	1,500.00		
Talladega	1,000.00								
Union Springs							300.00		
Uniontown	1,000.00								
Wetumpka									300.00
Totals	$6,400.00	$7,000.00	$5,350.00	$7,300.00	$9,000.00	$7,000.00	$10,000.00	$3,200.00	$4,300.00

—Ibid., p. 69.

At Dr. Sears' death (1881), Rev. J. L. M. Curry formerly of Talladega, once president of Howard College in Marion, and at the time of his election on the faculty at Richmond College, was unanimously elected to fill the office as agent of the fund. He remained in that post until he was made minister to Spain in 1885. Eleven years later (1896) he returned to the Peabody Fund. He spent much of his time urging legislatures to appropriate funds adequate to the needs of the schools. He was interested in new departures in education and when in Alabama he liked to make unannounced visits to Noble Institute in Anniston and the Alabama Girls' Industrial School in Montevallo. In January, 1898, he spent a day at the latter school, visiting each department and exhibiting much interest in what he saw.

School Attendance and Support

The tables Weeks has compiled vividly show the tortuous road of public schools in the post-war period. Even after making allowances for inaccurate statistics, the picture is less than heartening. The number of schools fluctuated considerably for no apparent reason. In 1868–69, for example, there were 2,824 but the next year there were only 1,845. However, in 1871 the number was 3,470 and in spite of fluctuations was by 1900 more than 6,000. According to Weeks, the average monthly salary in 1871 was $42.52; in 1878–79 it had fallen to $20.96 for whites but was $26.57 for Negroes; by the end of the century, the average monthly salary for white teachers was $25.05 but for Negroes was only $17.66. While monthly salaries were low, the annual income for teachers was even lower because of the short school terms. In 1869 the average length of the term for all children was 49 days; by 1900 the whites attended 68 days and blacks 62 days, but in the mid-eighties the number had been more than 87 days for children of both races. The number of children increased steadily and the state nearly doubled the money it set aside for public schools, yet the expenditure per child was even lower at the end of the century than it had been in 1868—$1.44 to $1.47. However, the lowest per child expenditure had been in 1875–76 when it was only 85 cents.

The Report on Public Schools for 1894–1895 breaks down the figures even more.

REPORT ON PUBLIC SCHOOLS
1894–95

Number of white schools	4,626
Number of colored schools	2,294
Total number of schools	6,920

Teachers in white schools, male	2,878
Teachers in white schools, female	1,826
Total teachers in white schools	4,706
Teachers in colored schools, male	1,322
Teachers in colored schools, female	966
Total teachers in colored schools	2,288
Total teachers employed	6,994
Total enrollment	319,526
Average monthly pay for white teachers	$24.03
Average monthly pay for colored teachers	$18.71
Average monthly pay for all teachers	$21.37
Average length of school in days, white	72½
Average length of school in days, colored	65⅓

—*Circular of Information from the Department of Education of Alabama* (Montgomery: 1898), p. 36.

These figures did not apply to schools in cities or to separate school districts. Nearly all of those systems maintained schools for nine months each year.

Public School Contract

The date of the following teacher's contract is slightly later than the period under consideration, but the form was standard for many years.

PUBLIC SCHOOL CONTRACT

The State of Alabama, *Clay* County.

THIS AGREEMENT, made this *27th* day of *Oct.,* 1906, between *Leona Thompson,* Teacher, and the County Board of Education in and for *Clay* County. Witnesseth: That the said *Leona Thompson* agrees to teach a *Third* Grade Public School for the *white* race at Schoolhouse No *1* in District No *59* for the term of *five* scholastic months, beginning on the *15th* day of *November* 1906.

The said *Leona Thompson* further agrees to exert the utmost of *her* ability in conducting said school and improving the education and morals of the pupils, to keep such register, and make such reports to the District and County Board of Education, as may be required of *her,* and in all respects to conform to the other requirements of law.

In consideration of these services, properly rendered, the County Board of Education agrees that the County Superintendent of Education of said county shall pay the said *Leona Thompson* Teacher, *Twenty eight dollars* Dollars per Month from the General School Fund *$28.00* and *all poll tax* dollars of Poll Tax apportioned to said race in said District, for the Scholastic Year ending September 30th, 190__, the payments to be made monthly, as prescribed by law.

_____ Teacher.

W. H. Griffin
J. D. Garrett
D. L. Campbell
F. G. McCain
County Board of
Education.

Approved by direction of County Board of Education, this *November 12th, 1906*

A. S. Ham
County Superintendent
of Education

—Contract is by the courtesy of Mrs. J. M. Deupree, Sylacauga, and Mrs. Jake Richerson, Goodwater.

The state had some normal schools before 1900, but most of its teachers received certificates upon examination by a county board of examiners. Mitchell B. Garrett, who grew up in the Hatchet Creek community, remembered the way teachers were examined and the methods they used in finding a position.

It was not difficult in the eighteen eighties and nineties to get a license to teach school in Clay County, Alabama. On the day appointed for the purpose the prospective teacher, usually a man, repaired to Ashland, the county seat, and took an examination prepared, supervised, and graded by the County Superintendent of Education, an official elected by popular vote. For a dozen years or more in succession the County Superintendent was A. S. Stockdale. "Col." Stockdale was not a teacher himself, but a mediocre lawyer and smooth politician, who knew how to keep himself in office by currying favor with the voters. Readily, on payment of the legally established fee, he handed out first grade, second grade, and third grade certificates by virtue of the authority in him vested by law and the tacit consent of the Board of Education.

After getting his license, the prospective teacher visited a community in need of a teacher and made a canvass of the situation. To each patron of the school he presented written articles of agreement stipulating the length of the term, the amount of his salary, and other conditions. Presently a meeting of the trustees and patrons was held at the schoolhouse to discuss and possibly to ratify the articles of agreement.

Usually the most serious problem was financial. How much of the public funds could be counted on for this school for the coming year? How much could be raised by subscription?

In the end, the candidate for the teaching job would probably be employed to teach a seven months school, beginning in November, for the sum, say, of $280. Since the school could hardly expect more than, say, $70 from the public funds, $210 would have to be raised by subscription. The newly appointed teacher was expected, of course, to

make the rounds of the community and collect the necessary pledges.—
Mitchell B. Garrett, *Horse and Buggy Days on Hatchet Creek* (University, Alabama: University of Alabama Press, 1957), pp. 136–37.

Once hired, teachers were given in-service training at teachers'
institutes (sometimes paid for by the Peabody Fund) such as the
one at Centreville.

PROGRAMME OF THE TEACHERS INSTITUTE TO BE HELD AT CENTREVILLE, AUGUST 18, 1883

10 A. M.	Statement of the objects and aims of the county institute by the President.
10:30 A. M.	Subject of discussion: What proportion of the pupil's time should be spent in the study of arithmetic? Opened by D. C. Logan.
11:15 A. M.	What studies should be pursued in the public schools? Opened by Sam'l Sellers.
2 P. M.	Should corporeal punishment be abolished in our schools? Opened by M. J. Greathouse.
2:30 P. M.	How can we elevate the standard of teachers? Opened by R. H. Pratt.
3 P. M.	What elements of character and attainments are necessary in the true teacher? Opened by H. K. W. Smith.
3:30 P. M.	What are the teachers' rewards? Essay by Miss Annie Kennedy.
4 P. M.	What are the teachers' trials? Essay by Mrs. M. L. Conwill. What should be the aim of the teacher in conducting a recitation? Opened by J. M. Langston.

Board of Education

Township superintendents are invited and requested to come.—*The Bibb Blade* (Six Mile), August 6, 1883.

As these institutes became more frequent and teachers began
forming associations, they and other school officials gave attention
to questions of common interest, especially those concerning curriculum and textbooks about which there was little agreement. The
first unified plans were at the county or local rather than the state
level. Gadsden was one of the leaders in the movement.

Gadsden adopted a graded system in the mid-1890's. Most schools
remained ungraded and the standards of achievement individualized
until much later.

FIRST COURSE OF STUDY 1895–96
FIRST GRADE

Reading	McGuffey's First Reader	Reading from chart and blackboard in script.
Spelling	No text	Phonic drills every day. Words selected from chart and reader.
Language	No text	Oral works, conversational, oral

		expressions and sentence build-ing, oral reproduction.
Writing	Copy Book	Slate work, pencil work, tracing.
Drawing	No text	Slate and blackboard work, form and color emphasized.
Geography	No text	Oral work. Develop the idea of direction and distance as ap-plied to the school grounds, the city, the county and state.
Numbers	No text	Counting to 100 by successive ad-ditions using 1, 2, 3, and 4 respectively. Mental and written addition, subtraction, multiplica-tion and division to 12. Writing numbers to 1000.

SECOND GRADE

Reading	McGuffey's Second Reader	
Spelling	No text	Phonic drills continued. Words se-lected from reader and other texts.
Language	No text	Oral and written. Conversation and picture lessons, reproduction of stories, letter writing.
Writing	Tracing books 2, 3, and 4	Using pen and ink.
Drawing	Bartholomew's, Books 1 & 2	
Geography	No text	Map of city, county, and State of Alabama to be drawn on black-board. Talk about the State, its boundaries, physical features, resources, cities, products, oc-cupations. Develop the idea of shape and surface of Earth.
Numbers	No text	Writing numbers to 1,000,000. The operation of addition and sub-traction. Multiplication tables.

THIRD GRADE

Reading	McGuffey's Third Reader	
Spelling	McGuffey's Speller	Also words taken from reader. Oral and written work.
Language	No text	Oral and written descriptions.
Writing	Spencerian Copy Books Nos. 1 & 2	
Drawing	Bartholomew's, Books 3 & 4	
Geography	Maurey's Elementary Geography	Beginning to Middle Atlantic States.
Numbers	Ray's New Elem. Arithmetic	To U. S. Money.
	New Intellectual Arithmetic	To fractions.

FOURTH GRADE

Reading	McGuffey's Fourth Reader	Pupils taught how to use dic-tionary.
Spelling	McGuffey's	Also words taken from texts.
Language	Long's Lessons in English No. 2	Oral and written descriptions, nar-ratives and short stories.
Writing	Spencerian Copy Books Nos. 3 & 4	
Drawing	Bartholomew's Books 5 & 6	
Geography	Maurey's Elementary Geography	Completed and reviewed.
Numbers	Ray's New Elem. Arithmetic	To decimal fractions.
	New Intellectual Arithmetic	To page 62.
Physiology	Cutter's Elementary	First half of book.

FIFTH GRADE

Reading	McGuffey's Fifth Reader	Memorized selections once each month.
Spelling	McGuffey's	Words from textbooks.
Language	Long's Lessons in English, No. 3	Composition and letter writing.
Writing	Spencerian Copy Books Nos. 5 & 6	
Drawing	Bartholomew's Books 7 & 8	
Geography	Maurey's Manual	First 59 pages.
History	No text	Oral instruction on the history of Alabama.
Numbers	Ray's Elementary Arithmetic	Completed.
	Ray's Practical Arithmetic	First 130 pages.
	New Intellectual Arithmetic	To page 90.
Physiology	Cutter's Elementary	Completed.

SIXTH GRADE

Reading	McGuffey's Sixth Reader	Reading newspapers and magazines at sight. Memorization.
Spelling	McGuffey's Speller	Completed. Also words from all textbooks.
Language	Holbrook's New English Grammar	Composition & letter writing. First half of book.
Writing	Spencerian Copy Books Nos. 7 & 8	
Drawing	Bartholomew's, Books 9 & 10	
Geography	Maurey's Manual	To page 101.
History	Normal History of the United States	First half of book.
Arithmetic	Ray's New Practical Arithmetic	Pages 130 to 219.
	Intellectual Arithmetic	Pages 90 to 134.
Physiology	Cutter's Advanced	First half of book.

SEVENTH GRADE

Reading	English Classics	
Spelling	No text	Words selected from Texts.
Language	Holbrook's English Grammer	Completed.
Writing	Spencerian Copy Books Nos. 9 & 10	
Drawing	Bartholomew's, Books 11 & 12	
Geography	Maurey's Manual	Completed.
History	Normal History of the United States	Completed.
Arithmetic	Ray's New Practical Arithmetic	Completed.
	Intellectual Arithmetic	Completed.
Physiology	Cutter's Advanced	Completed.

—1895—The Public Schools—1951 (Gadsden) (no copyright, no pagination, no date).

A few years later, Talladega County adopted a uniform course of study for the whole county. To show the comparison within a short geographical distance and span of time, the curriculum for the first two grades and the seventh grade is given here.

COURSE OF STUDY
Adopted by Board of Education for the
Public Schools of Talladega County

FIRST GRADE.
Holton's Primer.

Baldwin's First Reader.

Combining of numbers from 1 to 10, including addition, subtraction, multiplication and division.

Writing numbers to 1000; small fractions.

Geography—Cardinal points, directions and distance, use of inch, foot, yard, rod, mile, etc.

History—Myths, stories and legends interestingly told. The relation of personality to be made prominent.

Writing and drawing under direction of teacher.

Spelling—Selected words.

Supplementary Reader.

Graded Literature—Book One; "Hand in Hand with the Wise Men."

SECOND GRADE.

Baldwin's Second Reader.

Arithmetic—Combining of numbers from 1 to 100, as in the first grade.

Van Amburgh's "First Days in Numbers."

Geography—Develop maps of County, State, United States and Globe.

Spelling—Selected words Branson's First Book to page 65.

Copy Books, A. & B. (semi-slant.)

Language—Oral and written reproduction. Develop idea of one and more than one. Also idea of subject and predicate without naming them specifically.

History—Local biography, fairy tales.

Drawing—Book One.

Supplementary Reader.

Graded Literature—Book Two.

Eggleston's Stories of Great Americans.

SEVENTH GRADE.

Baldwin's Seventh Reader.

Spelling—Reed's Word Lessons, Reviewed; Blank Speller.

Language—Modern English Grammer completed from page 143.

Writing—Selected copies.

Arithmetic—Advanced completed; Mental arithmetic.

History—Higher of U. S. completed.

Geography—In connection with history and civics.

Civics—Peterman's Civil Government.

Supplementary Readers—Lamb's Tales from Shakespeare; Dicken's Christmas Stories.

—"Rules and Regulations and Courses of Study for the Public Schools of Talladega County by County Board of Education, October 10, 1904" (pamphlet), courtesy Mrs. J. M. Deupree and Mrs. Richerson.

Standardization in grading and textbooks was a luxury reserved for town schools or a rare progressive county. In the rural schools teaching methods had changed little for decades. A man who received his early education in Clay County described the school he attended which was typical of the rural, public school.

No law had ever been passed establishing a uniform system of text-books for the public schools of the state, but what the legislature had failed to do had been done, to all intents and purposes, by custom and tradition. In the schools of Clay County the basic textbooks were Webster's *Blue Back Speller* and *McGuffey's Readers.*

The first task of the beginning pupil was to learn the letters of the alphabet which were printed for his convenience on page 15 of the *Speller.* In the first two columns of the page were the Roman letters, small and capital; in the third and fourth columns were the Italic letters, small and capital; in the fifth column were the names of the letters spelled out, thus: *a, be, ce, de, e, ef, je, aytch,* and so on down to *wi* and *ze.* On page 16 were the Old English letters, small and capital; the letters in script, small and capital; and the arabic numerals in script. Fortunately the pupil was seldom required to learn much more than the Roman letters.

After the alphabet came the syllabarium which contained tables of nonsense syllables, two letters in length, such as: *ba, be, bi, bo, bu.* The pupil, with his eyes on the page and his index finger properly pointed, spelled each of these syllables orally and pronounced it. Then followed tables of three-letter syllables, such as: *bla, ble, bli, blo, blu,* and then tables of easy one-syllable words, such as: *bog, log, dog,* or *edge, wedge, hedge.* It was a proud day when the pupil reached two-syllable words, such as: *baker, shady, lady.*

Thus the pupil advanced from syllables to easy words, and from easy words to words that progressively became harder until he reached words of many syllables. Never was he allowed to forget that words are composed of syllables. When spelling a word of more than one syllable, he was required to pronounce each syllable when the spelling of that syllable was completed, then, dropping back, to pronounce the syllables spelled thus far, and, when the last syllable was spelled and pronounced, to bring his chant to a conclusion by pronouncing the entire word. Thus: I-N in, C-O-M com, incom, P-R-E pre, incompre, H-E-N hen, incomprehen, S-I si, incomprehensi, B-I-L bil, incomprehensibil, I i, incomprehensibili, T-Y ti, incomprehensibility.

Seldom did it happen that a pupil knew the meaning of a single word in his spelling lesson. But that did not matter. What do you want to know the meaning of words for?

Ordinarily during the first year of school the pupil had no other text-book than the *Blue Back Speller.* When he had spelled his way as far as *baker* on page 25, he was turned back to the syllabarium for a fresh start. On his second journey forward he probably advanced as far as *banquet* on page 34 before he was turned back for another fresh start. After his third fresh start he probably made his way as far as *luminary* on page 51 before he was again turned back. By this time he was eight years old and ready for *McGuffey's First Reader.* But he kept his spelling book and continued for two or three years more, if indeed he remained in school that long, to advance and retreat over its difficult pages, until he reached *cachexy* and *chalybeate* on page 124 and at long last the pictures and fables at the end of the book.

McGuffey's Readers were an improvement over the *Blue Back Speller* in that they were designed to combine the word method with the phonic method in teaching reading. The pupil was encouraged to recognize simple words or groups of words at first glance, but if he encountered a word which he did not recognize immediately he was required to spell and pronounce it before going on to the next word. In the first lessons of the *First Reader* words of only two or three letters were used. Gradually longer and more difficult ones were introduced as the pupil gained aptness in the mastery of words. At the head of each lesson was a list of words that had not been used in previous lessons. These new words were to be spelled, pronounced, and rendered thoroughly familiar before the lesson for the day was read. The carefully chosen pictures that accompanied the lessons were designed to arouse the interest of the pupil. Arithmetic . . . was a subject of which all the patrons of rural schools recognized the practical value. Even before a pupil had completed the *Second Reader,* he was usually introduced to Robinson's *Primary Arithmetic.* Here he learned how to write arabic numerals, how to use the plus and minus signs, the signs of multiplication and division and of equality, how to perform simple arithmetical operations. Here also he was likely to have his initial encounter with the bar sinister to the study of arithmetic, namely, the multiplication table. This multiplication table had to be learned by heart, a task which required several sessions of school and much drilling on the part of the teacher.

Robinson's *Practical Arithmetic,* which was taken up by the pupil in his early teens and pursued during the rest of his academic career, was the principal study of the whole curriculum. In the popular mind the teacher's qualifications were measured by the deftness and dispatch with which he could solve the hardest problems in this notable book, and the pupil's progress toward a practical education was measured by the number of pages which he covered. Parents' enthusiasm for the cause of education rose and fell with the degree of effectiveness with which arithmetic was taught in the school.

Problems in arithmetic were "figured out" on slates or on the blackboard.

Today the slate, with its soft stone pencil, has given way before the cheap scratch pad, but in the eighties and nineties it was the commonest article of the school child's equipment. The strongest argument against the use of the slate was hygienic. Fastidious teachers might show their pupils how to erase writing with a damp cloth or sponge, but to school children this seemed a long-way-around method of achieving results that could be just as efficaciously attained by saliva and a brisk rubbing with hand or coat sleeve.

The blackboard was the handiwork of some local carpenter. It consisted of three wide boards, from ten to fifteen feet long, smoothly planed and painted black, and held in place, edge to edge, by "tongue and groove" and by cross pieces which extended far enough on one edge to serve as legs. This clumsy contrivance, with its painted surface exposed to the room, was stood on its legs and leant against the wall in front of the recitation benches. Pupils wrote on the blackboard with chalk and used old rags and pieces of sheepskin for erasers.

It was with chalk and slate pencils that pupils learned to write. If a teacher should happen to be adept with his Spencerian pen, he might encourage his larger pupils to bring copybooks, pens, and inkstands to school and let him give them instruction in penmanship. But the initial enthusiasm was likely to wane quickly. The furniture of most rural schoolhouses, consisting, as it did, of long benches, like church pews, and rickety desks, made penmanship a difficult undertaking. The copybook was a quire of foolscap paper swathed for protection in a discarded newspaper; the steel pen which fitted snugly into its holder was easily ruined by unskillful handling or by an accidental drop, point downwards, to the floor; and the open inkstand was easily overturned by a careless gesture or the wobble of a rickety desk, to the detriment of desk, clothing, and the sweet disposition of all concerned. The overall result was that very few pupils ever learned to write with a pen.

No law of the state required parents to send their children to school. As a consequence, attendance was woefully irregular.—Garrett, *Horse and Buggy Days on Hatchet Creek, pp.* 137–39, 141–43.

In the 1960's an elderly man of Wilton recounted for a young neighbor his memories of a country school in the 1890's.

I started to school when I was seven. This was in 1894. It was called Elder School. It was three or four miles north of Six Mile in Bibb Country. It was just a country school. It was a log school house. It was about thirteen by twenty. It had just one room. There was one window in the back. It was just a hole in the wall. The only light came through this window and the door. It was heated by a fireplace. We had to bring in wood from the woods to burn. We didn't have desks. We sat on benches without backs. We had to write in our lap.

It was three miles from my house to the school. I walked it everyday. Nobody had anything to ride. The teacher even walked. We had to carry water and food to school with us. I remember we use to warm our biscuits or potatoes on the limestone in the fireplace that were used as firedogs. We just brushed the ashes off and laid them on the hot rock. It worked well.

We didn't have a ball field. We just played in the woods. We just ran up and down jumping ditches. We couldn't get out of sight of the school. School started at eight and lasted until four. We had to go about three months every year. Usually it was during November, December, and January. The only thing we had to write on was a slate. They were usually twelve inches by fifteen inches. We didn't have blackboards, maps, globes, or anything like that. Miss Belle Lightsey was my teacher. We used the McGuffey Reader and the Blue Back Speller. We just had reading, writing and some arithmetic. Every Friday evening we had a spelling test. There were children from seven to fifteen years old going to this school. There were about twenty-one in all. The little ones generally had spelling and reading. The older ones had harder reading and spelling, and also arithmetic. Sometimes summer schools were held. I went to summer school several times. We had a recess at 10:00 o'clock thirty minutes long. We got an hour for dinner. After dinner we had an hour play period. I went to Elder School off and on for five years. After that I went to Six Mile School.

Six Mile School was a two-story frame building. This was in 1899 or 1900. This school was a lot better. We had heaters that burned coal. We had glass windows in this building. We had plenty of light but there was no electricity. There were three rooms. We had desks with ink wells and a place for a pencil and a drawer under the top. The tops were smooth. We had a blackboard too. We would work our arithmetic problems on it.

When I went to Six Mile School, I had to get up at 4:00 o'clock in the morning to do my work and then get ready for school. School started at eight and ended at three. We went to school five or six months out of the year. . . .—Mr. A. C. McElroy to Benny Nash, interview (1967).

High Schools

Secondary education (preparation for college) was given in academies, usually designated as "male" and "female." Very few of them were coeducational. Green Springs Academy continued to function until Dr. Henry Tutwiler's death in 1884. Mt. Sterling Academy in Choctaw County was considered almost its equal and attracted students from several Southern states. Marion Military Institute, Noble Institute in Anniston, and many other institutes and seminaries at centers such as Athens, Mobile, Selma, Tuskeegee, provided preparation for college. The movement for free high schools did not reach Alabama until after the turn of the century (Dallas County High School at Plantersville was established in 1908, making it the oldest in the state) so that before that date high schools, by whatever name, were tuition schools.

ROCKFORD HIGH SCHOOL
Rockford, Ala., March 27, 1882.

The school, at this place, now numbers about sixty pupils, and is still growing. The building has been enlarged and is now quite a comfortable school-room.

The water is as good as any in the State. The health of Rockford is unsurpassed by any town in the South.

Board can be obtained for pupils at from $8 to $10 a month.

TUITION

1st Class	$1,50.
2d "	$2,00.
3d "	$2,50.

4th "	$3,00.
5th "	$4,00.

Those at a distance who wish to send their children to a healthy location to school, and where they will receive needed attention, can find no better place than Rockford.

Discipline strict, but mild. We promise you to discharge our duty fully toward your children, should they be placed under our charge.

Society here is first class. Two Sabbath schools under excellent management. No whiskey sold in or near the Town.

Feeling that should you give us a trial you will have no cause to regret it, I am

Very respectfully,
O. C. BENTLEY,
Principal.

—Handbill, courtesy Mrs. Deupree and Mrs. Richerson.

The curriculum in the first year in high school at Decatur included a variety of subjects.

EIGHTH GRADE or FIRST YEAR HIGH SCHOOL

Latin ....Harkness Introductory Grammar and Reader.
English ....Waddy's Composition and Rhetoric.
Arithmetic ....Ray's New Higher Arithmetic.
Algebra ....Ray's New Elementary.
Geography ....Maurey's Physical Geography.
History ....Montgomery's English History.
Civics ....Civil Government in the U. S.
Spelling ....Words Selected from Textbooks.

Talladega County schools offered similar courses.

EIGHTH GRADE.
Advanced Physiology.
Advanced Arithmetic, (Reviewed.)
Elementary Algebra.
English History, (Coman & Kendall's.)
Physical Geography, (Davis)
Lockwood's Composition and Rhetoric.
English literature.

NINTH GRADE.
Advanced Algebra.
Plane Geometry.
Lockwood's Composition and Rhetoric.
Myer's General History.
Gage's Physics.
American Literature.
Physiology should be taught orally in the first five grades.

Negro Education

Many problems of Negro schools were the same ones that white schools faced. The problems of the freedmen, however, were compounded by the fact that there had been no formal schools for them before 1865 and therefore there were no foundations on which to build, and by the fact that the whole question became political rather than educational. Radical Republicans made education for the blacks a main issue of their regime.

In the last years of the war and immediately thereafter the blacks exhibited considerable interest in schooling. The whole race seemingly wanted to go to school. Booker T. Washington later said old and young alike shared the universal desire for education. Furthermore, white Alabamians generally agreed that some form of education for the freedmen would have to be devised and newspapers and churches all over the state publicly supported the idea. It was generally accepted by both whites and blacks that whites would be the teachers and that school would be segregated.

There is little information about the schools before northern agencies moved in except that in a number of communities both races cooperated in erecting school buildings. It is uncertain whether there were any schools in actual operation before representatives of the Freedmen's Bureau and the various aid and missionary societies moved into the state. The original act establishing the Bureau made no provsion for educational activities, but General O. O. Howard convinced Congress that funds could be well spent in educating the freedmen. Consequently, on July 16, 1866, legislation was passed giving the Bureau this right. In theory the Bureau was to furnish school buildings and the aid associations the teachers, but they were unable to do so, and as a result the Bureau had to hire Northern teachers and what Southern ones they could induce to teach Negroes. Elizabeth Bethel says that Alabama was the only state where the Bureau paid teachers' salaries. It discontinued this practice after 1867. For their safety, Northern teachers were placed in schools near where troops were stationed. When it could do so, the Bureau used freedmen as teachers and principals; Troy and Wetumpka had Negro principals. In Greenville the whole staff of one school was Negro. Miss Bethel summarized the Bureau schools:

> The schools for freedmen prospered during the school year 1866–1867 more than at any other period of the Bureau's existence. The year opened with 68 teachers, and 3,220 pupils, and closed with 175 schools, 150 teachers, and 9,799 pupils. At the end of the year permanent schoolhouses were located at fourteen points in the state. The

Bureau's expenditures for the school years 1865–1866 and 1866–1867, respectively were $6,633.62 and $45,237.55, the principal items being $33,762.25 for teachers' salaries and $14,703.47 for school buildings.— Elizabeth Bethel, "Freedmen's Bureau in Alabama," *Journal of Southern History,* vol. 14, p. 70.

The American Missionary Association (AMA) was the most active of all the aid societies. In some other states its agents met opposition, but in north Alabama all was peaceful in 1866. Major J. Jones reported seven schools were in operation, three taught by native white men, three schools taught by seven Negroes, and two schools taught by ex-soldiers of the Federal army. In 1867 the AMA purchased a fine antebellum brick building overlooking the town of Talladega and established a primary school with four teachers and 140 pupils. From this grew Talladega College, the oldest institution for Negro education in continuous operation in the state. It has remained a respected liberal arts college.

Native Alabamians also ran schools for the freedmen in no way connected with the Bureau or any of the associations. In Montgomery a prominent citizen opened a night school that had 150 pupils; in Selma the Presbyterian Church sponsored a school with the pastor and his wife doing the teaching, and in the Black Belt there were some plantation schools. In 1867, with very few jobs available, there were graduates of the University of Alabama among the applicants to teach Negro schools.

Although there was widespread interest in rudimentary schooling for the freedmen, Superintendent N. B. Cloud found pockets of bitterness against public education for them. Much of the opposition centered on the "Yankee" teacher, although tales of floggings and murders seem to be greatly exaggerated. An unidentified Mount Holyoke graduate was visited by the Ku Klux Klan, which fired a "volley of beans" through her window while she was teaching. The incident was meant to frighten her away, but she stayed and the annoyances finally stopped. Warnings, such as the following to a teacher in Pike County, were fairly common—and often effective.

September 20, 1875

Mr. Banks we thought we would give you a chance to save yourself one of the worst scourings that a man ever got and you can do so by reading this note and acting upon its contents. You have set up a nigger school in the settlement which we will not allow you to teach if you was a full blooded negro we would have nothing to say but a white skin negro is a little more than we can stand you can dismiss the school immediately or prepar yourself to travail we will give you a chance to save yourself and you had better move instanter.

Our little band calls themselves The Writing Straitners and if you

dont leave this settlement with your negro children we will straten
you.—W. L. Fleming, *Documentary History of Reconstruction* (A. H.
Clark Co.: Cleveland, Ohio, 1906–07), vol. 2, p. 208.

The Northern white teachers were not the only ones with
problems; the southern black teachers had some too, as the following letter indicates.

Bluffton Ala
Oct the 29th 1874

HON. MR. BINGHAM
    Kind Sir   Address you for the perpos of noing wether we School
Teacher will get any pay for the terms of the Scholastic year for we
have not got nothing for the whole terms that have bin tought in
Chambers county.   the county tresure say the money was sent to
Montgomery he say that neere *$4,000* sent there so I thought I would
ask you   we the Teachers of Chambers County have not got any
money this hole year & now we are in debt & dont no how to get out
We owe for Board & the County Tresure tell ous that money was sent
to Montgomery & he dont no when we will get any   the Supt. give
orders but the tresure give no money I tryed to sell my warrent to
the Banker Shapard at opelika & he rote to the Tressure of Chambers
County How the case stood   So he return the Compliments stateing
that the money was in the hands of the Ratical at montgomery   So
he hand my warrent back to me saying that he would not give any
ting & it was not werth anyting pleas sir Be so kind as to Let me no
Something about
    I am at Bluffton ala.   please direct your Letter to West Point Ga

Your Obedent
H. C. CALHOUN (Col d)

—Ibid., vol. 2, p. 198, quoting Ms. letter in Alabama Archives, Montgomery.

In addition to the problems all teachers had in the postwar period,
teachers of Negro children had two that were especially frustrating
—lack of educational background on which to build, and irregular
and "fitful" attendance.

Tuskegee Institute

There was considerable debate about the best kind of education
for the freedmen. There was one school of thought that held that
it should be the same as that of the whites, which meant basically
classical. If the black man was to rise, it was argued, he must do
so with the same kind of education his former master had. Another
school of thought believed that the newly independent man must
be taught practical skills so that he could have his economic independence which, in turn, would lead to social recognition if not
equality. Tuskegee Institute embodies this last philosophy.

The town of Tuskegee, located in the heart of Macon County with its rich heavy soil, big plantations, and large black population, was a center of culture, wealth, and learning. Many of the leading families had Virginia aristocratic backgrounds, the stately ante-bellum mansions still standing testify to the wealth and good taste of its inhabitants, and its good schools indicated an interest in education. It is an irony of history that this lovely little city should be known for not these things but as the home of the leading college for Negroes in the deep South.

Tuskegee Institute is truly the "lengthened shadow" of Booker T. Washington, for few men have influenced an institution to the degree he did. Born a slave in Franklin County, Virginia, he worked his way through Hampton Institute and, after a few years teaching, went to Tuskegee (1881) to open a school for which the legislature had appropriated $2,000. He had been thoroughly indoctrinated with the philosophy of hard work and self-help at Hampton, which was founded and operated by New Englanders. This philosophy he believed was best for the Negroes, and he instituted it at Tuskegee. He described his manner of selling the idea to both the whites and the blacks in Macon County.

One of the first questions that I had to answer for myself after beginning my work at Tuskegee was how I was to deal with public opinion on the race question.

It may seem strange that a man who had started out with the humble purpose of establishing a little Negro industrial school in a small Southern country town should find himself, to any great extent, either helped or hindered in his work by what the general public was thinking and saying about any of the large social or educational problems of the day. But such was the case at that time in Alabama; and so it was that I had not gone very far in my work before I found myself trying to formulate clear and definite answers to some very fundamental questions.

The questions came to me in this way: coloured people wanted to know why I proposed to teach their children to work. They said that they and their parents had been compelled to work for two hundred and fifty years, and now they wanted their children to go to school so that they might be free and live like the white folks—without working. That was the way in which the average coloured man looked at the matter.

Some of the Southern white people, on the contrary, were opposed to any kind of education of the Negro. Others inquired whether I was merely going to train preachers and teachers, or whether I proposed to furnish them with trained servants.

Some of the people in the North understood that I proposed to train the Negro to be a mere "hewer of wood and drawer of water," and feared that my school would make no effort to prepare him to take his place in the community as a man and a citizen.

Of course all these different views about the kind of education that the Negro ought or ought not to have were tinged with racial and sectional feelings. The rule of the "carpet-bag" government had just come to an end in Alabama. The masses of the white people were very bitter against the Negroes as a result of the excitement and agitation of the Reconstruction period.

On the other hand, the coloured people—who had recently lost, to a very large extent, their place in the politics of the State—were greatly discouraged and disheartened. Many of them feared that they were going to be drawn back into slavery. At this time also there was still a great deal of bitterness between the North and South in regard to anything that concerned political matters.

I found myself, as it were, at the angle where these opposing forces met. I saw that, in carrying out the work I had planned, I was likely to be opposed or criticized at some point by each of these parties. On the other hand, I saw just as clearly that in order to succeed I must in some way secure the support and sympathy of each of them.

I knew, for example, that the South was poor and the North was rich. I knew that Northern people believed, as the South at that time did not believe, in the power of education to inspire, to uplift, and to regenerate the masses of the people. I knew that the North was eager to go forward and complete, with the aid of education, the work of liberation which had begun with the sword, and that Northern people would be willing and glad to give their support to any school or other agency that proposed to do this work in a really fundamental way.

It was, at the same time, plain to me that no effort put forth in behalf of the members of my own race who were in the South was going to succeed unless it finally won the sympathy and support of the best white people in the South. I also knew—what many Northern people did not know or understand—that however much they might doubt the wisdom of educating the Negro, deep down in their hearts the Southern white people had a feeling of gratitude toward the Negro race. . . . I felt confident that, if I were actually on the right track in the kind of education that I proposed to give them and at the same time remained honest and sincere in all my dealings with them, I was bound to win their support, not only for the school that I had started, but for all that I had in my mind to do for them. . . .

First, that I should at all times be perfectly frank and honest in dealing with each of the three classes of people that I have mentioned;

Second, that I should not depend upon any "short-cuts" or expedients merely for the sake of gaining temporary popularity or advantage, whether for the time being such action brought me popularity or the reverse. With these two points clear before me as my creed, I began going forward.

One thing which gave me faith at the outset, and increased my confidence as I went on, was the insight which I early gained into the actual relations of the races in the South. I observed, in the first place, that as a result of two hundred and fifty years of slavery the two races had become bound together in intimate ways that people outside tht South could not understand, and of which the white people and coloured people themselves were perhaps not fully conscious. More than that, I perceived that the two races needed each other and that for many years to come no other labouring class of people would be able to fill the place occupied by the Negro in the life of the Southern white man. . . .

I determined, first of all, that as far as possible, I would try to gain the active support and cooperation, in all that I undertook, of the masses of my own race. With this in view, before I began my work at Tuskegee, I spent several weeks travelling about the rural communities of Macon County, of which Tuskegee is the county seat. During all this time I had an opportunity to meet and talk individually with a large number of people representing the rural classes, which constitute 80 per cent of the Negro population in the South. I slept in their cabins, ate their food, talked to them in their churches, and discussed with them in their own homes their difficulties and their needs. In this way I gained a kind of knowledge which has been of great value to me in all my work since.

As years went on, I extended these visits to the adjoining counties and adjoining states. Then, as the school at Tuskegee became better known, I took advantage of the invitations that came to me to visit the more distant parts of the country, where I had an opportunity to learn still more about the actual life of the people and the nature of the difficulties with which they were struggling. . . .—Booker T. Washington, *My Larger Education* (Garden City, N. Y.: Doubleday, 1911), pp. 21–35 passim.

Washington became one of the best-known citizens Alabama had, and the Institute was the recipient of many large gifts. People throughout the world were interested in him and his work. The Rev. John Massey was the president of The Alabama Conference Female College in Tuskegee.

BOOKER WASHINGTON.

In my travels either North or South, when it becomes known that I live in Tuskegee, the question is sure to be asked: "What do you think of Booker Washington?" Almost every one is curious to look at this remarkable man through the eyes of a near neighbor. As I am giving reminiscences of people I have known, I will not avoid this question because there have been diversities of opinion in regard to the subject of it.

In the year 1880 Hon. W. F. Foster and Hon. Asa Brooks, respectively Representative and Senator from Macon County, had a bill passed through the Legislature of Alabama appropriating two thousand dollars annually for the maintenance of a normal school for the education of colored teachers. Four years later this appropriation was increased to three thousand. George W. Campbell, Esq., an honored citizen and the only banker in Tuskegee at that time, Lewis Adams, a colored man, a shoemaker and tinner by trade, and Raymond Threat, a colored carpenter, were appointed trustees of the school. They wrote to General Armstrong, of Hampton, Virginia, requesting him to send a man to take charge of the school. General Armstrong recommended Booker Washington, a young man about twenty-three years of age. He came in the fall of 1881, took charge of the school, and conducted it in an old church till better quarters could be provided. To supplement the State appropriation, contributions were solicited, mainly from Northern people, who alone had the money to give. But money did not come in large sums for some years. The school was often hard pressed for means to meet its expenses during its early history and was sometimes carried through its impecunious periods by Mr. Campbell, who never lost faith in Washington while he was endeavoring to gain the confidence of Northern friends. When Mr. Collis P. Huntington was first approached for a donation, he gave two dollars. Years afterwards, when he saw what Washington was doing, Mr. Huntington gave fifty thousand dollars.

As soon as Washington could get the means he started a brickyard and a carpenter shop and began trying to inculcate ideas of industry and orderly conduct among the negroes, some of whom had been too long waiting for "forty acres and a mule from the government." Thinking that it would be a good thing to help the industrial feature of the school, I suggested to Dr. Atticus G. Haygood, who was then the agent of the Slater Fund, that I believed a donation would be worthily placed at this point. Dr. Haygood visited the school, was pleased with the work, and induced his board to make an annual contribution, which was continued for a number of years.

Some years ago a grant of twenty-five thousand acres of mineral land came to this school through an act of Congress, which donated the same number of acres to the Girls' Industrial School, at Montevallo. Thus out of the State appropriation as its first support and the old church as its first home, the school has grown until it now has over one hundred public buildings, constituting a plant worth several millions, and an annual patronage of about sixteen hundred students.

How did Washington do this? In a conversation with an intelligent citizen about fifteen years ago we were discussing the growth of the Normal School. My friend was apprehensive that it would be a menace to the country when it got strong enough to show its real animus. I cited several facts showing the fine discipline of the school and the restraints which Washington preached and practiced. The gentleman replied: "Yes, he shows a tact and a self-control that are almost superhuman." Now, I do not believe that tact and self-control alone could ever have accomplished such results.

Some years ago Washington made a speech in Tuscaloosa. A gentleman who heard it said that he was at a loss to account for his influence over an audience; for, said he, "he is not an orator." The editor of the paper from which I read the account asked this question: "Wouldn't any man like to be able to exercise the influence which Washington has over an audience, whether of the most intelligent class or the ignorant and illiterate?"

While he may not have been considered an orator in the usual acceptation of that term, he had the power to state his thoughts in clear-cut, forcible language and to elucidate his meaning by apt illustrations and sprightly anecdotes—all pervaded by good humor and expressed by a voice, not particularly melodious, but of great carrying power. No doubt this faculty helped him in his work, but his oratory alone fails to account for his achievements. He could never by his eloquence, like George Whitefield, have induced Benjamin Franklin to empty his whole purse into the collector's dish. Something else besides his tact, his self-control, and his oratory is necessary to account for his success.

Now, with a full share of innate feeling against the amalgamation of the races, I have observed Washington and his work from the beginning. I have been, I think, ready enough to see any objectionable features that might crop out during this extraordinary growth. I have also been striving to be a fair and open-minded man, seeking to do the right thing by every human being.

During the last fifteen years I heard Washington speak in Charleston, South Carolina, in New Orleans, Louisiana, and in the North, as well as here at home. All these speeches were characterized by the same sentiment expressed in his Charleston speech, in which he exhorted his own race to cherish friendly feelings toward the white people among whom they live. He said he thanked God that he had so far gotten the victory over all malevolent prejudices that he would not harbor in his breast unkind feelings toward any man. So far as I have been able to judge, his actions at home and abroad have been in accord with this sentiment. No provocation threw him off this line of pacific conduct. In the language of my friend: "His tact and his self-control have been almost superhuman." This course has awakened the idea of justice that slumbers in the human breast, has appealed to the generosity of the benevolent, disarmed the prejudices of the unsympathetic, and opened the way for a success which has been wrought out by most untiring and unselfish labor.

On a former page I have mentioned the estrangement of the races as the most deplorable result of the Reconstruction period. Since the two races are to live here side by side, some amicable plan must be found upon which we can live in peace. Animosity always magnifies and multiplies evils, which dissolve and melt away under the power of good will like dismal fogs before the rising sun. I do not know any man who has done so much to blot out estrangement between the races and bring in an era of good feeling as Booker Washington. Dr. Washington modestly wore the highest honorary title conferred by the universities of this country; but his unselfish work, his peaceable conduct, and his law-abiding example far surpasses any complimentary title that can be conferred.

Born in slavery in 1858, he lived in poverty during his childhood,

worked in the coal mines in his boyhood, went to night schools, walked
to Hampton Institute, graduated with distinction. . . . He died on Sunday morning, November 14, 1915, at the age of fifty-seven, worn out
with overwork.—John Massey, *Reminiscences* (Nashville, Tennessee:
Publishing House of the M. E. Church, South, 1916), pp. 314–17.

Higher Education

THE UNIVERSITY OF ALABAMA

In the field of higher education, several of the antebellum colleges continued to operate, and some like the University reopened.
The University, which had been burned by Croxton's raid in 1865,
received a grant of 46,080 acres of public land in compensation. The
$90,000 from the sale of these lands eventually helped the Univer-
sity to rebuild its physical plant.

Because of delays in construction of the new buildings, the difficulty of assembling a faculty, and interferences by politicians,
the University did not open until 1871. Thomas C. McCorvey, one
of the students at the opening and later commandant for the University, set down his memories of that date some years later.

When the University threw open its doors in 1871, it found a clever
body of students ready made to hand—students who had already seen
something of college life under a variety of conditions. There was material for all the college classes; for several young men who elsewhere
had been advanced to within one year of graduation were eager for a
diploma from Alabama's University. I can now look back and see how
excellent a thing for this institution was this bringing together of students from a number of other colleges. We were all "taken out of
ruts." The traditions of no one college were here set up in student
life; but our intellectual habits as well as our college slang and our
college customs was a composite of the varying phases of student life
at a score of other institutions. . . .
As with students, so with Faculty. In the reorganization of that body a
variety of vigorous young blood had been infused into the college life.
Wyman and Vaughan and Meek, then young in years, but old in experience, remained from the former Faculty to pass on to the new
organization the traditions of a glorious past. Lupton and Parker and
Smith, trained in the great universities of the Old World, introduced
new habits of thought and methods of work; while in Garnett and
Hodgson and Griswold and Peck, we had men of affairs as well as
scholars—men who knew the great world outside the college walls.
It would be hard to estimate the stimulating effects of the conditions
mentioned upon the ambitious student.—Quoted in James B. Sellers,
History of the University of Alabama (University, Alabama: University
of Alabama Press, 1953), pp. 312–13.

Robert Somers, making a tour of the Southern states about the time McCorvey described, recorded his observations.

> . . . Tuscaloosa is the seat of the University of Alabama, where upwards of a hundred students, the flower of the State, were wont to spend or misspend, as the case might be, their golden hours. But the professors, at the close of the war, were put under the ban of political proscription like all other highnesses in the South, and new men of inferior attainments were set down in their chairs. The consequence is that Alabama has still a University, with buildings and libraries, and professors, and expenditure, but no students; and one wanders about this beautiful arboury, asking, "Where is the fruit?" The wise men of the North and East attribute this lack of fruit to the deep and inveterate disloyalty of the South, forgetting that while "one man may lead a horse to water a hundred cannot compel him to drink," and that three-fourths of the disloyalty in the South is the result of a too prolonged course of political injustice.—Robert Somers, *The Southern States since the War, 1870–71* (New York: Macmillan Co., 1871), pp. 159–60.

In answer to Somers' observation that the faculty was inferior to what it had been before the war, it must be admitted that there was no Michael Tuomey, Henry Tutwiler, Henry Hilliard, or F. A. P. Barnard on the staff. But on the other hand some very able men served the institution in many ways.

The University of Alabama had eight presidents from 1871 to 1901: Nathaniel Thomas Lupton, a scientist; Carlos Green Smith, a close friend of Henry Tutwiler; Josiah Gorgas, former chief of Ordinance for the Confederacy and former vice-chancellor of the University of the South whose career in Tuscaloosa was cut short by death; Burwell B. Lewis, a nephew of Judge George Shortridge, the Know-Nothing gubernatorial candidate of 1856; Henry D. Clayton, a judge and former legislator from Barbour County, and husband of Victoria V. Clayton, whose reminiscences of the old regime are often quoted; Richard C. Jones, a native Virginian who came to Alabama in his early childhood, later graduated from the University, served in the Confederate army and practiced law in Camden; and Jones K. Powers, an alumnus of the class of 1873, president of State Normal College at Florence and former president of the Alabama Education Association. As Dr. Sellers points out in his history of the University, all of these men were Southern born except Gorgas; all were mature men; four were educators, three were lawyers and one, Gorgas, was a soldier. Four were alumni, and all were awarded the University's honorary LL.D. degree before they left office. Each made a distinct contribution to the institution.

The faculty was not large in these years, but there were notable men among its members. Some of them served out their years there, and others, like Thomas W. Palmer, who was professor of mathematics from 1883 to 1907 and dean of the Faculty of Arts and Sciences after 1905, went on to Montevallo in 1907 to guide the Girls' Industrial School in its transition to a four-year, degree-granting, accredited college. And any record of these years at the university would be incomplete without mention of Amelia Gayle Gorgas, widow of Josiah Gorgas, who was librarian from the time of her husband's death in 1883 until 1907.

William G. Clark, a member of the Board of Trustees, described the organization of the University as it was in 1889.

ORGANIZATION AND GENERAL INFORMATION

There are now two general departments of instruction:
I. An academic department.
II. A department of professional education.

In the academic department are the following schools: (1) School of the Latin language and literature; (2) school of the Greek language and literature; (3) school of the English language and literature; (4) school of modern languages; (5) school of chemistry; (6) school of geology and natural history; (7) school of natural philosophy and astronomy; (8) school of mathematics; (9) school of philosophy and history; (10) school of engineering. Candidates for admission to the Freshman class must be at least sixteen years of age, and have such preparation as will enable them to pursue with advantage the course of study they may select.

There are four undergraduate courses of study: (1) The classical course; (2) the scientific course; (3) the civil engineering course; (4) the mining engineering course. The first two lead to the degree of bachelor of arts, the third to the degree of bachelor of engineering, and the fourth to the degree of bachelor of mining engineering.

Students who are unable or who do not wish to complete all the studies of either of the regular courses are allowed to select a course of study on certain conditions, and upon the completion of such course are entitled to a diploma of graduation in the schools selected, and are enrolled as alumni of the University. Students who have received the degree of bachelor of arts may attain the degree of master of arts by remaining one year longer at the University and pursuing advanced studies in at least three of the academic schools of the University. Bachelors of civil or mining engineering can attain the degree of civil or mining engineers by pursuing advanced studies in their respective courses one year longer. All matriculates in the courses mentioned become members of the Alabama Corps of Cadets, subject to military discipline, and are required to reside in the University halls.

In the department of professional education there are three schools: (1) The school of international and constitutional law; (2) the school of common and statute law; (3) the school of equity jurisprudence. The students of this department are not permitted to reside in the University halls, but are subjected to the same discipline, the military features excepted, as the academic students. The law course covers a period of two years, but a student may enter such advanced class as his acquirements on entering may justify. The degree of bachelor of laws is only conferred after the applicant has sustained a satisfactory written examination in all the studies of the course in presence of the Faculty of the University.

The Rules of Practice of the Supreme Court of Alabama authorize the graduates of this department to practise in all the courts of the State, on simple motion, without examination.

The course of instruction in the military department of the University embraces: (1) Military art and science; (2) military law; (3) elementary tactics.

The academic year is divided into three terms. Besides the daily examinations in the lecture-rooms there are two general examinations of each class held each year.

There are three literary societies connected with the University,—the Erosophic, the Philomathic, and the Pethonian, to each of which suitable rooms have been set apart and handsomely furnished by the trustees. These societies are considered, through their debates and literary exercises, of great advantage to the University, both in the individual benefit to the members and in the good influence they exert. Therefore every encouragement is given them by the Faculty and trustees. Each of these societies holds an annual celebration in the month of April, at which an oration is pronounced and a subject discussed. The Monday morning of each commencement week they hold an "inter-society debate" in Commencement Hall, which is always interesting and well attended.

The Society of the Alumni of the University holds its annual meeting on Tuesday of commencement week. These reunions are looked forward to with much interest. An oration is always delivered at each meeting, and last season a handsome banquet was given. The success of the entertainment led to the determination to make the banquet a feature of each annual gathering of the alumni.

"The society at its meeting in June, 1885, resolved to establish a fund for the assistance of meritorious students in narrow circumstances, who are seeking the benefits of a thorough education at the University. It is the purpose of the society to lend the income of the fund to students who may need pecuniary assistance during their residence in the University. A considerable amount has already been contributed to this fund, but there will be no income available for loans before the beginning of the fiscal year of the University, July 1, 1889. The management of this fund is confided to a board of trust appointed annually by the society. All contributions to the fund are to be invested by the board of trust in Alabama State bonds, under the general supervision of the society. It is confidently expected that every graduate of the University will contribute liberally to this fund. Former students of the University and all other friends of education in the State are likewise invited to contribute."—Willis G. Clark, *History of Education in Alabama, 1702–1889* (Washington: Government Printing Office, 1889), pp. 124–25.

Fees for a year cost $156.

AUBURN

Before the Civil War, higher education was provided by the University at Tuscaloosa and by several denominational colleges scattered throughout the state. In 1872, a new college opened its doors, the Agricultural and Mechanical College at Auburn.

Auburn already had a college, the East Alabama Male College owned and operated by the Methodist Church. It was chartered in 1856 and opened it doors in the autumn of 1859. The Rev. William J. Sasnett with a faculty of five instructed 80 college and 113 preparatory students. The curriculum was strictly classical. Although the village had two Federal raids during the war, the college building was never damaged and for two years it was used as a hospital. After the war the college faced declining enrollment and reduced income, but the faculty and trustees struggled on until 1871, hoping that times would improve. Alabama was able to use the land provided by the Morrill Act of 1862 by which each state was entitled to 30,000 acres of public land for each Senator and representative it had in Congress. Professor Charles W. Edwards describes the way in which the trustees of the college solved their problems.

The Board, in particular the Auburn and Opelika members, was determined to keep the College going. Events were leading to a solution. The Federal Congress in 1862 had passed the Morrill Act for the establishment of land-grant colleges. In 1868, the State of Alabama had accepted the federal grant and approved the establishment of a land-grant college. Land script for 240,000 acres was sold and the proceeds totaling $253,500 were invested in state bonds. Thus the State had funds for support of a college, but none for a building. The College had a building and equipment, but no funds for support. The Board, with the approval of the Conference, offered its property to the State. Although the University and Florence Wesleyan were bidding, Auburn had the best building and the best situation in all respects. Accordingly, on February 26, 1872, a bill introduced by Representative Sheldon Toomer was approved establishing at Auburn the Agricultural and Mechanical College of Alabama, the first land grant college set up in the South separate from a state university.—Charles Wesley Edwards, *Auburn Starts a Second Century* (Auburn, Ala.: Alabama Polytechnic Institute, 1958), p. 9.

The Agricultural and Mechanical College was the subject of considerable newspaper debate. When it was only three years old, President Isaac Taylor Tichenor (1872–1880) wrote Colonel Robert McKee, a Selma newspaperman.

We are much obliged to you for that part of your notice of our school which speaks in such kindly terms of the teachers &c. But we would have been much more obliged if you had left out what you said about the agricultural features. It may not be "any great thing" but it is the only thing, as a school, in the State which even proposes to give instruction in that Science and Art from which 86 per cent of our population make a living.

It would not be reasonable to expect it to be a great thing, as it is yet in its infancy. We are not yet old enough to graduate a class in agriculture. Our first class in that department graduates next summer and I am sure I do not overstate the case when I say that these young men will have acquired here a knowledge of scientific and *practical* agriculture which will surprise and gratify the friends of agricultural education. We would be very glad when you come up and see us. Come to our next commencement if you cannot come before. See what we are doing and what possibilities lie before us. You are Editor of one of the most influential papers in the State and I know you do not desire to cast your influence against anything that is benefitting or can be made to benefit the State. We are working faithfully and honestly for the good of Alabama and we want your aid and the aid of all good men in building up the interest of the state. There is no humbug about us. We are plain practical straight-forward men doing according to our judgment the best we can with the interest committed to our charge. . . . —Otcober 1, 1875, McKee Papers, Alabama State Archives, Montgomery.

President Tichenor reported to the Board of Trustees the advantages of the college to the state as he saw it.

The resources of our State are admitted to be beyond all computation. Our mountains of iron, our thousands of square miles of coal, our immense beds of marble, our splendid deposits of copper and of gold, together with a great variety of other minerals less known to our people, but scarcely less valuable; our numberless streams furnishing sites for the factories of a nation, running idly to the sea; our varied and fertile soils all await the science and skill to transform them into comfort and wealth for our people. The leading object of this college is to teach those sciences related to Agriculture and the Mechanic Arts, to fit young men to lead in all those enterprises designed to develop the industrial interests of the country. This is the education demanded by the wants of the country, and in it are to be found the forces which are to mould the new civilization of the South. For that purpose this

institution was organized, and its courses of study, the labors of its
faculty, and the whole spirit of the institution is directed to that end.—
Report to Board of Trustees, 1876, quoted in Edwards, p. 14.

The name was changed to Alabama Polytechnic Institute in 1899,
and on January 1, 1960, to Auburn University.

MONTEVALLO

What is now the University of Montevallo was established by
the state in 1896 as Alabama Girls' Industrial School. It was the
culmination of a lengthy campaign by various labor and farm
groups, educators and politicians. Miss Julia Tutwiler had long
agitated for such a school.

Senator Sol Bloch of Camden was largely responsible for getting
the bill creating the school passed in the legislature.

He, "realizing how long the girls of the State had been neglected,
and what a far-reaching effect the establishment of such a school
would have for the welfare of our people," gave this matter his
especial attention and finally procured the passage of the act.

The purpose was the establishment of "a first-class industrial
school for the education of white girls in the State of Alabama in
industrial and scientific branches. . . ." Courses were offered in
normal school education, telegraphy, stenography, photography,
phonography, typewriting, printing, bookkeeping, indoor carpentry, electrical construction, clay modeling, architectural and mechanical drawing, sewing, dressmaking, cooking, laundering, house,
sign and fresco-painting, home nursing and "other practical industries." When the first term was begun October 12, 1896, the total
expenses were $80 per term; by the second year the sum was raised
to $88. Captain H. C. Reynolds was acting president.

The activities of the young women in the Montevallo school, as
elsewhere, were hedged in by many restrictions. The uniform was
universally accepted.

UNIFORMS

It is our purpose to avoid all extravagances in dress. To reduce school
expense to a minimum, we require the day pupils, as well as the boarding pupils to have a uniform dress and hat.

The uniform dress is a navy blue Henrietta or serge. The young
woman can make her own dress and hat in the dressmaking department or she can have the dress made for $3.00.

The spring uniform is the same skirt, with a light blue chambray shirt
waist. The uniform hat is the Oxford cap, made of the dress material,
trimmed with white cord and tassel. The Commencement dress is of
white lawn, price not to exceed 20 cents per yard.

The goods for the uniforms are kept by two reliable firms here, viz;

George Kroell and S. A. Latham & Co. Should you desire to purchase before coming on, write to either of these firms and they will make you prices for the entire outfit.

Students are required to appear in uniform at church and at all public entertainments, whether in the town or in the college chapel.

No low neck or short sleeve dresses will be permitted on our school platform.

The uniform must be ready within three weeks after the pupil enters the schools.

There are two grades of the material, which cost 35 and 50 cents a yard, the entire outfit costing about $5.00 to $6.00. . . .

It is understood that pupils are not here to enter society, but to be educated, therefore they are not allowed to correspond with gentlemen, and visits from them is positively prohibited under penalty of expulsion. Also, that pupils cannot be withdrawn from school to attend theatres or other places of amusement and returned at will.—The First Annual Catalog of the Girls' Industrial School of Alabama, a Polytechnic Institute, 1896–97, p. 20.

In the early days it was only a high school, but it offered an opportunity for a unique education, combining a technical or industrial skill and a liberal education. It was never a vocational school in the true sense of the word, for along with telegraphy, sewing, millinery, and other vocational courses, the girls studied English, Latin, and other usual liberal arts subjects.

It opened on October 12, 1896, with 145 students and grew rapidly. Its role as a college came in the next century after the county high schools were authorized by legislation in 1908, and there was no further need for a state high school. The need now was for teachers to staff the high schools, especially the home economics departments.

Miss Julia Tutwiler

The name of Julia S. Tutwiler (1841–1916) is associated with many phases of social reform and social progress in this state. "Miss Julia," as she was familiarly called, was interested in many movements but her chief concern was the education of women. Besides establishing the normal school at Livingston and serving as the president and persuading the University of Alabama to admit women, she was instrumental in getting the state to establish the Alabama Girls' Industrial School at Montevallo, October, 1896.

She was active in prison reform and was instrumental in starting night schools in jails and prisons. At her death there was still much to be done but she had succeeded in beginning the classification of prisoners, the separation of the sexes, and the first juvenile reform school. She succeessfully urged the first law requiring the inspection of jails and prisons. In recognition of her activities, the state prison for women at Wetumpka is named for her.

In the fall of 1881 Miss Julia [Tutwiler] had her first opportunity for original work. There were few women in the state so well equipped for teaching as Miss Julia, and she was made co-principal with Dr. Carolos G. Smith of the Livingston Female Academy. The institution was a private one when she entered it, but one year later the state made an appropriation of two-thousand dollars for tuition and five hundred dollars for appliances to be used in adding to the academy a training school for teachers.

"This," says Miss Julia, "was the first and only gift which the women of the state had up to that time received from state or federal treasury."

A few years later the name was changed to that of the Alabama Normal College and Miss Julia was made the first president. Then Miss Julia began the work that laid the foundation for her state-wide fame. The new Normal School was planned by her carefully, lovingly, the course of study being based upon all that she had learned in America, in Germany, in France. Neglecting none of the academic studies, she managed to introduce something of industrial education, of art, and of science, although these things were regarded as innovations, perhaps dangerous for female minds. . . . Her own personal salary was five hundred dollars. . . .

. . . Miss Julia proved herself not only a good and great teacher, but a thoroughly alert business woman, when the appropriation was but two thousand dollars, she took hold of the boarding department, ran it so it paid a profit sufficient to furnish the salaries of several extra teachers and filled up the remaining gap in the faculty by doing the work of three herself.

. . . For many years she worked to get the University of Alabama to open its doors to her graduates but without avail. Then slowly, reluctantly, those doors did open. Miss Julia had by sheer persistency wearied the authorities until they gave her permission to use a vacant cottage on the University grounds. The experiment was regarded as hazardous by the trustees, faculty, and the people at large. It is safe to say that no ten young women who ever matriculated for a college course were as carefully coached on conduct as well as on subjects as the ten young women first sent to the University by Miss Julia. At the end of the year the trustees, the faculty and the people at large saw a triumphant Miss Julia and the downfall of their doubts. Her ten girls had won sixty-six per cent of all the honors given against the competition of several hundred young men. Their conduct was pronounced irreproachable by the most conservative of the professors, and they had done all the work of their cottage including their own cooking.—*The Pictorial Review,* April 1913.

In 1971 Alabama recognized her outstanding achievements by electing her to the Alabama Women's Hall of Fame at Judson College.

Not all higher education, of course, was given at state institutions. Denominational colleges continued to train men, especially those going into the ministry, and women. There was Spring Hill, a Catholic college in Mobile; Judson in Marion; Howard, which was moved to the Birmingham area in 1886; Southern University in Greensboro, which later would be consolidated into Birmingham-Southern College; Alabama Conference Female College in Tuskegee, the ancestor of Huntington College; and others less permanent. In comparison to twentieth century colleges and universities, they (as well as the state institutions) were small, their student bodies seldom, if ever, amounting to more than two-hundred fifty. In the difficult years after the war, all of these institutions were hampered by lack of adequate financial support. Yet in spite of that, they turned out many graduates who served their state and country well.

Evaluation

In assessing the progress of education in Alabama after the war, it is necessary to view it from two directions: within the state itself and in comparison with other states. The state, defeated and economically ruined in 1865, began rebuilding its public schools and with the aid of outside agencies initiated free education for Negro children. It increased the sums spent on public schools from $275,000 in 1870 to over a million dollars in 1900. More children were attending school, and the expenditure per child was also increasing. The length of the school term had been lengthened about twenty days or one whole month. But when Alabama is compared to the nation as a whole, it appears less progressive. In 1890 the national average expenditure per capita of population was $2.24; Alabama's was 59 cents; its average school term was 73 days while the national average was 131. The illiteracy rate in the whole nation was 13.3 percent, but Alabama's was 41. However, the state could be proud that in twenty years it had reduced it from 50.9 percent. Progress was being made, but it was very, very slow.

In assessing the poor showing Alabama made in these thirty-five years, Allen Going finds several factors responsible:

> The theory of free public education still did not go unquestioned, and too often were the schools regarded as charitable institutions or "objects of public contempt." Although Democratic leaders supported the cause of public education, their emphasis on strict economy prevented any large expenditures or additional revenues from new forms of taxation. The maintenance of separate schools for Negroes and whites imposed an additional burden on the educational system.—Allen J. Going, *Bourbon Democracy in Alabama, 1874–1890* (University, Alabama: University Press, 1951), p. 168.

In the field of education beyond the secondary level, the state had increased the number of normal schools to seven, revived the University, created the Agricultural and Mechanical College, and founded the Girls' Industrial School. The foundations were laid; there was some evidence of new life by 1900, but the great periods of educational development were not to be realized until the twentieth century.

Chapter 16

ECONOMIC DEVELOPMENT
AFTER THE WAR

It is a truism that the Civil War altered the economic life of the South. The plantation system based on slavery was replaced by the New South built on free labor and greater diversification. The industrial revolution, however, did not suddenly burst full-grown in 1865. In reality, the New South was built on foundations laid in the antebellum period. There had been mills and mines before the war, but they had been neither large nor influential. After the war they grew in importance although agriculture continued to dominate the economic life. Cotton was still the most valuable single product but coal, iron, and steel made up an increasing share of the state's wealth.

Agriculture and Tenant Farming

When Alabama began to revive after the staggering defeat in 1865, its people naturally turned to agriculture for their livelihood. The crop of that first year of peace was short because the men returned from the battlefield too late to plant a full crop. Furthermore, farm animals, tools and seed were often unavailable. But the greatest problem in the plantation area was the lack of labor. Robert Somers, an Englishman making a tour of the Southern states, spent some days around Livingston, "a respectable little place, spreading over a rising ground nicely embowered under rows of trees. . . ." There he found farming disrupted by the unavailability of labor.

Slavery was dense in this prairie region in the time before the war, and now there is a great scarcity of free negro labour. A spirit of roving, and the demand for labour on the railways, have carried away the blacks in thousands. The planters have been able to grow but small

587

patches of corn and cotton on their teeming lands. Hundreds of acres
on every plantation of rich arable soil are lying idle, and enjoying a
long fallow, which will probably make them richer and fatter still,
against the time when they may again be brought into use.—Robert
Somers, *Southern States Since tthe War* (New York: Macmillan Company, 1871), pp. 158–59.

It was not long, however, before some of the freedmen began
coming back to their former homes. This helped, but did not
solve, the whole problem. Since they were no longer slaves, they
had to find jobs. They had only their labor to sell. The planters
having lost their biggest investments (slaves and Confederate
money and securities) had only their. land. Within a short time,
a mutually beneficial system was worked out by which the landless
freedman and the land-poor planter could survive together. This
system was tenant-farming, which in many instances was share-
cropping. Robert Somers described it as he saw it.

The emancipation of the slaves is accepted with remarkable equanimity
when one considers the overturn of personal fortune, and all the bitterness of the war with which it was associated; and an expression of
gladness to have now done with slavery, and to have touched some
common ground of civilization, is often heard. But what the planters
are disposed to complain of is that, while they have lost their slaves,
they have not got free labourers in any sense common either in the
Northern States or in Europe; and, looking around here at Jonesboro
(Alabama, Tennessee Valley), after a calm and wide survey, one cannot but think that the New England manufacturer and the Old English
farmer must be equally astonished at a recital of the relations of land,
capital, and labour as they existed on the cotton plantations of the
Southern States. The wages of the negroes, if such a term can be applied
to a mode of remuneration so unusual and anomalous, consist . . . of
one half the corn and cotton, the only crops in reality produced. This
system of share and share alike betwixt the planter and the negro I
have found to prevail so generally that any other form of contract is
but the exception. The negro, on the semi-communistic basis thus established, finds his own rations; but as these are supplied to him by the
planter, or by the planter's notes of credit on the merchants . . . and
as much more sometimes as he thinks he needs by the merchants on his
own credit, from the 1st. of January onward through the year, in an-
ticipation of crops which are not marketable till the end of December,
he can lose nothing by the failure or deficient outcome of the crops,
and is always sure of his subsistence. As a permanent economic relation
this would be startling anywhere between any classes of men brought
together in the business of life. Applied to agriculture in any other part
of the world, it would be deemed outrageously absurd. But this is only
a part of the "privileges" (a much more accurate term than "wages")

of the negro field-hand. In addition to half of the crops, he has a free cottage of the kind he seems to like, and the windows of which he or his wife persistently nail up; he has abundance of wood from the planter's estate for fuel and for building his corn-cribs and other out-houses, with teams to draw it from the forest; he is allowed to keep hogs, and milch cows, and young cattle, which roam and feed with the same right of pasture as the hogs and cattle of the planter, free of all charge; he has the same right of hunting and shooting, with quite as many facilities for exercising the right as anybody else—and he has his dogs and guns, though, as far as I have discoverd, he provides himself with these by purchase or some other form of conquest. Though entitled to one-half the crops, yet he is not required to contribute any portion of the seed, nor is he called upon to pay any part of the taxes of the plantation. The only direct tax on the negro is the poll-tax, which is wholly set apart for the education of his children, and which I find to be everywhere in arrears, and in some places in a hopeless chaos of nonpayment. . . .

. . . The negro field-hand, with his right of half-crop and privileges as described, who works with ordinary diligence, looking only to his own pocket, and gets his crops forward and gathered in due time, is at liberty to go to other plantations to pick cotton, in doing which he may make from two to two and a half dollars a day. For every piece of work outside the crop he does even on his own plantation he must be paid a dollar a day. It may be clearing ditches or splitting rails, or anything that is just as essential to the crops as the two-inch plowing and hoeing in which he shambles away his time, but for all this kind of work he must be paid a dollar a day. While the landowner is busy keeping accounts betwixt himself and his negro hands, ginning their cotton for them, doing all the marketing of produce and supplies of which they have the lion's share, and has hardly a day to call his own, the "hands" may be earning a dollar a day from him for work which is quite as much theirs as his. Yet the negroes, with all their super-abounding privilege on the cotton field make little of it. A ploughman or a herd in the old country would not exchange his lot for theirs, as it stands and as it appears in all external circumstances. They are almost all in debt; few are able at the end of the year to square accounts with "the Merchant;" and it is rarely the planter can point with pride, and with the conscious joy of recording his own profit, to a freedman, who, as a result of the year's toil, will have a hundred or two dollars to the good. The soul is often crushed out of labour by penury and oppression. Here a soul cannot begin to be infused into it through the sheer excess of privilege and license with which it is surrounded.—Ibid., pp. 128–29.

Written share-cropping contracts were a legacy of the Freed-men's Bureau. Contracts differed from community to community and according to what each side furnished. This one was made between a partnership and a family.

Hamburg, Ala.
Jan. 14, 1897

This agreement or contract made and entered into at Hamburg, Perry County, Ala. this the 14th day of Jan. 1897, by and between J. L. Crenshaw, L. W. Crenshaw, parties of the first part, and the following described freedmen, parties of the second part, viz.

Mollie Johnson
Lizzie Johnson
Oscar Johnson
Peter Johnson

First, the said parties of the first part are to furnish the land, implements and the team and to feed team for farming purposes during the year 1897 and that parties of the second part must be responsible for all damages done to implements or team carelessly handled, and that the said parties of the second part must be responsible for ½ of the blacksmithing or repairs on implements for making said crop.

Second, in consideration of the above being carried out and after performing good and useful labor to parties of the first part, the parties of the second part are to receive for services ⅓ of the fodder or hay made by parties of the second part and ⅓ of the corn and ½ net products of the cotton after ginning, packing, and preparing for market and ⅛ of cotton seed.

Third, these parties of the second part have no right to terminate this contract only by consent of parties of the first part. If crop is found grassy and parties of the second part fail to work it properly, the parties of the first part are impowered to hire day labor and the expenses of same must come out of the earnings of the parties of the second part. We hereunto this day set our hands and seals.—Sheppard and Crenshaw, Account Book, 1892–1897. Original in private hands.

Dr. Eugene Allen Smith, professor of geology at the University of Alabama for many years, served as state geologist and made many significant surveys (often during summer vacation with volunteer help) of the resources of Alabama. One of these was a *Report on Cotton Production of the State of Alabama* based on the 1880 census.

The central cotton belt is generally a region of large farms or plantations, in which the laborers are chiefly negroes, as seen in the tables. As a rule, these laborers do not own the land, have no interest in it beyond getting a crop from a portion of it, which they rent either for a sum of money or for a share of the crop, and are not interested in keeping up the fertility, at least not to the extent of being led to make any attempt at the permanent improvement of the same. In the case of the owner of the land, while the conditions are different, the result is the same. He is, of course, interested in the improvement of his land; but to supply the fertilizers for a large plantation, when he cultivates it by hired labor, would cost more than he usually has to expend, and where the share system, or that of renting, prevails he is still further removed from personal care of the land; and thus from all causes there is an exhaustive cultivation of the land, without any attempt at maintenance or restoration of its lost fertility.

In addition to these, the system of advances or credit, so prevalent throughout the cotton-producing parts of the state, is not without its evil influence, for the laborer, and too often the owner of the land, is obliged to get advances of provisions from their merchants, for the payment of which the crop is mortgaged; and as cotton is the only crop which will always bring ready money, its planting is usually insisted on by the merchants making the advances and selected by the farmer as a means of providing for payment. In this way cotton comes to be the paramount crop, and there is little chance for rotation with other things. . . .

In the other agricultural regions of the state, and in most of the counties also of the Tennessee and Coosa valleys, the farms are, as a rule, small and cultivated by their owners, with the assistance of such labor as may be hired from time to time. In all these cases provisions are produced on the farm, and cotton is planted as a secondary crop. There is thus some chance for selection of the soils and for rotation of crops; and when a man cultivates his own farm fertilizers are in more general use, so that with the soils naturally much inferior to those of the main cotton-producing regions the average per acre is much higher in these regions of small cultivation. . . .

To recapitulate, the following conclusions seem, therefore, to be plainly taught by the discussion of the data contained in the tables presented; . . . .

1. That where the blacks are in excess of the whites there are the originally most fertile lands of the state. The natural advantages of the soils are, however, more than counterbalanced by the bad system prevailing in such sections, viz., large farms rented out in patches to laborers who are too poor and too much in debt to merchants to have any interest in keeping up the fertility of the soil, or rather the ability to keep it up, with the natural consequences of its rapid exhaustion and a product per acre on these, the best lands of the state, lower than that which is realized from the very poorest.

2. Where the two races are in nearly equal proportions, or where the whites are in only slight excess over the blacks, as is the case in all the sections where the soils are of average fertility, there is found the system of small farms worked generally by the owners, a consequently better cultivation, a more general use of commercial fertilizers, a correspondingly high product per acre, and a partial maintenance of the fertility of the soils.

3. Where the whites are greatly in excess of the blacks (three to one and above), the soils are almost certain to be below the average in fertility, and the product per acre is low from this cause, notwithstanding the redeeming influences of a comparatively rational system of cultivation.

4. The exceptions to these general rules are nearly always due to

local causes, which are not far to seek, and which afford generally a satisfactory explanation of the discrepancies.—Quoted in W. L. Fleming, *Documentary History of Reconstruction* (Cleveland, Ohio: A. H. Clark Company, 1906), vol. 2, pp. 323–24.

Not all tenant farmers were black nor were all blacks tenant farmers. Under the leadership of Tuskegee Institute, some Negroes were buying their own land and becoming prosperous farmers. In 1905, Tuskegee printed a book of success stories about their former students—lawyers, college presidents, teachers, ministers, mechanics, housewives, and others. Frank Reid was a planter. He and his brother Dow had attended the Institute but did not graduate. He tells their story.

We are located at a place called Dawkins, not more than twelve miles from the Tuskegee Institute, and immediately within its sphere of influence.

Our mother and father were born within a few miles of where we now live. Both of our parents, at the time I write, are living, and are each about sixty-five years of age; they were, for twenty-five years each, slaves. Neither can read or write. My brother and I each spent about three years at Tuskegee, and, in addition, he attended school for two years at Talladega College.

I had a very thorough course in carpentry, and my brother worked on the Institute farm. We married two sisters, Susie and Lillie Hendon. Shortly after my marriage my beloved wife Susie died, leaving me with one child. My brother's wife still lives; they have three children.

Until ten years ago we, with our father, were renters, all of us working together. But the Sunday evening talks at Tuskegee by Principal Washington, and his urgent insistence, at all times, that Tuskegee graduates and students should try to own land, led us to desire to improve our condition. We were large renters, however; for twenty-three years our father and his relatives had leased and "worked" a tract of 1,100 acres of land, having leased it for ten years at a time. We still lease this tract, and, in addition, rent an additional 480 acres in the same way, ten years at a time. We subrent tracts of this total of 1,580 acres to thirty tenants, charging one and one-half bales of cotton for each one-horse farm. We pay twenty-three bales for the rent of the 1,580 acres. My brother and I run a sixteen-horse farm, doing much of the work ourselves and paying wages to those who work for us. A number of others also work for us on "halves"—that is, we provide the land, furnish the seeds, tools, mules, feed the mules, and equally divide whatever is raised. This is largely done in all the country districts of the South.

About ten years ago we bought in our own right our first land, 320 acres. Since that time we have acquired by purchase another tract containing 285 acres. The first tract we paid for in two years; the other is also paid for. The total of 605 acres, I am glad to say, is without incumbrance of any kind.

The following statements may give some idea as to what we have been able to do since leaving Tuskegee:

During the year 1904 alone, we paid out $5,000, covering debts on land, fertilizers, and money borrowed with which to carry our thirty tenants.

We own sixteen mules and horses, fourteen head of cattle, thirty hogs, and have absolutely no indebtedness of any character.

My brother Dow lives in a good three-room house. My father and I live in a good six-room house, with a large, airy hall, and kitchen; it cost us to build, $1,500.

We conduct a large general store, with everything carried in a country store of this kind. The colored Odd Fellows use the hall above our store for their meetings.

The Government post-office is located in our store, and here all of the surrounding community come for their mail.

Our store does a large yearly business averaging about $5,000.

We have a steam-gin and grist-mill. We gin about 500 bales of cotton a season for ourselves and others living near; of the 150 bales got from the land owned and rented by us, 100 are ours, the other 50 belong to our tenants.

We raise large quantities of corn, potatoes, and peas, in addition to our cotton crop.

We are now trying to purchase the 480 acres we have been so long renting.

The church and the schoolhouse are on four acres of land immediately adjoining ours. The church is roomy, well-seated, ceiled and painted, in striking contrast with most of those in the country districts of the South. The schoolhouse has two rooms, and is but partially ceiled, though it is nicely weather-boarded. The school is regularly conducted for five months each year, and part of the time has two teachers. Mr. J. C. Calloway, a Tuskegee graduate, Class of '96, is principal of the school. We are cooperating with Mr. Calloway in an effort to supplement the school funds and secure an additional two months. We helped pay for the land, and gave a part of the money toward the schoolhouse, and have done all possible to help, keeping in mind Principal Washington's oft-repeated statement that "it is upon the country public schools that the masses of the race are dependent for an education."

My brother and I, with our father, it will be noted, own and rent 2,185 acres of land, but we try to help our tenants in every possible way, and, when they desire it, subrent to them such tracts as they desire for ten years, or less. We have established a blacksmith-shop on our land, and do all our own work and most of that of the whole community. . . .

This further statement may not be amiss: Under the guidance of the Tuskegee influences, the annual Tuskegee Negro Conferences, the visits of Tuskegee teachers, etc., the importance of land-buying was early brought to our attention, but because of the crude and inexperienced laborers about us, we found that we could, with advantage to all, rent large tracts of land, subrent to others, and in this way pay no rent ourselves, as these subrenters did that for us. We could in this way also escape paying taxes, insurance, and other expenses that naturally follow. We could, as many white farmers do, hire wage hands at from $7.50 to $10 a month, with "rations," or arrange to have them work on "halves," as I have already described.

But at last we yielded to the constant pounding received at Tuskegee whenever we would go over, that we ought to own land for ourselves; and then, too, it occurred to me that we might not always have the same whole-souled man to deal with, and that terms might be made much harder. My brother and father agreed, and we set about to purchase the first 320 acres. As I feared, rental values have increased; formerly we rented the 1,100 acres for three bales of cotton; now we give sixteen bales for the same land.

My brother, our father, and I have worked together from the beginning. We have had no disputes or differences; we have worked on the basis of a common property interest.—Booker T. Washington, ed., *Tuskegee and Its People: Their Ideals and Achievements* (New York: D. Appleton and Company, 1905), pp. 164–70.

Reid reported that several other farmers in his community owned their land. Turner Moore, a slave for twenty-five years, owned 210 acres; and James Whitlaw owned 1,137 acres. Reid emphasized in each case that the property was fully paid for.

Immigration

The difficulties of Negro labor and dissatisfaction with sharecropping led forward-looking citizens to seek other sources of labor and other means of using their lands. To many immigration seemed the answer. Many Southerners assumed that wherever the immigrants came from, whether the North or Europe, they would be white, energetic, and thrifty. Although officially the Democratic party was divided on a policy toward immigration, many local leaders and state officials took steps to advertise the states' attractions.

The work of Commissioner of Agriculture Reuben F. Kolb in advertising the state with his travelling exhibit of Alabama products, "Alabama on Wheels," has already been mentioned. There were several publications, including a handbook written by the Rev. Benjamin F. Riley called *Alabama As It Is: or The Immigrants' and Capitalists' Guide Book to Alabama* for which the state appropriated $1,500 for printing 5000 copies to be distributed wherever they would attract attention. Other writers dealt with the state topically but Riley described each county. His sketch of

Wilcox County emphasizes not only the physical resources but also the progressiveness of the inhabitants and their eagerness to have new settlers.

WILCOX COUNTY

This county derived its name from Lieutenant Joseph M. Wilcox. It was created as early as 1819, and has steadily maintained a reputation as one of the leading agricultural counties of the State. It is highly favored, both with respect to the character of its lands and the abundant supplies of water. Most of its lands, and especially its most tillable soils, lie well for cultivation. Its favorable climate, its diverse soils, its varied crops, make it a most desirable home for the man of limited means, as well as for the more extensive planter. Its area embraces 960 square miles.

Population in 1870, 28,377; population in 1880, 31,828. White, 6,711; colored, 25,117.

Tilled Land—161,228 acres. Area planted in cotton, 77,076 acres; in corn, 40,053 acres; in oats, 7,011 acres; in sugar-cane, 251 acres; in rice, 14 acres; in tobacco, 15 acres; in sweet potatoes, 1,597 acres.

Cotton Production—26,745 bales.

The general surface of Wilcox is uneven though it has much level land. Most of the land of even surface, whether found in the prairie districts, along the streams, or upon the table lands amid the hills, has been brought into cultivation. In the palmy days of the past, there could have been seen, in the most fertile sections of the county, especially upon its prairie and bottom lands, some of the most splendid and extensive plantations of the Far South. There is a variety of soil to be found in different parts of the county, and sometimes a variety in the same section. For instance, along the northern end of Wilcox, there are to be found all the varieties of black and red, with gray or white lands, with an occasional intervention of mulatto soil. All of this land is productive, however. This is a fair index of the diversity of soils prevalent throughout Wilcox. The gray and mulatto uplands are valuable for farming purposes, while the black prairie soils, and the rich alluvial bottoms which lie along the large creeks and Alabama River, sometimes embracing leagues of land in the great curves of that stream, are remarkable for their productiveness. Upon these, grows to rank luxuriance, the cotton of Wilcox, the yield of which, under favorable circumstances, is immense.

In portions of the county, notably in the southern part, the lands become thinner, being overlaid with a surface of dark sands. But beneath this sandy surface, there is usually a deep red, or yellowish clay subsoil, which proves an invaluable adjunct to the upper soil in the production of crops. Cotton, corn, oats, sweet and Irish potatoes, millet, sorghum, sugar-cane, and rice, are the principal products of the farm.

In some portions of Wilcox, the breeds of stock are being vastly improved, and this is leading to the cultivation of useful grasses, which flourish with only partial attention.

The native grasses in summer, and the cane which abounds along

the creeks and river at all seasons, furnish herbage for stock throughout the year. Enterprising parties are engaged in every portion of the
county in stock raising. Horses and mules are raised with ease and
scarcely at no expense. The dairy interest is exciting attention and
large numbers of improved strains of cattle have been introduced into
the county.

Large quantities of apples, peaches, pears, and plums, are produced
in great abundance every year. All the domestic berries, such as rasp-
berries and strawberries, produce quite satisfactorily, and quantities
are annually grown. All the wild fruits known to our southern lattitude,
grow in the waste places and through the forests of Wilcox.

The range of hills in southern Wilcox are admirably adapted to fruit
raising. From the orchards fruit comes to perfection earlier than in
any other section of the State. Grapes are easily and abundantly produced.

The timbers of the county are long and short-leaf pine, the different
varieties of oak, hickory, ash, elm, poplar, cedar, mulberry, beech,
magnolia, sycamore, and walnut. Some of the most splendid specimens
of timber found in Southern forests can be obtained in Wilcox. Perhaps
no county surpasses it in the abundance of its cedar growth. There is
also quite a quantity of excellent cypress timber. When this is removed,
and the land upon which it grows is thoroughly drained, it has been
found to equal any other in its capacity of production.

The Alabama River, Pursley, Pine Barren, Cedar Gravel, Bear,
Turkey, and Chilatchee Creeks, are the chief streams flowing through
the county, but like all large streams, they are fed by many smaller
ones, which drain different parts of the county. These and others afford
a sufficiency of water. The water of the springs and wells is either of
the coolest freestone, or purest limestone. Green sand marl has been
found at different points in Wilcox. Between Coal Bluff, on the Alabama
River, and the mouth of Pursley Creek, not a great distance above
Gullett's Landing, there are several occurrences of green sand along
the banks of the river. These extend to within a short distance of
Yellow Bluff, at McNeill's Shoals. Evidences of green sand prevail near
Lower Peach Tree. The productiveness of the lands which are embraced
in the great curves of the Alabama, is no doubt largely due to the
prevalence of these marls. The presence of green sand is also reported
from the neighborhood of Snow Hill. At Coal Bluff, on the Alabama
River, are traces of coal.

The places of interest are Camden, a beautiful town of 1,400 people,
and the county seat, Snow Hill, Allenton, Pine Apple, and Rehoboth.
Most of these places have superior educational facilities. All of them
have excellent church organizations.

Camden has been long noted for the superiority of its social advantages. It is a center of controlling influence in that section of the
State in which it is located. Besides an excellent male High School,
Camden has a Female Institute, which has long been established. Both
at Snow Hill and Pine Apple, are schools of superior grades. An excellent school is also sustained at Oak Hill. Wilcox is not excelled,

perhaps, by any other county in Alabama, in educational institutions of superior order.

Facilities for religious worship also abound throughout the county. There are many local industries, such as ginneries, grist and saw mills, and the number of these are annually increasing. For transportation, the people of the eastern end of the county rely mainly upon the Pensacola & Selma Railroad, which at present, extends from Selma to Pine Apple.

The Mobile & Birmingham Railroad, which has just been completed, traverses the western portion of the county. This has awakened great interest, as it furnishes this fertile section with an outlet to New Orleans and other Gulf ports. It also brings it into connection with the great railway systems at Selma, Montgomery and Birmingham. The Camden, Hayneville & Montgomery Railroad is in contemplation.

The Alabama River is an important channel of commerce to a large section of Wilcox county. This is regarded one of the finest waterways in the South, and in more prosperous days supported some of the most magnificent steamers found upon American rivers.

A telephonic line links together Camden and Snow Hill, where it connects with the Western Union Telegraph Company. The Vicksburg and Brunswick Railroad is projected through Wilcox, and is expected to pass the town of Camden.

Lands may be purchased in the county at prices ranging from $2 to $25, depending, of course, upon the locality and the fertility—the average price being from $3 to $5 per acre.

So eager are the people to have thrifty and energetic settlers locate in their midst, that they are willing to offer extraordinary inducements in the sale of lands and homes.

There are 3,380 acres of government land in Wilcox still untaken.

Detailed information concerning the county will be cheerfully furnished by Hon. Sol. D. Bloch, Camden, Ala.—B. F. Franklin, *Alabama As It Is: Or The Immigrant's and Capitalist's Guide Book to Alabama* (Atlanta, Georgia: Constitution Publishing Company, 1888), pp. 136–39.

Some 500,000 acres of land in north Alabama belonged to a group of English investors. In 1874–1875 when the Democrats adjusted the public debt, the English stockholders of the Alabama and Chattanooga Railroad were forced to exchange their bonds for the lands of the railroads. Although they protested loudly at these "illegal actions," nonetheless they realized that they had become the owners of some of the finest lands "on the face of the globe." The investors of course were eager to sell the lands and develop the region. One section of the report to the owners of the railroad lands stressed the advantages to English farmers.

This hill country of Alabama is now undeveloped and unsettled but . . . owing to its great mineral resources, it is destined to become studded with numerous townships and to be the home of a vast population engaged in the iron and coal industries; . . . it follows that it is exactly the place where the small industrious farmer cannot fail to prosper; for he will have an ever-increasing ready home market close at his doors and he will be free from the deadly competition which rages in other and more remote districts. . . .—*The Hill Country of Alabama, U.S.A.* (London: E. & F. N. Spon, 1878), p. 4.

Prospective immigrants were urged to go to Alabama for a first-hand look at the lands but if this was impossible and they felt competent to judge from the description of the land available in England, they were to address inquiries to the Secretary of the English Committees of Holders of Alabama 8 per cent Gold State Bonds of 1870, 17 Moorgate Street, London.

An excellent example of a local attempt to get skilled labor into the state was written by John W. Lapsley, president of the Shelby Iron Company. It was directed to the Reverend Albertus C. van Raalte, the founder of the Dutch colony in Holland, Michigan. The letter of which only a portion is given here is dated March 6, 1869.

I would not expect a colony to engage at once in any business requiring as much capital to start it as a cotton manufactury; but having become firmly established, capitalists among their own countrymen, or elsewhere, would doubtless be found (if the colonists should not possess the means among themselves) to furnish such means as would be necessary to establish this or some other valuable branch of manufactures. But independent of this, there isn't any doubt that a good large colony could on becoming established, with the remunerating employment which would be furnished by the Shelby Iron Company, become self-sustaining from the commencement. Some could locate on lands (of the company) already cleared, and prepare at once for cultivating the soil. Those who located on timbered lands, would find ample support from the products of the forest, in cutting wood and making it into coal, or in selling the wood if they preferred, either or both of which the company (as they intend [to] keep at least one furnace and perhaps more in operation with charcoal) will want in large quantities, and pay a fair price for; as before stated, give employment in the various branches of business. Among other things, the company require the manufacture of large quantities of brick; and will probably do so for several years in making the various improvements required in addition to the erection of furnaces. The company and employees about the works will furnish a good market for the farm and garden and orchard products raised in the vicinity of the works; and have a railroad from the works, connecting at Columbiana, six miles distant, with the Selma, Rome & Dalton Railroad, to send off any surplus not required at the works.—Printed in *The Journal of Southern History,* vol. 14, pp. 251–61.

Nothing came from this correspondence but there were some more successful attempts to interest outsiders. In the 1890's Baldwin County, for example, had attracted Italians, Germans, Poles, as well as immigrants of other nationalities. Chilton County had a Scandinavian settlement at Thorsby and Cullman a large number of Germans. While the definitive study of these immigrant-settlers has yet to be made, it is an accepted fact that they brought with them new and experimental ideas about fruit and vegetable growing.

Transportation

RAILROADS

Of all the forms of transportation, railroads were making the greatest progress in these years. From less than a thousand miles of track in operation in 1860, the mileage grew to 3,422 miles in 1890 and 4,226 miles in 1900. Railroads in this period were built with better roadbeds, more comforts for passengers, and better connections with other lines at common terminals. Railroads continued to be built by small companies and often extended relatively short distances between two given points. Summersell says that in 1892 there were 43 different lines in the state. However, railroads in Alabama were being consolidated into two large systems: the Louisville and Nashville, connecting the northern and southern parts of the state to each other and with principal cities like Nashville and New Orleans; and the Southern Railway, a product of the panic of 1893, which gave the state even wider connection with the markets outside the South. Each of these systems had many feeder lines so that most Alabamians now lived within a reasonable distance of a railroad.

WATER TRANSPORTATION

Trains were the chief rivals of river boats. Before 1860, railroads were feeders to river traffic; after the war, trains competed with steamboats for both passengers and freight service. While steam boats still plied the rivers and did considerable carrying trade, they waged a losing battle so that few survived after 1900. The condition of the streambeds contributed to the decline of river traffic. While generally rivers were as good as ever for boat travel, occasional sand bars prohibited passage. Sandbars, of course, were no new phenomenon but the inability to get rid of them was. The constitution of 1875 forbade the use of state money for internal improvements. Since clearing a river channel was too expensive for a company or local communities to finance, nothing was done until the late 1870's when a group of enterprising men appealed successfully to Congress for Federal aid to improve the Alabama River. A similar project for the Tombigbee-Warrior Rivers was approved in the next decade. This second undertaking was doubly expensive because it required locks and dams to make the river navigable.

When work began on the Warrior River in 1890, it was the result of the combined efforts over a period of years of leading citizens in west Alabama. As early as 1875, the Tuscaloosa Board of Industries sent a lengthy memorial to Congress, asking that $151,000 be appropriated for improvement of navigation on the Warrior River. On November 17, 1885, a mass meeting of interested citizens was called by the River Harbor Improvement Convention at the courthouse; all were called on to "lend their influence in behalf of this great and important enterprise." The work took about five years and was completed by January 1896. The local paper carried a full account of the festivities at the opening of the locks at Tuscaloosa.

THE FIRST TUGBOAT AND BARGE PASS THROUGH DRAW BRIDGE AND THREE LOCKS

At nine o'clock Saturday night, January 11, 1896 the first tugboat—the steamer "Baltimore" of Demopolis—passed under the drawbridge and into anchor at Lock No. 1.

Sunday morning a large party of Tuscaloosa and Northport people, ladies and gentlemen, small boys and girls, boarded the "Baltimore" at lock No. 1 and through the courtesy of Col. R. P. Knox, enjoyed the first trip of a tugboat to several mines along the river's edge [for several] miles from Tuscaloosa.

The "Baltimore" is the property of the Black Warrior Lumber Company of which Colonel Knox is president. To his public spirited brainy enterprise the city of Demopolis owes the tidal wave of her prosperity, to him the Tide Water Coal Company applied to organize a barge line to inaugurate a trade that is destined to make Tuscaloosa and Mobile great cities in spite of themselves. . . .

Tuscaloosa enters the contest [i. e. the rivalry with Pittsburg] with the following advantages: Tuscaloosa's water is less than 400 miles to tidewater . . . coal reaches Tuscaloosa from its mines by water of permanent, perennial, and minimum depth of six feet and from Tuscaloosa to the Gulf on six feet of water more than six months a year. . . . There is never a day that our coal mining or coal shipping is checked by cold weather. . . .

It was the special privilege and pleasure of one of our worthy townsmen, Capt. John P. Bartee to pilot the "Baltimore" on this trip. Christening, as it were, the great enterprise on the Warrior River to which he has long looked for with longing eyes and abiding faith. . . . Although he is no tyro in the handling of the wheel, yet on the night of the 11th of January, 1896, as the "Baltimore" followed the stream of its powerful arc lights swiftly through the drawbridge and into the first lock, his delicate touch of his wheel was with that anxious delight that fills the heart of the school boy as he tells his first tale of love. He was assisted in bringing the "Baltimore" from Mobile by Capt. Mage Garnett, whose steady hand guided many a craft to our city where he has a host of friends. . . .

Along the river bank on both sides was gathered a population in their best Sunday attire to do honor to the first boat to venture where no tug boat had ever been before. It was a sight to arouse the enthusiasm of the passengers, many of whom were business people of Tuscaloosa and Northport.

The approach of the boat frightened the cattle and horses browsing along the water edge, driving them into the hills. At the dock of the Tide Water Coal Company the whole surrounding region seems to have turned out to give an oration to that harbinger of prosperity and contentment. It was indeed an interesting sight to watch from the deck of the boat the happy things on the shore. The love sick swain and the blushing maidens were there in best bib and tucker, taking advantage of the occasion to steal sly glances at each other, and when the clatter of mining plants in that vicinity got under full headway, we may expect a matrimonial boom there if we are any judges of signs. . . .

Col. Horace Harding, the central figure in yesterday's gala occasion, surveyed with interest the perfect work which he had accomplished for the Government, as its engineer in charge of the Warrior River improvements.

He has expended in completing the three locks and dams and in opening out a channel through the reefs under the bridge, something like the sum of $520,000 and has on hand about $35,000 with which to begin the fourth lock. The work thus far finished affords six feet of water to about ten miles from Tuscaloosa and two and a half from about two miles farther up the river.

The locks are 322 feet long by 52 feet wide inside. The first lock has a lift of 14 feet at lowest stage of the water; the second lock, 8 feet and 6 inches. It requires about 15 minutes to fill a lock and 8 minutes to empty it.

The "Baltimore" is a splendidly built tow boat with capacity to carry four barges of 250 tons of coal each, and draws about 30 inches of water. . . . [Col. Knox] informs us that he is now shipping lumber from his large mills at Demopolis to London, England, on a through bill of lading, and a total cost of 35 cents per hundred freight less than it formerly cost to get lumber from the interior to tidewater. . . .

On that part of the river covered by the lock system, [plans] are now being pushed with energy and vim by three companies, preparing to do a large business. Already the pulse of Tuscaloosa trade beats faster by reason of money being paid out to employees by these several companies, and the business people and the working people generally can well afford to blow the trumpet loud and long in honor of the pioneers in the vast work just begun. . . . [The three companies described in the remainder of the article are: The Tidewater Coal Co., The Blair Coal Co., and The Miller Coal Company.]—Tuscaloosa *Times,* January 15, 1896.

Eventually, seventeen locks were needed for the Tombigbee-Warrior River; these were not completed until 1915, at a cost of $10,500,000. Locks were built on the Coosa and some improvements (usually dredging and removing snags) were done to the other rivers, but despite all efforts river transportation continued to decline.

In spite of available water traffic and rapidly expanding rail service, most people still traveled by horse and buggy or wagon. If a person needed to hire a horse and conveyance, he did so at a livery stable, the ancestor of the modern garage and filling station. W. H. Tisdale, who offered his business for sale, lived in Greensboro.

LIVERY STABLE FOR SALE

The undersigned offers for sale his Livery Stable, Stock and Vehicles. The stable building is substantially built and conveniently arranged with several sheds and a good stock lot. There are 28 head of horses, 17 vehicles with good harness. The horses are much above the average of livery stock. The vehicles are in good shape and well adapted to the business.

Wishing to engage in some other pursuit, I will sell at low figures.

W. H. TISDALE

Greensboro, Nov. 26, 1880
—*Alabama Beacon* (Greensboro), December 26, 1880.

Alabama roads were in a deplorable state, probably worse than they were before 1860. That less is heard about them than formerly is probably due to the fact that travelers could, if they chose, go by rail. Roads were of immediate concern to farmers, especially those some distance from a railroad line and the legislature spent considerable time listening to their complaints and trying to find a solution to them.

The legislature was powerless, however, to build or improve roads because the Constitution of 1875 forbade the state from engaging in such activities. Roads were the responsibility of the counties and communities where they were located. According to the road law, every able bodied man between eighteen and forty-five was to furnish ten days of labor on the public road to which he was assigned. The work was under the supervision of "apportioners" who were appointed by the county commissioners. The law was loosely enforced, supervision was lax, and, as a result, roads were not kept in good repair. In the 1880's, the legislature passed special road tax laws for fifteen counties but a general amendment to permit taxation for roads was defeated in 1886. Jefferson, Madison, and a few other counties had some good roads, but they would not be common until the advent of the automobile.

Cities and Industry

BIRMINGHAM

While Alabama remained predominantly rural, an outstanding feature of this period is urban growth. Cities and towns all over the state were increasing in size and importance. In 1900 while only ten municipalities had more than 5000 inhabitants, Mobile and Birmingham each had over 38,000.

Birmingham, of course, made the most remarkable growth. In 1865, there was no Birmingham at all; six years later it was an incorporated town; in 1880 it had 3,086 inhabitants and ten years later 26,178. It was developed by the Elyton Land Company on a site where iron, coal and limestone, in close proximity, promised great industrial growth.

Fortunately for the historian, some of the early settlers—members of the Pioneers' Club who according to the bylaws had to be residents in 1871–1873—wrote down and published some of their memories of the budding center. The author of the following passage was the wife of Alfred N. Hawkins, a well-known businessman, a partner in the firm of Cheek and Hawkins which had a store on 20th Street between Second and Third Avenues.

While on our way from Texas to Atlanta, we learned that there was to be a new town in Jefferson County, Alabama; a town that was to become a city of great expectations. My father, still an ambitious young man, made a detour for this promised city.

We arrived September 29, 1871. There was no shelter to be had for love or money so we camped in tents on Village Creek at the old Hawkins home, which is now Thomas Furnace. We waited there two weeks for a house to be near enough completed that we might be sheltered. We moved in October 10, 1871, occupying only one room which was incompleted, and would move from one side of the room to the other while it was being ceiled. Mr. Judd D. Kelley was the building contractor. This home was on 4th Avenue and 22nd Street, now the new News building.

The child was in her swaddling clothes, but had already been christened "Birmingham."

There was a well on 25th Street and 2nd Avenue—this furnished the water supply until more wells could be sunk. There were only four houses in the town. One was Allen's Grocery on 1st Avenue between 19th and 20th Streets. One was the tool house for the Alabama-Chattanooga Railroad and the L. & N., which were just being constructed. This tool house stood on the corner which is now Steiner's Bank. Another was Mrs. Watkins residence on the northwest corner of 3rd Avenue and 21st Street, now the Guarantee Building. The other was Webb's Saloon on the southwest corner of Second Avenue and 20th Street. Here a man was shot and killed the day we moved in.

Building kept a steady pace, still the people came faster than the building. November 10, 1871, Mr. McAnally, an engineer assisting the city engineer, moved his family into his tool house for lack of house to go into; this was on the northeast corner of 1st Avenue and 23rd Street. It was here that the first male child was born to Mr. and Mrs. Pat McAnally, November 11, 1871.

When we came in September it was not a fact that the city would be located just here. It possibly would go to Elyton, where the court house was. Therefore my father began investigations. He was told to see Colonel Worthington, who advised him to see the engineer who was surveying the railroad as he would determine whether the city would be here or in Elyton. The engineer had reached Morris Avenue and 20th Street with his survey, now where the L. & N. depot stands. "Here will be the city as the grade is too low toward Elyton," he said.

Then work began in earnest. Colonel Powell, whom we call the "Duke of Birmingham," was as busy as a bee, determined to have the city here and succeeded. He wrote to Birmingham, England, telling her of her namesake in Alabama and she sent him a knife made in Birmingham, England, but from Alabama iron. Then building began to grow as if by magic.

Twentieth Street was the center of the city as it is now. My father bought three lots on the southeast corner of 3rd Avenue and 20th Street. He built immediately the first drug house in the city. F. E. Taylor built on the northwest corner of 3rd Avenue and 20th, the first dry goods store. Mr. Paul built on the northeast corner of 3rd Avenue and 20th Street, a tinner's shop.

On July 4, 1872, Birmingham had her first fire. All of my father's buildings, with others, burned to ashes.

On the northwest corner of 19th Street and Morris Avenue was the Relay House. The northeast corner of 1st Avenue and 20th Street was Linn's Bank. The Southwest corner of 5th Avenue and 20th Street was Mr. Chas. Linn's residence. The south side of 1st Avenue between 19th and 20th Street was Linn's Park. Mr. Ed Linn's residence was on the northwest corner of 5th Avenue and 20th Street, now where the Southern Club stands. Southeast corner of 2nd Avenue and 21st Street was Mr. Oxford's Photograph Gallery. Northeast corner of 2nd Avenue and 21st Street was Mr. O'Connor's Furniture Store. The northwest corner of 2nd Avenue and 21st Street was Joe and Maurice Wilson's Grocery Store, now the Jefferson County Bank Building, (Comer Building). In the center of the street at 2nd Avenue and 20th Street was an open well of water. Major Marre had several buildings on northeast corner of 1st Avenue and 19th Street. Samuel Torrey had a bakery on the northeast corner of 2nd Avenue and 19th Street. Southeast corner of

Second Avenue and 19th Street was a mud hole. The city bell was placed on this corner. This mud pond afforded great sport for the city boys, especially did George Ward like to "sqush" the mud between his toes.

Doctor Maddox had a building on the northeast corner of 1st Avenue and 21st Street, now where the B. R. L. & P. (Birmingham Electric) building stands. This was a feed store. Next door to this building was the Bryant Building. It was here that the first school was taught by Mr. Clement, and in this house on Sunday any Christian minister might speak to the people. The house was usually crowded. We had Union Sunday School and most all the population joined in the services. I remember there were small collections and one minister, a Baptist (a Mr. Hillyer), planted out the first shade trees. . . .

Morris Avenue was named for Josiah Morris of Montgomery, who furnished funds for the Elyton Land Company. They had purchased most of the land in this vicinity. The court house at Elyton burned and Birmingham was accused of burning it. Then came the vote for the location for the new court house. We won, though Elyton gave us a good fight. Col. Powell understood human nature, he knew the way to a man's heart, so he gave to the people a fish dinner on the grounds where the new court house was to be built. He also knew psychology and mixed freely with his people, all day riding his calico pony and asking them in his winning way to "Vote for your country and your God." The voting place was in my father's building, corner 2nd Alley and 21st Street, where the News Building later stood for many years. We lived upstairs in this building and I watched the vote casting below.

Northeast corner of 2nd Avenue and 20th Street was the McDonald Building, now where the 1st National Bank stands. Southeast corner of 2nd Avenue and 20th Street was Mr. Dargan's Dry Goods Store. Southwest corner of 4th Avenue and 21st Street was the Calahan family residence. Northeast corner of 4th Avenue and 21st Street was the first church built in Birmingham. It was the Presbyterian Church. Mr. Kennedy was pastor. The next church was the Methodist, northeast corner of 6th Avenue and 21st Street. The third church was the Catholic Church, corner of 2nd Alley and 22nd Street. The fourth church was the Baptist, southeast corner of 6th Avenue and 22nd Street. The fifth church was the Cumberland Presbyterian, corner of 5th Avenue and 18th Street. The sixth church was the Church of the Advent, southeast corner of 6th Avenue and 20th Street. On the southside of 4th Alley and 22nd Street was a little school house where Miss Etta Hughes taught. Southeast corner of 4th Avenue and 22nd Street Mr. and Mrs. Pressley lived. Northwest corner of 4th Avenue and 22nd Street was Mr. Garrett's residence, now a hotel.

Then came 1873 with its epidemic of cholera. Many of our people left town. Some were courageous enough to stay through it all, some survived but many passed to the beyond. Then the Powell School was built with Professor Connelly, principal; Mrs. Thomas, Prof. Frank Grace, Prof. Felix McLaughlin and Miss Mary Calahan as teachers.

R. H. Roberts' was the first hardware store in the city, being located on 2nd Avenue.

In 1872 (I think) Mr. Fogarty bought several acres of land on Huntsville Road, built a residence and had such beautiful gardens. Mr. Paul also bought all the ground on Huntsville Road between 13th and 15th Avenues. He built a nice residence and had a peach orchard on the west side of the road and an apple orchard on the east side.

There was not much amusement for the young folks of that day so Sunday afternoons we would make up a party of six or perhaps a dozen and stroll out to see the new reservoir that was to contain the muddy water of Village Creek for our consumption, or we would go to Red Mountain but there were no beautiful terraced yards or handsome residences as there are now.

There was a place of amusement, however, a platform which was called the Crystal Palace. This was at Nabor's Springs on Southside where we had good times picnicing and dancing in the summer time.— Pioneers Club, *Early Days in Birmingham* (Birmingham: Privately printed, 1937), pp. 1–6.

One of the men principally responsible for the development of Birmingham was James R. Powell, president of the Elyton Land Company. A native of Virginia, he moved to Lowndes County, Alabama, in 1833. Ever an opportunist, he engaged in many different ventures. He owned and managed hotels; he operated a stage coach line out of Wetumpka; he served Coosa County as sheriff; he represented that county for two terms in the state senate; he packed a warehouse full of ice when the Alabama River froze over in 1863 (but refused to sell it, choosing instead to donate it to Confederate hospitals); and he bought extensive farming lands and raised cotton. He was living in Montgomery in 1870–71 when he saw the opportunities for a great industrial city in the Jones Valley district.

Some of the bustle and optimism of the early days in this "magic city" is caught in a letter by an unidentified contributor to the Montgomery *Advertizer* in the spring of 1872. Editors, he wrote, were not telling half the truth about the new city's growth "for fear of taxing the credulity of their readers to too great extent." But if they understood its great advantages, they could accept it more readily.

Atlanta, before the war, had no advantage of Birmingham in point of railroad facilities. Upon the completion of the South and North Railroad, Birmingham will be accessible to the great cities of the Northwest, having direct communication with Louisville, Nashville, Memphis, Cincinnati, and Chicago. It now has connection by the Alabama & Chattanooga Railroad, via Chattanooga, with Richmond, Washington, Baltimore, Philadelphia and New York; and via Meridian, with Mobile and New Orleans; and via Montgomery, with the Atlantic ports at Savannah

and Brunswick. This much Atlanta also had, and no more. In addition
to all these, Birmingham has rich and fertile agricultural lands around
it, and the finest mineral country in the world. The beds of coal, iron
and lime that surround it are simply inexhaustible. Enterprising men
from the North are being daily attracted to Birmingham by the wonderful stories told of its great wealth, now buried in the bowels of the
earth. When once on the spot, they find themselves spellbound by the
superior quality and quantity of the ores, and they at once resolve to
invest. Yet Atlanta, which twenty-five years ago was a mere wilderness,
is now a growing city of thirty-five or forty thousand inhabitants. I
remember well, as you doubtless do, Messrs. Editors, the contemptuous
remarks and sneers made at the predictions about Atlanta, and even
now there are those who will not believe Atlanta anything more than
a mushroom town—for, Convince a fool against his will,/He'll be of
the same opinion still.

So it is with Birmingham; but let any one who doubts, come and
see for himself, and like the writer, though his expectations may run
high, he will nevertheless be surprised. A little more than seven months
ago, the site of Birmingham was a cotton-field. There was not a hut
upon the place. When the founder, the indefatigable and enterprising
Col. Powell (the present Duke), with his surveyor, Mr. Parker, and
his clerk, Mr. Milner, landed at Birmingham to lay off the streets, they
were compelled to go into camps. On the 8th of August, 1871, the
foundation for the first house was laid, and on the 29th of August it
was ready for use. On the 19th of December thereafter, the city was
incorporated by the Alabama legislature, (application having been made
only three weeks before,) and a Mayor and City Council were immediately elected. Col. R. H. Henly, a talented young lawyer, and the
editor of the "Sun," has the honor of being the first Mayor of this
promising young city.

There are now over 300 buildings, 80 framed storehouses, 20 brick
stores and houses two and three stories high, and 40 brick stores under
contract, and to be built this summer. There are also two planing mills,
and sash and blind factories, two grist mills, one cotton factory, (being
built,) one foundry and machine shop, two hotels, five restaurants, ten
boarding houses, one Episcopal Church, eight brick-yards, two lime-
kilns, three stone quarries, two butcher pens, six physicians, six lawyers,
two newspapers, two job printing offices, one livery stable, three blacksmith and wagon shops, two paint stores, two news depots, five bar and
billiard saloons, three hardware stores, two furniture stores, and last,
but not least, a perfect Mohammed's paradise of lovely women. . . .

If you will take your map and follow me, I think I can show the
practicability, probability and vast importance of each and every one
of these roads. The S. & N. and the A. & C. Roads being already built,
we will begin with the Georgia Western Road. This road, it is conceded, will surely be built. Atlanta is bound, in self-defense to build it,
in order to open up the vast fields of iron and coal in N.W. Georgia
and N.E. Alabama. The road to West Point, known as the West Point
L. & B. (Narrow Gauge) Railroad, I am assured by the citizens of

West Point will soon be commenced. The Savannah & Memphis is being pushed forward by capitalists at the North, and there is not a shadow of a doubt as to its early completion. Selma, I learn, is determined, at all hazards, to have a direct communication with Birmingham, by means of an air line road from Ashby, a point on the Selma, Rome & Dalton Railroad a few miles south of Montevallo. Mobile will never allow the "Grand Trunk" to stop short of Birmingham. Now comes the Road of Roads, the one most important to the cities of Birmingham, Montgomery, St. Louis and Brunswick, Viz: the Elyton, Corinth & Tennessee River Railroad.

As you will readily perceive, this road will form almost an air line from St. Louis, via Birmingham and Montgomery, to Brunswick, Ga., on the Atlantic Coast. It will begin at Pittsburg landing, on the Tennessee River, and run through the counties of Walker, Winston, Marion and Franklin to Birmingham in Jefferson county. I have just had the pleasure of meeting Dr. A. M. Johnson, the Secretary, an intelligent and well-informed gentleman, who informs me that a survey of this road has been completed to Birmingham. It passes through the best coal regions of Alabama, as yet untouched, and will place Montgomery in as direct communication with St. Louis as it will shortly be with Louisville. It will therefore give us two outlets to the great North-west.

This road, shortening the distance, as it does, from St. Louis to the Atlantic Coast, at Brunswick, Georgia, by 80 miles or more, will afford us the great desideratum of our people, viz: direct communication with Europe. It will open to us the immense cribs and meat houses of the Queen City of the West, where we can deal with friends and sympathizers. When this matter is properly viewed by our own citizens, and the citizens of St. Louis, Brunswick and other places equally interested, I am forced to believe that this important road will be speedily built. It is a matter in which Montgomery is or should be deeply interested, because this road will afford two sources from which to draw her supplies, instead of one as now.—William Garrett, *Reminisences of Public Men in Alabama* (Atlanta, Ga.: Plantation Publishing Company Press, 1872), pp. 441–43.

T.C.I. Merger

Alabama industry had its earliest development under a number of independent companies (and usually with local capital) which were gradually consolidated into larger ones. The announcement of the merger of the Sloss and DeBardeleben interests with the Tennessee Coal, Iron, and Railroad Company was made on March 9, 1892.

ALABAMA IRON

THREE GREAT PRODUCING COMPANIES COME TOGETHER,
WITH A CAPITAL OF TWENTY FIVE MILLION DOLLARS
THE TENNESSEE, SLOSS AND DEBARDELEBEN FURNACES

New York, March 7.—Special.—It was announced on Wall Street today that the Tennessee Coal, Iron and Railroad Company would probably absorb the Sloss Iron and Steel company and the DeBardeleben Coal and Iron company of Alabama. The announcement caused a sharp advance in the stock of the Tennessee Coal, Iron and Railroad Company. The details of the consolidation of the three big companies have not all been arranged, but the name of the consolidated company will probably be the Tennessee and Alabama Coal and Iron Company, and the capital stock will be not less than $25,000,000. The three companies own a majority of the coke furnaces in Alabama and Tennessee and the best and largest of the coal and iron mines.

President Seddon of the Sloss company and President DeBardeleben of the DeBardeleben Coal and Iron company have been here for a week conferring with President Thomas C. Platt of the Tennessee Coal and Iron Company. They will probably complete their details of the consolidation of their companies in a few days.

It was said on Wall street that the low price of iron brought about the consolidation, which is expected to materially reduce the cost of production. It is expected that the big company will soon absorb all the coke furnaces in Alabama and Tennessee.

The officers of the three companies are holding a conference at the Fifth Avenue hotel tonight. I saw Mr. DeBardeleben a while ago, and he said the terms had not yet been agreed upon, and the indications were the conference would last until a late hour and might go on all day tomorrow. He said he could not make public any of the details until the consolidation was made.

The AGE HERALD several days ago first gave local currency to the important rumor concerning the consolidation of the three great iron properties of Alabama, and this was followed up by expressions of opinion from various financiers and business men of the city. Some of these expressed doubts as to the correctness of the rumors, but others in positions to form intelligent conclusions did not doubt that the rumors were based upon facts. It transpires that these latter were correct in their estimate of the situation.

It will be a gigantic enterprise, and promises to unmeasurably strengthen Birmingham's position in the iron trade.

"It will help this community abroad," said a leading banker last night. "In all probability the great company will build a steel mill of its own, and that is what we now need most."

It is pointed out that the new company will have to organize under the law of some other state, as the law of Alabama does not permit any corporation to organize with a capital exceeding $10,000,000.—Birmingham *Age-Herald*, March 9, 1892.

BOOM TOWNS

Birmingham, founded shortly before the Panic of 1873, did little more than survive until 1879. The Elyton Land Company, incorporated with capital of $200,000, sold shares at $100 each. Extensive work was done in developing the city site but the company did not prosper. At one point shares sold for $15 and the indebtedness amounted to $150,000. With the erection of the Alice Furnace in 1879, and shortly thereafter the Birmingham Rolling Mill, the future of the city was assured. From this time forward, as one writer said, "the success of the company reads more like a tale from *The Arabian Nights* than nineteenth-century business." In 1886, for example, the company paid 340 per cent dividends and almost that much in some other years.

The success of the Elyton Land Company in Birmingham encouraged other promoters to attempt similar developments in other places. These became known as "boom towns."

There were certain basic ingredients necessary for a "boom" town—reports on the coal, iron ore and other natural resources in a given area. When the promoters had selected a site, they bought up options on large tracts of land around it. This done, they printed some attractive literature about the resources and made extravagant predictions about future growth. They used every inducement to get industries to agree to move in. When all was in readiness for the "grand opening," the company tried to get the biggest possible crowd there for the first sale of lots. Some of these towns failed and others, although they made good beginnings, never achieved the grandiose plans of their founders. Fort Payne in De-Kalb County, promoted by several New Englanders, and Calera in Shelby County are among this latter group.

> One of the thriving manufacturing towns of the state is the pretty little city of Calera situated in the southern part of Shelby county at the point where the Louisville and Nashville road is crossed by the line of the East Tennessee, Virginia and Georgia system. The location of Calera for the purposes of manufacturing is unsurpassed. Warrior coalfield lying to the north, the Cahaba coalfield in the southern extremity of which it is situated, and the Coosa coalfield, which lies to the northeast, and which combined, comprise the richest deposit of coal on this continent. Calera is also within a very short distance of inexhaustible deposits of both red and brown hematite ores, while it is surrounded with masses of as fine a quality of limestone as can be found in the world, and in quantities sufficient to supply the demands for furnace purposes for all time to come.
>
> For many years Calera has been noted as a point at which a large amount of lime was provided annually, and for this reason it first commanded attention, and investments in the extension of old, and the erection of new kilns, resulted in calling the attention of capitalists to the possibilities of the place as a center for general manufacturing purposes and for the manufacture of pig iron especially.
>
> About two years ago a party of Montgomery capitalists organized the Calera Land Company and purchased some fifteen or twenty thousand acres of land adjacent to the little town. This company at once proceeded to develop the city, and build in it a line of industries and

manufactures which would cause it to become an important factor in the growth and development of the state. The city was laid out anew, streets were run in every direction and preparation made for the accommodations of a population of 100,000, to which the city bids fair to attain.

Inducements were offered by the land companies to capitalists, to secure the location of manufacturing enterprises. Sites were furnished and every aid possible was extended to parties who exhibited an intention to establish an institution calculated to add to the development of city. The result of this policy has been that Calera is now the seat of many manufacturing enterprises which are in a prosperous condition, and which, judging from the past, promise to enjoy an existence of unrivalled prosperity. Those enterprises are varied in their nature consisting of lime works, shoe factories, tanneries, spoke and hub works, handle factories, sash door and blind factories, saw and planing mills and other works for utilizing the timber product of the country around.

The company has interested itself in the upbuilding of Calera, and to that end began preparations for the manufacture of charcoal iron on an extensive scale. The first in this movement was the erection of about fifty charcoal ovens, with which will be operated a chemical plant whereby a superior article of wood alcohol will be made and the charcoal product of the ovens will be a net profit. After the erection of these ovens the company became aware that for their successful operation a plentiful supply of water was necessary, which Calera did not afford and in consequence, on the completion of the ovens no effort was made to operate them further than for the purpose of making a test, which proved entirely satisfactory, and then the company turned its attention to securing a supply of water. Work was begun on several artesian wells and this work was pushed without cessation until water was secured in four wells, capable of furnishing a supply of 8,500,000 gallons daily, which is sufficient to furnish water for the extensive system of waterworks laid out for the city, as well as for the operation of the chemical plant.

The successful operation of the chemical plant depended on obtaining a supply of water, and this obtained, the future of Calera is assured. The land company will at once begin to push the enterprises which it has already underway there, and every inducement possible will be offered to secure the location of other industries in this promising city. That other manufactures will come there is no doubt. Those already located there have met with a success far beyond the anticipations of their projectors, and this result will be the strongest argument that could be used in securing the location of other plants.—*The Daily Dispatch* (Montgomery), October 20, 1887. Clipping courtesy of Dr. Justin Fuller, University of Montevallo.

OTHER IRON AND STEEL

Most of the iron and steel production was centered in the Birmingham area, but there were also numerous other furnaces and factories scattered throughout north-central Alabama. To advertise local economic opportunities in 1892, Saffold Berney published a *Hand-Book of Alabama.* In it he listed all of the state's blast furnaces, rolling mills and iron and steel factories, giving a brief history and resumé of the products of each. For the sake of brevity, only the first five in each category are given here.

Blast Furnaces in Alabama.—Coke.—*Bay State Furnace Company.*— Fort Payne, DeKalb county; one stack, 65 x 14; partly built; begun in 1889; work suspended in 1890.

Cole Furnaces.—Alabama Iron and Railway Company; Sheffield, Colbert county; three stacks, each 75 x 18; built in 1887–8; ore, brown hematite; product, foundry pig iron; estimated annual capacity, 120,000 net tons.

DeBardeleben (The) Coal and Iron Company.—Bessemer, Jefferson county; seven stacks in Jefferson county, of which five are in Bessemer and two at Oxmoor; Bessemer—Nos. 1 and 2, each 75 x 17, built in 1886–7; Nos. 3 and 4, each 75 x 17, built in 1889–90; No. 5, or Little Belle, 60 x 12, built in 1889–90; Eureka—No. 1, 75 x 17, built in July, 1877, and rebuilt in 1883; No. 2, 75 x 17, built in 1876 and rebuilt in 1886; ores, brown hematite and red fossiliferous; product, foundry pig iron; total annual capacity, 210,000 net tons.

Edwards Iron Company.—Woodstock, Bibb county; one stack, 70 x 15; first blown in in 1880; remodeled in 1887 and in 1890; ore, red hematite; product, foundry and mill pig iron; annual capacity, 30,000 net tons.

Fort Payne Furnace Company.—Fort Payne, DeKalb county, one stack, 65 x 14; built in 1889–90; ores, red and brown hematite.— Saffold Berney, *Hand-Book of Alabama,* second edition (Birmingham, Ala.: Roberts and Sons, 1892), p. 465.

Charcoal.—*Attalla Furnace.*—The Southern Iron Company, Nashville, Tennessee; furnace at Attalla, Etowah county; one stack, 55 x 11, built in 1888–9; ores, red and brown hematite; product, car wheel pig iron; annual capacity, 15,000 net tons.

Bibb Furnace.—Alabama Iron and Steel Company, Brierfield, Bibb county; one stack; 55 x 12; built in 1863; rebuilt in 1881; re-modeled in 1886; ore, brown hematite; annual capacity, 14,000 net tons.

Clifton Furnaces.—Clifton Iron Company, Ironaton, Talladega, county; two stacks; No. 1, 55 x 13, built in 1883; No. 2, 60 x 14, built in 1889–90; ore, brown hematite; product, car wheel and malleable pig iron; total annual capacity, 33,000 net tons.

Decatur Charcoal Iron Furnace.—Decatur Land, Improvement, and Furnace Company, New Decatur, Morgan county; one stack, 60 x 12, built in 1887–8; blown in 1890; ore, red and brown hematite; estimated annual capacity, 18,000 net tons.

Gadsden Furnace.—Gadsden Iron Company, Gadsden, Etowah county; one stack, 64 x 12, built in 1882; blown in in 1883; ores, red and brown hematite; product, foundry and car wheel pig iron; annual capacity, 9,000 net tons.—Ibid., p. 467.

Summary.—Number of coke furnaces in Alabama, completed, 38; uncompleted, 1; total number, 39. Number of charcoal furnaces in Alabama, completed, 15; uncompleted, 1; total, 16. Total number of furnaces in Alabama, completed, 53; uncompleted, 2. Annual capacity of completed furnaces in Alabama, net tons, coke, 1,407,000; charcoal, 211,000; total, 1,618,000.—Ibid., pp. 468–69.

Rolling Mills and Steel Works in Alabama.—*Alabama Iron and Steel Company.*—Brierfield, Bibb County; built in 1863, rebuilt in 1882–83 and put in operation in 1883; product, merchant bar iron and nails; annual capacity, 9,000 net tons. Formerly called Brierfield Rolling Mills. See Furnaces.

Alabama Rolling Mill Company.—Birmingham, Jefferson county. Works at Gate City, Jefferson county. Built in 1887–8; product, bars, bands, hoops, light T rails, etc. Annual capacity, 15,000 net tons.

Anniston Rolling Mills.—Anniston Rolling Mills Company, Anniston, Calhoun county. Built in 1890–1, but not put in operation.

Bessemer (The) Rolling Mills.—Bessemer, Jefferson county. Built in 1887–8; product, bar, guide, plate, and sheet iron. Annual capacity, 30,000 net tons.

Birmingham Rolling Mill Company.—Birmingham, Jefferson county. Built in 1880. New mill added in 1887; product, bar, angle, sheet and plate iron, round edge tire, small T rails, tram rails and fish plates; car iron a specialty. Annual capacity, 50,000 net tons.—Ibid., p. 469.

There were ten rolling mills and steel works in Alabama. There were also five iron pipe works at Bessemer, Anniston, Bridgeport, and Pell City; five car wheel works and several other specialty iron works.

Too little is known about the scores of small businesses that sprang up all over the state. Therefore, the following family letter from E. G. Morris, Sr. is a welcome illustration of the ups and downs of an entrepreneuer in the early days of Alabama's industrial expansion.

* OFFICE OF *
THE MORRIS MANUFACTURING COMPANY
Successors to E. G. Morris & Sons
FOUNDERS, MACHINISTS AND MILLWRIGHTS
Manufacturers of the Morris Turbine Water Wheel
PULLEYS, SHAFTINGS AND COUPLINGS.
Special attention given to mill and gin machinery
Agents for the MEDART PATENT PULLEY
Morrisville, Ala., March 1, 1891

Mr. Isaac Morris, Sen.
Dear Uncle, I got a letter from Moses H. Morris a few days ago, that

informed me that you are still living and are 87 years old. I was afraid you were dead but was real glad to learn that you and Uncle Jesse are still living. I am almost ashamed to think that I had neglected to write to you for such a long time. The only excuse I have for not writing to you for such a long time is that my misfortunes have kept me on the rock, and so hard run to keep my head above the waves that I hardly had time to write. It seems that there has been a perfect stream of misfortunes attending me ever since the beginning of the War, I was about 41 years old when the war commenced. Although I had been burnt out two or three times I had made a considerable fortune and had put a large amount of my earnings in negro property and the balance in Iron Works consisting of Blast Furnace, Puddle Furnace and forge Hames for making bar iron and a Foundry for making hollow ware, and all kinds of mill and gin machinery. And had a large Machine shop with most all kinds of wood working, and some iron making machinery. Had a large interest in 2 or 3 saw mills and 4 flouring mills, the last named was up to 1868 the best paying property in the country. After the war I bought up 3 other mills and rebuilt them until I had 21 pair of burrs running. I had just finished the last one in August 1868. When the wheat crop was thrashed it did not turn out over 2 bushels of wheat to the acre, and the farmers became discouraged and quit sowing wheat until there is not now a bushel (of wheat) raised in Calhoun or Talladega Counties, that I know of.

I forgot to mention the Federal Army (Wilson's Raiders) burned out the Iron Works entirely, also a fine brick building that was built for a cotton factory but the cotton machinery had been sold out of the house before I bought it, but I had turned it into a fine ginning establishment. After the farmers quit raising wheat my mills all became a dead weight on me and would not make the tax I had to pay on them. I held on to them for several years and the repairs and taxes were about to eat me up, and I had to begin to sell them off and of course had to let them go for almost nothing, as it was plain to see there was no money owning them.

My next move was to start up a large furniture factory; made mostly bedsteads. Made over 8,000 bedsteads on one run, and for a time made big money at it but they began to get railroads all through our country and began to ship in cheap bedsteads and furniture made in the Northeast Penitentiaries and sell them for about what it would cost me to get the material to make them, so I had to pull out of that business.

The next move was, I invented a new turbine water wheel and had them made in Rome, Georgia but they charged me so high for making them that it left me but very little profit. By this time my boys had grown up and began to learn the trade so I got them to go in with me and we built up a Foundry and the machinery to make them (the turbine water wheels) at home where we could run by waterpower. We had to get started up and get a full stock of patterns for 10 different sizes of water wheels ranging as follows: 12 inch, 16 inch, 20 inch, 24 inch, 30 inch, 34 inch, 37 inch, 42 inch, 48 inch and 54 inch wheels. Just then my oldest son Shadrach Fulton died on the 21st day of Jany.

1884. (He married Tommie Fowler who is doing a fine job of rearing her children). But the other 3 boys, Elbert Green Jun., Lewis J., and John H. Morris concluded to go on with the business. Then on top of all other misfortunes there came a flood on the 14th of April 1884, caused by 5 water spouts falling at the head of the (Cane) Creek and came down on us and raised the water at the mill 21 feet 4 inches, more than twice as high as it had ever been before, and washed away everything we had that would make a nickel. It took the dam, the shops, the machine shop 40 x 90 feet, 2 stories high, and all our patterns worth at least $3,000.00 as well as all the machinery consisting of one large planer and matcher, one Dovil planer, one sack sticker, and one moulding machine, one morticing machine and a full line of cut off and rip saws, trim saw, jib saws, several boring machines, 4 wood lathes, 2 iron lathes, sash and blind machinery and a full set of chair machinery. It took also the iron foundry, saw mill, a covered bridge, the flouring mill which was as a fine a mill, if not the finest mill in the State of Alabama.

Well you can imagine we felt pretty blue, and for sometime we did not know what to do, but we looked around and found we had our land left and 2 of the best mill shoals in the country and a pretty fair farm, the best garden and orchard in the settlement, a good new dwelling house with 7 rooms and kitchen and smoke house, store house, 10 tenant houses for our hands to live in. So we thought the best we could do was to get as much of the old wreck as we could and try it again. So we have got our Foundry and machine shop and pattern shop and blacksmith shop rebuilt and are running ahead making wheels and all kinds of mill machinery for cotton gins that the country demands. . . .
—Courtesy of the late Mrs. B. A. Jenkins of Emelle, granddaughter of E. G. Morris, Sr.

With the rapid development of mines, accidents were inevitable. The explosion in the Pratt Mines in Jefferson County on May 22, 1891, was particularly disastrous. It should be noticed that many of the victims were convicts leased by the state to mine operators. The leasing of convicts became one of the hot political issues around the turn of the century but was not abolished until 1928.

PRATT MINES DISASTER [OF 1891]
AND THE CAUSES WHICH LED TO IT.
INEFFICIENT VENTILATION AND DANGEROUS GASES.
THE FULL OFFICIAL REPORT

Mine inspector Hooper today filed with the governor his official report of the mining disaster at Pratt Mines on May 22. Following is the full text of the report:

To His Excellency, Thomas G. Jones, Governor of the State of Alabama.

Dear Sir: In accordance with your directions to investigate thoroughly the explosion which occurred at Pratt Mines on May 22, I have done so.

It appears that at, or near, the place of this explosion gas had been observed for several days. On the day previous to the explosion men working in that vicinity had to leave their work for a short time owing to the amount of gas there. This explosion occurred in the left air course of the main heading of Rock slope, apparently about sixty feet this side of the eighth left, by that I mean back towards the air shaft and hoisting shaft. The scene of this explosion was about one mile under ground from the hoisting shaft. The men killed were: Phillip Page, larceny and burglary, Jefferson county; Bob Clay, murder, Jefferson county; Tom Hamilton, grand larceny, Montgomery county; Tom Hare, burglary and larceny, Jefferson county; Joe Hall, manslaughter, Calhoun county; Charles H. Robinson, forgery, Montgomery county; W. D. Mayfield, murder, Lawrence county; A. M. Hays, murder, Jefferson county; J. G. Davis, gaming and concealed weapons, Lamar county— all convicts; Thomas Moore, free man, working as carpenter in the mines. Of these J. G. Davis, W. D. Mayfield, A. M. Hayes and Tom Hare were burnt, though it is probable that all of these men were killed by the after-damp or gases following the explosion.

The air course in which this explosion occurred is an intake and receives part of the air at the fourth left, which comes through a mule stable and blacksmith shop, and the balance of it at the pump near the air shaft. The main heading is also an intake and these two intakes come together about 125 or 130 feet beyond the eighth left and return through the right hand air course as an outtake to the air shaft situated near the sixth right.

It appears that on the morning of this explosion the fire boss, to whose testimony I would call your particular attention, found gas there at about 3 o'clock a.m.; that he went back at 5 a.m. and still found gas there; that he met all the men that worked in that portion of the mine at the sixth right; that he waited until the under boss in charge of these men came down and told him that he had stopped the men from going in that portion of the mine, and not to let any of them work there until everything was clear; that Mr. DeLacey, this under boss, went to the eighth left about 8 or 8:30 o'clock and found gas there; that he stopped the men from working in the eighth left, but put other men that work in that portion of the mine to work; that he nailed up the door to the eighth left and wrote the word "Fire!" on it in big letters; that he warned all of the men working in that portion of the mine to keep out of the eighth left. This door to the eighth left was not a permanent mine door, being apparently only put there for temporary use. It had a crack of 3 or 4 inches open above it, and also open space at the bottom. It appears that he did not investigate this place thoroughly to see how much gas there was, but only to find that there was gas there in a dangerous quantity; he went back to the intake of this air course at the blacksmith shop and opened the door to increase the draft through this air course. He also went to the air shaft and built a fire to increase the circulation of the air. The natural consequence of this action would be that if there was gas in the left air course, that being an intake, in dangerous quantities, that it would bring it to the men working with naked lights, and who get part of their air from this air course. My opinion is clear that no men should have been put to work in that portion of the mine with naked lights when gas was known to exist in dangerous quantities in the left air course, which was an intake, and the men would have to work in air coming out of that place. I think, in justice to Mr. DeLacey, that I should say that his action in this matter was not the result of carelessness, but of ignorance of the nature and dangers of fire damp.

I was unable to find that the company had any rules or regulations for the removal of gas when found or that there was any one especially responsible for it.

I wish to say in regard to the fire boss, that if equal care had been taken by others in the discharge of their duties that he seems to have taken in regard to his, that this explosion would not have occurred.

J. G. Davis, convict, and Tom Moore, free man, were working at first brattice above eighth right, which is opposite first above eighth left. These men were put there to double this brattice and should have both been working on the same side, that is, on the air course side. After the explosion Davis was found in the cross cut on the slope side while Moore was found some ninety feet up the inside in the right hand air course. This seems to have been the scene of the greatest force of the explosion and is probably where it occurred. The force of the explosion occurred in the left air course and came across the main heading and into the right air course. From a profile of this heading which accompanies the map made by Mr. Hasket, you will see that this is the highest opening that there is on the left side of this air course, and it is probable that the accumulation of gas in the left air course or from its being stirred up by Mr. DeLacey's efforts to increase the draft by opening the intake and building a fire in the air shaft, that is tailed out through this brattice near eighth left and caught from the Davis lamp and thus lit the body of gas behind the brattices in the air course. There were three other men burnt in the main heading and some one of these four men certainly ignited the gas, and it is just as certain the body of the gas was in the left air course and that the great force of the explosion came from there.

This mine has no furnace or fan with which to create a regular and constant current of air and has to depend almost entirely upon natural ventilation; no regular system seems to be in force for distributing to the different cross entries the amount of air each should have according to the number of men and mules worked there. In driving their headings too much dependence seems to be had on the condensed air running in pipes up each heading and cross entry. This explosion was a very small one considering the disastrous results as regards loss of life, the mine track not being disturbed and mine cars not thrown off the track. In regard to this I have a separate paper to submit to you which, I think, gives the solution of this question, that it was largely conduced by inefficient ventilation and by gasses formed from the air passing through the mule stable and blacksmith shop, and that this was an improper arrangement as regards ventilation, to let air from the mule stable and blacksmith shop go to men to breathe, and entirely unnecessary.

In regard to the class of labor employed in this shaft, there are very few of what we call skilled miners, that is, miners familiar with the different styles of work in mining and the dangers incident thereto.

From my investigation of this occurrence I wish to say that if this explosion occurred as claimed by the officials of the Tennessee Coal and Iron company, as one of those unforseen accidents that could not be guarded against, then this is a dangerous and unfit place to work convicts, who are ignorant of the dangers of mining and not competent to protect themselves and who have no option as to where or when they shall go to any place to which they are ordered; that if this explosion could have been guarded against then there is very great neglect somewhere in the management of the parties in charge of shaft No. 1. I also wish to state that in view of the dangers incident to the working of gaseous mines and of the ignorance of the convicts, (who are generally recruited from the cotton fields of south Alabama) that no convict should be allowed to work in a gaseous mine; that this is especially dangerous from where there is only one avenue of escape from said mine and where the carelessness of one man may cause the loss of several hundred lives; that I do not consider an air shaft 360 feet deep which is crooked and in which the smoke stacks of underground boilers are placed, is an escape shaft; that the entrance from old slope No. 1, which comes in at the bottom of No. 1 shaft, is not, I think, a reasonably safe method of escape; that the Tennessee Coal and Iron company were well aware that this was a gaseous mine, as in the past two years two men have been killed and a number, I don't know how many, burned. I think in view of these facts No. 1 shaft is a dangerous and unfit place to work men who have but little knowledge of the dangers to be guarded against in mining. I have not expressed these conclusions without careful thought, as probably the best prison in the south is built at this point and of the management of the convicts above ground I cannot speak too highly, from what I saw while at the prison. I also wish to say in regard to and in justice to Mr. Ramsey, that the progressive plan of the work in the mines is good and that the trouble seems to be in the detail of the work in the mines, that I found it very difficult to get at the exact course of the currents of air and where they went, in many instances.

Respectfully yours,
J. DE B. HOOPER
Inspector of Mines.

—Birmingham *Age-Herald,* June 10, 1891.

TEXTILE MANUFACTURES

Cotton manufacturing was but a continuation of an industry begun before the war. For a time after 1865, it was of little more importance than it had been formerly. There were 12 cotton mills in 1850 and only 18 in 1880. However, they were larger and more important than the number indicates. The capital invested in these eighteen was $1,386,500, the labor force consisted of 444 men, 731 women and girls over 15 years of age, and 467 children; wages amounted to $283,189, which was pathetically low. Adult wages were small enough but child wages were even less. There is a documented case of a nine year old girl who worked an 11½ hour day for ten cents. The mills used raw materials and produced goods worth $1,352,090. A decade later, there were 36, most of which were located in the north and central parts of the state. The Chattahoochee River Valley with its abundant water power was rapidly becoming a center of textiles. The history of the industry there is essentially the history of the West Point Manufacturing Company and, as its president said in 1955, the history of the company is the history of the Lanier family. In an address to the Newcomen Society he recounted their growth and development.

On an August day in 1866, Robert M. Patton, newly elected Governor of Alabama, and Judge William Chilton, later Chief Justice of the Alabama Supreme Court, arrived in West Point to preside over ceremonies for the laying of the cornerstones of The Chattahoochee Manufacturing Company, at present-day Langdale, and The Alabama-Georgia Manufacturing Company, several miles farther down the river, at River View. In West Point, ante-bellum cotton center of east central Alabama and west central Georgia, some two thousand people had gathered for the occasion. Dignitaries from Georgia also were present. From the beginning, because of its geographical location, the industrial Valley has been a joint Alabama-Georgia enterprise. Amid colorful ceremonies, conducted by the Masonic Lodge of West Point, the cornerstone of the Chattahoochee mill was laid in the morning and, after a noonday barbecue, a similar ceremony was re-enacted at River View. In a speech prepared for the occasion, Governor Patton spoke with great earnestness of the plight of the South, its defeat, and depleted economy. As for slavery, its passing was a "blessing to the white man." He considered a balanced economy based on a sound agriculture and industry the only hope of the people. He declared that if the Southern people "only produced one-half of the former crop of cotton and manufactured it, even into yarns, the profits would be far greater than during the antebellum days of four million bales." The ceremony over, the leaders of The Valley started the long hard task of making their dream a reality.

Who were these first mill men in The Valley and from whence came their capital? The Chattahoochee mill was organized by a group of West Point businessmen and planters. The Alabama-Georgia mill was founded at River View by planters. Both mills secured capital from the sale of high priced cotton in Savannah and Augusta, before it could be illegally seized by Reconstruction agents. At these ports buyers for English cotton mills were eagerly awaiting cotton at the conclusion of the war. James W. McClendon, a local businessman, was the first president of the Chattahoochee mill. The Alabama-Georgia mill was incorporated under the leadership of George Huguley, an extensive planter who had been left an orphan while still a young boy. Because of the Huguley's initiative and drive, his mill was the first to begin actual operations. The founders dug the clay from their own grounds, made and baked their brick for the buildings. . . .

Both of these mills struggled with tremendous problems in the early years. The first machinery was secondhand, discarded by Eastern mills. Experienced labor was lacking and capital was scarce. The mills in the Chattahoochee Valley made osnaburgs, a type of coarse cloth for the local market. Profits on osnaburgs were always meager by comparison with those on finer goods made in the East. In 1870, a bale of osnaburgs from the Chattahoochee mill took the first premium at the Fair in Atlanta. At this time a local newspaper declared that "capitalists desiring to invest in a substantial institution would do well to visit West Point." However, in the Panic of 1873, since the market for cloth was local, both mills closed for a time.

It was during the panic [of 1873] that two young Confederate veterans, Lafayette Lanier and his older brother, Ward Crockett, neither of whom was an original stockholder in either of the companies, became interested in the Chattahoochee mill. No doubt they had inherited an interest in the industrial Valley from their father, Reuben Lanier, who operated a successful copper mine near West Point in the ante-bellum period. Like their cousin Sidney Lanier, who wrote the *Song of the Chattahoochee,* the Lanier brothers were interested in the river, but for a different reason. They dreamed of harnessing its power for industrial purposes. At the end of the War Between the States, the Laniers had established a mercantile business in West Point and then a bank. Lafayette Lanier had gained a family interest in the Alabama-Georgia mill when he married Ada Alice Huguley, daughter of the President of the company. The Chattahoochee mill, however, became his main interest. One of his first purchases of stock in the latter mill came during the panic of 1873, when he traded a piece of property to James W. McClendon for his stock in the shutdown mill. . . .

The machinery in the Chattahoochee mill, which was poor in the beginning, had worn out by the early 1870's. While others were curtailing expenses because of the panic, the Laniers, together with the new president, John D. Johnson, showed their confidence in the enterprise by making plans to re-equip and re-organize the mill. Through contact with an English manufacturer of mill machinery, they secured the services of William Lang, an experienced cotton mill man from Oldham, England. After Lang arrived in West Point, he made a survey of the mill, ordered new machinery, and supervised the repairing of other machinery by the local Lanier Iron Works. Lafayette Lanier decided that since the company had been losing money on osnaburgs it should convert to flat duck, a fabric in great demand on the frontier.

This product proved to be profitable and production increased steadily during the following years. Later, Thomas Lang, the father of William Lang, came from England to become superintendent of the Chattahoochee mill. William Lang then became superintendent of the Alabama-Georgia mill at River View. The Langs were experienced cotton mill men and brought the technical "know-how" to the industrial Valley in its formative years. This played no small part in the success of the enterprise. According to one account, Tom Lang got the "best production at the lowest cost of any other duck mill in the country."—Joseph L. Lanier, *The First Seventy-Five Years of West Point Manufacturing Company 1880–1955* (New York: The Newcomen Society in North America, 1955), pp. 8–11.

There were other enterprises similar to the West Point Company. Avondale Mills, founded by Braxton Bragg Comer in 1897, is another example of how one man with drive, using the help of bankers and eastern connections, could make a successful business.

In 1891, an Attalla paper reported on the existing cotton mills.

COTTON MILLS IN ALABAMA

A new cotton mill, with 42,000 spindles and 1,000 looms, is to be forthwith erected at Riverside, Ala.

A $1,000,000 cotton mill is being built at Huntsville, Ala.

The most extensive cotton yarn mill in the south is going up at Piedmont, Ala.

In each of these instances, the principal capitalists interested are northern cotton mill men.

The boom in iron development is to be followed by a boom in cotton manufacturing.

That the movement in cotton manufacturing in the south did not precede that in iron production is simply because northern iron makers perceived more quickly than northern cotton mill men the character of the competition which both these great northern industries were to meet from the south, and more promptly shaped their business to the inevitable.

Pennsylvania iron makers hurried to the ore beds of Alabama and the neighboring states, bringing their furnaces with them; and New England cotton spinners and cotton weavers, having delayed as long as they could with safety, are making haste to bring their spindles and looms from Massachusetts and thereabouts to the cotton fields.

Every well equipped and tolerably well managed cotton mill in the south has made money, and some of them which are not well appointed or efficiently conducted have been profitable.

The new mills now going up in Alabama, all of which are to be ready for operation within the calendar year, will be to those now in operation here what the new furnaces in the state are to those of ten years ago, and the results will be correspondingly more satisfactory.

The cotton mill alongside the field, saving freights, commissions, in-

surance, compress charges, warehousing, and other costs, has the choice
of the raw material, which hereafter it will itself handle through all the
processes is approximately equi-distant from Baltimore and New Orleans, from Boston and Galveston, and from Louisville to Cincinnati
on one side and Charleston and Mobile on the other.

A cotton mill in Piedmont, using the fine upland cotton of Calhoun,
Cherokee and Cleburne counties, is located to take instant advantage of
any local disturbance in the markets for yarns and fabrics in any part
of the country, north or south, and has means of speedy communication
with all parts. . . .—The *Attalla Vigil,* June 4, 1891.

In the late 1880's four woolen and knitting mills opened, all in
the southeastern part of the state.

In summarizing the extent of manufacturing in 1900, Dr. Charles
G. Summersell says there were in Alabama over 5,500 factories,
employing 53,000 and consuming more than $44,000,000 worth of
raw materials. Since 1870 industry had increased at an amazing
rate, providing more jobs, raising the per capita income, and improving the economic life in the state.

Organized Labor

Too little is known about organized labor in Alabama. None of
the standard histories or even those of Birmingham make the
vaguest reference to its existence. Only recently has any serious
work been done on labor history. Although it deals with a specific
incident, the best study easily available is Robert David Ward and
William Warren Rogers, *Labor Revolt in Alabama: The Great
Strike of 1894,* published by the University of Alabama Press.
Even they admit that the early history of the movement is shrouded
with secrecy and that consequently little information is obtainable.

There were strikes in coal mines in the 1870's but whether the
strikers were organized is not known. Apparently the first unioni-
zation was among coal miners in 1879–80 when the Knights of
Labor organized local assemblies at Helena, Jefferson, Pratt, New
Castle, and Warrior. The Knights, which were a relatively conservative organization in Alabama, increased in membership and
later declined in power at about the same rate as the national union
did. After 1886, it was of little importance to the hard-pressed
miners who wanted stronger support. In that same year, the National Federation of Miners and Mine Laborers was organized.
Four years later (January 25, 1890), when the United Mine
Workers of America was organized, Alabama was granted membership in District 20. This proved to be the most powerful union to
date and emboldened miners to engage in several strikes, most of

which they lost but in an occasional one they made some slight gains.

Miners here had not only the grievances of low pay (often cut without warning), dangerous working conditions, and the use of strikebreakers, which all labor had in common, but the added ones of convict labor in mines and factories and the competition of Negroes who were often used to break strikes.

Statistics on labor unions are lacking but news about their activities after 1890 when Jerry Dennis established the *Labor Advocate* in Birmingham is plentiful. The paper's purpose, so the masthead proclaimed, was to be "a mouthpiece of organized labor and an exponent of union principles." The following account of the "grand rally" gives some idea of the extent of labor activities of 1893.

A GRAND RALLY
of local Trades Unions called for March 26th
TINNERS' GRAND BALL ON MONDAY, April 3rd
STEEL MEN CELEBRATE IN GRAND STYLE

Organized labor took another long step to the front Sunday afternoon at the regular session of the Birmingham Trades Council in the affiliation of the Railway Carmen's National Association with the central body.

One by one the isolated unions are coming in and perfecting labor's great local clearance house and forming an unbroken and united front for the peaceful and harmonious solution of all their differences and an insurmountable bulwark of defense against the many insiduous encroachments of unfair and unjust conditions in the every day affairs of life.

ELECTION OF NEW OFFICERS

President Adams of the Tin, Sheet Iron and Cornice Workers, stated that it would hereafter be impossible for him to attend the meetings of the Council on Sunday and therefore begged leave to tender his resignation as financial secretary.

President Sexton, of the Journeymen Barbers, notified the Council of the resignation of Vice-President Eckert, and Messrs. Arrico, Marion and Brand were appointed tellers of the election for the Council to cast up its ballots for a choice to the vacant positions.

Several nominations were made for both positions; but Mr. Ed. Chapple, of the Railway Carmen, was finally declared elected and obligated as vice-president, and Mr. John C. McNulty, of the Boilermakers, financial secretary.

THE RAILWAY BROTHERHOODS

President Acton, of the Machinists, spoke urgently and well upon the affiliation of all the railway Brotherhoods, not only among themselves but with the great central body of organized trades as well, followed by others, and on motion Delegates Acton, McNulty, Chapple and Sutto were appointed a special committee to act with the committee on organization and affiliation and meet the railway men tomorrow (Sunday) morning at 9 o'clock in the Knights of Pythias hall of Third Avenue opposite the post office, and endeavor to have them form still closer relations with the rank and file of all the miscellaneous unions as represented in the local trades congress.

This would make a complete and perfect unification of all the bodies of labor in the city.

APPLICATION FOR PARDON

Delegate Conolly, of the local Bricklayers, spoke of the application for pardon that was being circulated in behalf of their comrade Lew Farrell undergoing imprisonment for manslaughter, and on motion Delegates Conolly, Chapple and Mullins were appointed a committee to confer with the railway unions, one of whom it is thought the deceased was a member, with power to act in the name of the Council.

REVIVAL OF INTERESTS

President John F. Marion, of the local Bricklayers, and chairman of the committee on organization and affiliation, said it was time the workers were brushing off their lethargy and inactivity and rousing up to a full realization of the severe economic conditions facing us on all sides and therefore called for

A GRAND RALLY

of all union men at the next session of the Council Sunday afternoon the 26th instant, which met with the heartiest approval of every delegate present, who were therefore instructed by the chair to so notify their respective fellow unionists.

BLUE LABEL CIGARS

Mr. Linkenfeter, of the local Cigarmakers, again took the floor and especially thanked the Amalgamated Association of Iron and Steel Workers for their persistent efforts in setting a good example for the business men of the city to follow in patronizing home industry by accepting nothing but our own home workmen's blue label cigar, their special brands being given as follows:

PATRONIZE HOME INDUSTRY

Pride of Birmingham,	Flora Extra,
Spanish Victor,	Pearl of Key West,
"Elegance."	

10 CENT BRANDS

Laciencia,	La Flora de Cuba.

TINNERS' GRAND BALL

The Tin, Sheet Iron and Cornice Workers gave notice of their second annual grand ball to be held in Erswell hall on the night of Monday evening April 3rd and at which they will present the young lady selling the most tickets with one of the handsomest parasols ever brought to the city, and the best lady dancer with a pair of Pearson & Wyatt Shoe Co's choicest slippers, both of which are now on exhibition in their handsome show windows on corner of First avenue and 21st Street.

Prof. Fred L. Grambs' full orchestra will furnish music for the occasion and every effort will be put forth to have it as brilliant and successful as our home people know how to make it.

Mr. J. J. Curran will preside as master of ceremonies and Messrs. Wm. Horan, Pat Fagan, John Jewell, John Schwenfurth and President James Adams are in charge of all arrangements.

The County Seat Town

Alabama's industry was growing rapidly with iron, steel, coal, brick, lime, and textiles playing an increasingly important role in the economy. Nevertheless, in 1900, eight out of every ten inhabitants still lived in rural settings or small towns. Here, as in all other Southern states, the county seat town has always been important. Usually, although not always, it has been the largest town within the bounds of the county. In addition to being the seat of government, it was (and still is) the economic and at times the social center of the area. In recognizing both the growing urbanization and the persistent ruralness of the state, it is easy to overlook the importance of towns like Greenville.

GREENVILLE, 1885

We have just carried the reader briefly over the gradual development of this pleasant little city. We shall now turn our attention to the Greenville of the present day.

Her corporate limits are about two miles square, and her officers claim 4,000 inhabitants, the majority of whom are whites. In a business point of view, she is generally considered the most important point on the Louisville and Nashville Railroad between Mobile and Montgomery, receiving more freight, and shipping more cotton and other produce.

The amount of trade carried on here can be estimated, and its character and quality determined, by the number and variety of stores, which may be classed thus: fifteen dry goods and grocery stores, four dealing in drugs, one in books and stationery, eight in family groceries, two in furniture, two in jewelry, four in hardware, three in notions, ten in confectioneries, and two in tinware. There are also three well-kept livery and feed stables, six warehouses for weighing and storing cotton, three gun-shops, two excellent carriage shops, two shops for the manufacture of bridles and saddles and all kinds of harness, two shops for making tinware, several good blacksmith and shoe-shops, eight liquor and billiard saloons, one poor-house, three bakeries, five millinery stores, etc. The names of the most important firms are: D. G. Dunklin & Co., H. Z. Wilkinson & Co., A. G. Winkler, Flexner & Lichten, Charles Neuman, Drum & Ezekiel, Steiner Bros. & Co., Long and Greenhut, Wimberly & Co., J. T. Perry & Co., A. Steinhart, Weatherly & Barrow, Payne & Burnett, Beeland & Co., and J. K. Seale. The only banking house here is owned by Joseph Steiner & Sons. H. Z. Wilkinson & Co. carry on some banking business, but do not keep a regular exchange.

The travelers stopping here have the privilege of choosing between three well-kept hotels—the Perry House, at the depot; the Holzer House, about the center of the business part of town, and the City Hotel, near the court-house. Persons so desiring can procure very good board at private boarding-houses at reasonable rates.

The people belong to nearly all the religious denominations found in Southern cities. The whites have five churches—Methodist, Missionary Baptist, Primitive Baptist, Presbyterian and Episcopalian. The Methodists and Presbyterians have very durable brick churches; the other denominations have neat frame buildings, sufficiently large for their present congregations. The colored people have four churches, all of which are made of wood.

The children and young people of Greenville enjoy the advantage of receiving instruction from any of the following schools: The Greenville Collegiate Institute, governed by a Board of Trustees appointed from members of the Methodist Church, and directly under the management of Professor S. P. Rice, male and female; the South Alabama Female Institute, now under the supervision of Mrs. M. E. Garrett, who is assisted by several competent teachers; the Greenville Male High School, with Professor George W. Thigpen as principal; the Butler High School, for boys and girls, with Professor E. L. Norris as principal; the Home School, taught by the Misses Farrior. There are a few other schools taught in private families. Besides these, the State and county pay for the teaching of a public school, free of tuition. Greenville could be made a great educational center, as it is healthful, conveniently located, with a favorable climate and a refined society.

The health reports from the Medical Board of the county show that Greenville is the most healthy city of its size in the cotton belt. Within three miles of the court-house are situated the celebrated Roper Wells, whose waters, upon analysis, are found to be very valuable for medical purposes. Water is shipped from these wells to all parts of the United States. Five miles west of the city are found the Reddock Springs, noted for their healing properties in cases of dyspepsia, dropsy, consumption, etc. Within the limits of the city the water is freestone, of the very best quality, and is found about forty feet from the surface of the earth. An artesian well is now being bored, and when completed will furnish the city with an abundance of water for all uses.

The city is governed by a Board of Councilmen, elected by the citizens, and the laws are enforced by a mayor, as chief executive officer, assisted by a marshal and several police officers. By this means the people have perfect order, and enjoy all the privileges of city life. The city owns the two-story brick building called the City Hall, which is located near the center of the city. The basement of this building is rented and used as a market-house; the second floor is used as the armory for the Greenville Light Guards, and for theatrical performances, balls, etc. All the revenue collected from the use of this building is turned into the city treasury.

Greenville has twelve pleaders at the bar, whose persuasive powers make them rank high in their noble profession, and no citizen need fear that he will not get his deserts in this locality, for these followers of Blackstone are ever ready to prosecute or defend those who may happen to be in need of their assistance and counsel. Those in need of medical advice have the privilege of naming one of eight skilled physicians, who are ever ready and willing to prescribe, to the best of their ability. Greenville is not wanting in the dental profession. Three of these happy relievers of human pain hang their signs in conspicuous places in her streets, and inform the public that all work in their line will receive prompt and careful attention.

The *Greenville Advocate,* the only paper printed in the county, is issued here, and employs a large number of men to do different kinds of work.

From what has been said, we see that nearly every profession and trade is represented in Greenville, so that no one need go from her salubrious shades in search of employment, for no city of the same size and importance has so great a diversity of work as the county-site of Butler.—John Buckner Little, *The History of Butler County, Alabama, 1815–1885* (Cincinnati, Ohio: 1885), pp. 95–99.

In conclusion, the economic life of the state continued to be based on the land, and most of the people lived in rural settings. By 1900 eight out of every ten inhabitants still lived in the country, but more and more of them were moving into towns which were increasing both in number and in size. Nevertheless, there were only ten municipalities with more than 5000 people, only Mobile and Birmingham having more than 38,000 each. Birmingham had experienced the most phenomenal growth. Considering the fact that it was not even founded until after 1870, it had experienced such rapid expansion that by 1900 it had 38,415 inhabitants.

The economic life of the cities was based on both trade and industry. By 1897 Birmingham alone had around 200 industrial plants. In addition to iron and steel, these plants produced cotton gin works, brick, brooms, furniture, clothing, and cotton seed oil. Iron and steel were the most valuable industrial products in the state. Lumber came next and cotton goods third. The vast deposits of iron, coal, and limestone in north central Alabama were appreciated fully only after 1865 but thereafter provided the base on which the state's industrial wealth developed, attracting investors, both American and foreign, into the mineral belt.

There were towns, however, that were trade, not industrial, centers. These towns, although they were growing in size and importance, differed little from their antebellum counterparts. The leading ones were usually the county seats where the best stores were located, the weekly paper was published, and the elected officials carried on the functions of government. They often had good schools and an active social life. Places like Greensboro, Monroeville, Greenville, Talladega, Clanton, Oneonta, Livingston, and dozens like them were really more typical of the whole state than was Birmingham.

EPILOGUE

While in 1900 Alabama still bore the scars of the 1860's and 1870's, the state was making remarkable strides in many fields, but especially in industry. Fortunes were being made in coal and iron mines, in industry, and in railroads. There was greater opportunity for wealth in these fields now than in agriculture, even though planters in the cotton areas were still making money. If the small farmer and especially the tenant farmer was sinking into despair, so were his counterparts all over the nation. Although factory wages were low and an intense form of paternalism existed in mill villages, this was also true in other parts of the South where the industrial revolution had spread. Conditions were no better and no worse here than in most other sections.

The fact that Alabama's history has been less turbulent than that of some of her neighbors has led to the erroneous belief that little has happened here. This is far from the truth. The same forces and often the same events cast their influences in this state as elsewhere. In fact, some of these forces have been intensified in Alabama. Nowhere else, for example, was the early international rivalry more keen than here. England, France, and Spain vied for the Indians' trade, friendship, and land. Eventually the English and their descendants, the Americans, won the land and removed the Indians from the scene, but only after a long struggle and considerable intrigue.

Furthermore, many of the events that shaped its individual history were nationwide in scope. Indian troubles, inflation, the panics of 1837, 1873, and 1893, slavery, the Civil War, Reconstruction, were common to the whole nation, and only the details differed. The industrial revolution, which came after 1865, was but a delayed phase of the movement that came to the Northeast half a century earlier.

Are there, therefore, no unique features to Alabama history? The answer is, of course, yes. Incidents at the local level are never exactly the same even though they are similar. Furthermore, there were several incidents based largely or wholly within this state. While Indian wars were common all over the country, the Creek War of 1813–1814 was fought entirely within Alabama. Likewise the Confederacy was organized in Montgomery and Alabama furnished most of the iron for the Confederacy. The foundries at Selma were the only ones functioning after the capture of the Tredegar Iron Works near Richmond and were therefore especially important. The close proximity of coal, iron, and limestone, and steel found in the Birmingham area is duplicated only in Pittsburgh. This list could be lengthened easily. However, the forces and events that have had the greatest influence in shaping Alabama's history have been those she shared with the region and the nation rather than those that were uniquely her own.

In 1900, with a new constitution being drafted, many people expected a new day in politics to dawn. Also many Alabamians were looking forward to new economic prosperity. For many people living at the close of the eighteen hundreds, 1900 was a significant date, if for no other reason than that it ushered in a new century.

APPENDIX I

Alabama Counties

Name of County	Date of Origin	Present County Seat	Population, 1970
Autauga	1818	Prattville	24,460
Baldwin	1809	Bay Minette	59,382
Barbour	1832	Clayton	22,543
Bibb (originally Cahaba)	1818	Centreville	13,812
Blount	1818	Oneonta	26,853
Bullock	1866	Union Springs	11,824
Butler	1819	Greenville	22,007
Calhoun (originally Benton)	1832	Anniston	103,092
Chambers	1832	Lafayette	36,356
Cherokee	1836	Centre	15,606
Chilton (originally Baker)	1868	Clanton	25,180
Choctaw	1847	Butler	16,589
Clarke	1812	Grove Hill	26,724
Clay	1866	Ashland	12,636
Cleburne	1866	Heflin	10,996
Coffee	1841	Elba	34,872
Colbert	1867	Tuscumbia	49,632
Conecuh	1818	Evergreen	15,645
Coosa	1832	Rockford	10,662
Covington (in 1868 named Jones)	1821	Andalusia	34,079
Crenshaw	1866	Luverne	13,188
Cullman	1877	Cullman	52,445
Dale	1824	Ozark	52,938
Dallas	1818	Selma	55,296
DeKalb	1836	Fort Payne	41,981
Elmore	1866	Wetumpka	33,535
Escambia	1868	Brewton	34,906
Etowah (originally Baine)	1866	Gadsden	94,144
Fayette	1824	Fayette	16,252
Franklin	1818	Russellville	23,933
Geneva	1868	Geneva	21,924
Greene	1819	Eutaw	10,650
Hale	1867	Greensboro	15,888
Henry	1819	Abbeville	13,254

630

Name of County	Date of Origin	Present County Seat	Population, 1970
Houston	1903	Dothan	56,574
Jackson	1819	Scottsboro	39,202
Jefferson	1819	Birmingham	644,991
Lamar (originally Jones, later Sanford)	1867	Vernon	14,335
Lauderdale	1818	Florence	68,111
Lawrence	1818	Moulton	27,281
Lee	1866	Opelika	61,268
Limestone	1818	Athens	41,699
Lowndes	1830	Hayneville	12,897
Macon	1832	Tuskegee	24,841
Madison	1808	Huntsville	186,540
Marengo	1818	Linden	23,819
Marion	1818	Hamilton	23,788
Marshall	1836	Guntersville	54,211
Mobile	1812	Mobile	317,308
Monroe	1815	Monroeville	20,883
Montgomery	1816	Montgomery	167,790
Morgan (originally Cataco)	1818	Decatur	77,306
Perry	1819	Marion	15,388
Pickens	1820	Carrollton	20,326
Pike	1821	Troy	25,038
Randolph	1832	Wedowee	18,331
Russell	1832	Phenix City	45,394
St. Clair	1818	Pell City	27,956
Shelby	1818	Columbiana	38,037
Sumter	1832	Livingston	16,974
Talladega	1832	Talladega	65,280
Tallapoosa	1832	Dadeville	33,840
Tuscaloosa	1818	Tuscaloosa	116,029
Walker	1823	Jasper	56,246
Washington	1800	Chatom	16,241
Wilcox	1819	Camden	16,303
Winston (originally Hancock)	1850	Double Springs	16,654

APPENDIX II

Governors of the State

Name	County	Year of Inauguration
William Wyatt Bibb	Autauga	1819
Thomas Bibb	Limestone	1820
Israel Pickens	Greene	1821
John Murphy	Monroe	1825
Gabriel Moore	Madison	1829
Samuel B. Moore	Jackson	1831
John Gayle	Greene	1831
Clement Comer Clay	Madison	1835
Hugh McVay	Lauderdale	1837
Arthur P. Bagby	Monroe	1837
Benjamin Fitzpatrick	Autauga	1841
Joshua Lanier Martin	Tuscaloosa	1849
Reuben Chapman	Madison	1847
Henry Watkins Collier	Limestone	1845
John Anthony Winston	Sumter	1853
Andrew Barry Moore	Perry	1857
John Gill Shorter	Barbour	1861
Thomas Hill Watts	Montgomery	1863
Lewis E. Parsons	Talladega	1865
Robert Miller Patton	Lauderdale	1865
William Hugh Smith	Randolph	1868
Robert Burns Lindsay	Colbert	1870
David Peter Lewis	Madison	1872
George Smith Houston	Limestone	1874
Rufus W. Cobb	Shelby	1878
Edward Asbury O'Neal	Lauderdale	1882
Thomas Seay	Hale	1886
Thomas Goode Jones	Montgomery	1890
William Calvin Oates	Henry	1894
Joseph Forney Johnston	Jefferson	1896
William Dorsey Jelks (Acting)	Barbour	1900
William James Samford	Lee	1900
William Dorsey Jelks	Barbour	1901
William Dorsey Jelks	Barbour	1903

Name	County	Year of Inauguration
Russell McWhorter Cunningham (Acting)	Jefferson	1905
Braxton Bragg Comer	Jefferson	1907
Emmett O'Neal	Lauderdale	1911
Charles Henderson	Pike	1915
Thomas Erby Kilby	Calhoun	1919
William W. Brandon	Tuscaloosa	1923
Bibb Graves	Montgomery	1927
Benjamin M. Miller	Wilcox	1931
Frank M. Dixon	Jefferson	1939
Chauncey Sparks	Barbour	1943
James E. Folsom	Cullman	1947
Gordon Persons	Montgomery	1951
James Folsom	Cullman	1955
John Patterson	Tallapoosa	1959
George C. Wallace	Barbour	1963
Lurleen B. Wallace	Barbour	1967
Albert P. Brewer (Acting)	Morgan	1968
George C. Wallace	Barbour	1971

APPENDIX III

United States Senators from Alabama

Name	Years in Senate	Birthplace
John W. Walker	1819–1823	Virginia
William R. King	1819–1844	North Carolina
William Kelly	1823–1825	Tennessee
Henry Chambers	1825–1826	Virginia
Israel Pickens	1826 (8 mos.)	North Carolina
John McKinley	1826–1831	Virginia
Gabriel Moore	1831–1837	North Carolina
Clement Comer Clay	1837–1841	Virginia
Arthur P. Bagby	1841–1848	Virginia
Dixon H. Lewis	1844–1848	Georgia
William R. King	1848–1853	North Carolina
Benjamin Fitzpatrick	1848–1849	Georgia
Jeremiah Clemens	1849–1853	Alabama (Madison County)
Benjamin Fitzpatrick	1853–1861	Georgia
Clement Claiborne Clay	1853–1861	Alabama (Madison County)

Alabama was not represented in the U. S. Senate during the Confederate period, 1861–1865.

Name	Years in Senate	Birthplace
George S. Houston	1865	Tennessee

(Elected to the U. S. Senate, but the Senate refused to seat him.)

Name	Years in Senate	Birthplace
Lewis E. Parsons	1865	New York

(Elected to the U. S. Senate, but the Senate refused to seat him.)

Name	Years in Senate	Birthplace
John A. Winston	1867	Alabama (Madison County)

(Elected to the U. S. Senate, but the Senate refused to seat him.)

Name	Years in Senate	Birthplace
Willard Warner	1868–1871	Ohio
George E. Spencer	1868–1879	New York
George Goldthwaite	1872–1877	Massachusetts
John T. Morgan	1877–1907	Tennessee
George S. Houston	1879	Tennessee
Luke Pryor	1880	Alabama (Madison County)
James L. Pugh	1880–1897	Georgia
Edmund W. Pettus	1897–1907	Alabama (Limestone County)

634

Name	Years in Senate	Birthplace
John H Bankhead	1907–1920	Alabama (Lamar County)
Joseph F. Johnston	1907–1913	North Carolina
Frank S. White	1914–1915	Mississippi
Oscar W. Underwood	1915–1927	Kentucky
Braxton B. Comer	1920	Alabama
J. Thomas Heflin	1920–1931	Alabama (Randolph County)
Hugo L. Black	1927–1937	Alabama (Clay County)
Dixie Bibb Graves	1937–1938	Alabama
John H. Bankhead 2d	1931–1946	Alabama (Lamar County)
Lister Hill	1938–1968	Alabama (Montgomery County)
John Sparkman	1946–	Alabama (Morgan County)
James B. Allen	1968–	Alabama (Etowah County)

APPENDIX IV

Alabama Representatives to the Congress of the Confederate States

Representative	*Congress and Session*
William P. Chilton	Provisional
	House, First Congress
	House, Second Congress
Clement C. Clay	Senate, First Congress
David Clopton	House, First Congress
	House, Second Congress
M. H. Criukshank	House, Second Congress
Jabez L. M. Curry	Provisional
Edward S. Dargan	House, First Congress
Nicholas Davis, Jr.	Provisional
James S. Dickinson	House, Second Congress
Thomas Fearn	Provisional
Thomas J. Foster	House, First Congress
	House, Second Congress
Stephen F. Hale	Provisional
Robert Jemison, Jr.	Senate, First Congress
H. C. Jones	Provisional
David P. Lewis	Provisional
Francis S. Lyon	House, First Congress
	House, Second Congress
Colin J. McRae	Provisional
James L. Pugh	House, First Congress
	House, Second Congress
John P. Ralls	House, First Congress
Cornelius Robinson	Provisional
John Gill Shorter	Provisional
Robert H. Smith	Provisional
William R. Smith	House, First Congress
Richard W. Walker	Provisional
	Senate, Second Congress
William L. Yancey	Senate, First Congress

BIBLIOGRAPHY

The books and articles included in this bibliography are readily available in most libraries.

The two most useful journals are *Alabama Review*, published by the Alabama Historical Association, and designated as *AR;* and *The Alabama Historical Quarterly*, published by the Alabama Department of Archives and History, and designated as *AHQ*.

Colonial Period

BOOKS

Alden, John R. *John Stuart and the Southern Colonial Frontier.* Ann Arbor, Mich.: University of Michigan Press, 1944.

Bartram, William, *Travels.* Mark Van Doren, ed. New York: Dover Publications, 1928.

Bossu, Jean Bernard. *Travels in the Interior of North America.* Norman, Okla.: University of Oklahoma Press, 1962.

Claiborne, J.F.H. *Mississippi As a Province, Territory, and State.* Baton Rouge, La.: Louisiana State University Press, 1964.

Crouse, Nellis M. *Lemoyne d'Iberville: Soldier of New France.* Ithaca, N.Y.: Cornell University Press, 1954.

Gipson, Lawrence H. *The Triumphant Empire: New Responsibilities Within the Enlarged Empire, 1763–1770.* New York: Knopf, 1956.

Hallenbeck, Cleve. *Alvar Núñez Cabeza de Vaca.* Glendale, Calif.: A.H. Clark Co., 1940.

Hamilton, Peter J. *Colonial Mobile.* Mobile, Ala.: First National Bank, 1952.

Holmes, Jack D.L. *Gayosa: The Life of A Spanish Governor in the Mississippi Valley.* Baton Rouge, La.: Louisiana State University Press, 1965.

Howard, Milo B., Jr. and Robert R. Rea, eds. *The Memoire Justifi-catif of the Chevalier de Monberaut: Indian Diplomacy in British West Florida, 1763–1765.* University of Alabama Press, 1965.

Johnson, Cecil. *British West Florida.* New Haven, Conn.: Yale University Press, 1943.

Pickett, Albert J. *History of Alabama.* Charleston, S.C.: Walker and James, 1851.

Romans, Bernard. *A Concise Natural History of East and West Florida.* Rembert B. Patrick, ed. Gainesville, Fla.: University of Florida Press, 1964.

ARTICLES

Abby, Kathryn, "The Intrigue of a British Refugee Against the Willing Raid, 1778," *William and Mary Quarterly,* January 1944.

Abby, Kathryn, "Peter Chester's Defense of the Mississippi after the Willing Raid," MVHR, June 1935.

Arnade, Charles W., "Tristan de Luna and Ochuse (Pensacola Bay), 1559," *Florida Historical Quarterly,* January-April, 1959.

Born, John D., Jr., "Charles Strachan in Mobile: The Frontier Ordeal of a Scottish Factor, 1764–1768," AHQ, Spring and Summer, 1965.

Brannon, Peter A., "The Coosa River Crossing of British Refugees, 1781," AHQ, Vol. 19, 1957.

Brown, J.A., "Panton, Leslie and Company: Indian Traders of Pensacola and St. Augustine," *Florida Historical Quarterly,* January, April, 1959.

DeLaney, Caldwell, "A Newly-Found French Journal, 1720," AR April, 1966.

Griffin, William B., "Spanish Pensacola, 1700–1763," *Florida Historical Quarterly,* January–April, 1949.

Griffith, Lucille, "South Carolina and the Fort Alabama, 1714–1763," AR, October, 1959.

Hamilton, Peter J., "British West Florida," *Publications of the Mississippi Historical Society,* Vol. 7.

Halbert, H.S., "Bernard Romans' Map of 1772," *Publications of the Mississippi Historical Society,* Vol. 6.

Holmes, Jack D.L., "Notes on the Spanish Fort San Esteban de Tombecbe," AR, October, 1965.

James, James A., "Oliver Pollock, Financier of the Revolution in the West," MVHR, Vol. 16, June, 1929.

Johnson, Cecil, "Expansion in West Florida," MVHR, March, 1934.

McWilliams, Richebourg G., "Iberville and the Southern Indians," AR, October, 1967.

Mowat, Charles L., "The First Campaign of Publicity for Florida," MVHR, December, 1943.

Mulcrone, Thomas F., "Antoine de Laval, S.J. at Dauphin Island (1720)," AR, January, 1967.

Pearson, Theodore B., "Early Settlement Around Historic McIntosh Bluff: Alabama's First County Seat," AR, October, 1970.

Rea, Robert R., "Madogwys Forever!" AHQ, Spring, 1968.

Rea, Robert R., "Graveyard for Britons: West Florida 1763–1781," *Florida Historical Quarterly*, April 1969.

Rea, Robert R., "Outpost of Empire: David Wedderburn at Mobile," AR, July, 1954.

Rea, Robert R., "The Trouble at Tombeckby," AR, January, 1968.

"Revolutionary Soldiers in Alabama," AHQ, Winter, 1944.

Ross, Edward H., and Dawson A. Phelps, eds., "A Journey Over the Natchez Trace, 1792," *Journal of Mississippi History*, October, 1953.

Rowland, Mrs. Dunbar, "Peter Chester, Third Governor of the Province of West Florida Under British Dominion, 1770–1781," *Publications of the Mississippi Historical Society*, Centenary Series, Vol. 5.

Taylor, Garland, "Colonial Settlement and Early Revolutionary Activity up to 1779," MVHR, December, 1935.

Thomas, Daniel H., "Fort Toulouse, The French Outpost at the Alabamos on the Coosa," AHQ, Fall, 1960.

Thomas, Daniel H., "Fort Toulouse—in Tradition and Fact," AR, October, 1960.

Whitaker, A.P., "The Muscle Shoals Speculation 1783–1789," MVHR, Vol. 13.

Miller, Carl F., "Life 8000 Years Ago Uncovered in an Alabama Cave," *National Geographic Magazine*, Vol. 110, October, 1956.

Miller, Carl F., "New Light on Stone Age Life," *National Geographic Magazine*, Vol. 113, March, 1958.

The Territorial Period

BOOKS

Abernethy, Thomas P. *The Formative Period in Alabama, 1815–1828*. Montgomery, Ala.: Brown Printing Co., 1922.

Bailey, Hugh C. *John Williams Walker: A Study in the Political Life of the Old Southwest*. University, Ala.: University of Alabama Press, 1964.

Baldwin, Joseph G. *Flush Times in Alabama and Mississippi*. N.Y.: Appleton, 1853.

Carter, Clarence E. ed. *The Territorial Papers of the United States*. Vols. 5, 16, 18. Washington: Government Printing Office, 1934.

Claiborne, J.F.H. *Mississippi as a Province, Territory, and State*. Baton Rouge, La.: Louisiana State University, 1961.

Royall, Anne. *Letters From Alabama.* Lucille Griffith, ed. University, Ala.: University of Alabama Press, 1969.

ARTICLES

"Annexation of West Florida Proposed," AHQ, Spring, 1946.

Brannon, Peter J., "The Pensacola Indian Trade," *Florida Historical Quarterly*, July, 1952.

Chappell, Gordon T., "John Coffee: Land Speculator and Planter," AR, January, 1969.

Chappell, Gordon T., "John Coffee: Surveyor and Land Agent," AR, July–October, 1961.

"Claiborne," AHQ, vol. 19 (Summer, whole issue, 1957).

Cobbs, Hamner, "Geography of the Vine and Olive Colony," AR, April, 1961.

Cox, I. J., "General Wilkinson and His Later Intrigues with the Spanish," *American Historical Review*, Vol. 19, July, 1914.

"Diary of Richard Breckenridge, 1816," *Transactions of the Alabama Historical Society, 1898–1899.*

Doster, James F., "Early Settlements on the Tombigbee and Tensaw Rivers," AR, April, 1959.

Dunbar, William, "Report of Sir William Dunbar to the Spanish Government at the Conclusion of His Services in Locating and Surveying the Thirty-first Degree of Latitude," *Publications of the Mississippi Historical Society*, Vol. 3.

"Establishment of the Alabama Territory," AHQ, vol. 24, Spring, 1962.

Gaines, G. S., "Letters . . . Relating to Events in South Alabama, 1805–1814," *Transactions of the Alabama Historical Society, 1898–1899.*

Gaines, G. S., "Notes on the Early Days of South Alabama," AHQ, Fall and Winter, 1964.

Gallalee, Jack C., "Andrew Ellicott and the Ellicott Stone," AR, April, 1965.

Hamilton, P. J., "St. Stephens . . . ," *Transactions of the Alabama Historical Society, 1898–1899.*

Haynes, Robert V., "Early Days in Washington County, Alabama," AR, July, 1965.

Haynes, Robert V., "Law Enforcement in Frontier Mississippi," *Journal of Mississippi History*, January, 1960.

Holmes, Jack D. L. (ed.), "Fort Stoddart in 1799: Seven Letters of Captain Bartholomew Schaumburgh," AHQ, Fall and Winter, 1964.

Jones, C. E., "Governor William Wyatt Bibb," *Transactions of the Alabama Historical Society, 1898–1899.*

Lightner, David, "Private Land Claims in Alabama," AR, July, 1967.

Lincecum, Gideon, "Autobiography," *Publications of the Mississippi Historical Society*, Vol. 8.

Lyon, Anne Bozeman, "Bonapartists in Alabama," AHQ, Fall and Winter, 1963.

Martin, Thomas W., *French Military Adventures in Alabama 1818–1828*, Birmingham, Ala.: Birmingham Publishing Co., 1940.

McCorvey, Thomas C., "The Highland Scotch Element in the Early Settlement of Alabama," AHQ, Spring, 1930.

McGroarty, William B., "Major Andrew Ellicott and Historic Border Lines," *Virginia Magazine of History and Biography*, January, 1950.

"Mobile Custom House Entries, 1817–1818," AHQ, Winter, 1958.

Moffat, Charles H., "Charles Tait, Planter, Politician, and Scientist of the Old South," *Journal of Southern History*, May, 1948.

Morgan, Madel J., ed., "Census of Washington County, Mississippi Territory, 1810," *Journal of Mississippi History*, January, 1952.

Phelps, Dawson A., "Colbert Ferry," AHQ, Fall and Winter, 1963.

Phelps, Dawson A., "The Natchez Trace in Alabama," AR, January, 1954.

Phelps, Dawson A., "Stands and Travel Accommodations on the Natchez Trace," *Journal of Mississippi History*, January, 1949.

Riley, Franklin L., "Location of the Boundaries of Mississippi," *Publications of the Mississippi Historical Society*, Vol. 3.

Riley, F. L., "Spanish Policy in Mississippi After the Treaty of San Lorenzo," *Publications of the Mississippi Historical Society*, vol. I.

Roberts, Frances C., "Dr. David Moore: Urban Pioneer of the Old Southwest," AR, January, 1965.

Roberts, Frances C., "Politics and Public Land Disputes in Alabama's Formative Period," AR, July, 1969.

Rowland, Mrs. Dunbar, "Marking the Natchez Trace," *Publications of the Mississippi Historical Society*, vol. XI.

Shepherd, William R., "Wilkinson and the Beginnings of the Spanish Conspiracy," *American Historical Review*, Vol. 9, 490–507, April, 1904.

Stephen, Walter W., "Andrew Jackson's 'Forgotten Army'," AR, April, 1959.

Summersell, Charles G., "Alabama and the Supreme Court: The First Case," AR, July, 1957.

"Towns in the Alabama Territory," AHQ, Spring, 1941.

"A Visit of President James Monroe to Alabama Territory, June 1, 1819," *Transactions of the Alabama Historical Society, 1898–1899*, Vol. 3.

Wallace, Katherine T., "Elk County, Alabama," AR, July, 1966.

Welsh, Mary, "Reminiscences of Old St. Stephens," *Transactions of the Alabama Historical Society, 1898–1899.*

Whitfield, Gaines, Jr., "The French Grant in Alabama," *Transactions of the Alabama Historical Society,* Vol. 4, 1899–1903.

Wilburn, Bessie Patterson, "A History of the Old French Gun of Demopolis," AHQ, Spring, 1944.

Indians

BOOKS

Adair, James. *History of the American Indians.* Samuel C. Williams, ed. Johnson City, Tenn.: Watauga Press, 1930.

DeVorsey, Louis. *The Indian Boundary in the Southern Colonies.* Chapel Hill: University of N. C. Press, 1966.

Swanton, John R. *The Indian Tribes of North America.* Washington: Government Printing Office, 1952.

Swanton, John R. *The Indians of the Southeastern United States.* Washington: Government Printing Office, 1946.

Swanton, John R. *Myths and Tales of the Southeastern United States.* Washington: Government Printing Office, 1929.

Swanton, John R. *Social Organization and Social Usages of the Indians of the Creek Confederacy.* Forty-Second Annual Report of the Bureau of American Ethnology. Washington: Government Printing Office, 1928.

Swanton, John R. *Source Material for the Social and Ceremonial Life of the Choctaw Indians.* Washington: Government Printing Office, 1931.

Woodward, Thomas S. *Woodward's Reminiscences of the Creek or Muscogee Indians.* Tuscaloosa, Ala.: Alabama Book Store, 1939.

ARTICLES

"Aboriginal and Indian Remains in Alabama," *Publications of the Alabama Historical Society,* Vol. 1, 1901.

Brannon, Peter A., "More About Mordacai," AHQ, Vol. 20, Spring, 1958.

Gatschet, A. S., "Towns and Villages of the Creek Confederacy," *Publications of the Alabama Historical Society,* Vol. 1, 1900.

Halbert, H. S., "Choctaw Indian Names in Alabama and Mississippi," *Transactions of the Alabama Historical Society, 1898–1899.*

Halbert, H. S., "Funeral Customs of the Choctaws," *Publications of the Mississippi Historical Society,* Vol. 3.

Halbert, H. S., "The Choctaw Creation Legend," *Publications of the Mississippi Historical Society,* Vol. 4.

Hamilton, Peter J., "Indian Trails and Early Roads," *Publications of the Alabama Historical Society,* Vol. 1, 1900.

Holmes, Jack D. L., "The Choctaws in 1795," AHQ, Spring, 1968.

Macy, Robert C., "The Indians of the Alabama Coastal Plain," AHQ, Winter, 1930.

Owen, Marie Bankhead, "Indian Chiefs," AHQ, Vol. 13, 1951.

Owen, Marie Bankhead, "Indians in Alabama," AHQ, Vol. 12, whole issue.

Owen, Marie Bankhead, "Rich Archeological Remains of the Mound-Builders Distinguish Alabama History," AHQ, Spring, 1930.

Owsley, Frank L., Jr., "Benjamin Hawkins, the First Modern Indian Agent," AHQ,

Plaisance, Father Aloysius, "The Choctaw Trading House, 1803–1822," AHQ, Vol. 16, 1954.

Street, O. D., "Cherokee Southern Boundary," *Publications of the Alabama Historical Society,* Vol. 1, 1900.

Tarvin, Marion Elisha, "The Muscogees or Creek Indians, 1519 to 1893," AHQ, Vol. 17, 1955.

Warren, Harry, "Chickasaw Traditions . . . ," *Publications of the Mississippi Historical Society,* Vol. 8.

Indian Wars and Removal

BOOKS

Foreman, Grant. *Indian Removal.* Norman, Okla.: University of Oklahoma Press, 1953.

Gatschet, Albert S. *A Migration Legend of the Creek Indians.* Philadelphia: D. G. Brenton, 1884–1888.

Motte, Jacob R. *Journey Into Wilderness.* Gainesville, Fla.: University of Florida Press, 1953.

Young, Mary Elizabeth. *Redskins, Ruffleshirts, and Rednecks: Indian Allotments in Alabama and Mississippi 1830–1860.* Norman, Okla.: University of Oklahoma Press, 1961.

ARTICLES

Austill, Jeremiah, "Jeremiah Austill," AHQ, Spring, 1944.

Austill, Margaret E., "Life of Margaret Ervin Austill," AHQ, Spring, 1944.

Bonner, James C., "Tustunugee Hutkee and Creek Factionalism on the Georgia Alabama Frontier," AR, April, 1957.

Brannon, Peter A., ed., "Journal of James A. Tait for the Year 1815," AHQ, Winter, 1940.

Brannon, Peter A., "Creek Indian War, 1836–1837," AHQ, Vol. 13, 1951.

Brannon, Peter A., "Indian Treaties," AHQ, Vol. 12, 1950.

Brannon, Peter A., "Indian Wars," AHQ, Vol. 13, 1951.

Campbell, John A., "The Creek Indian War of 1836," *Transactions of the Alabama Historical Society*, Vol. 3, 1898–1899.

Coley, C. J., "The Battle of Horseshoe Bend," AHQ, Vol. 14, 1952.

Coley, C. J., "Creek Treaties, 1790–1832," AR, July, 1958.

Doster, James F., "Letters Relating to the Tragedy of Fort Mims: August–September 1813," AR, October, 1961.

Dillard, A. W., "The Treaty of Dancing Rabbit Creek," *Transactions of the Alabama Historical Society*, Vol 3, 1898–1899.

Ethridge, George H., "Sam Dale," AHQ, Winter, 1945.

Foreman, Carolyn Thomas, "John Gunter and His Family," AHQ, Fall, 1947.

Guyton, Pearl V., "Sam Dale," AHQ, Spring, 1945.

Halbert, H. S., "Creek War Incidents," *Transactions of the Alabama Historical Society*. Vol. 2.

Halbert, H. S., "Some Inaccuracies in Claiborne's History in Regard to Tecumseh," *Publications of the Mississippi Historical Society*, Vol. 1.

Halbert, H. S., "The Story of the Treaty of Dancing Rabbit," *Publications of the Mississippi Historical Society*, Vol. 6.

Holland, James W., "Andrew Jackson and the Creek War: Victory at the Horseshoe," AR, October, 1968.

Hoole, W. Stanley, "Echoes From the 'Trail of Tears,' 1837," AR, April–July, 1953.

Jenkins, William H., "Alabama Forts, 1700–1838," AR, July, 1959.

Mahon, John K., ed., "The Journal of A. B. Meek and Second Seminole War, 1836," *Florida Historical Quarterly*, April, 1960.

McCorvey, T. C., "The Mission of Francis Scott Key to Alabama," *Transactions of Alabama Historical Society*, Vol. 4, 1899–1903.

Orr, W. G., "Surrender of Weatherford," *Transactions of the Alabama Historical Society*, Vol. 2, 1897–1898.

Owsley, Frank L., "Francis Scott Key's Mission to Alabama in 1833," AR, July, 1970.

Rowland, Mrs. Dunbar, "Mississippi Territory in the War of 1812," *Publications of the Mississippi Historical Society*, Centenary Series, Vol. 4.

Watts, Charles W., "Colbert's Reserve and the Chickasaw Treaty of 1818," AR, October, 1959.

Wright, J. Leitch, "Creek-American Treaty of 1790: Alexander McGillivray and Diplomacy of the Old Southwest," *Georgia Historical Quarterly*, Vol. 50, Dec., 1967.

Young, Mary E., "The Creek Frauds: A Study in Conscience and Corruption," MVHR, December, 1955.

Young, Mary E., "Indian Removal and Land Allotment: the Civilized Tribes and Jacksonian Justice," *American Historical Review*, Vol. 61, October, 1958.

Economics Before 1860
(Chapters 5–6)

BOOKS

Baldwin, J. G. *Flush Times in Alabama and Mississippi*. N.Y.: Appleton, 1853.
Benners, Alfred H. *Slavery and Its Results*.
Davis, Charles S. *The Cotton Kingdom of Alabama*. Montgomery, Ala.: Department of Archives and History, 1939.
Jordan, Weymouth T. *Antebellum Alabama: Town and Country*. Tallahassee, Fla.: Florida State University Press, 1957.
Jordan, Weymouth T. *Hugh Davis and his Plantation*. University, Ala.: University of Alabama Press, 1948.

ARTICLES

Brannon, Peter J., ed., "James M. Torbert's 1848 Day Book," AR, July, 1948.
Brantley, William H., Jr., "Henry Hitchcock of Mobile, 1816–1839," AR, January, 1952.
Chapell, Gordon T., "John Coffee: Land Speculator and Planter," AR, Jan., 1969.
Chapell, Gordon T., "Some Patterns of Land Speculation in the Old Southwest," *Journal of Southern History*, November, 1949.
Dale, William Pratt, "A Connecticut Yankee in Ante-Bellum Alabama," AR, Jan., 1953.
Daniel, Adrian G., "Navigational Development of Muscle Shoals, 1807–1890," AR, October, 1961.
Davis, Hugh C., "Hilary A. Herbert: Bourbon Apologist," AR, July, 1967.
Davis, Nan Greys, "Steamboat Days on the Alabama River," AHQ, Summer, 1945.
Draughon, Ralph, "Some Aspects of the History of Alabama Bond Issues," AR, July, 1953.
Essler, Elizabeth McTyeire, "The Agricultural Reform Movement 1850–1860," AR, October, 1948.
Griffin, Richard W., "Cotton Manufacturing in Alabama to 1860," AHQ, Fall, 1956.
Hoole, W. Stanley, ed., "Advice to an Overseer: Extracts from the 1840–1842 Plantation Journal of John Horry Dent," AR, January, 1948.

Hoole, W. Stanley, ed., "Elyton, Alabama, and the Connecticut Asylum: The Letters of William H. Ely, 1820–1821," AR, January, 1951.

Irons, George V., "River Ferries in Alabama Before 1861," AR, January, 1951.

Jordon, Weymouth T., "Agricultural Societies in Ante-Bellum Alabama," AR, Oct., 1951.

Jordon, Weymouth T., "Ante-Bellum Mobile: Alabama's Agricultural Emporium," AR, July, 1948.

Knapp, Virginia, "William Phineas Browne, Business Man and Pioneer Mine Operator of Alabama," AR, April, July, 1950.

Lightner, David, "Private Land Claims in Alabama," AR, July, 1967.

Partin, Robert, "A Connecticut Yankee's Letters from Conecuh County, Alabama, 1847–1866," AR, Jan., 1951.

Patterson, Ernest F., "Alabama's First Railroad," AR, Jan., 1956.

Peterson, Walter F., "Slavery in the 1850's: Recollections of an Alabama Unionist," AHQ, Fall, 1968.

Powell, George, "A Description and History of Blount County," AHQ, Spring and Summer, 1965.

"Principal Stage Stops and Taverns in what is now Alabama Prior to 1840," AHQ, Spring and Summer, 1955.

Russell, Robert H., "Gold Mining in Alabama Before 1860," AR, Jan., 1957.

Sellers, James B., "Free Negroes of Tuscaloosa County Before the Thirteenth Amendment," AR, April, 1970.

Small, Marvin B., "Steamboats on the Coosa," AR, July, 1951.

Smith, Warren I., "Land Patterns in Ante-Bellum Montgomery County, Alabama," AR, July, 1955.

Stewart, Edgar A., ed., "The Journal of James Mallory, 1834–1877," AR, July, 1961.

The Church Before 1860

BOOKS

Lazenby, M. E. *History of Methodism in Alabama and West Florida.* Privately printed, 1960.

Montevallo Baptist Church: One Hundred-eight years of Glorious Service. Montevallo, Alabama. Privately printed, 1963.

Riley, B. F. *A Memorial History of the Baptists of Alabama.* Philadelphia: Judson Press, 1923.

West, Anson. *A History of Methodism in Alabama.* Nashville, Tenn.: Methodist Publishing House, 1893.

ARTICLES

Bailey, Hugh C., "Alabama's First Baptist Association," AR, January, 1961.

Cobbs, R. H., "Statistics of the Protestant Episcopal Church in the Diocese of Alabama," *Transactions of the Ala. Hist. Soc.*, 1897–1898, Vol. 2.

Frazer, Mary Reese, "History of Methodist Episcopal Church at Autaugaville," AHQ, Fall, 1946.

Frazer, Mary Reese, "History of Auburn Baptist Church," AHQ, Spring, 1946.

Frazer, Mary Reese, "Ministers of Fellowship Baptist Church, Wilcox County, 1828–47," AHQ, Vol. 17, 1955.

Gardner, Robert, "A Tenth-Hour Apology for Slavery," *Journal of Southern History*, August, 1960.

Hall, J. H. B., "The History of the Cumberland Presbyterian Church in Alabama Prior to 1826," *Transactions of the Alabama Historical Society*, Vol. 4, 1899–1903.

Hunt, Emmie Martin, "Old Clay Bank Church," AHQ, Winter, 1930.

"Joseph F. Roper Diary, 1846–1853," AHQ, Vol. 19, Fall and Winter, 1957.

Lambert, Bess Stout, "Canaan Baptist Church, Oldest Church in Jefferson County," AHQ, Winter, 1940.

Lardent, Minnie L., "An Old Mother Celebrates Her Day (Valley Creek Church)," AHQ, Spring, 1941.

Lipscomb, Oscar Hugh, "Catholic Missionaries in Early Alabama," AR, April, 1965.

Newman, Anne Elizabeth, "History of Rock Springs Baptist Church, Chambers County, Alabama," AHQ, Spring, 1944.

Pennington, Edgar L., "The Episcopal Church in the Alabama Black Belt, 1822–1836," AR, April, 1951.

Rogers, Tommy W., "Frederick A. Ross: Huntsville's Belligerent Clergyman," AR, January, 1969.

Smoot, Joseph G., ed., "An Account of Alabama Indian Missions and Presbyterian Churches in 1828. From the Travel Diary of William S. Potts," AR, April, 1965.

Spencer, William M., "St. Andrew's Church, Prairieville," AR, January, 1961.

Stewart, Margaret, "Carmel Presbyterian Church, Cherokee County," AHQ, Summer, 1941.

Weaver, Oliver C., "Benjamin Lloyd: A Pioneer Primitive Baptist in Alabama," AR, April, 1968.

Whatley, George C., III, "The Alabama Presbyterian and His Slave, 1830–1864," AR, January, 1960.

Wilson, Harold, "Basil Manly, Apologist for Slavocracy," AR, January, 1962.

Wilson, S. W., "Some Events Bearing Upon the History of Concord Baptist Church," AHQ, Spring, 1946.

Woolley, David C., "Hosea Holcombe: Pioneer Baptist Historian," AR, January, 1961.

Antebellum Education

BOOKS

Clark, Willis G. *History of Education in Alabama: 1702–1889.* Washington: Government Printing Office, 1889.

Fulton, John. *Memoirs of Frederick A.P. Barnard.* New York: The Macmillan Company, 1896.

Nixon, Herman C. *Alexander B. Meek.* Auburn, Ala.: Alabama Polytechnic Institute, 1910.

Sellers, James B. *History of the University of Alabama.* University, Ala.: University of Alabama, 1953.

Weeks, Stephen B. *History of Public Education in Alabama.* Washington: Government Printing Office, 1915.

ARTICLES

Ellison, Rhoda C., "Caroline Lee Hentz's Alabama Diary, 1836," AR, October, 1951.

Owsley, Frank L., ed., "The Education of a Southern Frontier Girl," AR, Part I, October, 1953; Part II, January, 1954.

Pyburn, Nita Katherine, "Mobile Public Schools Before 1860," AR, July, 1958.

Sellers, James B., "Student Life at the University of Alabama Before 1860," AR, October, 1949.

Vallenweider, Roy W., "Spring Hill College: the Early Days," AR, April, 1954.

Watts, Charles W., "Student Days at Old La Grange, 1844–1845," AR, January, 1971.

Social Antebellum

BOOKS

Fry, Anna M. Gayle. *Memories of Old Cahaba.* Nashville, Tenn.: Publishing House of the M.E. Church, South, 1908.

Hammond, Ralph Charles. *Antebellum Mansions in Alabama.* New York: Architectural Book Company, 1951.

Jordan, Weymouth T. *Antebellum Alabama Town and Country.* Tallahassee, Fla.: Florida State University, 1957.

League of Pen Women. *Historic Homes of Alabama and Their Traditions*. Birmingham, Ala.: Birmingham Publishing Co., 1935.

Posey, Walter B. *Alabama in the 1830's As Recorded by British Travelers*. Birmingham, Ala.: Birmingham–Southern College, 1938.

Smith, Sol. *Theatrical Management in the South and West for Thirty Years*. New York: Harper & Brothers, 1868.

ARTICLES

Brannon, Peter A., "Dueling in Alabama," AHQ, Vol. 17, Fall, 1955.

Brannon, Peter A., "Medical Sources of the Confederacy," AHQ, Vol. 17, Spring–Summer, 1955.

Davidson, James D., "A Journey Through the South in 1836: Diary of James D. Davidson," *Journal of Southern History*, 1935.

DuBose, John W., "Chronicles of the Cane Brake, 1817–1860," AHQ, Winter, 1947.

Frazer, Mary Reese, "Early History of Auburn," AHQ, Fall, 1945.

"General LaFayette's Visit to Alabama in 1825," AHQ, Vol. 14, 1952.

Griffith, Lucille, "Anne Royall in Alabama," AR, January, 1968.

Jordan, Weymouth T., "Martin's Book: Household Hints," AHQ, Fall, Winter, 1940; Spring, Summer, 1941.

Kelly, Maud McLure, "Alabama's First Ladies," AHQ, Vol. 10, 1948.

Lee, Mary Welch, "Old Homes of Talladega County," AHQ, Vol. 10, 1948.

Lowry, Lucile Cary, "LaFayette's Visit to Georgia and Alabama," AHQ, Spring, 1946.

McCall, D. L., ed., "LaFayette's Visit to Alabama," AHQ, Vol. 17, Spring–Summer, 1955.

McWilliams, T. S., "The Marquis and the Myth: LaFayette's Visit to Alabama, 1825," AR, April, 1969.

Peterson, Walter F., "Rural Life in Ante-Bellum Alabama," AR, April, 1966.

Politics Before 1860

BOOKS

Bailey, Hugh C. *John Williams Walker: A Study in the Political, Social and Cultural Life of the Old Southwest*. University, Ala.: University of Alabama Press, 1964.

Brantley, William H. *Three Capitals*. Privately printed, 1947.

Denman, Clarence. *The Secession Movement in Alabama*. Montgomery, Ala.: Department of Archives and History, 1933.

Dorman, Lewy. *Party Politics in Alabama from 1850 Through 1860*. Wetumpka, Ala.: Wetumpka Publishing Company, 1935.

Garrett, William. *Reminiscences of Public Men in Alabama*. Atlanta, Ga.: Plantation Publishing Co., 1872.

Jack, Theodore H. *Sectionalism and Party Politics in Alabama, 1819–1842*. Menasha, Wis.: George Banta Publishing Company, 1919.

Jackson, Walter M. *Alabama's First United States Vice-president: William Rufus King*. Decatur, Ala.: Decatur Printing Co., 1952.

McMillan, Malcolm C. *Constitutional Development in Alabama, 1798–1901*. Chapel Hill, N.C.: University of N.C. Press, 1955.

Nuermberger, Ruth K. *The Clays of Alabama*. Lexington, Ky.: University of Kentucky Press, 1958.

Smith, William R. *Reminiscences of a Long Life*. Washington: William R. Smith, Sr., 1889.

ARTICLES

"Alabama Census Returns 1820 and an Abstract of Federal Census of Alabama 1830," AHQ, Fall, 1944.

Alexander, Thomas B., et al, "The Basis of Alabama's Ante-Bellum Two-Party System," AR, October, 1966.

Anderson, John C., "The Supreme Court of Alabama, Its Organization and Sketches of its Chief Justices," AHQ, Spring, 1930.

Atkins, Leah, "The First Legislative Session: The General Assembly of Alabama, Huntsville, 1819," AR, January, 1970.

Bailey, Hugh C., "John W. Walker and the 'Georgia Machine' in Early Alabama Politics," AR, January, 1970.

Bailey, Hugh C., "Israel Pickens, Peoples' Politician," AR, April, 1964.

Barbee, David R. and Milledge L. Bonham, Jr., editors, "The Montgomery Address of Stephen A. Douglas," *Journal of Southern History*, Vol. 5, November, 1939.

"Butler County, Alabama," AHQ, Spring and Summer, 1955.

Clarke, William Edward, "For My Children: Reminiscences of W.E. Clark," *Alabama Lawyer*, Vol. 18.

Draughon, Ralph B., Jr., "George Smith Houston and Southern Unity, 1846–1849," AR, July, 1966.

Gardner, Alto L. and Nathan Stott, "William L. Yancey: Statesman of Secession," AR, July, 1962.

Golden, B. G., "The Presidential Election of 1840 in Alabama," AR, April, 1970.

"Governor Bibb and the Times," AHQ, Vol. 19, Fall and Winter, 1957.

Harrison, Robert W., "Public Land Records of the Federal Government," *Mississppi Valley Historical Review*, September, 1954.

Haynes, R. V., "Early Washington County," AR, July, 1965.

Hicks, Jimmie, "Associate Justice John McKinley: A Sketch," AR, July, 1965.

Howard, Milo B., Jr., "The General Ticket," AR, July, 1966.

Jackson, Carlton, "The White Basis System and the Decline of Alabama Whiggery," AHQ, Fall and Winter, 1963.

Jones, Allen W., "Party Nominating Machinery in Antebellum Alabama," AR, Jan., 1967.

Jones, Virginia K., ed., "A Great Day for the Whigs of Alabama," AHQ, Fall and Winter, 1963.

Long, Durwood, "Alabama Opinion and the Whig Cuban Policy," AHQ, Fall and Winter, 1963.

Long, Durwood, "Economics and Politics in the 1860 Presidential Election in Alabama," AHQ, Spring and Summer, 1965.

Martin, John M., "John McKinley: Jacksonian Phase," AHQ, Spring and Summer, 1966.

Martin, John M., "The Senatorial Career of Gabriel Moore," AHQ, Summer, 1964.

Martin, John M., "William R. King: Jacksonian Senator," AR, October, 1965.

McMillan, Malcolm C., "Joseph Glover Baldwin Reports on the Whig National Convention of 1848," *Journal of Southern History*, August, 1959.

McMillan, Malcolm C., "Taylor's Presidential Campaign in Alabama, 1847–1848," AR, April, 1960.

McMillan, Malcolm C., "The Alabama Constitution of 1819: A Study of Constitution-Making on the Frontier," AR, October, 1950.

McPherson, James P., "The Career of John Archibald Campbell: A Study of Politics and the Law," AR, January, 1966.

McWhiney, Grady, "Were the Whigs a Class Party in Alabama?" *Journal of Southern History*, November, 1957.

Murphy, James L., "Alabama and the Charleston Convention of 1860," *Publications of the Alabama Historical Society*, Vol. 5, 1904.

Nuermberger, Ruth K., "The 'Royal Party' in Early Alabama Politics," AR, April, July, 1953.

Owen, Thomas M., ed., "Statistics of the Counties of Alabama," *Transactions of the Alabama Historical Society*, 1897–1898.

Owsley, Frank L., "The Clays in Early Alabama History," AR, October, 1949.

Owsley, Frank L., "John Williams Walker," AR, April, 1926.

Powell, E. A., "Fifty-five Years in West Alabama," AHQ, Winter, 1942.

"Proceedings of Alabama Legislature, Friday, December 8, 1920," AHQ, Vol. 18, Fall, 1956.

"Register of Gubernatorial Appointments, Civil and Military, 1818–1822," AHQ, Summer, 1944.

Roberts, Frances, "Dr. David Moore, Urban Pioneer of the Old Southwest," AR, January, 1965.

Rogers, William W., "Kossuth's Visit to Alabama," AR, April, 1964.

Scott, Sutton S., "The Alabama Legislatures of 1857–8, and 1859–60," *Publications of the Alabama Historical Society,* Vol. 5, 1904.

Steward, Luther N., Jr., "John Forsyth," AR, April, 1961.

Venable, Austin L., "William L. Yancey's Transition from Unionism to State Rights," *Journal of Southern History,* Vol. 10, August, 1944.

Williams, Clanton W., "Conservatism in Old Montgomery, 1817–1861," AR, April, 1957.

Williams, Clanton W., "Early Ante-Bellum Montgomery: A Black-Belt Constituency," *Journal of Southern History,* November, 1941.

The Civil War

BOOKS

Chadwick, Mrs. W. D. *Civil War Days in Huntsville.* Huntsville, Alabama: *The Huntsville Times,* n.d.

Cumming, Kate. *Kate: The Journal of a Confederate Nurse.* Baton Rouge, La.: Louisiana State University Press, 1959.

Denman, Clarence P. *The Secession Movement in Alabama.* Montgomery, Alabama: Department of Archives and History, 1933.

Hague, Parthenia A. *A Blockaded Family: Life in Southern Alabama During the Civil War.* New York: Houghton Mifflin, 1888.

Hodgson, Joseph. *Cradle of the Confederacy.* Mobile, Alabama: Register Publishing Co., 1876.

Holt, Thad, Jr., ed. *Diary of Miss Mary Waring of Mobile During the Final Days of the War Between the States.* Chicago: Wyvern Press, 1964.

Lytle, Andrew N. *Bedford Forrest and His Critter Company.* New York: G.P. Putnam's, 1931.

McMillan, Malcolm C., ed. *The Alabama Confederate Reader.* University, Alabama: University of Alabama Press, 1963.

Martin, Bessie. *Desertion of Alabama Troops from the Confederate Army.* New York: Columbia University Press, 1932.

Massey, Mary Elizabeth. *Refugee Life in the Confederacy.* Baton Rouge, La.: Louisiana State University Press, 1964.

Moore, Albert B. *Conscription and Conflict in the Confederacy.* New York: The Macmillan Co., 1924.

Richardson, James D., ed. *A Compilation of the Messages and Papers of the Confederacy.* 2 vols. Nashville, Tenn.: United States Publishing Co., 1905.

Smith, C. Carter, Jr., ed. *Two Naval Journals.* Chicago: Wyvern Press, 1964.

Sterkx, H. E. *Partners in Rebellion: Alabama Women in the Civil War.* Rutherford, N. J.: Fairleigh Dickinson University Press, 1970.

ARTICLES

"Alabama Conscript Laws, 1863," AHQ, Vol. 23, Summer, 1961.

Alexander, Thomas B., and Peggy J. Duckworth, "Alabama Black Belt Whigs During Secession," AR, July, 1964.

Anon., "Contemporary Account of the Inauguration of Jefferson Davis," AHQ, Spring, 1961.

Anon., "A Sketch of 12 Months Service in the Mobile Rifle Company," AHQ, Spring and Summer, 1963.

Bailey, Hugh C., "Disaffection in the Alabama Hill Country, 1861," *Civil War History,* June, 1958.

Bailey, Hugh C., "Disloyalty in Early Confederate Alabama," *Journal of Southern History,* November, 1957.

Bailey, Mrs. Hugh C., "Mobile's Tragedy: The Magazine Explosion of 1865," AR, January, 1968.

Bearss, Edwin C., "Rousseau's Raid on the Montgomery and West Point Railroad," AHQ, Spring and Summer, 1963.

Brannon, Peter A., "Cahawba Military Prison, 1863–1865," AR, July, 1950.

Carpenter, James A., "James D. Lynch in War and Peace," AHQ, Vol. 20, Spring, 1958.

Chadick, Mrs. W. D., "Civil War Days in Huntsville," AHQ, Summer, 1947.

Christian, Ella Storrs, "The Days that are No More," AHQ, Vol. 14, 1952.

Crenshaw, Captain Edward, "Diary," AHQ, Fall, Winter, 1940.

Curry, J. H., "A History of Company B, 40th Alabama Infantry, C.S.A.," AHQ, Vol. 17, Fall. 1955.

Donald, W J., "Alabama Confederate Hospitals," AR, October, 1962.

DuBose, Euba E., "Mt. Sterling: Civil War and Reconstruction," *The History of Mount Sterling,* AHQ, Fall and Winter, 1963.

Ely, Robert B., "This Filthy Ironpot," *American Heritage,* February, 1968.

Fornell, Earl W., "Mobile During the Blockade," AHQ, Spring, 1961.

Fleming, Mary Love, "Dale County and Its People During the Civil War," AHQ, Vol. 19, Spring, 1957.

"Fort Morgan in the Confederacy," AHQ, Summer, 1945.

Fretwell, Mark E., "Rousseau's Alabama Raid," AHQ, Vol. 18, Winter, 1956.

Griffith, Lucille, "Mrs. Juliet Opie Hopkins and Alabama Military Hospitals," AR, April, 1953.

Henry, Robert S., "Railroads of the Confederacy," AR, January, 1953.

Hoole, W. Stanley, ed., "The Battle of Athens and Letter from Cahawba Prison, 1864–1865," AR, April, 1962.

Howard, Milo B., Jr., "Sedition in Winston County," AHQ, Vol. 23, Summer, 1961.

Howard, Milo B., Jr., "Alabama State Currency, 1861–1865," AHQ, Spring and Summer, 1963.

Jones, Allen W., "A Georgia Confederate Soldier Visits Montgomery, Alabama, 1862–1863," AHQ, Spring and Summer, 1963.

Jones, Charles T., "Five Confederates: The Sons of Bolling Hall in the Civil War," AHQ, Spring, 1962.

Jones, James P. and William W. Rogers, "Montgomery as the Confederate Capital," AHQ, Vol. 25, Spring, 1964.

Jones, Virginia K., ed., "The Journal of Sarah G. Follansbee," AHQ, Fall and Winter, 1965.
"Contemporary Account of the Inauguration of Jefferson Davis," AHQ, Vol. 23, Summer, 1961.
"Letters of Rev. W. H. Mitchell, Jan., 1861," AHQ, Spring, 1961.

Krouse, T. J. "Clarke County Salt Works," AHQ, Vol. 20, Spring, 1958.

Letford, William and Allen W. Jones, "Action, Affairs, Attacks . . . in Alabama from 1861–1865," AHQ, Vol. 23, Spring, 1961.

"Letters of Jacob Faser, Confederate Armorer," AHQ, Summer, 1941.

Lipscomb, Oscar H., "Catholics in Alabama, 1861–1865," AR, October, 1967.

Long, Durwood, "Political Parties and Propaganda in Alabama in the Presidential Election of 1860," AHQ, Spring, 1963.

Manly, Basil, "Diary, 1858–1867," AR, April, July, October, 1951.

Meyer, Henry, "A Leaven of Disunion: The Growth of the Secessionist Faction in Alabama, 1847–1851," AR, April, 1969.

Monroe, Baskell, "Early Confederate Political Patronage," AR, January, 1967.

Newton, James K., "The Siege of Mobile," AHQ, Vol. 20, Winter, 1958.

Nichols, James L., "Confederate Engineers and the Defense of Mobile," AR, Jan., 1967.

Partin, Robert, "Money Matters of a Confederate Soldier," AHQ, Spring and Summer, 1963.

Rhett, Robert B., "The Confederate Government in Montgomery," *Battles and Leaders of the Civil War*, I, 99–111.

Roberts, Kate Q. N., "A War Time Foundry," AHQ, Winter, 1956.

Schmandt, Raymond H., and Josephine H. Schulte, eds., "Spring Hill College Diary, 1861–1865," AR, July, 1962.

"Secession," AHQ, Summer, 1941.

"Shelby Springs CSA Hospital," AHQ, Vol. 23, Summer, 1961.

Stephens, Walter W., "The Brooke Guns from Selma," AHQ, Vol. 20, Fall, 1958.

Still, William N., "Selma and the Confederate States Navy," AR, January, 1962.

Sterkx, H. E., "A Patriotic Confederate Woman's War Diary, 1862–1863," AHQ, Winter, 1958.

Stoxy, James O. A., "Pocket Diary for 1861," AHQ, Spring and Summer, 1966.

Vandiver, Frank E., "The Shelby Iron Works in the Civil War," AR, Jan., April, July, 1948.

Walter, Francis X., "The Naval Battle of Mobile Bay," AHQ, Vol. 14.

Watson, Elbert L., "The Story of the Nichajack," AR, Jan., 1967.

Woodward, Joseph H., "Alabama Iron Manufacturing, 1860–1865," AR, July, 1954.

Wooster, Ralph A., "The Alabama Secession Convention," AR, January, 1959.

Reconstruction

BOOKS

Fleming, Walter L. *Civil War and Reconstruction in Alabama.* New York: Columbia University Press, 1905.

Hunnicutt, John L. *Reconstruction in West Alabama.* Tuscaloosa, Ala.: Confederate Publishing Co., 1959.

ARTICLES

Alexander, Thomas B., "Persistent Whiggery in Alabama and the Lower South, 1860–1867," AR, January, 1959.

Belser, Thomas A., Jr., "Alabama Plantation to Georgia Farm: John Horry Dent and Reconstruction," AHQ, Spring and Summer, 1963.

Bethel, Elizabeth, "The Freedmen's Bureau in Alabama," *Journal of Southern History*, February, 1948.

Copeland, Kate Murphree, "Reconstruction Pike County, Political and Military," AHQ, Winter, 1960.

Cox, La Wanda, "The Promise of Land for the Freedmen," *Mississippi Valley Historical Review*, December, 1958.

Feldman, Eugene, "James T. Rapier 1839–1884," *Journal of Negro History*, December, 1956.

Griffin, Richard W., "Cotton Frauds and Confiscations in Alabama, 1863–1866," AR, October, 1954.

Keyes, Julia L., "Our Life in Brazil," AHQ, Fall and Winter, 1966.

McNair, Cecil E., "Reconstruction in Bullock County," AHQ, Vol. 15, 1953.

Moore, A. B., "Railroad Building in Alabama During The Reconstruction Period," *Journal of Southern History*, Vol. 1, November, 1935.

Myers, John B., "The Freedmen and the Law in Post-bellum Alabama," AR, January, 1970.

Partin, Robert, "Alabama Newspaper Humor During Reconstruction," AR, October, 1964.

Rhodes, Robert S., "The Registration of Voters and the Election of Delegates to the Reconstruction Convention in Alabama," AR, April, 1955.

Sloan, John Z., "The Ku Klux Klan and the Alabama Election of 1872," AR, April, 1965.

Sterkx, H. E., "William C. Jordan and Reconstruction in Bullock County, Alabama," AR, January, 1962.

Williamson, Edward C., "The Alabama Election of 1874," AR, July, 1964.

Wilson, Clyde E., "State Militia of Alabama During the Administration of Lewis E. Parsons," AHQ, Vol. 13.

Woolfolk, Sarah, "Amnesty and Pardon and Republicanism in Alabama," AHQ, Summer, 1964.

Woolfolk, Sarah, "The Political Cartoons of the Tuskaloosa Independent Monitor and Tuskaloosa Blade, 1867–1873," AHQ, Fall and Winter, 1965.

Woolfolk, Sarah Van, "George E. Spencer: A Carpetbagger in Alabama," AR, January, 1966.

Woolfolk, Sarah Van, "Alabama Attitudes Toward the Republican Party in 1868 and 1964," AR, January, 1967.

Woolfolk, Sarah, "Carpetbaggers in Alabama: Tradition versus Truth," AR, April, 1962.

Woolfolk, Sarah, "Five Men Called Scalawags," AR, January, 1964.

Social Life Since 1865

BOOKS

Garrett, M. B. *Horse and Buggy Days on Hatchet Creek.* University, Ala.: University of Alabama Press, 1957.

Henry, Mary D. *One Mile from Trinity*. Athens, Alabama: Strode Publishers, 1958.

Liddell, Viola G. *With a Southern Accent*. Norman, Okla.: University of Oklahoma Press, 1948.

Pannell, Anne G. and Dorothea E. Wyatt. *Julia S. Tutwiler and Social Progress in Alabama*. University, Ala.: University of Alabama Press, 1961.

Sulzby, James F. *Birmingham Sketches*. Birmingham: Privately printed, 1945.

Sulzby, James F. *Historic Alabama Hotels and Resorts*. University, Ala.: University of Alabama Press, 1960.

ARTICLES

Andrews, W. L., "Early History of Southeast Alabama," AHQ, Vol. 10.

Anderson, Mary Tutwiler, "Mountain People," *Tennessee Folklore Society Bulletin*, December, 1960.

Bigelow, Martha M., "Birmingham's Carnival of Crime, 1870–1910," AR, April, 1950.

Cobb, Buell, "The Sacred Harp of the South," *Louisiana Studies*, Summer, 1968.

Cobbs, Hamner, "Negro Colloquialisms in the Black Belt," AR, January, 1957.

Cobbs, Hamner, "Superstitions of the Black Belt," AR, January, 1958.

Cobbs, Hamner, "Tournaments in the Black Belt," AR, October, 1967.

Culp, D. P., "The Dud in Livingston, Alabama," AR, January, 1966.

Davis, Hugh C., "Edwin T. Winkler, Baptist Bayard," AR, January, 1964.

Palmer, Edward, "Alabama Notes Made in 1883–1884," AHQ, Vol. 22, Winter, 1960.

Parham, Wallace, ed., "Century of Presbyterianism in South Pickens," AHQ, Fall, 1945.

Partin, Robert, "A Black Belt Doctor's Diary, 1880," AR, April, 1954.

Partin, Robert, "Alabama's Yellow Fever Epidemic of 1878," AR, January, 1957.

Partin, Robert, "Dr. Jerome Cochran, Yellow Fever Fighter," AR, January, 1960.

Plaisance, Aloysius, "Benedictine Monks in Alabama, 1878–1956," AR, January, 1958.

Sisk, Glenn N., "Diseases in the Alabama Black Belt, 1875-1917," Vol. 24, Spring, 1962.

Sisk, Glenn N., "Social Life in the Alabama Black Belt, 1875–1917," AR, April, 1955.

"State at Large, 1878-1879," AHQ, Summer, 1945.

Sulzby, James F., "Blount Springs, Alabama's Foremost Watering Place of Yesteryear," AR, July, 1949.

Education Since 1865

BOOKS

Atchison, Ray M. *Richard Hopkins Pratt and the Six Mile Academy.* Birmingham, Ala.: Banner Press, 1965.

Alderman, Edwin A. *J.L.M. Curry.* New York: Macmillan, 1911.

Bond, Horace M. *Negro Education in Alabama.* N.Y.: Octagon Books, 1969.

Ellison, Rhoda C. *Huntingdon College, 1854–1954.* University, Ala.: University of Alabama Press, 1954.

Elliot, Lawrence. *George Washington Carver: The Man Who Overcame.* Englewood Cliffs, N.J.: Prentice Hall, 1966.

Griffith, Lucille. *Alabama College, 1896–1969.* Montevallo, Ala.: University of Montevallo, 1969.

Hughes, W. H. *Robert M. Morton of Hampton and Tuskegee.* Chapel Hill, N.C.: University of North Carolina Press, 1956.

Parks, Joseph H. and O. C. Weaver. *Birmingham–Southern College, 1856–1956.* Nashville, Tenn.: Parthenon Press, 1957.

Richardson, Jesse M. *The Contributions of John W. Abercrombie to Public Education.* Nashville, Tenn.: George Peabody College for Teachers, 1949.

Walker, Anne K. *Tuskegee and the Black Belt.* Richmond, Va.: Dietz Press, 1944.

Washington, Booker T. *My Larger Education.* New York: Doubleday, Page, 1911.

Washington, Booker T. *Up From Slavery.* New York: A.L. Burt Co., 1901.

ARTICLES

Brown, W.T., "Booker T. Washington as a Philosopher," *Negro History Bulletin,* November, 1956.

Chaffee, Mary L., "William E. B. De Bois' Concept of the Racial Problem in the United States," *Journal of Negro History,* February, 1956.

Du Bose, Euba E., "Mt. Sterling as an Educational Center," AHQ, Fall and Winter, 1963.

Harlan, Louis R., "The Southern Education Board and the Race Issue in Public Education," *Journal of Southern History,* May, 1957, Vol. 23.

Owen, Marie B., "Miss Julia Strudwich Tutwiler," AHQ, Vol. 14.

Rogers, William W., "The Establishment of Alabama's Land Grant College," AR, January, 1960.

Rosser, L. V., "Columbian Institute," *Transactions of the Alabama Historical Society*, 1897–1898, Vol. 2.

Sisk, Glenn N., "Denominational Schools and Colleges for White Students in the Prairie Section of Mid-Alabama, 1875–1900," *Peabody Journal of Education*, July, 1957.

Walden, Daniel, "The Contemporary Opposition to the Political and Educational Ideas of Booker T. Washington," *Journal of Negro History*, April, 1960.

Vance, W. Silas, "The Teacher of Helen Keller," AR, January, 1971.

Simms, L. Moody, "William Dorsey Jelks and the Problem of Negro Education," AR, January, 1970.

Politics after 1874

BOOKS

Clark, John B. *Populism in Alabama*. Auburn, Alabama: Auburn Printing Co., 1927.

Going, Allen J. *Bourbon Democracy in Alabama*. University, Alabama: University of Alabama Press, 1951.

Rogers, William Warren. *The One-Gallused Rebellion: Agrarianism in Alabama 1865–1896*. Baton Rouge: Louisiana State University Press, 1970.

ARTICLES

Abramowitz, Jack, "The Negro in the Populist Movement," *Journal of Negro History*, July, 1953.

Bailey, Hugh C., "Alabama and West Florida Annexation," *The Florida Historical Quarterly*, January, 1957.

Burnette, O. L., "John Tyler Morgan and the Expansionist Sentiment in the New South," AR, July, 1965.

Davis, Hugh C., "Hilary A. Herbert: Bourbon Apologist," AR, July, 1967.

Doster, James F., "Railroad Domination in Alabama 1885–1905," AR, July, 1954.

Doster, James F., "Were Populists Against Railroad Corporations? The Case of Alabama," *Journal of Southern History*, August, 1954.

Byer, J. P., "The Final Struggle for Democratic Control in North America," AHQ, Winter, 1930.

Going, Allen J., "Critical Months in Alabama Politics, 1895–1896," AR, October, 1952.

Going, Allen J. "The Establishment of the Alabama Railroad Commission," *Journal of Southern History,* Vol. 12, May, 1946.

Grantham, Dewey W., Jr., "The Progressive Movement and the Negro," *South Atlantic Quarterly,* October, 1955.

Hesseltine, William B., and Larry Gara, "Confederate Leaders in Post-War Alabama," AR, January, 1951.

Huggins, Louise, "John Tyler Morgan," AHQ, Vol. 14.

Johnson, Kenneth R., "The Troy Case: A fight against Discriminatory Freight Rates," AR, July, 1969.

Jones, Allen W., "Political Reforms of the Progressive Era," AR, July, 1968.

Jones, Thomas G., "The 1890–92 Campaigns for Governor of Alabama," AHQ, Winter, 1958.

Jones, Walter B., "William Calvin Oates," AHQ, Fall, 1945.

Radke, August C., "Senator Morgan and the Nicaraguan Canal," AR, January, 1959.

Roberts, Frances, "William Manning Lowe and the Greenback Party in Alabama," AR, April, 1952.

Rogers, William W., "The Alabama State Grange," AR, April, 1955.

Rogers, William W., "The Farmers' Alliance in Alabama," AR, January, 1962.

Rogers, William W., "The Negro Alliance in Alabama," *Journal of Negro History,* January, 1960.

Summersell, Charles C., "The Alabama Governor's Race in 1892," AR, January, 1955.

Summersell, Charles C., "Kolb and the Populist Revolt as viewed by Newspapers," AHQ, Fall and Winter, 1957.

Wiggins, Sarah Woolfolk, "The 'Pig Iron' Kelley Riot in Mobile," AR, January, 1970.

Wiggins, Sarah Woolfolk, "Press Reaction in Alabama to the Attempted Assassination of Judge Richard Busteed," AR, July, 1968.

Economics Since 1874

BOOKS

Armes, Ethel. *The Story of Coal and Iron in Alabama.* Birmingham, Ala.: Chamber of Commerce, 1910.

Comer, Donald. *Braxton Bragg Comer.* Birmingham: Privately printed, 1947.

Crane, Mary P. *The Life of James R. Powell, and Early History of Alabama.* Brooklyn, N.Y.: Brounworth & Co., 1930.

Duffee, Mary Gordan. *Sketches of Alabama.* University, Alabama: University of Alabama Press, 1970.

Lanier, Joseph L. *The First Seventy-Five Years of West Point*

Manufacturing Company, 1880–1955. New York: The Neucomen Society of North America, 1955.

Neville, Bert. *Steamboats on the Coosa River in the Rome, Georgia-Gadsden-Greenport, Alabama Trades, 1845–1920's*. Selma, Ala.: Privately printed, 1966.

Walker, Anne K. *Braxton Bragg Comer*. Richmond, Va.: Dietz Press, 1947.

Walker, Anne Kendrich. *Life and Achievements of Alfred Montgomery Shook*. Birmingham, Ala.: Birmingham Publishing Co., 1952.

Ward, David. *Labor Revolt in Alabama: The Great Strike of 1894*. University of Alabama: University of Alabama Press, 1965.

Young, Marjorie W., ed. *Textile Leaders of the South*. Columbia, S.C.: R.L. Bryson Co., 1963.

ARTICLES

Bailey, Hugh C., "Edgar Gardner Murphy and the Child Labor Movement," AR, January, 1965.

Cole, Houston, "Glimpses of Early Anniston," AR, April, 1967.

Doster, James., "Logging Railroads in Alabama, 1880–1914," AR, January, 1961.

_____ "Trade Centers and Railroad Rates in Alabama, 1873–1885: The Cases of Greenville, Montgomery, and Opelika," *Journal of Southern History*, Vol. 18, May, 1952.

_____ "Were Populists Against Railroad Corporations? The Case of Alabama," JSH, Vol. 20, August, 1954.

_____ "Wetumpka's Railroad: Its Construction and Early Traffic," AR, July, 1950.

Duffee, Mary Gordon, "Sketches of Alabama," AR, January, 1957.

Dykema, Frank E., "An Effort to Attract Dutch Settlers to Alabama, 1869," *Journal of Southern History*, May, 1948.

Farmer, Margaret Pace, "Furnishing Merchants and Sharecroppers in Pike County, Alabama," AR, April, 1970.

Fuller, Justin, "Alabama Business Leaders: 1865–1900," AR, October, 1963; Jan., 1964.

Fuller, Justin, "From Iron to Steel: Alabama's Industrial Revolution," AR, April, 1964.

Jay, John C., "General N. B. Forrest as a Railroad Builder in Alabama," AHQ, Vol. 24, Spring, 1962.

Johnson, Dudley S., "Early History of the Alabama Midland Railroad Company," AR, October, 1968.

Partin, Robert L., "Black Belt Grange, 1873–1877," *Agricultural History*, Vol. 31, July, 1958, pp. 49–59.

Rogers, William Warren, "The Alabama State Fair, 1865–1900," AR, April, 1958.

Rogers, William Warren, "The Agricultural Wheel," AR, January, 1967.

Sisk, Glenn H., "Negro Migration in the Alabama Black Belt, 1875–1917," *Negro History Bulletin,* November, 1953.

Torbert, James M., "Journal for 1857–1874," AHQ, Vol. 22, Spring and Summer, 1960.

Vandiver, Frank E., "Josiah Gorgas and the Brierfield Iron Works," AR, January, 1950.

Since 1900

BOOKS

Akens, David S. *Historical Origins of the George C. Marshall Space Flight Center.* Huntsville, Ala.: National Aeronautics and Space Administration, 1960.

Cosman, Bernard. *Five States for Goldwater: Continuity and Change in Southern Presidential Voting Patterns.* University of Alabama: University of Alabama Press, 1966.

Davis, Hazel B. *Uncle Hugo.* Amarillo, Texas: Privately printed, 1965.

Hackney, Sheldon. *Populism to Progressivism in Alabama.* Princeton, New Jersey: Princeton University Press, 1969.

Hubbard, Preston J. *Origins of the TVA: The Muscle Shoals Controversy, 1920–1932.* Nashville, Tenn.: Vanderbilt University Press, 1957.

Jones, Bill. *The Wallace Story.* Northport, Ala.: The American Southern Publishing Co., 1966.

Larson, James E. *Reapportionment in Alabama.* University, Ala.: University of Alabama Press, 1955.

Walters, Helen B. *Werhner Von Braun: Rocket Engineer.* New York: The Macmillan Co., 1964.

ARTICLES

Abrams, Richard M., "Woodrow Wilson and the Southern Congressmen, 1913–1916," JSH, November, 1956.

Alderson, William T., ed., "Taft, Roosevelt, and the U.S. Steel Case: A Letter of Jacob McG. Dickinson," *Tennessee Historical Quarterly,* September, 1959.

Allen, Lee N., "The Woman Suffrage Movement in Alabama, 1810–1920," AR, April, 1958.

Allen, Lee N., "The Underwood Presidential Movement of 1924," AR, April, 1962.

Bailey, Hugh C., "Edgar Gardner Murphy and the Child Labor Movement," AR, January, 1965.

Blassingame, Wyatt, "Fairhope by the Bay," *Southern Living,* March, 1969.

Daniel, Adrian G., "The Origins of Muscle Shoals Power, 1896–1906," AR, October, 1962.

Daniel, Pete, "Black Power in the 1920's: The Case of Tuskegee Veterans Hospital," *Journal of Southern History,* vol. 36, 1970.

Davis, Charles S., "Early Agricultural Demonstration Work in Alabama," AR, July, 1949.

Doster, James F., "Alabama's Gubernatorial Election of 1906," AR, July, 1955.

Doster, James F., "Comer, Smith and Jones: Alabama's Railroad War of 1907–1914," AR, April, 1957.

Ecroyd, Donald H., "The Alabama Governor's Primary, 1954: A Case Study," *Southern Speech Journal,* Spring, 1959.

Flynt, Wayne, "Dissent in Zion: Alabama Baptists and Social Issues, 1900–1914," JSH, November, 1969.

Flynt, Wayne, "Organized Labor, Reform, and Alabama Politics, 1920," AR, July, 1970.

Franklin, John Hope, "Legal Disfranchisement of the Negro," *Journal of Negro History,* Summer, 1957.

Gersh, Gabrile, "Recollections on the Scottsboro Affairs," *Negro History Bulletin,* May, 1957.

Gilbert, William E., "Bibb Graves as a Progressive, 1927–1930," AR, January, 1957.

Gomillion, C. T., "The Negro Voter in Alabama," *Journal of Negro History,* Summer, 1937.

Heacock, Walter J., "William B. Bankhead and the New Deal," JSH, Vol. 21, August, 1955.

Hoole, W. Stanley, "Alabama's World War II Prisoner of War Camps," AR, April, 1967.

Howington, Arthur F., "John Barleycorn Subdued: The Enforcement of Prohibition in Alabama," AR, July, 1970.

Johnson, Evans C., "Oscar W. Underwood and the Senatorial Campaign of 1920," AR, January, 1968.

Johnson, Evans C., "Oscar W. Underwood: A Fledgling Politician," AR, April, 1960.

Jones, Allen W., "Republicanism in Jefferson County, Alabama, 1952–1958," AHQ, Spring and Summer, 1960.

Jones, Walter B., "Constitutional Convention of 1901 and Poll Taxes," AHQ, Vol. 10, 1948.

Jones, Walter B., "Survivors' Constitutional Convention, 1901," AHQ, Fall, 1940.

Johnson, Evans C., "Oscar W. Underwood: An Aristocrat from the Bluegrass," AR, July, 1957.

Lewis, John E., "Repeal in Alabama," AR, October, 1967.

Link, Arthur S., "The Underwood Presidential Movement of 1912," JSH, Vol. 11, May, 1945.

Murphy, Laura Frances, "The Cajans at Home," AHQ, Winter, 1940.

Osborn, George C., "Woodrow Wilson Visits Mobile, October 27, 1913," AHQ, Spring, 1957.

Reagan, Hugh D., "Race as a Factor in the Presidential Election of 1928 in Alabama," AR, January, 1966.

Saloutos, Theodore, "The Alabama Farm Bureau Federation," AR, July, 1960.

Sandlin, Winfred G., "Lycurgus Breckenridge Musgrove," AR, July, 1967.

Segrest, J. L., "Resume of Alabama State Park History," AHQ, Vol. 10, 1948.

Sellers, James B., ed., "Alabama's Losses in the Korean Conflict," AR, July, October, 1960.

Sisk, Glenn N., "Post War Vigor and Industry in the Alabama Black Belt," *Mississippi Quarterly*, Spring, 1959.

Snell, William R., "Fiery Crosses in the Roaring Twenties: Activities of the Revised Klan in Alabama, 1915–1930," AR, October, 1970.

Stein, Waltrant, "The White Citizens' Councils," *Negro History Bulletin*, October, 1956.

Tanner, Ralph M., "Senator Tom Heflin as Storyteller," AR, January, 1962.

Taylor, James S., "John M. Patterson and the 1958 Alabama Gubernatorial Race," AR, July, 1970.

Thompson, Lawrence S., "Foreigners in Alabama, 1900–1950," AR, October, 1952.

Thornton, J. Mills, III., "Alabama Politics, J. Thomas Heflin, and the Expulsion Movement in 1929," AR, April, 1968.

Torodash, Martin, "Underwood and the Tariff," AR, April, 1967.

Walton, Norman W., "The Walking City, A History of the Montgomery Boycott," *Negro History Bulletin*, October, 1956, April, 1957.

Wiggins, Sarah W., "The Life of Ryland Randolph (1853–1903) as Seen Through His Letters (1900–1903) to John W. Dubose," AHQ, Fall, 1968.

Wright, Leslie S., "Henry Ford and Muscle Shoals," AR, July, 1961.

Books of General Interest

Brewer, Willis. *Alabama*. Montgomery, Ala.: Barrett and Brown, 1872.

Carmer, Carl. *Stars Fell On Alabama.* New York: Farrar and Rinehart, 1934.

Memorial Record of Alabama. 2 vols. Madison, Wisc.: Brant and Fuller, 1893.

Moore, Albert B. *History of Alabama.* Tuscaloosa, Ala.: University Book Store, 1950.

Moore, Albert B. *History of Alabama and Her People.* Chicago: The American Historical Society, 1927.

Owen, Marie B. *The Story of Alabama.* 5 vols. New York: Lewis Historical Publishing Co., 1949.

Owen, Thomas M. *History of Alabama and Dictionary of Alabama Biography.* 4 vols. Chicago: S. J. Clark Publishng Company, 1921.

Pickett, Albert J. *History of Alabama.* Sheffield, Alabama: Robert C. Randolph, 1896.

W.P.A. *Alabama: A Guide to the Deep South.* New York: Hastings House, 1941.

County and Town

BOOKS

Clanahan, James F. *History of Pickens County, 1540–1920.* Carrollton, Ala.: Clanahan Publications, 1964.

Comings, Lydia J. *A Brief History of Baldwin County.* Fairhope, Ala.: Baldwin Co. Historical Society, 1928.

Henley, John C. *This is Birmingham.* Southern University Press, 1960.

History of Jefferson County. Birmingham, Ala.: Teeple and Smith, 1887.

Ingram, William P. *A History of Tallapoosa County.* Birmingham, Ala.: Privately printed, 1951.

Jemison, E. Grace. *Historic Tales of Talladega Prior to the Twentieth Century.* Montgomery, Ala.: Paragon Press, 1959.

Leftwich, Nina. *Two Hundred Years of Muscle Shoals.* Tuscumbia, Ala.: Privately printed, 1935.

Moss, Florence H. *Building Birmingham and Jefferson County.* Birmingham, Ala.: Birmingham Printing Co., 1947.

Riley, B. F. *History of Conecuh County.* Columbus, Ga.: Privately printed, 1881.

Scott, Eva Clyde. *History of Henry County, Alabama.* Pensacola, Fla.: Privately printed, 1961.

Smith, Nelson F. *History of Pickens County.* Carrollton, Ala.. Pickens Republican, 1856. Reprinted, 1958.

Stewart, Margaret T. *Cherokee County History.* 2 vols. Centre, Ala.: Privately printed, 1958, 1959.

Sulzby, James F. *Birmingham Sketches.* Birmingham, Ala.: Birmingham Printing Co., 1945.

Walker, Anne K. *Back-Tracking in Barbour County*. Richmond, Va.: Dietz Press, 1941.

Walker, Anne K. *Russell County in Retrospect*. Richmond, Va.: Dietz Press, 1950.

Wyatt, Thomas E. *Chilton County and Her People*. Clanton, Ala.: Union-Banner Press, 1941.

ARTICLES

Anthony, J. D., "Cherokee County," AHQ, Fall, 1946.

Brewer, George E., "History of Coosa County," AHQ, Spring, Summer, 1942.

Cherry, F. L., "The History of Opelika and her Agriculture Tributary Territory," AHQ, Vol. 15, 1953.

Clarke County, "The Autobiography of Samuel Forwood," AHQ, Vol. 17, Spring & Summer, 1942.

Clinton, Thomas, "Early History of Tuscaloosa," AHQ, Spring, 1930.

Curry, J. L. M., "Reminiscences of Talladega," Spring, 1940, Summer, 1940.

"Early History of Tuskegee," AHQ, Vol. 18, 1956.

Farmer, Margaret Pace, "Early History of Pike County, Alabama," AHQ, Vol. 10.

Guinn, J. M. K., "History of Randolph County," AHQ, Fall, 1942.

Hardy, John, "History of Autauga County," AHQ, Spring, 1940.

James, R. L., "Colbertians," AHQ, Summer, Fall, Winter, 1945.

"Macon County," AHQ, Vol. 18, 1956, whole summer issue.

Malone, Thomas Smith, "Scraps Relating to the Early History of Limestone County," AHQ, Vol. 18, 1956.

Mims, Shadrack, "History of Autauga County," AHQ, Fall, 1946.

"Montgomery," AHQ, Vol. 18, Spring, 1956, whole issue.

Richards, E. H., "Reminiscences of Early Days in Chambers County," AHQ, Fall, 1942.

Rumph, Catherine H., "Reminiscences of Perote in Bullock," AHQ, Vol. 20, Fall, 1958.

"Russell County," AHQ, Vol. 21, 1959, whole volume.

Schribner, Robert L., "A Short History of Brewton, Alabama," AHQ, Vol. 11.

Taylor, Thomas Jones, "Early History of Madison County, and Incidentally of North Alabama," AHQ, Spring, Summer, Fall, Winter, 1930.

Taylor, Thomas Jones, "Later History of Madison County," AHQ, Fall, Winter, 1940.

Townes, S. A., "History of Marion, Perry County," AHQ, vol. 14.

Vandiver, John W., "Pioneer Talladega," AHQ, Vol. 16, 1954.

The Arts

Adams, Henry W. *The Montgomery Theatre 1822–1835*. University, Alabama: University of Alabama Press, 1955.

Arnold, Byron. *Folk Songs of Alabama*. University, Alabama: University of Alabama Press, 1950.

Ellison, Rhoda C. *A Check List of Alabama Imprints, 1807–1870*. University, Alabama: University of Alabama Press, 1946.

Ellison, Rhoda C. *Early Alabama Publications*. University, Alabama: University of Alabama Press, 1947.

Fidler, William P. *Augusta Evans Wilson, 1835–1909*. University, Alabama: University of Alabama Press, 1951.

Hammond, Ralph. *Antebellum Mansions of Alabama*. New York: Architectural Book Co., 1951.

Hentz, Caroline Lee. *Ernest Linwood*
> *Linda, or, The Young Pilot of the Belle Creole*
> *Marcus Warland, or The Long Moss Spring*
> *Delara, or The Moorish Bride*

Hoole, W. Stanley. *Alias Simon Suggs: The Life and Times of Johnson Jones Hooper*. University, Alabama: University of Alabama Press, 1952.

Ludlow, Noah M. *Dramatic Life as I Found It*. St. Louis: G. I. Jones and Co., 1880.

Weeden, Howard. *Shadows on the Wall*. Northport, Alabama: Colonial Press, 1962.

Wilson, Augusta Evans. *Beulah*
> *Inez: A Tale of the Alamo*
> *Mecaria, or Altars of Sacrifice*
> *St. Elmo*
> *Vashti*

ARTICLES

Abernathy, Cecil, "Lanier in Alabama," AR, January, 1964.

Browne, Ray B., "Negro Folktales from Alabama," *Southern Folklore Quarterly*, June, 1954.

Current-Garcia, Eugene, "Alabama Writers in *The Spirit*," AR, October, 1957.

Current-Garcia, Eugene, "Joseph Glover Baldwin: Humorist or Moralist?" AR, April, 1952.

Ellison, Rhoda C., "Mrs. Hentz and the Green-eyed Monster," *American Literature*, November, 1950.

Ellison, Rhoda C., "Propaganda in Early Alabama Fiction," AHQ, Fall, 1945.

Fidler, William P., "Augusta Evans Wilson as Confederate Propagandist," AR, January, 1949.

Figh, Margaret Gillis, "Alexander Beaufort Meek, Pioneer Man of Letters," AHQ, Summer, 1940.

Figh, Margaret Gillis, "Listen to the Mocking Bird, or the Treatment of Nature in Alabama Verse of the Nineteenth Century," AHQ, Winter, 1945.

Fisk, Sarah Huff, "Howard Weeden, Artist and Poet." AR, April, 1961.

Going, William T., "Alabama in the Short Story: Notes for an Anthology," AR, January, 1969.

Going, William T., "The Prose Fiction of Samuel Minturn Peck." AR, January, 1955.

Helmbold, F. Wilbur, "Early Alabama Newspapermen, 1810–1820," AR, January, 1959.

Hollingsworth, Annie May, "Johnson Jones Hooper," AHQ, Fall, 1930.

Hoole, W. Stanley, " 'Alabama': Drama of Reconciliation," AR, April, 1966.

Hoole, W. Stanley, "Jeremiah Clemens, Novelist," AR, January, 1965.

"John Gorman Barr: Forgotten Alabama Humorist," AR, April, 1951.

"Willis Brewer as a Novelist," AR, July, 1965.

Howard, Milo B., "John Hardy and John Reid: Two Selma Men of Letters," AR, Jan., 1969.

LeVert, Octavia, "Madam LeVert's Diary," AHQ, Spring, 1941.

McWilliams, Richebourg, "Penecaut as Alabama's First Literary Figure," AR, Jan., 1952.

O'Brien, Frank P., "Passing of the Old Montgomery Theatre," AHQ, Spring, 1941.

Rogers, William Warren, "Alabama Newspaper Mottoes From 1965 to 1900," AHQ, Vol. 20, Fall, 1958.

William, Benjamin B., "Alabama Civil War Poets," AR, October, 1962.

"Betsy Hamilton: Alabama Local Colorist," AHQ, Summer, 1964.

"Thomas Cooper De Leon: Alabama's First Professional Man of Letters," AHQ, Spring, 1961.

INDEX

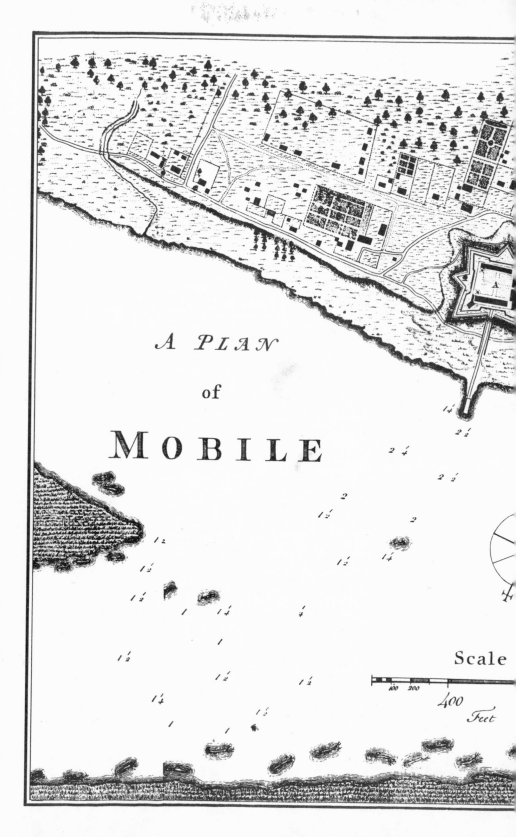

A PLAN

of

MOBILE

Scale

100 200

400

Feet